D1569809

Oxford Studies in British Church Music

General Editor
Nicholas Temperley, University of Illinois

Oxford Studies in British Church Music

Series Editor
Nicholas Temperley, University of Illinois

Goostly Psalmes and Spirituall Songes
English and Dutch Metrical Psalms from Coverdale to Utenhove, 1535–1566
Robin A. Leaver

The Succession of Organists
of the Chapel Royal and the Cathedrals of England and Wales from c.1538
Watkins Shaw

Restoration Cathedral Music

1660–1714

IAN SPINK

CLARENDON PRESS · OXFORD
1995

Oxford University Press, Walton Street, Oxford OX2 6DP
Oxford New York
Athens Auckland Bangkok Bombay
Calcutta Cape Town Dar es Salaam Delhi
Florence Hong Kong Istanbul Karachi
Kuala Lumpur Madras Madrid Melbourne
Mexico City Nairobi Paris Singapore
Taipei Tokyo Toronto
and associated companies in
Berlin Ibadan

Oxford is a trade mark of Oxford University Press

Published in the United States
by Oxford University Press Inc., New York

British Library Cataloguing in Publication Data
Data available

Library of Congress Cataloging in Publication Data
Spink, Iran.
Restoration cathedral music, 1600–1714 / Ian Spink.
p.   cm.—(Oxford studies in British church music)
Includes bibliographical references (p.   ) and index.
1. Church music—Church of England—17th century—Sources.
2. Church music—Church of England—18th century—Sources.
I. Title. II. Series. ML3166.S75 1995
781.71'3'0094209032—dc20   94-23774
ISBN 0-19-816149-2 (acid-free paper)

1 3 5 7 9 10 8 6 4 2

Typeset by Best-set Typesetter Ltd, Hong Kong
Printed in Great Britain
on acid-free paper by
Biddles Ltd, Guildford and King's Lynn

EDITOR'S FOREWORD

THE church music of Britain, like its church buildings and liturgical texts, is a national heritage that transcends religious controversy and the decline of faith. Unlike them—because of the ephemeral nature of music—it needs revival, interpretation, and advocacy if it is to be preserved and appreciated. Such processes must rest on a sound basis of fact and understanding. This series serves to encourage and present some of the best efforts of modern scholarship in the field.

The great Anglican cathedral tradition, with its roots in the Middle Ages, naturally takes the central place in this heritage. For centuries it has raised the music of worship to a high art, with its own style and history and its own series of composers, performers, and critics. It constitutes a school of musical art that is effortlessly distinctive, recognizably English, without being in the least nationalistic. Much though we may appreciate cathedral music as art, it also has a function in religious worship, and indeed in society. It shares this function with many other kinds of British church music—not all Anglican, not all English, not all achieving or even attempting high artistic value, but each playing a certain part in the life of a denomination and a community. The books in this series all, in their several ways, link developments in church music with the life of the individuals and societies that produced them.

The Restoration of Charles II stimulated one of the greatest triumphs of Anglican cathedral music. A group of gifted men, led by Henry Purcell, succeeded in transforming the carefully preserved and revived traditions of the Golden Age into a contemporary style that vigorously embraced the idioms of the French and Italian Baroque. But although perhaps a dozen masterpieces of the period remain in the cathedral repertoire, few of us can have had any idea of the riches and variety of music awaiting rediscovery.

Professor Spink is already well known as an authority on seventeenth-century English music. He has now carried out an extraordinary and completely new investigation of the musical sources of the period and of the archives of every cathedral and choral foundation. The result is not only a largely unfamiliar picture of the musical life and circumstances of choral foundations, from the Chapel Royal to remote Carlisle. He has also given us a fresh assessment of the music, taking in minor masters as well as the great men of the age. For the first time, perhaps, the true character and shape of the Restoration period of musical history is revealed.

NICHOLAS TEMPERLEY

Urbana, Illinois
March 1994

PREFACE AND ACKNOWLEDGEMENTS

THIS is a study of English cathedral music during the Restoration period; that is, from the return of King Charles II from exile in 1660 to the death of Queen Anne in 1714. I realized when I was writing my chapter on church music for *Music in Britain: The Seventeenth Century* (Oxford, 1992) that there was nothing dealing comprehensively with the subject, and it seemed to me that such a study was needed. Obviously, it would require investigation of the repertoire beyond what was available in print as well as exploration of the institutional background. Once I had finished the chapter I set about the research. That was in 1981. I cannot say that I have finished, but at least the ground has been surveyed.

In effect, the book was written in reverse order. I began with the music of the cathedrals and collegiate foundations of England, Wales, and Ireland (though there was little of concern beyond Dublin). This material forms the bulk of Part III, and for most readers it will be new. Part II deals with the music of the Chapel Royal, where composers like Humfrey, Blow, and Purcell were active, and where many cathedral composers were trained. Inevitably they looked to the Chapel Royal for their models, as we must do in order to establish critical norms. Finally, Part I was needed in order to introduce the subject and make sense of what followed.

Most earlier treatments of this music have been within a wider context. E. H. Fellowes devoted a chapter to it in his *English Church Music from Edward VI to Edward VII* (London, 1941; rev. J. A. Westrup, 1969) but his sympathies lay with the music of an earlier age, while J. S. Bumpus—who knew a great deal about the sources of Restoration church music and owned a number of important manuscripts now randomly dispersed—was just not musician enough to make the relevant sections of his *History of English Cathedral Music, 1549–1899* (2 vols., London, 1908) much more than an antiquarian's note-book. At the time I felt that the best general treatment of the period was in Kenneth Long's *The Music of the English Church* (London, 1972) but that what the music deserved, and could bear, was something along the lines of Peter le Huray's *Music and the Reformation in England, 1549–1660* (London, 1967; 2nd edn., Cambridge, 1978). Despite the existence of an excellent sequel to that book by Christopher Dearnley covering the period up to 1750, I decided to cast my net wider, and, in some respects, deeper. My object was not particularly to discover new masterpieces (though I may have done so), or to establish new criteria for their rehabilitation (though this may follow), but to map out the territory and expose its riches for others to exploit.

Two Victorian writers supplied a framework. John E. West's *Cathedral Organists Past and Present* (London, 1899; 2nd edn., 1921) listed some, though by no means all of the composers, and put them in context; Myles Birkett Foster's *Anthems and Anthem Composers* (London, 1901; repr. 1970) identified the anthem repertoire, more or less—actually, more *and* less. The first draft of this book was completed before the publication of Watkins Shaw's *The Succession of Organists* (Oxford, 1991), a thorough revision and up-dating of West's book that in some respects overlapped with what I had set out to do, though I have since pruned needless duplication and drawn on some of his discoveries. As I later became aware, Shaw had virtually finished his research before I started, and though our two books are essentially different, I am grateful for having benefited from private communication with him, and, of course, his scholarship over the years. Everyone working in the field owes him an enormous debt of gratitude for his work, which began as long ago as the 1930s and has now been crowned with this *magnum opus*.

I am indebted to many other scholars too—sometimes for a helpful letter in reply to a query, sometimes for much more. I now list them, not out of duty but with a real appreciation of their generosity (and hoping that I have left no one out): Mr Frank Atkinson, Mr R. M. Beaumont, Dr B. S. Benedikz, Canon R. J. W. Bevan, Mr Christopher Bornet, Dr Donald Burrows, Dr Vernon Butcher, Mr John Carter, Dr Ian Cheverton, Canon T. R. Christie, Mrs M. V. Cranmer, Mr John Crook, Dr Brian Crosby, Mr Roger Custance, Mr R. H. Davis, Mr Mark Dorrington, Mr John A. Emerson, Mrs Audrey Erskine, Miss Suzanne M. Eward, Dr Robert Ford, Mrs Patricia Gill, Mr J. P. Godwin, Mr Walter Goodman, Mr Andrew Goodwin, Mr David Griffiths, Dr W. H. Grindle, Dr Christopher Grogan, Dr George Guest, Canon E. C. C. Hill, Dr Mary Hobbs, Dr Timothy Hobbs, Mr Kerry Houston, Mrs Patricia Hughes, Miss Anne M. Jones, Mr B. C. Jones, Mrs Brenda M. Kipling, Mr Francis Knights, Dr Barbara Knowles, Dr Margaret Laurie, Mr John Lees, Mr Lowinger Maddison, Mrs Norah Maisey, Mrs Priscilla Manley, Dr Peter Marr, Prof. John Morehen, Dr Penelope Morgan, Canon Leslie Morley, Mr P. S. Morrish, Mr Howard Nixon, Mrs Dorothy M. Owen, Miss A. M. Oakley, Mr Peter Partner, Dr Lionel Pike, Mr Nicholas Plumley, Mr P. R. Quarrie, Mr Richard Seal, Canon John Simpson, Mr W. N. Thacker, Mrs Barbara Carpenter-Turner, Miss Joan Williams, Dr Ruth Wilson, Mr H. J. R. Wing, Dr Bruce Wood, Mr N. Yates, and Dr Percy Young. Comments and advice from Dr H. D. Johnstone and Prof. Nicholas Temperley in the later stages of preparation have been invaluable, as has Mr Bruce Phillips's encouragement. I should also like to acknowledge the help of the University of London Central Research Fund in supporting my research, and my college in granting me a year's leave in 1992–3 to complete it.

I mentioned above that my object in writing this book was not primarily the 'rehabilitation' of the music. Nevertheless, in the long term I believe this will happen. It will involve a change of taste principally as regards the verse anthem, leading to a recognition that this was the one indigenous and substantial musical form to achieve viability in seventeenth-century England. As such it represents a peak of the English Baroque comparable in richness and diversity with Wren's city churches, even, in some cases, with St Paul's itself. It may now seem something of an acquired taste—but, then, almost everything is. My hope is that, with the help of this book, the taste may be acquired more widely.

I.S.

Royal Holloway and Bedford New College
University of London
3 April 1995

CONTENTS

ABBREVIATIONS

PRINTED BOOKS AND MUSIC

Arnold   Samuel Arnold (ed.), *Cathedral Music*, 4 vols. (London, 1790)

Ashbee   Andrew Ashbee (ed.), *Records of English Court Music*, 6 vols. (Snodland, Kent, and Aldershot, Hants, 1986–93)

Boyce   William Boyce (ed.), *Cathedral Music*, 3 vols. (London, 1760–73)

Dearnley   Christopher Dearnley, *English Church Music 1660–1750, in Royal Chapel, Cathedral and Parish Church* (London, 1970)

DNB   *The Dictionary of National Biography*, ed. Leslie Stephen and Sidney Lee, 66 vols. (London, 1885–1900)

HMC   [Historical Manuscripts Commission] 'Papers Relating to Archbishop Laud's Visitations', *The Fourth Report of the Royal Commission on Historical Manuscripts* (London, 1874), 124–59

le Huray   Peter le Huray, *Music and the Reformation in England, 1549–1660* (London, 1967)

Long   Kenneth R. Long, *The Music of the English Church* (London, 1972)

MB   *Musica Britannica* (Royal Musical Association; London, 1951–)

NG   *The New Grove Dictionary of Music and Musicians*, ed. Stanley Sadie, 20 vols. (London, 1980)

Page   John Page (ed.), *Harmonia Sacra*, 3 vols. (London, 1800)

PS   *The Works of Henry Purcell*, 32 vols. (Purcell Society; London, 1878–1965)

Rimbault   Edward F. Rimbault (ed.), *The Old Cheque-Book or Book of Remembrance of the Chapel Royal from 1561 to 1744* (Camden Society, NS iii; London, 1872; repr. New York, 1966)

Shaw   Watkins Shaw, *The Succession of Organists of the Chapel Royal and the Cathedrals of England and Wales from c.1538* (Oxford, 1991)

MANUSCRIPTS

The following library sigla are used in footnotes and brackets within the text (omitting MS or MSS before the numbers). Note: British Library collections are given their own abbreviations; thus, *Eg.* = Egerton MS, *Harl.* = Harleian MS, *Lbl* = Additional MS, *RM* = Royal Music MS.

GB:

Bu	Birmingham, University Library (Barber Institute of Fine Arts)
Cfm	Cambridge, Fitzwilliam Museum
Ckc	Cambridge, King's College (Rowe Library)
Cjc	Cambridge, St John's College
Ctc	Cambridge, Trinity College
Cu	Cambridge, University Library
CA	Canterbury Cathedral
CH	Chichester Cathedral (West Sussex Record Office)
DRc	Durham Cathedral
Eg.	Egerton Collection (London, British Library)
EL	Ely Cathedral (Cambridge, University Library)
GL	Gloucester Cathedral
H	Hereford Cathedral
Harl.	Harleian Collection (London, British Library)
Lam	London, Royal Academy of Music
Lbl	London, British Library
Lcm	London, Royal College of Music
Lsp	London, St Paul's Cathedral
Lwa	London, Westminster Abbey
LF	Lichfield Cathedral
LI	Lincoln Cathedral
Mp	Manchester Public Library (Henry Watson Library)
NW	Norwich Cathedral (Chapter Records; Norwich and Norfolk Public Record Office)
Ob	Oxford, Bodleian Library
Och	Oxford, Christ Church
Ojc	Oxford, St John's College
Omc	Oxford, Magdalen College
PE	Peterborough Cathedral (Cambridge, University Library)
RM	Royal Music Library (London, British Library)
RO	Rochester Cathedral
SB	Salisbury Cathedral
WB	Wimborne Minster
WC	Winchester Cathedral
WO	Worcester Cathedral
WRec	Windsor, Eton College
WRgc	Windsor, St George's Chapel
Y	York Minster

US:

AUS	Austin, Texas, University of Texas (Stark Library)
BE	Berkeley, California, University of California (Music Library)

Cn   Chicago, Illinois, Newberry Library
LAuc   Los Angeles, California, University of California (William Andrews
       ˙Clark Memorial Library)

Manuscripts cited by title:
Berkeley Organ Book = *US-BE* 751
Bing–Gostling Partbooks = *Y* M.1.S
Flackton collection = *Lbl* 30931–3
Gostling Manuscript = *US-AUS*
Tenbury Partbooks = *Ob* Tenbury 797–803 and 1176–82
Tudway collection = *Harl.* 7337–42

OTHER ABBREVIATIONS

B   bass
Bc   basso continuo
C   countertenor
T   tenor
Tr   treble

PITCH DESIGNATIONS

Where necessary, precise pitches are indicated according to the following
system, using roman letters.

In the seventeenth century, however, notes below G (gamut) were designated
FF, EE, DD, CC, whereas they would now be written *F, E, D, C*. (Notes
above gamut carried their hexachord solmization to distinguish one octave from
another; thus, *c* was C fa ut, *c'* was C sol fa ut, and *c"* was C sol fa.)

MAJOR AND MINOR KEYS

Normally, a capital letter by itself indicates a major key (e.g. 'Service in A'
means A major); minor keys are written in full (e.g. 'Service in A minor').

MUSIC EXAMPLES

Music examples are transcribed from the sources indicated at pitch, with original note-values and time signatures. No collation between sources has been attempted except to correct mistakes, in which case the change is explained in a note. Original voice designations (but not clefs) have been shown. Countertenor parts have usually been transcribed in the 'transposed treble' clef, i.e. sounding an octave lower (as if they were tenors). To save space voice parts have been condensed on two or three staves (occasionally on one), though not all parts have been underlaid. In homophonic passages it should be clear how the words fit; in polyphonic passages, leading phrases have been underlaid, with slurs to show how the omitted text should be fitted. Texts have been modernized in spelling and punctuation. Editorial amendments to the music have been shown by footnotes, square brackets and the use of ⌢ for slurs and ties. Differences between basso continuo (tails down)and bass voice (tails up) have been shown on the same stave where possible, though sometimes a separate organ bass-line has been provided.

PART I

The Choral Service and Its Music

1

Liturgy and Chant

INTRODUCTION

On 26 May 1660 King Charles II and his brother James, Duke of York, landed at Dover. His first Sunday service was at Canterbury Cathedral the following day, and on 29 May—his thirtieth birthday—he entered London in triumph. The Restoration was an accomplished fact, and Charles resolved never to go on his travels again.

The Civil War, which had cost his father's life and throne, had broken out in August 1642. In religious terms the fight was between those who wanted a church with bishops and those who sought to establish the Presbyterian system. In January 1643 Parliament passed a bill 'for the utter abolishing and taking away all archbishops, bishops . . . deans and chapters . . . and all vicars choral and choristers, old vicars and new vicars of any cathedral or collegiate church . . . out of the Church of England', and in August the Westminster Assembly of 'Godly and Learned Divines' began to draw up a new Prayer Book.[1] An 'Ordinance for further demolishing of Monuments of Idolatry and Superstition' was enacted in May 1644, decreeing that 'all Organs, and Frames or Cases wherein they stand in all Churches . . . shall be taken away, and utterly defaced, and none hereafter set up in their places'.[2] In January the following year the 'Directory for Public Worship' was approved by Parliament and became the official liturgy of the Church of England.[3]

The rigour with which all this was enforced varied from place to place, and, in fact, the collegiate establishments of Oxford and Cambridge, Winchester and Eton were exempt. Nevertheless, Prayer Book worship was forbidden and could only be carried out in private. Towards the end of Cromwell's Protectorate breaches of the law became more flagrant, so much so that the government made a show of force to suppress services at Christmas 1657—an account of which Evelyn relates in his diary.[4] The chapel at Exeter House, where Peter

---

[1] William H. Hutton, *The English Church from the Accession of Charles I to the Death of Queen Anne (1625–1714)* (London, 1934), 127; quotation from Henry Gee and William J. Harding, *Documents Illustrative of English Church History* (London, 1910), 566.

[2] C. H. Firth and R. S. Rait (eds.), *Acts and Ordinances of the Interregnum, 1642–1660* (London, 1911), i. 425–6.

[3] Hutton, *English Church*, 128–9.

[4] *The Diary of John Evelyn*, ed. E. S. de Beer, 6 vols. (London, 1955), iii. 204.

Gunning preached and which both Evelyn and Pepys frequented, was only one of several known to the authorities. Gunning, who became Master of St John's College, Cambridge, after the Restoration and successively Bishop of Chichester and Ely, had links with the composer George Jeffreys, who composed a Gloria in excelsis 'at Mr Peter Gunning's motion, May 1652'.[5] This may be only one of a number of works by Jeffreys written for Gunning during the 1650s, but the extent to which music played a part in such clandestine services is unclear. One report mentioned that 'att some Churches in the citty there were as bad doinges, for the superstitious and ceremonious parte, as att the private places'.

Att one church by Garlick Hill [St James, Garlickhythe?] I hear they had gott some old Choristers and new taught singing boyes, and after the Common Prayer att length in all pontificalibus ended, a young canonicall votary went uppe into the pulpitt, and made an oration or sermon . . . often taking occasion to mencion the name of Jesus, he duck't even to within the pulpitt, and all the people bowed and cringed as if there had bin mass.[6]

Following the Declaration of Breda (1660) whereby Charles II promised 'liberty to tender consciences' a conference of Puritan and Anglican divines was called at the Savoy, to advise on what changes, if any, were needed in the Book of Common Prayer to meet the new situation. The Puritans were opposed to the reintroduction of the old Prayer Book as being too 'romish', but in the end—thanks in no small part to the arguments of Peter Gunning, 'ever zealous for Arminianism and formality and church pomp'—it was approved with something like six hundred mainly minor alterations and came into use officially on St Bartholomew's day [24 August] 1662. Twelve hundred dissenting ministers were forced to relinquish their livings by an Act of Uniformity, and were replaced in many cases by clergy who themselves had been dispossessed by the parliamentarians some years earlier. Most of the changes were in a Catholic direction, but from a musical point of view the result differed little from the Elizabethan and Jacobean liturgies.[7] For the first time, however, the rubric 'In Quires and Places where they sing here followeth the Anthem' was added after the third collect at morning and evening prayer, no doubt to safeguard a practice which, though it dated back to the Reformation, might otherwise have come under attack from Puritan quarters.

While Charles II was on the throne the Church of England was safe from those who wished to see a more Protestant form of worship. Various acts of

[5] Robert Thompson, 'George Jeffreys and the "Stile Nuovo" in English Sacred Music: A New Date for his Autograph Score, British Library Add. MS 10338', *Music and Letters*, 70 (1989), 332–3.

[6] C. H. Firth (ed.), *The Clarke Papers* (Camden Society, 3; London, 1899), 130.

[7] W. K. Lowther Clarke and Charles Harris (eds.), *Liturgy and Worship: A Companion to the Prayer Books of the Anglican Communion* (London, 1964), 190–7.

Parliament prevented toleration of Dissenters, but although Roman Catholics were equally legislated against, a Catholic queen and Catholics (or Catholic sympathizers) at court gave rise to fears of a Catholic take-over. The Test Act of 1673 allowed only members of the Church of England to hold office under the crown, but anti-Catholic sentiment increased in the following years, culminating in 1679–81 with bills to exclude James, Duke of York, the king's brother and a Roman Catholic, from succession to the throne. Though passed by the Commons they were never enacted, thanks to the king dissolving Parliament. Even so, the strength of Protestant opinion was evident and it did not augur well for James's eventual accession, which occurred in 1685.

With no great subtlety James sought to advance his own religion. Dispensing with the Test Act, he introduced Catholics into the government, the army, and the universities. At Oxford, the Catholic John Massey was appointed Dean of Christ Church, and a strong attempt was made to romanize Magdalen College. When, eventually, the king came to challenge the Church by commanding that a Declaration of Indulgence granting toleration to Protestant Dissenters and Catholics alike be read from pulpits throughout the country, he was defied by the majority of the clergy. Seven bishops were committed to the Tower of London, but acquitted in June 1688 to popular acclaim. Mounting opposition brought home to the king the fact that the country could not be governed in the way he wished. The High Church party, though opposing his attempts to subvert the Church, remained loyal to the king, but Parliament and the more Protestant faction in the country as a whole were intent on inviting William of Orange over from Holland to rule jointly with Mary, his wife and James's daughter. William arrived in England in November 1688 and James fled to France the following month.

This was the so-called 'Glorious Revolution'. The new king was unsympathetic to Anglicanism, and received little support in return. Indeed, a number of bishops refused to take the Oath of Allegiance on the grounds that they had already sworn allegiance to James II. But with so many Dissenters among William's supporters, an attempt to reform the Church of England in a more Protestant direction was set afoot. A bill for 'Protestant Comprehension' was passed in the House of Lords (1689) but failed in the Commons.[8] The king was petitioned to call a convocation to inquire into the forms and ceremonies of the Church and make recommendations acceptable to Dissenters and churchmen alike. When the commissioners met on 3 October 1689 one of the articles before them was 'that the chanting of divine service in cathedral churches be laid aside that the whole may be rendered intelligible to the common people'.[9]

[8] Hutton, *English Church*, 246–51.
[9] Edward Cardwell, *A History of Conferences and other Proceedings connected with the Revision of the Book of Common Prayer from the Year 1558 to the Year 1690* (3rd edn., Oxford, 1899), 429–32.

Hardly surprisingly, Henry Aldrich—the new Dean of Christ Church and, as we shall see, a talented amateur composer—was one of the commissioners who left in disgust early on, but although the remainder were prepared to make radical proposals, they were unable to carry them through. The High Church party virtually hijacked the proceedings and the Prayer Book survived unscathed.

Those bishops who had refused to take the Oath of Allegiance to King William were still unable to do so when Queen Anne came to the throne in 1702, for, ardent Anglican though she was, her father's son had a better claim to the throne in their eyes, Catholic though he might be. Nevertheless, Anne's reign saw a return to the high Anglicanism of Charles II's day, and rounded off a fifty-year period which, from some points of view (including the musical one), may be regarded as a golden age. The Stuarts had served the church well—perhaps too well.

THE RESTORED LITURGY

Under the Act of Uniformity (1662) divine service was to be performed daily in cathedrals and collegiate churches throughout the kingdom according to the 'Rites and Ceremonies of the Church' as set out in the Book of Common Prayer. The daily round began with morning prayer, followed by the litany on Sundays, Wednesdays, and Fridays, and Holy Communion (whether or not the sacrament was celebrated) on Sundays and holy days. Evening prayer was held in the afternoon. Morning and evening prayer followed much the same pattern. Both began with the introductory sentences, exhortation, general confession, and absolution—all said—followed by the Lord's Prayer. Then came the preces ('O Lord, open thou our lips', etc.) with responses sung kneeling and the Gloria Patri standing. The new Prayer Book divided the latter into versicle and response for the first time, the priest's 'Glory be to the Father . . .' being answered by the choir's 'As it was in the beginning . . .'. Also new was the response 'The Lord's name be praised' to the priest's 'Praise ye the Lord'.

At morning prayer the *Venite* followed 'except on Easter Day, upon which another Anthem is appointed: and on the nineteenth day . . . [when it was sung] in the ordinary course of the Psalms'. The 'anthem' in question was 'Christ our passover is sacrificed for us' (new to 1662) followed by 'Christ being raised from the dead' and 'Christ is risen from the dead', the texts now taken from the Authorized [King James's] Version, as the Puritans had requested, instead of Coverdale's 'Great Bible'. (The equivalent passages in the Great Bible which earlier prayer books had used began 'Christ rising again from the dead' and 'Christ is risen again'.) The rubrics continued: 'Then shall follow the Psalms in order as they are appointed' and so arranged that in the course of a month all 150 psalms were sung. 'And at the end of every Psalm . . . and likewise in the end of Benedicite, Benedictus, Magnificat, and Nunc Dimittis, shall be repeated, *Glory be to the Father*', etc.

After the first lesson from the Old Testament, the *Te Deum* or *Benedicite* was sung at morning prayer, the *Magnificat* or *Cantate Domino* at evening prayer; similarly, after the second lesson from the New Testament, the *Benedictus* or *Jubilate Deo* at morning prayer, the *Nunc dimittis* or *Deus misereatur* at evening prayer. The office continued with the singing of the Apostles' Creed 'by the Minister and the people standing' except that on major feasts the Athanasian Creed was sung instead. The suffrages, Lord's Prayer, and versicles and responses followed, the only change in 1662 being the treatment of 'Christ, have mercy upon us', etc., as a response, instead of all three petitions sung by the priest. The collects were followed by the anthem, then, except on 'Litany Days', by further prayers added in 1662 'for the King's Majesty', etc. Little need be said at this stage about the litany; essentially it consisted of a series of prayers and petitions to each of which the choir made some such response as 'Good Lord deliver us', 'We beseech thee to hear us, good Lord', etc.

The Prayer Book stipulated that on Sundays and holy days there should be a service of Holy Communion and a sermon. If the sacrament was not to be offered, the rubric stated that the service should skip from the prayer for the Church Militant to the final collect(s) and blessing—omitting the exhortation, general confession, comfortable words, preface, consecration, communion, and Gloria in excelsis. However, 'in Cathedral and Collegiate Churches . . . where there are many Priests and Deacons, they shall all receive Communion with the Priest every Sunday at the least, except they have a reasonable cause to the contrary'. This was an ideal which it seems was not generally observed, but there is no evidence that the service (as opposed to the sacrament) was any less frequent than the Prayer Book prescribed. The only references in the Prayer Book to singing in the communion service were with regard to the Creed, the preface beginning 'Therefore with angels and archangels' leading into the Sanctus, and the Gloria in excelsis—each of which could be 'sung or said'. Although the rubrics fail to mention the word 'sing' in connection with the Responses to the Commandments, it was normal for the choir to do so. 'Glory be to thee, O Lord' before the gospel, though not even prescribed in the Prayer Book, was also frequently sung.

The only other Prayer Book service in which music played an important part was the Burial Service. In the 1662 Prayer Book there was some rearrangement of material from earlier prayer books, and the introduction of two psalms, one or both of which were to be read. The opening rubrics stipulate 'Priest and Clerks meeting the corpse at the entrance of the Church-yard, and going before it, either into the Church, or towards the grave, shall say, or sing' the following funeral sentences: 'I am the resurrection and the life', 'I know that my redeemer liveth', and 'We brought nothing into the world'. After the reading of the psalms, and the lesson, there followed further verses said or sung at the grave side. These included 'Man that is born of a woman', 'In the midst of life', 'Thou knowest, Lord', and, after the burial, 'I heard a voice from heaven'. Most settings of the Burial Service group the processional verses together as a single anthem; similarly those sung at the grave, with the last forming a separate item.

Morning and evening prayer were performed daily by the choir in all English cathedrals as required by their statutes. In Wales (and Ireland, outside Dublin) the choral service was likely to be confined to Sundays and holy days, due in part to inadequate endowments for maintaining choirs. Cathedral dignitaries and canons were supposed to attend the services when resident. They had their terms to keep and their sermons to preach, but it was the function of the choir under the precentor or succentor to keep the services going, day in, day out. Times of service differed from place to place and with the seasons. Sunday morning service, which would include morning prayer, litany, Holy Communion, and sermon, was longer than on a weekday, and consequently an earlier start was usual. In winter, longer hours of darkness necessitated an earlier start for evening prayer. For example, at Chichester in 1678 (see Pt. III) the Chapter decided that on Sundays and holy days morning prayer should begin at 9 a.m., on litany days (Wednesdays and Fridays) at 9.45 a.m., and on other days at 10 a.m. In autumn and early spring (Michaelmas to All Saints and Candlemas to 1 March) evening prayer was to begin at 3.30 p.m., in winter (All Saints to Candlemas) at 3 p.m., and the rest of the year at 4 p.m. Early morning prayer, which did not involve the choir (other than a vicar choral to read it) was at 7 a.m. in the winter, and 6 a.m. at other times.

PERFORMING THE LITURGY

The early years of the Restoration saw the publication of a number of manuals dealing with music in the cathedral service. The first of these was Edward Lowe's *A Short Direction for the Performance of Cathedrall Service* (1661), which set out to inform 'Persons as are Ignorant if it, And shall be call'd to officiate in Cathedrall, or Collegiate Churches'.[10] It included the traditional psalm tones and chants for the responses which in essence go back to Merbecke's *Booke of*

---

[10] The following matters are dealt with in more detail in Ruth M. Wilson, 'Anglican Chant and Chanting in England and America, 1660–1811', (Ph.D. diss., University of Illinois, Urbana, 1988), 14–26; see also Dearnley, 97–8.

Common Praier Noted (1550). It also included some harmonized psalm tones 'to serve only so long, till the Quires are more learnedly Musicall', and some four-part 'Extraordinary Responsalls' for festivals, adapted from Byrd's second set of preces and Tallis's second set of responses. Lowe's source was presumably Barnard's *First Book of Select Church Musick* (1641); likewise 'The Letany in four parts' was also based on Tallis. As the title indicates, these harmonized versions were intended to be sung on feast-days, when they would be accompanied by the organ. At other times, psalms and responses were chanted unaccompanied.

Lowe had been organist of Christ Church, Oxford, before the Civil War, and was now one of the organists of the Chapel Royal. His book, however, pre-dates the 1662 version of the Prayer Book, and it was one of the purposes of the revised second edition, entitled *A Review of some Short Directions* (1664), to accommodate the changes, though these were not very significant musically. In addition he expanded the range of psalm tones from two (one for Sundays and one for weekdays) to one for every day of the week, with four others 'formerly in use for the Psalmes', adding for good measure a four-part setting of the Burial Service by John Parsons.

Complementing Lowe's work was James Clifford's *The Divine Services and Anthems* (1663 [Imprimatur 'Novemb. 20. 1622', i.e. 1662]), which contained a section headed 'Brief Directions for the understanding of that part of the *Divine Service* performed with the *Organ* in S. *Pauls* Cathedrall on Sundays and Holy-dayes'. Clifford was a vicar choral of St Paul's at this time, hence his model. A second edition was issued in 1664 (Imprimatur 'Jan. 16. 1663', i.e. early 1664), which included twelve psalm tones and three four-part harmonizations. Both editions also listed anthems sung in the king's chapel and the cathedrals and collegiate churches of England and Ireland—172 in the first edition, 406 in the second, showing how much progress there had been in little more than a year.[11] Ten years later, John Playford added a section to the 1674 edition of his *Introduction to the Skill of Musick* dealing with 'The Order of Performing the Divine Service in Cathedrals and Collegiate Chappels'. In addition to the traditional chant and psalm tones for each day of the week, he included a couple of harmonized psalm tunes. Significantly, he also gave six tunes 'sung in His Majesties Chappel with the Organ to the Psalms, Te Deum &c Compos'd by Mr John Blow and Mr William Turner' which are, in effect, the earliest printed Anglican chants. To these may be added an early eighteenth-century manuscript at Ely which provides musical notation for the priest's part in the morning service (see App. A). Making some allowance for its later date and local character, it confirms a fairly uniform practice.

[11] Le Huray, 367.

In the first part of the service (leading up to the *Venite*) there are minor variants between the sources. The opening sentences and exhortation do not seem to have been sung either by the priest or the choir, Ely stipulating a 'reading tone'. According to Playford the general confession and absolution were 'read by the Priest in one continued and solemn Tone', not specifically notated but pitched on *a* at Ely, where the rubric is 'Elevate your voice to a Moderate pitch & begin the confession . . . keeping your voice stedfast in the same tone'. Ely keeps *a* as the reciting note for all further versicles and responses, but Lowe and Playford vary it. (For the most part Playford follows Lowe, but sometimes carelessly.) Lowe, having finished the Lord's Prayer on *d* (or *a*—he uses F3 and C3 clefs together) begins 'O Lord, open thou our lips' on the note below, and moves up via *d* (*a*) to an *f* (*c′*) reciting-note for 'O God, make speed to save us'. From then on *f* (*c′*) remains the reciting-note. The ensuing doxology is given to the priest alone in the 1661 edition, but divided between priest and choir in the 1664 edition, adding the response 'The Lord's name be praised' to the priest's 'Praise ye the Lord'—all in conformity with changes in the 1662 Prayer Book.

The *Venite* and the proper psalms that follow are sung antiphonally. According to Playford the *Venite* 'is begun by one of the Quire, then sung by Sides, observing to mark the like break or Close in the middle of ev'ry Verse according as it is shorter or longer'. The psalm tones (harmonized and unharmonized) printed by Lowe, Clifford, and Playford were used not only for the psalms but also for canticles 'when more solemn composures are not used'. After the psalms Clifford observes that an organ voluntary is played, which Playford confirms. This was no doubt what happened at St Paul's, and seems to have been general, the organist leaving the choir and ascending the organ loft at this point, as at Westminster Abbey.[12] Following the first lesson the intonation for the *Te Deum* was sung, 'the Priest singing alone' according to Playford, and the choir joining in with 'We knowledge thee to be the Lord'. Playford gives the intonation derived from Merbecke's *Booke of Common Praier Noted* and ultimately from the Sarum chant (Ex. 1). This is clearly necessary when the setting of the *Te Deum* begins

Ex. 1. Te Deum intonations: (*a*) Merbecke, 1550; (*b*) Playford, 1674

'We knowledge thee', though redundant when the opening words are set. He goes on to say that the *Te Deum* is 'composed usually in 4 parts

[12] Jocelyn Perkins, *The Organs and Bells of Westminster Abbey* (London, 1937), 14.

for sides [cantoris and decani]', but may also be sung to the common tunes [tones] 'with the organ or without it'—likewise the *Jubilate* or *Benedictus* after the second lesson. The Apostles' Creed is sung by the whole choir 'in one continued solemn and grave Tone' or 'upon Festivals *Athanasius*'s Creed is sung in the same Tune by sides'. Alternatively it may be sung to one of the harmonized tunes, accompanied by the organ. Playford is alone in dropping the reciting-note of the Lord's Prayer to *d*, returning to *f* for the ensuing responses. Following the collects, to which the choir answers 'Amen', comes the anthem.

On 'litany days' came the litany, comprising the main body of petitions and responses down to 'Lord have mercy', with a concluding section beginning with the Our Father and ending with the grace. As with all unharmonized singing it would have been performed unaccompanied. The chant is pitched on *f* (or *c'*) in Lowe, falling a fourth at the Lord's Prayer and thereafter returning to *f* (or *c'*). Practice varied as to who sang the priest's part. Playford said that 'it is sung by two of the Quire' in the middle of the Church [between the choir-stalls] near the Bible desk', and this was generally followed (there being a stone in the middle of the choir at Lincoln with 'Cantate Hic' on it). At most places it seems as if lay clerks or lay vicars officiated, at least early on. At Lincoln in 1678 it was decreed 'that the Poor Clerks continue the reading of the Litany in their turnes'.[13] In some places a minor canon from one side and a lay clerk from the other went into the middle. At Ely a change was enacted in 1708 whereby 'one of the minor canons do always chant or sing that whole service at the desk . . . instead of lay clerks chanting part of it by former custom', the implication being that clerks had previously chanted the first part, a minor canon taking over at the Our Father.[14] At the end of the service Clifford indicates 'a *Voluntary* alone upon the Organ'.

As already mentioned, the sung portions of the Holy Communion (or 'second service' as it was sometimes called) usually consisted of the responses to the Commandments and the Creed, though the Sanctus often seems to have been sung between the end of the litany and the beginning of the communion, judging by its placement in the service books. Lowe is mostly clear on the subject. He says:

The Second Service is begun by the Priest who reads the Lords Prayer to one grave tone, the deeper (if strong and audible) the better: Then the Collect before the Commandements, and the Commandements in a higher tone, the whole Quire (if no singing to an Organ) answering *Lord have mercy upon us &c* after each Commandement in the same tone.

[13] A. R. Maddison, 'Lincoln Cathedral Choir, A.D. 1640 to 1700', *Lincoln and Nottingham Architectural Society*, 20 (1889), 47.
[14] *Cu* Ely, Dean and Chapter Records, 2/1/2 (Chapter Books, 1660–1729), 275.

'If no singing to an Organ' probably means 'unless the choir is singing a composed setting'—which would have been accompanied by the organ. Lowe continues:

Then the Priest reads the Prayers before the Epistle, the Quire answering *Amen*. When the Epistle is done and the Gospell named, the Quire sings *Glory be to thee, O Lord* as here set down.

The gospel would normally have been read by one of the minor canons (the 'gospeller') or senior clergyman present, the epistle by a lay clerk (the 'pistoler'). After the gospel 'the Priest (or whole Quire) say (or sing) the *Nicene Creed*. And after that the Priest reads the Prayer for *Christs Church Militant &c* and then goes on to the end of the morning service'.

Lowe's final sentence, like the last part of the service, is somewhat laconic. Clifford is even more so, merely adding 'After the Sermon, the last Anthem'. St Paul's was not alone in having this second anthem. Pepys noted that it was also the practice in the Chapel Royal, except in Lent: 'the chapel . . . being hung with black and no Anthemne sung after the sermon as at other times'.[15] In fact, as we shall see, it was the custom in some places for the congregation to sing a metrical psalm parochial fashion before the sermon (sometimes in the nave). Where this was not the case, however, it is unlikely the choir would have remained after the Creed, unless there was to be a celebration of Holy Communion at which the Sanctus and Gloria in excelsis were to be sung. These were not set regularly as part of a communion service; sometimes they survive among anthems rather than services.

Lacking a litany and communion (though on Sundays there was usually a sermon) the evening service was shorter, and this gave scope for longer and more elaborate music such as verse services and verse anthems.

COMMON TUNES AND THE BEGINNINGS OF ANGLICAN CHANT

Lowe, Clifford, and Playford included in their books a selection of unharmonized 'Common Tunes' to which the *Venite*, the proper psalms, and other canticles could be chanted.[16] Lowe gave two in 1661, one for weekdays, the other for Sundays, and in 1664 added others for specific days of the week, besides four more 'formerly in use for the Psalms' and one each for Ps. 136 and the Athanasian Creed. Clifford (1664) likewise gave thirteen, though they do not correspond with Lowe's, while Playford gave only seven (one for each day

---

[15] *The Diary of Samuel Pepys*, ed. R. C. Latham and W. Matthews, 11 vols. (London, 1970–83), iv. 69.

[16] Wilson, 'Anglican Chant', 27–34; see also Dearnley, 285–7; le Huray, 159–61.

in the week but not corresponding with either Lowe's or Clifford's). Most bear
a close resemblance to the old Sarum tones, especially their endings, which can
usually be matched, though the first half of a tone may not always correspond.[17]
Thus, Lowe's tune for Monday, Clifford's no. 1, and Playford's for Sunday is
the old Sarum tone 1; while Lowe's tune for Tuesday, Clifford's no. 6, and
Playford's for Monday (printed a third too high) seems to be a simplified version
of tone 3, or alternatively the first half of 2 or 7 with one of tone 3's endings
(see Ex. 2).

Both Clifford and Lowe state that although these tunes are written down in
measured notation 'yet they are not intended to signifie any *exact time*'
(Clifford's wording). Nevertheless, the longer note-values 'are to be sung slower
and more emphatically than the rest'. There is therefore some potential for
observing natural speech rhythm, or so one might think were it not for the
overstressing of some weak syllables in the examples overleaf. Table 1 shows the
correspondence between Lowe, Clifford, and Playford and their relationship to
the psalm tones (disregarding intonations).

Clifford, Lowe, and Playford each included some harmonized psalm tones in
four parts 'proper for Quires to Sing the *Psalms, Te deum, Benedictus* or *Jubilate*
to the *Organ*, or sometimes without it' (Playford). Those in Clifford and Lowe
are more or less clearly based on psalm-tone tenors, most obviously 'Christ
Church Tune', common to both and presumably the work of Edward Lowe,
the tenor of which is tone 1.iv (Ex. 3). Clifford has, in addition, a slightly
different setting of the same tenor with the title 'Mr. *Adrian Battens* Tune'.
Other harmonizations include 'Imperial Tune' (a simplified version of tone 8.
iv) in Clifford and Playford, and 'Canterbury Tune' (related to tone 5 or 8 but
without a differentiated ending). Lowe also has one 'For Boyes' which must
have sounded rather beautiful, using his Sunday tone in the lowest part. These
settings of psalm tones represent a practice that can be traced to before the Civil
War, if not further back.[18] Playford, however, marked a further development by
including not only 'Imperial' and 'Canterbury' (the latter with its psalm tone
now in the treble) but also 'six tunes . . . sung in His Majesties Chappel with the
Organ to the Psalms, Te Deum, &c Composed by Mr. *John Blow* and Mr.
William Turner . . .'. (Blow was responsible for one, no. 2 (in E minor), Turner
for the remainder.) These are not based on pre-existing tunes, but are freely
composed melodies harmonized in four parts, in which the first chord of each
phrase is used as a reciting-note. They were not written down in accordance
with the modern convention of presenting the rhythmic structure of the 'single'
chant—which is virtually what they are—but laid out under the first verse of the
Venite by way of example, as the Common Tunes had been.

[17] W. H. Frere, *The Use of Sarum: II. The Ordinal and Tonal* (Cambridge, 1901), pp. lxiv–lxxi.
[18] Le Huray, 158; see also Nicholas Temperley, *The Music of the English Parish Church* (Cambridge, 1979), i. 25; ii. no. 5.

Ex. 2. Common tunes and Sarum psalm tones

Lowe (1664) Monday

O come let us sing un-to the Lord: Let us hear-ti-ly re-joice in the strength of our Sal-va-ti-on.

Clifford (1664) No. 1

O come let us sing un-to the Lord: Let us hear-ti-ly re-joice, &c.

Playford (1674) Sunday

O come let us sing un-to the Lord: Let us hear-ti-ly re-joice in the strength, &c.

Sarum: Tone I,iv.

Di - xit do - mi - nus do - mi no me - o: se - de a dex - tris me - is.

Lowe (1664) Tuesday

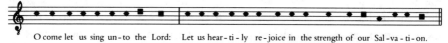

O come let us sing un-to the Lord: Let us hear-ti-ly re-joice in the strength of our Sal-va-ti-on.

Clifford (1664) No. 6

O come let us sing un-to the Lord: Let us hear-ti-ly re-joice, &c.

Playford (1674) Monday [printed a third higher]

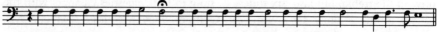

O come let us sing un-to the Lord: Let us hear-ti-ly re-joice in the strength, &c.

Sarum: Tone III,iii. (Frere, *Use of Sarum*, lxiv - lxxi)

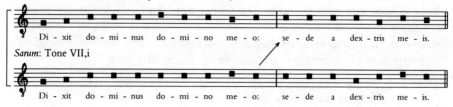

Di - xit do - mi - nus do - mi - no me - o: se - de a dex - tris me - is.

Sarum: Tone VII,i

Di - xit do - mi - nus do - mi - no me - o: se - de a dex - tris me - is.

Ex. 3. Christ Church tune in four parts (Clifford, *Divine Services,* 1664)

O come let us sing un - to the Lord: let us hear - ti - ly re - joice in the strength of our sal - va - ti - on.

As Playford implies, it was at the Chapel Royal that this method of chanting the psalms developed. By the early 1670s a sizeable repertory existed and soon spread to provincial centres. A manuscript (*Lbl* 17784) belonging to Dr John Butler, Precentor of St George's Chapel, Windsor, from 1670 contains twenty-one such chants, and this, or a common source, seems to have provided copies for Durham in 1674.[19] In all, the number of chants that can be assigned to the period before 1700 is not perhaps very great—Ruth Wilson has identified thirty or so that circulated quite widely, mostly composed by members of the Chapel Royal.[20] William Turner and Thomas Purcell (the composer's uncle) seem to have been most prolific, though other members of the Purcell family contributed, including Edward (Henry's elder brother) and Henry himself. Provincial composers were also active. Names such as 'Lincoln Tune' or 'Ely Tune' indicate the origins of particular chants that migrated from one cathedral to another, but local repertoires also existed; the 'Wells Tunes', for example, surviving in a manuscript from Wells (*Lcm* 673), include four chants by John Jackson, organist there from 1674 to 1688.

The most popular chants seem to have included those by Blow in E minor, Humfrey in C, and Turner in A (his favourite key). There are more by Turner than anyone else—sixteen alone in autograph at Christ Church, Oxford (MS 49), including one 'double' chant. Perhaps he should be regarded as the father of Anglican chant, though he was not the inventor. As a group his chants show above average harmonic interest. Some begin and end in different keys (a third above or below the tonic), and their enterprising modulations and chord juxtapositions bring colour to a form that was naturally and increasingly inclined to be pale.[21] Two printed by Playford in the 'Divine Service' section of his *Introduction to the Skill of Musick* (1674) are given in Example 4. The harmonic structure is particularly interesting; the first, beginning on B flat and ending in G minor with a D major / F major juxtaposition in the middle, the second with a half-way cadence on the supertonic major (dominant of the dominant).

[19] *DRc* MSS C 12, C 28; Wilson, 'Anglican Chant', 60.
[20] For a fuller treatment see Wilson, 'Anglican Chant', 58–66.
[21] Ibid. 72–6.

TABLE 1. *Correspondence between psalm tones and 'common tunes'* (reciting-notes are in italics; half verses are marked by colons)

Psalm tone	Lowe (1661)	Lowe (1664)	Clifford (1664)	Playford (1674)
1. iv *A* GA:*A* GFGA	Weekdays *A* GA:*A* GFGGA	Monday *D* CD:*D* CB♭CCD	1 *A* GA:*A* GFGGA	Sunday *A* GA:*A* GFGGA
2. i *F* GF:*F* ECD		Friday *C* D:*C* BGA	3 *F* G:*F* ECD	Wednesday G A: *G* F♯DE
3. iii *C* DCBC:*C* ACB		Tuesday *C* CD:*C* ACCB	6 *F* GF:*F* DFFE	Monday *F* GF:*F* DFFE[b]
4. vii *A* GAB [A]:*A* GABGE		Wednesday *G* FGA:*G* FAFFD	7 *F* B♭FG:*F* B♭GB♭B♭C	Thursday G F♯GA:*G* FAFFD
5. i *C* DC:*C* DBCA		Thursday *C* D:*C* DBCCA	8 *F* G:*F* GEFFD	Friday *A* GA:*A* FGAGGF
6 *A* GA:*A* FGAGF		'Other' 3 *E* DE:*E* CDEDDC	10 *A* GA:*A* FGAGGF	
7. i *D* FEDE:*D* EDCBA		'Other' 1 *D* FEDE:*D* EDCBA	0 (unnumbered) *D* FEDE:*D* EDCBA	Saturday G B♭AGA:*G* AGFED

8. iv
C DC:*C* BCAG

Peregrinus
A GB♭AGF:G DFED

Sundays
F GF:*F* DDC

'Other' 2
C BCD:*C* BCAAG

Ps. 136
A GGF:*A* GDDFED

Sunday
C DC:*C* AAG

Athanasian
G B♭AGA:G AGFFF

'Other' 4
C D:*C* ACDCC

Saturday
C DC:*C* BC

9
F EFG:*F* EFDDC

11 (Ps. 136)
E DCC:*E* DACBA

4
F GF:*F* DDC

12 (Athanasian)
G B♭AGA:G AGFFF

5
F G:*F* DFGFF

2
F EFG:*F* EF

Tuesday
A B♭GA:*A* FGED

---

[a] no ♮ in original
[b] printed 3rd too high
[c] F♯ in original

Ex. 4. William Turner, two chants (Playford, *Order of Performing the Divine Service,*
1674, nos. 1 and 5)

Mistakes have been tacitly corrected from *Lhl* 17784

As to the way the psalms were chanted, without the standardized seven-bar form, fitting the words to the music was a rather haphazard process. Roger North's strictures seem somehow familiar:

When performed decently, the organ presiding, the musick, tho' it chant most upon the key note, yet in vertue of the cadences which are artificiall, the harmony is exceeding good. But one may conceive how it might be much better . . . if the whole quire should pronounce the verse as well as the close in distinct counterpoint time, with respect to long and short syllables, and then come off in the cadence all exactly together. But [even] where the most deliberate chanting is, the pronunciation is at best a huddle unintelligible, as if all strove to have done first. And for this reason, where the organ is not used which keeps the quire upright, the chanting is scandalous, such a confused din as no one living not pre-instructed could guess what they were doing.[22]

There was, of course, no place in the cathedral service for congregational hymns, or even, strictly speaking, for metrical psalms. Hymns were beginning to be used in parish churches towards the end of the seventeenth century, but by and large congregational singing was confined to metrical psalms from the 'Old Version' of Sternhold and Hopkins (1562) or the 'New Version' of Tate and Brady (1696). Nevertheless, such collections as Henry Playford's *The Divine Companion* (1701, 1707, etc.) provide the source of some of the hymn tunes by Jeremiah Clarke and William Croft that are current today. Some cathedrals did,

[22] John Wilson (ed.), *Roger North on Music* (London, 1959), 269.

however, permit a psalm to be sung before and after the sermon, the choir moving into the nave where the sermon was preached in order to do so. Thus, at Chichester in 1695 it was ordered 'that the Singing Men and Choristers on Sundays, after Morning Prayers, when they go out of the Choir, do go into their seat in the body of the Church and joine in singing the Psalm before the Sermon, and continue there all the sermon time and till after the blessing pronounced'.[23] At Gloucester, in 1665, one of the lay clerks was paid an extra £2. 10s. for 'beginning the psalme before sermon',[24] while the same year at Lichfield, Bishop Hackett stipulated that the choir should sing a psalm rather than an anthem after the sermon, much to the annoyance of those who feared a return to Puritan ways: 'how nauseous church music and common prayer will again become if Hopkins and Sternhold's rhythms may jostle out our anthems, and a long pulpit-prayer seduce the devotions of the common people.'[25]

[23] R. H. Codrington *et al.*, *Statutes and Constitutions of the Cathedral Church of Chichester* (Chichester, 1804), 41.

[24] Suzanne Eward, *No Fine but a Glass of Wine: Cathedral Life at Gloucester in Stuart Times* (Salisbury, 1985), 136, 214.

[25] Ann J. Kettle and D. A. Johnson, 'The Cathedral of Lichfield', in *A History of the County of Stafford*, iii, ed. M. W. Greenslade (London, 1970), 181.

2

Services and Anthems

Detailed consideration of the dozens of service settings and hundreds of anthems (well over 1,500) that survive from the period 1660–1714 is neither possible nor appropriate here. Many will be dealt with later in the book when it comes to examining the work of individual composers in the context of their institutions. The present purpose is to paint the general picture and provide a perspective against which their work can be viewed.[1] Two basic techniques were involved in writing both services and anthems—'full' and 'verse'. The former used mainly the full choir, the latter used mainly solo voices in 'verses' for solo, duet, trio, or larger ensemble. Needless to say, things were not quite so straightforward as that, but it will be clearer if service settings are treated separately from anthems.

THE SERVICE

Services were written in varying degrees of completeness. A 'whole service' included settings of the morning and evening canticles, and the communion service—enough for a complete performance of the daily liturgy. The usual morning canticles were the *Te Deum* and *Benedictus* or *Jubilate* (the *Benedicite* as an alternative to the *Te Deum* was rarer); the usual evening ones were the *Magnificat* and *Nunc dimittis* (though the *Cantate Domino* and *Deus misereatur* were fairly common). A communion service included at least settings of the responses to the Commandments (often called Kyrie in musical sources) and the Creed. For some reason the *Venite* was never set in the Restoration period as it had been earlier in the century, but was chanted like a psalm. Settings of the Gloria in excelsis were also quite rare, while the Sanctus, if sung, usually seems to have served as a kind of introit to the communion service. Many services were not 'whole', however, and comprised only one or two of the subsets, designated morning service, communion service, or evening service as appropriate.

Restoration composers themselves recognized two categories of service: the 'full service' (not to be confused with 'whole service') and the 'verse service'. As its name suggests, the former employed the full choir, singing either as a whole

---

[1] Ian Spink, 'Church Music II: From 1660', in *Music in Britain: The Seventeenth Century*, ed. Ian Spink (Blackwell History of Music in Britain, iii; Oxford, 1992), 97–137, provides such a survey. See also Dearnley, 107–15; Long, 227–9.

or antiphonally between the precentor's side (cantoris) and the dean's side (decani) of the choir—liturgical north and south respectively. Homophonic writing predominated, often to the exclusion of any counterpoint other than perhaps in a doxology or Amen. Brief imitative points might occasionally be dovetailed into chordal passages, likewise a kind of 'staggered' homophony in which one part was rhythmically out of step with the other three.

This kind of service was sometimes called a 'short service'—an appropriate term since brevity and economy were its principal characteristics. It was simple, dignified, often dull: well suited to choirs of modest attainment. For the most part the words were clearly declaimed according to the reformers' principle of 'for every syllable a note',[2] though frequently syncopated to allow for cadential suspensions and to maintain urgency of movement. The short service had been prevalent before the Civil War, and is represented at its best by those of Byrd and Orlando Gibbons. It continued after the Restoration, formally little changed but with its harmonic language updated, until by the early eighteenth century it had became insipidly diatonic. William Child's Service in F, written for Charles II's coronation in 1661, is a typical example—homophonic throughout, with only alternations of cantoris and decani offering relief from continual full texture, and the occasional touch of harmonic colour. The opening of the Creed gives an idea of the utilitarian nature of his style, which, despite a tuneful treble part, tends to be fussy in harmony and word-setting compared with Gibbons's Short Service in the same key (Ex. 5).

The 'verse service' typically alternated full and verse sections; indeed, 'full with verse' by analogy with that type of anthem would be a better description of the form. Being longer and more elaborate than the short service, it was suited to festal occasions and good choirs. Both the full and verse writing were likely to be homophonic, but counterpoint might be a feature of either, bringing welcome variety to the texture (and increase in length). The full sections established the basic framework while the verse sections functioned as episodes, usually with reduced voice numbers (often a trio, TrTrC or CTB), though occasionally enlarged to six or more parts. Such contrasts were textural and colouristic; key and metre changes were other elements that contributed to the richness and variety of the effect.

As an example of the 'full with verses' type of service we may cite Child's E flat Service (Arnold, i)—the key itself is evidence that composers were beginning to recognize signatures of three or more sharps or flats. It makes virtually no use of imitative counterpoint, but exploits textural contrast to maintain interest and achieve a restrained dramatic effect. Composers were keenly aware of such possibilities, particularly in the *Te Deum* and Creed, which offered scope for varied treatment. Thus, in the *Te Deum* of Child's service, different orders

---

[2] Oliver Strunk, *Source Readings in Music History* (London, 1952), 351.

Ex. 5(*a*) William Child, Creed in F (*Cfm* 117)
 (*b*) Orlando Gibbons, Creed in F (*Cfm* 117)

of angels, represented by high voice-groupings, sing from opposite sides of the choir, coming together at the words 'Holy, holy, holy' (full). Likewise 'the glorious company of the apostles' (TrTrC cantoris), 'the goodly fellowship of the prophets' (CTB decani) and 'the noble army of martyrs' (CTB cantoris) unite at the words 'the holy church throughout the world' (full). Later passages dealing with the birth, death, resurrection, ascension, and second coming of Jesus are depicted in like manner; so too the contrast between the ethereal 'saints in glory' (TrTrC decani) and the lower-pitched Church Militant (CTB cantoris). Changes in vocal registration such as this are the most important expressive resource that Child had at his disposal, and in conjunction with colourful harmonic juxtapositions between the end of one section and the beginning of another (typically a third apart), it could create mood, and even changes of mood. Indeed, change from minor to major, or vice versa, was often enough. It was a technique known and practised by the madrigalists, though, by and large, madrigalisms are not a feature of Child's style, despite the fact that 'the sharpness of death' in the *Te Deum* never fails to be signalled by the introduction of a sharp in the music. (This was a convention that persisted a long time, and Purcell even contrived to give all three of his voices sharps at this point in his B flat Service.)

The musical merits of Child's in many ways restricted idiom can be demonstrated with reference to the *Magnificat* in the same service. The rhythms and accents of the words are sensitively handled, and it is difficult to imagine any lute-song composer improving the melody in a passage like Example 6, or, indeed, the harmony. Music such as this is dignified, expressive, and simple, and performs its liturgical function almost perfectly by keeping a balance between what it does itself and what it leaves the words to do.

Free-standing evening services 'for verses' were less inclined to treat the verses episodically. Such services were more analogous to the verse anthem, in which solos, duets, trios, etc., succeeded each other in a fragmented patchwork for which the support of an organ was essential. Frequently they began with a short organ introduction leading into the opening verse. Techniques included open-textured imitative ensemble writing, as well as declamatory or tuneful idioms. The differences between these verse services and those of Gibbons, Weelkes, and Tomkins earlier in the century are striking. In place of solo voices conceived polyphonically within a continuously unfolding texture there is now a heterogeneous soloistic treatment that depended for cohesion on a basso continuo. Why such treatment tended to be reserved for the evening canticles is uncertain. Perhaps the fact that the *Magnificat* and *Nunc dimittis* are more personal and reflective in character than the *Te Deum* and *Jubilate* had something to do with it; perhaps there was more time in the evening to take a leisurely approach. (Verse anthems were also favoured at evening prayer.)

The opening of the *Nunc dimittis* from Child's Evening Service in B flat 'for verses' (Ex. 7) shows the kind of thing that is found—very much an English adaptation of the 'concertato' style of Italian church music and a good example of the extent to which things had changed from the polyphonic verse style of the earlier part of the century.

Ex. 6. William Child, *Magnificat* in E♭ (*Cfm* 117)

In *Cfm* 117 this service is written in C with 'high clefs' (C3, C4, C5, F5), but is described as being 'in E la mi Flat'.

As might be guessed, any survey of the development of the service from 1660 to 1714 must begin with William Child, organist of the Chapel Royal and of St George's, Windsor, at the Restoration, and the most prolific composer of services in the period. He was 90 or so when he died in 1697, and his earliest work probably dates from the 1630s, if not before. At least four of his seventeen services had been written before the Civil War, but as will be seen when we consider his work in greater detail, the evidence of style and sources suggests that many, perhaps most of the others, were written after 1660, when there was an urgent need for new services in an up-to-date style that took account of the deficiencies of cathedral choirs. Of the older generation that began to compose again at the Restoration, Benjamin Rogers of Eton (later of Magdalen College, Oxford) and Albertus Bryne of St Paul's (later of Westminster Abbey) wrote services in the 'short' style. Rogers's 'Sharp Service' in D (Boyce, i) is a well-known example, modelled on Child's pre-war service of the same name, but

Ex. 7. William Child, *Nunc Dimittis* in B♭ (*Cfm* 117)

devoid of counterpoint. Though otherwise 'full', it has verses in the middle of the Creed (as has Child's). The change from major to minor at the words 'And was crucified also for us' is a simple, obvious, and effective expressive device that few composers at the time seem to have exploited. The use of a 'head-motif' linking the beginning of the *Te Deum*, *Magnificat*, and *Nunc dimittis* (and modified in the *Jublilate* and *Kyrie*) is worth noting as a unifying gambit sometimes encountered in canticles belonging to the same service. The use of a common Gloria Patri between movements, though not found in this service, is another fairly frequent cyclic device.

Younger composers who made important contributions to the service repertoire up to about 1680—that is to say, before Purcell—included Michael Wise, Pelham Humfrey, and John Blow. All were Children of the Chapel Royal in the early years of the Restoration, and must have been heartily sick of singing Child in this or that key. Additionally, Wise would have had plenty of exposure to Child at Windsor, where he worked after leaving the Chapel

Royal and before going on to Salisbury. His D minor Service is one of the best 'full with verse' services written under Child's influence, and is characterized by sound technique and solid musicality. By contrast, Humfrey's Service in E minor is rather crabbed and awkward; he was clearly happier writing anthems.

The 1670s, however, were dominated by John Blow, whose three important and widely disseminated services in A major (Boyce, i), G major (Boyce, i), and E minor (Boyce, iii) are the representative masterpieces of their type and time. Their scale is impressive, they do not eschew counterpoint, and all exploit the potential of 'full' and 'verse' contrast. The verse sections especially provide much harmonic richness and textural colour. The G major Service makes considerable use of canon (as had Child's 'Sharp Service'), and the E minor Service is interesting as an example of an increasingly common type, being almost entirely in triple time. Byrd's Third Service ('Mr Birds 3 minoms') had provided a precedent, but no doubt it owed more to the king's fondness for the 'step tripla', and the fact that it was a quick and relatively painless way of setting (and sitting through) lengthy texts, such as the *Benedicite* which this service contains.

The earliest of Henry Aldrich's four services also dates from the 1670s. Canon of Christ Church, Oxford, from 1681 and dean from 1689, his talents embraced mathematics and architecture as well as music. The G major Service (Boyce, i) is a 'short service', the F major 'full with verse', the E minor (Arnold, iii) in triple time throughout, and the A major (Arnold, i) alternates triple-time verses with full sections in common time. Thus they provide examples of the main species of service composition at the time.

Although Purcell's services (*PS* 23) do not compare in importance with his anthems, the B flat Service, dating from 1681–2, represents a peak in the development of the form. It is unusual in providing settings of all the morning and evening canticles, including the alternatives, as well as the communion service. He seems to have had in mind a work that would satisfy all possible liturgical occasions. In general, but particularly with respect to the use of canon, Purcell's inspiration may have been Blow's G major Service, which likewise seems to have been aimed at liturgical comprehensiveness.

Other composers who made significant contributions to the service repertoire in the latter part of the century were William Turner of the Chapel Royal, Henry Hall of Hereford, and James Hawkins of Ely. Among four by Turner, there is an impressive large-scale setting in A. Hall composed several services, but the pairing of his *Te Deum* in E flat with a *Jubilate* by William Hine of Gloucester (Arnold, iii) took his work to almost every English cathedral in the eighteenth century. No such fame attached to Hawkins. As many as seventeen services are attributed to him, including two 'chanting services'—a type seemingly of his own invention in which full sections sung to a four-part 'Anglican' chant alternate with freely composed verses. The only composer to take up this idea during the period was William Norris of Lincoln.

Hawkins was an indefatigable copyist of his own and other men's work, and supplied Thomas Tudway with some of the material for his great six-volume collection of English church music covering the years from the Reformation to the death of Queen Anne (*Harl.* 7337–42). The last two volumes of this work mainly contain music from Queen Anne's reign, and include services by (among others) John Goldwin, Child's successor at Windsor, Benjamin Lamb of Eton, Vaughan Richardson of Winchester, Anthony Walkeley of Salisbury, Richard Goodson of Christ Church, Oxford, Charles King of St Paul's, and Tudway himself. Most of these are of the 'short' or 'full with verse' type, following the pattern established in the early years of the Restoration, but in a more modern and, from a Purcellian point of view, less interesting harmonic style.

The Evening Service in B flat by which Tudway chose to represent himself in his collection reflects the final stage of development in the service 'for verses'. The text is set as a series of distinct movements, each characterized by key, metre, melodic style, and vocal colour, and contrasting with its neighbours in these respects. There is thus an analogy with the multiple-movement structure of the cantata. The *Magnificat*, for example, begins with a flamboyant counter-tenor solo, interspersed with echoes on the organ. Subsequent verses, mostly set as CTB trios, move from B flat though G minor, D minor, F major, D minor again, and back to B flat at the end. A bass solo is assigned to the verse 'He hath put down the mighty from their seat'; this, and the florid treatment generally, is typical of the new approach that Purcell himself had taken in his anthems, and had been adopted in the verse service. Marks of expression like 'Slow' (at 'the lowliness of his handmaiden'), 'Drag' (at 'the humble and meek'), and 'Soft' (at 'For mine eyes have seen thy salvation') are symptomatic of a conception and manner of performance that was becoming increasingly expressive, if not senti-mental. Benjamin Lamb's Evening Service in E minor is a similar case, with the 'Trumpet Stop' providing an appropriate accompaniment to a bass solo at the words 'with trumpet also and shawms' in the *Cantate Domino*. The vogue for operatic songs with trumpet obbligato in the 1690s was thus carried over into church music.

On the whole, however, a sense of propriety (and practicality) encouraged moderation in setting the liturgy; the anthem, after all, was the musical show-piece and elaborate solo verses, trios, and symphonies for organ in the canticles would have made services unbearably long. There was, indeed, a reaction against theatricality in church music in the early eighteenth century, and Blow's four late services, modelled on the 'short' services of a century earlier, are a reflection of this move in favour of simple dignity. Unfortunately, too often and especially in the years ahead, simple dignity degenerated into simple dullness—as the services of Charles King exemplify.

THE ANTHEM

For the first time in the Anglican liturgy, the 1662 Prayer Book made official provision for the singing of an anthem 'In Quires and Places where they sing'. The position chosen—after the third collect of morning and evening prayer—was no doubt traditional, for anthems had obviously been sung in cathedrals and collegiate churches since the Reformation. The Elizabethan injunctions of 1559, while counselling 'a modest distinct song, so used in all parts of the common prayers in the Church, that the same may be as plainly understood, as if it were read without singing', did, however, make a gesture towards those who wanted something more artistic:

Nevertheless, for the comforting of such that delight in music, it may be permitted that in the beginning, or in the end of common prayers, either at morning or evening, there may be sung an Hymn, or such like song, to the praise of Almighty God, in the best sort of melody and music that may be conveniently devised, having respect that the sentence of the Hymn may be understood and perceived.[3]

As to the 'sentence' of these anthems, well over a half of those written between 1549 and 1644 were taken from the Psalms (58%), a tenth were prayers or seasonal collects (10%), and another tenth metrical texts (11%).[4] With Restoration composers the proportion of psalm settings became a good deal higher, though in the early years collects and metrical texts continued to be set. Later, settings of collects dwindled considerably, while metrical settings diverged into what, for present purposes, amounted to a distinct form—the 'hymn' or sacred song aimed at domestic use, and typified by Purcell's settings of poems by John Patrick, William Fuller, and others.

The Restoration anthem may therefore be defined as a musical setting of a sacred text drawn from Scripture (most often from the Psalms) or from the Book of Common Prayer, and intended for performance in the cathedral service. (Anthems for parish choirs began to make their appearance around the end of the century.) Whole psalms might be set, a selection of continuous (or discontinuous) verses, even (especially later) composite texts drawn from a number of psalms. As with the service, two basic techniques were employed: 'full' and 'verse', each with subdivisions. The full anthem was either for full choir throughout, or 'full with verse', in which case one or more verse sections were introduced to lighten the texture in the middle and to provide variety. Four voices was the norm, mixing polyphony and homophony, sometimes alternating cantoris and decani antiphonally. The texture was complete in itself, though in practice the organ always accompanied. An accompaniment was,

---

[3] Le Huray, 33.

[4] John Morehen, 'The English Anthem Text, 1549–1660', *Journal of the Royal Musical Association*, 117 (1992), 64.

however, essential in the verse anthem since it consisted of a varied series of solos, duets, trios, or larger ensembles needing continuo support. Brief choruses might be introduced between verses, and were inevitable at the end, bringing many anthems to a close with rousing Hallelujahs. Some anthems written for the Chapel Royal, especially during the reign of Charles II, were furnished with additional 'sinfonies' and 'ritornellos' for strings—hence the term 'symphony anthems'—played before and between the verses, which were sometimes also accompanied by obbligato instruments. A further type of verse anthem, known as the 'solo anthem' and more characteristic of the later years of our period, consisted merely of a string of solo movements for a single voice ending with a chorus.

It is hardly surprising that in the early Restoration period the full anthem should follow closely the pre-war model. If anything there was greater emphasis on the melodic aspect of the top part, a more pronounced rhythmic squareness, and a growing sense of key governing the harmony. Despite current ideas of 'just note and accent', the underlay of the text often appears to have been subservient to musical considerations. Cathedral choirs were still building up their strength in the early 1660s, and this created a market for technically undemanding full anthems, free of contrapuntal elaboration, which Child, Rogers, and many local composers set out to satisfy. Child's *O Lord, grant the king a long life* (Boyce, ii) provides a good example—the witless Hallelujah apart. It is homophonic throughout, the phrase and harmonic structure well balanced, the only moment of disruption occurring at the words 'clothe them with shame'. On the whole one has to admire the rhythmic setting of the words, and, in the absence of counterpoint, acknowledge some harmonic interest. *O pray for the peace of Jerusalem* (Arnold, i) seems to have most of these virtues and fewer vices. It is 'full with verse'; the full sections judiciously mix chordal writing, staggered homophony ('they shall prosper'), and simple imitation ('I will wish them prosperity'), while the TrTrC verses offer contrast of sonority and characteristic chord juxtapositions—notably the move from G major to B major between the end of the opening section and the beginning of the succeeding verse (Ex. 8). The concluding Gloria shows Child at his best, with all the melodic, rhythmic, and harmonic elements nicely integrated. The simultaneous false relation and 6–5 progression at the approach to the final cadence provides a striking reminder of the continuity of the English tradition.[5]

As with the service, so with the full anthem; these short pieces by Child represent a point of departure for Restoration composers. His influence is plain to see in the work of Benjamin Rogers; for example, in *Teach me, O Lord, the way of thy statutes* (Boyce, ii). If anything the commitment to key is stronger and the rhythm even more square-cut; nevertheless its effectiveness cannot be

[5] Quoted Spink, 'Church Music', 111.

Ex. 8. William Child, *O pray for the peace of Jerusalem* (Bing-Gostling Partbooks)

denied, nor its obvious attraction to the 'politer' ears of the eighteenth century. In terms of general character and structure, the full anthem underwent little change during the remainder of the seventeenth century, though composers like Blow and Purcell expanded its technical and expressive range considerably. Like their contemporaries, however, they wrote many more verse anthems than full anthems—for reasons that hardly need elaborate explanation. For all that they were church musicians, their outlook was essentially 'modernist', and, except for solemn occasions, they preferred the musical variety and expressive potential of the verse anthem to the old-fashioned and, by the 1680s, somewhat dowdy virtues of the full anthem.

Towards the end of the century, however, the full anthem began to enjoy something of a revival. The move in 1689 towards 'Protestant Comprehension' and the threat to cathedral music, though defeated, may have forced composers into a recognition that there were meretricious elements in the verse anthem, and that the ancient 'solemn and grave style' was preferable. Henry Aldrich, a member of the commission that debated the future of cathedral music, gave practical support to the view not only through his own anthems in this style, such as *Out of the deep* (Boyce, ii), but in his adaptations of polyphonic works by Palestrina and others to English words. Blow, in turn, took up the old style again in *My God, my God, look upon me* (Boyce, ii) dating from 1697, and in more than a dozen anthems written in the last ten years of his life. He was old enough to have a real feeling for the style, and this showed in the freedom with which he handled it, especially in the rhythmic independence of the voices. For those like William Croft who came after him, such unselfconsciousness was impossible. In their hands the style became stiff and academic, although the opening sections of Croft's *Hear my prayer, O Lord* and *O Lord, rebuke me not* show that the older tradition still exerted an influence.[6] Both are 'full with verse' and this was the standard approach to the form in the early eighteenth century.

Nevertheless, the verse anthem remained in favour. Composers preferred it because it gave greater scope for contemporary techniques, which were essentially soloistic and expressive. And, for all its secularity, the words were likely at least to be intelligible. The verse anthem of the earlier part of the century had used solo voices within a polyphonic context, condensing various supporting contrapuntal strands into an organ accompaniment. With the advent of the continuo in a piece like Walter Porter's *O praise the Lord* (dating from before 1632),[7] a more monodic style became possible, involving declamatory text delivery and ornamentation. The presence of a continuo also permitted a looser form of imitative writing. Further developments along these lines took place during the commonwealth period in metrical psalm settings by Henry and

[6] Both in Croft's *Musica Sacra*, 2 vols. (London, 1724).
[7] *Treasury of English Church Music*, ed. G. H. Knight and W. L. Reed, 5 vols. (London, 1965), ii. 232–47.

William Lawes (*Choice Psalmes*, 1648), John Wilson (*Psalterium Carolinum*, 1657), and Walter Porter (*Mottets*, 1657). A similar collection, though non-metrical, had come out in 1639, composed by William Child: *Psalmes of III Voyces . . . with a Continuall Base . . . newly composed after the Italian way*, reprinted in 1650 and again as *Choise Musick* in 1656. Matthew Locke, too, made some similar settings. At the Restoration he began to develop the form further, together with Henry Cooke, Christopher Gibbons, Edward Lowe, and William Tucker. Locke and Cooke were especially involved in writing symphony anthems for the Chapel Royal; Gibbons, Lowe, and Tucker, though members of the chapel, cultivated the verse anthem with continuo accompaniment. Gibbons's *How long wilt thou forget me, O Lord* may be taken as a representative example of the work of these men (Ex. 9). Verses for two trebles and the simple declamatory style in both solo and ensemble are typical. It begins with a written-out organ introduction leading into a verse for two trebles, rounded off by a brief four-part chorus. The chorus begins homophonically, echoing material from the verse, breaking into imitation a few bars before the cadence. A second verse and chorus repeats the pattern and completes the work.

Such were the modest beginnings of the Restoration verse anthem, and the starting-point for the work of Michael Wise. Unlike some of his fellow choristers in the Chapel Royal—who included Humfrey, Turner, and Blow—he showed little interest in the most modern trends. Perhaps this was because his move to Windsor and then to Salisbury took him to places where the latest fashions had yet to be accepted. Compared with the work of his more famous contemporaries, his anthems are modest in scale and restrained in effect, but they circulated widely and must have been influential. The basic pattern is of alternating verse and chorus sections. Short introductory passages for organ are fairly common in opening verses, and the choruses which separate the verses are simply and effectively written. He favours the use of trebles in his verses—far from avoiding the use of boys' voices at this stage, as has sometimes been suggested, composers seem to have revelled in it—and the bass voice is sometimes used to dramatic effect. Most verses consist of dialogue-textured ensembles such as we have just seen, with natural and expressive text underlay, rarely given to 'affective' exaggeration.

Beyond the Chapel Royal almost every cathedral had one or two composers who cultivated this style of anthem. Of those with a numerically significant output born before 1660 the following should be mentioned: Daniel Henstridge of Canterbury, Richard Hosier of Dublin, Thomas Tudway of King's College, Cambridge, John Cutts and John Foster of Durham, John Ferrabosco of Ely, Henry Hall of Hereford, Richard Ayleward of Norwich, Henry Aldrich and William King, respectively of Christ Church and New College, Oxford, John Jackson of Wells, John Reading and Daniel Roseingrave of Winchester, and Richard Davis and John Badger of Worcester. Their work will be considered in

Ex. 9. Christopher Gibbons, *How long wilt thou forget me* (*Cfm* 117)

(1) written out organ part stops here.

connection with the cathedrals where they worked—or in the case of those who moved from place to place, under whichever seems most appropriate. Similarly, younger composers born between 1660 and 1685 and working in the provinces include James Heseltine of York, James Hawkins of Ely, Benjamin Lamb and John Walter of Eton, George Holmes and William Norris of Lincoln, Daniel Purcell of Magdalen College, Oxford, Anthony Walkeley of Salisbury, Vaughan Richardson and John Bishop of Winchester, and John Goldwin of Windsor.

Without much change in the general formal principles of the verse anthem, the last quarter of the seventeenth century saw some stylistic development nevertheless. The role of the chorus diminished and often survived only as a concluding section. Verses became longer and much more highly differentiated from each other, frequently achieving the status of independent movements. Most anthems included at least one more or less florid declamatory solo for bass or countertenor, while imitative duets and trios, and tuneful triple-time sections were common. In fact, triple time tended to predominate from the 1670s onwards. The trio combination of countertenor, tenor, and bass (or counter-tenor and tenor duet with continuo) was preferred, and stylistic similarities with the trio sonata became more pronounced. It was rare, however, for individual movements not to be in the tonic key, apart from switches to tonic minor from tonic major (or vice versa) in at least one movement. In the early years of the eighteenth century key schemes opened up to include excursions to tonalities related to both tonic major and tonic minor. Thus A minor and E flat major could cohabit through the former's relationship to C major and the latter's relationship to C minor. By this time, too, ground basses and ostinatos had been added to the range of forms which might be adopted in the verses, and many solos began with a 'motto' opening—a kind of false start in which instrumental introduction and the opening phrase of the voice part were repeated before being continued—so characteristic of the Italian aria. Italian influences were not strong enough to oust the typical Purcellian florid declamatory movement in favour of *recitativo secco*, however.

As an example of this later stage in the development of the verse anthem we may cite Tudway's *Thou, O Lord, hast heard our desires* (Arnold, ii), written in 1705. It so happens that nearly all of it is in triple time, but even so, the movements are clearly distinguished by contrasts of key and texture (Ex. 10). The first (*a*) is a trio in C minor, the second (*b*) a tenor solo in G minor, the third (*c*) a trio in C major changing to minor (*d*) and back again for a brief four-part chorus (*e*). The second half of the anthem begins with four bars of quasi-recitative in A minor for the countertenor (*f*) directly leading into an affective C minor 'aria'. The final chorus (*g*) brings the work to a conventionally jubilant close, with full and verse contrasts and brief ritornellos for organ imitating a pair of trumpets at the words 'let her crown flourish'. It is a work which needs no apology; the opening verse begins in a solemn and arresting manner, and the change from major to minor at the words 'Yea, and abundance of peace so long as the moon endures' in the third movement produces a striking change of atmosphere. Both the solo verses appeal by virtue of numerous Purcellian echos, some by no means unworthy of their original.

The solo anthem is a characteristic phenomenon of these later years, though isolated examples can be found throughout the period. In places where vocal resources were limited there were clearly reasons for using the best singer available throughout an anthem and consigning the rest to the chorus. Where the best singer was a virtuoso there was still more reason for doing so. Thus the great bass John Gostling was in all probability the singer for whom Purcell wrote the solo anthem *The Lord is king, the earth may be glad* in 1688 (PS 32) and Blow *The Lord, even the most mighty God* about the same time. A later star of the Chapel Royal was the countertenor Richard Elford, and it was for him that John Weldon wrote the anthems in *Divine Harmony* (1716). For the most part they consist of a varied sequence of solo movements ending with a chorus, and

Ex. 10. Thomas Tudway, *Thou, O Lord, hast heard our desires* (*Harl.* 7341)

(1) ₵ original time signature.

[C] In her time _____ shall the right - -

[T]

[B] In her time, in her time _____ shall the

- - - eous flour - ish

right - - eous flour - ish,

Verse a 3 voc.

[C]

[T]

(d) Yea, and a - bun - dance of ___ peace, of peace, so long, so long as the moon

[B]

6 6

Cho.

Her do - min - ion shall be al - so from the one sea to the oth - er,

can be appropriately described as 'cantata anthems' by analogy with the Italian cantata. Jeremiah Clarke's *How long wilt thou forget me, O Lord* (Boyce, ii) is another example.[8]

Undoubtedly Italian influences were about, making their effect felt in instrumental and vocal music. Purcell himself had succumbed, willingly, up to a point. But it was his own example and influence that was dominant in the twenty years after his death. No one could match the force of his particular brand of recitative, and attempts to do so frequently resulted in bathos. But triple-time lyrical movements were another matter, and in this respect things had moved on. Certainly there are too many such movements in the work of Clarke and Weldon, for example, but though the worst examples can seem rather empty, the best have a spaciousness that makes the equivalent sections in Purcell's anthems appear a trifle cramped. One might say that the 'air' has become the 'aria', and no doubt Italian influences were the cause even though the detail is not particularly Italianate.

It is the symphony anthem as practised by Locke, Humfrey, Blow, and Purcell that typifies Restoration church music for us today. In terms of quantity, of course, such works form only a small part of the repertoire, but it is undeniable that some of the most engaging and inspiring music of the period was of this type. Without doubt its finest examples show that English music in the second half of the seventeenth century was on a par with anything on the Continent. Unlike the forms of church music we have been considering—the service and other types of anthem—its development was more or less confined to the Chapel Royal (a few occasional pieces apart), and will be discussed in that context. Charles II took great pride in his chapel; he knew what he liked and encourged his musicians to supply it. Neither of his successors, for different reasons, was so enthusiastic, and it was not until the accession of Queen Anne in 1702 that some sense of pride in its tradition and purpose was restored. The symphony anthems of Clarke and Croft dating from the early years of the eighteenth century were, however, mostly written for services of national thanksgiving celebrating the Duke of Marlborough's victories in the Low Countries during the War of the Spanish Succession. Their usual venue was St Paul's Cathedral, newly completed and ideally suited to the mood of triumphalism that permeated the church music of Anne's reign.

In this connection some mention should be made of ceremonial settings of the *Te Deum* and *Jubilate* accompanied by trumpets and strings written during the last twenty years of our period. All are in the trumpet key of D major, and the earliest was Purcell's of 1694—written (according to Tudway) for the grand opening of St Paul's though this was still three years away. Its first performance was at the 1694 St Cecilia service, and it was followed in subse-

[8] Ibid., iii. 114–21.

quent years by settings by Blow (1695) and Turner (1696). In the same tradition, though not for the same purpose, came William Croft's *Te Deum* and *Jubilate* written to celebrate the victory at Malplaquet in 1709, and Handel's to mark the Peace of Utrecht in 1713. With the re-establishment of the Festival of the Sons of the Clergy at St Paul's from 1697, Purcell's *Te Deum* became a regular feature of the occasion until 1713 when Handel's 'Utrecht' *Te Deum* was given.[9] Thereafter, these two settings alternated until Maurice Greene came on the scene in the 1720s.

There was no vacuum in English church music after the deaths of Blow and Purcell, nor was there anything approaching the abject capitulation to Italian music that occurred in the secular field. Emerging as Croft's natural successor, Greene was heir to a tradition that was still strong, and which gave, even to Handel in his church music, more than it received.

[9] Ernest H. Pearce, *The Sons of the Clergy: Some Records of Two Hundred and Seventy Five Years* (2nd edn., London, 1928), 234.

3

Choirs and Places

Today's cathedral choirs are composed of lay clerks (sometimes called lay vicars) and choristers, but this is just the latest stage in a development that leads from the Middle Ages, via the upheavals of the sixteenth and seventeenth centuries, to the reforms of the 1840 Cathedrals Act, which set cathedral chapters and choirs on a new footing. The choirs of the great medieval 'secular' (as opposed to 'monastic') cathedrals were composed of vicars choral and choristers, but with the growth of polyphony in the later Middle Ages professional lay singers were introduced, so that by the time of the Reformation, three-tier structures of priests, laymen, and boys had come into being.[1] Many monastic cathedrals, too, had professional choirs by this time to provide music for non-conventual services.[2]

At the Reformation, the secular cathedrals of England and Wales were left constitutionally untouched, but monastic cathedrals were dissolved and re-established with new statutes. At the same time, the opportunity was taken to create five new sees, so that by Elizabeth's reign there were twenty-six in all: thirteen cathedrals of 'old foundation' comprising Chichester, Exeter, Hereford, Lichfield, Lincoln, London (St Paul's), Salisbury, Wells, and York, with Bangor, Llandaff, St Asaph, and St David's in Wales; and thirteen of 'new foundation'— Canterbury, Carlisle, Durham, Ely, Norwich, Rochester, Winchester, and Worcester, with Bristol, Chester, Gloucester, Oxford (Christ Church), and Peterborough raised to cathedral status. All these establishments were bound to perform the daily liturgy of the Church of England in choir, and their statutes made provision for a body of singers—still priests, laymen, and boys—to do so. Certain collegiate churches and chapels were also under the same obligation, notably the Chapel Royal and the Royal Peculiars of Westminster Abbey and St George's Chapel, Windsor; likewise, according to their statutes, some of the colleges of Oxford and Cambridge Universities, and the collegiate foundations of Winchester and Eton. Anomalously, a few parish churches had charters which also provided for a collegiate body to perform the choral service: Manchester, Ripon, Southwell, and Wimborne.

Cathedrals and collegiate churches, then, were multi-tiered establishments. At the highest level were the senior clergy comprising the Dean and Chapter

---

[1] Frank Ll. Harrison, *Music in Medieval Britain* (London, 1958), 2–4.
[2] Ibid. 185–93.

(canons in a cathedral, fellows in a college), and below them a rank of inferior clergy to perform their choir duties: vicars in cathedrals of the old foundation, minor (or 'petty') canons in those founded or refounded at the Reformation, and chaplains in colleges. Beneath them were the lay singers (lay vicars, clerks, or 'singing men'), and finally, the choristers. Such was the general arrangement, though details varied here and there. The major distinction was between those 'old' cathedrals whose continuity was not disrupted at the Reformation, and those ex-monastic foundations that were re-established following their dissolution in 1538–9. The latter acquired new statutes tailored to the new situation; in essence, simplified versions of the typical set-up as it survived in cathedrals of the old foundation. Thus, the three-tier organization of the choir was retained, but rationalized into priests, lay clerks, and boys in equal or roughly equal numbers. At the same time, the precentor (who in secular cathedrals had been a dignitary second only to the dean) became one of the minor clergy with responsibility for the cathedral music, and the organist became statutory. Nevertheless, to understand the nature of this rationalization and its significance, we need first to look at the role of the vicars choral in cathedrals of the old foundation.

VICARS CHORAL

Vicars choral were, as the name implies, the choir deputies of the cathedral canons. At first they were paid and kept individually by the canon whose duty they performed, but at a later date they were variously formed into corporations or colleges governed by their own statutes and confirmed by Royal Charter, living together in their own close, court, or cloister, and keeping 'commons' (eating communally) in their own hall.[3] These lesser clergy mirrored at a lower level the composition of the cathedral chapter, dignitaries such as the precentor, chancellor, and treasurer having their counterparts among the inferior clergy. Thus the precentor (or 'chanter', as he was called in the vernacular) had his succentor or 'subchanter' with responsibility for the music; the chancellor had his vice-chancellor with responsibility for administrative and disciplinary matters; and the treasurer had his subtreasurer or sacrist with responsibility for the plate, vestments, and so forth. At St Paul's, where minor canons corresponded to vicars choral, even the subdean was vicarial. Title and function might differ from place to place, but the same general principles applied, give or take a few anomalies.

[3] For the general picture see Mackenzie E. C. Walcott, *Cathedralia: A Constitutional History of Cathedrals in the Western Church* (London, 1865); John Jebb, *The Choral Service of the United Church of England and Ireland* (London, 1843); Kathleen Edwards, *The English Secular Cathedrals in the Middle Ages* (Manchester, 1949).

In theory there was a vicar for every canon, whether resident or not. They were correspondingly numerous, but in the later Middle Ages their numbers declined; for example, there were fifty-two vicars at Salisbury in the thirteenth century, but only thirty-one two centuries later.[4] At the same time their role was changing. Originally it had been to sing the plainsong of the mass and office: they had not been intended for, and, as constituted, were not suited for performing polyphonic music. As polyphony developed in the fifteenth century, lay singers were enlisted to provide some professional stiffening, either by incorporating them among the vicars (after taking minor orders) or as a separate body of lay clerks. With the abandoning of minor orders at the Reformation, some colleges of vicars, such as those at Exeter, Lichfield, Lincoln, and Wells, became mixed communities of priests and laymen, while at Chichester, Hereford, Salisbury, and York the laymen were excluded and became non-collegiate stipendiaries. In some places there persisted an intermediate grade between the choristers and vicars, known as 'secondaries' at Exeter, 'altarists' at Wells, and 'poor clerks' at Lincoln—a kind of limbo (if not purgatory) where choirboys with broken voices remained until they were ready to fill a vacancy among the vicars.

The income of a vicar was derived from several sources. Some of it, the largest portion, came from the rents and fines which the vicars received from the property they owned corporately. Some of it represented payments such as stall-wages, due to them from their canons, allowances for their diet, a share of mulcts and admission fees extracted from fellow vicars, and augmentations (simply to increase their salaries) out of the common fund of the cathedral. Other fees were received for performing the office of master of the choristers, organist, subchanter, vice-chancellor, or sacrist, or for services over and above their vicarial duties, such as reading early morning prayers, preaching sermons, etc. It is difficult to say what all this added up to, especially since vicars' accounts were kept separately from the cathedral treasurer's accounts, and rarely so methodically. At Lichfield in 1718 priest vicars were still receiving £14. 3s. 3d. as their share of the rents, the lay vicars £2 less. In addition, each received about £7. 17s. for their commons, stall-money, etc., making their basic income about £22 or £20 respectively.[5] These were below average figures, since the Lichfield vicars were not well off, but premiums payable for granting renewals of their leases (fines) considerably enhanced this amount, and may have doubled it in some years. Moreover, it was common for priest vicars to hold additional livings in nearby churches simultaneously with their cathedral posts, thus further increasing their income. Obviously, such a course was closed to lay vicars, but secular callings such as tradesman, shopkeeper, etc., were open to them.

[4] Harrison, *Music in Medieval Britain*, 8–9.
[5] Kettle and Johnson, 'The Cathedral of Lichfield', 185.

Whether or not they were in holy orders (the conferment of which might verge on a mere formality), vicars choral were by no means immune from the seven deadly sins, as records indicate over and over again. Although they continued to hold their estates and manage their affairs under their elected officers, jealously guarding their rights against encroachment from whatever quarter (particularly deans and chapters), their discipline and common life deteriorated. Married vicars naturally lived out, and many vicars sublet their houses. Meals in hall were abandoned at Exeter at the Restoration though maintained at Hereford until 1875, and generally the observance of their own rules, not to mention their attendance at services, became increasingly lax as the eighteenth century progressed.

To understand the way a corporation of vicars functioned in the latter part of the seventeenth century, we shall examine the situation at Lichfield, which may be regarded as typical, though differing in numerous details from elsewhere.[6] Both the cathedral statutes and the vicars' own domestic statutes tell us what should have been; reading between the lines we may get some idea of how it actually was. Chapter 8 of the cathedral statutes, which relates to the vicars choral, was probably framed in response to earlier articles of inquiry put to them by the dean, William Paul, in 1663 (see App. B).[7] Unfortunately, the replies have disappeared, but the implications of the questions help to fill out the picture with regard to the vicars' corporate affairs and their choir duties. For example, in asking about the subchanter's responsibilities, his involvement with the choir school is mentioned. Evidently he is answerable to the precentor for governing the 'musick School & children of the Quire' and for advising the master of the choristers. Early morning prayers are alluded to, though apparently not yet instituted. Lateness in choir is defined as entering 'after the first Gloria Patri', early departure as leaving 'before the blessinge', while observances regarding kneeling and turning towards the altar are specified in some detail. Senior vicars might wear a black tippet over their surplices. Apparently it was expected that the organist would play a voluntary before the first lesson, but of suitable gravity—'for ye know how he hath bin accused that hath bin in that office'. The questions clearly indicate the kind of conduct that was expected of the vicars: good behaviour in the choir, promptness and no absenteeism, regular partaking of the sacrament, respect for the canons, no bribery in electing new vicars. They were to be careful about the female company they kept, and selling ale in the close was frowned on.

[6] For accounts of vicars elsewhere see Philip Barrett, *The College of Vicars Choral at Hereford Cathedral* (Hereford, 1980); J. F. Chanter, *The Custos and College of Vicars Choral of the Choir of the Cathedral Church of St Peter, Exeter* (Exeter, 1933); Maddison, 'Lincoln Cathedral Choir'; W. D. Peckham, 'The Vicars Choral of Chichester Cathedral', *Sussex Archaeological Collections*, 78 (1937), 126–59; J. H. Srawley, *The Origin and Growth of Cathedral Foundations as Illustrated by the Cathedral Church of Lincoln* (Lincoln, 1965).

[7] Kettle and Johnson, 178–80.

When the statutes were finally promulgated in 1694, chapter 8 laid down that 'it is the Chief or Sole Office of the Vicars to attend the Celebrating the Divine worship, to apply themselves with diligence to the service of the Choire & to do their utmost in those parts of it which are appointed them in their places by the Precentor, or Subchanter' (App. C). The subchanter, in church as well as in hall, was the senior vicar choral. The rest took precedence from the canons whom they served. It was the subchanter's job to choose the services and anthems to be sung and, each Saturday by morning prayer, to draw up the duty roster for the following week. He was to appoint one of the priest vicars to officiate at all public services during the week, should the canon in residence be absent, and another to read the epistle at the communion service. The first lesson at morning and evening prayer was to be read by one of the lay vicars, while two others were assigned to chanting the litany as far as the Lord's Prayer. At the installation of a canon the subchanter received from him 6*s.* 8*d.* and a further 1*s.* 6*d.* for certifying the same.

Compared with the fees due to the sacrist (the fourth vicar choral) this was rather modest, for the latter performed all weddings, christenings, and burials in the cathedral and pocketed the fees. On the other hand, he was involved in some expenses. Not only did he have to provide the bread and wine for communion, coal for heating, and candles for lighting, he also had to see that the bells were kept in good order and rung at the proper times, that the furniture and ornaments were cleaned and repaired, the doors locked and unlocked, the church inside and the graveyard outside swept, etc. In this he was assisted by the subsacrist, to whom he paid £2. 8*s.* a year. The organist received £4 over and above his other emoluments as a lay vicar, with 6*s.* 8*d.* for the organ-blower. In those parts of the service which were not accompanied by the organ he was to sing in the choir in whatever stall was his by virtue of his canon's place among the canons.

All vicars were entitled to three days off each month, which must not include Sundays and holy days. The organist was always to provide a deputy, and there were never to be more than two vicars away on each side of the choir. Absence without leave, unless through sickness, was fined 1*s.* and attendance was to be reported to the weekly chapter meeting. A vicar coming into the choir after the psalms had begun, or leaving before prayers were finished ('unless he goes out to ease nature & comes in again') was to be counted absent. During the service they were to behave with decorum, bowing before the altar—and then to the bishop or dean if present—on entry, and wearing a surplice unless they had just arrived from out of town, or were about to depart. They were to look after their buildings in the close and not grant leases without the permission of the Dean and Chapter. They were each to receive commons of 3*d.* a day, and a free burial place in the cathedral churchyard. No vicar could be deprived of his stall except by a majority of the general chapter or, at least, the unanimous decision of the dean and all the residentiaries. To be so deposed he must have done something 'very ill' or committed the same fault three times, after being warned the first time and punished the second.

When it came to their own self-government, the vicars were bound by a set of 'Statutes of the Subchanter & Vicars of the Cathedral Church of Lichfeild' confirmed by the bishop, also in 1694 (App. D). First, the statutes set out the oath of loyalty to the subchanter and the rest of the community that all vicars were required to swear, and stipulated a fee of 20s. to be paid before any vicar could share in the common goods and profits. Then followed rules enjoining respectful behaviour to the subchanter and fellow vicars, the need for discretion regarding private matters, and avoidance of disharmony within the community. Slander and backbiting were forbidden, as were the carrying of weapons, threatening behaviour, and assault, against which the heaviest fines were to be levied. Among other misdemeanours were peeping and prying, litigiousness, gaming, keeping greyhounds and hunting dogs, and consorting with suspect women in the precincts of the close. Further statutes were concerned with the management of their property. They were to appoint a bailiff to collect and distribute their income, render proper accounts for the same, and safeguard their leases by depositing them in the muniments room. Finally, provision was made for a general meeting of all vicars to be held quarterly, at which their statutes were to be read aloud so that no one might be ignorant of them, Likewise, a copy was to be hung up in hall, where it could be read by everyone.

So much for the vicars of Lichfield. Terminology and practice differed from place to place, but the same general principles were common to all corporations of vicars, and distinguished their mode of life from the corresponding category of choirmen in the 'new' cathedrals—the petty canons.

MINOR CANONS AND LAY CLERKS

The term minor or 'petty' canon was already used in pre-Reformation times at St Paul's cathedral (also at St Patrick's, Dublin, and St George's, Windsor) to indicate a body of minor clergy forming part of the choir, additional and superior to the vicars choral. But the changed role of music in the reformed liturgy—in particular the disuse of plainsong other than psalm tones—pointed to the need for a different balance between the clerical and lay element. Ordained ministers were still required, but there was a need to increase the number of professional singers if the musical part was to be properly performed. In general, the formula arrived at—equal or roughly equal numbers of priests, lay clerks, and choristers—reflected and regularized the structure existing at that time in secular cathedrals, but the numbers of each were defined by statute. Thus there were six of each at Bristol and Gloucester, eight at Ely, Oxford, and Peterborough, and ten at Worcester. Elsewhere there was some inequality between the groups: 8–8–6 at Norwich, 8–4–6 at Carlisle, 6–6–8 at Chester and Rochester, 12–10–10 at Durham, and 12–12–10 at Canterbury, Winchester, and Westminster Abbey.[8]

The statutes of these 'new' cathedrals laid down the constitution of their choirs in some detail, to the extent that at Norwich the sixteen minor canons and lay clerks were to comprise five or six basses, five tenors, and five or six countertenors.[9] Separate headings dealt with the duties of minor canons, clerks, choristers, and the various officers. Among the minor canons, the precentor or 'chanter' was senior—no longer a cathedral dignitary but, like the subchanter in a cathedral of the old foundation, responsible for the music. Also drawn from the minor canons were the sacrist and gospeller, the latter, together with the epistoler, becoming increasingly vestigial in function as the seventeenth century progressed. As deacon and subdeacon respectively their pre-Reformation role in celebrating high mass continued still at Norwich, where, according to the Elizabethan statutes, the former was to 'read the gospel at every Communion within the cathedral church . . . as oft as it is to be sung or said', as well as to perform parochial duties for those living within the cathedral precinct. The epistoler was to read the epistle at every communion, to 'sing or say the Litany, so oft as it is to be sung or said', and read early morning prayers in the cathedral daily throughout the year. Other officers included the master of the choristers (one of the choir and either a minor canon or a lay clerk), charged with training the choristers and advising the precentor on musical matters. He might, or might not, also serve as organist.

Minor canons were normally expected to be in priest's orders and were thus the equivalent of priest vicars in cathedrals of the old foundation. Unlike vicars choral, however, they were not members of a self-governing corporation (except at St Paul's), and did not lead a collegiate life. They held no property from which to draw rents, but instead received a statutory stipend from the cathedral revenues. This varied from place to place, but, like vicars choral who were priests, they often held benefices in the town or nearby country. At Durham in 1668–9 the minor canons were paid £20 or £30 a year, depending on seniority, while at Norwich in 1685 they received only £10. Augmentations were frequently funded by keeping places vacant and dividing between them the stipend thus saved. They received extra for performing the duties of precentor, sacrist, gospeller, 'pistoler', or master of the choristers.

To fill in the detail of this general picture, the Restoration statutes of Ely cathedral may be referred to (App. E). Most cathedrals of the new foundation

---

[8] Le Huray, 14.

[9] Andrew Cornall, 'The Practice of Music at Norwich Cathedral, *c*.1558–1649' (M. Mus. diss., University of East Anglia, 1976), 156. For a translation of the Jacobean statutes see 152–61, from which the following information is derived. For the Elizabethan statutes see 139–45.

were still governed by statutes dating from the reign of Henry VIII, but some
had been revised more recently: those for Norwich, for example, in 1608,
Canterbury and Winchester in 1637 and 1638 respectively. In general these
revisions took some account of changed situations in cathedrals since the
Reformation with regard to the duties of certain officers, the balance between
clerical and lay members of the choir, and their remuneration, but for the most
part they followed the same lines as those they replaced. As was usual, the 1666
Ely statutes began by summarizing the establishment: one dean, eight canons,
five minor canons (the Henrician statutes had established eight), a scripture
reader, and four chaplains to look after Holy Trinity (the Lady Chapel of the
Cathedral) and St Mary's Church in the town, as well as Chettisham and
Stuntney just outside. There was to be a deacon (epistoler) and eight lay clerks,
a master of the choristers, an organist, and eight choristers. Also belonging to the
foundation were a master and an assistant master for the cathedral school, and
twenty-four boys 'to be taught grammar'.

Minor canons were to be priests; they and the lay clerks were to be chosen
by the dean, or in his absence by the vice-dean and chapter, and, so far as
possible, were to be well-educated, of good report, decent speech, and skilled
in singing—'a thing which we wish to be established by the judgement of those
in the same Church who are well versed in the Art of Music'. In their oath they
pledged observance of the statutes and deference, obedience and reverence to
the Dean and Chapter. Continual residence was obligatory, and three months'
notice was required before anyone could leave the choir. Unlike some other
cathedrals, no 'days off' in the month were specified, and official permission was
required for choirmen to be away for a day or more. Absence from services was
punishable by fine of a penny in the morning and a halfpenny in the evening.
The penalty for lateness (entering the choir after the end of the first psalm) was
a farthing. Petty offences were punishable by the dean, who could expel minor
canons and clerks for more serious breaches of discipline. Minor canons were
prohibited from enjoying other ecclesiastical benefices, but in practice they seem
to have shared the 'chaplaincies' of Holy Trinity, St Mary, Chettisham, and
Stuntney between them, the statutes being somewhat ambiguous on this point.

From among the minor canons the precentor and sacrist were to be chosen
by the dean. The former was to be of mature years and more distinguished than
his fellows. He was expected to ensure decorum in the choir and give a lead
with his voice. All the minor canons and clerks were to obey him 'so far as
concerns the business of the Choir'. The choice of music lay with him and he
was responsible for looking after the music books. He was to maintain a record
of attendance, not only of those in the choir but also ('without malice') of the
dean and canons, submitting it fortnightly to the Dean and Chapter. As to
stipends, the minor canons each received £15 a year, the lay clerks £10, the

organist £20, the master of the choristers £10, and the choristers £4 each. The precentor received a further 40 shillings by statute over and above his stipend as a minor canon, similarly the sacrist £6 and the epistoler £8. In addition, the treasurer's accounts make clear that a further £30 a year was payable to whoever held St Mary's and Holy Trinity, and £20 for Chettisham and Stuntney. The schoolmaster also seems to have counted as one of the minor canons, as did his assistant; their pay was £18 and £10 respectively.

From the Restoration onwards the musical performance of cathedral choirs was left more and more to laymen. Priest vicars and minor canons might, of course, be as skilful musicians as any layman, but the fact that many held benefices in addition to their cathedral posts necessitated their absence from the choir, especially on Sunday, and meant that lay clerks provided the backbone of the choir. Yet as the value of their stipends (fixed in many cases at the Reformation) declined, so did their standards, and many were forced to rely on what they could earn as artisans, tradesmen, and shopkeepers. As this happened the social homogeneity of the choir broke up, though less so in cathedrals of the old foundation where priest and lay vicars shared a common income and to some extent a communal life. Thus minor canons increasingly saw themselves as gentlemen amateurs, while the clerks, who should have been professionals, descended into amateurism of another kind.

As usual, Thomas Mace is eloquent on the subject.[10] He identifies two reasons why choirs were so poor in his day: first 'the *Paucity* or *small number* of *Clarks* belonging to *each Quire*', where 'there is but allotted *One Man to a Part*', and their further depletion through absence; second, 'the *Disability* or *Insufficiency* of *most of Those Clarks*'. He calls for more endowments to maintain and improve such choirs, and points out that whereas stipends 'not exceeding *eight, ten* or *twelve pounds a year*' may have been ample originally, they were now after 150 years scarcely '*One quarter* so much as may *sufficiently*, or *comfortably maintain such Officers*'—especially if they were to '*Sing chearfully unto God, and Heartily Rejoyce*'. How could anything better be expected from men on such wages? Indeed, they would starve were it not for the fact that they were forced 'to *Work* and *Labour* (otherwise) for Their necessary *Livelihoods*; some in *one Calling*, and some in *another*, viz. in the *Barbers Trade*, the *Shoe-makers Trade*, the *Taylors Trade*, the *Smiths Trade*, and divers other (some) more *Inferiour Trades* or *Professions*, (God knows).'

Now I say, *These Things* considered how certainly *True they* are, first in reference to the *Clarks Pitifull-poor-Wages*, and likewise to the general *Dead-heartedness*, or *Zeal-benumb'd-Frozen-Affections* in *These our Times*, towards the *Incouragement of Such Things*; how can it be imagined, that such *Clarks* should be *Fit and Able Performers* in *That Duty*, which

[10] Thomas Mace, *Musick's Monument* (London, 1676), 23–7.

necessarily depends upon *Education, Breeding,* and *Skill* in *That Quality of Musick,* which is both a *Costly, Carefull,* and a *Laborious-Attainment,* not at all acquirable (in its *Excellency*) by any *Inferior-low-capacitated Men.*

Despite his partiality, Mace may be allowed to have proved his point. But he is not finished yet, and goes on to tell an entertaining story by way of illustration that can hardly be omitted here.

I have known a *Reverend Dean of a Quire* (a very *notable, smart-spirited Gentleman*) *Egregiously Baffled* by one of the present *Clerks;* who to my knowledge was more *Ignorant* in the *Art of Song,* then a *Boy* might be thought to be, who had *Learn'd* to *Sing* but only *One month;* yet could make a shift to Sing most of the *Common Services* and *Anthems,* by long use and habit, (with the *Rest*) pritty well, (as *Birds* in *Cages* use to *whistle* their *Old Notes.*)

Yet I say, *This Dean* being known by *This Bold-Confident-Dunce-Clark* (who you must know took himself to be a kind of *Pot-Wit*) to have *No Skill* at all in the *Art of Musick; The Dean,* I say, upon a *Time* (after *Prayers*) coming out and following *This Great-Jolly-Boon-Fellow,* and as he was pulling off his *Surplice,* began to *Rebuke him sharply,* (and indeed very *justly*) for a *Gross Absurdity* committed by *Him* in *That very Service Time,* by reason of his *Great-Dunstical-Insufficiency* in *Singing* of an *Anthem* alone; in *which* he was so *Notoriously and Ridiculously Out,* as caused *All,* or most of the *Young People* then present, to burst out into *Laughter,* to the *Great Blemish* of the *Church-Service,* and the *Dishonour* of God, (at *That Time,* and in *That Place.*)

But *Thus* it fell out, (in short) viz. that after the *Angry Dean* had *Ruffled* him soundly in very *smart Language,* so that he thought he had given him *Shame enough* for his *Insufficiency* and *Duncery;*

How think ye *This Blade* came off?

Why, *most Notably,* and in such a manner as made all the standers by *Wonder* and *Admire Him;* venting himself in *These very Words,* (for I my self was both an Eye and Ear witness) with a most *stern Angry Countenance,* and a *vehement Rattling Voice,* even so as he made the *Church Ring* withall, saying, *Sir-r-r-r* (shaking his head) I'd ha' you know I Sing after the *Rate of so much a Year,* (naming his *Wages*), and except ye *Mend my Wages, I am resolv'd Never to sing Better whilst I live.*

Hark ye *Here, Gentlemen!* was there *ever* a more *Nicking* piece of *shrewd Wit,* so suddenly shew'd upon the *Occasion,* than *This was?* Yea, of *more Notable* and *Effectual* to the *Purpose?* as you shall hear, by the *Sequel.*

For the *Cholerick Dean* was so *fully* and *sufficiently Answer'd,* that turning immediately away from him, without *one word* more, He Hasted out of the *Church,* but *Never* after found the least *Fault* with *This Jolly Brave Clark;* who was *Hugg'd* more then sufficiently by *all the Rest* of the *Puny-Poor-Fellow-Clarks,* for *This* his *Heroick Vindication* and *Wit.*

Mace's 'Bold–Confident–Dunce–Clark' may not have been typical, but he was not exceptional. Indiscipline and defiant behaviour, drunkenness, licentiousness, swearing, and gaming were commonly reported in Chapter minutes, while incompetent individuals were repeatedly censured, yet suffered to continue, because it was impossible to get better at the price.

CHORISTERS AND THEIR MASTERS

From figures already given it will have been observed that the balance of voices between men and boys in the typical 8–8–8 choir was two to one in favour of the men. Even with absenteeism among the petty canons, and to a lesser extent among the clerks, we may be fairly sure that the modern top-heavy sound was then less evident in cathedral choirs.

The number of choristers varied from four in some of the smaller foundations, like St Asaph or Christ Church, Manchester, to as many as sixteen in certain Oxford and Cambridge chapels, where boys actually did outnumber the men. The Chapel Royal had twelve and Westminster Abbey ten—as did such well-endowed choirs as Canterbury, Durham, and Worcester among the 'new' foundations. Among the 'old' foundations, St Paul's and Exeter had ten, the remainder eight or six. These numbers were generally kept up throughout the period, for such places were not hard to fill—mainly because of the useful education the choristers received and the relief to parents that a chorister's pay (though small) provided, or his maintenance away from home.

In charge of the choristers was the master of the choristers, often called *Informator choristarum*. Cathedral statutes of the new foundation usually define him as 'one of good character and upright life, skilled in singing and in organ-playing, who would diligently apply himself to teaching the boys, to playing the organ at proper times, and to singing the divine offices'.[11] He was not always the organist, however. His responsibilities were extensive. According to the Jacobean statutes of Norwich, he was to board and lodge the choristers, and give them a basic education.

We also wish that this man should look after the health of the choristers and we wish that they live in whatever place he dwells, and we also entrust to his faith and industry their teaching and training in letters and in Scripture. Also we wish that in this place they should be accommodated at table and daily life. . . . If this man shall be found negligent or lazy in his teaching duties, after the third warning he must be removed from the office.[12]

For this he was paid £20 as organist, £8 as master, over and above whatever he received for his place in the choir (£10 if he was a minor canon, £8 if he was a lay clerk), and an allowance of £10 for each of the four choristers in his care.[13]

The Norwich statutes are typical in that they stipulate 'boys of tender age, and with tuneful voices, skilled in singing, who shall serve, minister, and sing in the choir and have instruction and training in playing various musical instru-

---

[11] Such was the wording at Durham; see Shaw, p. xix.
[12] Cornall, 'The Practice of Music', 157.
[13] Noel Boston, *The Musical History of Norwich Cathedral* (Norwich, 1963), 47–8, 54–5.

ments'.[14] The latter was an important aspect of their education and standard provision. A year's probation was normal, while parents or guardians may usually have been required to indenture them to the master, like apprentices. Indeed, from 1662 the Windsor choristers on admittance were 'bound apprentise for 7 yeares to some of the Church for the use of the Church or some other good security given to the Colledge by the parents that they will not take them from the service of the Colledge in 7 yeares'.[15] At Winchester, parents or guardians entered into a bond whereby the boy

shall dayly be at the singing Schoole of Mr Daniel Rosingrave master of the Choristers of the sd. Church at such houres & times as he shall appoint & not depart thence without the Leave of his sd. Master & shall from time to time observe the directions & instructions of his sayd Master until he shall be by the sd Dean & Chapter thence forth acquitted & discharged Then this Obligacion to be voyd & of none effect els to remain in full force & Virtue.[16]

Most boys were 8 or 9 years old when they entered. The average length of service was five or six years, but seven or eight was not uncommon. Sometimes they boarded with the master, or they might live with parents, relatives, or friends in the town. In the former case the master received an allowance for their maintenance, in the latter, the boys received a stipend of a few pounds a year. At Ely they received £4, at Lichfield and York the same, but it could be lower or higher; for example, at Salisbury the pay of the senior boys was increased from £8 to £12 in 1713.[17] These sums could be augmented by various extras such as 'spur money'—fines from challenging men wearing spurs in the cathedral.[18]

When they boarded with the master, he was responsible for their physical well-being in addition to their vocal and instrumental training, and was frequently entrusted with their religious and elementary education too. Once they were adequately grounded, the boys would enter the grammar school frequently attached to cathedrals of the old foundation or actually part of the establishment in most of the new ones. Their successors today are the King's Schools at Canterbury, Chester, Ely, etc.—though the link with the choir has not always been maintained. At Ely the choristers were eligible to be educated among the twenty-four poor boys 'of natural aptitude (so far as possible) for learning' and could be admitted to the school before the statutory age of 9. The objective was to acquire 'a reasonable knowledge of Latin Grammar . . . to speak Latin and write Greek: for this the space of six years will be allowed, or if the Dean and

[14] Cornall, 'The Practice of Music', 157.

[15] Neville Wridgway, *The Choristers of St George's Chapel, Windsor Castle* (Windsor, 1980), 46–7; Shelagh Bond, *The Chapter Acts of the Dean and Canons of Windsor, 1432, 1523–1672* (Windsor, 1966), 234. [16] Bond dated 28 Apr. 1690 in Chapter Library.

[17] Dora H. Robertson, *Sarum Close: A History of the Life and Education of the Cathedral Choristers for 700 Years* (London, 1938), 201, 228–9. [18] Wridgway, *Choristers*, 52.

Headmaster think fit, at the most seven and no more' (App. E). At the same time they were expected to attend the singing school 'three afternoons, at least, in every week'.[19] At Westminster, where the link between choir and school was broken in the 1840s, once the choristers could 'write moderately well and have learned the eight parts of speech' they attended the school for two hours each day.[20] At Lincoln, the choristers lived in their own house under a steward (one of the vicars choral). They were expected to attend the grammar school as well as practice in the music school daily—an arrangement which did not seem to be working smoothly in 1676 when it was observed that 'the Choristers are very remiss and negligent in resorting to the Free Schoole at the usuall times'. Consequently, they were admonished

to frequent the [early morning] Chappell Prayers and immediately after they are ended to get their breakfasts, and then to goe forthwith down to the Free Schoole, and there to stay and continue, untill nine o'clock, and then to come up to the Singing Schoole, and there to abide untill the belle ring in toe prayers. And that in the Afternoone they in like manner goe down to the Free Schoole at one a clock, and continue there so long as that they may bee at Evening Prayers.[21]

(Evening prayers were held at 3 p.m. in the winter, 4 p.m. in the summer.) The steward, John Blundeville, was warned 'to take care that their breakfast bee prepared against they return from Chappell Prayers'. From replies to visitation articles of 1718 it seems, however, that a somewhat different regime was in operation:

there is a Steward of ye Choristers by whome they are well ordered and provided for, they are instructed in vocal and Instrumental musick, and taught to write and read, and their Master is ordered to instruct them in ye principles of Religion, and when their voices fail, they are usually put out to trades or otherwise provided for by ye Dean and Chapter.[22]

Procuring an apprenticeship on behalf of a boy whose voice had 'failed' and who had done good service was fairly standard practice, as was the presentation of money or a suit of clothes on leaving the choir. At Winchester in 1667, £8 a year was set apart 'for the better encouragement of our present Choristers and Parents of such Youths . . . for the binding them out to be Apprentices'.[23] A parting gift of £5 seems to have been usual at Windsor after 1685,[24] while at the

[19] *Cu* Ely Dean and Chapter Records, EDC 2/1/2, dated 14 June 1698.
[20] [Maria Hackett], *A Brief Account of Cathedral and Collegiate Schools, with an Abstract of their Statutes and Endowments* (London, 1824), 54–5; Edward Pine, *The Westminster Abbey Singers* (London, [1953]), 74–6.
[21] Maddison, 'Lincoln Cathedral Choir', 46–7.
[22] Christopher Wordsworth, *Statutes of Lincoln Cathedral*, 3 vols. (Cambridge, 1897), iii. 659.
[23] John Crook, *A History of the Pilgrim's School and Earlier Winchester Choir Schools* (Chichester, 1981), 11.
[24] Wridgway, *Choristers*, 46.

Chapel Royal at the turn of the century it was £20 and a suit of clothes.[25] For promising lads, however, there was the possibility of continuing until a place fell vacant among the clerks. Indeed, many spent the rest of their lives in the choir, moving up via altarist or secondary (if such grades existed in their church) to clerk or lay vicar, and beyond—at least in the earlier years when 'class' and gentlemanly breeding were less important—to priest vicar or minor canon.

ORGANISTS

The post of organist was not identified in medieval cathedral statutes since there was really no need for one. There may, indeed, have been organs in such cathedrals, increasingly so as time went on, but they were played either by one of the choir or by someone specially hired to do so who was no part of the endowed establishment.[26] Thus, a separate post of organist was slow to establish itself and seems to have been regarded as somewhat inferior in that the master was likely to be a priest and the organist a layman. New statutes, such as those at Lichfield in 1694 (App. C), do specify an organist, however. He was to be 'a lay Vicar in our Cathedral Church, that in those parts of the Services which are onely to be sung he may joyn with the rest, & in those where the organ is to be used he may play upon that . . . for salary the Organist shall yearly receive from the Dean & Chapter of Residentiarys four pound' (in addition to his income as a vicar).

As we have already seen, when cathedrals of the 'new foundation' were given their statutes by Henry VIII, the form of words used implied that the master of the choristers was also to be the organist. Subsequent revisions do not generally alter the emphasis, though it is sometimes envisaged that the two jobs could be separate. The 1638 Winchester statutes, for example, use the standard phraseology in defining the role of the master of the choristers, but continue:

howbeit, forasmuch as it may sometimes come to pass that one of the minor Canons or Clerks is better fitted than the Organist, and sometimes that the Organist is better fitted than the minor Canons or Clerks to train the Choristers, we will that the Dean and Chapter, or in the Dean's absence the Vice-Dean and Chapter, have power of choosing either the Organist or one of the minor [Canons or] Clerks for this duty according to merit.[27]

In practice, this was what usually happened elsewhere. Sometimes both jobs were done by one man, sometimes they were separated, though the tendency was for them to be combined. In this way cathedrals could attract musicians

---

[25] e.g. Ashbee, ii. 79, 80, etc.

[26] Harrison, *Music in Medieval Britain*, 202–18; see also Shaw pp. xviii–xxiv.

[27] Arthur W. Goodman and William H. Hutton, *The Statutes Governing the Cathedral Church of Winchester Given by King Charles I* (Oxford, 1925), 54–5.

with something approaching the required all-round skills by offering a reasonable salary based on a place in the choir and additional payments for being organist and master of the choristers. Thus Daniel Henstridge at Canterbury in 1705 officially received £18 a year as lay clerk, £14 as master of the choristers, and £22 as organist,[28] while at Ely the same year James Hawkins was paid £30 as organist and £10 as *informator choristarum*—to which, somehow, the cook's stipend of £6 was added as a sinecure.[29] (In the accounts Hawkins, as organist, always appears among the minor canons, his salary being the equivalent of two of their places; as *informator* he appears among the lay clerks, his salary being the equivalent of one of their places, though additional to the statutory eight.)

The reason for the organist's increased status since Reformation statutes had been drawn up is not hard to fathom. The century following had seen the instrument becoming larger and acquiring a more defined role in accompanying the choir and playing voluntaries. It demanded greater expertise, and this was even more the case during the Restoration period, especially after 1680 when Father Smith and Renatus Harris were building their instruments. Surprising as it may now seem, many organists were extremely young when first appointed—often still in their teens. Precocious youngsters, who had displayed talent under the tutelage of the previous organist, and were experienced in the ways of a particular place, no sooner dropped out of the chorister lists than they re-appeared as organists. In this respect, Henry Purcell, organist of Westminster Abbey at 20 (though not a chorister there), is by no means exceptional. Less happily, there were others who were barely competent, as we shall see when we turn to individual institutions.

As to what the organist was required to do, the little detailed evidence that exists seems to point to a fairly standard practice.[30] At Westminster, for example, he was supposed to 'come into the quire at the beginning of Prayers in his surplice and betake himself to his stall till toward the end of the Psalms except on festival days when the answers [responses] are to be performed with the organ; then to go up the stairs leading from the quire and perform his duty'.[31] At Lichfield, this entailed playing a voluntary 'grave and apt' before the first lesson—this seems to have been general—and presumably remaining at the organ to accompany the rest of the service (App. B). Usually it seems that part-music sung by the choir was accompanied by the organ, whereas unison chant was unaccompanied. According to Clifford's *Divine Services* (1663/4) a second voluntary was played between the end of the litany and the beginning of the communion service at St Paul's Cathedral. A concluding voluntary was probably

---

[28] *CA* Treasurer's Accounts, 1705.

[29] *Cu* EDC 3/1/4, 1705.

[30] Geoffrey Cox, *Organ Music in Restoration England*, 2 vols. (London and New York, 1989), i. 1–16.

[31] Perkins, *Organs and Bells of Westminster Abbey*, 14.

also general, for one of the misdemeanors of Stephen Jefferies at Gloucester was, at the end of morning prayer on 8 February 1689—a thanksgiving service 'for making the Prince of Orange [King William III] the instrument of the king-doms delivery from Popery and arbitrary government' no less—to 'play over upon the Organ a Comon Ballad in the hearing of fiftene hundred or two thousand people to the great scandall of Religion, prophanation of the Church, and greivous offence of all good Christians'. For good measure he did the same again after evening prayer 'insomuch that the young gentlewomen invited one another to dance, the strangers cryed it were better that the Organs were pull'd downe then that they should be so used'.[32] In view of the date and occasion, it is probable that the ballad was *Lillibulero*.

This sort of thing lends colour to what we know of these men. In varying degreees, seventeenth-century cathedral organists seem to have been a trouble-some bunch, frequently quarrelsome and insubordinate, or simply lazy and incompetent, sometimes apparently pathogically defiant of authority and morally depraved. Of course, archives usually give only the Dean and Chapter's side of an argument; blameless behaviour was likely to go unmentioned, and, in any case, there must often have been aggravating circumstances. Nevertheless, such men as Thomas Mudd and Daniel Roseingrave seem to have caused trouble wherever they went. Sometimes the authorities were content to endure an unruly organist, as with Stephen Jefferies above, at other times they were driven to dismissal—as happened with Nicholas Wootton at Canterbury, Paul Heath at Bristol, Edmund White at Chester, and Richard Henman at Exeter. We need not, here, look at the details of such cases, but we can easily imagine their causes: frustration at poor pay, difficult colleagues, and officious authority within a narrow community all helped to exacerbate natural prickliness and, in some cases, mental instability.

---

[32] Eward, *No Fine but a Glass of Wine*, 186; Shaw, 122, dates the incident a year earlier.

4

Organs and Organ Music

The restoration of cathedral organs after 1660 was a two-stage process which we shall find repeated again and again throughout the sections dealing with each institution. First there was a need to get something working as quickly and cheaply as possible, either the old organ made serviceable where it had survived, or a temporary one installed. It was a matter of honour that its sound should be heard again, for just as the dismantling or destruction of cathedral organs in the Civil War had symbolized the demise of Anglicanism, so their re-erection symbolized its triumph. In most cathedrals the next stage was the installation of a large permanent instrument. The process was liable to be lengthy, but by 1666 or so it had usually been achieved, with a new, rebuilt, or enlarged organ placed commonly on the screen, or in a gallery on the north side of the choir.[1]

THE EARLY ENGLISH ORGAN

In design, this first generation of organs was still very much of the pre-war type.[2] The largest were 'double organs', comprising great and chair organs, with a dozen or more stops between them, but no pedals. Such organs lacked reeds and mixtures, and were based on diapasons and flutes of metal or wood, with octave, twelfth, fifteenth, and twenty-second above, the lower ranks often duplicated. From its position on the screen the great organ spoke westwards into the nave and eastwards into the choir (one reason for having sets of identical pipes), while the chair organ was positioned behind the organist and faced the choir directly. But although 'chair' later became 'choir', the word probably derived from 'chare', implying a turning aside, away, or back (see *OED*) and was thus analogous with the 'Rück' in *Rückpositiv*.[3] It appears that even in Dallam's Restoration organ at St George's Chapel, Windsor, the organist still had to turn round to play the chair organ.[4]

---

[1] Stephen Bicknell, 'English Organ Building, 1642–1685', *Journal of the British Institute of Organ Studies*, 5 (1981), 5–22.

[2] Cecil Clutton and Austin Niland, *The British Organ* (London, 1963), 53–68.

[3] William L. Sumner, *The Organ* (4th edn., London, 1973), 161–3; Bernard B. Edmonds, 'The Chayre Organ: An Episode', *Journal of the British Institute of Organ Studies*, 4 (1980), 19–33.

[4] Clutton and Niland, *British Organ* (1963), 188; Sidney Campbell and W. L. Sumner, 'The Organs and Organists of St George's Chapel, Windsor Castle', *The Organ*, 45 (1965–6), 148.

Robert Dallam had succeeded his father Thomas as the leading organ-builder before the Civil War; Ralph and George Dallam were presumably younger brothers.[5] Up to 1629 Thomas Dallam built many of the most important organs in England, including that of King's College, Cambridge (1605–6), the case of which still survives, and the Worcester organ of 1613; in his turn, Robert was responsible for new instruments at York (1632), Magdalen College, Oxford, and Lichfield (1636). During the Civil War and Commonwealth period he worked in Brittany, and on his return seemed at first inclined to introduce French influences. His 1662 specification for the organ of New College, Oxford, with its 'simbale', 'furnitor', 'sagbot', and 'cleron', shows him aiming for a more colourful tonal scheme, but in the end conservative taste prevailed.[6] He or his brother Ralph was responsible for the 1660 organ for St George's Chapel, Windsor; his brother George got the contract at Durham the following year. Robert Dallam's last organ was for the Chapel Royal at Whitehall, costing £650; he died in May 1665, but the money was not actually paid until the following year.[7] Thomas Harris, his brother-in-law and father of the great Renatus, built important organs for Gloucester (1663), Worcester (1666), and Salisbury (1668–9).

Other makers active at the time included Lancelot Pease of Cambridge, who built a chair organ for King's College in 1661 and a large double organ for Canterbury in 1662–3, before moving to Dublin, where he was responsible for the Christ Church organ of 1667.[8] Thomas Thamar, also of Cambridge (at least, for a time), provided 'a faire, substantial, good and perfect double organ' for Winchester in 1665 and a new great organ for King's College, Cambridge, in 1673.[9] Robert Taunton of Bristol erected a chair organ in the cathedral there in 1661 at a cost of £150 and a new double organ for Wells in 1662 costing up to £800.[10] Further west, John Loosemore built an organ at Exeter in 1665 with the longest pipes in England (20 ft. 6 in.).[11] The average price of such instruments was just over £500 for a double organ, depending on how much of the old case and pipe-work could be used again; a chair organ cost about £150.

As an example of the conservatism of English organs at this time, Harris's Worcester organ of 1666 may be cited—a virtual replica of his grandfather's instrument of 1613. The agreement signed with the Dean and Chapter on 5 July 1666 stipulated that he should 'within the space of eighteen months next ensuing the date hereof at his or their proper costs and charges make and set up in the Quire of the said Cathedral Church over the entry to the Quire [i.e. on

[5] Betty Matthews, 'The Dallams and the Harrises', *Journal of the British Institute of Organ Studies*, 8 (1984), 58–68.

[6] Bicknell, 'English Organ Building', 19; Michel Cocheril, 'The Dallams in Brittany', *Journal of the British Institute of Organ Studies*, 6 (1982), 68; Andrew Freeman, 'The Organs at New College, Oxford', *The Organ*, 9 (1929–30), 152–3.

[7] Ashbee, i. 69–70.   [8] Sumner, *The Organ* (1973), 131–3.

[9] Ibid. 123–5.   [10] Ibid. 128–9.   [11] Ibid. 122–5.

the screen], A Double Organ consisting of a Great Organ and a Chair Organ with such number of stops and pipes and in such manner and form as followeth':

In the Great Organ the faces East and West, both Diapasons in sight and some of the Principals, Two Open Diapasons of Metal, A ten foot pipe as at Sarum and Gloucester, following the proportion of eight inches diameter in the ten foot pipe, and four inches diameter in a pipe of five foot. The Great Organ Case to be designed after the manner of Windsor Church before the wars. . . . Two Principals of metal. Two Fifteenths of metal, One Twelfth metal, One Recorder metal, One place for another stop: In the Chair Organ, one Principal of metal, in front according to the design of Windsor before the wars. . . . One Stopt Diapason of wood, One open Diapason of wood, saving nine pipes towards the Bases beginning in A re, One Fifteenth of Metal, One Two and Twentieth (as they call it): The Bellows, Soundboards and all the timber and iron as at Sarum and Gloucester, or whichsoever is the fairest. The Case of such wainscot as shall be judged by expert ones to equal those of either Sarum or Gloucester.[12]

The absence of mixtures and reeds is to be noted, as well as mutation stops other than a twelfth. Also typical were the doubled ranks of diapasons, principals, and fifteenths on the great so that the east and west faces of the organ looked and sounded the same. The chair organ, which faced only the choir, consisted of single ranks up to a twenty-second, and included both wooden and metal pipes, whereas all those of the great organ were metal. The difference in the tone quality of each organ can be imagined.

The cost was to be 'four hundred pounds of lawful English money in manner following, That is to say':

The sum of forty pounds in hand at the ensealing and delivery of these presents; The sum of eighty pounds immediately after the setting up the Chair Organ Case; and the lower part of the Great Organ Case; the sum of one hundred pounds at such time as the said Chair Organ will be finished and set up; The sum of one hundred pounds more at such time as the forefront of the said Great Organ so to be made as aforesaid be perfected. And fourscore pounds at such time as both the said Organs shall be fully perfected finished completed and set up. Further it is provided that if the Dean and Chapter (being advised or informed by expert men) shall judge or estimate the aforesaid Double Organ not to be worth the aforesaid sum, that then it shall be lawful for them to default and detain the sum of forty pounds out of or from the last payment above mentioned, payable otherwise to the said Thomas Harris.

Discussion of the Worcester organ raises the question of pitch in these early organs, for one of the archaic features that seems to have been reinstated at the time was that of a transposing keyboard whereby a 'C keyboard' (lowest note C = 'CC fa ut' according to the gamut) operated ranks of pipes whose pitch was based, nominally, on the F above (='FF fa ut') using 5' principals, or an octave

---

[12] A. Vernon Butcher, *The Organs and Music of Worcester Cathedral* (Worcester, 1981), 11–12.

lower using 10′ diapasons. We know that Thomas Dallam's 1613 Worcester organ had been like that—'double F fa ut of the quire pitch' being equivalent to 'double C fa ut according to the keys'[13]—and so, apparently, was Harris's replacement. The reference in his specification to an 'open Diapason of wood, saving nine pipes towards the Bases [i.e. *C–G♯*] beginning in A re' implies a C keyboard in an organ based on 10′ diapasons. Similar instruments were built at Salisbury and Gloucester, and, indeed, it is likely that most 'ten-foot' organs were transposing instruments in the early Restoration. At Winchester Cathedral, Thomas Thamar's organ was to be 'Gam ut in D sol re', which also suggests a transposing organ.[14]

Such organs, while they continued to exist, required the organist to transpose anthem accompaniments up a fifth (using 10′ diapasons) or down a fourth (using 5′ principals). This was done either by writing out the accompaniments a fifth higher, as found in several organ-books dating before and after 1660,[15] or by reading substitute clefs that had the same effect. For example, by imagining a G clef in place of a C clef in the right hand, and a C clef in place of an F clef in the left hand, the required transposition was produced automatically. It seems also that several of Dallam's organs had a stop that was tuned to choir pitch. The York organ (1632) had a recorder stop 'unison to the voice', the Lichfield organ (1636) a 'flute of wood to sing to', and the one he built for New College, Oxford, in 1663 a 'flute or singing stoppe'—perhaps the 'antheme stop' in his original specification.[16] The change from organs 'in F' to organs 'in C' was probably effected, in most cases, in the later 1660s and 70s, though it was not until 1713 that the New College organ was converted 'from Gamut in D sol re to Gamut proper', in other words, ceased to be transposing.[17]

Quite apart from whether these early Restoration organs were transposing or not, their pitch was generally sharp. Theoretically, a pipe ten feet long (regarded by the organ builders as *F*) sounds about *A♭* at modern pitch, though the diameter of the pipe makes a difference. Examination of surviving pipes from the organs at Exeter, Worcester, and New College has suggested, however, that they were probably only a semitone above today's pitch. This was the pitch that Bernard Smith favoured for his organs later in the century (about $a' = 474$), whereas Renatus Harris preferred a lower pitch (about $a' = 428$).[18]

[13] Dominic Gwynn, 'Organ Pitch in Seventeenth-Century England', *Journal of the British Institute of Organ Studies*, 9 (1985), 67; J. Bunker Clark, *Transposition in Seventeenth-Century English Organ Accompaniments and the Transposing Organ* (Detroit, 1974), 23–37.

[14] Betty Matthews, *The Organs and Organists of Winchester Cathedral* (3rd rev. edn., Winchester, 1975), 6.

[15] e.g. *Och* 88, 427, 438; *Ojc* 315; *DRc* A.4; *GL* 110; *Ckc* 9. In turn these suggest that the organs of Christ Church, Oxford, St John's College, Oxford, and the cathedrals of Durham, Gloucester, and Norwich were also 'transposing' instruments.

[16] Gwynn, 'Organ Pitch', 75.

[17] Freeman, 'Organs at New College', 153.

[18] Gwynn, 'Organ Pitch', 66–73; Arthur Mendel, 'Pitch in Western Music since 1500', *Acta Musicologica*, 50 (1978) 28.

BERNARD SMITH AND RENATUS HARRIS

The last two decades of the seventeenth century were a period of change in the history of English organ-building, and saw the emergence of 'Father' Smith from 1667, and Renatus Harris from 1674, as leaders of their craft. In their work Continental influences begin to assert themselves, from Holland and North Germany in Smith's (which is where he probably came from), from France in Harris's (where his father and uncles had worked during the Commonwealth). Both benefited from the second wave of organ-building which gathered pace about 1680, and to some extent they helped to determine the path it took. At this time many cathedrals were facing the problem of whether to repair or replace their old organs. Christ Church, Oxford (1680?), may have been Smith's first two-manual cathedral organ; its thirteen stops, including a three-rank sesquialtera, a four-rank cornet from middle C♯ upwards (possibly the first in England), and a trumpet on the great show the direction in which things were going.[19] The organ he built for Durham between 1683 and 1685 was larger still. The specification of the great organ included twelve stops:

viz., Two open diapasons of Mitall containing one hundred and eight pipes. A stop diapason of wood containing fifty four pipes. A principall of Mitall containing fifty four pipes. A cornet of Mitall containing nynety six pipes. A quinta of Mitall containing fifty four pipes. A super Octave of Mitall containing fifty four pipes. A Holfluit of wood containing fifty four pipes. A block flute of Mitall containing fifty four pipes. A small Quint of Mitall containing fifty four pipes. A mixture of three ranks of pipes of Mitall containing one hundred and sixty two pipes. A trumpett of Mitall containing fifty four pipes

while the Chair had five:

A principal of Mitall in the front containing fifty four pipes. A stop diapason of wood containing fifty four pipes. A voice Humand [voix humane] of Mitall containing fifty four pipes. A holfluit of wood containing fifty four pipes. And a super octave of Mitall containing fifty four pipes.

Being placed on the screen, it was necessary that the great organ sound both to the nave and the choir, though now only one rank of pipes was duplicated. Thus,

Item it is agreed . . . that the sd great Organ shall have a back front towards the body or west end of the Church which shall be in all things and respects like to the fore front both in pipes and carving. And all the pipes belonging to the two diapason stops shall speak at will in the sd back front as in the fore.[20]

The cost of the organ was to be £700, and as usual the payments were to be staged, one-third on signing the contract, one-third on bringing the organ into

---

[19] Clutton and Niland, *British Organ* (1963), 71–2.
[20] Andrew Freeman, *Father Smith* (Oxford, 1977), 72–4.

the church prior to setting up, and one-third on completion (when the old organ was to become Smith's to dispose of as he pleased). Painting and gilding the pipes in both fronts of the great organ, and the front of the chair organ, were to cost a further £50. This was Smith's largest organ to date, and the ways in which it differed from the Dallam type of organ are obvious. Instead of expensive duplications and consequent waste of space, more varied tone colours were introduced. In addition to diapasons, various types of flute, both metal and wood, were on the great, where also there were two mutation stops (a quint and its octave), two mixtures (one a four-rank cornet), and a trumpet. Another reed stop that was becoming fashionable, the voix humaine, was included on the chair. It was said to be one of two organs made by Smith employing what he called 'quarter nots'—divided keys (and separate pipes) for E♭/D♯ and A♭/G♯, so that each could be properly tuned within the mean-tone system. (In fact, the number of pipes does not support this, though Smith may have exceeded his brief in this respect.) The other was his organ for the Temple Church, which he was working on concurrently; it had twenty-three stops, his first with three manuals—the third an 'echo' organ enclosed in a box to give the impression of distance—and the one that was to make his reputation.[21]

The climax to Smith's career came with the commission to build the organ for the new St Paul's Cathedral (1695–7). This was an even larger and more colourful instrument with twelve stops on the great including cornet, sesquialtera, and trumpet, nine on the chair including a cimball, voix humaine, and crumhorne, and six on the echo. The case was designed by Wren and the carving done by Grinling Gibbons. A few years later he built another sizeable instrument for the Banqueting House chapel at Whitehall (1699), and smaller ones, though still with three manuals, for Eton College (1700–1) and Trinity College, Cambridge (1708). He also had a hand in building or enlarging organs at Rochester (1668), Manchester (1681), Canterbury (1684), Chester (1684), and St David's (1704–5), and had charge of the organ at Westminster Abbey at various times from 1667 onwards.

Renatus Harris, once the restraining influence of his father Thomas had passed, was prepared to outdo Smith with even more lavish specifications and mechanical improvements. Beginning modestly enough at Chichester (1677), his organ for Bristol (1683–5) cost £950 and had three manuals; a great organ with twelve stops, including a three-rank sesquialtera, five-rank cornet, trumpet (8′) and clarion (4′), an echo organ with hautboy and cremona among its seven stops, and a chair organ retained, in all probability, from the earlier instrument by Taunton.[22] Nothing is known of the specification of his Hereford organ

[21] Freeman, *Father Smith*, 24–6; for the 'Battle of the Organs' see John Hawkins, *A General History of the Science and Practice of Music* (2nd edn., London, 1875), 691–2.
[22] Laurence Elvin, 'The Organs of Bristol Cathedral', *The Organ*, 42 (1962–3), 72; John Speller, 'Bristol Organs in 1710', *The Organ*, 57 (1978–9), 85–7.

(1686), but at both King's College, Cambridge (1686) and Winchester Cathedral (1694) he built new great organs to go with already existing chair organs, and, for St Patrick's, Dublin, a new two- or three-manual instrument (1697). (The following year he was able to off-load part of his unsuccessful Temple Church organ on Christ Church Cathedral in the same city.)

The peak came with his four-manual, 'fifty-stop' organ for Salisbury cathedral (1710).[23] The reason for its fourth manual was due to Harris's system of 'communication', or borrowing, whereby most of the stops on the great organ could also be played independently from this fourth manual. There were therefore only thirty-three ranks (plus a drum pedal to accompany the trumpet in martial effects), but nevertheless it was the largest in England. The fifteen stops on the great comprised three open diapasons, two stopped diapasons, a principal, flutes (including twelfth, fifteenth, tierce, and larigot), a four-rank sesquialtera, and a five-rank cornet, with trumpet, clarion, crumhorn, and vox humana reeds. Eleven of these were duplicated in the echo organ. In addition to six diapasons and flutes of various sorts, the chair organ was also provided with a bassoon. Even so, this was as nothing compared with the grandiose proposals he published in 1712 for a ceremonial organ at the west end of St Paul's, 'for the Reception of the Queen on all public Occasions of Thanksgiving for the good Effects of Peace and War, upon all State Occasions', etc. This was to 'consist of Six entire sets of keys for the hands, besides Pedals for the feet . . . the sixth to be adapted to the emitting of Sounds to express Passion by Swelling any Note as if inspir'd by Human Breath; which is the greatest improvement an organ is capable of except it had Articulation'.[24] Though nothing came of the scheme immediately, it very much reflected new thinking.

Mechanical improvements were in the air and had perhaps been there for some time. Even before 1676 Thomas Mace had a chamber organ with 'a *Hooboy Stop*, which comes in at any Time, with the *Foot*',[25] and it seems improbable that such a useful contrivance can have been completely forgotten in the intervening years. At the same time that Harris was boasting about his device for 'Swelling any Note', Abraham Jordan was building a four-manual organ for St Magnus-the-Martyr, near London Bridge, the first in England with a swell box.[26] By 1721 Smith's organ at St Paul's had both a swell ('the Loudning & Softning') and pull-down pedals ('six large Trumpet Pipes . . . to be used with a pedal or without') fitted by Christopher Shrider, his son-in-law and successor.[27] Smith died in 1708, Harris in 1724.

As for the tonal qualities of their organs, it is difficult to judge at this distance, since surviving pipe-work is so rare. Smith is generally praised for his diapasons and the sweetness of his wooden pipes, Harris for his reeds and mixtures. The

[23] Clutton and Niland, *British Organ* (1963), 146–7; Sumner, *The Organ* (1973), 152–3.
[24] Clutton and Niland, 80–1; Sumner, 151–2.   [25] Mace, *Musick's Monument*, 245.
[26] Sumner, *The Organ* (1973), 191–2.   [27] Ibid. 183.

judgement of history may be that, on the whole, the seventeenth century got it wrong in preferring Smith to Harris—as organ-builders, if not as men. For all their innovations, the design of their organs was still limited compared with those of France, Holland, and Germany, especially in lacking a pedal department. Nevertheless, from about the turn of the century composers began to exploit various timbre qualities in their verse anthem accompaniments and in their voluntaries.

ORGAN ACCOMPANIMENTS AND VOLUNTARIES

As we have seen, the organ was used to accompany the choir in anthems and services, and when canticles and psalms were sung to harmonized chants, but not apparently when they were chanted in unison. The organist played from an organ-book, which early in the Restoration period differed little from what had been used before the Civil War—indeed in some cases they were the same books with additions, as at Durham (MSS A.3 and A.5). Where the organ was at F pitch this necessitated transposing the accompaniment up a fifth (which may have been written out already) or imagining clefs a fifth higher. The music in front of him was a more or less complete short score of what was being sung, arranged on two six-line staves with regular bars. The text was not underlaid, but the opening words of each section were entered as a guide with indications of 'Full' or 'Vers[e]', C [= cantoris], or D [= decani]. Increasingly the texture was likely to be reduced to the top and bottom part with significant entries sketched in and perhaps a few figures in the bass. Sometimes a figured bass alone sufficed. John Ferrabosco's organ-books at Ely (the earlier parts of *Cu* Ely MSS 1 and 4) are like this, as is John Reading's section of the Berkeley Organ Book (*US-BE* 751), which hails from Winchester. Moving away from a full towards a more skeletal texture are Daniel Henstridge's Gloucester organ-books (MSS 111 and 112), while John Jackson's from Wells (*Lcm* 673) is basically all 'top and bottom' supplemented with figuring. The same is true of the Ely organ-books in the hand of James Hawkins (parts of MSS 1–3). By this time five-line staves had become the norm.

Detailed indications of how the organist was to accompany a piece are rare. Occasionally passages are marked 'loud', 'soft', or 'echo' (not at this early period a reference to an echo organ), or more specifically 'full organ', 'double organ', '2 Diapasons'—the latter encountered frequently enough to suggest that it was the standard accompanying tone for the full choir, and presumably implied the use of both open and stopped diapasons without the octave. In verse anthems a few bars of organ introduction might be ornamented—most commonly with the double-stroke shake and sometimes with the single-stroke slide—but thereafter ornaments were written in rather sparingly as a general rule, whatever may have been done in performance. It seems likely that the typical organist would have added a certain amount of ornamentation, perhaps profusely. Nevertheless, a few examples of written-out ornamentation seem so elaborate and highly wrought as to represent versions intended as voluntaries rather than accompaniments. One is of Orlando Gibbons's Short Service at Magdalen College, Oxford (MS 347), another is of the *Te Deum* and *Jubilate* from Tallis's 'Dorian Service' in George Holmes's organ-book (*Lbl* 31446; Ex. 11). Since there is no evidence that they were used *alternatim* with the choir, or as an Anglican 'organ service' analogous with the Continental 'organ mass', the only possibilities seem either that they are specimen accompaniments (with uncomfortable tempo implications perhaps) or independent organ pieces in which service settings are transformed into voluntaries. The presence of text incipits may support the former.

For the remainder of the period organ parts normally consist of the top part above a figured bass. When the organ was intended to play by itself 'organ' (or 'ritor[nello]') is marked, 'solo', 'verse', or 'cho[rus]' indicating the vocal sections, usually with a textual incipit. After 1700 interpretative directions become frequent, not only for manual changes like 'loud', 'soft', 'Great Organ', 'Echo', etc., but also for mixed manual and solo effects, such as 'loud organ left hand', 'trumpet', 'cornet', 'sex[quialtera]', etc. Tempo indications such as 'drag', 'grave', 'brisker', etc., are also common. Set beside the sober effects of forty years earlier, they show the importance of colour and variety as an ingredient of the 'high Baroque' style.

The same kind of development characterized solo organ music during the period. The voluntary was the typical form of English organ music, and might be played at various points in the service—before the first lesson at morning and evening prayer, after the litany, at the offertory in the communion service, and after the final blessing. It seems likely that such works were usually improvised; the paucity of the surviving repertory is otherwise difficult to account for, though it should not be forgotten that just as pre-Restoration anthems and services remained in the cathedral repertoire, so the organ music of Byrd, Bull, and Gibbons probably retained some currency. Surviving manuscripts leave little doubt that a certain amount of continental, mainly Italian, organ music was also known. Girolamo Frescobaldi, or 'Frisco Baldy' as he is called in William Ellis's organ-book (*Och* 1113), seems to have been the most widely represented.

There are more than forty manuscripts containing Restoration organ music, but the total number of surviving works is quite small.[28] Apart from thirty anonymous pieces, many of which are substantial and thoroughly competent

---

[28] Much of what follows depends on Cox, *Organ Music in Restoration England*, which includes a thematic catalogue of extant pieces (App. A, 295–367), details of manuscript sources (App. E, 483–522), and sixty-seven representative transcriptions (vol. ii), including all the anonymous ones. See also Barry Cooper, *English Solo Keyboard Music of the Middle and Late Baroque* (London and New York, 1989); John Caldwell, *English Keyboard Music before the Nineteenth Century* (Oxford, 1973); Francis Routh, *Early English Organ Music from the Middle Ages to 1837* (London, 1973).

Ex. 11. Thomas Tallis, *Te Deum* in D minor: (*a*) First Service (EECM 13);
(*b*) keyboard accompaniment (*Lbl* 31446)

technically, there are thirty-three by Blow, but scarcely two dozen by other composers, including Christopher Gibbons, Locke, and Purcell. It was not until Croft and Hart came on the scene in the early eighteenth century that the numbers began to build up. The following are among the main sources:[29]

[29] Cox, i. 487, 494–8, 509, and 514.

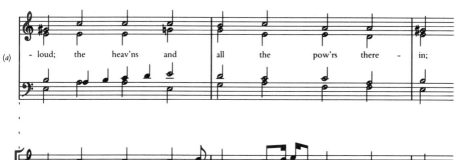

1. Oxford, Christ Church, MS 47; dating from before 1677, and containing organ accompaniments for anthems by pre-Commonwealth composers, and organ music by Orlando Gibbons (3), Christopher Gibbons (4), John Blow (2), John Hingeston (1), and 'anon.' (3).

2. London, British Library, Add. MS 31403; the earlier part dates from before the Commonwealth (Bull, Gibbons, etc.). Later additions include organ pieces by Blow (5) and 'anon.' (9), also harpsichord pieces.

3. London, British Library, Add. MS 31446; once apparently inscribed

'George Holmes, his Book, 1698, at my Lord Bishope of Durham's'. In addition to some harpsichord pieces, it contains organ music by Blow (13), C. Gibbons (2), Purcell (2), 'anon.' (7), and Michelangelo Rossi (3). Holmes later became organist of Lincoln cathedral (1705–20); however, there is no reason to suppose that he was the author of any of the anonymous items.

4. London, British Library, Add. MS 31468; inscribed 'Will Davis [of Worcester] / Eius Liber' and dating from the early eighteenth century. It contains organ music by Blow (17), C. Gibbons (2), and Purcell (1), as well as a number of harpsichord pieces.

5. London, British Library, Add. MS 34695; compiled by Nicholas Harrison in the early eighteenth century using Add. MS 31446 as one of his sources. It contains organ music by Blow (17), C. Gibbons (4), Purcell (3), Hart (3), Bryne (1), Croft (1), and 'anon.' (6), as well as some harpsichord pieces.

Manuscripts which have direct links with cathedral (or collegiate) establishments include the following:

1. Wimborne Minster, MS P.10; dated '1670'. In addition to organ accompaniments of anthems and services, it contains pieces by C. Gibbons (1), Richard Portman (1), and Frescobaldi (4).

2. Hereford Cathedral, MS 30.B.II; dating from the early eighteenth century and probably in the hand of Henry Hall (organist 1688–1707). It contains organ parts to anthems, and pieces by Blow (3), 'anon.' (2), Johann Kaspar Kerll (1), and Sebastian Scherer (1).

Voluntary and 'verse'—the titles are interchangeable—were terms now preferred to 'fancy' or 'fantasia' for organ music, but they retained the contrapuntal approach of the old fantasia, despite the encroachment of modern idioms.[30] They usually consisted of one or two imitative sections, beginning in a vocal style though embellished after the fashion of keyboard music, and becoming increasingly enlivened with passage-work towards the end. The counterpoint did not necessarily maintain a consistent number of parts, nor were the parts strictly confined to a specific range. Virtually no use was made of the *stile brisé* characteristic of harpsichord music; this and the absence of dance elements more or less defined the idiom. A few preludes consisting largely of keyboard figuration supported by chords comprise the only other type of organ music.

Some voluntaries, called 'double voluntaries', exploited the fact that many organs had two manuals, and could therefore provide contrast between the great and chair organs, and make a theme in the bass stand out by being played on the 'loud organ'.[31] Double voluntaries date back to the earlier part of the century, though Orlando Gibbons's 'Fancy for a double Orgaine'—usually regarded as the first—may not have been conceived as such originally. As

[30] Cox, i. 172–205.   [31] Ibid. 206–58.

instruments began to acquire solo stops such as the cornet, sesquialtera, and trumpet around 1680 (and, later still, echo organs), composers began to put these resources to use in the voluntary. Even without two manuals, divided stops enabled a solo to be played in either the treble or bass register of the organ. Thus cornet voluntaries and trumpet voluntaries (not to be confused with 'trumpet tunes' such as Jeremiah Clarke's famous piece) came into existence. These developments meant sacrificing counterpoint to some extent in favour of solo and echo effects, and in the end brought the demise of the old fantasia style. By the early eighteenth century the voluntary had become a two- or three-movement form, analogous to the sonata, usually beginning with a slow introduction and ending with some kind of fugue or piece for solo stop.

The earliest group of composers of voluntaries includes Christopher Gibbons and Matthew Locke, neither of whom lived long enough to take advantage of the sounds offered by the new type of organ. The former was organist of Westminster Abbey (q.v.) and one of the organists of the Chapel Royal at the Restoration; the latter was organist to the queen, Catherine of Braganza, from about 1662. Seven voluntaries are attributed to Gibbons, eight to Locke, and one each to Albertus Bryne, Benjamin Rogers, and John Hingeston. Three of Gibbons's are called 'verse', and of the remaining four, three are voluntaries for double organ; an eighth is a keyboard version of one of his father's three-part viol fantasias.[32] The first two, respectively in A minor and D minor, survive in shorter and longer versions, the latter inclined to ramble towards the end and stylistically at odds with what has gone before. The shorter versions (nos. 1 and 2) are certainly more convincing musically, and with their 'great' and 'chair' contrasts raise fewer questions regarding the capabilities of the early Restoration organ than the longer versions (nos. 1a and 2a), which indicate passages for 'cornet' (right hand), 'sesquialtera' (left hand), and 'trumpet' (both hands). In fact, Gibbons can hardly be responsible for these extensions, which in the case of no. 2a includes a quotation from no. 1, part of one of Blow's D minor voluntaries (no. 27), and—more surprisingly from the tonal point of view—a section from an anonymous trumpet voluntary in C major (which also appears in no. 1a).

Gibbons's original versions of these pieces are basically diatonic, but by no means bland; their counterpoint is sufficiently irregular to place them firmly in the second half of the century. In this respect, however, they cannot match the seven organ pieces which Locke published in *Melothesia* (1673) along with thorough-bass rules and keyboard suites. Taken together (nos. 62–8) they show typical distortions of line and harmony that probably owe as much to

---

[32] Christopher Gibbons, *Keyboard Compositions*, ed. Clare G. Rayner, rev. John Caldwell (Corpus of Early Keyboard Music, 18; Neuhausen-Stuttgart, 1989). See also Cox, i. 81–90; Cooper, 196–200; Routh, 143–6; and Julie Bray's review of the Rayner/Caldwell edition in *Early Music*, 21 (1993), 121–7.

Frescobaldi and Froberger as to his English predecessors.[33] (Froberger was in London during the 1650s.) All but one begin imitatively and last no longer than necessitated by one or two statements of the theme beyond the opening point, and some suitable concluding gestures. The longest, no. 3 (64), takes up two themes in succession and ends with toccata-like passage-work, while no. 2 (63) is alone in beginning chordally before moving into imitations and lively figuration before the close. Its two-part structure (like Gibbons's no. 3) prefigures that of the eighteenth-century voluntary. Number 7 'For a Double Organ' (68) presents both mixed manual and echo effects, the latter contributing to the general excitement of the last page.

The fantasias of Bryne, Hingeston, and Rogers show their composers in a respectable light.[34] The opening of Hingeston's Double Voluntary in A minor is quoted to illustrate the kind of counterpoint which composers of this period employed in their fantasias (Ex. 12). It continues rather loosely, sticking closely to the tonic key and taking up several points of imitation in rather desultory fashion before breaking into semiquavers towards the end. The absence of ornamentation is unusual.

Blow's surviving voluntaries (or verses—the term he seems to have preferred) outnumber those of all his contemporaries by more than two to one, and the number continues to increase as sources are investigated. The tally now stands at thirty, with another three doubtful.[35] Typically they begin imitatively and end with passage-work. Their average length exceeds Locke's, but most of them are quite short nevertheless, based on a single subject but becoming freer towards the end. Some, however, are clearly in two movements: no. 2, for example, is virtually a prelude and fugue, while nos. 9, 10, 14, and 16 divide into two complementary but self-contained sections. Some, such as nos. 3, 14, and 19, are in canzona style, others, like nos. 13, 15, and 24, have more solemn subject-matter, though note-values tend to diminish as the work gets under way. Number 18 is based on a chromatically descending subject of a type common in Italian keyboard music; no. 2 begins with nine bars from a toccata by Frescobaldi—not the only such quotation as it happens, since no. 29 (one of the best) incorporates six bars from another Frescobaldi toccata in the middle, and no. 7 is a version of Frescobaldi's setting of the hymn *Iste confessor* (fourth verse)

---

[33] Matthew Locke, *Melothesia*, ed. Christopher Hogwood (Oxford, 1987); Matthew Locke, *Organ Voluntaries*, ed. R. T. Dart (Early Keyboard Music, 7; 2nd edn., London, 1968); also Matthew Locke, *Seven Pieces (Voluntaries) from 'Melothesia' (1673)*, ed. Gordon Phillips (Tallis to Wesley, 6; London, 1957); Cooper, 200–3; Routh, 146–7.

[34] See Beniamin Rogers, *Complete Keyboard Works*, ed. Richard Rastall (Early Keyboard Music, 29; London, 1972); also Cox, ii. 160–3 and 208–14.

[35] John Blow, *Thirty Voluntaries*, ed. Watkins Shaw (rev. edn., London, 1972), does not include Cox's nos. 31–6 (329–31), and sometimes omits the second part of a voluntary. For discussion of the music see Caldwell, 166–9; Cox, i. 95–114; Cooper, 203–15; Routh 147–50. See also Barry Cooper, 'Problems in the Transmission of Blow's Organ Music', *Music and Letters*, 75 (1994) 522–47.

Ex. 12. John Hingston, Voluntary (*Och* 47)

from his *Toccate, canzoni* (1627). At first sight it may be difficult to explain these 'borrowings', since, while it may be acceptable to take the opening of a pre-existing piece as a point of departure, incorporating second-hand material in the course of a piece seems to need justification. However, in discussing 'The Excellent Art of Voluntary', Roger North says: 'he that hath most musicall passages drawne off from the musick of others and in most variety to be put together with extempore connection, is the best furnished for voluntary'.[36]

There are four voluntaries for double organ (nos. 25–7 and 29) in which the great organ is used to 'bring out' the theme, whether in left or right hand, against accompanying voices on the chair organ. On the other hand, the two cornet voluntaries (nos. 8 and 28) seem to have been composed originally for a single manual with cornet 'half stop' above middle C or C♯ (as was usual), the accompaniment being restricted to the lower half of the keyboard; a certain amount of rewriting subsequently led to the two-manual versions we now have.[37] In the case of the voluntary on the 'Old Hundredth' (no. 30) the reverse process seems to have been at work. From the layout of the music it seems that two manuals were originally required, but that, in revising it, Purcell—if it was he—improved some of the detail, at the same time making it playable on a single manual, using a 'half stop' in the lower register for the first verse, and a cornet in the upper for the second. It is the only known organ piece by an English composer of this period which adopts the technique of the 'chorale prelude', and though no early source survives, the attribution to 'Mr Blow' implies a date not later than 1677, the year Blow was awarded his doctorate.[38] The first line of the psalm tune is introduced imitatively, continuing with successive lines of the tune in the left hand (= great) with brief interludes and accompanying voices in the right hand (= chair). The second verse places the tune in the right hand (= great) with two-part accompaniment in the left hand (= chair). Three manuals are needed for the voluntary for cornet and echo (no. 32).

Blow is the most important composer of organ music in the period, his usual rough edges notwithstanding. Several are impressive pieces by any standard, and taken together they exhibit a wide range of style. Whether they can be ordered chronologically in terms of progressive development over a period of forty years or so remains to be seen. The sources, being mostly later, do not help much, and the superficially attractive notion that the canzona types are later than those of a more sober cast, while possibly true up to a point, needs to be further refined.

Purcell's output is small by comparison, and has been made smaller by reattributions, though recently the toccata in A has landed back on his doorstep

---

[36] Wilson (ed.), *Roger North on Music*, 141–2.
[37] Cox, i. 228–39.   [38] Caldwell, 171–5.

until a more likely home is found.[39] Apart from the voluntary on the 100th psalm already discussed in connection with Blow, there is a verse in F which Caldwell describes as 'a short fugal piece of no particular distinction', a voluntary in C which the same author is inclined to question, and another in G which begins with an introduction somewhat in the style of a Frescobaldi toccata and concludes with a vigorous canzona.[40] There is also a trumpet voluntary which may or may not be by him—or only in part.[41] That leaves the voluntary in D minor, which survives in two versions, a longer and a shorter one (Z. 718 and Z. 719). They share a common opening down to the furious left-hand passage in bars 17–19, after which the shorter one tails off rather aimlessly, though the theme is heard once more in the bass. The longer version for 'Duble Organ' continues in more disciplined fashion, introducing a new, leaping theme towards the end which is worked in stretto before the final dominant pedal. It is a piece that makes one regret how few organ works by Purcell there are. Cox surmises that it may have been written (or rewritten) soon after the Westminster Abbey organ acquired its second manual in 1694.[42]

In comparison, the voluntaries of eighteenth-century composers seem tame, hardly mitigated by exploiting contrasts between great, chair, and echo organs, and the colours of cornet, sesquialtera, trumpet, and cremona solos. Philip Hart's remarkable *Fugues for the Organ or Harpsichord* (1704) are an exception to the general blandness, and further works in manuscript enhance both his output and reputation.[43] These additional works include two further fugues (so called) and a canzona, three two-movement voluntaries (one for trumpet and echo), two toccatas (one with two movements, the other with three), and one two-movement lesson. Hart was organist of St Andrew Undershaft church in London from 1697 and no doubt found inspiration in the Harris organ recently built there.

Other city organists to add to the repertoire included John Barrett and John Reading; both were pupils of John Blow, but his influence left little mark. Barrett's voluntary in C is a two-movement work, once thought to be by Purcell (Z. D241a), with cornet solos and echos in the first section, and what might pass for a fugue to finish with. Reading's voluntary in G is a single movement—a good example of how voices freely come and go in a fugue, with

---

[39] Henry Purcell, *Organ Works*, ed. Hugh McLean (2nd edn., 1967). Cox, i. 115–19; Cooper, 218–31; also id., 'Keyboard Music', in *Music in Britain: The Seventeenth Century* (Blackwell History of Music in Britain, iii, ed. Ian Spink; Oxford, 1992), 364–6.

[40] Caldwell, 169–71.

[41] Barry Cooper, 'Did Purcell Write a Trumpet Voluntary?', *Musical Times*, 119 (1978), 791–3, 1073–5; also Cox, i. 250–1.

[42] Cox, i. 116.

[43] Ibid. 348–54; Caldwell, 191–2; see Philip Hart, *Organ Works*, ed. Frank Dawes (Tallis to Wesley, 37; London, 1973).

textural support added (or subtracted) at will.[44] William Croft was a more significant contributor to the form, and may be seen as beginning a new tradition, which passed to Maurice Greene and John Stanley. Some of his twelve voluntaries surviving in a late eighteenth-century manuscript (*Lbl* 5336) are single-movement works, but others point to the characteristic two-movement (slow–fast) form of the eighteenth century. Yet others show that it has arrived. Best of these, perhaps, is no. 12, which begins with a slow chordal section leading to a stirring double fugue.[45]

Thereafter, parish church organists like Thomas Roseingrave and John Stanley outnumbered cathedral organists in the production of voluntaries—not only in quantity. A rich city parish could pay its organist well and many organists were able to hold two posts at the same time yet still have most of the week free for professional engagements and teaching. Moreover, a large new organ was something of a status symbol for a parish church, and the organist himself was likely to be valued in a way which was not often the case with cathedral organists. It is one of the symptoms of the decline of cathedral music in the eighteenth century, and in itself a reflection of the atrophy afflicting cathedral life compared with the burgeoning vitality of the city church.

[44] Both are in Gordon Phillips (ed.), *John Blow and his Pupils John Barrett and John Reading* (Tallis to Wesley, 21; London, 1962). See Cox, i. 309–11; Caldwell, 191–2.
[45] William Croft, *Complete Organ Works*, ed. Richard Platt (rev. edn., London, 1980).

5

Sources and Performance

PARTS AND SCORES

Cathedral choirs sang from partbooks. In the first half of the century a set usually consisted of ten—treble or 'mean'; first and second countertenor, tenor, and bass, on both the cantoris and decani sides of the choir—and an accompaniment book for the organ. Four parts rather than five becoming the norm after 1660, a set would include eight (treble, still sometimes called 'mean', especially when the CI clef was used, countertenor, tenor, and bass), again with an organ-book. Compared with scores, partbooks saved space and time in copying, but were liable to contain and reproduce scribal errors which were not easy to correct.

Despite the destruction of choir music during the Civil War, more must have survived than we are now aware of, since the works of so many local composers who died before the Restoration continued to be performed after 1660. Thus, at Ely, the early Restoration partbooks contain numerous anthems by John Amner (d. 1641), only a few of which occur in his *Sacred Hymns* (1615). They are therefore likely to have been transcribed from earlier partbooks, and there is little doubt that this happened in many places. Here and there we have an indication of the extent of surviving material. An inventory at Norwich mentions fifty-four choirbooks in 1668, most of which must have dated from before the Civil War,[1] while at Lincoln, the '10 old Anthem books' rebound in 1664 can hardly have been recent.[2] Neither at Norwich nor Lincoln are there any remains of this material now, though at Durham twenty of the fifty pre-war partbooks listed in an inventory of 1664 are still extant—the most extensive collection to survive in place.[3]

Whatever may or may not have survived to the Restoration, an early priority of many choirs—especially where material had been destroyed—was to buy John Barnard's ten-volume set of *The First Book of Selected Church Musick . . . 1641*. Barnard's original intention had been to publish two books, the first to include works by composers dead at the time of publication, the second works

---

[1] Boston, *Musical History of Norwich Cathedral*, 58.

[2] Ian Cheverton, 'English Church Music of the Early Restoration Period, 1660–c.1676' (Ph.D. diss., University of Wales, Cardiff, 1985), 272.

[3] Brian Crosby, 'A Seventeenth-Century Durham Inventory', *Musical Times*, 119 (1978), 169; see also id., *A Catalogue of Durham Cathedral Music Manuscripts* (Oxford, 1986), pp. xii–xv.

by those 'now living'. As it happened (and the troubled times undoubtedly had something to do with it), the second book never came out, though the manuscript collection on which it was based (*Lcm* 1045–51) contains works that probably would have been included.[4] It was, of course, the wrong time to publish any such book, and apart from the title-page and the dedication to King Charles I there is no evidence to suggest that it saw the light of day before 1660.[5] What probably happened was that the collection had been set up by 1641 and was printed then or soon after, but in view of the threatening political situation the sheets were stored to await the return of more propitious times. Had things been different this might have been within a year or two; as it was it took eighteen years, by which time John Playford may have acquired the stock. He is known to have sold two sets to Canterbury in 1661 at £28 the pair, and a set to Westminster Abbey the same year for £13. 10s. Gloucester, Hereford, Lichfield, Salisbury, and Worcester were also among cathedrals that bought sets at this time, not necessarily (though probably) from Playford.[6]

Without doubt 'Barnard' supplied a useful repertoire, though there were perhaps too many services and not enough anthems suited to the purposes of 1660. It included services by Tallis, Strogers, Bevin, Byrd, Gibbons, Munday, Parsons, Morley, Giles, and Ward, with preces by Tallis, Byrd, and Gibbons, and Tallis's litany. Among composers of full anthems the most frequently represented were Tallis, Byrd, Gibbons, and Batten (a colleague of Barnard's at St Paul's); among composers of verse anthems, Byrd, Tye, Parsons, and White belonged to the oldest generation of composers of English church music, Weelkes, Gibbons, and Batten to the youngest (apart from those still alive). Inevitably it was a conservative repertoire, but it provided a core round which new repertoires could be built—literally at Canterbury, Gloucester, Hereford, Lichfield, Salisbury, and Worcester, where new music was added to blank pages bound up with Barnard's partbooks. These early Restoration sources will be explored in more detail when we come to deal with individual institutions.

Apart from Barnard's book, the only printed source of church music that became available to choirs in the early years was *Musica Deo Sacra* (1668), a posthumous collection of Thomas Tomkins's services, anthems, preces, and psalms, probably prepared for publication by his son Nathaniel. Unlike Barnard, it comprised four books for the voices with cantoris and decani parts to the left and right of an opening, plus a *Pars Organica*. For the books to be usable in choir, one set for each side was needed (despite a redundant organ-book) and this was what Canterbury seems to have acquired in 1668, paying £6. 12s. 7d.

---

[4] J. Bunker Clark, 'Adrian Batten and John Barnard: Colleagues and Collaborators', *Musica Disciplina*, 22 (1968), 207–29.

[5] John Morehen, 'The Sources of English Cathedral Music, *c.* 1617–*c.* 1644' (Ph.D. diss., University of Cambridge, 1969), 287–99; but see Cheverton, 227–41.

[6] Cheverton, 242–92.

'for a set of Service Bookes in 10 volumes Mr Thomas Tomkins's with 9 quires of ruled paper added to them and binding together with carriage'.[7] The sums paid at Chichester, Gloucester, and Lichfield were roughly half of this so they may only have bought a single set, copying the extra parts into their choirbooks as required.[8] This would have been normal procedure in any case, for even at Canterbury, one book between the five boys on each side would have been insufficient, though we do not know to what extent they sang from memory. At St George's, Windsor, two complete printed sets on each side were in use.[9] No choir, however, not even at Worcester, where local loyalties might have persisted and the choir was large, can have sung more than a small fraction of the total contents of five services and ninety-four anthems—many multi-voiced and elaborately contrapuntal.

The process of copying new anthems into old partbooks, and of compiling new ones, can be followed in many cathedrals through payments made to copyists. At Ely in 1663, for example, the organist 'Mr Ferrabosco shall have (in consideration of his pains in pricking out of Bookes) ten pounds'.[10] In addition, many cathedrals acquired music from contacts further afield, and in this way services and anthems spread from one establishment to another, particularly outwards from London. Still from the Ely accounts one reads in 1664: 'Mr [Zachary] Irish of Windsor for a Service and some Anthems of Dr. Child's £1. 3s.',[11] and at Peterborough in 1663: 'bought a set of Song Booke with Anthems prick'd £2 . . . for bringing them down from London by the Carrier 3s.'.[12] A few years later £3. 2s. was paid 'for a dozen anthems procured by Mr Dean and transcribed by Mr Tucker of Westminster'.[13] William Tucker, singer and copyist at both the Chapel Royal and Westminster Abbey, was seemingly much in demand for copies of recent anthems by London composers—including his own, if the widespread circulation of his anthems is anything to go by. The fact that he died on 28 February 1679 provides a *terminus ante quem* for the music in his hand, including some of Purcell's earlier anthems.[14]

It was common for partbooks to be filled up from both ends, with full anthems at one end, verse anthems at the other (reversed), or services at one end, anthems at the other. Although few cathedrals still possess partbooks dating from the early years of the Restoration, many can produce one or two—never a complete set, unfortunately—from towards the end of the century or the beginning of the next. The depredations of continual use and rough handling by the boys especially have taken their toll, but even in their incomplete state they tell us much about local repertoires and are often helpful in dating works—for

---

[7] Ibid. 249.   [8] Ibid. 296.   [9] Ibid. 288.   [10] Ibid. 259.
[11] Ibid.   [12] Ibid. 280.   [13] Ibid.
[14] Tucker's hand has been identified in the following MSS: *RM* 27.a.1–6 (Chapel Royal), *Lbl* 50860, *Cfm* 152, Tokyo Nanki Library N-5/10, *Lwa* 'First Set' of partbooks; see Watkins Shaw, *A Study of the Bing–Gostling Part Books in the Library of York Minster* (Croydon, 1986), 107–15.

example, by noting dates of entry, progress payments for copying, special occasions on which they were performed, or whether Child, Christopher Gibbons, Rogers, Blow, Aldrich, Turner, Tudway, or Croft are 'Mr' or 'Dr'. Later filling-up of blank or half-empty pages and rebinding may frequently obscure the chronological order, however.

One 'eight-plus-one' set from Norwich, now in the Rowe Library, King's College, Cambridge, is complete as to the number of books, though sections are missing. Of much greater importance, however, is the 'Bing–Gostling' set at York Minster—not intended for choir use but as a master set—comprising eight partbooks but unfortunately no organ-book. It provides the best source for many early Restoration full anthems, but the lack of the organ part hampers the reconstruction of the verse anthems. Most of the contents are in the hand of Stephen Bing, a minor canon of St Paul's before the Great Fire, and a vicar choral at Lincoln from 1669 to 1672, after which he returned to London to resume his place at St Paul's, and take up a clerk's place at Westminster Abbey. He died in 1681, whereupon John Gostling, the great bass singer recently come to St Paul's and the Chapel Royal, and a prolific copyist, acquired the set and made further additions up to about 1698.[15] He used the contents in compiling the late seventeenth-century sets at St Paul's Cathedral.[16] Two later sets of Gostling partbooks (again, a private record) dating from the first decade of the eighteenth century belong to the Tenbury collection, now in the Bodleian Library, Oxford. Though incomplete, they are nevertheless extremely valuable, since one contains a mixture of cantoris and decani parts for treble, counter-tenor, tenor, and bass, supported by three organ-books (MSS 1176–82, compiled between c.1700 and c.1713), while the other lacks only a cantoris treble, but has no organ part (MSS 797–803, compiled c.1712–c.1715).[17]

The surviving Chapel Royal partbooks have been studied in detail by Watkins Shaw and, more recently, Margaret Laurie.[18] The earliest set (*RM* 27.a.1–15) includes four cantoris, three 'subdecani', and three organ-books, and a cantoris verse-book, two cello continuo-books, and another (figured) for the lute. These are largely in the hand of John Church, who started copying for the Chapel Royal about 1700 or soon after, but include pages from an earlier set by William Tucker dating from the mid-1670s and continued by Edward Braddock in the 1680s. Interestingly, Tucker distributes the verses between both sides of the choir, while Braddock allots them to the decani; presumably the best singers

---

[15] Tucker's hand has been identified in the following MSS: H. Watkins Shaw, *A Study of the Bing–Gostling Part Books*, 3–18.

[16] Robert F. Ford, 'Minor Canons at Canterbury Cathedral: The Gostlings and Their Colleagues' (Ph.D. diss., University of California, Berkeley, 1984), 276–84.

[17] Ibid. 294–8.

[18] H. Watkins Shaw, 'A Contemporary Source of English Music of the Purcellian Period', *Acta Musicologica*, 31 (1959), 38–44; Margaret Laurie, 'The Chapel Royal Part-Books', *Music and Bibliography: Essays in Honour of Alec Hyatt King*, ed. Oliver Neighbour (London, 1980), 28–50.

were placed there in his time.[19] Church seems to have made separate books for verse singers and chorus, which was a sensible arrangement for a large choir.

Reconstructing the music from incomplete sets of partbooks obviously presents problems. Occasionally, however, an organ-book may help to supply a missing treble part, since organ parts usually consist of the bass plus whichever part was on top, sometimes with other detail sketched in. Nevertheless, comparatively few anthems can be reassembled in this way; one really needs scores, which are rare for the early years but increasingly frequent from the 1680s onwards.

Early autograph scores include a collection of anthems and odes by Cooke, Humfrey, Blow, and Purcell now at Birmingham University (MS 5001),[20] and more by Purcell and others in a similar compilation by William Flackton in the eighteenth century, now in the British Library (Add. MSS 30931–3). The most important autograph sources of anthems by Purcell, however, are (*a*) an early score-book in the Fitzwilliam Museum at Cambridge (MS 88) dated 1677–82, which also contains anthems by Locke, Humfrey, and Blow in his hand, together with earlier music by Byrd, Gibbons, etc., and (*b*) a collection of his symphony anthems in the Royal Library (*RM* 20.h.8) dated 1682–5.[21] A number of autographs by John Blow are known (among them *Och* 628), but nothing so comprehensive.[22] Instead we must rely on the great manuscript anthologies of church music made between 1680 and 1720, not only for most of Blow's work, but for the repertoire in general.

Only the most important sources will be discussed here—principally those compiled by Isaack, Gostling, Hawkins, and Tudway. (Others will be dealt with later in connection with the music of particular institutions.) The earliest, and one of the most extensive, of these manuscripts is Cambridge, Fitzwilliam Museum MS 117, a collection of services and anthems in the hand of William Isaack, lay clerk and minor canon of Windsor between 1671 and 1703 (he was also at Eton)—a prolific copyist of secular as well as sacred music.[23] It is important not only for its size and early date, but because its readings are reliable, and because it includes instrumental movements to anthems by Humfrey and Blow. Bruce Wood has drawn attention to other sources in the same hand, and pointed out that the attribution of Blow's E minor Service to 'Mr' Blow in the body of the manuscript (pp. 103–23 'service end')—though

---

[19] Laurie, 35.

[20] H. Watkins Shaw, 'A Collection of Musical Manuscripts in the Autograph of Henry Purcell and Other English Composers, *c*. 1665–85', *The Library*, 5th ser., 14 (1959), 126–31.

[21] Nigel Fortune and Franklin B. Zimmerman, 'Purcell's Autographs', in Imogen Holst (ed.), *Henry Purcell, 1659–1695* (London, 1959), 108–10, 112–15.

[22] H. Watkins Shaw, 'The Autographs of John Blow', *Music Review*, 25 (1964), 85–95.

[23] Bruce Wood, 'A Note on Two Cambridge Manuscripts and Their Copyists', *Music and Letters*, 56 (1975), 308–12; Peter Holman, 'Bartholomew Isaack and "Mr Isaack" of Eton', *Musical Times*, 128 (1987), 381–5.

not in the table of contents—suggests that its compilation had begun before the award of Blow's doctorate in December 1677. Both the table at the 'anthem end' and the one at the 'service end' are dated 1683, and it is probable that the manuscript was almost complete by that time, since the end of Blow's *Hear my voice, O God*, the last anthem to be entered in the main body of the manuscript, is dated 'July the 18th 1683'.

A Windsor provenance for MS 117 is compatible with the strong representation of Child's anthems and services in the early pages of the manuscript, and the fact that among the last pieces to be entered were anthems by John Goldwin and John Walter, and a service by Goldwin. Goldwin was Child's successor as organist of Eton; Walter was organist of Eton. A further manuscript in Isaack's hand at Christ Church, Oxford (MS 94), containing the service and twenty anthems by John Goldwin strengthens the connection.

The main body of the manuscript contains 128 anthems and twenty-nine services or parts of services in score. The anthems have been entered at one end, the services at the other. The anthem end begins with twenty-eight pages in the same hand as the rest of the manuscript but not paginated consecutively with it. Starting with some pieces by Tallis and Byrd, it continues with symphonies to anthems by Humfrey found elsewhere in the manuscript. A verse anthem by Christopher Gibbons (*How long wilt thou forget me, O Lord*) and an anonymous setting of *Let thy merciful ears* (adapted from Robert White's (?) *O how glorious art thou*) ends this section. Only the anthem by Gibbons has been entered into the table of contents, but with page number '00'.

The next section begins with forty-three anthems, mainly by contemporaries of Byrd and Orlando Gibbons but with eighteen by William Child, three more by Christopher Gibbons and an early work by Michael Wise. Then follows seventy-six anthems by various composers associated with the Chapel Royal in the period up to 1683, mainly Blow, Humfrey, and Purcell, but also Child, Locke, Wise, and Turner, and including one by 'Mr B Isaack'—the scribe's brother, Bartholomew. The last anthem of this group is Blow's *Hear my voice, O God*, which, as has already been stated, carries the date 18 July 1683. Then come fifteen pages containing 'The Symphonyes to some of the foregoing Anthems', and a further twelve which, since they include four by John Goldwin (born about 1667), were probably added a year or two later. Their first lines have been squeezed into the table of contents rather as an afterthought.

Reversing the manuscript to open at the 'service end', one finds first of all another table of contents, in which the services are listed by key. Rather surprisingly, pages '01–04' consist of the printed edition of Locke's communion service in F major (printed and defended in *Modern Church-Musick Pre-accus'd; Censur'd, and Obstructed in its Performance . . . 1666*) paginated consecutively with the next section, which contains the short services of Tallis and Bevin (pp. '05–028'). The contents table shows that Child's evening service in B flat originally followed at this point, but in fact the evening canticles from Byrd's First Service come next (on different paper), followed by Aldrich's Service in G. Neither of these is entered into the table of contents, so they presumably became part of the manuscript after 1683, perhaps considerably later. The fact that the Gloria in excelsis from Aldrich's service is inscribed 'The Lady Trelawneys' suggests an earliest possible date of 1684, assuming the lady in question to be the wife of Sir Jonathan Trelawney. (Trelawney, who married that year, became Bishop of Bristol, Exeter, and Winchester in succession; as he was a prominent benefactor of Christ Church, Oxford—Aldrich's college—the identification seems likely.)

The next section of the manuscript begins on page 6, which actually consists of the last page of the service by Child that should have begun on page '029', crossed out. From now on we are in the main section of the manuscript (reversed), and there follows a series of ten services by Child, paralleling the anthems by him which dominate the corresponding pages at the other end. Blow's services in E minor, G major, and A major are interrupted by various ones by Gibbons, Giles, and Byrd, and lead to Humfrey's Service in E minor— its only complete source. After two communion services by Wise comes Purcell's B flat Service, without, at this stage, the alternative canticles. This point probably equates with the dated anthem by Blow (1683) at the other end of the manuscript. The remaining services seem to have been added later, judging by the way they have been entered into the table of contents. They include additional movements for Blow's G major Service, and the rest of Purcell's. Apart from Morley's First Service, the only other is Goldwin's in F. Again, it seems unlikely that this can have been entered into the manuscript before 1685, in view of Goldwin's probable date of birth. Table 2 may help to clarify the various layers of the manuscript.

The importance of Fitzwilliam Museum MS 117 can hardly be overestimated in relation to the work of Humfrey, Blow, and to a lesser extent Purcell, especially considering its date and authoritative readings. Clearly it represents, for the most part, the Chapel Royal repertoire on either side of 1680. One would have guessed that the scribe was a gentleman of the Chapel Royal, or a close acquaintance, but the Windsor provenance is not surprising in view of the number of services and anthems by Child, as well as the presence of works by John Walter and John Goldwin. There is no problem in accounting for transmission, for several of the choir of St George's were also members of the Chapel Royal in the early 1680s—Leonard Woodson, Josias Boucher, and Nathaniel Vestment, among them—and every summer between 1678 and 1683 the gentlemen of the chapel went down to Windsor in attendance on the king.[24] The fact that the royal band came with them may even suggest that symphony anthems were a feature of Sunday services during that period.

---

[24] Ashbee, i. 180–207.

TABLE 2. *Summary of contents of Cambridge, Fitzwilliam Museum, MS 117*

section	pages	contents
		Anthem end
		'A Table of all the Full Anthems . . . 1683'
		'A Table of all the Vers Anthems . . . 1683'
1	[i–xxviii]	anthems by Tallis (2), and one each by Byrd, C. Gibbons, and White (anonymously), with instrumental symphonies for four of Humfrey's anthems
2a	1–122	anthems by Child (18), Byrd (5), O. Gibbons (3), C. Gibbons (3), Giles (2), Hooper (2), Tallis (2), and one each by Batten, Bull, W. Mundy, Parsons, Tomkins, Weelkes, White, and Wise
2b	122–449	anthems by Blow (29), Humfrey (14), Purcell (14), Child (5), Locke (4), Wise (4), Turner (3), and one each by Hall and Bartholomew Isaac. (Also the 'Club Anthem' by Blow, Humfrey, and Turner.) This section ends with the date 'July the 18th 1683'
2c	450–64	instrumental symphonies for six anthems by Blow and four by Humfrey
2d	465–514	further anthems by Blow (4), Goldwin (4), and one each by Aldrich, Purcell, and Walter
		Service end
		'A Table of all the Services . . . 1683'
1a	01–04	Locke's *Modern Church-Musick* . . . 1666 (printed but bound in and entered in the original 'Table')
1b	05–044	psalms by Tallis, and a service each by Tallis, Bevin, Byrd, and Aldrich
1c	045–047	(different paper) Sanctus and Gloria of Aldrich's G major Service ('The Lady Trelawny's')
2	5–244	services by Child (10), Blow (3), Byrd (2), O. Gibbons (2), Giles (2), and one each by Humfrey, Wise, and Purcell
3	244–86	later addition of services (or parts of services) by Blow, Purcell, Goldwin, and Morley

John Walter, organist of Eton from 1681 to 1705, was another important copyist, especially for the transmission of Blow's work. In this connection a manuscript in his hand at King's College, Cambridge (Rowe MS 22) provides an important source, though certain items may have been copied from Fitzwilliam 117, or vice versa.[25]

[25] Wood, 'A Note'.

We have already observed John Gostling as an industrious copyist of partbooks. Even more important are the scores in his hand, particularly the so-called 'Gostling Manuscript' now in the library of the University of Texas at Austin, and its sequel in the Newberry Library, Chicago (MS 7A/2).[26] The former contains sixty-four anthems, with dates between 1686 and 1705. This was possibly the period of compilation, though Robert Ford puts its commencement at about 1690.[27] Most of the dates are, in effect, dates of performance and are often accompanied by interesting details of the particular occasion. Thus, for example, Purcell's *Behold, I bring you glad tidings* carries the footnote 'Composed by Mr Henry Purcell For Christmas day 1687', while the one which follows, Purcell's *Blessed are they that fear the Lord*, gives even more information: 'Composed by Mr Henry Purcell. Jan: 12. 1687[8]. For the Thanksgiving— Appointed in London & 12 miles round, upon her Majesties being with Child. & on the 29 following, over England'. (The heading to the anthem adds that the Thanksgiving was 'appointed Jan: 15th', so Purcell was working to a tight schedule.) Starting at one end are twenty-six symphony anthems by Blow (9), Purcell (8), Humfrey (3), Turner (3), Tudway, and Clarke, etc.; at the other end, thirty-eight full and verse anthems by Blow (15), Purcell (10), Locke (3), Clarke (3), Tudway (2), Child, Wise, Humfrey, Turner, etc. Emanating from the Chapel Royal and St Paul's, these versions are invaluable in providing good texts of works by Blow and Purcell in the absence of autographs.

The Newberry Library manuscript begins more or less where the Austin manuscript ends, and continues up to about 1715. The first item, Croft's *O clap your hands together*, is inscribed 'Anthem on the Thanksgiving June. 27. 1706' and the second is Blow's *Blessed is the man*, dated a month later. Croft is accorded his doctorate from no. 30 onwards, so the last third of the manuscript must date from after July 1713, and, since no. 26 is dated 1708, it may have been completed fairly quickly after a fallow period. In all there are forty-eight anthems, with Croft (23 plus three unfinished), Clarke (5), Church (4), Weldon (4), and Blow (3) the main composers represented, and two early works by Greene in the later section. Again some interesting details are appended, particularly with regard to anthems performed to commemorate Marlborough's continental victories. Thus Clarke's *The Lord is my strength* was written 'In memory of the victory at Ramillies. Thanksgiving Anthem June 17, 1706', while the same composer's *The Lord is king, the earth may be glad* is described as 'Union Anthem for May the first 1707' (the Act of Union between England and Scotland was passed in March 1707). More than in the earlier collection Gostling gives details of performers; thus, Blow's *O clap your hands together* has

---

[26] Franklin B. Zimmerman (ed.), *The Gostling Manuscript* (facs. edn., Austin, Texas, 1977); see also id., 'Anthems of Purcell and Contemporaries in a Newly Rediscovered "Gostling Manuscript"', *Acta Musicologica*, 41 (1969), 55–70; Ford, 'Minor Canons', 288–94.

[27] Ford, 294; contents listed 893–9.

parts marked for Richard Elford, John Church, John Freeman, Daniel Williams, Charles Barnes, and Gostling himself, while towards the end of the manuscript Francis Hughes, Bernard Gates, and Samuel Weely make their appearance.

Gostling's scores and partbooks are the most important sources we have for the period 1685–1715. As the leading bass singer of his time and a member of the choirs of both the Chapel Royal and St Paul's (where he was also subdean) he transmits an essentially metropolitan repertoire, as does his colleague Charles Badham, a minor canon at St Paul's between 1698 and 1715. Unfortunately, Badham's scores tend to be defective.[28]

Over the same period James Hawkins, organist of Ely from 1682/3 to 1729, was engaged in compiling a more provincial repertoire no less industriously—indeed, rather too industriously for the Dean and Chapter, who in 1693 'ordered that the Organist shall not be allowd any bill for pricking books . . . unless his design shall be first allowd, before he performs it'.[29] Hawkins seems to have been a compulsive copyist, but the Chapter's strictures failed, fortunately, to deter him from compiling scores of the music that came his way. Whether paid for or not, many remained in the cathedral library and are now housed in the Cambridge University Library. Although a printed catalogue has existed since 1861 there are many points of uncertainty attaching to these manuscripts that deserve more attention than has been given to them so far.[30] Those scores which are entirely or mainly in Hawkins's hand include MSS 5–7, 9–12, 14, and 16–21, to which may be added British Library, Add. MSS 31444–5. These volumes carry comparatively few indications of date, but, judging by their contents, MS 5 is probably the earliest. It could have been begun as early as 1684, but in the absence of any works later than Aldrich's Service in G and the *Cantate Domino* and *Deus misereatur* from Purcell's B flat Service, little more can be said on the subject. Interestingly, it contains numerous pieces of local origin, including anthems by Tye, White, Farrant, Fox, Barcroft, and Amner (successively Ely organists between 1562 and 1641), scored up, presumably, from cathedral partbooks that were still surviving in the 1680s. A service and two anthems by Dr William Holder represent the early Restoration period, Holder being one of the canons at the Restoration.

The rest of the scores are probably considerably later, and it will be more convenient to deal with them in numerical than chronological order, since the latter is uncertain. So far as MS 6 goes, it was probably begun between 1705 and 1713, if attributions to 'Dr Tudway' and 'Mr Crofts' are to be taken at their face value. Among its twenty-eight anthems are works by Purcell (10) and Blow (9),

---

[28] Badham's scores include *Ob* Mus. c. 38–40, Mus. Sch. B.7, Tenbury 1031 and 1258.

[29] *Cu* EDC/2/1/2, 204.

[30] W. E. Dickson, *A Catalogue of Ancient Choral Services and Anthems, Preserved among the Manuscript Scores and Partbooks in the Cathedral Church of Ely* (Ely, 1861).

with others by Turner, 'Golding' (Goldwin), and Hawkins himself.[31] Nowhere among the remaining scores at Ely does Croft ever appear without his doctorate, and it must be assumed that all those which contain works by him are to be dated later than 1713.

Hawkins freely transcribed his own works along with those of other composers in the volumes he was compiling, but MS 7 is entirely devoted to them. It contains fifty-six anthems and six services (at the end), and seems to date from after 1714, judging by the inclusion of *O Lord grant the king a long life* among the full anthems in the middle. The idea of making a comprehensive collection of his own work would have been one to appeal towards the end of his life, and for this reason we may suppose a date some years later. Perhaps there was an intention to publish such a collection in emulation of Croft's *Musica Sacra* (1724).

Rather than mixing services and anthems in a jumbled sequence, or beginning with one at the front and the other at the back (reversed), Hawkins usually opens a volume with one or two services and continues with anthems. Thus, MS 9 begins with his Morning Service in C and 'chanting service' in D. Among the fifty-eight anthems which follow are thirteen of his own, and a wide representation of other composers, including Blow (8), Humfrey (5), Tudway (4), Purcell (3), and one or two each by Clarke, Croft, Golding, Greene, Hall, Henman, Hawkins Jnr, Norris, Turner, Walkely, Weldon, and Wise. The manuscript certainly dates from after 1714. Bound in with it is an organ-book (reversed), the first part of which is in Hawkins's hand and contains accompaniments to services by Tallis, Byrd, Child, Gibbons, Patrick, Portman, and John Ferrabosco—the latter Hawkins's immediate predecessor at Ely.

Pride of place in MS 10 is given to Croft's *Te Deum* and *Jubilate* with trumpets, oboes, and strings, followed by Hawkins's Service in A also with orchestral accompaniment. Conceivably, it may have been written for his B. Mus. exercise in 1719. Among the anthems are three each by Golding and Hawkins, and one by 'J: Hawkins Junr Organist of Peterborough'—an appointment which dates from 1714. MS 11 is devoted entirely to the work of Thomas Tudway, beginning with the service he wrote for the inauguration of Lord Harley's chapel at Wimpole in 1721. As the most prominent church musician in nearby Cambridge, Tudway was clearly someone for whom Hawkins had considerable respect. We know that Hawkins supplied copies for Tudway's own manuscript anthology of church music, and in this instance the process must have been reciprocated. Apart from the Wimpole service, there are twelve anthems.

---

[31] Goldwin is consistently called Golding by Hawkins, though he was generally known as Goldwin by fellow musicians, including his colleagues at Windsor. The Dean and Chapter of Windsor, however, referred to him as Golding.

The first item in MS 12 is Handel's 'Utrecht' *Te Deum* and *Jubilate* (1713), followed by anthems by Blow (4), Purcell (4), Hawkins (3), and Turner (2) among others. Passing over MS 14, which is another copy of the Utrecht *Te Deum*, MS 16 begins with yet another 'big' service, the York composer Valentine Nalson's Service in G. The same volume also includes parts of Purcell's Service in B flat and Goodson's in C, together with anthems by Nalson (3), Purcell (2), and Weldon (2), and single pieces by Clarke and George Holmes of Lincoln.

The next three volumes, MSS 17–19, are all inscribed 'John Hawkins Jnr 1726'. Presumably they passed into his hands at that time, though how or why they returned to Ely is not known. Most of MS 17 is not actually by the elder Hawkins, who seems only to have been responsible for adding two anthems by Philip Hart and a handful of his own. Several services and anthems by Hawkins are also featured in MS 18, along with a service by John Ferrabosco and a variety of other pieces (including some by Locke and earlier composers). At the end occurs a note, 'Dr Tudway desires you to send them to him as soon as you receive any thing from me Yours Benj Lam'—presumably asking Hawkins to forward certain copies of music to Tudway, who was then compiling his Harleian collection. In fact, although Lamb, who was organist of Eton from 1705 until 1733, is represented in the fifth and sixth volumes of Tudway's collection, Hawkins does not seem to have included any pieces by him in his own. MS 19 begins with Hawkins's Morning Service in G followed by his Chanting Service in C minor. In addition to four of his anthems, it contains works by Tudway (2), Croft (2), Purcell, Turner, Clarke, and William Norris of Lincoln. The end of the volume is signed and dated '6 Oct 1718'.

The repertoire of MS 20 is in most respects typically Restoration, with anthems by Humfrey (8), Blow (5), and three each by Aldrich, Hall, Purcell, and Hawkins himself, but the presence of pieces by Golding (3) and Valentine Nalson (1) suggests a date after 1700, while an attribution to 'Dr' Tudway in the middle of the manuscript dates that part 1705 at the earliest. It may be that the presence of Aldrich's *O Lord, grant the* king *a long life* as the third item points to a date of 1714 or later; on the other hand, the absence of anthems by Croft and Clarke is rather surprising for such a date. MS 21 was probably started about 1724 since the second item, Tudway's *Hearken unto me*, carries that date. It is notable for the inclusion of anthems by 'Mr' Greene—five in number and more than any other composer.

The Hawkins manuscripts in the British Library (Add. MSS 31444–5) are probably earlier than most of those at Ely, dating from 1695 to 1700. The first contains anthems by Blow (15) and Tudway (7) among others; Tudway is 'Mr' throughout, which he ceased to be in 1705. The last item is Blow's *Lord, remember David*, composed for the opening of the Banqueting Hall chapel

'December the 9th [1698]'. The omission of the year may suggest that it was copied that year. The second manuscript includes five anthems each by Blow, Purcell, and Turner, and others by Norris (3), Humfrey, Tudway, Hart, and Daniel Purcell. Turner begins as 'Mr' but ends as 'Dr', a change which occurred in 1696. The sixth item from the end is Blow's *I was glad*, written for the opening of St Paul's Cathedral in December 1697.

Hawkins at Ely was not far from Thomas Tudway at King's College, Cambridge, and as we have seen, he supplied Tudway with some of his material. We can follow Tudway's progress in compiling the enormous six-volume Harleian anthology for Edward, Lord Harley—the son of Queen Anne's minister, Robert Harley, Earl of Oxford—through his correspondence with Humphrey Wanley, Harley's librarian, beginning in 1715.[32] The successive dedications of each volume also show us how the collection developed (see App. F). According to Tudway it was Harley's 'Pious designe of rescuing from the dust & Oblivion, our Ancient compositions of Church Musick', and he continued to pander to Harley's antiquarianism by extolling the excellency of 'our Ancient compositions' in subsequent volumes, though Tudway himself, as a composer, was modernistically inclined. He also sought to reassure his patron that in the past many of royal and noble birth had been musicians themselves, or well disposed towards the art (King Henry VIII among them), and that to be so was quite compatible with being a gentleman—witness Dr Aldrich, Dr Holden, and Dr Creighton.

This first volume has a printed title-page dated 1715; it covered the period 'from the Reformation to the Restauration of K. Charles II', beginning with Tallis and ending with William Lawes. Perhaps this was all Harley originally wanted, but Tudway anticipated a second volume (showing 'how we are come to a Kind of Theatrical, & Secular way, in our Modern Compositions of Church Musick') towards the end of the first dedication. Volume ii bears the date 1716. The intention seems to have been to include only music written during Charles II's reign—the latest work is Purcell's *My song shall be alway* of 1688 (though Tudway may have thought it somewhat earlier)—and to bring the anthology down to the accession of Queen Anne in a third and final volume. The main composers represented in volume ii are Child with six services and four anthems, Humfrey with parts of his service and twelve anthems, Aldrich with sixteen anthems (all adaptations from Latin works by earlier composers), Blow with a service and three anthems, and Purcell with three anthems. There are services by Bryne, Creighton, Ferrabosco, Holder, Loosemore, Rogers, and

[32] Christopher Hogwood, 'Thomas Tudway's History of Music', in C. Hogwood and R. Luckett (eds.), *Music in Eighteenth-Century England* (Cambridge, 1983), 19–47; see also Edward Turnbull, 'Thomas Tudway and the Harleian Collection', *Journal of the American Musicological Society*, 8 (1955), 203–4; William Weber, 'Thomas Tudway and the Harleian Collection of "Ancient" Church Music', *British Library Journal*, 15 (1989), 187–205.

Wise; the volume ends with two orchestral anthems by Tudway himself, written for his Bachelor of Music exercise in 1681.

Volume iii (1716) and volume iv (1717) provide an amplification of the first two. At the end of the second volume Tudway had mentioned that 'after I had begun this volume, there [came] to my hands a great many important peices of the Ancient Church way of Composition; & allso an Anthem of Harry the 8ths Composing for his own Chappell'.

I judg'd it necessary therupon, to begin my 3d volume. with a Royal Composure, & with such other peices of Ancient Church Music, as were come to my hands before, & then proceed to add such further Modern Compositions, as I had not room for, in this.

Thus, volume iii begins with *O Lord, the maker of all things*, mistakenly attributed to King Henry VIII instead of William Mundy. It continues, however, with works mainly by Restoration composers, including Wise (a service and four anthems), Blow (a service and six anthems), and Purcell (part of the B flat Service and seven anthems). Blow and Purcell are also strongly represented in volume iv (Blow with another service and eight anthems, Purcell with more of his B flat Service and five anthems) along with Henry Aldrich (a service and five anthems). In addition, it contains a number of sixteenth-century works traceable back to Hawkins. The presence of William Norris and Jeremiah Clarke among the composers indicates that the scope of the volume had been expanded 'down to the Accession of Queen Anne'.

The last pair of volumes (1718 and 1720) contains works 'Compos'd Cheifly, in the Reigne of her Majesty, Queen Anne'. Volume v opens with Purcell's 1694 *Te Deum* and *Jubilate*, but otherwise may be true to its word in containing works written between 1702 and 1714. Nothing that we know about the remainder of the contents—predominantly by younger composers such as John Church, William Croft, George Holmes, Charles King, Benjamin Lamb, Vaughan Richardson, Thomas Wanless, John Weldon, etc.—indicates that they are earlier than 1702, which may support a similar dating for pieces in the volume by Hawkins, Tudway, and Turner. Tudway continues to copy his own work, and that of Hawkins, into volume vi, adding more by Church, Croft, etc., and bringing in younger composers such as Thomas Roseingrave, William Broderip, and Anthony Walkeley. Early anthems by Maurice Greene are also included, and the volume ends with 'Mr Hendale's' Utrecht *Te Deum* of 1713.

Tudway's texts are of variable quality. His copies came from a variety of sources and he was inevitably at their mercy, though he could also be careless. As we have seen, he was supplied with copies from Hawkins at Ely, while John Church and William Croft provided him with up-to-date works by London composers. Tudway's reward was 30 guineas a volume and posthumous fame that would never have come his way as a composer.

ASPECTS OF PERFORMANCE

Several matters relating to performance have already been touched on in the course of this study. The composition and balance of choirs was considered in Chapter 3, while the tonal quality and pitch of organs were dealt with in Chapter 4, as was evidence regarding organ accompaniments. Without too much repetition, it is proposed here to summarize some of this material and explore one or two areas in rather more detail—particularly that of choral sound, solo voices and ornamentation, questions of dynamics and tempo (already anticipated in dealing with organ-books), and the use of instruments.

Cathedral choirs varied in size from about eighteen men and boys in less well-endowed cathedrals like Bristol and Gloucester to thirty or more in grand places like Canterbury (34), Durham (32), and Worcester (30). The fact that men outnumbered boys two to one must have resulted in a balance rather different from today's. The blend, too, would have been different, especially if countertenors were 'natural' rather than 'falsetto'.[33] There is no hint in the written descriptions of the time that such voices were 'false' or 'feigned', and when the latter word was used (as when Matthew Locke described how 'Cornets and Mens feigned Voices' were used in the Chapel Royal immediately after the Restoration, 'there being not one Lad ... capable of singing his Part readily') it indicated men singing a *treble* part falsetto.[34] Charles Butler in *The Principles of Musik* (1636) does not regard the countertenor as extraordinary in any way, other than being rare (or, to be more precise, rarely well sung). He calls it 'the highest part of a man' and defines it thus:

The Countertenor or *Contratenor*, is so called, becaus it answereth the Tenor; though commonly in higher keys: and therefore is fittest for a man of a sweet shrill voice. Which Parte, though it have little Melody by it self ... yet in Harmony it hath the greatest grace: specially when it is sung with a right voice: which is too rare.[35]

Thomas Tudway at the end of our period also regards it as rare:

The devideing the scale into, Base part, Tenor, Contratenor, & Treble, were all contriv'd for Church Music, And Adapted to each part of the scale, according to the

[33] On the question of 'natural' or 'falsetto' countertenors see Frederic Hodgson, 'The Contemporary Alto', *Musical Times*, 106 (1965), 293; Roland Stuart Tatnell, 'Falsetto Practice: A Brief Survey', *The Consort*, 22 (1965), 31–5; G. M. Ardran and David Wulstan, 'The Alto or Countertenor Voice', *Music and Letters*, 48 (1967), 17–22; Olive Baldwin and Thelma Wilson, 'Alfred Deller, John Freeman and Mr Pate', *Music and Letters*, 50 (1969), 103–10; David Wulstan, 'Vocal Colour in English Sixteenth-Century Polyphony', *Journal of the Plainsong and Medieval Music Society*, 2 (1979), 19–60; Peter Giles, *The Counter Tenor* (London, 1982).
[34] Matthew Locke, *The Present Practice of Musick Vindicated* (London, 1673), 19.
[35] Charles Butler, *The Principles of Musik in Singing and Setting* (London, 1636; facs. edn., New York, 1970), 41–2. Butler's 'reformed' spelling has been un-reformed.

Naturall voices of men; some voices being fitted Naturally to sing the Base, or lowest part; others the Tenor; others, thô very few, the Contratenor; The Treble, or highest part, is always sung by Boys, or women, and hereby, is the whole scale compleated.[36]

Perhaps the passage 'some voices being fitted Naturally to sing . . . thô very few', contains the nub of the matter.

Such voices were highly prized, especially in the Chapel Royal, where men like John Abell, Josiah Boucher, Alexander Damascene, Richard Elford, John Freeman, John Howell, Francis Hughes, and William Turner were the leading soloists, once the heyday of the great bass John Gostling had passed. They were England's answer to Italian castratos like Siface and Tosi, who had recently made their appearance in this country, but what we know of the quality of their voices and their ranges tells us little about their actual methods of voice production. It may be that it was a voice which has virtually been lost in England since the eighteenth century. Possibly the voices of some cathedral choristers, especially those kept singing during puberty, never actually 'broke' (in the sense of collapsing an octave) but gradually dropped a fourth or fifth below their treble range. According to Burney, Turner's voice settled as a countertenor when it broke, adding that it was 'a circumstance which so seldom happens *naturally* [his italics], that if it be cultivated, the possessor is sure of employment'.[37] Others, breaking to a light tenor, may have developed the high tenor range, as did their French counterpart, the *haute-contre*. On the other hand, John Evelyn's description of Abell's voice—'one would have sworne it had been a Womans it was so high'[38]—hardly sounds as if it were merely a high tenor, though it does not seem to have gone above top C.

In the general repertoire (as represented by the contents of the countertenor partbook *Ob* Tenbury 1177, which includes anthems from the whole period) the normal countertenor range was a to a', with most of the music lying above middle C (c'). Top B♭ and B♮ were, however, quite often asked for, top C only rarely. At the other end, a or g marked the usual limit, though sometimes notes down to d were written. We are therefore looking at a voice that by modern pitch standards had an extreme range of $d\#$ to $c\#''$, with maximum flexibility between $c\#'$ and $a\#'$. Falsetto is certainly a possibility in some cases, but with a different tradition and training there could have been other ways of getting as high.

A similar analysis of the treble partbook in the same set (*Ob* Tenbury 1176) shows that with the G2 clef the treble range was mainly between d' and f'' or $f\#''$, c' below and g'' above being required on rare occasions. With the C1 clef f'' was the highest note. It would be hazardous to say what this might mean

[36] See App. F(iv).

[37] Charles Burney, *A General History of Music from the Earliest Ages to the Present*, ed. Frank Mercer, 2 vols. (London, 1935), ii. 361.

[38] Evelyn, *Diary*, iv. 270; 28 Jan. 1682.

with regard to tone production, but at least the boys were not expected to sing above (modern) top A♭.

The question of ornamentation also arises with regard to solo singers in the choir, who without doubt were expected to embellish their parts extempore. Most scores and even partbooks are therefore fairly reticent about what was actually done, but here and there we get an idea of the kind of thing that was added in performance. The flamboyant anthems of the 1690s and 1700s were, of course, by their very nature highly ornamented, but among the additions one finds trills or shakes, and forefalls and backfalls (appoggiaturas from below or above indicated by a stroke sloping upwards or downwards, though the former might be read as a slide beginning on the third below). Oddly, the Purcellian ⋎ is not explained in any of the usual sources, but it is obviously a trill of some sort. John Goldwin's *O Lord, my God* provides an example of the florid style (Ex. 13). The same embellishments were also added to works from earlier in the century, where the scope was, if anything, greater because of the simpler lines. On pp. 66–7 we saw an example of an ornamented organ part for Tallis's 'Dorian service'; vocal lines too were subject to the same process. The opening verse of Orlando Gibbons's *Behold thou hast made my days*, as notated by Gostling early in the eighteenth century, provides an illustration which actually may not be very different from the way it was sung in Gibbons's time (Ex. 14).

Ornamentation was both decorative and expressive, and there is no evidence to suggest that singers were any less inclined to employ it in sacred than in secular music—at least in principle. Playford's *Introduction to the Skill of Musick* (1664) mentions that the Italian style of vocal ornamentation had been introduced into the Chapel Royal 'above this 40 years . . . and now is come to that Excellency & Perfection there, by the Skill and furtherance of the Orpheus of our time, Henry Cooke, Gentleman and Master of the Children of His Majesties Chappell'.[39] This was, in fact, the method propounded in Giulio Caccini's *Le nuove musiche* (1602) and would only have been possible in verse anthems, where ornaments such as the *trillo* and *gruppo* would have been introduced along with expressive vocal and rhythmic nuances according to the taste and skill of the singer. So far as actual dynamic markings go, these are rare in the sources but are reflected in organ accompaniments where, for example, 'loud organ' or 'echo' (= soft) must indicate a corresponding dynamic level in the choir. 'Full' and 'verse' contrasts, as also of cantoris and decani semi-choirs, are other aspects of the dynamic variety provided by such music.

A comparison of Orlando Gibbons's *Behold thou hast made my days* (Ex. 14) with his son Christopher's *How long wilt thou forget me* (Ex. 9) reminds us that early in our period a change took place in church music from minim beats to

[39] Ian Spink, 'Playford's "Directions for Singing after the Italian Manner"', *Monthly Musical Record*, 89 (1959), 130–5; see also Peter le Huray's Introduction to *MB* 38, pp. xvi–xviii, and Bruce Wood's to *MB* 50, pp. xxi–xxiii.

Ex. 13. John Goldwin, *O Lord, my God (Och 94)*

(1) The version in T 1176 has 𝄿 at these points.

crotchet beats, irrespective of whether the time signature was **c** or **¢**. Side by side with works in an older style moving mainly in minims and crotchets, composers wrote music that moved in crotchets and quavers. The implication of this with regard to tempo and tempo relationships needs to be examined, for though the sense of the words was an important factor in determining the speed of a piece (as were, no doubt, the acoustics of a particular place and the number of performers taking part), some residual ideas relating time signatures and note-values to a tactus measured against the human heartbeat persisted well into the seventeenth century.

In the absence of tempo indications, beats were still related to a notional 'standard tempo' which in turn was equated with the human pulse. Thomas Ravenscroft's observation that '*Time* according to the discretion of the *Singer* (and according to the *Measure*) may be sung swifter, or slower'[40] implies that the 'Measure', or tactus, established a basic speed which could then be modified by

[40] Thomas Ravenscroft, *A Briefe Discourse of the True (but Neglected) Use of Charact'ring the Degrees* (London, 1614; facs. edn., New York, 1976), 21.

Ex. 14. Orlando Gibbons, *Behold, thou hast made my days* (*Ob Tenbury* 1176 - 82)

other considerations, presumably mainly expressive. Thus, the Tenbury organ part of Tomkins's *Musica Deo Sacra* (1668) contains a note to the effect that a semibreve equals two heartbeats, or the oscillation of a pendulum two feet long ('Sit mensura duorum humani corporis pulsum, vel globuli penduli, longitudine duorum pedum a centro motus');[41] in other words, a minim equals a heartbeat (= *c*.76). This applies to music in the 'old' style where the minim beat operates. Quite independently, Christopher Simpson (beating crotchets) says in his *Com-*

---

[41] Denis Stevens, *Thomas Tomkins, 1572–1656* (London, 1957), 73–4; also le Huray, 109–12.

pendium of Practical Musick (1667) that 'some speak of having recourse to the motion of a lively pulse for the measure of *Crotchets*', and equates the semibreve with a 'leisurely' reading, or pronunciation, of the words '*One, Two, Three, Four*'.[42] (If we take a 'lively pulse' as beating about eighty times a minute we have then the same figure that Quantz gives in the middle of the eighteenth century.[43]) This, then, may be taken as a basic speed for abstract music, or music where words were of neutral import, before other aspects affecting tempo were brought into play.

As for tempo markings, later manuscripts are quite freely supplied with words like 'drag', 'quick', 'slow', 'brisk', etc., though opening tempos are rarely indicated. In their absence there are some general principles that may be applicable, or at least ought to be considered. According to contemporary theory, and as a corollary of the idea of tactus, time signatures provide a clue to the appropriate tempo for a piece. Purcell, in revising the relevant section in Playford's *Introduction to the Skill of Music* (1694), states that

the first and slowest of all is marked thus ℭ: 'Tis measured by a *Semibreve*, which you must divide into four equal Parts, telling *one, two, three, four*, distinctly, putting your Hand or Foot down when you tell *one*, and taking it up when you tell *three*. . . . The second sort of *Common-Time* is a little faster . . . having a stroak drawn through it, thus ₵. The third sort of *Common-Time* is quickest of all . . . thus ₵; you may tell *one, two, three, four*, in a Bar, almost as fast as the regular Motions of a Watch.[44]

Unfortunately, there is so much inconsistency regarding the first two that it would be dangerous to read too much significance into the use of one or the other in a particular context; in fact, ₵ is used almost universally whether the movement of the music suggests crotchet beats or minims. Again, the heartbeat should probably suggest the basic tempo, modified by considerations of verbal expression and textural clarity.

It seems likely, however, that 'retorted' common time (₵) must have some notational significance, since it is so much rarer and would thus have been written with due awareness of its implications. Some authorities were more specific about the degree to which it was quicker than other types of common time. Editions of Playford's 'Introduction' before 1694 say it is 'as swift again as the usual Measure'.[45] Even so, it is sometimes oddly used; for example, the passage 'and the peace of God which passeth all understanding' in Purcell's *Rejoice in the Lord, alway*, where a slower rather than a quicker tempo would

---

[42] Christopher Simpson, *A Compendium of Practical Musick* (2nd edn., London, 1667), 22; mod. edn. by Phillip J. Lord (Oxford, 1970), 10.

[43] J. J. Quantz, *Versuch einer Anweisung die Flöte traversiere zu spielen* (Berlin, 1752); English trans. by Edward R. Reilly (London, 1966), 288.

[44] John Playford, *Introduction to the Skill of Musick* (12th edn., London, 1694; 'Corrected and Amended by Mr. Henry Purcell'), 25–6.

[45] e.g. 1674 edn. (facs., Ridgewood, N.J.), 34; see also Simpson (ed. Lord), 17–18.

seem more appropriate (or, at least, that crotchet should equal crotchet in view of the quavers in bar 168 and thereafter).

The change-over from minim to crotchet beat happened later with triple time than common time. Until $\frac{3}{2}$ and $\frac{3}{4}$ made their appearance in church music towards the end of the century the standard indication was a somewhat tautologous $\frac{C}{31}$ (sometimes 3–1 only) used at first with three minims to the bar but later with three crotchets. The implication was that the three minims or three crotchets took the same time as two common-time minims in 'old' music, or two common-time crotchets in 'new' music. In both cases, therefore, triple time was 'quicker' than common time by a ratio of 3:2. Indeed there does not appear to have been any slow church music in triple time until $\frac{3}{2}$ came on the scene; previously it had always introduced a note of levity. Thus, if the common-time crotchet had a value of 80 to the minute, the triple-time minim (at first, but later the triple-time crotchet where there were three to the bar) had a value of 120 to the minute. This assumes that the medieval system of proportions was still so some extent operative, and though this would be a dangerous assumption applied inflexibly, there is evidence that some kind of vestigial proportionality between duple and triple time survived, no doubt with decreasing force, up to the time that modern time signatures and written tempo indications were introduced. By 1694 Playford (or Purcell) could talk about triple time without relating it to duple time, and in doing so he distinguished two sorts: 'the first and slowest of which is measured by three *Minims* in each Bar. . . . This sort of *Time* is marked thus $\frac{3}{2}$. The second sort is faster . . . so that a Bar contains three Crotchets . . . 'tis marked thus 3 or thus 3 1.'[46] He goes on to mention that 'sometimes you will meet with three *Quavers* in a Bar', but this is virtually unknown in church music of the time. On the other hand there was a lot of quick music with three minims to the bar written after 1700.

The truth is that time signatures are much less help in determining the tempo of a piece than the notation and style of the music itself. Nevertheless, the idea of a standard tempo and proportional relationship between triple and common time needs to be understood and considered before it can be overridden.

The use of instruments other than the organ to reinforce and support choirs also merits some discussion. There is evidence involving wind instruments before the Civil War;[47] at Canterbury, for example, 'in leiw of a deacon and sub-deacon . . . are substituted two corniters & two sackbutters, whome we do most willingly maintaine for the decorum of our quire' (confirmed in Laud's statutes of 1637).[48] At the Restoration, four such musicians were listed in the

[46] Playford, *Introduction* (1694 edn.), 27.

[47] Le Huray, 125–9; Andrew Parrott, 'Grett and Solompne Singing; Instruments in Church Music before the Civil War', *Early Music*, 6 (1978), 182–7.

[48] HMC, 125; Ford, 'Minor Canons', 9.

treasurer's accounts, but they were not replaced when they died, and by 1670 they had disappeared. There was a cornett-player up to 1664 at Westminster Abbey,[49] while Durham had four cornetts and sackbuts on the establishment until well into the 1680s (they did not die out until the 1690s).[50] There, as at York and Carlisle, Roger North reported that 'they have the ordinary wind instruments in the Quires, as the cornet, sackbut, double curtaile and others, which supply the want of voices, very notorious there.'[51] If the boys were not up to standard, he was of the opinion that 'nothing can so well reconcile the upper parts in a Quire . . . as the cornet (being well sounded) doth; one might mistake it for a choice eunuch'. Exeter and Gloucester also had cornetts and sackbuts in the early years of the Restoration; one of the Exeter vicars, Henry Travers, was sent to London in 1664 to buy some at a cost of £19.[52]

It is possible that other places could also have used wind instruments to support the choir, if not as part of the establishment then played by local waits or superannuated choirboys who had learned to play as choristers. But it is probable that all cathedrals would have outgrown the practice well before the end of the century, for it was essentially old-fashioned and becoming more so. It may have rounded out the sound of a full anthem very satisfactorily, but the modern verse anthem offered little scope. As the century neared its end, taste was becoming too 'polite' for such sounds as the cornett and sackbut.

Even the Chapel Royal used wind instruments to support the choir at the Restoration; that was how things had been done before the war, and how—for a few years, at least—it continued. There is evidence that it lasted until at least the mid-1660s, but already the strings were taking over. As Evelyn noted in his diary (21 December 1662): 'now we no more heard the *Cornet*, which gave life to the organ, that instrument quite left off in which the English were so skillful.'[53] Instead there were string symphonies 'after the *French* fantastical light way', about which further discussion will follow in Ch. 6. Wind instruments were also occasionally involved: for example, in Blow's *Lord, who shall dwell in thy tabernacle*, which has parts for flutes as well as strings (including a 'Double Base'), and *Sing unto the Lord, O ye saints*, which employs tenor 'Hoboys' (with flutes alternating) and strings.[54] After about 1695 obbligato trumpet parts began to make their appearance in celebratory pieces. Blow's *I was glad*, written for the opening of St Paul's Cathedral in 1697, is an example.[55]

---

[49] Pine, *Westminster Abbey Singers*, 114, 121.

[50] Brian Crosby, *Durham Cathedral Choristers and their Masters* (Durham, 1980), 23.

[51] Wilson, *Roger North on Music*, 40, 286.

[52] Betty Matthews, *The Organs and Organists of Exeter Cathedral* (Exeter, [n.d.]), 2.

[53] Evelyn, *Diary*, iii. 347–8; Peter Holman, *Four and Twenty Fiddlers: The Violin at the English Court, 1540–1690* (Oxford, 1993), 393–8.

[54] Respectively in Zimmerman (ed.), *The Gostling Manuscript*, 24, and *MB* 50, no. 3; see Holman, 408–10.

[55] *MB* 50, no. 2.

Outside the Chapel Royal (and St Paul's) the symphony anthem had no currency, other than for exceptional occasions such as the thanksgiving service for the Peace of Utrecht at Great St Mary's, Cambridge, when Tudway's *My heart rejoiceth in the Lord* was performed. Chapel Royal anthems, when sung in cathedrals, were shorn of their instrumental symphonies and had substitute ritornellos played by the organ alone.[56]

In addition to the organ, the Chapel Royal also seems to have used a continuo group of cello and lute in the early years of the eighteenth century. As has already been mentioned, surviving partbooks include two for cello (*RM* 27.a.10–11, not duplicates) and one (27.a.12)—a copiously figured bass part—said to be for lute, though seemingly not labelled as such. Begun before Tudway took his doctorate (1705) and finished before Croft took his (1713), it must have been in use prior to 1717, when places for a lutenist and a violist were officially established in the chapel.[57] The question of whether the lute appointment was anything more than a sinecure thus seems to be answered, especially by a rubric in one of the organ-books (*RM* 27.a.14) attached to *Rejoice in the Lord* by Bernard Gates: 'Note, that the lower notes (where the notes are double [i.e. stems up and stems down]) is the Organ Part in the following Verse; the Upper dividing Base being for the Lute which the Organist may play when the Lute is not use'd, as he shall think proper.' Admittedly the work in question probably dates from after 1724, but the manuscript itself implies that the lute had a definite function in the chapel from at least 1705.

Performance is ultimately about ends, not means. Therefore, whatever it was about a particular work that strongly affected its contemporaries can tell us something about what we, in our turn, should aim at. To help define the aesthetic framework, Thomas Tudway's comments on two very different pieces by Purcell, typifying in themselves the two stylistic extremes in the church music of the period, are relevant. Writing of the *Te Deum* in D (1694) he had this to say:

there is in this Te Deum, such a glorious representation of the Heavenly Choirs, of Cherubins & Seraphins, falling down before the Throne & Singing Holy, Holy, Holy &c As hath not been Equall'd, by any Foreigner, or Other; He makes the representation thus; He brings in the treble voices, or Choristers, singing, To thee Cherubins, & Seraphins, continually do cry; and then the Great Organ, Trumpets, the Choirs, & at least thirty or forty instruments besides, all Joine, in most excellent Harmony, & Accord; The Choirs singing only the word Holy; Then all Pause, and the Choristers repeat again, continually do cry; Then the whole Copia Sonorum, of voices, & instruments, Joine again, & sing Holy; this is done 3 times upon the word Holy, only, changing ev'ry time

---

[56] For example, see *MB* 64, 165–72. The orchestral anthem after 1700 is dealt with in Monte Atkinson, 'The Orchestral Anthem in England, 1700–1775' (Ph.D. diss., University of Illinois, Urbana, 1991).

[57] Rimbault, 28.

the Key, & accords; then they proceed altogether in Chorus, with, Heav'n, & Earth are full of the Majesty of thy glory; This most beautiful, & sublime representation, I dare challenge, all the Orators, Poets, Painters &c of any Age whatsoever, to form so lively an Idea, of Choirs of Angels Singing, & paying their Adorations.[58]

Clearly, dramatic contrast and sheer sonority were important elements in moving an audience. The key word is 'sublime'—here inspired by massive (for the time) choral and instrumental effects. At another level, restraint could produce the same result. *Thou knowest, Lord, the secrets of our heart*, written for the funeral of Queen Mary in 1695 (and sung later that year at Purcell's own), overwhelmed in another way.

I appeal to all that were present, as well such as understood Music, as those that did not, whether they ever heard anything so rapturously fine, & solemn, & so Heavenly, in the Operation, which drew tears from all; & yet a plain, Natural Composition; which shows the Pow'r of Music, when tis rightly fitted and Adapted to devotional purposes.[59]

The pathetic and the sublime are the two aesthetic extremes of Restoration cathedral music. As we shall see, the former was easier to achieve than the latter.

[58] See App. F(vi).   [59] See App. F(iv).

PART II

The Chapel Royal and Its Composers

6

The Older Generation:
Lawes, Cooke, and Locke

Strictly speaking, the Chapel Royal was not a building, but a body of men and boys whose job was originally to sing the daily service wherever the king happened to be. Whitehall being the usual royal residence, the chapel was there too, but following a fire in January 1698, it moved briefly to St James's Palace, then back again at the end of the year to Whitehall after the Banqueting House had been converted for use as a chapel. In 1703 Queen Anne decided that the Chapel Royal should return to St James's, where it has remained ever since.[1]

Charles II attended Divine Service 'only upon Sundays in the Mornings, on the great festivals, & days of offerings',[2] but the chapel itself maintained choral services, morning and evening, throughout the year, just like a cathedral. Indeed, it was more lavishly endowed with musicians than any cathedral in the kingdom. Already in the reign of Edward IV (c.1478) it consisted of a dean, twenty-four 'chapelenes and clerkes', and eight boys, but by the middle of the sixteenth century it numbered thirty-two gentlemen and twelve boys, which is how it remained for most of the Restoration period. In 1669 the first edition of Edward Chamberlayne's *Angliae Notitiae* describes it as follows:

By the Dean are chosen all other officers of the Chapel, viz. a Subdean or *Praecentor Capella*, 32 Gentlemen of the Chappel, whereof 12 are Priests. . . . The other 20 Gentlemen, commonly called Clerks of the Chappel, are with the aforesaid Priests to perform in the Chappel the office of Divine Service in Praying, Singing, &c. One of these being well skilled in Musick, is chosen Master of the Children, whereof there are 12 in Ordinary, to instruct them in the Rules and Art of Musick for the Service of the Chappel. Three other of the said Clerks are chosen to be organists, to whom are joyned

---

[1] For further details of the Chapel Royal see David Baldwin, *The Chapel Royal: Ancient and Modern* (London, 1990), 188–97; Dearnley, 19–60, 278–80; John Harley, *Music in Purcell's London* (London, 1968), 78–95; Long, 225–6. For details of appointments, etc., see Rimbault. As to the buildings themselves: at various times there were three chapels in Whitehall (the chapel 'proper' destroyed by fire in 1698, King James's 'popish' chapel elsewhere in the palace, and the Banqueting House), and two at St James's Palace (the original 'Protestant' chapel and, somewhat larger, the 'Catholic' chapel designed by Inigo Jones, used by the consorts of Charles I, Charles II, and James II). There was also a Catholic chapel at Somerset House, where Catherine of Braganza resided following the death of Charles I's widow, Henrietta Maria. Holman, *Four and Twenty Fiddlers*, 389–93, deals in detail with the musical layout of Whitehall Chapel.

[2] Tudway, see App. F(ii).

upon Sundayes, Collar dayes, and other Holydayes, the Saickbuts and Cornets belonging to the King's Private Musick, to make the Chappel Musick more full and compleat.[3]

By the twelfth edition (1679) sackbuts and cornetts had been replaced by 'Consort'—meaning string band—but this merely recognized a change that must have occurred some years earlier. Before the Civil War the practice had been for the king's wind musicians to attend the chapel by roster, except that 'the whole Company shall wayte on all the solemn Feasts & Collar dayes of the yeare'.[4] This arrangement continued in the early years of the Restoration, and as late as 1665 the wind-players were still required 'to give theire Attendance in his Majesty's Chappell Royall . . . as the Master of the Musique shall request', though nothing is heard on the subject thereafter.[5] The earliest mention of strings was in August 1662 when Robert and Edward Strong were ordered to attend 'with their double Curtolls', together with Thomas Bates and William Gregory 'with their violls, every Sunday and Holy day, and all the rest to wayte in their turnes'.[6] Who, what, or how many the rest were is uncertain, but on 14 September 1662 Pepys reported: 'thence to White Hall chapel . . . and I heard Captain Cooke's new musique: This was the first day of having violls and other instruments to play a Symphony between every verse of the Anthem; but the Musique more full then it was the last Sunday, and very fine it is.'[7] From 1667 a four-man group (two violins and a bass plus theorbo?) was ordered to attend the chapel as often as required by Captain Cooke, and in 1670 rosters of the king's violins were drawn up—fifteen of them divided into three ensembles of five (two violins, viola, and bass plus theorbo?) 'soe that each person attend every third moneth'.[8] From 1673 until the end of the reign a total of twenty musicians were involved (four groups of five, presumably) at an annual cost of £400.[9] According to Peter Holman, the instruments were placed in a gallery next to the organ loft where the solo singers were positioned.[10]

Instruments apart, the Chapel Royal was like a cathedral choir, with a subdean (under the dean) and a three-tier choir of priests, laymen, and boys. There was, however, no difference in salary between priests and laymen; all were 'gentlemen' and received £70 a year, raised from £40 in 1663 and further increased to £73 in 1713.[11] The master of the choristers received the same, with additional allowances 'for the diett, lodging, washing, and teaching of the Children'.[12] The organists normally numbered three (two after Child's death), and in 1699 a post of 'Composer to the Chapel Royal' was created, its first

---

[3] Ashbee, v. 280. Collar days were ceremonial days when knights wore the chains and insignia of their orders.

[4] Ibid., iii. 94–5.   [5] Ibid., i. 64; Holman, 394.   [6] Ashbee, i. 35.

[7] Pepys, *Diary*, iii. 197.   [8] Ashbee, i. 76, 98.

[9] Ibid. 113, 124; Holman, 393–414, discusses the use of instruments and the beginnings of the symphony anthem in the Chapel Royal.

[10] Holman, 392–3, 398–9.   [11] Rimbault, 95–8, 234; Ashbee, v. 288–9.

[12] Rimbault, 97.

occupant being John Blow.[13] In due course this place was also doubled so that by 1715 William Croft and John Weldon each enjoyed places as Organist and Composer.[14]

From time to time various orders were promulgated 'for the better regulating of the Divine Service in his Majesties Chappel Royall'. A chapter held on 19 December 1663 laid down that attendance was required by all the gentlemen on Sundays and holy days with their eves; otherwise, half sang one month, the other half the next. They were to come 'decently habited in their gownes and surplices (not in cloakes and bootes and spurrs) . . . at the hours of ten and foure on weeke days, and at nine and foure on Sundayes and Sermon dayes'.[15] Absences and lateness were noted and fined, though substitutes were allowed in the case of sickness or good reason with permission of the subdean. One rule which seems frequently to have been dispensed with was the requirement that 'no man shalbe admitted a Gentleman of his Majesties Chapel Royall but shall first quit all interest in other quires'; for, as has already been indicated, some were also in the choir of St Paul's, others at Westminster Abbey, while a few were in both. No doubt such pluralism was a way of rewarding gentlemen who were particularly deserving, or especially valuable as musicians. How they managed to fulfil their duties is not entirely clear. In practice it seems likely that their attendance at the chapel was rostered, so that the full choir was not, in actual fact, present every Sunday ('extraordinary' appointments may have helped to make up the numbers). Records at Windsor show that choirmen there who were also gentlemen of the Chapel Royal were marked absent from St George's when, presumably, they were on duty at the chapel (see Pt. III under St George's, Windsor). Conversely, they must have been absent from the chapel when they were marked present at Windsor.

The master of the choristers had the power to take his choristers from anywhere in England. In view of the likely benefits that could accrue to their children, it was a power few parents objected to, however much the Dean and Chapter of Windsor might resent 'the insolencyes of mr Cooke (master of the Kings boys) . . . in his stealing away two of our Choristers without any speciall warrant'.[16] Especially in the early years of the Restoration when the re-establishment of the chapel was a matter of urgency, Cooke made frequent forays into the country for this purpose. Thus in July 1661 he received payment 'for fetching five boys from Newark and Lincoln for his Majesty's service', among them presumably the young John Blow from Newark and John Blundeville from Lincoln.[17]

There was no choir school as such attached to the Chapel Royal, merely a 'musick room' off the chapel where the boys practised. Some boarded with the master himself, who clothed and fed them, nursed them when they were ill,

---

[13] Ibid. 23.   [14] Ibid. 27–8.   [15] Ibid. 81–4.
[16] Bond, *Chapter Acts of . . . Windsor*, 249.   [17] Ashbee, i. 19, 98, etc.

paid for them to be taught 'to write, learn and speak latin', and to receive tuition on various musical instruments.[18] Many payments to Cooke are recorded in which he was reimbursed—more than adequately, it might be supposed, though often in considerable arrears—for the expenses involved, likewise his successors as master, Pelham Humfrey, Blow, and Croft. Judging by the results, they did their job well, for most of the important church musicians in the country were brought up as boys in the Chapel Royal—not only Humfrey, Blow, Purcell, and Croft, but Clarke, Hall, Norris, Daniel Purcell, Richardson, Tudway, Turner, and Wise, among others.

In earlier times, when choristers' voices broke, they could be sent to Oxford or Cambridge and there maintained 'tylle the king may otherwise advaunse them'.[19] For the period up to about 1685 the normal procedure was for a lad to be given a suit of clothes and maintenance for a year or two until a suitable job could be found. Thus, when Blow and Blundeville left the chapel in 1665, each was granted 'suits and other clothing' and £30 a year maintenance.[20] (Blow became organist of Westminster Abbey in 1668; Blundeville lay clerk and informator at Ely in 1669.) Later, £20 and a suit of clothes became standard; for example, when William Norris's voice broke in 1686, warrants were issued to provide 'the usual clothing' and pay him £20. That was on 3 June.[21] By September he was a junior vicar at Lincoln (q.v.) and four years later master of the choristers.

The organ that had been in the chapel before the Civil War was working again by June 1660, thanks to John Hingeston, 'Keeper and Repairer of His Majesty's Instruments'. But by Easter 1664 it had been taken down and 'a faire Double Organ' installed at a total cost of £909. 15s. Of this £600 was due to Robert Dallam 'for makeing the great Organ' and another £50 for 'an Addition to the said Organ and a new Stopp with Conveyances and another sett of keyes'.[22] Further work on the organ was carried out by Bernard Smith in 1674–5 (lowering the pitch by a semitone at the same time), but in all probability Dallam's organ lasted until the fire of 1698.[23] The following year Smith built a new organ costing £1,500 for the Banqueting House chapel with ten stops on the great, five on the chair, and four on the echo organ.[24]

By this time some of the splendours of Charles II's chapel had dimmed, for, as a Catholic, James II had his own private chapel elsewhere in Whitehall, and did not frequent the Chapel Royal. During his reign the number of boys in the chapel was reduced from twelve to ten and the number of gentlemen from thirty-two to twenty-four.[25] Anthems with elaborate instrumental accompani-

---

[18] Ashbee, i. 31, 39, etc.   [19] Rimbault, iv.   [20] Ashbee, i. 63.

[21] Ibid., ii. 8–9.   [22] Ibid., i. 69–70; Freeman, *Father Smith*, 113–15.

[23] Ashbee, i. 156–8; Freeman, 13.

[24] Ashbee, ii. 63–4; Freeman, 38–9, 138–9; H. Watkins Shaw, 'Some Stray Notes on "Father" Smith', *The Organ*, 51 (1971–2), 25.

[25] Compare the coronation lists of 1685 and 1689, Rimbault, 129–30.

ments ceased to be regular Sunday fare, though when Princess Anne (later Queen) was present, the string band was required to be in attendance.[26] Nor were William and Mary inclined to revive former glories, requiring only that 'the King's Chapel shall be all the year through kept both morning and evening with solemn musick like a collegiate church'.[27] Indeed, there seems to have been a deterioration in standards about which even the queen complained. In 1693 extra fines were imposed on gentlemen for failing to attend practices on Saturdays, or eves of holy days, when an anthem was due to be sung the following day before the king or queen. Public admonition, suspension, and deprivation were threatened if the offences continued.[28] Hoping to improve the music, the queen at this time may have intended to create a new post of composer-in-ordinary to the chapel, though nothing came of it until Blow was appointed in 1699.[29] It is difficult to see how this could have been expected to improve standards, however, unless by requiring him to compose easier pieces. More likely the problem was one of morale. Some new blood was needed, and fortunately this was what the new century brought.

The anthems and services sung in the Chapel Royal in the early years of the Restoration consisted largely of the old pre-war repertoire with a sprinkling of modern works added as they became available.[30] In view of the king's 'utter detestation of Fancys' and fondness 'for the step tripla',[31] the old-fashioned polyphonic repertoire was probably relegated to occasions when he was not present, and new works pandering to his taste put in their place when he was. The second edition of Clifford's *Divine Services and Anthems usually Sung in His Majesties Chappel* gives us an idea of what these new works were: it lists 20 by Henry Cooke, 10 by Henry Lawes, 9 by Edward Lowe, and 4 by Matthew Locke, as well as 6 by Robert Smith, 5 by Pelham Humfrey, and 3 by Blow— children of the Chapel Royal. The imprimatur on Clifford's book provides a date (16 January 1663/4) before which its contents must have been in existence.

HENRY LAWES

The most senior of these composers was Henry Lawes, a gentleman of the Chapel Royal since 1626.[32] Born at Dinton in Wiltshire in 1596, he was the son of Thomas Lawes (a lay vicar of Salisbury from 1602) and brother of William

---

[26] Ashbee, ii. 15–16.

[27] Ibid. 43; see Public Record Office, RG 8/110, 24ʳ–25ᵛ, also R. Doebner, *Memorials and Letters of Mary, Queen of England* (Leipzig, 1886),12.

[28] Rimbault, 86–7.   [29] Ibid. 23; Hawkins, *History*, ii. 740.

[30] Harl. 6346 (texts only) contains the pre-Restoration repertoire with additions by Lawes and Cooke.

[31] Wilson (ed.), *Roger North on Music*, 350.

[32] Willa McClung Evans, *Henry Lawes, Musician and Friend of Poets* (New York, 1941).

Lawes. He died in 1662. His reputation was principally as a songwriter; as such he was acquainted with many of the greatest poets of the day, and the dedicatee of Milton's sonnet 'To my Friend Mr. *Henry Lawes*'. In addition to well over 400 songs, he wrote at least nineteen anthems, and published two collections of metrical psalms, *A Paraphrase upon the Psalmes of David* (1638) and *Choice Psalmes* (1648). Though he was not primarily a church composer, some of his work may be seen as anticipating that most characteristic product of Charles II's chapel, the symphony anthem. The music of only six of his anthems survives complete; another three are incomplete and ten are known only from their texts. Clifford gives the words of two in the first edition of *Divine Services* (1663) and seven more in the second (1664), including *Zadock the priest*, written for the coronation of Charles II in 1661.[33] A simple homophonic setting only thirty-three bars long, it can hardly have added much splendour to the occasion, yet it established itself as a feature of successive coronation services, retaining its place at James II's musically much more magnificent ceremony, and possibly also at those of William and Mary in 1689, and of Anne in 1702.

Among the additional items in Clifford's 1664 edition are *Sitting by the streams that glide* and *My soul, the great God's praises sing*, both of which are to be found in British Library, Add. MS 31434. Interestingly, these same texts were printed, without music, in *Select Psalmes Of A New Translation, To be Sung in Verse and Chorus of five Parts, with Symphonies of Violins, Organ, and other Instruments, November 22, 1655. Composed by Henry Lawes, Servant to His late Majesty*, and since the description seems appropriate to the music, it seems likely that here we have pieces for a Commonwealth St Cecilia concert,[34] and—more importantly—models for the Restoration 'symphony anthem'. Both are in C minor, but otherwise they have little in common with each other. *Sitting by the streams that glide* is actually a full anthem with introductory symphony, in all only a few bars longer than *Zadok the priest* and clearly nothing remarkable. *My soul, the great God's praises sing*, however, is quite an extended work (225 bars), and falls, like many early symphony anthems, into two parts, the first consisting of two verses each rounded off with a chorus, the second comprising a longer verse and extended final chorus. The chorus is in five parts (TrTrCTB) but the part-writing is rather inept. The symphonies are notated in two-part organ score, but the idiom is violinistic and seems to imply a trio texture. The vocal declamation recalls that of his songs and the overall impression is somewhat reminiscent of the C minor movements for verse and chorus which he wrote for William Cartwright's play *The Royal Slave* (1636).[35] Passages like Example 15 introduce a dramatic element into church music, which budding young composers in the chapel—Humfrey in particular—were to seize and turn to their own use.

The two other anthems in the manuscript are of the same type and may have been written about the same time. Neither *Hark, shepherd swains*—a charming

---

[33] Sources include the Bing–Gostling Partbooks (*Y* M.1.S).
[34] Evans, 211.   [35] *MB* 33, nos. 43, 46.

Ex. 15. Henry Lawes, *My soul, the great God's praises sing* (*Lbl* 31434)

Christmas piece—nor *Thee and thy wondrous deeds, O Lord* seem to have been in the repertoire of the Chapel Royal. Nevertheless, works such as these, though written for private or public performance during the Commonwealth, can be seen as the prototype of the symphony anthem—a missing link between the pre-war verse anthem with organ accompaniment and the verse anthem with strings introduced into the Chapel Royal by Henry Cooke.

HENRY COOKE

Lawes and Cooke were in close contact during the later years of the Commonwealth, and indeed collaborated with each other and Matthew Locke in composing the vocal music for the first English opera, *The Siege of Rhodes* (1656), in which Cooke sang the part of Solyman. According to Wood he had been 'bred up in the Chapel' of Charles I, the son perhaps of John Cooke, 'a basse from Litchfield' who 'was sworne pisteler' in 1623, but died two years later.[36] Henry served in the Royalist forces during the Civil War, was commissioned captain, and became an important figure in London's musical life during the 1650s. Having already demonstrated qualities of leadership, he was no doubt well suited to his appointment as Master of the Children of the Chapel Royal at the Restoration, and the brilliant achievements of the years up to his death in 1672 bore this out.[37]

[36] Rimbault, 10–11; *Ob* MS Wood D.19(4).

[37] *NG* iv. 708–9 (Peter Dennison); see also Ian Cheverton, 'Captain Henry Cooke (c. 1616–72): The Beginnings of a Reappraisal', *Soundings*, 9 (1982), 74–86; Richard McGrady, 'Captain Cooke: A Tercentenary Tribute', *Musical Times*, 113 (1972), 659–60; Joseph C. Bridge, 'A Great English Choir Trainer, Captain Henry Cooke', *Musical Antiquary*, 2 (1910–11), 61–79.

Cooke is known to have composed more than thirty anthems, of which only thirteen survive—ten in autograph at Birmingham University (MS 5001).[38] In all probability most, if not all, were written in the first few years of the Restoration, but the fact that the choir may still not have been up to standard did not inhibit him from using the trebles freely. He himself would have taken the important bass solos. According to Tudway it was the king's idea to introduce string symphonies and ritornellos into these anthems, and both Pepys and Evelyn comment on the innovation, each in his characteristic way. Pepys's 'and very fine it is' sums up the man's enthusiasm, whereas Evelyn, less inclined to embrace novelty, noted regretfully that 'instead of the antient grave and solemn wind musique accompanying the *Organ* was introduced a Consort of 24 Violins between every pause, after the *French* fantastical light way, better suiting a Tavern or Play-house than a Church'.[39]

There was no established tradition of anthems with strings in England, either in cathedrals or the Chapel Royal. The English consort anthem of the earlier part of the century, supremely exemplified in Orlando Gibbons's anthems with viol accompaniment, was essentially a domestic performing tradition which, as such, had survived into the Commonwealth. But this was hardly Charles's taste. He had probably heard motets by Jean Veillot, Louis XIV's *sous-maître*, performed with strings in the French royal chapel, or the early *grands motets* of Henry Dumont, and these would have been more to his liking. For immediate native models Cooke could turn to the 1655 psalm settings of Henry Lawes just mentioned. In any event, Pepys was not strictly correct in dating the first symphony anthems from September 1662, for among those in Cooke's autograph is *Christ rising again from the dead*, which must have been performed at Easter 1661 or 1662, since that particular text was changed in the 1662 Prayer Book to 'Christ being raised from the dead'. (The new Prayer Book was ready by the end of 1661 though not enforced by the Act of Uniformity until St Bartholomew's day, 24 August 1662.) Another candidate for the first symphony anthem is *Behold, O Lord our defender*, written for Charles II's coronation, held on St George's day, 23 April 1661. Like most of Cooke's work it shows a certain amateurishness mixed with forward-looking ideas. Its introductory 'synphonye'—a vigorous four-part binary movement (Ex. 16*a*)—is followed by a verse which immediately resorts to triple time (Ex. 16*b*), and turns again to common time and a more declamatory style at the words 'O how amiable are thy tabernacles' (Ex. 16*c*). A short chorus uses the same material to round this section off. The second part of the anthem begins with an eight-bar instrumental prelude followed by a triple-time Alleluia for treble and bass, with interjections from the chorus and instruments in common time, broadening out to a final Alleluia chorus.

[38] Shaw, 'A Collection of Musical Manuscripts', 126–31.
[39] Pepys, *Diary*, iii. 197 (14 Sept. 1662); Evelyn, *Diary*, iii. 347–8 (21 Dec. 1662).

Here, in essentials, are the main formal and stylistic features, the 'blue-print' (as Dearnley puts it) of the Restoration symphony anthem.[40] Within a few years Cooke's gifted pupil Pelham Humfrey had expanded it into something much more formidable, both in size and expressive content. Cooke's other anthems show little sign of further development. Some are longer and larger, but, if anything, this tends to show up their deficiencies. Still, the colour contrasts between three high and three low voices in *O give thanks* are effective, and some of his solo declamatory writing for bass gives a further foretaste of Humfrey. It is not, however, the more advanced aspects of his style that are most satisfying, but rather the simple four-part writing found in some of the concluding choruses, or in his unaffected yet eloquent setting of the Burial Service in B flat, his favourite key.

Cooke's achievement in the chapel, judged by results, was quite remarkable. As a composer he may not have provided much inspiration, but he was undoubtedly an excellent teacher and choir-trainer, and somehow, perhaps only by offering encouragement and opportunity—he had the support of the king in this, as we shall see—the talents of his boys developed prodigiously.

MATTHEW LOCKE

What role the example of Matthew Locke played is hard to estimate. As the leading composer of the time his influence must have been inescapable, but as a Catholic he was barred from office in the Chapel Royal, serving instead as organist to the queen, Catherine of Braganza, in her chapel at Somerset House. Born in Exeter about 1621 and brought up a chorister there, his work covers the instrumental field as well as opera and church music, both Latin and English.[41] Some small-scale Latin pieces published in Playford's *Cantica Sacra* (1674) may have been written for use in the queen's chapel, as also some of the larger ones with string accompaniment, such as *Super flumina Babylonis*.[42] His English anthems were also performed in the Chapel Royal, where he had close connections and many friends—and some, perhaps, who were less than friendly, in view of the incident recounted in the preface to his *Modern Church-Musick Pre-accus'd, Censur'd, and Obstructed in its Performance before his Majesty, Aprill 1. 1666*. Apparently some of the choir had objected to his having set the responses to the

[40] Dearnley, 186–90, includes excerpts from *We will rejoice in thy salvation* and *We have sinned and committed iniquity*; see also Peter Dennison, *Pelham Humfrey* (Oxford, 1986), 13–17, and Cheverton, 'Captain Henry Cooke'.

[41] The church music is listed in Rosamond E. M. Harding, *A Thematic Catalogue of the Works of Matthew Locke* (Oxford, 1971), nos. 1–15 (English anthems), nos. 21–32 (Latin motets). Motets and anthems are in *MB* 38.

[42] *MB* 38, no. 6. Some were performed at (or written for) Oxford music meetings, e.g. *Ad te levavi* (no. 1) in Nov. 1665.

Ex. 16. Henry Cooke, *Behold, O God, our defender* (Bu 5001)

Commandments in his communion service ten times over, instead of contenting himself with the traditional tenfold repetition of the same music. Presumably it was not an April Fool's joke that misfired; an objection that the music was dull (*pace* Pepys's 'excellent good'[43]) would have been more to the point.

[43] Pepys, *Diary*, viii. 413.

Locke's anthems are another matter. From a musical point of view they are of absorbing interest, packed with surprising and sometimes uncomfortable harmonic and melodic effects that, considered individually, might raise questions as to his technical competence, but taken together persuade one that he was a genius—though of a peculiar and almost perverse kind. In all more than thirty anthems by him are known. Fourteen are 'chamber anthems' of a type probably intended for private devotions and possibly dating from the 1650s. They are in an autograph manuscript (*Lbl* 31437) and all for men's voices. This fact suggested to Rosamund Harding that they could date from the first year of the Restoration, before the boys in the chapel were up to scratch. The absence of the texts from Clifford's *Divine Services* does not support this, however, and the male-voice medium points strongly to private music-making.

Locke's anthems proper include five or six symphony anthems and five others with organ alone.[44] The former were probably composed in the years up to and including 1666, and it may be that with Humfrey's return from France in 1667 Locke's contribution to this genre ceased, though he lived for another ten years. Earliest from an evolutionary point of view if not in actual chronology are *The Lord hear thee* and *When the son of man*. With what is, in effect, a 'first singing part' and a four-part accompaniment for viols or violins (or cornetts and sackbuts, according to Peter Holman), these pieces adopt the technique of the consort anthem, almost as if Locke were back in pre-war Exeter, where 'viols and other sweet instruments' were reported to accompany the anthems in

---

[44] All in *MB* 38, nos. 7–16.

1635.[45] The idiom, needless to say, is hardly that of 1635, and is, indeed, so idiosyncratically Locke's that one hesitates to put a date on it. The absence of overtly Restoration traits may even suggest a date before 1660. The wonderful opening verse of *The Lord hear thee*, or the bass solo 'Come ye blessed of my father' in *When the son of man*, present an unparalleled richness in English church music of the time, and give cause for mild regret that this was not the direction the symphony anthem was to take, though Locke himself seemed inclined to follow it, albeit more feebly, in *I will hear what the Lord will say*. The fact that this is probably the second part of *Lord, thou hast been gracious*, attributed to Blow in table of contents in *Lbl* 31444 but bearing Locke's name in Clifford's *Divine Services*, enables us to date it earlier than 1664.[46] Significantly, Purcell transcribed all three anthems (but not *Lord, thou hast been gracious*) into his score-book (*Cfm* 88).

The direction the symphony anthem ultimately did take—i.e. string symphonies and ritornellos rather than full string accompaniments—is well and truly reflected in *O be joyful in the Lord all ye lands*, one of four known from the inclusion of its text in Clifford to have been written by 1664. The lively dance rhythms of the opening symphony and verse typify one aspect of the Restoration verse anthem, which sought to gratify the king's fondness for the 'step tripla'. Similarly, the use of CTB trio for two of the verses points to what later became standard practice, though at this stage Locke was still attracted to the idea of verses for treble solo or duet.

His writing for the Chapel Royal reached its apogee with *Be thou exalted, Lord*, described in the manuscript as 'A Song of Thanksgiving for his Majestys Victory over the Dutch . . . 1666 And Perform'd befoer his Majesty on the 14th of August . . .'.[47] It begins with a 'Grand Chorus' employing three four-part choirs and a five-part band of violins laid out for treble violin, three violas, and a bass in the French manner, with what are, in effect, concertino passages for a 'consort' comprising 'violins, theorbos and viols'. A swaggering triple-time symphony introduces a verse for two trebles ('The king shall rejoice') building up over a number of movements to verses in seven and eight parts and a final repeat of the opening chorus. It is a work of splendid panache and vitality which Pepys, who was present in the chapel on the occasion, noted as 'a special good Anthemne'.[48]

By contrast, the texts of Locke's anthems with organ accompaniment are penitential in nature. Two at least, *Lord, let me know mine end* (Boyce, ii) and *Not unto us, O Lord*, were in the repertoire of the Chapel Royal, and widely sung

[45] Matthews, *Organs and Organists of Exeter Cathedral*, 2; Holman, *Four and Twenty Fiddlers*, 394.

[46] Bruce Wood, 'John Blow's Anthems with Orchestra' (Ph.D. diss., University of Cambridge, 1977), 432–3.

[47] Holman, 403–4; *MB* 38, 154.   [48] Pepys, *Diary*, vii. 245; Holman, 403–5.

Ex. 17. Mathew Locke, *Turn thy face from my sins* (Cfm 88)

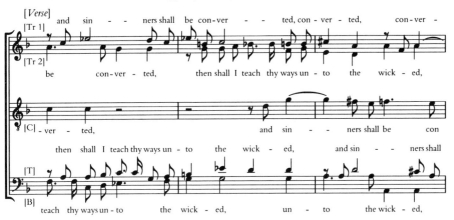

beyond. Again there is a profusion of riches, both in the verse and full sections, which never fail to make an effect, and seem to raise technical problems only to overcome them. It is hardly surprising that Purcell found so much of interest in them, and the lessons he learned from the final Alleluia of *Not unto us*, particularly the conclusion in eight parts, were not lost in his own writing. Similarly, *Turn thy face from my sins*, which he also copied into his score-book, represents a point of departure for Purcell's anthems of the late 1670s. Although it begins cautiously (for Locke), towards the end of the verse section (bars 44–58) the five-part writing becomes crammed with false relations, chromatic twists, augmented chords, unprepared discords, suspensions against notes of resolution, and clashing passing notes (Ex. 17). No wonder Purcell copied it into his score-book. A work like *Lord, how long wilt thou be angry* shows how well he learned the lesson.

7

Captain Cooke's Boys: Humfrey, Blow, and Turner

Cooke's first set of choirboys included Michael Wise, Pelham Humfrey, John Blow, Robert Smith, and William Turner. As has already been mentioned, Clifford includes the words of six anthems by Smith, five by Humfrey, and three by Blow in the 1664 edition of *Divine Services*. The encouragement given to these lads came from none other than the king, as Thomas Tudway (who had experienced it) reports.

Some of the forwardest, & brightest Children of the Chappell, as Mr. Humfreys, Mr. Blow, &c, began to be Masters of a faculty of Composing; This, his Majesty greatly encourag'd, by indulging their youthfull fancys, so that ev'ry Month at least, & afterwards oft'ner, they produc'd something New, of this Kind; In a few years more, several others, Educated in the Chappell, produc'd their Compositions in this style, for otherwise, it was in vain to hope to please his Majesty.[1]

Of these, Robert Smith seems, in the end, to have made no mark as a composer of church music, despite the early lead he established over Humfrey. He is not known to have written any anthems other than the six in Clifford, and of these nothing survives; instead, he became a popular composer of songs for the theatre, dying in 1675.[2] Michael Wise's voice had already broken by 1664. On leaving the chapel he became a lay clerk at St George's, Windsor, where his anthems were soon in the repertoire. In 1668 he moved to Salisbury as organist, and became in 1676 a Gentleman of the Chapel Royal as well.[3] His work will be considered under Salisbury.

Some idea of the repertoire of the chapel in the 1670s can be gathered from 'A Catalogue of Severall Services & Anthems' transcribed into the Chapel Royal partbooks between 1670 and midsummer 1676, and a supplementary list covering the period up to Christmas 1680.[4] Among the services are four by Child and four by Rogers, while more modern settings include one each by Humfrey, Tucker, Wise, and Aldrich, and three by Blow. Anthems by Tucker and Wise (11 each) outnumber those by Blow (9), Locke (7), and Humfrey (6), while Turner (3) and Holder (2) are among composers who were members of the

---

[1] See App. F(ii).   [2] *NG* xvii. 418 (Peter Dennison).
[3] *NG* xx. 462 (Watkins Shaw).   [4] Ashbee, i. 162–4, 193–4.

chapel. Remains of the original partbooks containing some of these services and anthems are now in the British Library (*RM* 27.a.1–15).[5]

PELHAM HUMFREY

The most precocious of the younger composers was Pelham Humfrey.[6] Born in 1647, his period as a chorister in the chapel lasted until Christmas 1664, when he was sent abroad with £200 from secret service funds 'to defray the charge of his journey into France and Italy'.[7] Over the next two and a half years he received a further £250, returning to take up his place as a gentleman of the Chapel Royal in October 1667.[8] Pepys met him on 15 November and found him 'an absolute Monsieur, as full of form and confidence and vanity, and disparages everything and everybody's skill but his own'.[9] He succeeded Cooke as master of the children on 14 July 1672, an appointment he was to enjoy for only two years—to the day. He died on 14 July 1674 'in the twenty seventh year of his age'.[10]

Including the 'Club Anthem' (*I will always give thanks*), which Humfrey, Blow, and Turner composed in collaboration while they were choristers, Humfrey's church music consists of a Service in E minor and eighteen anthems—all of them verse anthems.[11] Questions of authenticity arise in connection with two or three of these, however. Dennison has doubts about *O praise God in his holiness* (which he does not include in his edition), and Don Franklin queries *Hear my prayer, O God*, as well as the so-called 'first version' of *Have mercy upon me, O God*, which is probably by Richard Henman.[12] It may therefore have been the 'second version' that Pepys heard in the chapel on 22 November 1663, commenting (inaccurately) that it has been 'made for five voices by one of Captain Cookes boys, a pretty boy'.[13] It is one of only two anthems without strings by Humfrey, the other being *Hear, O heavens*. Both are in C minor, but very different in style. Whether the detectable influence of Carissimi in the latter indicates an earlier or later date is difficult to say, but the

---

[5] Shaw, 'A Contemporary Source', 39–41; and Laurie, 'The Chapel Royal Part-Books', 29–32. See also Watkins Shaw, 'A Cambridge Manuscript from the English Chapel Royal', *Music and Letters*, 42 (1961), 263–7.

[6] For details of Humfrey's life and work see Dennison, *Pelham Humfrey*.

[7] Rimbault, 213.   [8] Ibid. 14.   [9] Pepys, *Diary*, viii. 529.

[10] Ashbee, i. 117–18; Rimbault, 15–16; Dennison, 8–9.

[11] *MB* 34–5, ed. Dennison. For a discussion of Humfrey's church music see Dennison, *Pelham Humfrey*, 56–75, and id., 'The Church Music of Pelham Humfrey', *Proceedings of the Royal Musical Association*, 98 (1971–2), 65–71; also Long, 251–3; and Dearnley, 199–207.

[12] See Don Franklin's review of Dennison's edition of Humfrey's church music (*MB* 34–5) in *Journal of the American Musicological Society*, 28 (1975), 148, and further, ibid. 31 (1978) 541–3; also Robert F. Ford, 'Henman, Humfrey and "Have mercy"', *Musical Times*, 127 (1986), 459–62; and Dennison, *Pelham Humfrey*, 117.

[13] Pepys, *Diary*, iv. 393.

complete absence of triple time may suggest the former. Another early anthem, again in C minor but this time with instrumental symphonies, is *Haste thee, O God*; the sole survivor of the five anthems credited to him by Clifford and therefore dating before 1664. Other early anthems may include the contents of two sources: Birmingham University MS 5001 furnishes the autograph of *Almighty God, who mad'st thy blessed son*, a setting of the collect for the Feast of the Circumcision; and Durham Cathedral MS B.1 includes six anthems attributed to Humfrey, two that have already been mentioned, and four others—*Like as the hart, Lord, teach us to number our days, O praise the Lord*, and *O praise God in his holiness*. What may be a collection of later anthems is in one of Blow's autographs (*Och* 628); the widest selection is in Cambridge, Fitzwilliam Museum MS 117, which contains fifteen.

Having identified a group of eight possibly early works, we may then compare them with the others to see if there are any pronounced divergencies between the two groups. In terms of melodic and harmonic idioms, and general features such as balance of triple and common time, voice combinations, instrumental procedures, etc., there seems little to distinguish them in any consistent way. It is noticeable, however, that the longest anthems are in the second group, and while this may be the result of setting longer texts (perhaps a growing tendency in general, or a sign of Humfrey's own increasing ambition and self-confidence as a composer), it may also reflect a stylistic development. Statistical investigation of 'word-density' (expressed as words per bar, excluding independent instrumental movements and disregarding repeated vocal sections) seems, for all its undoubted crudity, to show a correlation between early works and compressed word-setting, and, so far as they can be identified, later works and a more expansive vocal style. The inference that Humfrey made greater use of word repetition and/or an increasingly spacious melodic idiom as he developed seems reasonable, and it may not be going too far to suggest that by arranging the anthems in decreasing order of word-density we are revealing their chronological order, or something like it. Not too much should be read into the exact position of any particular anthem in Table 3 (the 'Club Anthem' is an exceptional case, for good reason), but in general it may reflect a trend from earlier to later work.

Where to place Humfrey's continental visit (1665–7) in this list is a matter for speculation. Pepys's note that he heard 'a fine Anthemne, made by Pellam (who is come over) [recently from France]' at the Chapel Royal on All Saints' Day, 1667,[14] suggests a number of possibilities among anthems suitable for such a feast-day, though nothing obvious. On the other hand, it seems likely that the 'good anthem of Pelham's' which he heard on 29 May 1669 (the day celebrating the king's birthday and Restoration) was *The King shall rejoice*.[15]

---

[14] Ibid., viii. 515. [15] Ibid., ix. 563.

TABLE 3. *Humfrey's anthems in decreasing order of 'word density'*

words/bar	title	key
1.72	Hear, O heavens, and give ear	c
1.38	Hear my prayer, O God[a]	g
1.13	Have mercy upon me, O God I[a]	c
1.12	Like as the hart[c,d]	f
1.03	Have mercy upon me, O God II[c]	c
1.00	Haste thee, O God[b,c,f]	c
0.97	Almighty God, who mad'st[d,e]	e
0.94	O Lord my God, why hast thou[d]	f
0.91	Lord teach us to number our days[f]	a
0.90	O be joyful in the Lord	a
0.86	Lift up your heads[f]	a
0.82	O praise God in his holiness[a,c]	C
0.76	By the waters of Babylon[d]	f
0.75	I will always ('Club Anthem')[b]	e
0.68	O praise the Lord, laud ye[c,f]	c
0.63	The king shall rejoice[f]	d
0.63	Rejoice in the Lord, O ye righteous	B♭
0.54	O give thanks unto the Lord[f]	B♭
0.50	Thou art my king	c
0.41	Hear my crying, O God[f]	a

[a] of doubtful authenticity
[b] pre-1664 (Clifford)
[c] *DRc* B.1
[d] anthems with symphonies, where sections in ¢ and 3 are separated
[e] *Bu* 5001
[f] anthems with bipartite ¢:3 symphonies

In some ways Humfrey's anthems do not correspond to the popular idea of the typical Restoration verse anthem, nor to our impression of the musical ethos of Charles II's court. Admittedly, much of the writing is in triple time and close to dance music, and there is little counterpoint as such. Nevertheless, the texts themselves are mainly sombre, and even when festive are often in minor keys; indeed, only three (or four) are major. Most surprisingly, perhaps, there are no final Hallelujahs (except in the suspect 'first setting' of *Have mercy upon me, O God*). Dennison has drawn attention to the expressive elements in Humfrey's harmony and melody, and suggested foreign influences.[16] An anthem like *O give thanks unto the Lord* may approach the manner of the *grand motet* (and there may

---

[16] Dennison, *Pelham Humfrey*, 10–31.

be echoes of Carissimi in *Hear, O heavens*), but overall his anthems owe much more to Locke and Cooke than to Lully and Carissimi. For all that he returned 'an absolute Monsieur', first-hand French influences are hard to pin-point. It is true that seven of the above anthems have bipartite introductory symphonies—serious opening sections in broad common time followed by lively saraband movements—as found in the overtures to a few of Lully's earliest ballets (e.g. *L'amour malade*, 1657) and unprecedented in the anthems of Locke or Cooke, but it was a type that Humfrey had already adopted in *Haste thee, O God*, written in his teens before he went to France. It follows that his sojourn there may not have been so influential as has sometimes been supposed.

Haste thee, O God is in C minor throughout. The adherence to the home key in all movements is typical, though some larger ones (*O give thanks* and *O Lord my God*, for example) embrace a wider tonal spectrum. The four verses alternate triple and common time in a varied combination of soloists, sometimes singing alone but frequently joining together towards the end of a verse. Choruses in the middle and at the end of an anthem articulate an overall bipartite structure. Thematic material tends to be based on the outline of the tonic chord, and this gives a kind of unity that has more to do with Humfrey's style in general—or the key he is using—than with attempts at thematic integration. This can be seen by comparing the melodic material of all the C minor anthems (except for *Hear, O heavens*); it is virtually interchangeable.

But though thematic resemblances may be largely accidental, his use of recall and recapitulation, where it occurs, is clearly intended as a unifying device. Several anthems might be cited in this connection, but *Thou art my king, O God*, a much more mature anthem in C minor, provides an excellent example, as the annotated movement plan shown in Table 4 makes clear.

TABLE 4. *Movement plan of* Thou art my king, O God

section	metre
A Symphony	3
1 Verse: 'Thou art my king, O God' (CTTB), ending with a ritornello (a) derived in rhythm from the last 12 bars of A	3
2 Verse: 'Through thee will we overthrow our enemies' (CTT)	
A Repeat of opening symphony	¢
3 Verse: 'For I will not trust in my bow' (CT), ending with ritornello (a)	3
4 Verse: 'But it is thou that sav'st us' (TB), ending with ritornello (a)	3
1 Repeat of opening verse, including ritornello (a) Chorus (TrCTB): 'We make our boast of God'	¢ and 3

Here, elements of two-part structure (outlined by the symphonies) and three-part structure (established by the return of the opening verse at the end) are brought together into a whole by means of the ritornello refrain and final chorus.

Another example of Humfrey's innate sense of form is provided by *Like as the hart*, one of the F minor anthems. The whole falls into two sections: the first introduced by a common-time symphony in F minor, the second by a triple-time movement in C minor. The balance of tonality and structure is evident. There is symmetry and at the same time a sense of progression, most obviously in the move towards the dominant in the middle and the return to the tonic at the end, but also in the cumulative handling of textures in each half. Despite the nature of the form, which can easily seem fragmentary and diffuse, the two main sections are dependent and complementary by virtue of the tonal plan, though there are no recapitulated sections. On a lower level too, an appreciation of the way the tonal system functions is evident. The opening symphony provides a good example, with harmony that for all the false relations is basically as clear and firmly directed as Corelli's. He was in advance of his English contemporaries in this respect, and it helps to make his musical language more effective. Clearly he was drawn to C minor and F minor because they provided the right 'colour' and harmonic resource for his expressive technique. False relations, augmented chords, chromaticisms, and free discords are present on virtually every page, yet the firm tonal underpinning enables them to make their impact without being vitiated by confused or tortuous harmony. (This does not mean that he never loses his way, however.) The depth of feeling which the composer was capable of expressing is well illustrated in the following declamatory passage, which achieves its force partly through the rhythmic energy of the declamation itself, partly through the wide leaps of the vocal line and its harmonic implications (Ex. 18*a*).

It is the solo declamatory writing which is perhaps the most remarkable feature of these anthems—that, and the rich vitality of his symphonies and ritornellos. His use of triple time in both instrumental and vocal movements, though not excessive by later standards, is very much a pointer to the future. Although it represents the invasion of the sacred domain by the dance, only rarely is the effect disconcertingly secular. So far as the vocal music is concerned, it lightens the mood at appropriate points and introduces a lyrical element. Verbal repetitions are used to create a regular phrase structure that results in what are virtually short airs, usually at moments when the text takes a more optimistic or joyful turn. For instance, the verse 'Now when I think thereupon, I pour out my heart by myself' is set as a kind of recitative, turning to tuneful triple time for the words 'In the voice of praise and thanksgiving among such as keep holy day' (Ex. 18*b*).

After Humfrey's anthems, the Service in E minor comes as a disappointment. Variety of pace and texture, which was so much a part of his approach to the anthem, is denied him by the very nature of the short-service form, and the effect is crabbed and stilted. Dating from before 1672, it is probably the first service to show signs of the modernistic trends associated with the Chapel Royal. String symphonies and declamatory solos are hardly to be expected, and there is only one triple-time verse—in the *Nunc dimittis*. But the harmony is strikingly modern and this affects everything else. Free discord treatment and chromaticism add a new dimension to text expression in a service setting. There is no mistaking its originality; indeed, nothing quite like it had gone before or was to follow. It was Blow, however, who showed the direction the service was to take in the second half of the seventeenth century.

JOHN BLOW

Humfrey's verse anthems, together with some of Locke's, have size, weight, technical accomplishment, and expressive force enough to be regarded as the first masterworks of the English Baroque. Their stylistic break with the past is complete, and they provide both the model and inspiration for later works by Blow and Purcell. Blow was no more than a year or two younger than Humfrey, and though he contributed his portion to the 'Club Anthem' he played second fiddle to Humfrey while the latter was alive. Born at Newark and baptized 23 February 1649, he was probably one of the 'five boys from Newark and Lincoln' whom Captain Cooke fetched to serve in the Chapel Royal in 1661.[17] By the end of 1664 his voice had broken, but he seems to have remained at the fringes of the chapel until 1668 when he became organist of Westminster Abbey in succession to Albertus Bryne.[18] By 1671 he was listed as an organist of the Chapel Royal, though he was perhaps standing in for Christopher Gibbons, whose 'scholar' he was, since he was not sworn in as a gentleman until 16 March 1674.[19] In July that year he was admitted Master of the Children of the Chapel Royal and composer-in-ordinary to the private music for voices, in the place of Pelham Humfrey.[20] Three years later, in December 1677, came the award of a 'Lambeth' Doctor of Music degree—recognition of his status as a church musician, though it was odd that neither university honoured him in that way.[21]

This was the period when Henry Purcell first began to reveal his prowess, and in 1679 Blow stood down as organist of Westminster Abbey in favour of the younger man.[22] Nevertheless, he continued to acquire positions: almoner of St Paul's in 1687 (relinquished to Jeremiah Clarke in 1703), organist (again) of

---

[17] Ashbee, i. 19.　　[18] Ibid. 63; Shaw, 331.　　[19] Ashbee, i. 109; Rimbault, 15; Shaw, 9.
[20] Ashbee, i. 140.　　[21] Shaw, 9.　　[22] Ibid. 331–2.

Ex. 18. Pelham Humfrey, *Like as the hart* (Cfm 88)

Westminster Abbey from 1695, and newly created 'Composer of the Chapel Royal' in 1699. He died on 1 October 1708.[23]

Though Purcell's superior genius was generally admitted, Blow was widely recognized as the leading church composer of his time. In addition, he wrote organ and harpsichord pieces and numerous odes for the court. Many songs

[23] Shaw, 9, 333.

Verse Now when I think there-up - on, I pour___ out my heart___ by my - self
for I went with the mul - ti - tude, and brought them forth in - to___ the house of
God. In the voice of praise and thanks - gi - ving a - mong such as keep ho - ly___
day, in the voice of praise, in the voice _ of praise and thanks - gi - ving a - mong
such as keep ho - ly ___ day.

were printed in Playford's songbooks, and he published his own collection *Amphion Anglicus* (1700) in emulation of Purcell's *Orpheus Britannicus* (1697). His masque *Venus and Adonis* was given at court in the early 1680s, and is in some repects the model for Purcell's *Dido and Aeneas*. By virtue of his position in the Chapel Royal his pupils included many of the younger generation of church composers, including William Croft and Jeremiah Clarke.

Blow's output of services and anthems spans more than forty years. The ninety-two or so extant anthems comprise twenty-four full, forty verse, and twenty-eight symphony anthems, give or take a few doubtful cases.[24] Some can be dated from the known occasions for which they were written, or because they are dated in the sources. For others, a study of the order they were entered into successive manuscripts between 1670 and 1710 by William Tucker, Stephen Bing, and John Gostling suggests a reasonably convincing chronology.

In all, about thirty anthems are attributed to 'Mr Blow' and can therefore be dated before 1678. These years, his twenties, were the most creative of his whole life. His later decline in productivity may, perhaps, be explained by his time-consuming duties at the chapel from 1674, and, conceivably, by an unwill-

---

[24] Blow's anthems are discussed in Dearnley, 212–18, and Long, 258–68.

ingness in one 'not . . . totally free from the imputation of pride'[25] to enter into competition and suffer by comparison with Purcell. Among the early full anthems are *God is our hope and strength, O God, wherefore art thou absent, Save me, O God,* and *The Lord hear thee* (all in Boyce, ii). In this company the last is the odd man out, for it is a surprisingly bland and cheerful piece, its opening bearing a resemblance to Locke's setting of the same words in the same key. Its use of the three-quaver up-beat pattern at 'and strengthen them', though little enough to go on, may possibly suggest a very early work. The other three show Blow as a traditionalist steeped in the English polyphonic style. It is not Child that he looks back to but Byrd, especially in the rhythmic freedom of vocal lines that are mutually independent yet complementary. Their often jagged outlines and, of course, the harmony they make is another matter. It is almost as if he colours Byrd's textures with his own highly individualistic species of *musica ficta*. Apart from *The Lord hear thee* all are 'full with verse' and the full sections especially reveal his feeling for polyphony. The opening section of the eight-part *God is our hope and strength* is a *tour de force*, grand and devotional in effect, while in the final section the excitement generated by the dotted-note passages with syncopated word-underlay going down to bottom D and E in the bass is wonderfully stirring (Ex. 19a). The central verse opposes trios of high and low voices, and it is only at the words 'the waters thereof rage and swell' that the harmony comes unstuck (Ex. 19b). Why he chose colouristic rather than motivic treatment for this passage is difficult to say; such words normally called forth pictorial images.

Blow's use of augmented chords and diminished intervals for expressive purposes is much in evidence within the five-part polyphony of *O God, wherefore art thou absent*. It is a work which, both in texture and harmonic colouring, may have inspired some of Purcell's early full anthems. The return of the opening at the end is a device which Blow was to repeat years later in *My God, my God, look upon me* (Boyce, ii). *Save me, O God* is a more modest work, yet in some ways the best. It is in four parts, and unlike the other two begins chordally, though it soon breaks into free imitations. The rhythmic flow and shape of each line reveals the true polyphonist, especially the way in which accents are liable to occur on different beats of the bar. (See, for example, the phrase 'for the waters are come in', or 'I wept and chasten'd my soul'.) Augmented and diminished intervals are again pervasive, particularly in the verse 'I am weary of crying', but for the most part the harmony is not disconcerting. However, it gets derailed moving from G major to F sharp minor in the passage beginning 'my sight faileth me'. Likewise, C major and F sharp minor are too close together in the final section; the wrench comes at 'Hear me, O God, in the multitude of thy mercies', where D major and F sharp major chords are

---

[25] Hawkins, *History*, 743.

juxtaposed, though the effect undoubtedly imparts a sense of urgency to the words.

Turning to the verse anthems, the earliest that can be dated is *O Lord, I have sinned* (Boyce, iii), written for the funeral of General Monck in Westminster Abbey in 1670. (Three earlier anthems listed in the second edition of Clifford's *Divine Services* are no longer extant.) Formally it is what one would expect at that date, with open-textured verses and loose-knit imitations between the soloists, each verse rounded off by full sections which echo and sometimes reuse material from the end of each verse. Most of the other anthems display more modern features, such as a tendency to drop into triple time when the text lightens in tone, to adopt declamatory idioms approaching recitative in common-time solo verses, and to dispense with the chorus except at the end of a piece. The dramatic gestures that were to characterize Blow's and Purcell's anthems for John Gostling were still several years away; nevertheless we get a foretaste of them in *O Lord, thou hast searched me out* (Boyce, iii) for two solo basses. Some passages come close to true recitative, heightening the intensity of the words by repeating phrases at higher pitches, while others reflect the implications of movement and direction in the text, in a way which, far from being naïve, is absolutely thrilling (Ex. 20).

Twenty-four of Blow's twenty-eight symphony anthems were written for Charles II's chapel and may be regarded as a more or less homogeneous body of work.[26] The period 1670–85 overlaps with the activity, first of Humfrey, then of Purcell, in the same field. Blow basically accepted Humfrey's definition of the form, especially the structural role of the instrumental movements. In some respects, Locke too seems a powerful presence, while in the absence of precise dating Purcell's influence cannot be ruled out in some cases. Indeed, Dennison has noted the influence of all three composers—Locke, Humfrey, and Purcell—on *O sing unto the Lord . . . let the congregation.*[27] In general, Blow's work is less stereotyped than either Humfrey's or Purcell's, and there is a greater sense of continuity and organic growth. One element in this is the crucial linking role of the ritornellos, but whether instrumental or vocal, much of it can be put down simply to the higher proportion of triple time, which exceeds that of both the other composers. Far from being 'courtly' or 'galant', however, it is robust and vigorous. Tremendous rhythmic impetus is generated, fuelled by syncopations and hemiolas, swept along by phrase effects and harmonic twists that avoid points of cadential repose.

As an early example we may take *And I heard a great voice*, dating from 1674.[28] Not counting repeats, it extends to 362 bars, of which the only passages in

---

[26] See Wood, 'John Blow's Anthems'; see also *MB* 50, pp. xv–xx, and 64, pp. xix–xxvii.

[27] Review of Wood's edition of orchestral anthems by Blow (*MB* 50) in *Music and Letters*, 67 (1986), 100.

[28] *MB* 7, p. 62.

Ex. 19. John Blow, *God is our hope and strength* (Gostling MS)

common time are three brief episodes adding up to a mere sixteen bars. As is often the case, there are moments of thematic recall and internal repetition, but the overall effect is of freely evolving triple-time melody, interrupted only by the passages of common time—the first two being declamatory bass solos, the third a short Alleluia for CTBB verse. The CTBB grouping is Blow's preferred verse combination, and whereas Purcell's CTB or TTB trios tend to be homophonic, Blow's CTBB verses frequently subdivide into 'three plus one' or are treated in free dialogue style. The greater flexibility of texture resulting from this voice-grouping is one of the most notable features of Blow's verse-writing, as is his greater willingness to mix instruments with voices. He favours the two-movement symphony less than either Humfrey or Purcell, and instead prefers an introductory prelude leading directly into the opening verse, as in *Thy mercy, O Lord* and *Sing unto the Lord, O ye saints*.[29] The latter is especially noteworthy on account of the pair of tenor oboes (alternating with flutes, i.e. recorders) that augment and enrich the band. In respect of its CTBB verses and the predominance of triple time it is a thoroughly characteristic work, despite Purcell's misattribution to Locke in his autograph score-book (*Cfm* 88)[30]—full of irrepressible energy, though unfortunately lacking the end of the final Alleluia in all its sources.

Another anthem that is completely in triple time (apart from the opening section of the symphony) is *O give thanks unto the Lord, for he is gracious*. It is

---

[29] *MB* 50; respectively nos. 7 and 6.   [30] Ibid., p. 180.

Ex. 20. John Blow, *O Lord, thou hast searched me out* (Gostling MS)

(1) ♮ from *Cfm* 117   (2) no ♭ in *Cfm* 117; indistinct in Gostling

particularly interesting on account of various indications as to the disposition of the singers given in one of its sources (*Cfm* 117). The opening verse carries the rubric 'This anthem is sung some part in the singing loft, & som part below in the Quire', and has two solo groups (TrTrB and CTB) marked 'above', and a four-part group (TrCTB) marked 'below'. Even though the existence of two distinct solo groups 'above' might seem to imply separation, reference to a single 'singing loft' must presumably be taken at face value. Nevertheless, the performance directions provide tangible evidence of a spatial element in the conception and performance of at least one such anthem, and it was perhaps not unusual to have soloists separated from the choir (by being in the organ loft, or 'singing loft' as here), with the strings in their own gallery.

Blow's symphony anthems seem to cater for the presence of John Gostling in the chapel choir after 1679 less obviously than Purcell's. However, judging by the range, *Thy mercy, O Lord* was one that needed Gostling, even though, somewhat perversely, the phrase 'reacheth unto the heav'ns' goes down to bottom D. Later, propriety is restored when, at 'thy righteousness . . . standeth like the strong mountains', the bass goes up to top E, and at 'thy judgements are like the great deep' down to bottom D.[31]

God spake sometime in visions, written for the coronation of James II in 1685, brings Blow's early symphony anthems to a climax.[32] Comparison with its companion piece, Purcell's *My heart is inditing*, demonstrates the difference between the two composers' development up to this point.[33] Whereas Purcell introduces his work with a new type of overture (so far as his anthems go), Blow begins with a more old-fashioned one-movement symphony, bristling with false relations and leading directly into the opening eight-part chorus with strings, massive and almost apocalyptic in its grandeur. Purcell, indeed, writes for the same forces, but with more discipline and control, whereas Blow surges forward from one splendid moment to another as the spirit moves him.

Blow wrote at least ten services, the most important of which are the three early verse services in A major, E minor, and G major, dating from before 1678 in their original forms.[34] All three circulated widely. Their scale is impressive, with imitative points freely introduced and 'full' and 'verse' contrasts exploited imaginatively, the verse sections especially providing harmonic richness and textural colour. The morning and evening canticles of the G major Service are probably the earliest (Boyce, i). A head-motif links the *Te Deum*, *Magnificat*, and *Nunc dimittis*, and all sorts of canons are displayed, perhaps in emulation of Child's 'Sharp Service'. Thus, in the *Jubilate* at the verse 'O go your way into his gates', where Child has a canon 'four in one', Blow has one 'four in two', and at the doxology another 'four in one'—'enough to recommend him for one

---

[31] *MB* 50, no. 7. [32] *MB* 7, p. 1.
[33] *PS* 17, p. 69. [34] For a brief discussion see Long, 268.

of the Greatest Masters in the World', according to Purcell.[35] This may have been the one sent to Cardinal Philip Howard in Rome, and sung, so it was reported, in St Peter's:

> His *Gloria Patri* long ago reach'd *Rome*,
> Sung, and rever'd too in *St Peter's Dome*;
> A *Canon*—will outlive Her Jubilees to come.[36]

The Glorias of the *Magnificat* and *Nunc dimittis* are respectively 3 in 1 and 2 in 1, and far from sounding like academic exercises, they are alive and glowing. Indeed, the evening canticles show Blow at his best, steeped as he was in the English polyphonic tradition. A passage like 'For he hath regarded the lowliness of his handmaiden' came second nature to him (see Ex. 21*a*)—each part needs to be sung individually for its independent character to be appreciated. On the other hand, he could not resist a brief 'step tripla' before concluding the *Nunc dimittis* (Ex. 21*b*).

At a later date Blow completed the service by adding a Kyrie, Creed, Sanctus, and Gloria, using the head-motif for the Kyrie. Then, about 1682, he recomposed both movements in triple time, again using the head-motif as a starting-point for the Kyrie. At a later date he added a *Benedictus, Cantate Domino*, and *Deus misereatur* to complete the service. A third setting of the communion service and a second verse setting of the *Magnificat* and *Nunc dimittis* (in G) are also extant; the *Magnificat* begins like the earlier *Magnificat* but continues quite differently.

Triple-time services (the tradition of which stretched back at least to Byrd's Third Service) were becoming increasingly popular in the 1670s. Possibly the vogue began in the Chapel Royal at this time in deference to the king's taste, and Blow may have pandered to it by writing much of his E minor Service (Boyce, iii) in triple time, notably the *Benedicite*—the work is sometimes referred to as his 'Benedicite Service'. It had the added advantage that tuneful homophony, which was the inevitable vehicle for such word-setting, disposed of the text more quickly than any other way—no small recommendation when it came to the *Benedicite*, the length of which taxed any composer's resourcefulness. Blow managed to keep interest alive with rapid changes in vocal scoring, but even plentiful syncopations could not disguise the monotony that was inevitable over such a long stretch of text. Canon is completely absent from the E minor Service, but again there are thematic linking devices between the movements, including a motto opening and shared Glorias in the morning and evening canticles. A later *Te Deum* in E minor, written as a substitute for the *Benedicite*, is unrelated thematically to the rest of the service. The A major Service (Boyce, i) has no

---

[35] Purcell, in Playford's *Introduction* (1694 edn.), 141.

[36] John Blow, *Amphion Anglicus* (1700), 'A Pindarick Ode, On Dr. Blow's Excellency in the Art of Music. By Mr. Herbert.'

Ex. 21. John Blow, *a. Magnificat* and *b. Nunc dimittis* from the Service in G (*Harl.* 7339)

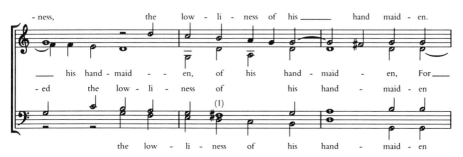

(1) ♯ from *Y* M.1.6, *Cfm* 117, *etc.*

internal links, and except towards the end of the Creed is devoid of triple time. There are numerous examples of Blow's disconcerting harmony in this work, but the end of the Creed and evening canticles especially make a grand effect.

More than any other works of Blow, it is probable that these three works established his position as the leading church composer. They may be regarded as the representative masterpieces of their type and time; and together with two or three services by Child, and later Purcell's in B flat, they provided the staple 'modern' fare of most cathedrals for the rest of the century, and for much of the next.

Blow's work for the Chapel Royal after 1685 includes twelve or so substantial verse anthems (nearly all contained in the Gostling Manuscript) and fifteen full anthems (all but one in the Gostling Tenbury Partbooks).[37] In addition, there are three anthems for the coronation of William and Mary in 1689, and a number of big occasional pieces mostly written for St Paul's, among them *Awake, awake, utter a song* to celebrate the Battle of Blenheim in 1704. Two incomplete verse services in C and D are almost certainly late, as are the 'short' services in A minor, D minor, F major, and G minor.[38] The ceremonial *Te Deum* and *Jubilate* for trumpets and strings was written for the St Cecilia service of 1695, in emulation of Purcell's of the previous year.[39]

Blow appears to have written no symphony anthems for the chapel during this period, apart from the 1689 coronation anthem *The Lord God is a sun*.[40] To the extent that such pieces were still required during the reign of James II, it seems as if Purcell and Turner provided them, while Blow continued to supply verse anthems with organ accompaniment. Two solo anthems for bass show the direction both he and Purcell were taking at the time. *The Lord, even the most mighty God* and *O Lord, thou art my God*, composed respectively in 1687 and 1688, are both 'cantata anthems' in which declamatory sections in common time alternate with contrasting song-like sections in triple time.[41] Unlike the Italian cantata, however, the main vocal emphasis is on 'recitative' rather than 'aria', and though the latter might contain florid passages, it was the former that was characterized by elaborate word-painting and affective ornamentation. Clearly Gostling's virtuoso capabilities were borne in mind; a fine and by no means wildly extravagant example is to be found in the second verse of *The Lord, even the most mighty God* (Ex. 22).

Following the death of Charles II, there were fewer occasions for symphony anthems in the chapel. Thus Blow's *We will rejoice in thy salvation*, a fine and typically energetic anthem 'made upon the discovery of the plot against King William [and] Sung April 16: 1696 the Thanksgiving Day', had ritornellos for organ, as did *Lord, remember David*, composed for the opening of the new chapel in the Banqueting Hall on 9 December 1698.[42] The only symphony anthems Blow is known to have written during these years are *I was glad* for the opening of the choir of St Paul's in 1697, *Blessed is the man that feareth the Lord* for the Festival of the Sons of the Clergy, also held at St Paul's the following year, and *O sing unto the Lord a new song . . . the whole earth* for 'Mr [Cavendish] Weedon's musical meeting' at Stationers' Hall, 31 January 1701.[43] Traditionalist though he may have been by temperament, Blow could not avoid the flamboyant, ceremonial style of the late seventeenth century, typified by virtuoso solo writing, florid trumpet parts, and grand, almost Handelian, choral effects. Indeed, *I was*

---

[37] *US-AUS*, *Ob* Tenbury 797–803 and 1176–82.
[38] All in *Cfm* 116 (organ score), and *Lbl* 31559.   [39] *Lbl* 31457, 17835.
[40] *Lcm* 1097.   [41] Both are in the Gostling Manuscript.
[42] Both are in the Gostling Manuscript.
[43] For dating see Wood, 'Blow's Anthems with Orchestra', 21–6; the first and third are in *MB* 50, nos. 2 and 5.

Ex. 22. John Blow, *The Lord, even the most mighty God* (Gostling MS)

glad is the musical equivalent of St Paul's itself, and it was appropriate that he should exploit the full range of characteristic devices. What the state of the famous echo was then we can only imagine, but it would seem that the opening tonic and dominant pedals and the pealing trumpets of the first section were designed for it. From Purcell's 1694 *Te Deum* he had learned how dramatic changes of texture, contrast of movement, and pathetic juxtapositions of major and minor could be exploited. Countertenors called to each other across the choir, long notes swelling and erupting in dazzling cascades of sound, with vocal flourishes matched by echoing trumpets (Ex. 23).

Yet for all the grandeur of the conception Blow's technique was still not quite up to it, and among the numerous untidy details that seemed not to worry him were some clashes between trumpets and voices in the final chorus (e.g. bars 295, 300, and 305) which he could easily have remedied, though few perhaps would have noticed them in the general clangour. Nevertheless, they raise doubts about how alert Blow's ears and eyes were. He appears to have been even more at sea in the anthem written for Weedon's music meeting. Gostling's score may be faulty, but the fact that neither he nor the modern

Ex. 23. John Blow *I was glad* (Gresham College MS 452)

editor could be sure what the composer really intended reflects the composer's own uncertainty as to the effect he was after.[44]

Parallel with these anthems, which, if not uncongenial to his taste, were not ideally suited to his talent, are the full anthems, written, so far as we can tell, in

[44] MB 50, no. 5; pp. 163–72, 178–9; see also Dennison's review (above, n. 26), 101.

the last ten years of his life. Fifteen are in an early eighteenth-century organ-book at Cambridge (*Cfm* 116). Apart from the well-known *My God, my God, look upon me*, the rest occur as a group in Gostling's Tenbury Partbooks, among them *My days are gone like a shadow*, *Be merciful unto me, O Lord*, and *Praise the Lord, ye servants*. Whether these anthems are to be regarded as the immediate fruits of his appointment as Composer of the Chapel Royal in 1699 can only be surmised, but they do not seem to have been entered into the chapel partbooks. The 'solemn and grave style' was becoming recognized as a kind of ideal for church music at this time, and it was an opinion that Blow himself probably shared. There may also have been an element of nostalgia underlying these late works—on the part of Blow for the Golden Age of Byrd and Gibbons, and on the part of the church (or at least high churchmen) for its Jacobean heyday. Yet in reverting to the textures and idioms of the early seventeenth century, Blow maintained his idiosyncratic harmony to the end. Without doubt his view of the polyphonic style was not shared by the eighteenth-century practitioners who followed him. Indeed, there is much that seems crude in these anthems, yet at the same time moments of strange beauty leave one wondering whether they are the result of genius or happy accident. *My days are gone like a shadow*,[45] for example, has wonderfully expressive passages at 'and I am withered like grass' and 'Arise, O Lord, and have mercy upon Sion' that are fine from the polyphonic point of view—especially in terms of the contour and rhythm of individual parts—but where the discord treatment is a law unto itself. Not that one would settle for a seventh, fourth, or second fewer in these particular instances, though what one ought to make of the false relation at 'For it is time *that* thou have mercy upon her' (if it was intended) perhaps only Blow could say.

The only one of these late anthems that can be dated precisely is *My God, my God, look upon me* (Boyce, ii), signed 'J. Blow at Aspinden Hall Sep. the 6th 1697' in the holograph (*Lbl* 30932). The sense of anguish is conveyed less by harmonic asperities, more by the semitonal rise and fall of the Phrygian subject and the suspensions that are generated as the polyphony unwinds. The return of the opening at the end is a device that satisfies the formal balance of the piece and intensifies the pathos.

The Cambridge organ-book containing these anthems also includes the four short services in A minor, D minor, F major, and G minor—all without communion settings but supplied with single chants in the appropriate key for the Venite and proper psalms. A mid-eighteenth-century score in the hand of John Christopher Smith (*Lbl* 31559) makes up for the deficiencies of the organ-book, and shows that, like the anthems, these services mark a return to the short-service style of a century earlier. Indeed, consciously or unconsciously,

---

[45] Ed. Heathcote Statham (London, 1955).

Ex. 24. John Blow, (*a*) *Magnificat* and (*b*) *Nunc dimittis*
from the Service in D minor (*Lbl* 31559)

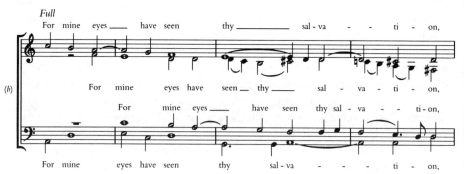

Blow quotes Gibbons's First Service (the treble opening of the Gloria to the *Nunc dimittis*) in the corresponding passage of the F major Service without any sense of incongruity.[46] The pastiche aspect is even more pronounced in the so-called 'Dorian' Service in D minor. Of course, there are many things in it which Gibbons could not have written, but in terms of texture and rhythm the influences are unmistakable. The underlay in homophonic sections is characteristically fluid, and genuine polyphonic movement gives rise to cross-accents in such passages as 'in the imagination of their hearts' from the *Magnificat* (Ex. 24*a*), or at the words 'For mine eyes have seen thy salvation' in the *Nunc dimittis* (Ex. 24*b*). Typically, in contriving an old-fashioned 'English' cadence, Blow throws up a pair of consecutive fifths quite unnecessarily.

In the dedication to *Amphion Anglicus* (1700) Blow said that he was preparing to publish 'as fast as I can ... my *Church-Services* and *Divine Compositions*', but although he lived another eight years, there is no evidence that he took any steps to do so. Had he, we would have authoritative texts but little more, for his music has maintained an honoured place in the cathedral repertoire from his day

---

[46] Compare *Treasury of English Church Music*, iii. 82, with *Orlando Gibbons, 1583–1627* [*Services and Anthems*] (Tudor Church Music, 4; London, 1925), 67.

to ours, and his reputation remained high, despite Burney's strictures.[47] Burney's general view was that 'some of his choral productions are doubtless in a very bold and grand style; however, he is unequal, and frequently unhappy in his attempt at new harmony and modulation'. Remove the grudging tone and one can hardly dissent from such a judgement; yet, taken overall, his virtues undoubtedly outweigh his vices. He may have been uneven, but a composer does not have to be justified by every work. Old and new often sit uncomfortably together, his ear sometimes lets him down, self-criticism may be lacking; even so, there is enough originality, imagination, vigour, expressive power, and, indeed, technique, for half a dozen composers. We sense a massive presence and a formidable achievement, one which, somehow, not even Purcell quite measured up to in his church music.

WILLIAM TURNER

The third member of the 'club' was William Turner.[48] Born in 1652, a native of Oxford (according to Anthony Wood), he began as a chorister at Christ Church under Edward Lowe. Later he entered the Chapel Royal, but by 1666 his voice had broken and he was put in the care of Captain Cooke until he obtained preferment. This came on 28 November 1667 when he was sworn master of the choristers of Lincoln Cathedral, aged 15 or 16, if his age at death is correctly recorded. He remained there for two years, returning to become a Gentleman of the Chapel Royal on 11 October 1669, when he was described as 'a countertenor from Lincolne'. Later he became one of the vicars choral of St Paul's as well (1683) and a lay clerk of Westminster Abbey (1699). In 1696 he was made Doctor of Music by Cambridge University, 'Purcell alone being more learned' (but dead). He composed New Year and birthday odes for the court and an ode, now lost, for St Cecilia's Day, 1685. As a singer he frequently took part in those of Blow and Purcell. Unless there was another singer of the same name, he was still performing publicly in 1716, when he would have been well into his sixties. He died on 13 January 1740 at the age of 88.

Four services and more than forty-three anthems are attributed to Turner in contemporary sources, and we have seen that he was one of the earliest composers to contribute substantially to the Anglican chant repertoire (see Ch. 1). Compared with his fellow choristers, Blow, Humfrey, and Wise, his music did not circulate so widely, and, beyond London, only at Lincoln is it signifi-

---

[47] Burney, *History*, ii. 350–6.

[48] For biographical details, stylistic discussion, and catalogue of anthems see Don Franklin, 'The Anthems of William Turner (1652–1740): An Historical and Stylistic Study' (Ph.D. diss., Stanford University, 1967); the list of anthems is amended in *NG* xix. 281–2 (Franklin). The anthems are also dealt with briefly in Dearnley, 222–5, and Long, 256–7.

TABLE 5. *List of Turner's anthems in chronological order of sources*

---

before 1664 (Clifford, *Divine Services*, 2nd edn.)

    I will always give thanks (with Humfrey and Blow) (v)

1668–70 (Bing–Gostling Partbooks; hand of Stephen Bing, d. 1681); 'made at Lincoln in the years 68, 69 & 70'

    Behold, God is my salvation (v)

    By the waters of Babylon (v) I (D minor)

    O be joyful in God, all ye lands (v)

    O praise the Lord, for it is a good thing (v) I (C major)

    Sing, O daughter of Sion (f)

    Sing unto the Lord, O ye kingdoms (v)

    The earth is the Lord's (v)

    This is the day which the Lord hath made (v)

before 1676 (Chapel Royal list)

    O Lord God of hosts, hear my prayer (f)

    Lord, thou hast been our refuge (v)

    Lord, what is man that thou art mindful? (v)

before 1679 (Nanki Library, Tokyo, N-5/10, hand of William Tucker, d. 1679)

    Hold not thy tongue, O God★ (v)

    O praise the Lord, for it is a good thing★ (v) II (F major)

before c. 1680 (Berkeley Organ Book)

    If the Lord himself had not been on our side (v)

    O Lord, the very heavens, (v) I

    Praise the Lord, O my soul (v)

before 1683 (Fitzwilliam Museum MS 117)

    I will magnify thee, O Lord (v)

before c. 1683 (Worcester Cathedral partbooks)

    Rejoice greatly, O daughter of Sion (MS 3.4) (v)

c. 1685 (Gostling MS)

    God sheweth me his goodness★ (v)

before 1686

    Behold now praise the Lord★ (v) (*Harl.* 7341: 'Composed in King Charles's time')

1686

    Preserve me, O God (v) (Gostling MS: 'Aug: 24th 1686')

1687

    O sing praises unto the Lord (v) (Gostling MS: '1687')

1696 (Henry Watson Library, MS 130, HD4, v. 235)

    O give thanks unto the Lord★ (v) ('June the 15th: 1696')

    O Lord, the very heavens★ (v) II (C major) ('June 1696')

before 1697 (attributed to 'Mr' Turner)

    By the waters of Babylon★ (v) II (G minor)

1697

    The king shall rejoice (v) (*Harl.* 7339: 'St Cecillia's Day, 1697')

TABLE 5 (*cont.*)

c. *1697* (Bing–Gostling Partbooks; Gostling's additions, after 1696)
  Hear my prayer, O God (f)
  Try me, O God (v)
c. *1698* (St Paul's partbooks, hand of Gostling, *c.*1698?)
  My soul truly waiteth (f)
  The Lord is king (v)
1702
  The queen shall rejoice (v) (*Harl.* 7341: 'Queen Anne's coronation, 23 April 1702')
c.*1705* (Tenbury Partbooks, MSS 1176–82, 707–803, hand of Gostling)
  Hear the right, O Lord (v)
  Judge me, O Lord (v)
  Plead thou my cause, O Lord (v)
Other anthems where the earliest attribution is to 'Dr' Turner (therefore probably
late, possibly after 1696)
  Arise, thy light is come (v)
  Deliver me from my enemies (v)
  Deliver us, O Lord our God (v)
  O God, thou art my God (v)
  Righteous art thou, O Lord (v)
  The Lord is righteous (v)
No date (*Bu* 5001, autograph)
  God standeth in the congregation★ (v)

★ = symphony anthem
f = full
v = verse

cantly represented—for obvious reasons. In Table 5 an attempt is made to
present his anthems in something approaching chronological order based on the
earliest sources in which they occur. Though several may be earlier than
appears, one can be reasonably confident about the general pattern which
emerges.

The earliest anthem in which Turner had a hand was the 'Club Anthem'
composed in collaboration with Humfrey and Blow sometime before 1664. His
contribution was the shortest of the three, but needs no apology for being the
work of a 12- or 13-year-old.[49] Otherwise his earliest surviving anthems seem to
date from his period in Lincoln. In the Bing–Gostling Partbooks there is a
section headed 'A Collection of Such Anthems for verses as have bin made at

---

[49] *MB* 34, no. 8, bars 90–106.

Lincoln in the years 68, 69 & 70' which includes nine attributed to Turner[50] (of which *Behold, how good and joyful* is probably by John Hutchinson of York). As might be expected, they are modest in scale, but in other respects bear clear evidence of his professionalism.

Of perhaps slightly later date (certainly before midsummer 1676) are two anthems that circulated widely, and by which he was best known in provincial centres. *Lord, what is man* and *Lord, thou hast been our refuge* (Boyce, iii) are excellent examples of the verse anthem as it was practised in the early 1670s.[51] Both have CTB verses rounded off by four-part choruses in the manner of the time. An excerpt from the latter shows Turner's ability to match the music sensitively to the words, avoiding awkwardness of line and harmony (Ex. 25). In this he shows a good deal more polish than either Humfrey or Blow.

Anthems written in the 1680s show certain advances in style. Movements are longer, solo writing becomes emancipated, and triple time predominates, but compared with Blow and Purcell Turner is rather restrained, even in symphony anthems. There are several of these from about this time; two—*Hold not thy tongue, O God* and *O praise the Lord, for it is a good thing*—date from before 1677.[52] His approach to the opening symphony is variable, like Blow's. Introductory preludes in three or four time are found, while Humfrey's usual bipartite movement is rare, *God sheweth me his goodness* being an example. *Hold not thy tongue* follows Humfrey's occasional practice of separating the common-time opening from its triple-time sequel with intervening verses. *God standeth in the congregation*, which survives in autograph (*Bu* MS 5001), adopts Purcell's post-1685 device of following the slow introduction with a quick fugal movement, *Behold, now praise the Lord* is interesting as an example of a symphony anthem built throughout on a three-bar (six minim) ground bass. The opening symphony in common time leads into a duet for tenor and countertenor with obbligato violin. A short ritornello intervenes without disrupting the flow, and this in turn is followed by a trio with rising chromaticism at 'the Lord that made heaven and earth'. The last two sections of the anthem comprise a triple-time ritornello over the same bass (now dotted minims) and a Gloria for the chorus which reverts to common time. The writing shows considerable skill and some nice effects, but the fact that the bass remains in the same key from beginning to end precludes any sense of development.

By 1685 Turner had established his position relative to Blow and Purcell by contributing two anthems for the coronation of James II—one fewer than Blow and the same number as Purcell (but without being asked for a symphony anthem). Unfortunately, his full settings of *Come holy ghost* and *The king shall*

[50] Shaw, *Bing–Gostling Part Books*, 29–30.

[51] *Lord what is man* is in the supplement to A. Lindsey Kirwan, *The Music of Lincoln Cathedral* (London, 1973).

[52] Wood, 'Blow's Anthems with Orchestra', 35.

Ex. 25. William Turner, *Lord, thou hast been our refuge (Cfm 117)*

(1) ♯ in source (absent in other sources)

Ex. 26. William Turner, *Judge me, O Lord* (*Ob Tenbury 797 - 803, 1176 - 82*)

rejoice are lost, though it is possible that in writing *The queen shall rejoice* (*Harl.* 7341) for the coronation of Queen Anne in 1702 he merely adapted the words of the earlier piece. In the years following the accession of James II he continued to supply the Chapel Royal with symphony anthems, though they were now less in demand. *Preserve me, O God,* dated 24 August 1686 in the Gostling Manuscript, and *O sing praises unto the Lord* of the following year are bold and simple in character, owing little to Purcell and less to Blow, but like them exploiting the range and dramatic power of Gostling's voice in bass solos.

Symphony anthems were discontinued in the chapel from 1691, but for the annual St Cecilia service trumpets and strings were in fashion. Turner's *Te Deum* and *Jubilate* of 1696 was next in line after Purcell's (1694) and Blow's (1695) for this occasion, and in 1697 his *The king shall rejoice* for the same orchestral forces was performed. This splendid piece was given again at a concert in Stationers' Hall on 31 January 1701 together with Blow's *O sing unto the Lord a new song* and a second anthem by Turner, said to have been a setting of *The heavens declare*,[53] but conceivably a mistake for *O Lord, the very heavens*, which survives with accompaniment for trumpet and strings.

The opening of St Paul's in 1697 seems to have coincided with a new and final burst of creative energy on Turner's part. The Chapel Royal may have been in the doldrums, but Wren's magnificent building needed filling with sound, and somehow its scale caused Turner to overcome his inhibitions at last. Gostling included several of Turner's late anthems in the Tenbury Partbooks, and most display a marked increase in scale, and a more extravagant approach to solo writing. *Judge me, O Lord, according to thy righteousness*, for example, has two bass solos, two tenor solos, one for countertenor (himself?), and a couple of elaborate CTB trios to begin and end with, the latter leading into a six-part chorus. In all, the seven sections amount to 219 bars, and show numerous up-to-date features, including a florid bass verse ('O let not them that are mine enemies triumph', Ex. 26a), and one for tenor which follows immediately and adopts the typical Italian 'motto' opening, in which the first phrase of the subject is interrupted by the ritornello, and then repeated before continuing (Ex. 26b). Contrasts of tonic major and tonic minor highlight the changes of mood between verses, which, instead of following their proper order in Ps. 35, are

53 Wood, 'Blow's Anthems with Orchestra', 12.

Ex. 27. William Turner, *Jubilate* from the Service in A (*Harl.* 7339)

(1) F♯?

rearranged to provide more scope for expressive variety; thus, verse 24 (C minor) is followed by verse 19 (also C minor), then verses 23 (C major), 26 (C minor), 27 (C major), and 28 (C minor). Changes of key such as this are a feature of these later anthems, lightening or darkening the mood as appropriate, but they mark the limit of Turner's tonal adventurousness, which rarely (if ever) extended to introducing movements in related keys.

Apart from the D major *Te Deum* and *Jubilate*, three other services survive: a four-part setting in E, a big six-part setting in A, with an accompanying six-part anthem in the same key (*My soul truly waiteth*), and another service in D, surviving incomplete at Durham (MS A.33), also with a companion anthem (*Deliver us, O Lord, our God*). Both the E major and A major Services are found in the St Paul's partbooks later than 1698, and scored up in Tudway's collection (*Harl.* 7340–1). Especially in the A major Service we see Turner relishing the sonority that St Paul's no doubt provided, even in its unfinished state. The opening of the *Jubilate* gives a taste of the richness and splendour of its full writing, as well as its confident technique (Ex. 27), but there is plenty of variety in the verse sections as well.

There is no evidence that Turner composed any church music after about 1705 despite the fact that he was still at the height of his powers and had another thirty-five years to live. His work thus covers the same chronological span as Blow's. Like Blow he adopted the flamboyant late Baroque style in the 1690s and was to show himself at home in it, more so than Blow, for he had always been modernistically inclined. And unlike Blow, or even the younger Purcell, he seems to have had little trouble handling the tonal system, though he lacked enterprise in exploiting it. His technique was certainly adequate to the ends he had in view; his harmony was usually well behaved and his vocal writing grateful to sing. What was missing was strength and energy, or any real sense of exaltation. In this he had many followers in the eighteenth century.

8

Henry Purcell

Purcell's church music amounts to three services, sixty-five anthems, and a set of funeral sentences.[1] Though some were written for Westminster Abbey, and others—probably the majority—for the Chapel Royal, his output will be considered more or less chronologically, irrespective of function and place except in so far as these are inherent in the chronological sequence. Thus, the works may be roughly divided into three fairly distinct groups: first, early anthems, many of them full anthems written before 1682 and probably intended in the first instance for the abbey; second, symphony anthems, beginning about 1678 and written specifically for the Chapel Royal of Charles II; third, later works, mostly for the chapel, dating from the last ten years of his life.

EARLY WORKS, UP TO 1682

Henry Purcell was one of the Children of the Chapel Royal under Captain Cooke.[2] A few months after Cooke's death in July 1673, Purcell's voice broke—he was probably still only 14—and he was issued with the customary suit of clothes, and '£30 by the year, to commence Michaelmas 1673'.[3] In the years following, he received payments for tuning the Westminster Abbey organ and copying music. In 1679 or 1680 he succeeded Blow as organist of the abbey,[4]

---

[1] See *The Works of Henry Purcell* (London, 1878–1965; rev. 1974–); the anthems are in vols. 13, 14, 17, 28–30, and 32, the services in vol. 23; for a catalogue see Franklin B. Zimmerman, *Henry Purcell, 1659–1695: An Analytical Catalogue of His Music* (London, 1963), nos. 1–65, N66–9 (anthems), nos. 230–2 (services). There are surprisingly few extended discussions of Purcell's church music; they include G. E. P. Arkwright, 'Purcell's Church Music', *Musical Antiquary*, I (1909–10), 63–72, 234–48; Peter Dennison, 'The Stylistic Origins of the Early Church Music [of Purcell]', in F. W. Sternfeld, Nigel Fortune, and Edward Olleson (eds.), *Essays on Opera and English Music in Honour of Sir Jack Westrup* (Oxford, 1975), 44–61; Anthony Lewis, 'English Church Music: Purcell', in Anthony Lewis and Nigel Fortune (eds.), *New Oxford History of Music*, v (Oxford, 1975), 526–37; Long, 269–84; Robert Manning, 'Purcell's Anthems: An Analytical Study of the Music and of Its Context' (Ph.D. diss., University of Birmingham, 1979); J. A. Westrup, *Purcell* (rev. edn., London, 1968), 197–221; Zimmerman, 'The Anthems of Henry Purcell'.

[2] The most detailed 'life' is Franklin B. Zimmerman, *Henry Purcell, 1659–95: His Life and Times* (London, 1967; rev. edn., Philadelphia, 1983).

[3] Ashbee, i. 131–2.   [4] Shaw, 332.

but already his music was being sung there, for the 'first set' of partbooks contains anthems by Purcell dating from before December 1677 (that is, they were entered while Blow was still 'Mr').

Westminster Abbey (First Set)

I will sing unto the Lord (f)
O God, the king of glory (f)
O Lord our governor (v)
Blow up the trumpet (v) ('1681' in a later hand)
Let God arise (v)
Blessed be the Lord my strength (v)
(f) = full, (v) = verse

To these may be added *Lord, who can tell*, which survives in a Chapel Royal manuscript of similar date, and two anthems in the earlier layer of the Bing–Gostling Partbooks dating from 1679–81—*Give sentence with me, O God* and *O praise the Lord, all ye heathen.*[5]

Another group of early anthems by Purcell, this time autograph and in score, are the twelve in Cambridge, Fitzwilliam Museum, MS 88.[6] Begun in 1677 as an anthology of anthems by other composers, he later used it—probably in 1682—to record fair copies of his own work. The reverse end bears the enigmatic legend 'God bless Mr Henry Purcell / 1682 September the 10th', but whether this was written before, during, or after the copying process is not known. The date is probably, in effect, a *terminus ad quem*, and points to 1677–82 as the period of composition.

Fitzwilliam Museum, MS 88

Save me, O God (f)
Blessed is he whose unrighteousness (v)
Hear me, O Lord, and that soon (v) II
Bow down thine ear (v)
Man that is born of a woman (f) (including *In the midst of life*)
Remember not Lord, our offences (f)
O God, thou hast cast us out (f)
O Lord, God of hosts (f)
O God, thou art my God (f)
Lord, how long wilt thou be angry (f)
O Lord, thou art my God (v)
Hear my prayer, O Lord (f)

One thing is noticeable immediately about this list: it contains none of the anthems in the Westminster partbooks—something that might have been

---

[5] Shaw, *Bing–Gostling Part Books*, 108.
[6] Fortune and Zimmerman, 'Purcell's Autographs', 108–10.

expected had he been making a collection of his work to date. In all probability they were already in another book or books, now lost or dismembered. Indeed, an unfinished version of *Hear me, O Lord, and that soon* is in an earlier autograph (*Lbl* 30930); perhaps some of those in the Flackton collection came from yet another score-book, obvious candidates being the following, which are all early:

Flackton collection (*Lbl* 30931–3)

Out of the deep (v)
In the midst of life (f) (from Burial Service)
Thou knowest, Lord (f) (from Burial Service)
Who hath believed our report (v)

The two funeral sentences, in fact, pre-date the Fitzwilliam versions, which contain revisions as part of *Man that is born of a woman*.[7]

The early group of six Westminster Abbey anthems are a remarkable set, not merely for a composer of 18. With the exception, perhaps, of *O God, the king of glory*, they are not just student works; they have their rough edges—awkward harmonic progressions and word underlay—but they show striking individuality, too. Obvious models in the work of Locke, Humfrey, and Blow do not readily present themselves, though occasional details may be traced to one or the other. Already a personal note is sounded, as when major turns to minor, triple time to common time, and 'full' to 'verse' at the words 'As for us sinners, they shall be consumed out of the earth' in *I will sing unto the Lord* (PS 28); still more, the eerie juxtaposition of A major with C minor in *Let God arise* (PS 28) at the words 'The earth shook'. Indeed, the signs of things to come in this anthem were strong enough to prevent Zimmerman from accepting a date earlier than 1683 for it, because of its Italian features elsewhere and the fact that 'florid passage-work for two tenors . . . is more consistent with the style of Purcell's later works'.[8] Such writing, and some of the descriptive gestures, may well reflect Italian influences; the point to be made is that he was already experimenting with them before 1678. So too with his technique of affective chromaticism, exemplified by the setting of 'Like as the wax melteth at the fire', in the same anthem. The introduction of flats into a melodic line at moments of pathos or anguish was to become a hallmark of his mature expressive language.

Another pointer to the future is the flamboyant writing for bass voice in *O Lord, our governor* (PS 29). It is true that there was already something of a tradition of this sort, but it was one which Purcell was soon to exploit with relish in his Chapel Royal anthems for John Gostling. Here the range is merely

[7] See Robert F. Ford, 'Purcell as His Own Editor: The Funeral Sentences', *Journal of Musicological Research*, 7 (1986), 47–67.

[8] Zimmerman, *Analytical Catalogue*, no. 23.

from top E♭ down to bottom G and the semiquaver runs are modest, but the signs are there. Most remarkable, perhaps, of these early anthems is the ten-part *Blow up the trumpet* (PS 28). Much of its effect comes from the echo treatment of high and low voices and the kaleidoscopic cantoris and decani combinations. The opening begins with pompous trumpet figures in C major, but there is a dramatic reversal at the words 'sanctify a fast' where the key changes to the minor and it becomes clear that, far from being a call to rejoice, it is one to repent. One passage in particular deserves to be quoted as illustrating the full range of Purcell's expressive devices in these early years—augmented triads, false relations, chromaticisms, major chords turning to minor (and vice versa), and passing notes against harmony notes resulting in momentary chords with three or more adjacent diatonic notes in them (see Ex. 28). It is a *tour de force* of dissonant writing remarkable in a composer of his age. After a short emphatic chorus to 'Spare thy people, O Lord', the work continues imitatively with perhaps too loose a texture to make as strong an effect as it should, but forceful enough at the end with off-beat cries of 'Where, where, where is their God'. The scale of the work implies a great occasion, a day of national fasting and penance, to judge from the text, though nothing in 1676 or 1677 immediately suggests itself. Actually, the anthem bears the date 1681 in both the Westminster Abbey and the Bing–Gostling Partbooks, but this cannot be the date of composition, whatever else it may signify.

When we turn to the first few anthems in Fitzwilliam MS 88, no startling advances are apparent, but there is considerable evidence of increasing maturity as we work through the volume. Admirable though it is in its way, it would be surprising if *Save me, O God* (PS 13) showed much stylistic progress, dating as it does from before 1678. But we can see the direction in which he was moving from the revisions of earlier pieces which the manuscript contains—specifically the funeral sentences *Man that is born* and *In the midst of life*, and the first section of *Hear me, O Lord* (PS 13). In general, the part-writing is smoother, dissonances are softened (though far from eliminated), and the composer shows more control over his material, with undoubted artistic gains.

But it is Purcell's polyphonic technique which impresses most in the later anthems in MS 88. Such works as *O God, thou hast cast us out* (PS 29) in six parts, *O Lord God of hosts* (PS 29) and *Hear my prayer, O Lord* (PS 28), both in eight parts, represent a peak of contrapuntal writing combined with harmonic expressiveness. During the summer of 1680 he had schooled himself in this field by writing his four-part fantazias, and no doubt he had learned something by transcribing anthems by Tallis, Byrd, and Gibbons into the early pages of MS 88. Far from pastiche, the result is a revitalization of the polyphonic style. In his handling of texture—integrating homophony and polyphony, dovetailing sections, combining motifs in double counterpoint—there is a mas-

Ex. 28. Henry Purcell, *Blow up the trumpet in Sion* (Bing – Gostling Partbooks)

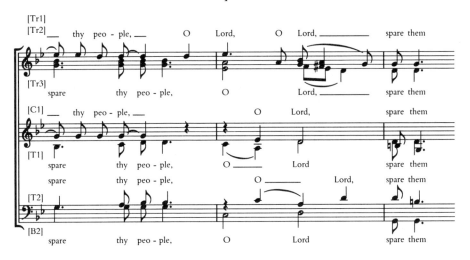

tery that does indeed recall the 'golden age', and a spaciousness that far outstrips the cramped style of his immediate predecessors. His counterpoint may lack the rhythmic fluidity of Elizabethan and Jacobean composers, but for all his concern for harmonic detail he never sacrifices his sense of line, highly individualistic though it may be. Indeed, it produces the discords in many cases.

Almost without exception these works are sombre in mood and incite the composer to some of his most expressive harmonic effects. Technically and artistically, nothing could be finer than *Hear my prayer, O Lord*; unfortunately, only the first section of what was presumably intended to be a longer work was completed. The other eight-part anthem, *O Lord God of hosts*, is less intense—A major instead of C minor—but demonstrates the full range and variety of his style with, if anything, greater skill. The opening point is based on a rising arpeggio answered by a mirror image of the theme in the upper voices. Grafted into this stately beginning is a new theme to the words 'how long wilt thou be angry' leading to a cadence on the dominant. The verse which follows for three low voices (CTB) expresses with pathetic harmony 'the bread of tears', echoed a fifth above by three high voices (TrTrC). The full choir returns, at first homophonically, but taking up a rather stereotyped imitation at the words 'and our enemies laugh us to scorn', it begins to show how, even upon such material, Purcell stamps his individuality—particularly at the cadence, sprinkled with dissonances. Then, at the words 'turn us again', comes one of those magic moments achieved simply by changing from major to minor, full to verse, common to triple time. The harmony at one point is almost like Grieg (bars 64–6); then follows a piece of pure Purcell (b. 68) where a B♭, functionally gratuitous, revives memories of the English cadence and the mannerisms of the Golden Age, even though the context is thoroughly modern. The final full section provides further examples of the antique flavour of false relations, while numerous discords, arising from glancing blows between parts as they jostle each other, bring strength and determination to the phrase 'and so we will not go back from thee'. Again there is contrast of texture; the lower voices plead 'O let us live', the upper voices promise 'and we shall call upon thy name', and when the two come together we have virtually what amounts to the simultaneous expression of two opposite 'affects'—entreaty and affirmation. Ultimately the mood of confidence triumphs, but in working out this conflict Purcell does something that was beyond the scope of even his greatest predecessors. Indeed, he looks forward to Handel. For all its 'harmonical license', Burney was justified in describing it as 'one of the finest compositions of the kind which our church, or perhaps any church, can boast'.[9]

Also belonging to this period is the B flat Service. As we have seen, it is unusual in that it comprises all the morning and evening canticles, including the alternatives, and the Kyrie and Creed from the communion service. Why he aimed at being so comprehensive can only be guessed, but perhaps he was keen to do something that no one had done since Child's pre-war G major Service, not even Blow in his G major Service (which may have been in the process of enlargement at this time but, in any case, never acquired a *Benedicite*). In fact, the B flat Service (usually so called) comprises two services: a 'first service' with Te Deum, Benedictus, Kyrie, Creed, Magnificat, and Nunc dimittis, and a 'second service' consisting of the remaining morning and evening canticles. The first service, if not also the second, dates from before Michaelmas (29 September) 1682, when payments were made for copying 'Mr Purcell's service and anthems' into the Westminster Abbey partbooks.[10] The presence of its companion piece, the anthem *O God, thou art my God*, towards the end of the Fitzwilliam autograph also points to 1682 as the year of composition. The earliest score of all ten movements of the service is in Fitzwilliam MS 117, but the original table of contents, dated 1683, lists only the movements of the first service; the rest were added only a few pages further on, though there is no way of knowing just how much later.

Because of the preponderance of triple time, the second service is lighter in character than the first. Both, however, are linked thematically by the use of head-motifs, seen most obviously in the opening of the Benedictus, Kyrie, Magnificat, and Nunc dimittis of the first service, and *O God, thou art my God* (labelled in *Cfm* 117 'To Mr Purcell's B mi service').[11] However, the *Deus*

---

[9] Burney, *History*, ii. 384.

[10] Information supplied by Dr Margaret Laurie; see also Zimmerman, *Analytical Catalogue*, no. 230.

[11] Franklin B. Zimmerman, 'Purcell's "Service Anthem" *O God, thou art my God* and the B-flat Major Service', *Musical Quarterly*, 50 (1964), 207–14.

misereatur in the second service uses a similar beginning (compare the *Nunc dimittis*), and a common bass progression relates the opening of the *Benedicite* (at its simplest) with the *Jubilate* and *Cantate Domino*, as well as the *Te Deum*. But the most striking feature that unites the service—at least in concept—is the use of canon. Child in his 'Sharp Service' and Blow in his G major Service had made considerable use of canon in similar contexts, and it may have been friendly rivalry that persuaded Purcell to turn this service into a kind of 'art of canon'. In all there are ten canons at various points in the service: canon 2 in 1 direct (*Benedicite*) and by inversion (*Benedictus*), canon 3 in 1 direct (*Magnificat*) and by inversion (*Cantate*), canon 4 in 1 direct (Creed and *Benedictus*) and by inversion (*Deus misereatur*), and canon 4 in 2 direct (*Te Deum* and *Nunc dimittis*) and by inversion (*Jubilate*).

Most of the canons are settings of the doxology, but at 'O go your way into his gates' in the *Jubilate*, following Child's canon 4 in 1, and Blow's canon 4 in 2, he took the trick with one 4 in 2 by inversion ('per arsin et thesin'). Some achieve wonderful effects of contrapuntal richness and daring part-writing; for example, the canon 4 in 1 at 'And thou, child, shalt be called the prophet of the highest' in the Benedictus, and the Gloria to the *Magnificat* (Ex. 29), which creates a marvellous sense of growth as the imitations work their way up through the texture, and generates tremendous harmonic intensity in the process. The full sections mix polyphony and counterpoint in about equal portions and give rise to much interesting detail. Purcell's harmonic language is still 'unreformed' and the dissonance treatment is very free, with many false relations. The verses are for various trio combinations, not always chosen for their expressive associations, it would seem. Thus, in the *Te Deum*, while three high voices seem appropriate for the incarnation ('When thou tookest upon thee to deliver man') and three low ones for the crucifixion—where at 'the sharpness of death' he contrives a sharp not just in one part but in all three (E major chord in B flat major)—the scoring of the equivalent passages in the Creed is reversed.

The B flat Service brings this early period of Purcell's creativity to a climax, yet without overtopping some of the peaks already revealed in the anthems. Angular lines, unprepared and irregularly resolved dissonances, augmented chords, clashing passing or unessential notes, and conflicting diatonic and chromatic progressions are a long way from classical polyphony, but the technique is fundamentally Renaissance—perhaps one might almost say 'mannerist'. However surprising the sound, it can usually be explained in terms of the movement of individual vocal lines. On the other hand, without much detriment to these lines they might often have taken other forms that would not have given rise to such sounds. Hence these characteristics are not there solely by accident; they are contrived, and the question arises, what is their

Ex. 29. Henry Purcell, *Magnificat* from the Service in B flat (*Cfm* 117)

purpose? The easy and, so far as it goes, the obvious answer is that they are there for reasons of expression. But this explanation will not do entirely, since they are also found in contexts where an immediate expressive function seems absent or at least somewhat tenuous. Sometimes they seem no more than a *jeu d'esprit*: a sign of youthful high spirits. Perhaps we cannot come closer to understanding the phenomenon than by recognizing that Purcell, almost from the first, possessed a highly idiosyncratic language that went well beyond what Locke, Humfrey, and Blow provided by way of a model. For some reason, in his early years he turned aside from the main current of harmonic thinking that was already pointing towards classical tonality, to explore whatever the transitional harmony of the mid-century could still offer in terms of technique and expression, rather than accept the new diatonic system with its simplifying tendencies and the associated aesthetic of restraint. Ultimately he conformed, as we shall see, but while it lasted it was magnificent.

PURCELL'S CHAPEL ROYAL ANTHEMS UP TO 1685

Although Henry Purcell was not officially appointed to the Chapel Royal until he became organist in 1682, he had many links through family and friends, as well as being an ex-chorister. Already his work was being performed there, for *Lord who can tell* had been copied into the chapel's partbooks by 1678 and one or two of his string anthems must date from about the same time. In the period up to the death of Charles II in 1685, he wrote fifteen or more such works for the chapel. The principal sources are the Flackton Collection and a mainly autograph 'Score Booke Containing Severall Anthems wth Symphonies' (*RM* 20.H.8) entered over the period 1681–5, probably more or less in chronological order.[12]

Flackton collection (*Lbl* 30931–2)

My beloved spake
Behold, now praise the Lord

British Library: Royal Music (MS 20.h.8)

It is a good thing to give thanks
O praise God in his holiness
Awake, put on thy strength (partial autograph)
In thee, O Lord, do I put my trust[a]
The Lord is my light[b]
I was glad when they said[b]
My heart is fixed[b]
Praise the Lord, O my soul, and all
Rejoice in the Lord alway (incomplete)
Why do the heathen?
Unto thee will I cry
I will give thanks unto thee, O Lord (incomplete)
They that go down to the sea (incomplete)
[*I will give thanks unto the Lord*][c]
[*O Lord, grant the king a long life*][c]
My heart is inditing ('one of the Anthems Sung at the Coronation of King James the 2d')[d]

[a] earlier autograph in *Ob* c.26
[b] earlier autograph in *Bu* 5001
[c] included in the index at this point but not copied in
[d] copied in but not included in the index

[12] Fortune and Zimmerman, 112–15.

It is probable that both *My beloved spake* and *Behold now praise the Lord* were written before 1679.[13] For the remainder there is little evidence for precise dating, though the spring of 1685 for *My heart is inditing* probably establishes a *terminus ante quem* for those that precede it in the list. Thus early 1685 seems about right for *They that go down to the sea*, and is not incompatible with the anecdote connected with it, related by Hawkins.[14]

Viewing these anthems as a whole, it would seem that Humfrey rather than Locke provided Purcell with his model. Significantly, it was the former's two-movement type of symphony that Purcell generally favoured, whereas (as we have seen) Blow preferred Locke's single introductory movement. These two-movement symphonies are frequently likened to French operatic overtures, and to the extent that the first section is slow and arresting in style, the second quick and in triple time, this is true. But they are far removed from Lully. Not only are they in four (or three) parts rather than five, the Englishness of the opening section is unmistakable, with its rich counterpoint and dense harmony. While Charles II was alive, Purcell never followed it with a fugue—always a dance, buoyant in rhythm and shot through with false relations. Sometimes, however, a single movement sufficed—a lively tripla in the case of *My beloved spake*, or a ground bass in *Rejoice in the Lord* and *In thee, O Lord, do I put my trust*. Rather surprisingly, *My heart is fixed* lacks an opening symphony, though several ritornellos occur during the course of the anthem. As frequently happens with Humfrey, the second section of a symphony is usually repeated somewhere in the middle of an anthem (sometimes the whole symphony), thus dividing the work into two halves and establishing the basis for an overall symmetry.

Purcell's debt to Humfrey is most obvious in these instrumental pieces. When it comes to the vocal music the differences are more obvious, for example, in the treatment of the verses and particularly the solos. There is more triple time and dotted figuration in Purcell—sometimes, indeed, there is almost no relief. It is one of the main reasons for the charge of secularity brought against his Chapel Royal anthems, and there is really no alternative but to admit the charge and plead in mitigation that the age, and particularly the court, was a secular one.

Untypical though it is in some respects, *My beloved spake* epitomizes the spirit of Purcell's symphony anthems. Clearly it was written to please the king, who could not tolerate the old-fashioned style and had a penchant for the 'step tripla'. The text, moreover, was not one that was likely to trouble his con-

---

[13] Two other early symphony anthems (*If the Lord himself* and *Praise the Lord, ye servants*) are known from incomplete sources in the hand of William Tucker (d. 28 Feb. 1679); see Zimmerman, *Analytical Catalogue*, N66 and N68, and Shaw, *Bing–Gostling Part Books*, 114–15.

[14] Hawkins, *History*, ii. 693.

science, and might even be regarded as congenial. In marked contrast to Humfrey's preference for the penitential mood, none of Purcell's symphony anthems could have raised qualms in the royal breast. Ultimately their tone is confident and reassuring. Why this should be so is an interesting question, for it is unlikely to reflect differences of temperament between the two composers. Perhaps it was a tactful response to the king's hardening cynicism. The mood is predominantly one of self-righteousness, and whatever disquiet there may be evaporates in complacent Hallelujahs. (Nearly all of Purcell's symphony anthems conclude thus, as do Blow's, yet none of Humfrey's do.) When God's enemies cry out for mercy, it is the king's enemies that are to be understood; the wicked and ungodly are those who have offended the king, and whose reward it may be to receive his magnanimous pardon or suffer his just punishment. Seen against the background of the Exclusion Crisis and the Rye House plot, the political message of *Why do the heathen* (PS 17), for example, is unmistakable: Divine Right and Passive Obedience.

On the other hand, one cannot avoid the suspicion that texts were often chosen with an eye to their suitability as vehicles for displaying the phenomenal range and histrionic power of that 'stupendious bass' John Gostling, and perhaps the king encouraged it since he was such an admirer of the singer.[15] Gostling joined the Chapel Royal in February 1679[16] and it is significant that early works such as *My beloved spake* and *Behold now praise the Lord* (both in PS 13) do not have extravagant bass parts. Purcell's 'uncle' Thomas wrote to Gostling on 8 February saying 'tis very Likely you may have a summons to appear among us sooner than you Imagin' and that his 'sonne' Henry was composing something 'wherin you will be cheifly consern'd'. A joking postscript adds 'F fa ut: and Double E la my are preparing for you' (that is, top F and bottom E), though it was not until *I will give thanks unto thee, O Lord* (PS 17) that Purcell took Gostling up to f'.[17] He frequently went below *E*, however, and beginning with *It is a good thing to give thanks* (PS 14) onwards, bass solos with a range of two octaves or more are normal. Most are declamatory in style, and words like 'glorious', 'furious', etc., are treated with exaggerated affect, while 'height' and 'depth', and similar words, are exploited in what now seems an almost comic manner, but must then have seemed quite awesome. Indeed, it is easier to imagine than reproduce the striking effect of what may have been Gostling's first solo in a Chapel Royal anthem by Purcell. The

[15] Wilson, *Roger North*, 270; also *NG* vii. 565 (Watkins Shaw).   [16] Rimbault, 16.

[17] Westrup, *Purcell*, 303–4, comments that the postscript refers to Gostling's 'exceptional low notes', whereas Zimmerman points out 'these are not low notes . . . but actually correspond either to the "E and F" just above middle C or the same notes an octave lower' (*Purcell: Life and Times* (2nd edn.), 399). Neither is right. 'F fa ut' is the F above middle C, 'Double E la mi' is the E below the bass stave.

congregation must have been spellbound (Ex. 30*a*). Soon, no doubt, they began to expect more, and in *I will give thanks* they got it—two octaves and a fourth (Ex. 30*b*).

Even a reflective work like *In thee, O Lord, do I put my trust* (PS 14) could not do without a verse like 'O what great troubles and adversities' to make use of Gostling's talents. Not all such writing is declamatory. *Why do the heathen*, for example, offers three solos in tuneful triple time (one with obbligato violin) that, nevertheless, do not neglect the potential of such phrases as 'furiously rage', 'laugh them to scorn', or 'uttermost parts of the earth', likewise, the opening verse of *They that go down to the sea* (PS 32). The proportion of such texts among these anthems could hardly have been so high had not 'the Gostling factor' been a consideration in their choice.

The solo role of countertenor and tenor was comparatively unimportant in these anthems, the latter especially, though they frequently sang together in

Ex. 30 Henry Purcell, (*a*) *It is a good thing to give thanks* (RM 20.h.8)
(*b*) *I will give thanks unto thee, O Lord* (RM 20.h.8)

duets, and of course, participated in CTB trios. The writing may be tuneful, declamatory, contrapuntal, or florid, much of it derived from the trio sonata— then preoccupying Purcell—and showing a similar polarity between bass (texted or not) and paired upper parts. One recognizes in the notation and textures the equivalents of movements that would be marked 'allegro', 'adagio', or 'largo' (not a slow tempo) in his sonatas. Optimistic or reassuring sentiments are most commonly conveyed through tuneful homophony, nearly always in triple time with frequently accented second beats after the manner of the saraband. Again, the harmony is liable to be peppered with false relations and squirming with quirkish progressions—not necessarily with any expressive intent, but because they were natural to Purcell. In common time the mood was likely to be more earnest, with imitations between the two upper voices in which the bass might participate, pointing more strongly to parallels with the trio sonata.

The choruses tend to be rather perfunctory and do little more than bring an anthem to a close with conventional Hallelujahs. It might be thought that such an insignificant role for the chorus (and the infrequency of verses with solo treble parts) indicated deficiencies in the main body of the choir, for which reliance on 'star' soloists was an easy way out. Certainly it would have saved rehearsal time, but more likely it was the king, and the prevailing ethos, that preferred soloists to full choir, and modernistic solo idioms to more traditional choral writing. Moreover, when it came to mixing boys and men in verses, there would have been problems of blend and balance, not to mention discrepancies of technique. Verse anthems were semi-operatic display pieces for the leading singers of the chapel, and treble voices would probably have detracted from the essential professionalism of the entertainment. Once or twice, however, Purcell allowed the chorus a more important role, and in the final section of *O praise God in his holiness* (PS 14) he demonstrates the technique of multi-voiced writing, already seen in his full anthems. Here three-part strings, four-part verse (CTBB), and four-part chorus are handled with masterly effect.

One of the best anthems from the period before 1685 is *Praise the Lord, O my soul, and all* (PS 14). The opening section of the symphony is in dotted quaver movement throughout, but unusual in that it is imitative in style. Although it begins in F major the tonality wavers (bars 8–10) and an influx of flats causes it to end in the minor. The tripla which follows (bars 16–45) reverts to the major and is enlivened with some witty harmonic details; it is composed of three eight-bar phrases, the first ending in the dominant and marked to be repeated, the second ending in the relative minor, and the third in the tonic (the last four bars repeated as an echo or *petite reprise*). The opening verse into which the symphony leads without a break is an impressive movement. Although the voices are solo, the conception is grand but simple, and brilliantly executed. The three high voices (TrTrT) and the three low voices (TBB) form semi-choirs which answer each other antiphonally and come together in elaborate six-part counterpoint and massive homophony with 'soft' echoes. A four-part string ritornello intervenes before the process begins again, this time extended and moving further away from the tonic. One group responds to another a semitone higher in the excitement (bars 97–9); ponderous hemiolas fill out the cadences; solo voices are answered by one group, then the other, then both together; a concluding ritornello maintains the exhilaration to the end.

At this point the tonic moves down from F to D minor; the mood changes, as does triple to common time (b. 168). A trio (TTB) sings 'The Lord is full of compassion', and expressive harmonies and suspensions on 'long-suffering' add a touch of pathos. A note of reassurance is sounded by a return to F major and triple time in the next section (b. 181). Regular four-bar phrases and melodic parallels between the first eight bars and the next eight make this, in effect, a binary air—a good example of a common device to lighten the mood, though tuneful symmetries would not have been possible without textual repetition.

As in several other anthems, the second half of the work is inaugurated by a reprise of the tripla from the opening symphony (b. 204). This marks a return to the mood of confidence, and makes the bass solo which follows all the more dramatic by contrast (b. 233). However, the range falls short of Gostling's two octaves plus, and the style is less extravagant than usual, given the potential of the line 'For look, how high the heaven is in comparison of the earth'. The last verse (bar 254) employs similar antiphonal effects to the opening, but in a more straightforward style that is nevertheless still full of verve. Syncopations abound, and the five-bar phrases towards the end are almost intoxicating. A concluding ritornello forms a link to the final chorus, the first time the full choir has been heard, but a mere fourteen bars long and somewhat disappointing after what has gone before. (For once there is no Hallelujah.) This apart, the work shows Purcell at his best, particularly the opening and closing verses which by simple means create a magnificent effect that puts one in mind of Handel, though the music itself could only be by Purcell.

The two anthems which Purcell listed in the contents of his score-book but never got round to entering (perhaps because of preparations for James II's coronation) are an odd pair. Both *I will give thanks unto the Lord* (PS 28) and *O Lord, grant the king a long life* (PS 29) have symphonies and ritornellos in three parts (two violins and bass), and thus form a group with *They that go down to the sea*, their companion in the table. On the other hand, both begin with single triple-time movements and thus hark back to *My beloved spake*, and Blow's more usual practice. Nor do they appear to contain solos specially written for

Gostling; indeed, their general effect is somewhat lightweight. Their position in the table, however, suggests a date in early 1685, and this is probably where they belong—perhaps the first few weeks of James's reign before he was crowned. *O Lord, grant the king a long life* would certainly have been appropriate at that time, and the fact that the king took little interest in the chapel could account for the routine quality of both anthems.

Purcell may also have had more important things on his mind—such as the anthems he had been commissioned to write for the coronation on 23 April. There were to be two: a full setting of *I was glad when they said unto me* sung by the choir of Westminster Abbey as an introit (probably the version that has generally been attributed to Blow[18]), and *My heart is inditing* (PS 17), 'performed by the whole Consort of Voices and Instruments' while the queen was being conducted to her throne after her crowning.[19] The latter is quite unlike the symphony anthems we have been considering and, significantly, marks the point at which Purcell, in his anthems, abandoned dance for fugue in the second movements of his symphonies. It is written for the same forces as Blow's magnificent companion piece *God spake sometime in visions*, which was sung at the distribution of the king's largesse. *My heart is inditing* is really a full anthem with verses and symphonies, and its choral writing invites comparison with the big multi-voiced anthems of four or five years earlier. In that respect it shows neither diminished contrapuntal skill nor harmonic amelioration. It embraces wonderful polychoral effects in the full sections and meets the challenge of eight real parts head on, producing a monumental sonority bursting with false relations and clashing part-writing. Although hardly a typical Chapel Royal anthem, it brings to a climax the first phase of Purcell's career as a composer for the chapel.

PURCELL'S LATER CHURCH MUSIC, 1685–1695

The great days of the Chapel Royal came to an end with the death of Charles II, though on the evidence of James II's coronation no one would have foreseen it. As a Catholic, James did not attend the chapel, and instead had his own 'popish' chapel—a 'world of mysterious Ceremony the Musique playing & singing', as Evelyn described it.[20] Nevertheless, services according to the liturgy of the Church of England continued as they were bound to by the Act of Uniformity, and when his daughter Princess Anne was present—she was not a

[18] Bruce Wood, 'A Coronation Anthem, Lost and Found', *Musical Times*, 118 (1977), 466–8.
[19] Zimmerman, *Purcell: Life and Times* (2nd edn.), 123–4; *MB* 7, pp. xii–xv.
[20] 29 Dec. 1686; Evelyn, *Diary*, iv. 534–5.

Catholic—it was ordered that the instruments also were to attend 'as formerly they did'.[21] However, the tradition of the Sunday symphony anthem was broken. There were still occasions when lavish music was required, but when it was, the manner was likely to be more ostentatious than in King Charles's day. Significantly, Purcell gave up writing sarabands for the second section of his symphonies after Charles's death; fugues were more solemn. Thus, Blow's and Purcell's symphony anthems became fewer after 1685 and took on the character of occasional pieces. So far as Purcell's own career was concerned, he remained organist of the chapel and Westminster Abbey up to the time of his death— which was only ten years away—but increasingly he sought musical fulfilment in the theatre, where, ultimately, his greatest achievements were to lie.

Before considering the anthems of Purcell's last period, some mention of his Evening Service in G minor (*PS* 23) should be made since it is difficult to date stylistically and has no obvious niche in his output. It belongs to a type which we have already encountered in the works of Wise, Blow, and Aldrich—that of the triple-time service. It is thus rather lightweight in character, but neatly put together with full sections separated by verses alternating high (TrTrC) and low (CTB) voices. It survives with a common-time Gloria to the *Nunc dimittis* 'compos'd by Mr [Ralph?] Roseingrave Jr' beginning as a canon 4 in 2, but the original version probably shared its Gloria with the *Magnificat*. In terms of its source pedigree Purcell's claim to the service is not strong, since the few sources there are all emanate from York after Purcell's death. It is probably safe to say that if it is by him, it is not an early work.

Autographs of Purcell's post-1685 anthems are almost completely lacking. Many, of course, exist in non-autograph sources, among which the Gostling Manuscript has the best selection.[22] It contains twelve anthems from this period, some with dates, the 'orchestral anthems' at one end, the 'choral anthems' at the other.

Gostling Manuscript ('Orchestral Anthems')

Behold I bring you glad tidings ('For Christmas day, 1687')
Blessed are they that fear the Lord ('Jan: 12. 1687[8] For the Thanksgiving . . . upon her Majesties being with Child')
Praise the Lord, O my soul, O Lord my God ('1687')[a]
Thy way, O God, is holy ('1687')[a,b]
O sing unto the Lord ('1688')

Gostling Manuscript ('Choral Anthems')

Blessed is the man that feareth the Lord ('Anthem for ye Charterhouse sung upon ye Founders day')[c]
O give thanks unto the Lord ('1693')[d,f]

---

[21] Ashbee, ii. 15–16. [22] Zimmerman (ed.), *The Gostling Manuscript.*

The way of God is an undefiled way ('November ye 11th 1694, King William then return'd
   from Flanders')
Sing unto God, O ye kingdoms of the earth ('1687')
My song shall be alway[d,e]
The Lord is king, the earth may be glad ('1688')
Blessed is he that considereth the poor
  [a] probably these dates are 'old style' i.e. before 25 March 1688
  [b] not actually a symphony anthem
  [c] follows a piece by Blow dated 30 June 1688, and precedes one dated Aug. 1693
  [d] has instrumental movements elsewhere
  [e] dated 'Sep: 9/90' in *Ob* Mus Sch. c. 61
  [f] *Cfm* 152 autograph '1693'

This list includes most of the anthems known to have been written by Purcell
after 1685, though notably absent is *Praise the Lord, O Jerusalem* (PS 17), written
for the coronation of William and Mary in 1689. Such works as *Behold, I bring
you glad tidings* (PS 28) and *O sing unto the Lord* (PS 17) are among his most
splendid. They have symphonies in a new style, with heavy chordal opening
sections introducing quick fugal movements, neither of which are in triple time.
The first begins with a tremendous verse for bass solo (Gostling again) accompanied by strings. No less striking is the 'Glory to God on high' section,
particularly the sudden change from major to minor, common to triple time,
chorus to verse at the words 'and on earth peace', and the juxtaposition of C
minor and A major—already encountered in *Let God arise*—where the angels'
message is taken up again the second time (b. 177). Unfortunately, he was
unable to reach this form again in time for the thanksgiving anthem marking the
queen's fateful pregnancy on 15 January following. Whatever Purcell's feeling
regarding this threat to the Protestant succession, *Blessed are they that fear the Lord*
(PS 28) lacks inspiration.

   O sing unto the Lord, however, is one of his most accomplished pieces of
church music. In places it foreshadows Handel, particularly at 'Tell it out among
the heathen', but elsewhere the mixture of intimacy and grandeur is typically
Purcellian. The opening section of the symphony suggests weighty matters to
follow; the ensuing fugue maintains its momentum and thematic interest to the
end. The whole demonstrates Purcell's conversion to the Italian 'sinfonia' style
of the late Baroque, where all is conditioned by the tonal framework yet
without any sense of harmonic impoverishment which one often gets with
the Italians. A short verse for 'upper Bass' introduces the first chorus—a
Hallelujah in which voices and instruments alternate. Neither this, nor the
balancing Hallelujah at the end, is in the slightest perfunctory, and there is much
elsewhere that claims attention; for example, the declamatory bass solo which
leads into the chorus 'Glory and worship are before him' and the F minor
section ('O worship the Lord in the beauty of holiness') with its pathetic
treatment of the words 'let the whole earth stand in awe of him'. Less successful

perhaps is 'The Lord is great', a duet for treble and alto on a three-bar ground, which alone betrays traces of Purcell's earlier harmonic waywardness. With this exception the work maintains its distinction, both from the expressive and technical aspect.

The coronation of William and Mary on 11 April 1689 was a more modest affair than the previous one—as well it might be in the circumstances.[23] Likewise the work Purcell wrote for it, *Praise the Lord, O Jerusalem* (PS 17), lacked the scale and splendour of *My heart is inditing*; to that extent it is disappointing, although its intrinsic musical quality is still high. One wonders, though, why he chose the minor key in view of the words and the occasion.

In the reign which followed there was little call for Purcell's talents in the chapel. The king, though a Protestant, was an infrequent attender, partly owing to his absences campaigning abroad, and partly because when at home, he preferred the less polluted air of Kensington Palace and Hampton Court because of his asthma. It may have been on William's return from the Irish campaign in September 1690 that *My song shall be alway* (PS 29) was performed, if the inscription 'H.P. Sep: 9/90' in *Ob* Mus. Sch. c. 61 is anything more than the date of copying. On the other hand, in the Gostling Manuscript it is sandwiched between two anthems dated 1687 and 19 June 1688, and this would put it back in the reign of James II, where it would probably be happier. A solo anthem for bass after the current fashion, it begins with Purcell's new type of symphony, and continues with a lengthy series of solo movements requiring formidable technical ability, though not in this case Gostling's range. The work displays a number of features characteristic of Purcell's anthems in the late 1680s. Clear divisions and pronounced contrasts between movements justify the useful modern term 'cantata anthem' to describe such works. A sign of the times, too, is the use of tempo indications such as 'slow', 'faster time', and 'fast' for these movements. Moreover, certain movements complement each other, rather like the recitative-aria pairs of a cantata: for example, the declamatory section 'O Lord, God of hosts' followed by 'Thou rulest the raging of the seas' (Ex. 31*a*–*b*). Another late feature is the presence of a free ground-bass movement ('Thou hast a mighty arm'), beginning in C major but modulating to the dominant, and then to its dominant, before retracing its steps (Ex. 3*c*). Other late anthems maintain the ensemble tradition and make imaginative use of the chorus, for example, *O give thanks unto the Lord* (PS 29), which at the same time provides a splendid example of the composer at his most Italianate, particularly in the duet 'Who can express'.

Purcell's last verse anthem, written to celebrate the king's return from Flanders in 1694, is *The way of God is an undefiled way* (PS 32), a rather empty

[23] Bruce Wood, 'John Blow's Anthems', 7–8.

Ex. 31. Henry Purcell, *My song shall be alway* (Gostling MS)

example of his late style. The opening verse begins with a puny symphony for organ, five bars long, with a trumpet ritornello later on. The text is appropriately martial, the key D major, and the solo bass (Gostling again) blusters in response to a pair of countertenors singing sweetly in thirds. Things improve towards the end, especially in an expressive D minor verse for the two countertenors ('They shall cry, but there shall be none to help them'), but the composer's lack of conviction cannot be disguised.

Towards the end of that year Purcell composed his *Te Deum* and *Jubilate* in D for trumpets and strings (*PS* 23). Its first performance was at St Bride's, Fleet Street, for the St Cecilia service of 22 November 1694, and later (on 9 December) 'before their majesties in the Chapel Royal'.[24] Given the occasion and the key, it could hardly avoid bombast, but some of the quieter sections in minor keys, such as the verse 'Be ye sure that the Lord he is God' in the *Jubilate*, are genuinely affecting. For better or worse the piece became the model for successive ceremonial *Te Deums*, not only for those written by Blow and Turner for the St Cecilia festivals of 1695 and 1696, but for subsequent thanksgiving services to which Croft, Handel, and Greene were called to contribute. Tudway reported that it had been commissioned 'principally against ye Opening of Pauls',[25] and in the event this might have been what happened, though the fact that Blow's *I was glad*, sung at the opening on 5 December 1697, was for trumpets in C, whereas Purcell's *Te Deum* uses trumpets in D, raises a doubt. In any case, a few days later it was performed at the Festival of the Sons of the Clergy, now re-established at St Paul's, where it became a regular part of the proceedings.[26] The edition of 1707 also mentioned that it had been 'perform'd before the Queen, Lords and Commons, at the Cathedral-Church of St. Paul, on the thanksgiving day for the glorious success of Her Majesty's army last campaign'.

Purcell's late church music shows a completely different outlook from his earlier work for the Chapel Royal. The anthems he wrote for the chapel up to 1685, for all their extravagance, have an intimacy, warmth, and even good humour that is lacking in those he wrote for James or William. There is something haughty and less human about them. Perhaps in this they reflect the style of the monarchs as much as the occasions for which they were written. Mixed in with this, so that one can hardly disentangle cause and effect, went a change in his own style, wherein imaginative richness acquired greater intellectual discipline, and youthful exuberance grew to mature brilliance. Technically speaking, older elements gave place to new, French idioms were supplanted by Italian, and idiosyncratic harmony succumbed to the higher demands of the tonal system. The revolution was not completed in his lifetime—old habits died

---

[24] Zimmerman, *Purcell: Life and Times* (2nd edn.), 238.   [25] App. F(vi).   [26] See Ch. 2.

Ex. 32. Henry Purcell, *Thou knowest, Lord, the secrets of our hearts*: (*a*) *Cfm* 88; (*b*) *Och* 794 and *Lbl* 31444

hard and he died young—but was on the point of being achieved. It was left to Croft and the succeeding generation to carry it through.

His last anthem was not, however, a verse anthem for some special occasion of celebration, but a setting of *Thou knowest, Lord* for the funeral of Queen Mary in March 1695.[27] Comparison between it and a previous setting, fifteen or more years earlier, gives an indication of the extent to which Purcell's musical language had changed, and the direction in which he had moved. Clearly the final bars of each represent a very different aesthetic: the one intense and full of

---

[27] At the Oxford Purcell Conference in 1993 Bruce Wood advanced convincing arguments to suggest that Purcell's *Thou knowest, Lord* ('third' setting) was sung in conjunction with Thomas Morley's burial service at Queen Mary's funeral.

anguish, the other classically restrained (Ex. 32). There is no doubt which the eighteenth century preferred. Croft in making his own setting of the Burial Service could not bring himself to set the same words for reasons 'obvious to every Artist', and incorporated it instead.[28] Eight months after Queen Mary's funeral *Thou knowest, Lord* was sung at Purcell's own funeral.

[28] William Croft, *Musica Sacra* (1724), i. 3–4.

9

The Younger Generation: Clarke, Weldon, and Croft

For the last ten years of his life Purcell was recognized as the most gifted church musician of his time. Not only were younger men like Clarke and Croft influenced by him, so were his seniors Blow and Turner, who had been in the chapel since the earliest years of the Restoration. Rightly, Blow was honoured as doyen, and composers brought up in the chapel acknowledged their debt to him, but it was Purcell's late anthems that provided them with their models.

With the accession of Queen Anne in 1702, the chapel enjoyed a surge of optimism. Unlike King William, the queen was a staunch Anglican, and expected the chapel to function as it had done in her uncle Charles II's day (though with fewer singers and without instruments). Under successive subdeans Ralph Battell and John Dolben morale was high, and there was some capable new blood among the gentlemen. Admittedly the new organist, Francis Pigott from Magdalen College, Oxford, had no great reputation, but on his early death in 1704 the opportunity was taken to appoint Jeremiah Clarke and William Croft as joint organists in his place. Clarke dying in 1707, Croft was left to enjoy the full place, and on Blow's death the following year became master of the choristers and composer, John Weldon succeeding Blow as organist.[1] Together with such singers as Richard Elford, John Freeman, and John Howell, they were a body of musicians to be reckoned with. Elford, indeed, seems to have inspired composers with his countertenor voice to almost the same degree as Gostling had done with his bass.

From October 1703 the chapel was established at St James's Palace, where the queen had been living since 1696. Bernard Smith had already been ordered to 'make a small new organ to be set up in her Majts Chappel at St James', which 'when completed by putting in the trumpet stop and that called Cremona' was to cost £690. As it turned out the organ was 'incapable of containing the Trumpet stop' so the bill was reduced by £100.[2]

The repertoire of the chapel is reflected in a word-book printed in 1712 entitled *Divine Harmony, or a New Collection of Select Anthems us'd at Her Majesty's Chappels Royal*, though not exclusively, since anthems from 'Westminster Abby

---

[1] Shaw, 9–11, 20, 175–6.   [2] Ashbee, ii. 76; Freeman, *Father Smith*, 139.

[*sic*], St Paul's, Windsor, both Universities, Eaton, and most Cathedrals in her Majesty's Dominions' were also included. Not only does it provide a useful dating tool for its contents, it identifies numerous occasional pieces written for thanksgiving services celebrating Marlborough's victories. Its compiler was probably John Church who, besides being a member of the choirs of the Chapel Royal and Westminster Abbey, was also copyist at both places. His Chapel Royal partbooks (*RM* 27.a.1–15)[3] reveal the repertoire of the chapel during the queen's reign—in effect, anthems entered side by side with those attributed to 'Mr' Croft, whose doctorate was awarded in 1713. It appears that several by Tallis, Byrd, and Gibbons were still being sung, but Restoration composers provided the basic fare. Blow and Aldrich, of the older generation, were the most frequently included, but Humfrey, Tucker, and Wise were not forgotten, nor were Turner and Tudway (who were still alive) and, of course, Purcell. Services included Farrant's 'High' Service, and others almost as ancient, such as the short services of Byrd and Gibbons. Among more recent repertoire works were a few of Child's, the three popular ones by Blow, two by Aldrich, and Purcell's in B flat. The most modern was Church's F major Service, but rather surprisingly nothing of the kind by Clarke, Weldon, or Croft, at least in these particular partbooks. In any case, the main musical focus of the chapel service was the anthem, and in this department the collection is thoroughly up to date. Most prolific was Croft, but Clarke and Weldon were also productive, as was Church, whose work will be considered in connection with Westminster Abbey. Apart from some keyboard music, Pigott is known only as the composer of a setting of *I was glad* in the Gostling Manuscript—probably the one sung at the queen's coronation on St George's day, 1703.

JEREMIAH CLARKE

Among the choristers of the Chapel Royal who took part in the coronation of James II in 1685 was Jeremiah Clarke.[4] By April 1692 he had left the chapel and was granted the usual clothing and £20 allowance.[5] From 1692 to 1695 he was organist of Winchester College,[6] but left to pursue a career in London as a theatre composer—Purcell's death having left something of a vacuum. He was appointed vicar choral and organist of St Paul's on 6 June 1699, and succeeded Blow as almoner and master of the choristers in November 1703.[7] Croft and he were appointed jointly to the Chapel Royal on 7 July 1700 'to succeed as Organists . . . when any such place shal fall voyd'. This happened in May 1704

³ Laurie, 'The Chapel Royal Part-Books', 35–9.
⁴ *NG* iv. 446–8 (Watkins Shaw and Christopher Powell); see also Dearnley, 237–9; Long, 290–1; Zimmerman, *Purcell: Life and Times*, 125.
⁵ Ashbee, ii. 45.   ⁶ Shaw, 398–9.   ⁷ Ibid. 175–6.

when Francis Pigott died.[8] Clarke's own death on 1 December 1707 was by suicide, supposedly caused by an unhappy love affair.

Like Purcell, he led the double life of a church and theatre composer, making a success of both artistically and financially—at his death his income was reputed to be £300 a year.[9] His church music includes two morning services, a Sanctus and Gloria (Arnold, i), and about twenty anthems.[10] Possibly the three anthems at Wimborne Minster were written while he was at Winchester College before 1695 and may thus be among the earliest. They include *How long wilt thou forget me* (Boyce, ii) and the first setting of *I will love thee, O Lord my strength* (Boyce, iii). The latter is also one of four by Clarke in volume iv of Tudway's Collection (*Harl.* 7340), and therefore likely to have been written before Queen Anne came to the throne. *Praise the Lord, O Jerusalem* (Boyce, ii) was written for her accession, and several thereafter can be dated as occasional pieces, among them the second setting of *I will love thee, O Lord my strength*, written 'for the Victory & Success in Flanders, in passing the French lines', and sung before the queen at the thanksgiving service on 23 August 1705 at St Paul's, and *O be joyful in the Lord all ye lands* for the Festival of the Sons of the Clergy (26 November 1706).

By far the most widely circulated anthem by Clarke was the first setting of *I will love thee, O Lord*. No doubt its dramatic choral centre-piece, 'The earth trembled and quaked,' with its tremolo diminished sevenths was largely responsible for this. Overall it provides a fine example of trends around the turn of the century. Four of its seven movements—in all 181 bars out of 215—are in triple time. The divisions between the movements are clear cut and the tonal scheme wide-ranging but symmetrical, beginning in A minor (some sources are a tone higher), with 'sorrowful' D minor (Ex. 33*a*) passing through 'trembling' A minor (Ex. 33*b*) to 'thundering' C major (Ex. 33*c*) before returning to the original home key. In it we can see the move towards the 'emancipation of the aria' with motto openings and incipient ritornello structure. As it happens, neither the big D minor bass solo ('The sorrows of death') nor the C major duet for tenor and bass ('The Lord also thundered out of heaven') quite realize the full potential of their beginnings; nevertheless, their dimensions are impressive—not the result of mere inflation but the structural principles of tonality at work. This anthem typifies Clarke's more extended verse anthems, among which *Praise the Lord, O my soul* (1705) and *The Lord is my strength* (1706) are equally interesting.

Apart from two insignificant contributions to Playford's *Divine Companion* (1701)—simple anthems for country choirs—all Clarke's anthems are verse anthems. (The full anthem *O Lord, God of my salvation*, sometimes attributed to

---

[8] Rimbault, 23, 25.   [9] *DNB.*

[10] Thomas F. Taylor, *Thematic Catalog of the Works of Jeremiah Clarke* (Detroit, 1977); see also H. Diack Johnstone's review in *Music and Letters*, 59 (1978) 55–7.

Ex. 33. Jeremiah Clarke, *I will love thee, O Lord* (Gostling MS)

him, has a more likely author in Vaughan Richardson, though one cannot be sure; a possible Winchester provenance could lie behind the mix-up.) Both the morning services are melodious, but the G major setting is less resourceful than the C minor in its verse-writing, as well as textural and metrical variety. Rimbault dated them 1693 and 1698 respectively, without citing any evidence.[11] Unusually, a manuscript of the latter in the Royal Academy of Music, London (MS 99) provides intonations to both the *Te Deum* ('We praise thee, O God' = *c, eb, f, g, c*) and the Creed ('I believe in one God' = *c, d, eb, f, g, c*) which bear a superficial but probably fortuitous resemblance to Merbecke's traditional incipits.

It is difficult to see what Hawkins meant when he described Clarke's anthems as 'remarkably pathetic'; nor do they seem particularly to 'preserve the dignity and majesty of the church style'.[12] Clarke certainly does not favour pathetic texts, though he readily responds to individual words and phrases when they offer themselves. As for 'dignity and majesty', this may only be Hawkins's way of saying that Clarke was closer to Blow and Purcell than was Croft. Things might have been different had he lived longer; as it is, one recognizes a composer who, at least, was not content to be dull or deal in trifles.

JOHN WELDON

According to Hawkins, Weldon 'was a very sweet and elegant composer of church music'.[13] He was born in Chichester on 19 January 1676, and was a chorister at Eton under John Walter. For a time he was also a pupil of Purcell before becoming organist of New College, Oxford, in 1684. He was sworn 'gentleman extraordinary' of the Chapel Royal on 6 June 1701, and succeeded to Blow's place as organist in 1708, as we have seen. He was admitted second composer-in-ordinary in 1715, but seems to have written little church music after that date. Concurrently with his chapel appointments, he was organist of St Bride's, Fleet Street, from 1702 and of St Martin-in-the-Fields from 1714. He died 'at his house in Downing St Westminster' on 7 May 1736.[14]

About thirty anthems by him are known, and there is a service in D major.[15] The latter survives in a set of parts (*Lcm* 2043, partly autograph) bearing the names of Chapel Royal singers of the period 1714–17, among them the basses 'Mr [Thomas] Baker' (appointed 1714) and 'Mr [Leonard] Woodson' (died March 1717). Unfortunately, the parts are not complete enough to allow the

---

[11] Edward F. Rimbault (ed.), *Cathedral Music* (London, [1847]), 63, 226.

[12] Hawkins, *History*, ii. 784.   [13] Ibid. 784–6.

[14] *NG* xx. 331–2 (Margaret Laurie); Shaw, 10–11, 20, 390.

[15] The service lacks a communion service, but a Sanctus and Gloria in E-flat were printed in *The Choir*, ed. E. F. Rimbault, nos. 49–50 (London, 1864). Earlier sources have not been traced.

reconstruction of the verse sections. The full sections are written in a straight-forward style, though the treble is ornamented in the source.

Two-thirds of the anthems, however, are complete.[16] Two easy anthems for parish choirs were published in Playford's *Divine Companion*, and six solo anthems 'Performed by the late Famous Mr Richard Elford' in the Chapel Royal were brought out by Walsh and Hare in *Divine Harmony* [c.1716–17]— a collection of anthems not to be confused with the word-book of the same name already mentioned. Anthems which Weldon may have written while at New College cannot be identified with certainty, but it is possible that the six which begin Simon Child's score (*US-BE* 173), dated 1716, were copied from sources already at New College, since Child was Weldon's immediate successor there as organist, and his versions are independent of those in *Divine Harmony*. Apart from minor variants, Child's earlier versions (if that is what they are) are longer, and in two cases pitched a tone lower for a tenor rather than a countertenor. (In fact, to accommodate Elford's range, the notation of the voice part stays the same except for a change of clef from C4 to G2). Features of his mature style are already present in these pieces, notably the highly affective declamatory writing for solo voice, often involving chromatic progressions modelled on Purcell's (though without his harmonic audaciousness) and the clear-cut rhythmic and tonal structure of the tuneful sections, frequently spun out by sequences and passages of coloratura. *Blessed be the Lord my strength* provides examples of both; the former in the verse 'Thou hast given victory unto kings' with its portentous opening and pathetic chromaticism at 'the peril of the sword' (Ex. 34a), the latter in the ensuing 'air', which is full of confidence (Ex. 34b). Anthems such as this consist, basically, of an alternating series of expressive declamatory sections and triple-time airs ending with a brief chorus. The tuneful sections frequently exhibit a melodiousness and regularity of phrase more characteristic of secular than sacred music.

By 1712, ten of Weldon's anthems were probably in the repertoire of the Chapel Royal. All were verse anthems, several of them for solo voice of the kind just described, and best represented by *Have mercy upon us, O Lord*. In more extrovert mood *O praise the Lord, laud ye the name of the Lord* is a splendid anthem for two voices and trumpet, typical of its genre with trumpet ritornellos, echoing phrases between voice and instrument, long-held notes in one part against movement in the other, etc. Whether it was for a real trumpet or merely a trumpet stop is not clear from the score, but the latter seems more likely. Some anthems were written for services to celebrate Marlborough's victories, among them *Rejoice in the Lord, O ye righteous* ('compos'd for the Thanksgiving on *Feb.* 17th. 1708[9] for the successes of that Year') and *O give thanks unto the*

---

[16] Dearnley, 239–41; Long, 294–5.

Lord, and call upon his name ('compos'd for the Thanksgiving Nov. 22. 1709').
From the contents of the 1724 edition of *A Collection of Anthems* (sequel to the
1712 word-book) it appears that a further ten anthems had entered the repertoire in the intervening years, four of them full anthems. By and large Weldon
showed little interest in the latter. Bold choral effects seem to have made little
appeal to him, and even his ostensibly 'full' sections have an openness of texture
more characteristic of multi-voiced verse-writing. This can be seen in the full
anthems *Hear my crying, O God* and *In the Lord have I put my trust* (both in
Boyce, ii). The first was the most widespread of Weldon's anthems in the early
eighteenth century, and the only one, verse or full, which Tudway included in
his collection (*Harl.* 7341).[17] Whether this neglect—which extended to most
provincial cathedrals—reflected Tudway's disapproval of Weldon's 'theatrical'
manner we can only guess, yet even here there is a curious lack of fibre in the
choral sections. For all its false relations and final fugue one senses a gentleness
almost that is at odds with the gravity of the 'antient stile'. The fugue itself
shows promise at the beginning, but entries peter out disappointingly and fail to
build up to anything substantial, as the optimism of the text might seem to
require. The final bars do, at least, offer a splash of harmonic colour in the form
of a 'German' sixth after numerous diminished sevenths, before finally closing
with a pair of perfunctory Amens.

Among his occasional anthems dating from the later years of Queen Anne's
reign are *The princes of the people*, written 'upon the Prospect of approaching
peace [of Utrecht]' and *O God, thou hast cast us out*, written 'for a publick Fast'
(Arnold, i). The latter has a beautifully expressive opening section, and although
all the movements are in A major or minor, the work shows an advance on the
solo anthems already mentioned, especially the 'arias', which are more extended
and motivically developed. Significantly, two are 'motto' arias which to all
intents and purposes could serve as the main sections of da capo structures. The
chorus plays a more important role than usual in this anthem, and the work as
a whole may be regarded as an example of Weldon at his best.

Weldon's verse anthems contrast strikingly with Croft's, and these days,
perhaps, may have a particular appeal, despite lapses into exaggerated coloratura
and sequences. The declamatory writing is more affective—often elaborately
so—and the tuneful sections at their best have a melodic elegance and lyric
quality that Croft rarely attains. Expressive chromatic touches abound and, in
general, the harmony is rich and adroitly handled—though the overall tonal
structure of his anthems is often unenterprising. His choral writing lacks Croft's
strength, and there is little sense of grandeur. There is, indeed, a kind of
'effeminacy' (as the eighteenth century might have regarded it) which was felt

[17] Rev. edn. H. Watkins Shaw (London, 1960).

Ex. 34. John Weldon, *Blessed be the Lord my strength* (US - BE 173)

at the time to be inappropriate to church music, but which is nevertheless attractive. Certainly the way in which his reputation has suffered in comparison with Croft's seems a trifle unjust.

WILLIAM CROFT

Three years younger than Weldon, William Croft (or Crofts, as his name is often given early on) was christened on 30 December 1678, and brought up as a chorister in the Chapel Royal under Blow. Describing himself as 'Your

youngest Off-spring, not the least endear'd' in a poem prefixed to Blow's *Amphion Anglicus* (1700), he signed himself 'Organist of St Anne's [Soho]'.[18] As we have seen, he and Jeremiah Clarke were sworn 'gentlemen extraordinary' of the chapel in July 1700 with right to succeed as and when there was a vacancy.[19] That event occurred on the death of Francis Pigott in 1704, but following Clarke's suicide in 1707, Croft had the reversion of the full place.[20] In due course Croft became Master of the Children and Composer in Ordinary as well as organist of Westminster Abbey after Blow's death.[21] He was made Doctor of Music by Oxford University in 1713, and in 1724 published his *Musica Sacra*, containing thirty-one anthems and the burial service in score. (Unless otherwise

[18] *NG* v. 55–7 (Watkins Shaw); Shaw, 10.
[19] Rimbault, 23.   [20] Ibid. 25.   [21] Ibid. 26.

stated the anthems discussed below are in that collection.) It was the first publication of its kind and, as well as being a useful innovation in itself (compared with singing from parts the advantages are obvious), it helped to give his anthems wide currency. He also published a considerable quantity of secular music, instrumental and vocal. He died on 14 August 1727 and was buried close to Purcell in Westminster Abbey.

Croft wrote four services and at least eighty-two anthems in addition to the famous burial service.[22] The services include a *Te Deum* and *Jubilate* in D with accompaniment for trumpets, oboes, and strings, composed for the victory at Malplaquet in 1709 and 'Perform'd twice before her most Gracious Majesty Queen Anne at the Chapell Royall at St James's on dayes of Thanksgiving, & thrice, at St Pauls, on the like Occasions', according to Tudway (*Harl.* 7342). It follows in the tradition of similar works by Purcell, Blow, and Turner, and is transitional in style between theirs and Handel's 'Utrecht' *Te Deum*. Too many short sections prevent it from developing much momentum, but some of the longer movements are rewarding in themselves, especially the expressive countertenor solo 'Vouchsafe, O Lord'. Also noteworthy is the remarkable setting of 'The father of an infinite majesty', in which four countertenors rapturously pile dissonant suspensions on top of each other. The *Jubilate* has the advantage of a shorter text and can thus afford to take a more expansive approach, with particular benefit to the choruses.

Other services include morning and communion services in A major and B minor (Arnold, i) and a morning and evening service in E flat, which has a *Cantate Domino* that begins like his well-known hymn tune, St Anne ('O God our help in ages past').[23] This service is dated 19 March 1719/20 (*Lbl* 38668) and is the most interesting of the three. The other two are probably earlier—not that much can be deduced from conservative traits in the general run of such settings. However, the Sanctus and Gloria from the B minor Service are found attributed to 'Mr' Croft (*Ob* Tenbury 797–803) and this suggests that the rest of the service, too, may date from before 1713. The *Te Deum* in particular is an admirable piece with an opening that converts the major of Purcell's B-flat *Te Deum* into B minor (Ex. 35) and continues with plenty of variety in the verses, which sometimes expand to six or eight parts treated antiphonally. The five-part verse with two trebles setting the text 'When thou took'st upon thee to deliver man' is especially attractive, and the withdrawl of the two trebles at the words 'When thou had'st overcome the sharpness of death' produces a strikingly effective change of colour. For all the limitations such a work imposes on a composer, Croft shows his class. He had the technique and he had the imagination; he needed the anthem to provide more scope for both.

---

[22] Long, 291–4; Dearnley, 241–8; also Robert L. Scandrett, 'The Anthems of William Croft (1678–1727)' (Ph.D. diss., University of Washington, 1961).

[23] The services are in *Lbl* 17844, 17848–9, and 38668.

Ex. 35(*a*) Henry Purcell, *Te Deum* from the Service in B flat (*Cfm* 117)
 (*b*) William Croft, *Te Deum* from the Service in B minor (*Lbl* 17844)

The extant anthems include ten full and seventy-two verse anthems, five of which are orchestral. The earlier anthems date from around 1698 and include those in Gostling's Tenbury Partbooks (1179–82). Broad indications of the date of later anthems may be determined by their presence in the word-books of 1712, 1724, and 1736, while thirty or so attributions to 'Mr' rather than 'Dr' Croft imply composition not later than 1713. It is these we shall be concerned with here.

Most of the full anthems are early works and all are of the 'full with verse' type. The outer sections are invariably contrapuntal, often in a style that owes more to the eighteenth-century idea of the *stile antico* than to Purcell. The treatment of the central verse sections is less stereotyped, providing contrast of key, metre, and texture. The fact that they are usually in triple time gives them more of a Restoration feel, especially when dotted rhythms are employed. The texture may contract to three parts or expand to six or eight, in which case antiphonal effects between different solo groups are often a feature. But the main weight of these anthems lies in their opening and closing sections. Here Croft is committed to the formalities of fugal writing, using stiff academic subjects; *God is gone up with a merry noise*, dating from about 1706, is a familiar example.[24] Instances might be multiplied—in *Sing praises to the Lord*, for example, or *O Lord, grant the queen a long life*—though an exception must be made of the opening and closing choruses of *We will rejoice in thy salvation*, which have a Handelian vigour that sweeps them along.

The more voices Croft has at his disposal, the less mechanical these movements seem. Undoubtedly he possessed a capable technique, and had an ear for rich counterpoint. Thus the opening section of *Hear my prayer, O Lord* in five parts (later becoming eight), and *O Lord, rebuke me not* in six show him at his best. Instead of a regular fugal exposition, the voices enter as they might in a polyphonic motet, and the themes themselves are less strongly tonal and more fluid rhythmically than those mentioned above. *Hear my prayer*, indeed, recalls Purcell's setting of the same words, not only in key but thematically as well (Ex. 36). *O Lord, rebuke me not* also contains echoes of Purcell, particularly in its use of augmented triads and false relations.[25] Among many fine passages, perhaps the build-up to the cadence at 'neither chasten me in thy displeasure' deserves special notice, as does the simple urgency of 'Have mercy upon me' that follows. A few bars later, a further reversion to homophony and a harmonic move from D major to B flat major at the words 'O Lord, heal me' is no less affecting, while the intensity of the closing bars with their swooning ninths is a match for anything in Purcell.

Quite a number of the verse anthems can be dated through the occasions for which they were written, in particular those for the thanksgiving services held at St Paul's Cathedral for Marlborough's victories. When the queen attended, St Paul's became a kind of public Chapel Royal—a veritable national shrine. There are a dozen or so anthems by Croft of this type. Thus, *I will give thanks unto thee, O Lord* was 'Composed . . . for the Thanksgiving on the glorious Victory at Blenheim', and others for Ramillies (1706), Oudenarde (1708), and Mons (1709), and finally, the Peace of Utrecht (1713). These anthems are surprisingly free from bombast, and, though uneven in quality, are not dull. Indeed, they are musically rather satisfying. Even *O praise the Lord, ye that fear him* ('Composed . . . for the Thanksgiving *November* 22. 1709 upon the Victory obtain'd near *Mons*'), though in jubilant D major, avoids militaristic idioms, and offers a considerable amount of minor key contrast in its nine movements, including ground basses in B minor and D minor. *Sing unto the Lord*, written 'for the Thanksgiving *Febr.* 1708[9] upon the great Success of that year', attempts some grand effects; so too does *Rejoice in the Lord, O ye righteous*, a symphony anthem written for Ramillies. The final chorus has a Handelian grandeur that, according

---

[24] *Treasury of English Church Music*, iii. 140–51.   [25] Ibid. 124–39.

Ex. 36. William Croft, *Hear my prayer, O Lord* (*Musica Sacra*, 1724)

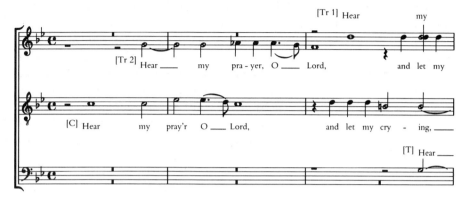

N.B. Bass figuring omitted.

to Burney, 'must shew Crofts in the light of a man of genius, who, without leaning, or preying upon the abilities of others, dared to advance farther into the dark recesses of latent effects than his predecessors'.[26]

In more reflective vein, *Out of the deep* is a good example of Croft's ordinary work for the Chapel Royal. Burney found 'little to remark' in it, but for John Wesley it was one of the essential experiences that went to make up the day of his conversion (24 May 1738)—he heard it at St Paul's that afternoon.[27] It is in B minor and falls into eight sections, the first and second, third and fourth, and sixth and seventh linked by Phrygian cadences. The first pair consists of a bass solo, elaborately affective in style and pedantically censured by Burney for misaccentuating the word 'of' (Ex. 37*a*), leading into a 3/2 ostinato movement ('If thou, Lord, wilt be extreme', Ex. 37*b*–*c*). The next pair comprises a short expressive duet for bass and countertenor in common time ('For there is mercy with thee'), and a further 3/2 lyrical movement with a typically Corellian 'andante' bass ('Therefore shalt thou be feared'). Another ostinato movement follows, this time more Purcellian in character and based on a vigorous two-and-a-half-bar ground in E minor ('I look for the Lord'). The third pair of movements begins with a florid declamatory passage for countertenor ('My soul fleeth unto the Lord'), which Burney thought bordered too much on 'theatrical levity' because of the treatment of the word 'fleeth', followed by another duet ('O Israel, trust in the Lord'), the voices echoing each other above what begins as if it is to be yet another ground bass, though it changes its character half-way through. The final chorus reworks the thematic material of the previous movement, and brings the anthem to a majestic conclusion without any false heroics.

The characteristic features of Croft's verse anthems are to be seen in this work. Harmonically they are strong and show the unmistakable influence of Corelli's sonatas, particularly in lyrical 3/2 movements, and motivic common-time movements full of suspensions and sequences. Purcell's legacy may be seen, first in the loosely imitative ensemble verses, secondly in the florid word-painting and expressive chromaticism of many declamatory solos, and thirdly in ubiquitous ostinato basses—rarely strict grounds—driven by motifs that propel the bass through a circle of related keys. Such movements, whether ostinatos or more freely composed, usually begin with a 'motto' opening, moving towards either the dominant (or relative major if the key is minor) where either the

[26] Burney, *History*, ii. 484–5.

[27] Actually, Wesley notes the anthem's text in his journal without naming the composer, but the 1736 word-book (*A Collection of Anthems as the same are now sung . . .* 1736) shows that only settings by Croft and Aldrich were then in the repertoire (Purcell's therefore seems unlikely). As quoted by Wesley the text is closer to Croft's than Aldrich's, which is a full setting and much shorter; see *The Journal of the Rev. John Wesley, A.M.*, (London, 1827), i. 97.

Ex. 37. William Croft, *Out of the deep* (*Musica Sacra*, 1724)

(a)

material reappears as it would in a ritornello aria, or new material begins the return journey to the tonic (as in Examples 37*b* and *c* above).

There does not seem to be any positive indication as to where Croft's Burial Service comes in his output, or for whose funeral it was written. One might guess that it was written for Queen Anne (or the Duke of Marlborough, who died in 1722), but the composer himself drops no such hint in the preface of *Musica Sacra*, where there is a paragraph about the work. His funeral anthem for the queen (*The souls of the righteous*) is in C minor, a key not incompatible with

(b) If thou, Lord,   will be — ex - treme to mark what is

2 Diapasons upon the great Organ with the left hand

done a - miss, —

(c) O —   Lord, who — may, who —

may a - bide it.

the burial service, whose movements all close on G, but this is hardly proof one way or the other. As is well known, Croft's simple homophonic version incorporates the setting of *Thou knowest Lord* written by Purcell for the funeral of Queen Mary almost twenty years before.

The Reason why I did not compose that *Verse* a-new, (so as to render the whole *Service* entirely of my own Composition,) is obvious to every Artist; in the rest of That *Service* composed by me, I have endeavoured, as near as possibly I could, to imitate that great *Master* and celebrated *Composer*, whose Name will for ever stand high in the Rank of Those, who have laboured to improve the *English Style*.[28]

[28] Croft, *Musica Sacra*, i. 3–4.

Croft may fairly claim a place among those 'who have laboured to improve the English Style', even though, as Purcell himself found, this involved learning from the Italians. He is the most important figure in English church music between Purcell and Greene, and though his output is substantial it never falls below a certain level of technical competence or descends into bathos. Burney may be right in saying that he 'never reaches the sublime'—for him to have done so would have been virtually impossible by late eighteenth-century criteria—'yet he is sometimes grand, and often pathetic', and, if one may add something, rarely feeble.[29] Were it not for Handel he might have achieved still more and exerted even greater influence. As it was, his music provided Handel with a point of departure for his own English church music.

[29] Burney, ii. 486.

10

Postscript: George Frideric Handel

Handel visited London for the first time in the late autumn of 1710 and returned to Hanover the following summer, having had great success with his opera *Rinaldo* in the mean time. Towards the end of 1712 he was in London again, this time prepared to settle and ambitious to produce further operas. Within a month he had composed an ode for the queen's birthday (6 February), and on 19 March his 'Te deum (to be sung when the Peace is proclaim'd) was rehears'd at the Banqueting House at Whitehall, where abundance of Nobility and Gentry were present'.[1] In due course the treaty was signed on 31 March, and the 'Utrecht' *Te Deum* performed at the thanksgiving service held at St Paul's on 7 July. Why Handel's setting, rather than one by Croft, was sung is difficult to understand on grounds of custom if not of musical worth, but Handel had friends in high places and was in favour. Croft had to be content with writing the anthem *This is the day which the Lord hath made* for the occasion.

Dating from these early years are two anthems by Handel written for the Chapel Royal (others later than our period will not concern us here).[2] Both *O sing unto the Lord a new song* and *As pants the hart* were reworked and expanded a few years later into Chandos anthems (nos. 4 and 6 respectively), but singers known to have taken part in performances of the earliest versions included Richard Elford, who died on 29 October 1714. *As pants the hart* (HWV 251a) was probably composed soon after Handel's return to London in 1712. In this form it was conceived as an ordinary Chapel Royal anthem without instrumental accompaniment (though with right-hand obbligato for organ in the verse 'Now when I think thereupon').[3] By contrast, *O sing unto the Lord* (HWV 249a) has parts for flute, oboes, trumpets, and strings, and was presumably written for a special occasion. It has been suggested that it may have been performed together with the so-called 'Caroline' *Te Deum* (HWV 280) at

[1] Michael Tilmouth, *A Calendar of References to Music in Newspapers published in London and the Provinces (1660–1719)* (*RMA Research Chronicle*, 1 (1961)), 84.

[2] *Georg Friedrich Handel: Anthems für die Chapel Royal*, ed. Gerald Hendrie (Hallische Handel-Ausgabe, III:9; Kassel, 1992); see also Donald J. Burrows, *Handel and the English Chapel Royal* (London, [1984]).

[3] Donald J. Burrows, 'Handel's "As pants the Hart"', *Musical Times*, 126 (1985), 113–14; see also id., 'Handel and the English Chapel Royal during the Reigns of Queen Anne and King George I' (Ph.D. diss., Open University, 1981), i. 71.

George I's first attendance at the Chapel Royal, six days after his arrival in London.[4]

Neither anthem fully conforms to the English tradition. For one thing, each begins and ends in a different key; for another, each has a recitative (*secco* in *As pants the hart*, *accompagnato* in *O sing unto the Lord*) quite foreign to the florid declamatory style as handed down by Purcell. On the other hand, Handel seems to have taken the trouble to find out and exploit the vocal strengths of his English singers. The second movement of *As pants the hart* ('Tears are my daily food') was clearly written to show off the expressive quality of Elford's voice, with swelling long notes on the word 'tears' and pathetic chromaticisms in the bass (Ex. 38). The first movement of *O sing unto the Lord* is another for 'Mr Eilfort', this time in the bravura style with oboe obbligato. A later solo for him ('Sing unto the Lord') has parts for 'traversiere' and unison violins, and the *accompagnato* for 'Mr Baker' ('The Lord is great') goes up to top E and down to bottom E as if it had been intended for Gostling. (Thomas Baker had been in the chapel only since the beginning of 1714.[5]) The bass solo which follows ('Glory and worship') is a typical ostinato piece, while Corellian suspensions unwind themselves in the duet between him and Elford ('O worship the king in the beauty of holiness'). Chorus and instruments enter towards the end against more held notes for Elford rising sequentially from f' to g' to a'—an exciting passage which lost something in the slightly fussy revision it underwent for Cannons. The words here are 'Let the whole earth stand in awe' and, interestingly, Handel treats the word 'whole' every time as if it had two syllables (who-le)—a sign that his English was still uncertain.

It is sometimes suggested that Handel's 'Utrecht' *Te Deum* (HWV 278) was modelled on Purcell's of 1694, but there is little to support this and their differences fully reflect the years between. Handel would certainly have known Purcell's *Te Deum* (it was in print and he would have heard it at the 1710 and/ or 1712 Festival of the Sons of the Clergy). It gave him an idea of the sort of thing that was expected, but within those terms of reference he did it in his own way. He could hardly have made a better début as a composer of English church music. It is so much in advance of Purcell's or Croft's 1709 setting that no one could have mistaken the arrival of a genius.

Disregarding the historical and doctrinal divisions of the text, he allows its emotional shape to determine the major divisions. The work begins and ends with substantial D major sections, each relieved by a verse for soloists in a minor key—respectively F sharp minor and B minor. The sense of symmetry is strengthened by the pronounced stylistic parallels between the opening and

[4] Otto Erich Deutsch, *Handel: A Documentary Biography* (New York, 1955), 63; Graydon F. Beeks, *The Chandos Anthems and the Te Deum of George Frideric Handel (1685–1759)* (Ann Arbor, Mich., 1981), 468–71.

[5] Ashbee, v. 103.

Ex. 38. G. F. Handel, *As pants the hart* (*Lbl* 30308)

closing sections. The lengthy middle section is more fluid from the tonal point of view, moving away from the tonic through related keys in a series of mostly short movements varying in independence. The main points of focus are the verse 'The glorious company of the apostles' in A minor (and, for the first time in the work, triple time), the fugue 'Thou art the king of glory, O Christ' in F major—centre-piece of the whole work—and the quartet 'We believe that thou shalt come again' in G minor. Thus balance and contrast are achieved overall, even if a rather piecemeal effect cannot be avoided due to so many short sections.

Without doubt there is a rich profusion of ideas in this work, especially in the solo sections, but most of them cannot be developed for lack of time. One movement which does achieve the scale its material demands, and for that reason (as well as for its intrinsic beauty) may be regarded as perhaps the most satisfying, is 'The glorious company of the apostles'. Here the text works in Handel's favour, for the four verses parallel each other in form and content, and are thus suitable for treatment within a single movement. Like many composers before him, but in quite a new way, Handel characterizes the succession of apostles, prophets, martyrs, and 'the holy church throughout all the world' differently from each other. Thus, the apostles are represented by tenor accompanied by oboe, the prophets by bass with strings and oboe, the martyrs by two trebles and strings alone—a ravishing sound made still more ethereal by a modulation to C major at this point—and finally, the whole church by full chorus, woodwind, and strings at the words 'The holy church throughout all the world'. Scarcely less effective is the verse 'We believe that thou shalt come again' with accompaniment for strings and 'traversa', and the artless moment that depicts the incarnation.

The *Jubilate* (HWV 279) mirrors the form of the *Te Deum*, but though Handel has the opportunity here to expand, the text being shorter, inspiration is at a lower level. Particularly in the solo sections the text did not stimulate his musical imagination as the *Te Deum* had done. The opening movement, for all its exploitation of Richard Elford's virtuosity as a singer (and presumably John Shore's as a trumpeter), is less impressive than the opening of *Laudate dominum*, written some years before in Italy, from which Handel borrowed the thematic material. Some of the fugal writing in the choruses is stiff and mechanical, though 'O go your way into his gates' is, of its kind, admirable. Not for the last time did he introduce a long-note cantus firmus in combination with the main subject in 'Serve the Lord with gladness'. Despite the rather routine final fugue, the Gloria perhaps offers the best moments. Among them are the opening section, with its instrumental premonitions of 'Glory to God in the highest' in *Messiah*, while the eight-part chorus broadly proclaims the first verse of the doxology; and at the end, one of Handel's dramatic strokes, simple yet grandly imaginative, opening up visions of eternity at the words 'world without end'.

Handel had little ambition to be a church composer, yet works to follow included four more *Te Deums*, among them the 'Caroline' *Te Deum* already mentioned, ten Chandos anthems (which include, in addition to revisions of the two earliest Chapel Royal anthems, the 'Utrecht' *Jubilate* served up again as *O be joyful in the Lord*), several written for the Chapel Royal after 1717 (some of them based on Chandos anthems), and other occasional pieces, most importantly the four anthems for George II's coronation in 1727. Clearly he was a composer who wrote for special occasions with great effect, and, with hindsight, it is easy to see why he was preferred to Croft. Yet he had little influence on the general development of English church music over the next half-century. Excerpts from his oratorios may have been sung as anthems in many cathedrals at a later date, and the popularity of his music in the middle of the century could hardly fail to make its mark on church composers—even such a sturdy and traditional character as William Boyce. But the true succession passed from Croft to Greene more or less unaffected by Handel's presence in the country.

PART III

Cathedrals and Collegiate Foundations

Bristol

Despite the fact that Bristol was one of the largest cities in England, the musical establishment of the cathedral was one of the smallest. It was in its parish churches that the importance and prosperity of the city was reflected, there being according to Lieutenant Hammond in 1634 '18 Churches, which all are fayrely beautify'd, richly adorn'd, and sweetly kept, and in the major part of them, are neat, rich, and melodious Organs, that are constantly play'd on'.[1]

The cathedral was poorly endowed at the Reformation, and throughout the Restoration period its music lacked prestige. The Henrician statutes called for a choir of six minor canons, six lay clerks, and six choristers with a master, but before the Civil War it had been the custom to keep two of the minor canons' places vacant in order to augment the stipends of the remaining four from £10 to £15 a year. Other offices also remained unfilled for the same purpose; thus, the master's salary was increased from £10 to twenty marks (£13. 6s. 8d.), 'the six singing men from twenty nobles [£6] to eight pounds a piece', and the choristers from five marks (£3. 6s. 8d.) to £4.[2] Laud's visitation of 1634 also elicited the information that 'our singing men are, some clerks of parishes in the city, some organists, whereby their ordinary attendance in our church is much hindred, especially on Sunday mornings. We very seldome or never have the Letany sung on Sunday morninges cathedraliter.'[3]

By 1663 there were only three petty canons installed, although the other places had been filled.[4] Thomas Deane, the pre-war organist, was among those reinstated, but whether Dallam's pre-war double organ survived is not known. It probably did, and, with some attention from Robert Taunton, a local organ-builder, served until Harris's three-manual organ was erected in 1683–5. According to a later organist, Stephen Jefferies, writing in 1710, this organ 'cost 900 and 50£, the chaire organ was Built before, by one Mr. Taunton, of this citty, wich cost one hundred & fifty pounds'.[5] How, or whether, the old organ from Gloucester cathedral, bought by Deane in 1663 for £65, fits into this history is difficult to determine.[6]

---

[1] L. G. Wickham Legg (ed.), *A Relation of a Short Survey of 26 Counties . . . 1634* (London, 1904), 92.

[2] HMC, 141.   [3] Ibid. 143.   [4] Cheverton, 'English Church Music', 64.

[5] Speller, 'Bristol Organs in 1710', 85.

[6] Suzanne Eward, *No Fine but a Glass of Wine*, 132; Elvin, 'Organs of Bristol Cathedral', 71–2; Speller, 85–7; Andrew Freeman, 'The Organs of Bristol Cathedral', *The Organ*, 2 (1922–3), 66–7.

No music from the period now survives at Bristol, but it seems likely that works by Elway Bevin, the pre-war organist, would have been sung, and there may have been some interchange of repertoire with Gloucester. Fragments of services at Lichfield and Worcester attributed to Thomas Deane are more likely to be by a lay clerk of the same name who was at Worcester early in the next century.[7] Nor is Paul Heath, who succeeded Deane in 1669, known as a composer. He did, however, create a lot of trouble and was dismissed in 1682 after 'severall admonitions for keeping a Disorderly Alehouse, Debauching the Choirmen . . . and neglecting the service of the Church.'[8] By this time the stipend of the organist had been increased to £22, but there is no record of who followed Heath until the appointment of Joseph Gibson in 1686.[9] After Gibson came Stephen Jefferies in 1700. He was not quite twenty, and had been a chorister and lay clerk at Gloucester, where his father was organist.[10]

Things may have looked up with the arrival of Nathaniel Priest in 1710. He had been one of the children of the Chapel Royal for some years prior to 1705, and may have been the Priest who became organist of Bangor later that year. His attempt to move from Bristol to St George's, Windsor, in 1719 was perhaps a trifle ambitious, however.[11] A verse service in F by him circulated quite widely, and is competently written.[12] There are some expressive moments in F minor, but others which are empty and pretentious. The Josias Priest who was organist of nearby Bath Abbey from 1711 to 1725 was probably his brother (a son was christened Nathaniel), but the relationship with the more famous Josias Priest of Chelsea, though likely in view of the names, has yet to be established.[13]

---

[7] *NG* v. 290 (Watkins Shaw).   [8] Shaw, 38.   [9] Ibid.   [10] Eward, 194–5, 214.

[11] Edmund H. Fellowes, *Organists and Masters of the Choristers of St George's Chapel in Windsor Castle* (Windsor, 1939), 56.

[12] *Och* 40.

[13] David Falconer, *Bath Abbey: Its Choirs and its Music* (Bath, 1984), 13; id., 'The Two Mr Priests of Chelsea', *Musical Times*, 128 (1987), 263.

Cambridge

The title-page of an anthem word-book printed at Cambridge in 1706 informs us that at King's College the choral service was sung daily throughout the year; at Trinity, St John's, and Jesus Colleges 'upon Sundays and Holy Days', and at Peterhouse, Pembroke, Christ's, and Emmanuel 'upon Extraordinary Occasions'. Services were also sung 'before the University, in Great St. *Mary's* Church, upon the chief Festivals of the Year'.[1] How long this arrangement had been operating is unclear. The King's foundation statutes established a choir of ten chaplains, six clerks, and sixteen choristers;[2] the Elizabethan statutes of Trinity stipulated four chaplains, six clerks, and ten choristers with a master of the choristers who was also to play the organ.[3] The short-lived choral foundation at Peterhouse which had existed before the Civil War seems not to have been revived at the Restoration, but at St John's 'a Music Master and six Choristers were added to the former establishment'.[4] Other choirs, so far as they existed, must have depended on students, senior college members, and outside assistance, perhaps involving singers from the main choral foundations. All the above colleges had organs in their chapels, and presumably employed organists. Thomas Tudway, in addition to being organist of King's, was also organist of Peterhouse and Pembroke. The latter appointment was made in 1706 (at £20 a year) and required him 'to instruct the Scholars in singing so far as to enable them to chant the Psalmes in tune to the Organ, & perform with decency all the other parts of the service to be chanted; & also, the Conducts or others whose duty it shall be to read prayers, in a tunable way of chanting them according to the capacity of their voices . . .'.[5]

KING'S COLLEGE

In the early years of the Restoration there were two organ-builders based in Cambridge, Lancelot Pease and Thomas Thamar. At King's, Pease was paid

---

[1] *A Collection of all the Anthems Daily Us'd in Divine Service, throughout the Year . . . in Cambridge* (Cambridge, 1706). The situation at these colleges before the Civil War is thoroughly dealt with in Ian Payne, *The Provision and Practice of Sacred Music at Cambridge Colleges and Selected Cathedrals, c.1547–c.1646* (New York and London, 1993), 93–109, *et passim*.

[2] J. Saltmarsh, 'King's College', in J. P. C. Roach (ed.), *A History of the County of Cambridge and the Isle of Ely*, iii (London, 1959), 382.

[3] Ian Payne, 'Instrumental Music at Trinity College, Cambridge, c.1594–c.1615', *Music and Letters*, 68 (1987), 128.   [4] Maria Hackett, *A Brief Account of Cathedral and Collegiate Schools*, 9.

[5] Payne, *Provision and Practice*, 98, 108.

£200 for a chair organ in 1661,[6] but after his departure for Ireland in the mid-1660s, Thamar took over and built a new great organ (*altioris organi*) in 1673–4 at a cost of £130.[7] Then, in 1686–7, Renatus Harris built a new organ costing £350, to which further stops were added in 1688, a trumpet in 1695, and a new diapason in 1710.[8]

During that period there were only two organists, Henry Loosemore and Thomas Tudway—indeed, between them their periods of office added up to ninety-nine years. The former had been organist of King's since 1627 and served until his death in 1670.[9] He is credited with two services and about thirty anthems, the most famous of which, *O Lord, increase our faith*, was once attributed to Orlando Gibbons. Most were written before the Civil War, and thus fall outside the scope of this study, though sources suggest that *Praise the Lord, O my soul, while I live* and *The Lord hath done great things* may date from after 1660.

With Thomas Tudway, King's acquired one of the most famous names in Restoration church music. His father (also Thomas) was a lay clerk at St George's, Windsor, and young Thomas was probably a chorister there before entering the Chapel Royal in 1664. By 1668 his voice had broken and the master, Captain Cooke, was allowed '£30 a year . . . for the keeping of Thomas Tedway'.[10] He was appointed organist of King's in 1670 and held the post until his death in 1726, apart from a brief period in 1706–7 when he was suspended from his degrees and offices for a slighting reference to Queen Anne.[11] In due course he recanted and was reinstated, though he seems to have suffered again for political reasons in 1714, when he complained that he had been 'barbarously used by the late ministry . . . all of my subsistance taken from me . . . turned out of my house . . . a livelihood to seek at near three-score years of age'.[12] He had taken the Cambridge Bachelor of Music degree in 1681 and the Doctorate in 1705, when he was appointed Professor of Music in the University.

Tudway is known primarily as the compiler of six large manuscript volumes of English church music copied between 1715 and 1720 for Edward, Lord Harley, son of the politician and statesman Robert Harley, Earl of Oxford, and now in the Harleian collection of the British Library (*Harl*. 7337–42; see Ch. 5). Together they contain seventy services and 244 anthems by eighty-five composers ranging from Henry VIII (supposedly) to 'Mr Hendale', including an Evening Service and eighteen anthems by Tudway himself. (Unless otherwise stated, works by him mentioned below are all to be found in this collection.) A total of three services, twenty-four anthems, and a Burial Service by him can be

---

[6] Andrew Freeman, 'The Organs at King's College, Cambridge', *The Organ*, 8 (1928–9), 132.
[7] Ibid.   [8] Ibid. 132–3.   [9] *NG* xi. 222 (John Morehen).
[10] Ashbee, i. 89.   [11] Shaw, 358.
[12] Turnbull, 'Thomas Tudway and the Harleian Collection', 203; also Weber, 'Thomas Tudway and the Harleian Collection'.

traced. Early anthems include three in the Bing–Gostling Partbooks datable before 1678. All are unpretentious works, but *My God, My God* he thought worthy of including in his own collection. Dated 1675 and subtitled 'A verse Anthem on ye Passion', its key of F minor brings harmonic anguish to the setting without becoming extravagant. In style and technique it owes more to the neat workmanship of William Tucker than the expressive intensity of Locke or Humfrey. More indebted to Humfrey is the symphony anthem *The Lord hear thee*—part of the exercise for his Bachelor's degree. Also with string symphonies and ritornellos is *The Lord hath declared*, written 'on the Thanksgiving for the discovery of the Rye House Conspiracy . . . 1682', in which the temptation for the bass to bluster at the verse 'The enemy hath not been able to do him violence' is successfully resisted (Ex. 39), though it might have been different fifteen or twenty years later.

Tudway's later work follows the contemporary trend towards a more florid verse style, with interpolated organ passages and ritornellos. Among anthems attributed to 'Mr' Tudway, and therefore written before 1705, a comparatively early date may be assigned to *Let us now praise worthy men* and *Not unto us, O Lord*, both of which are rather restrained, and a somewhat later date to *O how amiable* and *Is it true that God will dwell*, where there is a more expansive approach. The latter, in fact, is reported to have been sung 'before Queen Ann at Windsor July 12, 1702 by Dr Turner, Mr Damascene & Jo Gostling'[13]— though Tudway, unaccountably and confusingly, said that it was 'design'd for the opening of St Pauls Church [i.e. Cathedral] and Sung at the opening of Kings College Chapel'.[14] The latter presumably refers to the reopening of the choir following its paving with black and white marble in 1702.

Increasing flamboyance was, of course, in line with stylistic tendencies at large, and in Tudway's case was likely to be exaggerated by the celebratory nature of most of his later anthems. A few days before his anthem had been sung at Windsor, he had petitioned the queen for a place as organist of her chapel, saying that Charles II had promised him the next vacancy back in 1682, but that on Purcell's death the place had not been filled.[15] (Actually, Francis Pigott had been appointed, and this was probably the reason why nothing could be done officially about a post for Tudway.[16]) Nevertheless, he does seem to have enjoyed, or assumed, some kind of unofficial laureateship during Queen Anne's reign, with the real or imagined duty of writing anthems to mark the great occasions of state. These include *I will sing unto the Lord* in thanksgiving for Marlborough's victory at Blenheim in 1704, *Behold how good and joyful* for the Act of Union in 1707, *O praise the Lord, for it is a good thing* for the battle of

---

[13] Gostling Manuscript, 181.   [14] *Harl.* 7341, fo. 35.

[15] Robert P. Mahaffy (ed.), *Calendar of State Papers, Domestic Series, 1702–3* (London, 1916), 435 (6 July 1702).

[16] Rimbault, 21.

Ex. 39. Thomas Tudway, *The Lord hath declared* (Harl. 7340)

Oudenarde in 1708, and *Give the Lord the honour due* and *My heart rejoiceth* for the Peace of Utrecht in 1713. (Marking a rather different category of state occasion is *Plead thou my cause*, which he wrote for the Chapel Royal on 'the change of the Ministry, & the insolence of the Faction thereupon'—presumably in grateful thanks for the appointment of the Tory ministry of Harley and St John.) Hardly surprisingly, these anthems attempt to do justice to the events they celebrate by adopting the full panoply of 'heroic' clichés—brilliant vocal flourishes and dotted rhythms on such words as 'triumph', 'glorious', 'joyful', etc., with symphonies and ritornellos for the organ and prominent use of the recently acquired trumpet stop at King's. Movement structure is emphasized by contrast of mood and key between sections, though most individual movements are still quite short and triple time predominates. Despite his advancing years he was clearly trying to keep pace with Croft and Clarke in the Chapel Royal, but for all his professionalism there is a lack of memorable musical events. Nevertheless, *My heart rejoiceth*, which was 'perform'd in St Marys Church before the University', makes a stirring effect with its string symphonies and accompaniments.

Other anthems written for special occasions at Cambridge include *Thou, O Lord, hast heard our desires* sung before the queen in King's College chapel on 16 April 1705, and what must presumably be one of his last works, *Hearken unto me*, for the laying of the foundation stone of James Gibbs's new building at King's College, 25 March 1724 (*Ckc* 108).

Contrasting with all this pomp and circumstance is Tudway's burial service, performed on 24 February 1703 at the obsequies of Charles Churchill, Marquis of Blandford, a student of King's College, and only surviving son of the Duke of Marlborough. The graveside sentences beginning *Man that is born of a woman* had been written for the funeral of Dr Beaumont, Regius Professor of Divinity and Master of Peterhouse, which took place in November 1699. Ten years earlier Beaumont had been a member of the Royal Commission that had saved 'the cathedral service' (see Ch. 1), and, in all probability, friendship and a sense of gratitude prompted Tudway to compose this service. Sombre texts are rare with him, but he was capable of unaffected solemnity. Rather unusually, the setting of these sentences is in verse style; the key is C minor and there are some moving moments in the last section, where verse and chorus echo each other at the words 'But spare us, O Lord, most holy'.

The funeral service for the duke's son provided an occasion to expand the service to include the opening sentences, beginning *I am the resurrection*, and a setting of the anthem *I heard a voice*. These are quite different from each other: the former is in G minor and adopts—for the only time in his whole output—a simple full style; the latter is in E minor, and is a dramatically conceived verse anthem. The opening countertenor solo is answered by the organ and joined by tenor and bass urging 'write from henceforth'. Then all is calm G major and the trio sings 'Blessed are the dead which die in the Lord'. There is a lovely feeling of repose at this point, achieved by the simplest means. Perhaps this is the 'memorable event' that was lacking so far in Tudway's output.

Two Evening Services in A and G, both incomplete and attributed to 'Mr Tudway', are at Worcester (1684 or earlier) and St John's College, Cambridge, respectively (*Cjc* O.12). The Service in B flat is probably considerably later. Indeed, the *Te Deum* is dated 1721, and was intended for the consecration of the chapel at Lord Harley's house at Wimpole, near Cambridge. Tudway may have seen himself in relation to Harley as Handel to the Duke of Chandos—even to the extent of choosing B flat for his 'Wimpole' *Te Deum* as Handel did for his 'Chandos' *Te Deum*. Both works are accompanied by strings (with a pair of oboes or trumpets in Tudway's case, a single oboe in Handel's) and, following the introductory symphony, they begin with virtually the same opening gambit (Ex. 40), though in other respects they are very different.

The *Magnificat* and *Nunc dimittis* in B flat, though elaborate in style, has an accompaniment for organ rather than orchestra, and the fact that it is included

Ex. 40(*a*) Thomas Tudway, *Te Deum* from the Service in B flat (*Cu* Ely 11)
       (*b*) G.F. Handel, *Te Deum* ('Chandos') (*RM* 20.d.7)

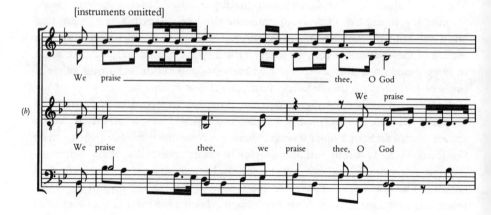

in volume V of Tudway's collection (*Harl.* 7341) probably places it in Queen Anne's reign. Whether Tudway regarded the rest of the 'Wimpole Service' as completing it or as something separate is academic; the fact is that the orchestral accompaniment to the Te Deum, Jubilate, Kyrie, and Creed establishes an altogether grander scale. The only comparable work of the period is Hawkins's orchestral Service in A minor, and it may be that Hawkins, a friend and near neighbour of Tudway's at Ely, sought to emulate him in making a similarly imposing setting of the liturgy. Significantly perhaps, the manuscript containing 'Dr Tudways Musick for the Opening the Lord Harleys Chappell at Wimple' is in Hawkins's hand (*Cu* Ely 11).

From the introductory essays to the volumes of his collection (see App. F) it is clear that Tudway disapproved of modern church music as 'light & Airy Compositions' decked out with 'all ye Flourish of interludes & Retornellos' (vol. ii). In the absence of full anthems from his output, and such 'as are Grave, solemn & fitted to devotion' (ibid.), this comes as a surprise, and confronts us with an apparent contradiction between theory and practice. By maintaining that works written for great public occasions were 'not stricktly call'd Church Music, although they are upon the same divine Subject' he rationalized his position (vol. vi). Otherwise he was not given to excess. Unlike Purcell's, his solo writing is generally modest and devoid of extravagant conceits, exaggerated expressive devices, and recondite harmony. In choral passages he favours naturally declaimed homophony with little contrapuntal elaboration. All this is supported by adequate technical resources, but not enough imagination.

Contemporary with Tudway at King's, and also a member of the choirs at St John's and Trinity, was Charles Woolcott. Tudway included a *Te Deum* in G, and an anthem *O Lord, thou hast cast us out* by him in his collection (*Harl.* 7341). The *Te Deum* flows agreeably enough in its triple-time verses, but is marred by some very turgid four-part writing in common-time sections, including a canon 4 and 1 at the words 'Thou sittest at the right hand' that outstrips his technique. Another composer attached to King's at this time was John Bishop, lay clerk and master of the choristers in 1688, who became organist of Winchester College (q.v.) in succession to Jeremiah Clarke in 1695.[17]

ST JOHN'S COLLEGE

With the appointment of Peter Gunning as Master of St John's in 1661, music had a friend in high places who supported 'better provision of more voices for the Quire, whereby God's service may be more solemnly performed and decently sung'.[18] Dallam's pre-war organ was re-erected and put in charge of

---

[17] Shaw, 399.
[18] See William L. Sumner, 'The Organs of St John's College, Cambridge', *The Organ*, 36 (1956–7), 29.

Thomas Thamar, who, by 1669, seems to have added a chair organ.[19] The organist at this time was 'Mr Lusmere'[20]—probably George Loosemore rather than his older brother Henry. The fact that George's organ-book (*Lbl* 34203) passed to Thomas Williams, his successor at St John's, suggests as much, as does the fact that Williams was appointed in 1682, the year of George's death. However, it will be more appropriate to deal with the music of George Loosemore in connection with Trinity College, and pass on here to Thomas Williams, leap-frogging over the year 1681–2, when it appears that a certain Mr Hawkins was paid for teaching the choir. This was almost certainly James Hawkins, who became organist of Ely (q.v.) the following year.[21]

Williams's tenure at St John's lasted from 1682 until 1729,[22] but according to Tudway, whose collection contains a *Magnificat* and *Nunc dimittis* in A minor by him (*Harl.* 7341), he was also a member of the choir at King's and Trinity. There is an organ-book at St John's (MS K.2), largely in his hand, with two morning services by him, one in E and the other in G, as well as two anthems, *Come, Holy Ghost* and *O clap your hands*. The latter also occurs in an autograph score at King's College (MS 23) but is of little musical interest. Apart from a rather jejeune tenor solo ('God is gone up') it is in triple time throughout, as are all but eight bars of *Arise, shine*, a rambling Epiphany anthem in an Ely organ-book (*Cu* Ely 3). There is likewise a great deal of triple time in the evening service, but also more coherence. Word-painting is a feature of the *Magnificat*, and the Gloria which ends both canticles is reassuringly competent.

TRINITY COLLEGE

The organ at Trinity College was either repaired or a new one installed by Thomas Thamar in 1662 at a cost of £110.[23] The organist at this time was George Loosemore, younger brother of Henry Loosemore and, as we have just seen, probably organist of St John's also.[24] He had been organist of Jesus College before the Civil War, but it is likely that most if not all of his church music dates from after his appointment at Trinity in 1660. There is a medius partbook in the college library (MS R.2.58) copied by him in 1664, containing eleven 'Graces'—settings of collects for the principal feasts of the church. As a sign of the times, five of them are in triple time.[25] Another manuscript in his hand is the organ-book, already mentioned, which probably represents the repertoire at Trinity College (and St John's) towards the end of his life, about 1680.[26] It

[19] Sumner, 'The Organs of St John's College'.

[20] Ethel M. Hampson, 'Choir Schools', in L. F. Salzman (ed.), *A History of the County of Cambridge and the Isle of Ely*, ii (London, 1948), 337.

[21] Sumner, 'The Organs of St John's College', 35; Shaw, 362.　　[22] Shaw, 362.

[23] Sumner, *The Organ* (1973), 124.　　[24] *NG* xi. 222 (John Morehen).

[25] Contents kindly communicated by John Morehen.　　[26] Clark, *Transposition*, 171–3.

Ex. 41. Charles Quarles, *Out of the deep* (*Cathedral Magazine*, iii [*c.*1775])

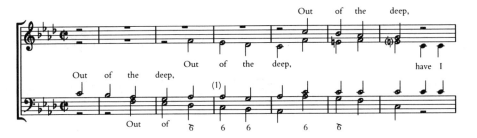

(1) Tenor has been 'corrected' from *b* to *a* by hand.

contains music by 'Dr' Blow, Humfrey, 'Mr Pursol', Tucker, and Wise of the Chapel Royal, and also local men such as Tudway, Ferrabosco of Ely, John Thamar (son of the organ-builder and a member of the Trinity choir), as well as the Loosemore brothers. Attributed to 'G.L.' are a setting of the Athanasian Creed and four anthems, among them *How doth the city sit solitary*. A much later source (*Ob* Tenbury 1021) includes three others, each in sober, four-part chordal style with simple imitations, appropriate for collects and solemn texts, but rather lame for the 150th psalm. A fourth 'anthem' is *O that mine eyes*, a rhymed meditation on the Passion, well known at the time through Thomas Brewer's setting.[27] Loosemore may well have written it for private devotional purposes during the Commonwealth; nevertheless it is quite widely distributed among liturgical sources (including the Bing–Gostling Partbooks). Each of its three stanzas is set as a verse for treble and bass in declamatory style, the final couplet echoed in a four-part chorus.

While Tudway and Williams were occupying their respective organ lofts at King's and St John's, Trinity had three organists—and three (or four) organs. Thamar's 1662 organ was repaired by Smith in 1686, enlarged in 1694 for £160, and rebuilt in 1708.[28] The ferociously named Robert Wildbore succeeded

[27] Ian Spink, *English Song: Dowland to Purcell* (2nd edn., London, 1986), 121–2.
[28] Freeman, *Father Smith* (1977), 31, 34, 44.

Ex. 42. John Bowman, *Show yourselves joyful* (Harl. 7341)

(The repeat is witten out in the original)

Loosemore in 1682 but served only six years.[29] He is represented in Tudway's collection by *Almighty and everlasting God* (Harl. 7340), a full setting of the collect for Trinity Sunday dated 1683, somewhat in the Loosemore mould but more awkwardly written. His successor, Charles Quarles (who may also have been organist of Pembroke College), took the Bachelor of Music degree in 1698, and seems to have continued until his death in 1717.[30] Thus, the Charles Quarles who was organist of York from 1722 to 1727 may have been a son, but the attribution of *Out of the deep*[31] to him rather than the older composer is probably erroneous, since this is one of two anthems in the Worcester partbooks appending 'of Cambridge' to the composer's name. On the other hand, it sounds as if it could be later than 1717. A full anthem (with verse) in F minor, it is typically eighteenth-century in its combination of archaic texture and 'modern' harmony, including augmented sixths, diminished sevenths, and minor ninths, and a triple-

[29] Shaw, 366.   [30] *NG* xv. 497–8 (Watkins Shaw).
[31] 'Mr Charles late Organist at York'.

time verse for two trebles singing mainly in thirds. Whatever the case, Edward Naylor's observation, quoted by West, that if the mistakes were rectified 'the Anthem might be considered a fair composition' seems reasonable comment (Ex. 41).[32] Three further anthems attributed to Quarles are in the Cambridge anthem word-book of 1706.

From 1709 Quarles shared his duties at Trinity with John Bowman, who took over completely in 1717 and continued until 1730.[33] His anthem *Show yourselves joyful* (*Harl.* 7341) was probably written to celebrate the Peace of Utrecht, and displays most of the clichés found in such occasional pieces. The technique is up to date but limited. The bass solo 'He maketh wars to cease' begins in the manner of a motto-aria but merely repeats the opening statement rather than using it as a springboard for further development (see Ex. 42).

[32] John E. West, *Cathedral Organists Past and Present* (2nd edn., London, 1921), 121.
[33] Shaw, 367.

Canterbury

As befitted the dignity of the primatial see, Canterbury was one of the richest cathedrals of the new foundation. By the Henrician statutes the choir consisted of twelve minor canons in priests' orders, twelve lay clerks, and ten choristers. Although it was a large choir, almost from the first the problem of finding so many priests sufficiently skilled in music to serve as minor canons led to the introduction of lay 'substitutes'. The change was officially recognized in Archbishop Laud's statutes of 1637, whereby the choir was established at 'six Minor Canons, six Substitutes, one Organist, as the custom has long obtained in the Church, twelve Lay Clerks, one Master of the Choristers, ten Choristers ... two Sackbutters and two Corniteers ...'.[1]

Thus it was at the Restoration. King Charles II landed at Dover on 23 May 1660, and his first Sunday was spent at Canterbury, where the service was conducted according to the Book of Common Prayer. Enough of the choir—boys excepted—survived for it to have been a choral service. By the summer of 1661 the choir was complete, except for one minor canon and one substitute, whose vacancies were soon filled.[2] There were even four wind musicians, though they were allowed to die out until, by 1670, there were none left. By that date the salaries of the minor canons had been increased from £3. 16s. 8d. a quarter to £4. 11s. 8d. (further augmented to £5 early in the eighteenth century); that of the substitutes from £3. 5s. to £3. 12s. 6d.; the lay clerks from £3. 15s. to £4. 10s., and the boys from £1 each to £1. 5s. In 1670 the master of the choristers received £3. 5s. a quarter, and the organist £5. 10s., in addition to their lay clerk's pay. Thus, over the years, the status of the substitutes had undergone a change, whereby instead of being, in effect, lay minor canons they had become inferior lay clerks, so that by 1723 'the Salary of these Substitutes being the least of any, and their Duty and Attendance now the same with the Lay-Clerks; the present Manner is to choose Candidates, first into the Place of Substitutes, and afterward, upon Vacancies, to promote them to that of Lay-Clerks'.[3]

Although the old organ at Canterbury had not been completely destroyed during the rebellion (only 'the keys and bellows ... cut and spoiled'), in July

[1] Ford, 'Minor Canons at Canterbury Cathedral', 9.
[2] Details of personnel, stipends, and periods of service are derived from the series of Treasurer's Books in the Chapter library covering the period (with a few gaps) from 1660 onwards.
[3] Ford, 25.

1662 the Dean and Chapter entered into an agreement with Lancelot Pease of Cambridge to replace it at a cost of £600, plus the old organ as a 'trade in'.[4] The chair organ of six stops was to be finished by Christmas, the great with thirteen stops by Christmas 1663. Rather than being put on the screen, for which it was probably too large, it was placed in a gallery straddling the north choir aisle. Twenty years later it was showing its age and, in 1684, Bernard Smith contracted to rebuild it. The result was a smaller instrument replete with mixtures after the current fashion—a four-rank cornet and a three-rank furniture on the great—to which a trumpet stop was added later.[5] The organists up to this point were Thomas Gibbs (in 1661–2), Richard Chomley (*c.*1670–5), and Robert Wren (1675–91), followed by Nicholas Wooton (1692–8) and Daniel Henstridge (1699–1736). The last three were masters of the choristers in addition, the post having been held separately by William Pysing until 1684.[6]

It appears that none of the pre-war music-books survived at the Restoration. To remedy matters two sets of Barnard's *Church Musick* (1642) were bought for £28 from John Playford in 1661, each volume already bound up with blank music manuscript paper for additions to be made.[7] Only one volume now remains at Canterbury (MS 1a); another is in the British Library (K.7.e.2).[8] These additions were made over quite a long period, since some are in the hand of Henstridge, who did not become organist until 1699, but those from the early Restoration period include a few items by local composers dating back to before the Civil War; for example, George Marson and John Ward, and John Heath of Rochester. In due course a set of Tomkins's *Musica Deo Sacra* (1668) was bought, but meanwhile the first set of post-Restoration partbooks was being compiled, now represented by a tenor decani book (MS 1).[9] Many anthems were transcribed from Barnard, but the post-war repertoire included work by mainstream composers from 'Dr' Rogers to 'Dr' Croft and, again, local men, with anthems by Henstridge, Charles and Robert Wren, and a Service in C minor by Humphrey Brailsford, a minor canon. Some of the other partbooks (MSS 2–8) may have been begun in the 1680s, but replacements, repairs, and rebindings have largely destroyed the chronological order. The contents of three organ-books (MSS 9–11) are less disturbed, however. The first contains a selection of the usual services, but also one by Henstridge in D minor and an Evening Service in C by 'Mr Smith'—possibly the John Smyth who was a lay clerk between 1662 and 1664. The second contains anthems, four by Henstridge, one by Brailsford, with nothing later than Purcell's generation. The third is mainly in the hand of Henstridge, as are parts of the previous two, with anthems at one end and services at the other. Interesting items by local composers include anthems by Wooton, the Wren brothers, and, again,

[4] S. W. Harvey, 'The Organs of Canterbury Cathedral', *The Organ*, 3 (1923–4), 3–6.
[5] Ibid. 6–7; Freeman, *Father Smith*, 27, 125–9.   [6] Shaw, 46–8.
[7] Cheverton, 'English Church Music', 237.   [8] Ibid. 322–6.   [9] Ibid. 327–8.

Henstridge himself. The extent and diversity of this repertoire is hard to reconcile with the Chapter order of 1696, quoted by Shaw, 'that every Sunday morning Tallis his Te Deum and Creed be used, and the Jubilate chanted, and that in the evening Batten's Service be sung.'[10] Perhaps the aim was for the Sunday congregation to learn these pieces through repetition; on weekdays, when there was little or no congregation, the choir could ring the changes.

An inventory drawn up by one of the lay clerks, John Knott, in 1713 lists 123 anthems and twenty-six services in use. Composers with three or more anthems to their credit were Aldrich (16), Blow (15), Purcell (7), Humfrey and Wise (6), Rogers and Tucker (5), Child, Christopher Gibbons, Hawkins, Henstridge, and Robert Wren (4), Raylton, Tudway, and Turner (3)—a conservative repertoire on the whole, with some up-to-date local work, but as yet no more than two each by the young Chapel Royal composers Church, Clarke, and Croft. Slightly later are a set of six partbooks in which John Gostling had a hand (MSS 12–17). Gostling, in addition to being subdean of St Paul's and a Gentleman of the Chapel Royal, was also a minor canon of Canterbury, and, significantly perhaps, the bass decani book (MS 12) is almost entirely in his hand.[11] Contents conform closely to the repertoire already outlined. It was not until William Raylton became the principal copyist (MSS 18–26) that Croft gained a firmer footing and the work of Maurice Greene was introduced. Services and anthems by Raylton himself figure fairly prominently and there is a small local representation from William Flackton, mention of whom leads to a consideration of 'Anthems Ancient & Modern . . . collected by William Flackton' in the British Library (Add. MSS 30931–3). This is a three-volume manuscript collection of anthems and services in various hands, including numerous autographs of Blow and Purcell, but otherwise with a strong Canterbury connection. Numerous items are in the hands of Henstridge and Raylton, including some of their own compositions. Also of local interest are anthems by Sargenson, Wooton, and 'Mr Bowers'—presumably Robert Bowers, organist of Rochester from 1699 to 1704. Flackton himself was a chorister in the cathedral from 1718 to 1726, and later combined trade as a bookseller in Canterbury with being organist of Faversham parish church, not far away.[12]

As will already have become apparent, Canterbury—like Worcester, another well-endowed cathedral—sported quite a number of local composers among its choirmen and organists. John Sargenson emerged early in the period, serving as a minor canon from 1663 until his death in 1684, at which time he also held the benefices of St Mildred's, St George's, and St Mary Magdalen's in the town.[13] Born at Coventry in 1639, he took his BA at Cambridge in 1659, and in the early years of the Restoration was one of the chaplains in the choir at King's College. Parts of a Service in B flat, a *Benedicite* in D and four or five anthems

---

[10] Shaw, 47. [11] For contents see Ford, 902–8.
[12] *NG* vi. 622 (Watkins Shaw). [13] Ford, 102–26.

Ex. 43. John Sargenson, *O God, the strength of all them* (*Lbl* 30932)

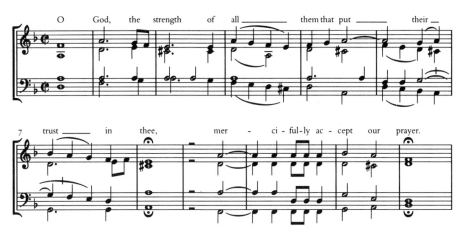

survive at Canterbury. The *Te Deum* and *Jubilate* in B flat even enjoyed some currency further afield during the eighteenth century, for they were entered into the Lichfield partbooks about 1680 (due, no doubt, to his Coventry connections), and from there spread to Lincoln and Peterborough; all three cathedrals had them in their service lists as late as 1824. At Canterbury they had been copied by 1673, though the Evening Service (and revisions to the Morning Service) may date from the 1680s. Judging from Henstridge's organ score, the work is a run-of-the-mill short service. Ford quotes some tedious sequences from the *Te Deum*.[14]

The anthems make the most of his limitations, however, especially the full settings of *Let thy merciful ears* (collect for the tenth Sunday after Trinity) and *O God, the strength of all them* (collect for the first Sunday after Trinity). Both are in D minor and are in Flackton's collection. The first is predominantly contrapuntal and a trifle graceless in an old-fashioned way; the second uses passages of chordal declamation in a manner well suited to the petitionary nature of the text, and there is melodic, harmonic, and contrapuntal interest, too. The piece is perhaps too long for its material, yet it makes a good effect overall—simple, yet eloquent (Ex. 43).

Charles and Robert Wren were choristers at Canterbury in the early years of the Restoration. Charles served from 1661 to 1664, becoming organist of Rochester about 1668 and of Gloucester in 1673; Robert served from 1663 to 1671, continuing as a lay clerk until his death in 1691. As we have seen, he was appointed organist in 1675. Among the Canterbury partbooks are an incomplete Service in E flat and two anthems, both of which are in the Gostling Tenbury

---

[14] Ibid. 119.

Partbooks (MSS 1176–82). *I will love thee, O Lord* is a five-part full anthem characterized by dissonance treatment that probably owes more to accident than design, though sometimes the stray seconds that spice his harmony seem to be a calculated, indeed sophisticated, effect that recalls Purcell, and makes one think again. Whatever doubts may be raised, the verse anthem *Teach me, O Lord* confirms that we are dealing with an otherwise unremarkable composer. Wren's successor as organist was Nicholas Wooton, a chorister from 1672 to 1684, and lay clerk from then until 1698. In 1690 he was listed as master of the choristers while Wren was still organist, but from the latter's death in 1692 he enjoyed both places. Trouble with the Chapter in April 1698 led to his removal, but this did not prevent his burial in the north aisle two years later.[15] The cathedral partbooks contain two services and four anthems by him, one of which, *Give ear, O heavens* in the Flackton Collection, is a rather routine verse anthem, though capably enough written.

Another minor canon who was something of a composer was Humphrey Brailsford.[16] He inherited Sargenson's place in the choir and was likewise vicar of St Mildred's (and All Saints). He came originally from Southwell, where he was born in 1658 and was a chorister at the Minster. Graduating from Cambridge in 1679, he became in rapid succession a minor canon at Peterborough (1681), Rochester (1682), and Canterbury (1684), but served in the choir only until 1692. He continued vicar of St Mildred's until 1707, when he returned to his native Nottinghamshire, eventually becoming a prebendary of Southwell in 1721. He died in 1733. Little of his music survives complete, though his verse service in C minor can be reconstructed more or less satisfactorily, and some idea of *God standeth in the congregation* can be gained from an organ score—without making a particularly favourable impression. The service remained in the repertoire at Canterbury during the eighteenth century, and no doubt its tuneful triple-time sections and bland trio-writing made an appeal. An Evening Service in B flat and another anthem are known, while the sacred song *Full of wrath*, generally attributed to Purcell (Z. 185) is more likely to be by Brailsford.[17]

Undoubtedly the most important of this group of composers is Daniel Henstridge, though Gloucester and Rochester might also claim him by virtue of his being organist successively at both places. He was a chorister at New College, Oxford, in 1664, and moved to Gloucester two years later.[18] There, soon after 1670, he entered his *Out of the deep, I will give thanks*, and *Thy word is a lantern* into an organ-book (MS 111); his morning service in D minor can be dated about the same time. Other early works include *Behold how good and joyful, Save me, O God*, and *Consider and hear me*, which occur in the Hereford

[15] Shaw, 47; West, *Cathedral Organists*, 12.   [16] Ford, 132–54.
[17] Robert F. Ford, 'A Sacred Song not by Purcell', *Musical Times*, 125 (1984), 45–7.
[18] Cheverton, 719.

'Barnard' set now at Christ Church, Oxford; they probably got there from Gloucester, though it is odd that they and the other group of anthems should be mutually exclusive. Works not in either of these sources, and which may thus date from his years at Rochester (1674–98) or Canterbury, include *Blessed be the Lord God, O be joyful, O come hither and hearken,* and *The Lord is king,* all of which are at Canterbury, while *Hear me when I call, O the vast change from life to death,* and *Thou God the father* are in the Flackton Collection. Whether the fact that they do not occur at either Gloucester or Canterbury indicates that they may date from his Rochester days is a possibility worth airing.

The Service 'for verses' in D minor, incomplete at both Gloucester and Canterbury (also in Flackton), seems a straightforward, workmanlike piece, mercifully free from amateurishness and, in the *Te Deum* at least, maintaining interest through contrast of full and verse texture, common and triple time, major and minor mode. Likewise his early anthems, dating from Gloucester, though modest in scale, are capably written—the sort of thing that might be expected from a pupil of William King. All but one are verse anthems, and though the partial nature of the sources makes reconstruction problematical, one can get an impression of their general style from the Gloucester organ-book. They begin with short introductions for organ and continue with mildly declamatory verses for one, two, or three voices, separated by brief, homophonic choruses (Example 44 from *Out of the deep* is typical). Less sense can be made of the verse anthems in the Hereford 'Barnard' set owing to the absence of an organ score, but the full anthem *Behold how good and joyful* seems neither very good nor very joyful. It also survives at Canterbury and was probably one of his most popular.

Whether or not the other anthems at Canterbury are later, the versions in Henstridge's autograph organ-books (MSS 10 and 11) show little stylistic advance. One of them, *The Lord is king,* also in Flackton and listed in *Divine Harmony* (1712) along with an otherwise unknown setting of *Blessed is the man,* is a straightforward setting in C major, full at the beginning, middle, and end with verses in between. Also in Flackton are two 'hymns', one a solo setting of *Thou God the Father* in three rhymed stanzas addressing the persons of the Trinity respectively.[19]

It is surprising that Tudway completely overlooked Henstridge's work in compiling his collection of church music. The reason can only be surmised, for his work is respectable and as organist of Canterbury he ought to have been represented. Although he lived on until 1736, his music belongs very much to the early Restoration. It does not draw on the polyphonic tradition, yet the modernistic trends of the 1670s are present to only a limited extent. He seems to have given every satisfaction to the authorities at Canterbury throughout his

---

[19] An earlier setting by Henry Lawes is in his *Second Book of Ayres and Dialogues* (1655).

Ex. 44. Daniel Henstridge, *Out of the deep* (GL 111)

(1) ♪. in source

long career. His salary as lay clerk, organist, and master of the choristers totalled £53 a year, but in 1718 he resigned the mastership to William Raylton (who effectively took over as organist as well), continuing to hold his lay clerkship up to his death.[20]

Raylton had been a chorister at Canterbury from 1698 to 1708, and at the same time a pupil of William Croft.[21] He is listed among the substitutes from 1708 to 1720 when he became a lay clerk. Having succeeded as master in 1718, he finally inherited the organist's post officially in 1736. Seven anthems, three services, and a burial service are known. Two anthems in Flackton bear early dates: 'November the 8th 1710' for *Behold I bring you glad tidings*, presumably anticipating the coming Christmas, and 'March the 8th 1712/13' for *Behold, O*

[20] Shaw, 48.
[21] A book of keyboard music given him by William Croft in '170[o]' is in the Nanki Music Library, Tokyo, MS N-3/35; see Cox, *Organ Music in Restoration England*, 516. 'The organ book of William Raylton when under Dr Croft's tuition' is in the Henry Watson Library, Manchester (Shaw, 48).

Ex. 45. William Reylton, *Behold, O God, our defender* (*Lbl* 30931)

God our defender, written to celebrate the anniversary of the queen's accession. (He actually signed it on 3 March.) *Great is the Lord* must also belong to the same period as all three anthems are listed in the 1713 inventory. Their style is unremarkable: triple-time verses for CTB predominating with much conventional jauntiness. Other than that, the potentialities of the Christmas text are hardly realized, but the accession anthem is stronger and offers an interesting sequence of varied movements, though each is short (Ex. 45). It was felt worthy of publication in volume i of *The Cathedral Magazine* (*c.*1775), adapted 'For the King's Birthday'.

Lift up your hearts, the fourth 'anthem' in Flackton's Collection, is, in fact, not an anthem at all, but a setting of the Preface to the Communion, in which a bass sings 'Lift up your hearts', tenor and countertenor responding 'We lift them up unto the Lord'. The chorus continues 'It is very meet, right', etc., followed by 'Therefore with angels and archangels' leading into the Sanctus. It is all in triple time, awkwardly underlaid and hardly music to inspire devotion. Though not in conformity with Prayer Book rubrics, it was presumably sung at Canterbury to enhance the solemnity of the communion. Raylton's service in the same key, G major, does not, however, contain settings of the Kyrie or Creed.

None of Raylton's services are listed in the 1713 inventory so they are probably later. The A major Service remained in the Canterbury repertoire throughout the eighteenth and nineteenth centuries. Judging by the consistent conjunction of the communion and evening canticles in E flat with Hall and Hine's *Te Deum* and *Jubilate*, it would appear that Raylton joined William Hayes and others in seeking to complete this torso—a worthy task, as it may then have seemed, but in retrospect surely a work of supererogation.

It has also been suggested that Raylton's setting of the opening sentences of the Burial Service was intended to complement Purcell's, the key being C minor and the items not duplicating each other.[22] The hint may have come from Flackton's note in Add. MS 30931 (fo. 55ᵛ): 'NB Mr Purcell's 2d part of the Burial Service, See No 26' (i.e. Raylton's *In the midst of life*), which might imply some such relationship. The simple chordal style is certainly very different from Purcell's early setting, and resembles more the later version of *Thou knowest Lord*, which, by Raylton's time, had become an ideal model for such things.

[22] Vincent Novello published them as an appendix in *Purcell's Sacred Music*, iv. 1828–32; see West, 12.

Carlisle

Even before the Civil War it was said, somewhat derogatorily, of the music in Carlisle Cathedral that 'the Organs and voices did well agree, the one being like a shrill Bagpipe, the other like a Scottish Tone'.[1] In view of the extreme geographical situation and modest musical establishment of eight minor canons, four lay clerks, and six choristers, such a comment is hardly surprising. For the same reason it would have been too much to expect a sudden blossoming of music after the Restoration. The cathedral itself had been partially destroyed by the Scottish army in 1646 and was still a ruin in 1676 when Roger North reported 'the east end onely and very little if any more of it standing'.[2] He added that—as in Durham and York—wind instruments such as the cornett and sackbut were used in the choir 'to supply the want of voices'.[3] John Howe is mentioned as organist in 1665, and it was during his period of tenure, in 1684, that the cathedral acquired a new organ of nine stops, including a sesquialtera of three ranks and a cornet of four ranks, the gift of the dean, Thomas Smith (who almost immediately became bishop).[4] Apparently John Howe was mayor of Carlisle in 1683, but in September 1692 he was 'solemnly admonished because as Organist he had for several years past neglected to attend the duties of his office', whereupon 'being sensible of his inabilities through age and other infirmities' he resigned, both as organist and petty canon, 'voluntarily and freely'. He was succeeded by his son Timothy, who served from 1692 until 1734.[5]

It seems that most of the old music-books were thrown out and burned about 1856 'except a few which were rescued as mementos'—one, a bass partbook (now lost) dating from the reign of James II, containing anthems and services.[6] There is also an alto cantoris partbook now in the Cumbria Record Office, which seems to have belonged to a later set.[7] (The third item, however, is attributed to 'Mr' Tudway.) Although the most frequently represented com-

---

[1] Legg (ed.), *A Relation of a Short Survey*, 37.
[2] Wilson (ed.), *Roger North on Music*, 40.   [3] Ibid. 286.
[4] Reginald Whitworth, 'The Organs in Carlisle Cathedral', *The Organ*, 15 (1935–6), 65–6.
[5] Ibid. 71; also Shaw, 55.
[6] James W. Brown, 'Caroline Music Books from Carlisle Cathedral', in *Round Carlisle Cross— Old Stories Retold* (Carlisle, 1921), 38; id., 'An Elizabethan Song-Cycle', *Cornhill Magazine* (1920), 574.
[7] Cheverton, 'English Church Music', 328–32.

poser is William Tucker with nine anthems, in general the repertoire shows strong Durham links, with anthems by John Foster (3), John Nicholls (1), and William Greggs (1), and three by 'Mr' [Thomas?] Mudd who died there. Significantly perhaps, Timothy Howe was attending the Durham choir school in 1679.[8] The only work included by a local composer is *They that put their trust in the Lord* by John Howe.

[8] Shaw, 55.

Chester

The Henrician foundation at Chester established a choir of six minor canons, six 'conducts' or lay clerks, a master of the choristers, and eight choristers.[1] It was thus one of the smaller of the new foundations, and tended during the Restoration period to be a musical satellite of Lichfield, lacking prestige for a mixture of historical, geographical, and financial reasons—the latter especially. Its endowments were inadequate, and from 1677 onwards the Chapter resorted to borrowing, with inevitable loss of morale and decline in standards, despite the best endeavours of the dean, Henry Bridgeman.[2]

Immediately prior to the Civil War the organist had been Randolph Jewitt, but at the Restoration he went to St Paul's (as master of the choristers), and, after the Great Fire, to Winchester.[3] Of the pre-war petty canons only three remained in 1660, and of the conducts two, but by 1664 the choirmen were up to strength.[4] Peter Stringer, a chorister between 1627 and 1631, and conduct since 1637, was made a minor canon in 1662; the offices of precentor, organist, master of the choristers, and cathedral treasurer were added in due course.[5] At this time the petty canons were paid £15 a year, the conducts £10, the master of the choristers £10, the organist £12, and the choristers £3. 6s. 8d.—so Stringer enjoyed quite a sizeable income.[6] He seems to have performed his multifarious duties with complete satisfaction, judging by the Chapter order dated 25 June 1673, soon after his death, whereby his places were conveyed to his son, John:

Whereas It hath pleased God to take out of this life our faithfull & beloved Chanter Mr Peter Stringer Petty Canon of this Church Organist & Mr of the Choristers which offices hee hath discharged with great fidelity on his part & Approbation on ours & who for his good discretion & knowledge in the Revenue & affaires of this Church hath for severall yeares last past bee[n] thought worthy to bee our Receiver & Treasurer of the Revenue thereof which administration hee hath very laudably executed . . . wee having

---

[1] B. E. Harris, 'Chester Cathedral', in *A History of the County of Chester* (VCH Cheshire), iii, 188; Joseph C. Bridge, 'The Organists of Chester Cathedral', *Journal of the Architectural, Archaeological and Historical Society for Chester and North Wales*, 19 (1913), 63.
[2] Harris, 191–2.   [3] Bridge, 81–90.
[4] R. V. H. Burne, 'Chester Cathedral after the Restoration', *Journal of the Architectural, Archaeological and Historical Society for Chester and North Wales*, 40 (1953), 27–30; also Cheverton, 'English Church Music', 64.
[5] Bridge, 91–7.   [6] Burne, 30.

a very good opinion of Mr John Stringer son of the said Deceased wee doe for our parts substitute & appoint him ... to continue his said fathers trust in the said offices of Receivor and Treasurer untill the next Audit and doe further conferr uppon him the office of Organist of our Church together with the office of Master of the Choristers together with all the respective salaryes & profitts thereunto belonging hee behaving himself diligently in the discharge of the same ...[7]

Although five anthems by the elder Stringer are listed in the 1664 edition of Clifford's *Divine Services*, none survives. The only other anthem known by a Chester composer of this period is *Have mercy upon me, O God* by 'Mr Ottey' in the Lichfield partbooks. William and Thomas Ottey were vicars at Lichfield before moving to Chester in 1664, where William became master of the choristers in 1683.[8] Meanwhile, Thomas had moved on to become organist of St Asaph in 1668.[9]

The organ, new or refurbished by Lancelot Pease and John Frye, had been installed by 1665,[10] but neither choir nor organ pleased a visitor on 28 June 1666, who became 'so wearie as I went in the mid[d]le of their service'.[11] The standard of the choir gave concern throughout the period, and practice times were laid down for the choir in 1675: half an hour after morning service and an hour after evening service for the boys, but only an hour a week for the men.[12] The authorities rather frowned on elaborate music because it tended to exclude the congregation. A Chapter minute of 1674 reads:

Whereas every one cominge to the publicke services of God ought to join and bear part therein, yet when full services and anthems are sung few of those who either are not skilled in music or have not copies thereof pricked out can join in the said worship or be edified therby; it is ordered that instead of full services after each lesson either verse services of the hymns [i.e. canticles] shall be sung wherein one or two singing at once, the words may be the more strictly attended to and in heart joined with by the congregation, or the said hymns shall be sung in the ordinary chanting tune which all who frequent cathedrals may easily bear a part in, and instead of full anthems verse anthems shall be also used for the reason before suggested and before each anthem one of the singing men shall audibly declare what portion of scripture is then to be sung.[13]

Thus, the congregation was expected to join the choir in chanting the canticles, and verse anthems were to be preferred to full anthems so that the words could be clearly heard.

Despite financial problems the Dean and Chapter were prepared to lay out £310 for a new single-manual organ of ten stops from Bernard Smith in 1684, though in doing so they were forced to borrow £150.[14] The choir continued

---

[7] Bridge, 97–8.   [8] Burne, 31; Cheverton, 437–8.   [9] Shaw, 243.
[10] Andrew Freeman, 'The Organs of Chester Cathedral', *The Organ*, 13 (1933–4), 131.
[11] Steven E. Plank, 'An English Miscellany: Musical Notes in Seventeenth-Century Diaries and Letters', *The Consort*, 41 (1985), 69.
[12] Burne, 40.   [13] Ibid. 39–40.
[14] Harris, 192; Freeman, 132; Watkins Shaw, 'Some Stray Notes', 26.

to give cause for concern, however, and in 1687 the situation was such that the precentor was threatened with dismissal for neglecting the services.[15] A succession of undistinguished organists and choirmasters did not help. Following the younger Stringer came William Kay (or Keys) in 1686, previously of Manchester Collegiate Church and St Asaph's Cathedral,[16] then John Monnterratt in 1699 and Edmund White in 1705.[17] To the latter name only scandal attaches and he was finally dismissed in 1715. In all this the impression of general slackness and incompetence is very strong. Skilful singers were difficult to find, and in 1711 the Chapter proposed a scheme to provide a year's singing instruction for newly appointed choirmen who were 'too meanly skilled'. If, thereafter, they failed to 'answer the end of their Instruction, they shall be dismissed and the Church be no longer burthened with them'.[18] There was no sign of any immediate improvement, however.

[15] Harris, 191.   [16] Bridge, 99; Shaw, 65–6.
[17] Bridge, 99–101; Shaw, 66–7.   [18] Burne, 49.

Chichester

By September 1661 the vacancies in the choir at Chichester had been filled to the statutory complement of four vicars choral, four 'Sherburne' clerks, four lay clerks, and eight choristers—an establishment of average size but far from lavishly endowed.[1] As at Salisbury and York, the vicars were exclusively priests, and despite the fact that the clerks were often called lay vicars, they did not belong to the college of vicars and thus did not share in its revenues. In addition, the vicars enjoyed 'stall wages' and 'bread money', houses in the vicars' close, and an augmentation of £3. 13s. 4d. from the common fund to supplement their individual share of the rents. The Sherburne clerks, however, were a separate foundation going back to Bishop Sherburne's 'donation' of 1526, and each received £10. 16s. 8d. a year. Though lay, they were considerably better off than the other clerks, who were paid only £4 a year (and lived in hope of promotion).[2] From 1685 one Sherburne clerk's place was added to the organist, while another was split between the remaining two, in order to increase their stipends.[3] There were thus six clerks in all, and by 1710 the choristers had been reduced to the same number.[4]

It seems likely that the pre-war organist, Thomas Lewes, took up the post again after the Restoration. His successor, Bartholomew Webb, an ex-chorister from Winchester, served from 1668, but on his death in 1673 Lewes was reappointed, perhaps only as a stopgap. He died little more than a year later and was replaced by John Reading, from Lincoln, where he had been master of the choristers. Reading, however, soon moved to Winchester, and was succeeded in 1677 by Samuel Pearson, who remained organist until his death in 1720.[5] From 1678 he had the benefit of a new organ by Renatus Harris, though a modest, single-manual one, with eight stops, including a three-rank sesquialtera and a

---

[1] Details of personnel, services, etc., below are from Chapter Act Books B (1660–1710) and C (1710–39), now in the West Sussex County Record Office, Chichester; dates provide references.

[2] For the vicars see Peckham, 'The Vicars Choral of Chichester Cathedral', other details from Cheverton, 'English Cathedral Music', 127, 146.

[3] F. G. Bennet et al., Statutes and Constitutions of the Cathedral Church of Chichester (Chichester, 1804), 49.

[4] Peckham, 144.

[5] For above details of organists see Nicholas Plumley and John Lees, The Organs and Organists of Chichester Cathedral (Chichester, 1988), 46–7; and Shaw, 75–7, who is inclined to believe in more than one Lewes and Reading.

five-rank cornet.[6] During this period at Chichester the normal time for morning prayer was 10 a.m., but on litany days it began a quarter of an hour earlier, and on Sundays and holy days at 9 a.m., no doubt to allow for the sermon, when the choir was expected to 'go into their seat in the body of the Church and joine in singing the Psalm before Sermon, and continue there all the sermon time and till after the blessing pronounced'. Evening prayer was at 3.15 p.m. during the winter (All Saints to Candlemas), at 3.30 p.m. from Candlemas to 1 March and from Michaelmas to All Saints, and at 4 p.m. the rest of the year. The vicars took it in turn, week by week, to perform the duty of the succentor, and thus to choose the anthems and services in consultation with the organist.[7]

The earliest musical source now at Chichester is a countertenor partbook which must have been begun before 1685 since it contains William Cranford's *O Lord make thy servant* Charles. Generally speaking, the book is rather a mess, with entries in several hands spread over many years and with numerous pages missing. It does, however, contain anthems by Webb, Lewes, and Reading, and a setting of *Hear my crying, O God* by John Cock—a vicar choral from 1670 to 1676—which remained in the repertoire until well into the next century. Later sources give some emphasis to the work of Vaughan Richardson, organist of nearby Winchester at the turn of the century, and to that of Thomas Kelway, organist at Chichester from 1720 (and a chorister from 1704). A treble partbook originating from Chichester and now in the British Library (Eg. 3767) includes five anthems and four services by him, and a service by Dr [Thomas] Manningham—more likely to be the Dr Manningham who was cathedral treasurer from 1712 (Doctor of Divinity, 1724) than his father who was the bishop. Since Child's *O Lord, grant the* king *a long life* is among the contents of the book, it cannot be earlier than 1714, but with anthems by 'Dr' Croft (6), Clarke (4), Turner (4), Richardson (3), and Weldon (2), as well as Wise (4) and Blow (4), it may be taken as representing the early eighteenth-century repertoire of the choir. Interestingly but perplexingly, Manningham and Kelway come together in one of the latter's services where, in the C major *Te Deum*, the passage in C minor at the words 'We believe that thou shalt come again' is marked 'Slow Dr. M'. Possibly Kelway incorporated at this point material which Manningham had composed.

---

[6] Cecil Clutton, 'The Organ at Chichester Cathedral', *The Organ*, 11 (1931–2), 72; Plumley and Lees, 1–3.

[7] Chapter Acts, 2 May 1678, 27 Apr. 1680; also Bennet, 41.

Dublin

Despite the fact that the bulk of the population of Ireland was Catholic, the Prayer Book was re-established there as in England, and, at least in the fifteen or so cathedrals with vicars choral, the full cathedral service should have been restored. But it was really only in Dublin, with its two cathedrals—Christ Church, a monastic foundation re-established in 1541, and St Patrick's, an 'old foundation'—that anything comparable with England was to be found. For the rest, money, men, and motivation were lacking, though here and there an effort was made to maintain modest establishments.[1] Thus, at Limerick during the reign of Charles II, certain glebes and tithes were granted 'for the constant support and maintenance of a sufficient and able choir to serve the cathedral', and at Cork a new endowment of 1679 was intended to support one of the four vicars 'and as many singers and choristers as the rents . . . extend to, and that each of them shall daily officiate in the said Cathedral or choir'.[2] Four years later the bishop had to remind the choir to attend the cathedral daily, and perform the service 'in the best melodies that they can', while in 1723 the 'master of song', Edward Broadway, was ordered to prepare a variety of solo anthems to be sung on Sunday afternoons and 'provide two boys and instruct them . . . to join with him in singing the said anthems'.[3]

The problem was that most Irish cathedrals lacked funds to pay lay singers and choristers, and as the musical role of the vicars choral went increasingly by default, so choirs withered away. Only in Dublin were effective steps taken to put the musical establishments on a sound footing. By English standards the choirs of Christ Church and St Patrick's were extremely well financed, and consequently were able to carry out a policy of attracting good, if frequently troublesome, musicians from across the water. Among those who came were the organists Peter Isaac and Daniel Roseingrave, both from Salisbury, and Robert Hodge, from Wells.

At St Patrick's the choir consisted of minor canons and vicars choral—as at St Paul's, London.[4] In 1640 the number of vicars had been set at twelve (five at least to be priests), and there were to be six choristers. In the early years of the

[1] W. H. Grindle, *Irish Cathedral Music: A History of Music at the Cathedrals of the Church of Ireland* (Belfast, 1989).
[2] Ibid. 75, 33.   [3] Ibid. 34, 51–2.
[4] Hugh J. Lawlor, *The Fasti of St Patrick's, Dublin* (Dundalk, 1930), 32–7.

Restoration the forces at Christ Church were enlarged to virtually the same—six vicars (two to be priests), six stipendiaries or lay clerks, and six choristers.[5] In practice, most of the personnel were the same at each cathedral, and the double emoluments they enjoyed put them among the highest-paid church musicians in the two kingdoms. The combined rents from the old estates of the vicars choral of St Patrick's and the 'augmentation estate appropriated to the Vicars and Choir-men of both Cathedrals' amounted to £643. 4s. 8d. in 1701—in other words, more than £50 each, not including stall-wages and profits on fines, etc.[6] Exactly how they split their time between the two institutions is not at all clear, for it seems as if anthems and services may only have been sung at Christ Church on Sundays. That, at least, is the implication of an order made by the Dean and Chapter in 1702 (and again in 1715), 'that the Vicars Choral, Stipendiaries and Choristers do meet in the said church on every Saturday at five of the clock in the afternoon to practise the anthems and service to be performed the day following'.[7]

Respectable salaries did not make the choirmen any less cantankerous than their opposite numbers in England. They were equally difficult to discipline, and reading between the lines of the 'Orders and statutes . . . of the Cathedral church of St Patrick, Dublin, for the government of the Viccars Choralls' (1692) it is not hard to guess their misdemeanours.[8] These orders deal with the necessary qualifications of a vicar (musical skill and moral rectitude), behaviour at divine service (correct attire, regular attendance, punctuality, marks of respect towards the dean, etc.), behaviour to each other ('he that strikes another eyther with hand or foote, or any other way, in the church, shall be expelled'), behaviour abroad ('noe Vicar is to haunt ale-houses or tavernes or suspicious scandalous places, or be out of his lodgeing or house, or colledge, att unseasonable times of the night, that is after ten att night, under paine of punishment'). Notwithstanding these strictures, Jonathan Swift, dean of St Patrick's from 1713 to 1745, still had problems with his choir. As he wrote to Alexander Pope in 1715: 'my amusements are defending my small dominions against the Archbishop and endeavouring to reduce my rebellious choir'.[9] As elsewhere, absenteeism and neglect of duty were frequent abuses.

The succession of organists at the two cathedrals is roughly the same for both, though here and there they were out of step, and sometimes a name appears in one and not the other. Each cathedral seems to have had its own master of the choristers, however.[10] As for the organs, a new one costing £160 was built at Christ Church between 1663 and 1667 by George Harris. In the latter year,

[5] Grindle, 19, 29.

[6] W. Monck Mason, *The History and Antiquities of the Collegiate and Cathedral Church of St Patrick's near Dublin* (Dublin, 1820), 94.

[7] Grindle, 30–1.   [8] Mason, 91–3.

[9] *The Correspondence of Jonathan Swift*, ii, ed. Harold Williams (Oxford, 1963), 177.

[10] Shaw, 410–11, 418–21; see also Lawlor, 249–50, Grindle, 222–5.

Lancelot Pease, who had built the organ at Canterbury in 1663, arrived in Dublin, joined both choirs, and contracted to add a chair organ of five stops to Harris's instrument at a further cost of £80. Pease was also commissioned to make a great organ at St Patrick's in 1678, but if it was ever built it was replaced between 1695 and 1697 with a new one by Renatus Harris costing £505, an allowance of £65 being made for the old pipes. This instrument was a double organ with thirteen stops, though within two months additional stops were ordered, constituting, perhaps, a new echo organ and costing a further £350. Not to be outdone—though the same organist, Daniel Roseingrave, was to play it—Christ Church approached Bernard Smith for a new organ, but he seems to have done nothing about it despite an advance of £100. The Dean and Chapter then contacted Harris, recent looser in 'the Battle of the Organs' for the Temple Church, London, who now had a spare instrument on his hands. Half of it went to St Andrew's, Holborn, the other half to Christ Church, Dublin, at a cost of £700, where it was installed in 1698 and put under the care of Jean-Baptiste Cuvillie, an immigrant French organ-builder. In the course of installation, Cuvillie added a tremulant in order 'to adorn [the voix humaine] and make it appear like a humaine voice'.[11]

The early Restoration repertoire of Christ Church is set out in a word-book of *Anthems to be sung at the Celebration of Divine Service in the Cathedral Church of the Holy and Undivided Trinity* [Christ Church] *in Dublin*, published in 1662. It lists fifty-one anthems, of which more than half are anonymous, but among those attributed are some by Randolph Jewitt (3) and Benjamin Rogers (2), both organists of Christ Church before the war. These represent a local repertoire, while works by Byrd, Bull, and Gibbons, among others, are from the mainstream. The only anthem that can be dated after 1660, however, is Richard Hosier's *Now that the Lord hath readvanced the crown*, which carries the rubric 'After the Consecration'. Set to a dismal text by William Fuller, Dean of St Patrick's, it was written for the great service on 27 January 1660/1, at which twelve new bishops were consecrated by the primate, Dr Bramhall. Coming after the years of Cromwellian repression, it must have been a magnificent occasion, intended as a demonstration of loyalty to the king as much as a replenishment of the Irish hierarchy.[12] The lords justices and nobility of Ireland progressed to St Patrick's in their coaches, preceded by horse- and foot-guards; the mayor, aldermen, sheriffs, and common council went on foot, likewise the Irish parliament led by the speaker. Then, as the procession of choir and clergy of the two cathedrals entered the church, a Te Deum was sung. Behind came the twelve bishops-elect, the primate, and four consecrating bishops, followed by the pro-vice-chancellor, provost, deans, and doctors of divinity of Trinity

[11] The above paragraph is based on Grindle, 134, 139–41; see also R. A. D. Pope, 'Organs of St Patrick's Cathedral, Dublin', *The Organ*, 15 (1935–6), 201.
[12] Mason, 192–4.

College. Once seated, the dean of St Patrick's officiated at morning prayer, and as Jeremy Taylor, one of those to be consecrated, moved to the pulpit to preach the sermon, the choir sang *Praeveni nobis*—presumably a setting of the collect 'Prevent us, O Lord'. After the sermon a further anthem was sung, and while the organ continued to play, the bishops took their places in the sanctuary. During their vesting in rochets and chimeres the choir sang the *Veni creator*, and after the consecration the specially composed anthem by Hosier. Holy Communion followed and after the blessing the procession moved towards the west door, the choir singing *Laetificetur cor regis*.

Richard Hosier, the composer of the 'Consecration Anthem', was an important figure in the Restoration scene at both cathedrals. He had been a gentleman of the Chapel Royal in 1641 and before that, in 1637, one of the choir of King's College, Cambridge. He may have been the same Richard Hosier who was deprived of his place as a stipendiary of Christ Church (Dublin) in 1634 for wilful absence. Admitted vicar choral of St Patrick's in 1660 and Christ Church in 1661, his career prospered thereafter, for he was promoted minor canon of St Patrick's in 1669, and, sometime before his death in 1677, master of the choristers.[13] The 'Consecration Anthem' is one of six anthems by him surviving in a score now at Durham cathedral (MS B.1),[14] and is laid out as a dialogue between treble and bass in rather stiff declamation. The choruses are in plain four-part harmony (sprinkled with consecutive fifths) though the concluding Hallelujah has some rudimentary imitative writing towards the end. All his anthems are rather similar in style. They begin with short organ introductions (bass only in the score), and, except for a brief passage in the Consecration Anthem, only *Unto thee do I cry*, has any ensembles. For the rest, treble and bass alternate their solos, the declamatory formula ♩♪♪♪ being much in evidence. Triple-time sections are rare and the choruses are short and homophonic.

Despite the strong representation of music from the Chapel Royal in Durham MS B.1, its connection with Dublin is clear, not only from the presence of Hosier's anthems, but also of two by other composers known to have been vicars at St Patrick's during Hosier's time: John Blett's setting of the metrical text *Thou art, O Lord, my strength*, and Walter Hitchcock's *Bow down thine ear, O Lord*. The latter, unlike the other contents of the manuscript, seems to be in Hitchcock's own hand, and is dated '[16]69'. The rest of the manuscript (or most of it) appears to be Hosier's autograph, and shows from its contents that works by Cooke (2), Christopher Gibbons (2), Humfrey (6), Tucker (3), and Wise (2) were known in Dublin in the period up to 1677. How the manuscript

---

[13] Lawlor, 201, 257; Henry Cotton, *Fasti Ecclesiae Hibernicae: The Succession of the Prelates and Members of the Cathedral Bodies in Ireland* (Dublin, 1849), ii. 84, 197, 205; see also Ashbee, iii. 110, 123.

[14] Brian Crosby, 'An Early Restoration Liturgical Music Manuscript', *Music and Letters*, 55 (1974), 462–3; id., *Catalogue of Durham Cathedral Music Manuscripts*, 23–4.

got to Durham is possibly to be explained by the signature on the inside cover, that of 'John Blunderfild'—perhaps the John Blundeville, vicar of St Patrick's from 1678 to 1680, who is encountered first as a chorister at Lincoln in 1660, then as one of the children of the Chapel Royal until Christmas 1664. He reappears as lay clerk and informator at Ely from 1669 to 1674, whence he moved first to Lichfield (1676), then Dublin. While there he may have acquired Hosier's anthem-book (Hosier being recently deceased), taking it with him to York, where he was master of the choristers from 1682 to 1692, and finally to Durham where he died in 1721.[15]

The above account admittedly leaves a few loose ends, and some interesting questions regarding the contents of this manuscript—for example, the authorship of the anonymous anthems, in particular three symphony anthems: *The voice of my beloved*, *O sing praises unto our God*, and *Sing, O daughters of Sion*. It is unlikely that these can have been composed locally.

In addition to the local composers represented in the Hosier manuscript, another name which occurs among the vicars of both cathedrals is that of Bartholomew Isaack, known from other sources as the composer of two anthems. A boy in the Chapel Royal up to 1676, he disappears from view until his appointment at Christ Church in 1684 and St Patrick's the following year. Two years later he was dismissed for neglect of duty (as was his brother Peter in 1688, though he later returned as organist). Bartholomew, in his defence, said that he had become a convert to Catholicism, and even had the support of the king in seeking to retain his place—but to no avail.[16] It is likely that his anthems were already written by this time. They form a contrasted pair: *Come unto me, saith the Lord* (*Cfm* 117), consisting mainly of loosely written ensembles, and *I will love thee, O Lord* (*Lbl* 17840), comprising a straightforward series of alternating treble solos and choruses. Both are in C minor, rather long and inclined to ramble, but not incompetent—as may be seen from the beginnings of the first two verses of *I will love thee, O Lord* (Ex. 46a–b).

Given the extent of contact and mobility between Dublin's cathedrals and those in England, it is probable that their repertoire was as up to date as anywhere in England. A list of music brought back from England by the organist of St Patrick's, Robert Hodge, in 1697 certainly suggests as much, though most of the items are anonymous; only *God is our hope and strength* and *I was glad when they said* are attributed—both to Blow. The latter was of very recent composition, having been written for the opening of St Paul's that very year. *My God, my God, look upon me*, listed among the full anthems and likewise by Blow, is of the same date. Services by Aldrich, Blow, Child, and Purcell were also brought back.[17]

[15] Crosby, 'An Early Restoration Liturgical Music Manuscript', 463–4.
[16] Ashbee, i. 166; Lawlor, 239–40. For his later career see Holman, 'Bartholomew Isaack', 383–4.　　　　　　　　　　　　　　　[17] Grindle, 32–3; for Hodge see Shaw, 420.

Ex. 46. Bartholomew Isaack, *I will love thee, O Lord my strength (Lbl 17840)*

Hodge was followed at St Patrick's by Daniel Roseingrave, whose chequered career can be traced in these pages from Gloucester in 1679, to Winchester in 1682, to Salisbury in 1692, and, finally, to Dublin in 1698. On 2 September the Dean and Chapter of Christ Church agreed 'that for the Encouragement of Mr Rosingrave organist coming over hee shall have when he comes the sallary due to the organ viz £25 yearly and a stipendiary's place which is £15 per annum, in all £40 per annum'.[18] Later that year he was admitted vicar choral and

[18] Grindle, 28.

organist of St Patrick's in addition, Having secured their man, the Chapter at
Christ Church decided to make life easier for him by declaring 'that Mr Daniel
Rosengrave organist ought not to do any other duty belonging to the church as
a stipendiary thereof but only attend to the organists place'. The honeymoon
was soon over, however. In 1699 he got involved in a tavern brawl with his
predecessor Robert Hodge, and on investigation was found to be 'the first and
chief agressor', fined £3, and ordered 'to beg publick pardon' of Hodge. He
was in trouble again in 1700, this time at Christ Church, where he and his
predecessor there, Thomas Finell, drew swords against each other. Both men
were suspended, but reinstated later with loss of salary: the Chapter subsequently
enacted 'that from henceforth no Vicar or Stipendiary of this church do wear a
sword, under penalty of expulsion'.[19]

Strangely, the choirbooks at Christ Church do not contain any of
Roseingrave's work, despite the fact that he was organist there for almost thirty
years. Possibly the explanation of his lack of productivity has something to do
with his 'difficult' personality, middle-age frustrations, or ill health. Petitioning
for his son Ralph to succeed him as organist at St Patrick's in 1719, he claimed
that he could no longer 'attend the doeing his Duty . . . without endangering his
health'.[20] As a result Ralph was appointed vicar choral, but not—at least,
officially—organist until his father's death in 1727.

Because of the apparent total separation between Roseingrave's activity in
England and Ireland, his music will be discussed in connection with Winchester
(q.v.), where most of it seems to have been written. That some of his later
music may have been misattributed to his sons is a possibility that needs to be
investigated, but in general their style is much too modern to be mistaken for
someone's whose formative years were the 1670s. His eldest son, Daniel,
became organist of Trinity College, Dublin, in 1705, but is not known as a
composer. His second son, Thomas, went to Italy in 1710 with ten guineas from
St Patrick's 'to improve himself in the art of music . . . that hereafter he may be
useful and serviceable to the said Cathedral'.[21] His large-scale symphony anthem,
Arise, shine, for thy light is come, was written to celebrate the Peace of Utrecht,
and according to Tudway was 'compos'd at Venice Xber [i.e. December] 1712'
(*Harl.* 7342). Other anthems by Thomas are hardly relevant to this study;
likewise the two services and numerous anthems by Ralph in Christ Church
Cathedral library. He is probably the 'Mr. Roseingrave Jr' who is credited with
the canonic Gloria to the *Nunc dimittis* of Purcell's G minor Service at York.

---

[19] Shaw, 411, 420–1.   [20] Grindle, 29.
[21] Chapter Act, 14 Dec. 1709, quoted in *Grove's Dictionary of Music and Musicians*, 5th edn., ed.
Eric Blom (London, 1954), vii. 233 (L. Dix).

Durham

According to the 1554 statutes of the cathedral: 'there shall be for ever in the said Church one Dean, twelve Canons, twelve Minor Canons, one Deacon, one Subdeacon, ten Clerks who may be either laymen or priests, one Master of the Choristers, ten Choristers . . .'.[1] It was thus one of the most lavish of the new foundations, as befitted the seat of a prince-bishop, comparable in size with Canterbury, Westminster Abbey, and Winchester (prior to its 1634 statutes). The numbers were not maintained in the Restoration period, however; something closer to 10–10–10 seems to have been aimed at. Thus, in 1675, there were seven minor canons, nine clerks, and ten choristers; in 1695, ten minor canons, eight clerks, and nine choristers—not counting the master of the choristers.[2] Minor canons were paid £20 or £30 a year depending on seniority, lay clerks £13. 6s. 8d. or £20 likewise. The choristers received £3. 6s. 8d. each and the master £40.[3] There was also an emolument for two sackbut- and two cornett-players of £6. 13s. 4d.—the equivalent of two clerks' places. First introduced about 1625, they were retained until 1680, but the last cornett-player did not disappear until 1698.[4] No doubt this was what lay behind Roger North's report of 1676 that at Durham and York 'they have the ordinary wind instruments in the Quire, as the cornet, sackbut, double curtaile and others, which supply the want of voices, very notorious there',[5] though 'want of voices' is difficult to explain in view of the size of the choir, and what is known of the repertoire.

As the statutes indicate, the master of the choristers was usually additional to the minor canons and lay clerks; in most cases he was also the organist. The first after the Restoration was John Foster, a chorister before the Civil War and organist and choirmaster from 1660 to 1677.[6] His successor as organist (but not as master) was Alexander Shaw, one of the first batch of choirboys after the

---

[1] J. Meade Falkner (ed.), *The Statutes of the Cathedral Church of Durham* (Durham, 1929), 85–6; also 131–3.

[2] For these figures and data regarding personnel, pay, and periods of service, I am indebted to Dr Brian Crosby, who generously gave me copies of material used in the preparation of his *Catalogue of Durham Cathedral Music Manuscripts*. For the history of the choir during the period 1660–1715, see his *Durham Cathedral Choristers and Their Masters*, 22–6.

[3] These figures are for 1668–9, but were unchanged at the end of the century.

[4] Crosby, 'A Seventeenth-Century Durham Inventory', 169; id., *Choristers*, 23.

[5] Wilson (ed.), *Roger North*, 40.   [6] Crosby, *Choristers*, 20, 22–3; Shaw, 91.

Restoration. He became one of the sackbuts in 1664 when his voice broke, and for some years before 1677 seems to have been organist of Ripon. In the latter year he returned to Durham, but in 1681 he was dismissed 'ob contumaciam'. He died in 1706.[7] During his time as organist the master of the choristers was John Nicholls, a lay clerk from 1661.[8] In 1682 both posts were reunited in the person of William Greggs—a singing man at York from 1670 and master of the choristers there from 1677 until his move to Durham. He, too, may not have given complete satisfaction, for in 1686 he was granted leave to go to London for three months to improve his skill, and in 1704 was admonished to take more care in teaching the choristers. His memorial indicates that he died on 15 October 1706 'in the 48 year of his Age'—though he must have been a good deal older.[9] James Heseltine, a pupil of Blow at the Chapel Royal, succeeded to the post in 1711 'at £70 per annum', and continued for more than fifty years until his death on 20 June 1763.[10]

All those mentioned so far are known to have been composers and have left examples of their work in the cathedral partbooks.[11] These are the richest survivals of their kind in England, comprising numerous organ-books and partbooks from before the Civil War, as well as after the Restoration. Their contents indicate how attached Durham was to its own composers. Men like Edward and William Smith, Thomas Wilkinson, Richard and John Hutchinson, and John Geeres, active in the earlier part of the century, all maintained a strong place in the repertoire after 1660. This was only one aspect of a generally prevailing conservatism, which Durham shared with its musical 'dependencies' Carlisle, Ripon, and even York to some extent. It may be explained partly by the fact that Foster and Shaw were local lads, partly by the fact that Durham was such a long way from London and the latest fashions, but principally by the attitude of Dr John Cosin—Laudian high churchman, prebendary of Durham and Master of Peterhouse, Cambridge, before the Civil War—now Bishop of Durham. For him the 1630s had been the high-water mark of the church and music was essential to its worship (as evidenced by his establishment of a choral foundation at Peterhouse). Now he intended to revive the old order, and in this he was zealously supported by successive deans.

It was Cosin who brought from London the small organ which did duty in the early years of the Restoration.[12] The pre-war Dallam organ had been vandalized by Scottish soldiers in 1641, and though the pipes were saved, the case was used for firewood in 1650.[13] Cosin's organ was set up in a loft on the

---

[7] Crosby, *Choristers*, 23–4.   [8] Ibid.

[9] Ibid. 25; Shaw, 82; Conrad Eden, *Organs Past and Present in Durham Cathedral* (Durham, 1970), 10.

[10] Crosby, *Choristers*, 26; Shaw, 92–3.   [11] See Crosby, *Catalogue*.

[12] Eden, 6; John H. Grayson, 'The Organs of Durham Cathedral', *The Organ*, 13 (1933–4), 66; Crosby, *Choristers*, 22.

[13] Eden, 5–6.

south side of the choir, while George Dallam built a 'fare double organ' over the screen at a cost of £550. The instrument was ready by the end of 1662 and should have been played for the first time on Christmas Day, though for some reason this was delayed until next day.[14] A list of stops in one of the organ-books in use after the Restoration (MS A.5) may be the specification of this organ: if so—and it is certainly of an early Restoration type—it had eight stops on the great (an open diapason, two principals, a stopped diapason, a fifteenth, twelfth, twenty-second, and furniture), and five on the chair (a principal, fifteenth, twenty-second, diapason, and flute).[15] Little more than twenty years later a new organ was being planned. Bernard Smith and Renatus Harris submitted rival bids in 1683, and Smith's design was chosen despite the fact that, at £700 (plus the old organ), it was dearer. It was to be ready by May 1685, and contain twelve stops on the great and five on the chair (see Ch. 5). Smith later said that he had 'out gon the pris, for this I declare that it cost mee above a thousant pound, lett anny boddy think or say what the[y] plees'. Some years later, possibly in 1691, he may have added an echo manual.[16]

The cautious development of the cathedral repertoire in these years can be conveniently followed through the contents of successive sets of partbooks and organ-books, particularly MSS A.3 and A.4 among the latter.[17] Most of A.3 is in the hand of John Foster, while A.4 was begun by Alexander Shaw and finished by William Greggs. The only recent pieces in A.3, however, are by Henry Loosemore, Albertus Bryne, Thomas Hearsdon of Lincoln, and Foster himself. Manuscript A.4 takes over where A.3 leaves off; the first 104 pages of the 'anthem end', and the first ninety-two pages of the 'service end' had been copied by Shaw, and paid for, by 30 October 1679. In addition to numerous older pieces it contains anthems by Child, Tucker, Tudway, Shaw, and Hawkins, while at the other end are services by Child, Tucker, and Shaw. Greggs's additions include more anthems by Child, Wise, Tucker, and Greggs himself, and two more services by Child.

A service sheet for the month of June 1680 shows some of this material in use.[18] Morning and evening prayer were sung by the choir daily, with anthems at each service except (usually) Wednesday and Friday mornings—perhaps to save time for the litany. Not every item in the list can be identified, but of those which can (and allowing for repeat performances), twenty-one different services and forty-seven anthems were sung. Most of the services were standard 'short' services, such as Tallis, Gibbons, etc., with one or two of more recent vintage by Bryne, Loosemore, and Child (4). Short services by Nicholls and Shaw, and

[14] Eden, 6; Crosby, *Choristers*, 22.
[15] Clark, *Transposition in Seventeenth-Century English Organ Accompaniments*, 155.
[16] Eden, 6–12; Freeman, *Father Smith*, 28–9, 71–4.
[17] See Crosby, *Catalogue*, 12–13; also Clark, 61–4, 134–59.
[18] Brian Crosby, 'A Service Sheet from June 1680', *Musical Times*, 121 (1980), 399–401; Dearnley, 282–4.

Foster's 'Second [verse] Service' characteristically provided a local flavour. Of the anthems, only seventeen were verse anthems, mostly sung at evening services. Again, the repertoire is old-fashioned—sixteenth-century rather than seventeenth-century—with Child (3), King, and Tucker representing early Restoration composers beyond Durham, and Foster (2) and Nicholls (2) the local product.

Two further organ-books in Gregg's hand are MSS A.33 and A.25.[19] The former was begun before 1696 and virtually completed by 1700. For the first time the repertoire is contemporary, though there is nothing after Purcell from the mainstream. Manuscript A.25 is slightly later and includes pieces by Croft (3), Clarke, and Holmes, and Norris (2) of Lincoln, in addition to Blow (14), Purcell (8), Tudway (5), Humfrey (4), and Greggs (4).

A discussion of work by Durham composers in the Restoration period naturally begins with John Foster, whose 'First' and 'Second' Services are dated 1638 and 1671 respectively. There are ten or eleven anthems by him in the Durham books, some of which can be reconstructed. On the evidence of the full anthem *When the Lord turned again*—one of those performed in June 1680— his style is conservative and somewhat dour, with an imitative technique that cannot quite do justice to his material. The verse anthem *Set up thyself* is, if anything, even more old-fashioned, for the word-setting is undeclamatory and the organ part contrapuntal. Both could well have been written in the 1630s.[20] John Nicholls is represented by a Service in G and two anthems. His full setting of *O pray for the peace of Jerusalem* shows a more capable technique than Foster's, especially in mixing homophonic and polyphonic textures, and perhaps deserved its double appearance in the June music list (see Ex. 47).[21] Alexander Shaw has two services and two anthems in the pre-1679 portion of MS A.4, but it is difficult to deduce much from them.[22]

William Greggs is credited with six anthems in all. He added two early ones to MS A.4 soon after his arrival at Durham, one of which, *My heart is inditing*, may have been composed to mark the coronation of King James II in 1685. Later anthems are found in MS A.25, among them *I will sing a new song*, written for the Thanksgiving for the Peace of Ryswick in 1697, an elaborate piece with symphonies and ritornellos in the modern style. *Hear my prayer* and *If the Lord himself* are in a more restrained, pre-Purcellian idiom.

Other Durham composers of this period known from the presence of their work in the cathedral partbooks include Elias Smith, minor canon from 1628 and precentor from 1661 until his death in 1676, whose verse anthem *How is the gold become dim* was written for the feast of King Charles the Martyr, newly instituted at the Restoration.[23] Another was Francis Forcer, an ex-chorister and

Ex. 47. John Nicholls, *O pray for the peace of Jerusalem* (DRc C1, 7, 11, 17)

private organist to the Bishop of Durham prior to 1669, when he ran off to London, to become organist of St Sepulchre's, Holborn, a prolific composer of songs, and lessee of Sadler's Wells.[24] Robert Hodge, a minor canon between 1691 and 1693, previously of Wells, later of Dublin, has two anthems to his credit, while Thomas Allinson, successively chorister and lay clerk between *c.*1682 and 1693, and later organist of Lincoln Cathedral (q.v.), has four.

To these may be added two early eighteenth-century divines, Theophilus Pickering, prebendary from 1692 to 1711, and Philip Falle, prebendary from 1700 to 1742, each with a single anthem in the partbooks. The latter, however, has fourteen anthems in a manuscript in the British Library (Add. MS 31586), including *Hear, O thou shepherd of Israel*, which was 'Set to Musick upon Occasion of Dr Sacheverel's Tryal' (for High Church anti-government views) in 1710. It is a substantial piece with ritornellos, though particular instruments are not specified. Falle, born in 1656,[25] was an amateur composer not quite in the class of Aldrich or even Creighton, but with a technique that was at least capable of getting him from bar to bar respectably. His harmony has moments of interest, but on the whole the palette is rather colourless, due perhaps to limited modulatory ability—though it should be remembered that he was of

[24] Crosby, *Choristers*, 23; Donovan Dawe, *Organists of the City of London, 1660–1850* (Padstow, Cornwall, 1983), 98; *NG* vi. 704 (Ian Spink).
[25] See Joseph Foster, *Alumni Oxonienses, 1500–1714* (Oxford, 1891).

Ex. 48. James Heseltine, *Praise the Lord, ye servants* (*Ob Tenbury* 821)

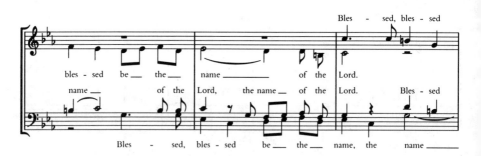

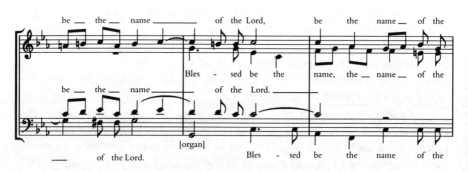

Purcell's generation, not Croft's. His work is surprisingly free of clichés, and even triple time is rather rare. Full writing lacks contrapuntal interest, but homophony is blandly effective. Word-setting and repetitions tend to be awkward; the texts themselves are somewhat atypical. Perhaps, as a clergyman, he was drawn to passages of scripture that were less hackneyed when it came to musical settings. For example, *Though I speak with the tongues of angels*, which he set as a solo anthem, does not seem to have been set by anyone else.

With the appointment of James Heseltine as organist and master of the choristers in 1711, Durham seemed at last to put its provincialism behind it. He had been a boy in the Chapel Royal until 1707,[26] where the main contemporary influences on him must have been Croft and Clarke. He was appointed organist of St Katherine by the Tower [of London] in 1709, and was allowed to keep this post during his fifty-three years at Durham, the former duty being performed by a deputy.[27] Despite his long tenure, the Durham books contain only four anthems by him. Probably there was something in Hawkins's assertion that 'having, as he conceived, been slighted, or otherwise illtreated by the dean and chapter, he in revenge tore out of the church-books all his compositions that were there to be found'.[28] The words of seven anthems by him are in *A Collection of Anthems . . . Durham* (1749) and a few are known from other sources—eleven in all. Earliest is a setting of *Unto thee will I cry*, which must have been composed while he was still in the Chapel Royal, according to its date '17 September 1707' (*Lbl* 30860). Another early anthem is *We have a strong city*, listed in *Divine Harmony* (1712). Of those now at Durham, *Praise the Lord, ye servants* is probably not much later. It survives in score there (and with three others in the Tenbury collection, *Ob*), and reveals the composer writing confidently in an up-to-date style. Verses for various CTB combinations form a sequence of contrasted movements begining and ending in C major, with excursions to C minor, F major, D minor, and A minor. The second movement is a fugue that owes something—as does much else—to Croft (see Ex. 48).

---

[26] Ashbee, ii. 91.   [27] Dawe, 109.   [28] Hawkins, *History*, ii. 800.

Ely

The Henrician foundation of Ely in 1541 stipulated a dean, eight prebendaries eight minor canons, eight lay clerks, and eight choristers, but the 1666 statutes (see App. E) amended the numbers in the choir to five minor canons, eight lay clerks, eight choristers, and an organist and master of the choristers—the latter paid for by savings from the three minor canons' places.[1] Minor canons were to be priests, of whom 'one more mature in years' was to be precentor. Their stipend was £15 a year; that of the lay clerks was £10, while the organist and master of the choristers—not always the same person—received £20 and £10 respectively, and the boys £4. Most of these sums were augmented in some way, and especially so in the case of the minor canons. The statutes bestowed on four of them the vicarages of Holy Trinity (the Lady Chapel of the cathedral) and St Mary in the town—each worth a further £30—and Chettisham and Stuntney just outside—worth £20 each. Sometimes, too, they served as head-master (£18) and undermaster (£10) of the school, as well as precentor (£2), sacrist (£1. 6s. 8d.), and epistoler (£8) within the cathedral.

With so many jobs to perform, the temptation for minor canons to absent themselves from divine service was no doubt great, and time and again the Dean and Chapter tried to enforce the statutes. In 1698 abuses were such that it was even found necessary to prohibit them from serving as minor canons or in any similar capacity at other cathedrals simultaneously 'upon pain of the loss of their place in this Church'.[2] With other cures to attend to, Sunday mornings were a problem, and it was frequently enjoined that minor canons, unless excused by the dean or subdean, 'perform the Service in the Quire at the usuall houres upon every Sunday morning in like manner as on other dayes'.[3] Precise details as to how they were to sing the prayers and responses are set out in an early eighteenth-century manuscript (see App. A),[4] though the practice of lay clerks

---

[1] James Bentham, *The History and Antiquities of the Cathedral and Conventual Church of Ely* (London, 1771), App., 40–1. The 1666 Statutes are in the Ely Dean and Chapter records (EDC) now on deposit in Cambridge University Library, and translated here in App. E. Details of personnel, periods of service, and stipends below are taken from the Treasurer's Accounts, 1660–1724 (EDC 3/1/2–4); dates identify the reference. Other details are from the Chapter Books, 1660–1729 (EDC 2/1/2). The pre-war situation is covered in Payne, *Provision and Practice*, 191–8, 252–6, etc.

[2] EDC 2/1/2, 14 June 1698.   [3] Ibid., 25 Nov. 1668.
[4] EDC 10/12b; 'O Ld save the Queen' indicates a date of 1702–14.

singing the first part of the litany, implied in the manuscript, was ended when the Chapter insisted that 'one of the Minor Canons do always chant or sing that whole Service at the Desk on Litany days instead of Lay Clerks chanting part of it by former custome'.[5]

Following the Restoration, minor canons and lay clerks were up to strength by Christmas 1661. As organist and master of the choristers, Robert Claxton resumed his immediate pre-war posts, but he was replaced by John Ferrabosco in 1662 while continuing as a lay clerk until 1668.[6] Ferrabosco in his turn was followed in 1682–3 by James Hawkins, whose tenure lasted until 1729, and whose vast industry as a copyist both of his own and other composers' work forms the basis of the Ely collection of church music, now deposited in Cambridge University Library (see Ch. 5). As for the organs these men had charge of, £65 had been disbursed in 1661 'for the Organe bought for the use of the Quier and for the bringing of it down to Ely', but this was probably a stopgap while the old organ was put into better repair.[7] Details of this latter instrument are lacking, but it would appear from one of the early organ-books (MS 1, p. 140 *bis*) that it had two manuals, in view of the direction "Eccho chaire Organ' ('eccho' referring to the musical effect at this point, not to an 'echo organ'), followed by '2 principles: Double Organ'. Then in 1682, Dr William Holder, subdean of the Chapel Royal and a prebendary of Ely, made a gift of money 'to compleat the Great Organ'.[8] There is a tradition that Renatus Harris built a new organ in 1685, but it seems more likely that if a new organ was built, then the builder was Gerhard Smith.[9] In 1690, Smith had been paid £130 for refurbishing the old chair organ, and the following year he agreed, for the sum of £300, 'to make new the Great organ in the case now standing in the choir of Ely. And shall put in the said new organ ten new stopps.' Though it included two four-rank mixtures and a cornet of five ranks, rather surprisingly for the date it lacked a trumpet stop—a deficiency which was not remedied until 1736. According to James Hawkins, the organist, writing to Thomas Tudway in the early eighteenth century, this organ was '3 quarters of a note higher than the pitch of organs now'.[10]

As already mentioned, the Ely collection contains important sources of Restoration church music, the earliest being two organ-books largely in Ferrabosco's hand (MSS 1 and 4) and a tenor partbook (MS 28).[11] Attributions

---

[5] EDC 2/1/2, 25 Nov. 1708 (starting next Candlemas—2 Feb. 1709).

[6] For organists see Anthony J. Greening, *The Organs and Organists of Ely Cathedral* [Ely, 1972], 11–12; Shaw, 99–102.

[7] Reginald H. Gibbon, 'The Account Book of the Dean and Chapter of Ely, 1604–1677' *Church Quarterly Review*, 115 (Jan. 1933), 226.   [8] EDC 2/1/2, 14 June 1682.

[9] W. E. Dickson, 'Early Organs in Ely Cathedral', *The Organ*, 1 (1921–2), 63; Greening, 5–6 (omits a Principal from the specification as given in EDC 10/12c).   [10] Greening, 7.

[11] See Dickson, *Catalogue of Ancient Choral Services*; Clark, *Transposition in Seventeenth-Century English Organ Accompaniments*, 64–5, 159–70; also Cheverton, 'English Church Music', 314–22 and 449–53.

to 'Dr' William Child and 'Mr' Benjamin Rogers date much of their content
between 1663 and 1669. Later partbooks include MS 29 with services at one end
mainly copied in the 1670s, and some in Hawkins's hand, among them MSS 3
and 25 dating from the 1690s. In addition, there are numerous scores which
Hawkins compiled, particularly MSS 5, 6, and 9, which give a wide selection of
contemporary work, and MS 7, containing 532 pages devoted to his own
compositions (see Ch. 5).

For present purposes the main interest of this collection is the way it reflects
the Ely repertoire, especially the work of local composers—John Amner, organist and choirmaster before the Civil War, his successors Ferrabosco and
Hawkins, and others connected with the cathedral, such as William Holder, and
the elder and younger Thomas Bullis. From nearby Cambridge came Henry
Loosemore, from Norwich, Richard Gibbs, and from Peterborough, Thomas
Mudd and Francis Standish.

Ferrabosco, as we have seen, was appointed to Ely in 1662. It is likely that he
was the king's wind musician of that name in 1631, but given 1626 as his date
of birth, this must have been a sinecure to provide for his upbringing following
the death of his famous father in 1628.[12] Nothing is known of him before his
arrival at Ely, beyond his place in the King's Musick. In 1671 he was made
B.Mus. of Cambridge University by letters patent from the king; from 1677
illness may have interfered with the performance of his cathedral duties. Eight
services and eleven anthems by him are known besides a Burial Service and one
or two miscellaneous pieces, such as a Kyrie to George Barcroft's G minor
Service. Most were written between 1663 and 1669. The services survive
incomplete in the partbooks, but two are in a score (MS 13) transcribed by
Thomas Kempton, Hawkins's successor. Both are full services, in A minor and
B flat major respectively, severely homophonic but with antiphony between the
two sides of the choir, bringing variety and a sense of movement to the texture.
However, another eighteenth-century copy at Cambridge contains the jaun-
diced comment that they were 'exceeding indifferent Musick, and not worth
the trouble of copying . . . I have corrected several particulars, which were
copyists faults, but many more have been obliged to leave as incorrigible'.[13] The
movements of each service are frequently interrelated by head-motifs, and the
fact that the anthem *The King shall rejoice* begins like the canticles in the B flat
Service suggests that it belongs to that service—and therefore, in view of the
words of the anthem, that both may have been written for the visit of the king
to Ely in 1669 (see Ex. 49a–c).[14]

The remaining anthems are all verse anthems. At times their style seems very
old-fashioned, with written-out organ parts providing a contrapuntal background against which the solo voices deliver their phrases. Sometimes, however,

---

[12] *NG* vi. 484 (John V. Cockshoot).   [13] Dr John Worgan (1758) in *Ckc* 106.
[14] Reginald H. Gibbon, 'Small Beer of History', *Church Quarterly Review*, 113 (Oct. 1933), 105.

Ex. 49 John Ferrabosco, (*a*) *Te Deum* (*Cu* Ely 18)
    (*b*) *Nunc dimittis* (*Cu* Ely 18)
    (*c*) *The king shall rejoice* (*US - BE* 751 and *Cu* Ely 3 and 28)

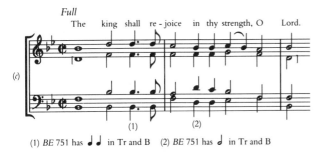

(1) *BE* 751 has ♩♩ in Tr and B   (2) *BE* 751 has ♩ in Tr and B

passages of more animated declamation and awkward moments in the harmony
remind us that Ferrabosco belongs to a younger generation than Gibbons or
Tomkins. Both these features are observable in the opening verse of *Behold, now
praise the Lord*, which can be recovered from the organ score (MS 1). Here the
organ introduction is shorter than usual; the brief, chordal, four-part chorus
which rounds off the verse is typical (see Ex. 50).

In attempting to reconstruct these anthems from the organ score there are
problems both in identifying the word-bearing parts and fitting the words to
them. Comment on expressive technique is therefore hazardous, but it does not
seem as if *By the waters of Babylon* or *Like as the hart*—two settings that might be

Ex. 50. John Ferrabosco, *Behold, now praise the Lord* (*Cu* Ely 1)

(1) Seems to be *f*♯ in original.

expected to offer potential from this point of view—contain any out-of-the-ordinary passages. The Burial Service (MS 8), on the other hand, perhaps because of its restrained simplicity, makes a deep effect. Its sombre G minor homophony is lit by numerous touches of harmonic colour, sometimes merely the substitution of major for minor chords, which bring a consoling warmth to the music.

Music at Ely benefited from the presence there of William Holder, a prebendary from 1660, also of St Paul's Cathedral from 1672, and subdean of the Chapel Royal from 1674, where his stern discipline earned him the title of 'Mr Snub Dean' from Michael Wise.[15] His links with Ely were not severed, however, for we have already seen that in 1682 he contributed towards the completion of the organ. Brother-in-law of Christopher Wren and a man of wide scientific interests, he was an early member of the Royal Society, and published tracts on *The Elements of Speech* (1669) and *A Treatise on the Natural Grounds and Principles of Harmony* (1693). As a composer, he is represented in the Ely collection by ten anthems copied before 1669, and a verse Service in C major. The service and two of the anthems also survive in one of Hawkins's scores (MS 5), and in Tudway's collection; most of the remaining anthems are in Ferrabosco's organ-book (MS 1), so some general view can be gained of them. All are verse anthems, mainly for three voices, with homophonic four-part choruses at the end of each verse. Without being a modernist Holder had an ear for the idioms of his time. An excerpt from *Out of the deep* provides a typical example of his style, and obviates the need for further comment beyond the general observation that it seems well adapted to achieve its modest aims (see Ex. 51).

Many of the anthems as they appear in MS 1 (though not *Out of the deep*) begin with organ introductions and have elaborate accompaniments to the verses. Not closely imitative, the texture is nevertheless filled out in some detail (and sprinkled with consecutives). Holder seems to have favoured penitential texts, and the overall impression his music makes is thus rather solemn. Triple-time sections are few and welcome when they come.

During the period of Ferrabosco's ill health, his duties as master of the choristers were performed by Thomas Bullis, senior (1627–1708), a lay clerk from 1661—and much else besides in and out of the cathedral. His son, likewise Thomas (1657–1712) and a lay clerk from 1677, served as organist between the death of Ferrabosco and the arrival of James Hawkins, receiving £5 'for his services during the vacancy of the Organists place' in 1683.[16] There are four anthems and a Short Service in G minor by the elder Bullis, all dating from the early or mid-1660s. The old-fashioned style of *O Lord, holy father* is obvious from the surviving organ score (MS 4), as is the service in the same source, predominantly chordal and modal in character, with head-motif beginnings to each canticle.

The younger Bullis wrote in a much more modern style. No fewer than three services and seven anthems by him are known. A *Benedicite* Service in G minor survives only in a single partbook (MS 29), and there are organ scores of an

---

[15] *NG* viii. 644 (Michael Tilmouth); also *DNB*.

[16] Frederick Hudson, 'Thomas Bullis, Father and Son', *Musical Times*, 114 (1973), 420; see EDC 2/1/2, 14 June 1683.

Ex. 51. William Holder, *Out of the deep* (*Cu* Ely 1, 28 and 29)

(1) MS 1 has *f* ' ♯

(2) As in MS 1. In the interest of clarity, mutually contradictory underlay of tenor (MS 28) and bass (MS 29)
    has not been shown.

evening verse Service in G and a whole Service in A (MS 4). So far as one can
judge they are of little musical interest, though the evening service contains
amiable stretches of triple time untroubled by harmonic incident, but now and
again stirred to life by dotted rhythms ('With trumpets also and shawms' in the
Cantate Domino, for example). As for the A major Service, one hopes that some

at least of its peculiarities are due to a corrupt text. Like Child in his 'Sharp Service' he essays a canon 4 and 1 at the words 'O go your way into his gates' in the *Jubilate*, but it is an arid contrivance, increasingly devoid of sense as it progresses. The full anthem *O clap your hands* has been published in modern times and is similar in style to the A major Service. To the extent that it makes a more convincing effect, this is largely due to the way it is carried along by its triple time.[17] By contrast, the setting of *O Lord, rebuke me not* shows a less facile idiom and solid competence in the declamatory verse style. The fact that it also survives in a score from Peterborough Cathedral (*Ob* Tenbury 789) suggests that his contemporaries may have regarded it quite highly.

By far the most important Ely composer was James Hawkins. He was probably a chorister at Worcester (q.v.), moving briefly to St John's College, Cambridge, as organist in 1681–2, before taking up the post at Ely. (His tombstone described him as '46 Years Organist of this Church', which suggests that he took up his appointment in 1682–3.)[18] From the absence of evidence to the contrary we may conclude that his life was fairly uneventful. His wife bore ten children (one, also James, became organist of Peterborough), but otherwise there was a great deal of composing and copying, and, of course, cathedral duties combined with visits to the country to teach. Thus, in 1684 the Dean and Chapter gave him permission 'to be absent at Bury [St Edmunds] for the teaching of Children there in Musick three days in a fortnight and no more. Provided that he take care for the supply of his two places of Organist and Informator.'[19] Some years later they forbade such excursions 'unless he carefully teach the Choir at home Three afternoons, at least, in every week; and unless the proficiency of the quire be very evident, and a sensible progress be made'.[20] Nevertheless, looking back over many years of service in 1727, the Chapter agreed 'that twenty Guineas be given to Mr Hawkins Our Organist in consideration of his present difficult circumstances, & of his long Service to this Church'.[21] What these difficult circumstances might have been can only be guessed. Two years earlier the accounts show him in receipt of £30 a year as organist, £10 as master of the choristers, £6 as 'cook' (a sinecure), and £6. 13s. 4d. as one of the six almsmen, besides £2 'for playing the Psalms [before the sermon] on Sundays' and another £1 'for his singing school'.[22] He died 18 October 1729.

Hawkins was nothing if not prolific. Dickson's catalogue lists seventeen services and seventy-five anthems by him, figures which may be taken as approximately correct, though some are misattributed or counted twice. One of his scores (MS 7), already alluded to, contains seven services and fifty-six anthems, and may have been compiled with a view to publication, prompted

[17] ed. Frederick Hudson (London, 1973).   [18] Bentham, App., 50; Shaw, 101–2, 362.
[19] EDC 2/1/2, 14 June 1684.   [20] Ibid., 14 June 1698.
[21] Ibid., 25 Nov. 1727.   [22] EDC 3/1/5 (1725).

Ex. 52. James Hawkins, *Nunc dimittis* from the Service in E flat (*Cu* Ely 7)

perhaps by Croft's *Musica Sacra* (1724). Whatever the reason, it probably represents what he himself regarded as his best work. With its revisions and
corrections it doubtless provides the most authoritative texts. Unless otherwise
stated it is the source of all the music considered below.

In view of his sizeable output, any discussion of his work is likely to be
tentative for the present. His earliest services are probably the evening canticles
in A and E flat, which, from their presence in the Worcester partbooks (e.g. MS
A.3.1.), may date from 1683 or earlier, certainly from before December 1684.
Of the two, that in E flat is simple and somewhat insipid, but the opening of
the *Nunc dimittis* is attractive (see Ex. 52). The Services in B minor, E minor,
the *Benidicite* in A, and most of the Service in F are in triple time—no more
need be said. However, the C major Service has a vigour that almost compen-
sates for its often routine moments, its all too obvious harmonic progressions,
and facile modulations. (On the other hand, the move to E minor, with D♯ and

F♯ at 'the sharpness of death', is just plain awkward, though its purpose is clear.) The most rewarding music is to be found in the verses, particularly those like 'Vouchsafe O Lord' (in the *Te Deum*), which provide contrast of key and a more intimate expression to set against the extrovert C major of the full sections. Tudway chose to represent Hawkins by Services in G and A in his collection (*Harl.* 7341–2), and no doubt he thought they did him justice. The former is 'full' throughout, after the manner of Child in such works; homophonic passages alternate with short-winded imitations rather mechanically worked out, sometimes taxing the composer's technique. There is not a single bar in triple time from start to finish, and this, together with the absence of verse sections, gives it an old-fashioned sound despite its latish date. By contrast, the A major Service seems more modern, though its relationship with the earlier 'Worcester' Service needs elucidating.

At Worcester only the *Magnificat* and *Nunc dimittis* are to be found, but in the Ely versions (MS 3) these canticles are grouped with a *Te Deum* and *Jubilate*, making a set having all its Glorias in common. However, comparison of this service with another in A having alternative evening canticles (MS 7) shows that the *Te Deum* and *Jubilate* are the same, though extensively revised. The most striking differences between the earlier and later versions of the morning canticles are the substitution of new sections for 'The glorious company of the apostles' in the *Te Deum*, and the opening of the *Jubilate*. The aim seems to have been to make them more modern by introducing 'affective' idioms such as dotted rhythms and stereotyped 'jubilation' figures representing 'glory', 'praise', 'joyful', etc., where previously the music had been more neutral from the expressive point of view (compare Ex. 53*a* and *c*).

Presumably these tarted-up settings were not intended for everyday use at Ely, but for holy days and special occasions. Something more utilitarian was appropriate at other times, especially to get evening prayer over as quickly as possible. For such circumstances Hawkins devised his 'chanting services', in which the verses of a canticle were sung by full choir 'chanting' in alternation with three- or four-part verses for soloists.[23] It was a species of *alternatim* performance, similar in principle to that practised before the Reformation but using Anglican chant instead of plainsong psalm tones. Hawkins wrote two such services, and from Ely the idea spread to nearby Norwich, Peterborough, and Lincoln, where William Norris adapted the idea to the morning canticles. Hawkins's Chanting Service in C minor sets the *Magnificat* and *Nunc dimittis* by alternating a four-part chant (by Croft) with three-part verses in triple time. The *Cantate* and *Deus misereatur* in D (MS 9), though described as a chanting service by the composer, is rather freer. Indeed, for most of the *Deus misereatur* the *alternatim* principle is abandoned, with, duets and trios, sections in four parts, and

---

[23] Ruth Wilson, 'Anglican Chant', 126–40.

Ex. 53. James Hawkins, *Jubilate* from the service in A: (*a*) and (*b*) *Cu* Ely 3;
        (*c*) and (*d*) *Cu* Ely 7

Ex. 54. James Hawkins, *Magnificat* from the Chanting Service in C minor (*Cu* Ely 7)

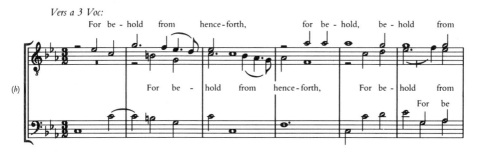

solos bursting into coloratura at the usual provocation (e.g. at the words 'O let the nations rejoice and be glad'). Such writing can hardly have hurried the service along or given the choir an easy time. The opening verses of the C minor *Magnificat* illustrate the method at its simplest (see Ex. 54).

In this survey of Hawkins's services, one further setting demands notice—his A minor verse service, with five-part chorus and strings. It is a work on a considerable scale, taking up 127 pages of score. One can hardly imagine the circumstances (if any) for which it was written, since not only does it contain morning and evening canticles, but also a communion service complete with responses to the Commandments. The fact that the normally intoned beginning of the Creed is also set points to some unusual purpose in writing the piece. Perhaps it was Hawkins's exercise for his Cambridge B.Mus. degree taken in 1719. Whatever the reason for its composition it is a remarkable piece, with no antecedents among his own output and little in common with any English church music of the period. It must certainly be a late work, and has some excellent passages; for example, 'Vouchsafe, O Lord' in the *Te Deum*, where invertible chromatic counterpoint testifies to a reasonable technique and some imagination. Performance indications are explicit as to the effects he was aiming at. The *Te Deum* is marked 'Devout and Grand', the passage just referred to has 'Very Slow and Devout' written above it, and the verse 'He hath shewed strength' in the *Magnificat* is marked 'Grave & Majestick'. What the overall effect of the piece would be is difficult to judge. It seems rather mean to suggest that it may not be interesting enough for its length; on the other hand, if he wrote it for his degree, one would have expected it to pass.

Most of Hawkins's full anthems are homophonic and in triple time, with lively syncopated rhythms. Sometimes there is a verse section in the middle, sometimes a concluding Hallelujah. The general style may be described as 'extrovert Restoration', and it served him well throughout his career. For more serious texts he inclined towards the old-fashioned imitative style, and appears to have had a real feeling for it. However, the fact that the first twenty-eight bars of *Bow down thine ear* are the same as Wilbye's *Draw on, sweet night* makes one wonder if there are not other borrowings elsewhere—the beginning of *Hear my prayer*, for example, looks suspicious, though the technique would probably not have been beyond him (see Ex. 55).

Among the verse anthems there are also some which, though signed James Hawkins, are attributed elsewhere to other composers. Thus, to mention only three, *O praise the Lord, all ye heathen* is actually by Purcell, and *Behold how good and joyful* and *Behold now praise the Lord* (MS 2) are more likely to be by William Norris of Lincoln. It seems unlikely, however, that they were deliberate attempts to pass off other men's work, for his ability to turn out ordinary, run-of-the-mill anthems by the dozen is not in question, and these particular ones are no better than he himslf was quite capable of. Possibly, understandably even, he may have become confused about exactly what he had written towards the end of his life, especially as in a few cases he set the same words twice. Nevertheless, consciously or unconsciously, one does find echoes of other composers in his work. The opening phrase of *Lord, thou hast been our refuge* is

Ex. 55. James Hawkins, *Hear my pray'r, O Lord (Cu Ely 7)*

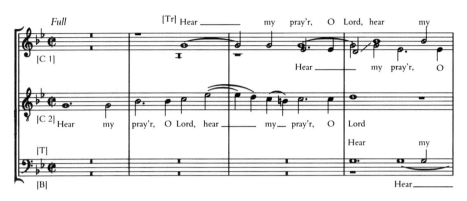

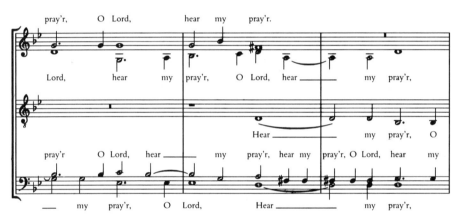

(1) Originally *d '* in C2.

clearly a memory of Turner's setting, though the subsequent handling is different, while the 'Glory be to God on high' in *Rejoice in the Lord alway* is blatantly
lifted from Purcell's *Behold, I bring you glad tidings*.

Lest we regard him as a mere plagiarist, it might be a good idea to look a little
more closely at *Rejoice in the Lord alway*, since it sets a text that is a conflation
of two of Purcell's best-known anthems, *Rejoice in the Lord alway* and *Behold I
bring you glad tidings*, both of which Hawkins transcribed. It is interesting to
observe points of similarity and difference, and see to what extent Hawkins is
able to take an independent line despite reminiscences of Purcell that must have
kept crowding in. Hawkins sets the opening verse as a duet between treble and
tenor (see Ex. 56a), Purcell as a trio. Both are in strongly syncopated triple time,
but this is a commonplace of the period, and while it leads to certain similarities
between the two, these were probably difficult to avoid owing to the prosody
of the text. Unlike Purcell, Hawkins employs dotted-quaver rhythms, but the
repetition of 'and again' towards the end does recall a similar device which
Purcell introduces when reworking the material for the chorus. (However, both
composers would have regarded the idea of an echo as appropriate to the sense
of the words.) Following a brief Hallelujah chorus, Hawkins moves forward
from the third Sunday in Advent to Christmas Day for the second part of
the anthem. A solo treble declaims the angel's message 'For behold I bring you
glad tidings'. Purcell's setting of these words is, of course, one of the most
magnificent things he wrote, exploiting as it does the full range of Gostling's
bass voice. For him the Christmas message is so powerful that it will change the
world. For Hawkins, it is the pathos of the child born in the stable that comes
across (see Ex. 56b). Both composers celebrate the 'glad tidings' with a change
to triple time, bold arpeggios expressing the idea of 'great' with Purcell, dotted
quavers the idea of 'joy' with Hawkins (see Ex. 56c). In the latter case, a short
treble recitative leads to the angels' chorus which, as has already been pointed
out, begins like Purcell's though its continuation is different. In no way is it a
match, but it does point the contrast between 'Glory be to God on high' and
'on earth peace, good will towards men' nicely, with echoes on 'peace' (see Ex.
56d).

The purpose of this comparison is not to demonstrate Purcell's superiority,
but to show something of Hawkins's method, and the way in which he uses the
idioms of the day competently and, at times, imaginatively. On the whole, the
contents of MS 7 do not show much variety in treatment. The main ingredients
of his style are tuneful verses in triple time for one, two, or three voices, and
common-time sections of a more declamatory nature, loosely imitative. In solos,
stereotyped affective motifs and descriptive flourishes highlight or draw out the
significance of particular words; likewise, chromaticism and exotic keys may be
used for expressive purposes. In general, his technique can cope with all this,

Ex. 56. James Hawkins, *Rejoice in the Lord alway* (*Cu* Ely 7)

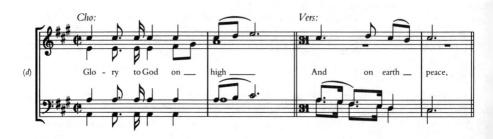

though side by side with really excellent passages one finds disconcertingly weak moments.

There are no symphony anthems among the contents of MS 7 though both the Burial Service and *O give thanks unto the Lord, for he is gracious* survive in other sources with instrumental symphonies. Worlds apart, and probably twenty-five or thirty years later, are two large-scale anthems, *Whoso dwelleth under the defence of the most high* and *O be joyful in the Lord all ye lands*, ostentatious in style and presumably written for some important occasion. The instrumental resources of the former (and the key of A major) may possibly connect it with the 'orchestral service' mentioned earlier, though the absence of trebles from the chorus (CCTB) is, in any case, perplexing. *O be joyful* has only an organ accompaniment but makes plentiful use of trumpet and crumhorn stops (and 'Voix humaine' at the end)—none of which the Ely organ possessed at this time. It is unusual in having a section actually marked 'Recitative' which is, for church music, quite operatic, and unlikely to have been written before the second decade of the eighteenth century.

In these late works Hawkins adopts the full-blown late Baroque style. To some extent they show an old dog performing new tricks, and it is perhaps surprising that they are as convincing as they are. On the whole, however, the idioms of the 1680s were more congenial to him. He was certainly talented, but a backwater like Ely was not the place to get the best out of him. Except for Tudway at Cambridge there was no one to provide informed criticism or set a challenging example, no incentive to do other than repeat himself. It remains to be seen whether further study will reveal more of interest. On the face of it, the effort could be worth making, for at the very least there are good reasons for dissenting from Watkins Shaw's comment that he 'is in no way significant as a composer'.[24]

[24] *NG* viii. 322 (Watkins Shaw).

Exeter

Lieutenant Hammond and his party visiting Exeter in 1634 noted 'a delicate, rich and lofty organ' in the cathedral, with pipes 'of an extraordinary length and of the bigness of a man's thigh'. He observed further that 'with their viols and other sweet instruments, the tunable voices and the rare organist, together make a melodious and heavenly harmony, able to ravish the hearer's ears'. With the entry of the parliamentary troops into the city during the Civil War all that was soon changed: 'they brake downe the organs, and taking two or three hundred pipes with them in a most scorneful and contemptuous manner, went up and downe the streets piping with them; and meeting with some of the Choristers of the Church, whose surplices they had stolne before . . . scoffingly told them: Boyes, we have spoyled your trade, you must goe and sing hot pudding pyes'.[1]

By 1660 the boot was on the other foot. Soon the Dean and Chapter were buying back the pipes of the former organ, and engaging John Loosemore, their clerk of works, for 'perfectinge the new organs'.[2] This was a temporary instrument, but in 1663 he began to build a much larger instrument which by 1665 had been erected on the screen.[3] Like its predecessor it had pipes that were the largest in the country (the bottom note, sounding about *GGG* at modern pitch, was 20' 6" long), though Roger North 'thought them made more for ostentation, than use'.[4] The instrument cost £847. 7s. 10d. and Loosemore was paid £15 a year for looking after it. Beyond that, little was done to the instrument until 1713, when Christopher Shrider (Father Smith's son-in-law) overhauled it and added several new stops.[5]

Equally important was the re-establishment of the choir. At Archbishop Laud's visitation in 1634 there had been fourteen vicars choral (four priests and ten laymen), twelve secondaries (an intermediate body between the choristers and lay vicars), and fourteen choristers—though three secondaries' places had been left vacant to increase the salaries of the rest.[6] From 1660 the new establishment seems to have been twelve vicars (four priests and eight laymen) and twelve choristers, with secondaries' places sometimes joined to vicars' in

[1] Andrew Freeman, 'The Organs of Exeter Cathedral,' *The Organ*, 6 (1926–7), 102; Matthews, *Organs and Organists of Exeter Cathedral*, 2. For the musical situation at Exeter before the Civil War see Payne, *Provision and Practice*, 177–80, 231–5, 289–90, etc.

[2] Matthews, 2–4, Freeman, 102.   [3] Matthews, 4–6; Freeman, 102–4.

[4] Wilson (ed.), *Roger North*, 39.   [5] Matthews, 6–7; Freeman, 104–5.

[6] HMC, 136–7.

order to increase their stipends.[7] For a time, too, instruments may have been in use, for in August 1664, £19 was paid 'for shagbutts and Cornetts procured att London . . . for the use of the Church'.[8] On paper, at least, it was a large choir, several members of which had worked themselves up through its various levels—William Wake, for example, who at the time of his death in 1682 had served the cathedral for seventy-two years. In 1640 he had been appointed a lay vicar, and was promoted priest vicar in 1666. Already on 9 July 1661 he had been made subchanter: '£20 per year to be payd unto him for his paynes in teaching the choristers and to continue so long as he shall do the same, and . . . to have the singing school for him and his wife to live in for the better performance of his place and office'.[9]

However, the communal life of the vicars was not revived at the Restoration. Many of the vicars' houses in the close were sublet, and even their quarterly dinners lapsed. But the Dean and Chapter continued to pay for the Christmas feast, and various pieces of plate surviving from the period testify to a measure of continuing conviviality in the hall, where, in the middle of the eighteenth century, the same benefactors provided a harpsichord for the vicars' musical evenings.[10]

No choir music survives at Exeter from the period. Works by local pre-war musicians such as Edward Gibbons, John Lugge, Robert Parsons (a vicar choral until 1676), and Greenwood Randall would, doubtless, have supplemented Barnard's *Church Musick*, and it is possible that anthems by Matthew Locke—a distinguished ex-chorister and friend of Wake—were also sung. Few of the organists had reputations as composers, however. First after the Restoration was William Hopwood, but he left to join the Chapel Royal as a bass in 1664.[11] His successor, Thomas Mudd, held the post for only a few months and is dealt with in connection with Peterborough, though he had brief periods at Lincoln and York in addition. Following Mudd came Theodore Colby, 'a German' according to Wood, who was previously organist of Magdalen College, Oxford.[12] His appointment in 1665 was at a salary of £50, increased to £60 two years later—a very large sum for playing a very large organ. In August 1674 he was dismissed for absenting himself, and it was ordered 'that Mr Henry Hall should be admitted into the said organists place'. Hall, an ex-chorister of the Chapel Royal, and temporary organist of Wells in the summer of 1674, served until 1678, when he moved to Hereford (q.v.).[13] Alone of the organists of Exeter he has a claim to being considered an important composer. His work will be dealt with in the context of Hereford, but some early anthems, among them *God standeth in the congregation* and the widespread *By the waters of Babylon*, were written before he went there.

[7] Chanter, *Custos and College of the Vicars Choral*, 27, 45–6, 49–50.   [8] Matthews, 2.
[9] Chanter, 27.   [10] Ibid. 26–31.   [11] Matthews, 23; Shaw, 109–10.
[12] Matthews, 23; Shaw, 111, 381.   [13] Matthews, 23–4; Shaw, 111, 288, 137–8.

Ex. 57. Henry Travers, *Shall we receive good* (*Cu* Ely 9)

One of the vicars at this time, Henry Travers, also seems to have been a capable composer, judging by his anthem *Shall we receive good* preserved in score (*Cu* Ely 9). Appointed lay vicar in 1663 and promoted priest vicar in 1676, he died early in 1679. It was he who in 1664 had been sent to London to buy cornetts and sackbuts, and (apparently) to learn how to play them.[14] The anthem is a sombre piece in F minor, with written-out organ accompaniment. Though specifically for organ in the manuscript, its style suggests the possibility of viol or (in view of the particular circumstances) cornett accompaniment. The tenor solo 'Wherefore I abhor myself' gives a good idea of its conservative, yet expressive idiom, as does the four-part verse 'Naked came I out of my mother's womb' (Ex. 57). Parts of 'an Anthem upon the Martyrdome of King Charles the first' by 'Hen: Trevors' survive at Lichfield.

Peter Passmore, an Exeter chorister whom the Chapter sent to London in 1676 to study with Blow, succeeded Hall as organist, though he was none too eager to heed their recall, and did not finally take up his place until the middle of 1679. In 1694 he was promoted from lay to priest vicar, resigning as organist

[14] Chanter, 27, 45, 49.

and becoming clerk of works. He died in 1708.[15] Two anthems by him, *O remember not our old sins* and *O praise the Lord*, are in eighteenth-century Exeter partbooks.

[15] Matthews, 24; Shaw, 111–12.

Passmore's successor, Richard Henman, caused problems from the start. He had been a chorister at Rochester, and then at the Chapel Royal under Blow. At Exeter, the choir complained of his 'unfittness' within a year. He was 'admonished to make himself capable & to qualify himself for his continuance'; later he was in trouble for absence and bad language. Nevertheless, it was not until 1741 that he was finally dismissed 'for his long absence and disorderly life'.[16] His only known work, *Have mercy upon me, O God*, survives in one of the Ely manuscripts (MS 9). An earlier version with introductory string symphony suggests that it may possibly have been written while he was a boy in the Chapel Royal, hence reminiscences of Humfrey's setting in the opening verse.[17] The similarity does not extend very far, however.

[16] Matthews, 24; Shaw, 112–13.

[17] Both settings are assigned to Humfrey in *MB* 34, nos. 4a and 4b. Humfrey's authorship of 4a was questioned (and tentatively ascribed to Richard Hosier) by Don Franklin in a review for the *Journal of the American Musicological Society*, 28 (1975) 143–9; for a more convincing attribution to Richard Henman see Ford, 'Henman, Humfrey and "Have mercy"'.

Gloucester

Charles II's coronation day, 23 April 1661, was celebrated at Gloucester with bonfires, the ringing of the cathedral bells, and a special service at which the lay clerks sang.[1] The following month a set of Barnard's *Church Musick* was bought for £15. 5s.,[2] and by the end of the year the choir stood at three minor canons, six lay clerks, and eight choristers.[3] But for there being three minor canons instead of six, this was as the statutes required; and, in fact, at no time during the Restoration period were there ever more than four minor canons.[4] Perhaps their salaries were diverted initially to pay for 'two Sackbutts & two Cornetts, for the use of our Singinge Service & anthems'.[5] The full complement of lay clerks and choristers was, however, maintained. The clerks were wretchedly paid at £6. 13s. 8d. a year, and the minor canons not much better off at £10, though the salary of the organist and master of the choristers was £22. 10s. in 1666, later raised to £30. Gloucester was one of the poorest of the new foundations, and this probably had a bearing on the problems some of their organists caused.

Whether John Okeover, organist of Gloucester in 1640, actually resumed his post at the Restoration is uncertain. He is usually regarded as being the same person as the John Okeover who overlapped for a time as organist of Wells (q.v.), but there is no positive proof of this. Indeed, some conflicting details make more sense if the two are regarded as father and son, the former dying before 1649 (when 'widow Oker' was living in the choristers' house at Wells), the latter succeeding his father there at the Restoration. Whatever the case, there is no evidence that Okeover took up his position again at Gloucester in 1660, though he did receive £5 in 1662 for 'pricking of Anthems to the Organ'.[6] For a year or two there was no officially designated organist; in 1663 the new master of the choristers, Robert Webb, was described as 'probationer

---

[1] Eward, *No Fine but a Glass of Wine*; 118–19; this book contains a great deal of musical information over and above what follows, including lists of minor canons, precentors, lay clerks, choristers, and organists, 336–9. Details of personnel, stipends, and periods of service below are either from Eward or from my own examination of the Treasurer's Accounts (D 936 A 1/2–5) in the Gloucester County Record Office.

[2] Cheverton, 'English Church Music', 239 and 340–1; Eward, 124.   [3] Eward, 336–7.

[4] H. G[ee], *The Statutes of Gloucester Cathedral* (London, 1918), 7.   [5] Eward, 129.

[6] Ibid. 128–9; Brian Frith, 'The Organists of Gloucester Cathedral', in *The Organs and Organists of Gloucester Cathedral* (Gloucester, 1971), 51–2; Shaw, 119–20; see Roger Bowers et al., *The Organs and Organists of Wells Cathedral* (7th edn., Wells, 1979), 19.

organist', but he died early in 1664.[7] He was succeeded by Thomas Lowe from Salisbury the following year, but his period of tenure was also short, and he left in 1666, perhaps to return to Salisbury, or possibly London.[8]

By this time the old Dallam organ had been made serviceable. In 1662 it was bought back from the person to whom it had been sold during the Interregnum, and the next year 'Mr Taynton' (i.e. Robert Taunton) from Bristol was paid £10 for 'tuninge & settinge up the Organ'.[9] Plans were soon put in hand, however, to commission an instrument from Thomas Harris, and by the end of 1665 it had been installed in a gallery above the south side of the choir. The Bishop of Oxford contributed £10 'towards the Furniture stop'. Otherwise its specification is not known, but in some respects the Worcester organ which Harris was about to build is supposed to have been modelled on it.[10] In December it underwent trial by William King of New College, Oxford, and Thomas Deane of Bristol.[11]

On 6 December 1666, Daniel Henstridge, ex-chorister from New College, became organist,[12] doubtless with King's backing. He left Gloucester for Rochester in 1673, and later for Canterbury (q.v.), where he died at a ripe old age. In effect, his move to Rochester was an exchange of posts with Charles Wren, who had been organist there since about 1668. Wren was admitted at Gloucester on 19 January 1673/4 at a salary of £30, but his tenure was cut short by death in 1678.[13] Then, again briefly, came Daniel Roseingrave, who departed for Winchester (q.v.) in 1682 *en route* for Salisbury and Dublin.[14] He had been admonished 'for beating and wounding John Payne, one of the singing men' in 1679, and also blotted his copy-book by marrying the subdean's daughter.[15]

Surviving manuscripts at Gloucester give us an idea of how the repertoire developed during the years following the Restoration. Additions to the Barnard set suggest an input from both Wells and Salisbury.[16] Tenor and bass partbooks (MSS 106–7) include seven services and twenty-five anthems by William Child, while William King is strongly represented in several organ books (MSS 109–12), the earlier parts of which show by their transpositions that the organ was tuned to the old 10' pitch.[17] The principal hand is that of Henstridge, who has

---

[7] Eward, 129; Frith, 52–3; Shaw, 120–1.

[8] Eward, 133–4; Frith, 53; Shaw, 121. Thomas Lowe is listed in 1664 and again in 1668 as one of the vicars choral at Salisbury. Thomas Low, joint editor of *New Ayres and Dialogues* (London, 1678) with John Banister, and described as 'one of the vicars choral of Saint Pauls' may be the same man, though his appointment at St Paul's does not appear in the surviving records.

[9] Eward, 129–30; Michael Gillingham, 'Organs and Organ Cases of Gloucester Cathedral', in *The Organs and Organists of Gloucester Cathedral* (Gloucester, 1971), 3–4. The Worcester organ was to contain 'Two Open Diapasons of Metal, A ten foot pipe as at Sarum and Gloucester'; see Butcher, *Organs and Music of Worcester Cathedral*, 4.

[10] Eward, 130–3; Gillingham, 6–9.   [11] Eward, 133; Gillingham, 8.

[12] Eward, 134; Frith, 54; Shaw, 121.   [13] Frith, 55; Shaw, 121.

[14] Frith, 55; Shaw 121–2.   [15] Eward, 134; see also *DNB*.

[16] Cheverton, 340–3, 381–2.   [17] See above, n. 9.

Ex. 58. Charles Wren, *O give thanks* (*Ob Tenbury* 1176 - 82)

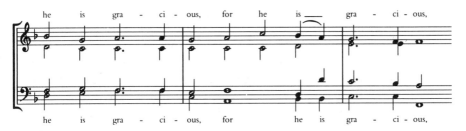

(1) Tenor has *c' c'* in original.

three anthems in MS 111. Wren has two in MS 112; *O give thanks unto the Lord*, dated 1672 and presumably written while at Rochester, is a full anthem alternating four-part homophony with simple points of imitation. Gostling, as a fellow Cantaburian, thought it worth transcribing into one of the Tenbury sets of partbooks (MSS 1176–82; Ex. 58). The other piece, *Look shepherd, look*, is a Christmas dialogue between an angel and two shepherds, written in a rambling, old-fashioned declamatory style. *I beheld, and lo*, attributed to 'Mr Wren' at Worcester, may, for geographical reasons, be by this composer, rather than his brother Robert, who was organist at Canterbury from 1675 to 1691.

Having got rid of one troublesome organist in the shape of Daniel Roseingrave, the Dean and Chapter proceeded to appoint another. Stephen Jefferies was, if anything, even more incorrigible than Roseingrave, yet he managed to hang on to his job for thirty years. His memorial stone in the east cloister gives his date of death as 25 January 1712/13 and his age as 54. He was a chorister at Salisbury under Wise, a lay vicar from 1673, and deputy organist in 1677 during Wise's absences.[18] He took up his position at Gloucester on 17 May 1682 and over the years his eccentric behaviour plagued the authorities. He was frequently admonished for neglecting his duties, and the famous occasion in 1689 when he gave offence by playing a 'common ballad' as a retiring voluntary has already been mentioned (see p. 56). Nevertheless, Jefferies survived another twenty years or so in the post without completely mending his ways. To this day, the cathedral bells play a tune by him.[19]

Parts of a *Magnificat* and *Nunc dimittis* in E minor and four anthems by him are in the cathedral library. Unfortunately, little can be made of them because of their fragmentary nature, though the service is in triple time throughout, and, as one might expect, alternates verse and chorus sections. Conflicting attributions to both Jefferies and Michael Wise raise a doubt as to its authorship, but the fact that it survives only at Gloucester favours Jefferies as the composer. Of the anthems, the most substantial are a coronation anthem, *O Lord save the queen*, presumably written in 1702, and a thanksgiving anthem for the battle of Ramillies, *I will love thee, O Lord my strength*, dated 27 June 1706. The latter is a suitably jubilant work in which the opening triple-time passage returns several times as a refrain, with solo verses for tenor, bass, and countertenor.

Jefferies may have been incapacitated towards the end of his life, for already in 1708 William Hine was described as 'the new organist' even though his official appointment did not take place until 1710.[20] Born at Brightwell, Oxfordshire, in 1687, he had been a chorister and lay clerk at Magdalen College, Oxford, whence he was dismissed 'propter fornicationem, manifestam et scandalosam'. He later went to London to study with Jeremiah Clarke. Unlike his two predecessors at Gloucester, and despite his somewhat blemished early reputation, Hine was a success with the Dean and Chapter, who voluntarily raised his stipend in appreciation of his personal and musical qualities (according to his memorial). He died 28 August 1730.

His widow published by subscription a collection of his work entitled *Harmonia Sacra Glocestriensis* [1731], including three anthems and the well-known *Jubilate* written as a companion piece to Henry Hall's *Te Deum* in E flat. It is difficult to see what it was about Hall's piece that prompted Hine to join his own—a somewhat bigamous liaison in any case, since there was already a legitimate partner back in Hereford. Modest competence apart, it is even more difficult to see why the resulting pair known as 'Hall and Hine' became so popular, and even spawned bastard progeny by Hine's pupil William Hayes, and by William Raylton of Canterbury (see under Canterbury). Hine's *Jubilate* has none of the older harmonic features of Hall's *Te Deum*, and lacks its occasional

---

[18] Eward, 184–5, 216–17; Frith, 55–7; Shaw, 122, 263.
[19] Eward, 193.   [20] Ibid. 215–17; Frith, 57–8; Shaw, 123.

Ex. 59. William Hine, *Save me, O God, for thy name's sake*
(*Harmonia sacra Glocestriensis*, 1731)

richness—all is bland. The full sections adopt a tuneful triple time, but the
common-time verses get caught in sequences a bit too easily—most lamentably
at the passage 'we are his people and the sheep of his pasture'. The anthems,
however, are more interesting. At least two of them, the solo anthem *Save me,
O God* and *Rejoice in the Lord, O ye righteous*, can be dated before 1720. In
general, they exhibit neo-Purcellian features inherited second-hand via Croft,
though on a smaller scale. He is fond of ground basses (not always capably
managed) and of lyrical triple-time solos and duets in minor keys (which usually

are). His familiarity with Purcell's vein of expressive recitative, toned down, is illustrated by the opening of *Save me, O God* ('for a Boy Solo'), particularly its melodic line and points of harmonic colour (Ex. 59). The B minor modulating ground which follows also has a Purcellian flavour, despite clumsy moments. A brief chorus intervenes before two triple-time verses respectively in E minor and E major. It is here that the influence of Jeremiah Clarke may be detected, especially in the smoothly unfolding vocal line, tastefully embellished with brief passages of coloratura. At such times Hine pleases most; similarly in the anthem *Rejoice in the Lord*, at the G minor duet ('The counsel of the Lord shall endure for ever'), which, for all its predictability, is charming. Elsewhere, there is a good deal of dotted-note cheerfulness and some bass bluster. In *I will magnify thee, O God my king*, C major and florid trumpet figuration emphasize the bombastic element, while two C minor movements towards the end provide a welcome change of mood—a trio with strong echoes of Purcell over a chromatically descending bass ('The memorial of thine abundant kindness') and another ground, this time with Handelian overtones ('The Lord is gracious'). The return to C major at the trio 'All thy works praise thee' leading into the concluding Alleluia makes a fine effect. Indeed, the work as a whole is impressive, and though it may falter here and there, its confidence carries the day.

Hereford

Although there were twenty-seven vicars choral of Hereford when they were incorporated in 1395 (and, a century later, twenty-seven small two-roomed houses to accommodate them in the vicars' cloister), their numbers were reduced in the sixteenth century.[1] The statutes of 1637 confirmed this state of affairs:

We ordain that there always be chosen twelve Vicars Choral, four sub-Canons, whom anciently they used to call Deacons and sub-Deacons, one to teach the boys Music and play upon the Organ, seven singing-boys whom they call Choristers, of such skill in Music as may suffice for performing that duty . . .[2]

The vicars were to be in holy orders, but the sub-canons 'by our authority may be laymen'.[3] Of the vicars, six were expected to sing in the choir, among them two 'Diddlebury vicars' (so called after the parish whose revenues they enjoyed). Of the boys, five were maintained by the Dean and Chapter, and two by the vicars from their income.

The vicars lived a collegiate life at Hereford longer than anywhere else in England and it was only in 1875 that their common table was discontinued. (The corporation itself was not disbanded until 1937.) In addition to their lodgings in the cloister, their buildings included a chapel with library above, and hall with various offices pertaining. At their head they elected a custos, and from among their number appointed two collectors of rents, two auditors, and two clavigers to manage their financial affairs. One of the vicars was 'steward of the buttery', and college servants included a butler, cook, brewer, and baker. Married vicars did not live in college and their rooms were sometimes leased to laymen, for example, to the sub-canons, who were regarded as commoners of the college. Despite the vicars being in holy orders, their moral reputation was not always high: cards, gambling, and drinking (or worse) gained them a reputation for 'conviviality and worldliness'. They also pursued more innocent

---

[1] Barrett, *College of Vicars Choral at Hereford Cathedral*, gives a brief history of the college of vicars from 1395 to 1937.

[2] J. Jebb and H. W. Phillott, *The Statutes of the Cathedral Church of Hereford, promulgated A.D. 1637* (Oxford, 1882), 41; Arthur T. Bannister, *The Cathedral Church of Hereford* (London, 1924), 166; Barrett, 8–9, 19–20. See also Payne, *Provision and Practice*, 181–4, etc.

[3] Jebb and Phillott, 13.

pleasures, and their music club in the early eighteenth century may have contributed to the foundation of the Three Choirs Festival.[4]

At the Restoration seven vicars were still alive and five more were promptly appointed, including John Badham, the new organist.[5] His admission dates from September 1660, but what there was then, or was to be, by way of an organ is hard to establish. Probably the pre-war Dallam organ was made serviceable, and various payments record the effort to keep it so.[6] Badham died in 1688, but from 1679 he seems to have been assisted by Henry Hall, one of Purcell's contemporaries as a chorister of the Chapel Royal, briefly organist of Wells and latterly of Exeter (q.v.). On 27 June he was granted £20 a year for 'assisting the organist, instructing the choristers thrice a week and assisting in the choir'. By the end of 1679 he had taken holy orders and been admitted vicar choral, but his official appointment as organist did not take place until 15 September 1688.[7] By this time the Renatus Harris organ of 1686 had been built at a cost of £515, with a further £70 for the case. Apart from the fact that it was a two-manual instrument, nothing is known about its specification, though some time later Harris may have added a trumpet stop.[8]

Hall died on 30 March 1707 'in his 51st year' and was succeeded by his son, Henry Hall the younger, 'from Ludlow', whose tenure lasted only until 1714. He died on 21 January that year, aged 27 or 28. Unlike his father he was not a vicar choral, nor was his successor Edward Thomson, who left Hereford to become organist of Salisbury Cathedral in 1718.[9]

There are now no partbooks at Hereford earlier than the first decade of the eighteenth century, but a set of Barnard's *Church Musick* at Christ Church, Oxford (MSS 544–53), came originally from Hereford and contains many manuscript additions reflecting the repertoire prior to Hall's period as organist.[10] Local composers represented include Badham and Hugh Davies, his predecessor before the war, each with three anthems, and James Read, a vicar choral until 1686, with one. Other anthems are by Worcester composers, Richard Browne (3) and Richard Davis (3), and from Gloucester, Daniel Henstridge (3). Services by Hugh Davies, Badham, Read, and Mr Broad—either John or Thomas, both were vicars[11]—are also present. (John Broad was expelled from the college in 1670 'for living incontinently with one Elizabeth Fletcher' and allegedly fathering her child; an anthem by him is at Gloucester.[12] The fragmentary nature of the sources and especially the absence of an organ part make it difficult to assess this music, but so far as Badham is concerned, one might say that the payment of 10s. to him in 1666 'for encouragment for making an anthem' was an over-

[4] The above paragraph is based on Barrett.

[5] F. T. Havergal, *Fasti Herefordenses* (Edinburgh, 1869), 92; Shaw, 136–7.

[6] Watkins Shaw, *The Organists and Organs of Hereford Cathedral* (Hereford, 1976), 15.

[7] Shaw, 137–8.   [8] Shaw, *Organists*, 28–9.   [9] Shaw, 138.

[10] Cheverton, 'English Church Music', 408–12.   [11] Havergal, 92.   [12] Barrett, 22–3.

optimistic gesture.[13] Perhaps the verses 'for 3 boys' in *O Lord, thou hast searched me out* created an attractive sonority; it is difficult to say more.[14]

Later sources at Hereford include a number of organ-books dating from the early eighteenth century, some in the hand of Henry Hall, senior, and all representing him strongly. The repertoire includes anthems by the usual Restoration composers, Wise, Humfrey, Blow, Purcell, and the like, and contemporary works by Clarke, Croft, and Weldon. Apart from Hall, the only local composer seems to be 'Mr Husbands'—presumably William or Thomas of that name; both were vicars—whose Service in D minor is in MS 30.B.X.[15] Most of the books have anthems at one end, services at the other, but two also contain organ voluntaries by Blow, Froberger, Kerll, Pollaroli, etc.[16]

In Henry Hall, Hereford acquired a real composer—the most distinguished between John Bull and S. S. Wesley. At least twenty-eight anthems by him survive in the books at Hereford, Gloucester, and Worcester, and in scores further afield, as well as five services and a *Benedicite*. As we have seen, his period at Hereford began in 1679, and during his years there he built up a reputation, not only as a musician, but also as a witty poet, a convivial fellow, and a 'rank Jacobite'.[17] Wistfully he reflected on what he was missing (and had to put up with) so far from London in his commendatory poem to Blow's *Amphion Anglicus* (1700):

> Thus while you spread your Fame, at Home I sit,
> Amov'd by Fate, from Melody and Wit,
> Whe[re] *British* Bard on Harp a *Treban* plays,
> With grated Ears I saunter out my days.
> *Shore*'s most Harmonious Tube, ne'er strikes my Ear,
> Nought of the Bard, besides his Fame, I hear:
> No Chaunting at St. *Paul*'s, regales my Senses,
> I'm only vers'd in *Usum Herefordensis*.

As a composer of services, Hall is something more than senior partner in 'Hall and Hine'—a pairing of Hall's E flat *Te Deum* with a *Jubilate* by William Hine of Gloucester that seems to have come about early in the eighteenth century, and achieved wide circulation (Arnold, iii). Two or three composers, William Hayes and William Raylton among them, even saw fit to complete the service by adding evening canticles and a communion setting (see under Canterbury and Gloucester). Despite a few false relations, the *Te Deum* is mild enough to

[13] Shaw, 137.

[14] Badham's *Defend us, O Lord* is reconstructed in Cheverton, 'English Church Music', Musical Supplement, 49–51.

[15] Havergal, 92.

[16] Barry Cooper, 'Keyboard Sources in Hereford', *Royal Musical Association Research Chronicle*, 16 (1980), 135–9.

[17] Barrett, 22.

account for its attractiveness to eighteenth-century composers. Ironically, MS 30.A.XXX actually contains, not only the *Te Deum*, but a companion *Jubilate* by Hall himself, so Hine and others might have saved themselves the trouble. A morning and evening Service in F, and a *Magnificat* and *Nunc dimittis* in G are in MS 30.B.X, and the score of a B flat *Cantate* and *Deus misereatur* in MS 30.B.II. Tudway's collection includes a hybrid 'Service in E flat', consisting of the famous *Te Deum*, a *Benedicite* in C minor mainly in triple time, and the B flat canticles in question (*Harl.* 3740). The composer can hardly have intended them to go together, but the *Cantate* and *Deus misereatur* clearly form a pair since they share the same Gloria. A further Service in G minor survives almost complete in the hand of John Walter of Eton.[18] Judging by the names of singers involved—Barnes, Edwards, Howell, and Williams—it must have been sung in the Chapel Royal early in the eighteenth century.

Early anthems by Hall can be identified in a number of manuscripts beyond Hereford. Prior to 1678 Stephen Bing had entered two into his partbooks (*Y* M.1.S)—*By the waters of Babylon* and *God standeth in the congregation*. *My soul is weary* had been copied into Cambridge, Fitzwilliam Museum MS 117 by 1683, and six further anthems had been entered into the Worcester partbooks before 27 March the same year, including *I will cry unto the Lord*, *O be joyful in God*, and *When the Lord turned* (MS A.3.5). These are not the only anthems known to be early, but they have been mentioned because they survive in score. *By the waters of Babylon* was the one that circulated most widely, and one of the earliest. The text was a poignant reminder of Charles II's exile, as also of the church's during the Interregnum. This may be why it was set so frequently. Hall's setting invites comparison with the settings of Wise and Humfrey, although not directly modelled on either (Ex. 60).[19] Stylistically it falls somewhere between the two. The declamation is bolder than Wise's, yet conceived more melodically than Humfrey's. The harmonic language, too, goes beyond Wise's and is more or less on a par with Humfrey's. On the whole the setting lacks the latter's dramatic feeling; nevertheless it makes a very positive impression.

Hall's subsequent development mirrors the change that anthem-writing underwent in the 1680s and 1690s. It is not difficult to recognize the end-point of the process, but without hard evidence as to dating, transitional works may be identified only tentatively. It is probable that *O Lord, rebuke me not* (*Cu* Ely 20) is one such work. The declamation in the verse 'My soul is also troubled' is particularly fine and shows a marked development beyond the technique of *By the waters of Babylon*, without, as yet, much hint of the florid style (Ex. 61). The word-setting is expressive and natural, as is the harmony—particularly the intensification of feeling caused by the rising chromaticism at the repeated

---

[18] Chichester, Cap. VI/I/I (West Sussex Record Office).
[19] For Wise's see Michael J. Smith, 'The Church Music of Michael Wise' (D.Mus. diss., University of Edinburgh, 1970), ii. 44–52; for Humfrey's see *MB* 34, 6–21.

Ex. 60. *By the waters of Babylon* (a) Michael Wise (*Lbl* 39032);
     (b) Pelham Humphrey (*Harl.* 7338);
     (c) Henry Hall (*Harl.* 7340)

phrase 'how long'. In general, the anthem is still somewhat restricted in its gestures, however. Later works show expansionist tendencies, such as more variety in the verses, a wider harmonic range, and more flamboyant character.

Of the anthems surviving in score, seven are probably late works: two are in Tudway's sixth volume (*Harl.* 3742) and five in Flackton's collection (*Lbl* 30931). Tudway's are a well-contrasted pair. *The souls of the righteous* adopts the pathetic style, with plenty of drooping thirds and sixths between countertenor and tenor over the bass, while *Comfort ye my people* is much grander, with many striking things in it, as well as some that jar.[20] The choral writing is in five and six parts (unprecedented for Hall), and, though his technique can barely cope, the use of high and low semi-chorus in contrast with the full choir produces an exciting effect. Inevitably he tries something special for the passage 'And the voice said, cry, What shall I cry? All flesh is grass', etc. The chromaticism on

[20] *Comfort ye* has been edited by Percy Young (New York, *c.*1977).

Ex. 61. Henry Hall, *O Lord, rebuke me not (Cu* Ely 20)

'cry' is, perhaps, just crude, though the reason for it is clear. However, the dramatic concept of what follows is gripping; a tenor sings 'All flesh is grass, and the goodliness thereof is as the flower of the field', while his companions reiterate the question 'What shall I cry?' separately and together. In turn they lament 'The grass withereth', repeating the phrase a tone higher each time, as if the thought was becoming increasingly unbearable, until reassurance comes with triple time at the words 'But the word of our God shall stand for ever.'

Signs of early eighteenth-century bombast are evident in the Flackton anthems, particularly *Why do the heathen* and *The Lord even the most mighty God*—the latter a solo anthem for treble with some florid descriptive passages that it is difficult to imagine a boy doing satisfactorily. Perhaps the most successful is *Blessed be the Lord my strength*. The belligerent text suggests that this may have been a thanksgiving anthem for one of Marlborough's victories. The opening bass solo in F minor is another fine piece of declamation, while in the verse 'Bow the heavens' the same voice vividly portrays the passage 'touch the mountains, and they shall smoke. / Cast forth thy lightning, and tear them: shoot out thine arrows, and consume them', though by Purcell's standards the effect is almost restrained. The chorus 'Thou hast given victory unto kings' continues the warlike mood, but at the words 'and hast delivered David thy servant from the peril of the sword' there is a change to triple time and a more lyrical expression. Unusually for Hall, though no doubt appropriately, there is a concluding Hallelujah chorus, rather four-square, but punctuated with some dramatic pauses.

Hall's music deserves more attention than has been possible here; undoubtedly it will repay further study. The fact that roughly half his anthems survive in score suggests that his work was widely admired, not only *By the waters of Babylon*. His son, too, was a composer—and, like his father, something of a poet. There is doubt as to which of them one or two anthems should be attributed, but in any case there are no more than four in all, and none in score.

Lichfield

Lichfield probably suffered more than any other English cathedral in the Civil War. The precincts were besieged three times, and on the third occasion, in 1646, the central spire was destroyed—as was the organ. At the Restoration, the chapter house and vestry were the only parts that were still roofed. But under John Hacket, bishop from 1662 to 1671, great progress was made in repairing the edifice, so that by 1666 the roof was on and the spire complete. An organ was ordered at a cost of £600, 'to be called the Ladies' Organ . . . because none but the honourable and most pious of that sex shall contribute to that sum'. Traditionally, this organ has been claimed for Bernard Smith, but in view of the fact that, according to Hackett writing in 1668, 'the maker of our organ . . . is detained about the organ of Whitehall', it was probably one of the Dallams. (Robert Dallam had built the cathedral's 1639 organ.) By Christmas 1669 all was ready for the service of rededication.[1]

By that time, too, the vicars choral were up to establishment. Already by 1661 there were seven, by 1663 nine, and by 1664 fourteen.[2] Under statutes formulated in the 1660s though not promulgated until 1693, there were to be twelve vicars of whom five were priests and the remainder—including the organist—laymen.[3] The number of choristers was set at eight. The daily round began with early morning prayers in the Lady chapel at 6 a.m. in the summer and 7 a.m. in the winter, read by one of the priest vicars. Morning prayer was sung at 10 a.m. followed (on litany days) by the litany. Evening prayer was at 4 p.m.[4]

We know a good deal about the vicars of Lichfield from several lists that survive and from records of appointment.[5] Their role, both in the cathedral and as an independent corporation, has already received attention in Chapter 3, and various relevant documents will be found in Appendices B–D. They were not over-generously remunerated, for Lichfield was modestly endowed. However,

---

[1] The above paragraph is based on Kettle and Johnson, 'The Cathedral of Lichfield', 174–6, 180–1. For the organ, see Freeman, *Father Smith*, 182–3, and Herbert Snow, 'The Organs of Lichfield Cathedral', *The Organ*, 12 (1932–3), 98.

[2] Kettle and Johnson, 175.   [3] Ibid. 185.   [4] Ibid. 180.

[5] Lists dated 1683, 1688, 1690, and 1694 are in the cathedral library's countertenor decani copy of Barnard's *Church Musick*. Dates of appointment given below are from Vicars Choral Bonds, 1630–96 (Lichfield and Staffordshire Record Office, D.30.V.1) and Chorister Bonds, 1661–99 (D.30.V.2).

under William Lloyd, bishop from 1692 to 1700, an attempt was made to improve their finances, mainly by raising rents as leases expired. Low incomes forced many vicars to seek extra employment such as additional livings for those in orders and outside jobs for the laymen. The aim was to reduce the necessity for this by raising their basic pay to £40 a year. In fact, the rents alone were nowhere near enough to provide such an income; even with 'extras' priest vicars received only about £22 in 1718, and lay vicars about £20. These sums, however, might be doubled or even trebled in a good year through fines levied when leases came up for renewal. Whatever the vicars' corporate annual income might be, it was divided equally among them, save that a differential of £2 was preserved in favour of the priest vicars. The master of the choristers, however, received an extra £10 for teaching the boys, and the choristers were each paid £4 a year.[6]

Despite its limited resources, the cathedral music was probably in good shape for most of the period. It could boast a wide repertoire, drawn from the mainstream, supplemented by works from other provincial cathedrals and its own musicians. As to standards of performance we have Roger North's opinion, formed on a visit to Lichfield in 1676, that 'the service in that church was performed with more harmony, and less hudle, than I have knowne it in any church in England, except of late in St Paul's'.[7]

As far as we know, the first Restoration organist at Lichfield was William Lamb, though it is possible that 'Rich[ard] Hind organist', as he appears in the cathedral partbooks, may have served in the early years. (He was probably a relation of Henry Hinde, the pre-war organist, who died in 1641.) Following Lamb's appointment the succession remained firmly in the family until John Alcock took over in 1750. Lamb died in March 1688, when his son, also William, succeeded to the post. The latter had been a chorister from 1672 and is listed as the most junior vicar in 1683. By 1712 he had been followed, in turn, by his son George, a vicar since 1709, and said to have led 'a wicked unchaste life'.[8] In the mean time, the organ had been enlarged by Bernard Smith in 1680, at a cost of £100, and again in 1714 by Christopher Smith, this time by the addition of a new trumpet stop and a five-rank cornet costing £80. At the same time the opportunity was taken 'to make the organ regularly pitched, by sinking its tone a note lower'.[9]

Music from this period now in the cathedral library includes, most importantly, seven volumes of Barnard's *Church Musick*, with a considerable amount of manuscript music of the Restoration period bound in.[10] In addition, there

[6] Financial details from Kettle and Johnson, 179–80, 185.
[7] Wilson (ed.), *Roger North*, 41.   [8] Shaw, 147–8.
[9] Kettle and Johnson, 176; Snow, 99; see also Lichfield and Staffordshire Record Office, DC/P4.
[10] Cheverton, 'English Church Music', 38–9.

are numerous partbooks which follow on and cover the end of the century and the beginning of the next. Unfortunately, the incomplete and disorderly nature of these sources makes the task of assessing this music extremely difficult except when other sources can supply missing material. The Barnard set was acquired in 1662, bought in London on the instructions of Zachariah Turnpenny, the subchanter, by the antiquary Elias Ashmole, himself an ex-chorister of the Cathedral.[11] The manuscript additions include services by Aldrich, Blow, Bryne, Child, Humfrey, Loosemore, and Rogers, as well as others by out-of-the-way composers such as Beckinshaw, Loggins, Sargenson, Scattersgood, and Spencer—the last two, at least, local men. 'Scattersgood' was probably Samuel Scattergood, vicar of St Mary's, Lichfield, from 1678 to 1681, and from 1682 to 1696 one of the cathedral prebendaries.[12] His Service in F minor is dated 1679, and it may have been his standing as a well-connected cleric that recommended it to neighbouring Worcester, where it also survives. Sampson Spencer, who is represented by a Morning and Evening Service in C and an Evening Service in E minor, was a vicar choral from 1665 and one of the copyists responsible for these additions to Barnard. As for the others, we have already met John Sargenson as a minor canon of Canterbury; Beckinshaw may or may not be the quack-theorist John Birchensha, said to have been able to 'teach men to compose that are deaf, dumb and blind';[13] and Loggins was probably John Loggins, a chorister in the Chapel Royal up to 1666.[14] Although his name does not appear on the lists of vicars mentioned above, the presence of a service and two anthems in the cathedral partbooks may, in the absence of indications to the contrary, suggest a period of service at Lichfield before 1683. One of the anthems, *Be thou my judge, O God*, occurs in Durham MS B.1, in the hand of Richard Hosier of Dublin (q.v.), and reveals quite an accomplished composer having something in common with his erstwhile colleague Pelham Humfrey. The anthem is in two major sections, each ending with a chorus, and the verses alternate declamatory duets for tenor and bass with tuneful, triple-time solos—the latter characteristically ending with echoes of their closing phrases ('sing this repetition soft'). Technical competence apart, however, there is nothing strikingly memorable about the setting; the beginnings of the first two verses give a good idea of their capable style (Ex. 62).

Other anthems by local composers include three, plus a Burial Service, by Michael East, master of the choristers before the war, and three by Ralph Swift, Turnpenny's predecessor as subchanter. There are three anthems by Richard Hinde, about whom we have already speculated, and one by John Hinton, organist of Newark—a mainly chordal setting of *I will magnify thee, O God my*

---

[11] Ibid. 346–54.   [12] *DNB*.
[13] *NG* ii. 727–8 (Christopher D. S. Field).   [14] Ashbee, i. 74–6.

Ex. 62. John Loggins, *Be thou my judge, O God (DRc.* B.1)

king.[15] More recent work includes three anthems by William Lamb, one a setting of *Except the Lord build the house* which may have been written for the 1669 service of rededication, and another, *O Lord, make thy servant Charles*, also attributed to his son. It is difficult to separate the work of the two William Lambs, and not only the younger's from the elder's; a note against Beckinshaw's service says 'Mr Lamb [junior] stole this service and put his own name to it'.

The next set of partbooks (MSS 14–18) dates from *c.*1685–1715, and contains services and anthems by the usual Restoration composers up to and including Clarke and Croft. Among earlier pieces with local connections is *Have mercy upon me, O God* by 'Mr Ottey'—either Thomas or William, both briefly vicars in 1663 before moving on to Chester, and *O Lord, to whom vengeance belongeth* by Thomas or John Rathbone (the latter, son of Thomas, was a choirboy in

---

[15] Cheverton, 611–14; the Musical Supplement includes a reconstruction of Hinton's anthem, 159–60. Hinton, described as 'a rare musician and an excellent composer, and one who hath the reputation of a very sober, civil and quiet person', had been an unsuccessful candidate for the organistship of Lincoln in 1663 (Maddison, 'Lincoln Cathedral Choir', 43).

Ex. 63. Mathew Haines, *O praise the Lord, for it is a good thing* (LF 21)

Great   is   our   Lord,   and   great ___ is _ his _ pow'r, ___ yea his

wis - dom,   his   wis - dom,   yea his   wis - dom is in -   fin - ite.

- ite.   The   Lord set - teth up   the meek, ___ the   Lord set - teth up   the meek, ___

1685, later becoming a lay clerk at Chester and organist of Bangor in 1712). Services by Sargenson and Loggins were still being sung, and two further anthems are ascribed to William Lamb, without being more specific. Additions made after 1709 include two anthems by 'Mr C Bassano', who may be connected in some way with the Richard Bassano who was a vicar in 1680.

A later set of partbooks (represented by MSS 21 and 24), begun before Croft received his doctorate (i.e. 1713), brings another local composer, Matthew Haines, to our attention. Haines had been a chorister from 1685 and was appointed vicar in 1695, being 'a sober person and of a good life and conversation'. In 1728, however, the organist George Lamb, alleged that he was debauched and a drunkard, and 'for above these twenty years, has been guilty of that notorious practice of buggery, and has attempted it very lately'.[16] Six anthems by him are in these books. Again, reconstruction is problematical, but judging by the bass solo in *O praise the Lord, for it is a good thing*, which has a surviving organ part, Handel had made his mark in the Midlands (Ex. 63). The violinistic figuration makes a nice change from the trumpet idioms that composers were besotted with at this time, but sustaining and developing such a promising beginning was more than Haines could be expected to manage.

---

[16] Letter of George Lamb, 4 Oct. 1728; Lichfield and Stafford Record Office, DC/P3.

Lincoln

In pre-Reformation times the choir at Lincoln consisted of vicars choral (divided into seniors and juniors, or those of the first and second forms), poor clerks, and choristers. So rich and magnificent a cathedral could support a large choir, which in 1506 comprised at least twenty-six vicars, nine poor clerks, and twelve choristers.[1] The senior vicars were priests, the junior vicars were in minor orders, and the poor clerks (like the secondaries at Exeter) were often ex-choristers on the way to becoming vicars. Gradually, following the Reformation, the distinction between junior vicars and poor clerks began to disappear, and it became customary to augment a lay vicar's income with a poor clerk's place. In effect, the end result was the establishment of the typical three-tier arrangement of priest vicars, lay vicars (incorporating poor clerks), and choristers—some of whom were designated Burghersh chanters, since their endowment derived from the revenues of the Burghersh chantry, suppressed at the Reformation.[2] In 1600 there were four priest vicars, eight junior vicars, seven poor clerks (four of whom were also junior vicars), a master of the choristers, six choristers, and six Burghersh chanters.[3] Lieutenant Hammond's visit in 1634 mentions twelve singing men and eight choristers: 'the Organs, with other Instruments, suited to most excellent voyces, were all answerable to such a famous Cathedrall'.[4]

By the spring of 1661 the choir was up to strength, and numbers were maintained (more or less) throughout the Restoration period.[5] At the 1718 visitation the state of the musical establishment was as follows:[6]

1 There are four Senior Vicars which are in Priests Orders, Seven Junior Lay Vicars, and One Organist, four Choristars and seven Burghurst Chanters . . . whose places are all filled excepting one Junior Vicar . . .

6 There is a Steward of the Choristars by whom they are well ordered and provided for, they are instructed in vocal and Instrumental musick, and taught to write and Read,

---

[1] A. R. Maddison, *A Short Account of the Vicars Choral, Poor Clerks, Organists and Choristers of Lincoln Cathedral* (London, 1878), 70–89; further references are to Maddison, 'Lincoln Cathedral Choir', 41–55. See Payne, *Provision and Practice*, 185–7.

[2] Kirwan, *Music of Lincoln Cathedral*, 5; Srawley, *Origin and Growth of Cathedral Foundations*, 13.

[3] Payne, 186.   [4] Legg (ed.), *A Relation of a Short Survey*, 6–7.

[5] Maddison, 'Lincoln Cathedral Choir', 42; Kirwan, 9.

[6] Henry Bradshaw and Christopher Wordsworth, *Statutes of Lincoln Cathedral* (Cambridge, 1892–7), iii. 657–9.

and their Master is ordered to instruct them in the principles of Religion, and when their voices fail, they are usually put out to trades or otherwise provided for by the Dean and Chapter . . .

Both senior and junior vicars were members of the college of vicars: lay vicars were not excluded from vicarial offices, for although the precentor's nomination of John Blundeville as his succentor in 1665 was contested on the ground that he was a layman, it did not prevent him from becoming vice-chancellor.[7] The old vicars' houses had been demolished during the Civil War, and rather than rebuild them, it was decided to convert certain property to tenements for the junior vicars.[8]

Soon after the Restoration, a new house was built for the choristers, who lived there with their master and steward.[9] The former was responsible for teaching them 'to write, cast accounts, and prick song', but in 1690, following the unsatisfactory way the master had been performing his duties, the post was divided between masters of vocal and instrumental music.[10] It was also proposed 'that for the encouragement of Instrumental Music two public consorts may be performed, one in every Easter week, the other in the Audit week, to be directed by the Sub-Chaunter and the masters of vocal and instrumental music'. The sum of forty shillings was 'to be divided among such as perform their parts therein'.[11] Daily life for the choristers began with early morning prayers in the cathedral at 5 a.m. in summer (6 a.m. in winter), after which they returned to their house for breakfast, thence to the free grammar school until 9 a.m. They then went to the song school, practising until morning prayer. At one o'clock they returned to the grammar school where they remained until time for evening prayer at 3 or 4 p.m., depending on the season.[12]

Even before the Civil War, the organ at Lincoln had been described as 'old and naught'.[13] There is no record of it having been destroyed during the troubles, however, or of substantial refurbishment after the Restoration. Edward Darby, a local organ-builder, was at work on it in March 1663, and by October the time had arrived 'to painte and guild the fronts of both the organs and the Loft on which they stand . . . for the sum of £50'.[14] Hollar's engraving of the Lincoln choir about 1672 shows a double organ in a loft on the north side above the choir stalls. Whether this organ lasted until the repair and removal to the screen by Gerhard Smith in 1702 is not known.[15]

The pre-war organist, John Wanless, resumed his appointment, after the Restoration, but survived only to 1662. His successor was the ne'er-do-well Thomas Mudd, lately of Peterborough (q.v.), whose short stay at Lincoln

---

[7] Maddison, 44–5.   [8] Ibid. 45.   [9] Kirwan, 9.   [10] Maddison, 45, 50.
[11] Ibid. 51.   [12] Ibid. 46; Kirwan, 9.
[13] Andrew Freeman, 'The Organs of Lincoln Cathedral', *The Organ*, 2 (1922–3), 194.
[14] Ibid.; Maddison, 44.
[15] See Kirwan, pl. 9; Clutton and Niland, *British Organ* (1963), 165 and pl. 10.

culminated in March 1663 with his abuse of the precentor 'above hope of Pardon' and drunkenly interrupting a sermon so 'that now wee dare trust him no more with our organ'.[16] In his place, the dean, Michael Honywood, who had spent some of the Interregnum in Leiden and Utrecht, immediately introduced a Dutch organist, Andrew [Andreas] Hecht. He served until his death in March 1693, whereupon his son Thomas was offered the job at a salary of £30 a year.[17] However, he left almost immediately to become organist at Magdalen College, Oxford, and instead Thomas Allinson, a lay clerk from Durham, took up the post at £40 a year.[18] Following his death in February 1705, he was succeeded by George Holmes, also from Durham, who died in 1712.[19]

Contemporary with them was a succession of masters of the choristers that also contains some quite well-known names; for example, William Turner, who on leaving the Chapel Royal in September 1666 was sworn in as master in November 1667, when he can have been no more than 15 or 16—a sign of powerful court backing and support for a precocious talent.[20] Two years later he returned to London as a countertenor in the Chapel Royal, where he remained for the rest of his long life. His place at Lincoln was taken by John Reading, junior vicar and poor clerk since 1667,[21] who moved on to Chichester in 1675, thence to Winchester (q.v.) the following year. His successor was William Holder (not the one who was subdean of the Chapel Royal), and after him, John Cutts from 1684 to 1689, whose unsatisfactory teaching of the boys has already been alluded to.[22] The incident which finally caused his removal from office occurred in November 1689, when John Jameson, the vestry clerk, reported that 'on the 31st Oct. last, when Mr Thomas Wanlesse [an ex-chorister and soon to be organist of York Minster] was playing on the organ he [Jameson] went into the Quire to hear him play, and found Cutts with his dog there. On remonstrating, Cutts swore at him, had raised his cane, and would have struck him, had not Mr Henry Wanlesse been present, and prevented him'.[23] Cutts nevertheless remained a junior vicar and was retained as master of the instrumental music, his place as master of the choristers being taken by another junior vicar, William Norris.[24] Like Turner, Norris had been a chorister of the Chapel Royal.[25] His period as master lasted from 1690 until his death in July 1702, whereupon John Reading, junior, succeeded him.[26] Reading too had been trained in the Chapel Royal, and after a period as organist of Dulwich College returned to Lincoln in 1702 and took up the post his namesake (father or uncle?) had held thirty years earlier. Apparently the job of a city organist appealed to him more, however, and in 1705 he returned to London,

[16] Maddison, 42–3; Shaw, 159–60.   [17] Maddison, 44, 51; Shaw, 160–1.
[18] Maddison 51; Shaw, 161.   [19] Shaw, 161; Srawley, 13.
[20] Franklin, 'Anthems of William Turner', 13–15.   [21] Maddison, 45; Shaw, 76–7.
[22] Maddison, 49.   [23] Ibid. 49–50.   [24] Ibid. 51.
[25] Ashbee, ii. 8, 9, 138.   [26] Shaw, 161.

becoming organist of St John's, Hackney, in 1708 and of other city churches later.[27]

Most of the names already mentioned are represented in Restoration partbooks still surviving at Lincoln, none of which can be dated before about 1685. An earlier repertoire, however, is reflected in the contents of the Bing–Gostling Partbooks now at York Minster, mainly in the hand of Stephen Bing, a senior vicar at Lincoln between 1667 and 1672.[28] Bing had been a minor canon at St Paul's before the great fire, and returned to London in 1672 to become a lay vicar at Westminster Abbey, retaining at the same time his place at St Paul's until his death in 1681. From the present point of view the most significant section of these partbooks is that marked 'A Collection of such Anthems for verses as have bin made at Lincoln in the years 68, 69 & 70', which includes anthems by Turner (9), Hecht (6), and Cutts (4). The collection as a whole contains seven by Hecht and nine by Cutts, all of which were probably entered during Bing's time at Lincoln. Two anthems by Thomas Heardson, an ex-chorister and junior vicar, are also included.[29] The fact that there are eight partbooks in the set means that a considerable number of full anthems can be reconstructed, though the lack of an organ-book is a serious deficiency when it comes to the verse anthems.

The early partbooks now remaining in the cathedral library do not, unfortunately, include any complete sets. Earliest are a pair of bass partbooks (MSS 48 and 49) which, from time to time, were examined, signed, and dated by the succentor; thus we can follow the development of the repertoire over the years. Anthems by Blow, Turner, Wise, Hall, and Humfrey—but none by Purcell—had been introduced by 1686. Over the next five years several more by Blow were added, and a number by local men such as Norris, Hecht, Cutts, and Blundeville. By 1693, Purcell's *Blessed is the man, O Lord, rebuke me not*, and *Be merciful unto me, O Lord* had been entered, along with more by Norris, and others by Blow, Humfrey, Turner, etc. Croft had made an appearance with *The Lord is king* by 1698, and Clarke with *The earth is the Lord's* by 1700. Other Chapel Royal composers of the younger generation, such as Weldon and Church, continued to be added in the early years of the century, side by side with the work of local composers.

There is thus a sizeable repertory of music by Lincoln composers. Leaving aside William Turner, whose work has been considered earlier, the early Restoration period is represented by Hecht, Cutts, and Heardson,[30] the later by Norris, Allinson, Reading, and Holmes.

As we have seen, Andrew Hecht came from Holland in 1663 and served as organist for thirty years. Nine anthems by him are known, all but one verse

---

[27] Ibid. 77, 161; Dawe, *Organists of the City of London*, 136.

[28] Shaw, *Bing–Gostling Part Books*, 4–7; Maddison, 45.

[29] Maddison, 42, 47–8.   [30] Cheverton, 'English Church Music', 626–33.

anthems in a rather desultory style. On the other hand, a full anthem, *O God, whose never failing providence*, is both affecting and eloquent while it maintains the simple, chordal style of the opening—which, happily, is most of the time.[31] Unfortunately, the introduction of imitation towards the end at the words 'Through Jesus Christ our Lord' thins out the texture too much, and causes the piece to sag, though the situation is retrieved in time for the final, broad Amen. The effectiveness of his homophonic writing is well illustrated in a chorus from a verse anthem, *Haste thee, O God* (Ex. 64).[32] The duet for countertenor and bass which follows nicely conveys the feeling of confidence which the text introduces at this point, by moving into triple time and adopting a flowing melodic style. With the reversion to a more despondent mood in the next verse the declamatory imitative style takes over.

So far as one can tell from the sources, the anthems of John Cutts do not measure up to Hecht's, though their general style is similar. Twelve anthems, mostly verse, are known, and two at least found their way to Durham. *I give you a new commandment* is a full anthem with rather dull counterpoint, though it begins effectively enough.[33] In verse anthems, triple-time solos and duets are more coherent than those in common time; full sections are mainly homophonic.[34] The two anthems by Thomas Heardson in Bing's partbooks are both full. The opening of *Keep, we beseech thee, O good Lord*, in particular, promises much by way of expressive homophony, but loses its sense of direction as it progresses—indeed, 'progress' soon becomes 'meander'.[35]

Taken together, these composers comprise a modest group of musicians only mildly influenced by modern trends, despite Turner's presence among them. The second group of composers, led by William Norris, presents a very different aspect. As already mentioned, he was an ex-chorister of the Chapel Royal, and was listed among those singing at the coronation of King James II in 1685.[36] Within a few months his voice had broken; by September 1686 he was a junior vicar at Lincoln and four years later master of the choristers.[37] The cathedral partbooks include more than twenty anthems by him, all copied between August 1686 and April 1703. Nine of them occur elsewhere in score, mainly in British Library Add. MSS 31444 and 17840—the latter probably originating close to the composer (if not from the composer himself, in view of the initials 'W.N.' which sign some of the anthems). Over the years between 1687 and 1702 they develop from such works as *God sheweth me his goodness* and *Behold now praise the Lord*, with their modest dimensions, uniform tonality, and pre-

---

[31] Cheverton, 'Musical Supplement', 7–8.   [32] Ibid. 67–70.   [33] Ibid. 1–2.

[34] Payne, 294, identifies a John Cutts who was a lay clerk at Trinity College, Cambridge, from 1661 until his death in 1665. It seems unlikely that this Cutts could have been the composer of these anthems, but one of them (*My days are gone*) is found in a MS in the hand of George Loosemore, organist of Trinity College up to 1682 (*Lbl* 34203).

[35] Cheverton, 'Musical Supplement', 6.

[36] Zimmerman, *Henry Purcell: Life and Times* (1967), 125.   [37] Maddison, 51.

Ex. 64. *Andrew Hecht, Haste thee, O God* (Bing - Gostling Partbooks)

(1) Passages in square brackets are editorial.

dominant triple time, to the full-blown style of *I will give thanks*, dating from 1701–3, with its extended movement structure embracing related keys, expansive text treatment, and incipient recitative–air pairings.[38] This feature is especially noticeable in solo anthems such as *Blessed are those that are undefiled* (later published in the second book of *Divine Harmony* in 1717 but entered into the cathedral partbooks fifteen years earlier), in which declamatory verses alternate with more lyrical 'songs' employing patterned ostinato bass lines or strict ground basses. The work is in seven sections (the first and last in C major, the rest in C minor) and provides a good example of what has been called the 'cantata anthem'. The beginning of the third pair of movements is given in Example 65.

Norris's anthems are transitional between those of Purcell and those of Croft, while retaining some of the awkwardness one finds in Blow's attempts at the modern style. He was also the composer of two 'chanting services'—a species of service apparently invented by James Hawkins of Ely (q.v.), in which canticles were sung by alternating a harmonized chant (full) with varied verse sections. Norris's D major setting of the *Cantate* and *Deus misereatur*, in fact, consists of the verses from Hawkins's chanting service in the same key, but with a new chant by Norris. His Morning Service in G minor applies the principle to the *Te Deum* (modified to cope with the long text) and *Benedictus*.[39]

Norris's contemporary as organist was Thomas Allinson. He had been a chorister at Durham in the 1680s, and a lay clerk there from 1690 before coming to Lincoln in 1693.[40] The Lincoln partbooks contain two anthems by him, while the Durham partbooks supply parts of four others. Those that appear in Durham but not Lincoln were presumably written before 1693; those in Lincoln but not Durham are presumably later—but since all the sources are incomplete little more can be said. Judging by its date, the thanksgiving anthem *I will bless thee at all times* may have been written to celebrate the Battle of Blenheim in 1704.

By then, John Reading had become master of the choristers. Two anthems by him are in the Lincoln partbooks; one, *Unto thee, O Lord, will I lift up my soul*, reappears in his *Book of New Anthems . . . with a Thorough Bass figur'd for the Organ or Harpsichord with Proper Ritornels*, published about 1715, after his return to London. The contents include six capably written, multi-movement solo anthems in an up-to-date style, with elaborate ritornellos. In general, they are more typical of the kind of anthem sung in a London parish church than a provincial cathedral, and mention of the harpsichord on the title-page suggests an attempt to widen the market by inviting chamber or concert performances.

---

[38] The anthem was copied twice by Tudway (*Harl.* 7340 and 7341); see Frank Dawes, 'Philip Hart and William Norris', *Musical Times*, 110 (1969), 1074.

[39] Wilson, 'Anglican Chant and Chanting', 138–9.

[40] Crosby, *Catalogue of Durham Cathedral Music Manuscripts*, 103.

Ex. 65. William Norris, *Blessed are those that are undefiled* (*Divine Harmony*, ii[1717])

The most important Lincoln composer of this period is undoubtedly George Holmes. Before succeeding Allinson as organist in 1705, he had been organist to the bishop of Durham from 1698, and a chorister there before that.[41] A manuscript of keyboard music in his hand (*Lbl* 31446), compiled when he was organist to the bishop of Durham, has already been considered in Chapter 4. At least six anthems by him were copied into the Lincoln partbooks in the years following his appoinment, all of which (plus a Burial Service) are to be found in two score books of John Barker, now at Lichfield (MSS 10 and 12). Why Barker—who at the time of Holmes's death in 1721 was still a boy in the Chapel Royal—copied these works is a mystery, but the fortunate result is that, perhaps uniquely for such a composer, all his known anthems survive in score. According to dates in the partbooks, the earliest is *I will love thee, O Lord* (1707–8) with an almost Brahmsian opening in B flat—bass, tenor, and countertenor in dialogue with each other (Ex. 66a–b). The rest of the work is rather more typical of its period, with a short but vigorous G minor recitative for bass ('He hath delivered me from my strongest enemy') and an easy-going CTB trio in triple time ('He hath girded me with strength'). The treble solo 'Great prosperity gives he unto his king' presents some late-Purcellian pomposities, while the final chorus (which also occurs in the middle of the anthem) sings more than perfunctory praises.

This was one of two anthems by Holmes which Tudway included in the fifth volume of his collection (*Harl.* 7341); the other was *Arise and shine* (also in Page, iii), written about the same time to celebrate the 1707 Act of Union between England and Scotland. It too shows a confident manner and technique. It is a more spacious work, and—like many such occasional works—inclined to bluster, though at least it forgoes the trumpet syndrome. The overall key scheme begins in F and moves through movements in D minor, B flat major, G minor, and back to B flat before returning to the home key. *Hear my crying*, an anthem for treble solo, is from about the same time. It begins plaintively in A minor, but ends triumphantly in A major, with coloratura Hallelujahs that would have taxed any boy. There is plenty of florid writing too in a later solo anthem, *I will sing of thy power*, and some Purcellian 'recitative' (Ex. 67).

For the coronation of King George I in 1714 Holmes composed a setting of *Blessed is thy people*. Once again there is an impressive opening verse, followed by a varied series of movements including solos for tenor and bass, the latter built on a one-bar modulating bass ostinato with a right-hand organ part—again, very reminiscent of late Purcell. By contrast, *Hear my prayer, O God* is a full anthem in sombre C minor, mainly homophonic and highly expressive harmonically. The change from common time to triple at the words 'O that I had wings like a dove' introduces—surprisingly for this device—a feeling, not so

[41] Crosby, *Catalogue of Durham Cathedral Music Manuscripts*, 173.

Ex. 66. George Holmes, *I will love thee, O Lord, my strength* (LF 12)

much optimistic and reassuring, as urgent, almost ecstatic, partly the result of a quickening pulse, partly the change from G minor to G major, and partly the threefold repetition of the exclamation 'O!'. The same key, mood, and style characterize Holmes's fine setting of the opening sentences of the Burial Service,

Ex. 67. George Holmes, *I will sing of thy power* (LF 12)

which in its simple eloquence rivals Croft's. Possibly it was written for the burial of James Gardiner, bishop of Lincoln, in 1705.

Enough has been said here to suggest that Holmes's best work bears comparison with that of his London contemporaries, Clarke, Croft, and Weldon. There is little sign of clinging to old ways in his music; late Purcell represents his point of departure, and there is a boldness about his music that is compelling. But whereas his verse anthems are confident examples of a form and taste that await 'rediscovery', works like *Hear my prayer, O God* and the Burial Service enshrine a continuing ideal.

London

London's cathedral was St Paul's—a great medieval secular foundation and in 1660 the largest Gothic church in Europe. Just over a mile up-river was Westminster, where the abbey church of St Peter, dissolved at the Reformation, had been re-established in 1560 as a 'Royal Peculiar' with Dean and Chapter and a lavish choral and educational foundation. A few hundred yards to the north was the palace of Westminster, where the king had his court and Chapel Royal. And though it was there that the best musicians in the country were drawn, neither St Paul's nor the Abbey were thereby put in the shade; indeed, some of the leading lights of the chapel—Blow, Turner, Purcell, Clarke, and Croft—held appointments at one or the other institution in addition to their chapel places, and some of the best singers were members of all three choirs.

The music of the Chapel Royal has already been covered so far as the work of its major figures is concerned. It would have confused matters to have tried to split Purcell and Croft between the chapel and Westminster (and at the same time to have dealt with such minor figures as William Tucker, Christopher Gibbons, and John Church, who were also members of both establishments), or to divide Turner and Clarke between the chapel and St Paul's—not to mention Blow, who served all three institutions. It will now be possible to deal with the Abbey and St Paul's individually, and allow their separate characters to emerge. For each had a distinct and symbolic nature (as well as an independent musical life), the Abbey serving almost as a royal parish church where great ceremonies of state such as coronations and royal funerals took place, St Paul's—at least in its rebuilt state—providing a religious focus for a rich and populous city and, in a sense, the whole country.

WESTMINSTER ABBEY

The Abbey's musical establishment comprised six minor canons, twelve lay clerks and ten choristers, a master of the choristers, and an organist. Before the Civil War, and perhaps for a year or two after the Restoration, there had been cornetts and sackbuts too, the last cornettist dying in 1666. Records of individual payments indicate that the lay clerks received £10 a year, the master of the choristers a further £7. 5s., and the organist £18, but additional fees for numerous special occasions augmented these sums considerably.[1] In all probability the choir was up to strength for Charles II's coronation on St George's day (23 April) 1661, with Christopher Gibbons as organist, and the elder Henry Purcell as master of the choristers.[2] Already £120 had been spent in setting up the organ, and on 30 December 1669 Pepys noted 'the great confusion of people that came there to hear the organs'.[3] As happened elsewhere, the organist was expected to sing in the choir 'till towards the end of the Psalms (except on festival dayes when the Answeres [responses] are to bee performed with the Organ) then to goe upp the stayers leading from the quire to the organ and performe his duty',[4] though Gibbons, 'a grand debauchee' according to Wood, was said often to be asleep when it came to that point at morning prayers.[5] On the death of Henry Purcell senior in 1664, he became master of the choristers as well as organist, but retired from both posts two years later. His successor as master was Thomas Blagrave of the Chapel Royal; the new organist was Albertus Bryne, whose post at St Paul's had become something of a sinecure since the Great Fire.[6] John Blow succeeded him in 1668, but stepped down in favour of the younger Henry Purcell in 1679, only to take over again on Purcell's death in 1695.

The previous year, Bernard Smith had been ordered to refurbish the organ and 'add thereto a double sett of keys and 4 new stops, vizt, one principall of mettle, one stop diapason of wood, one nason of wood and one fifteenth of mettle'.[7] Despite the late date, this sounds like the addition (rather than replacement or enlargement) of a second manual to the old organ, making what must have remained rather a modest instrument, considering the importance of the institution. Blow continued as organist until his death in 1708 (concurrently with his appointments at the Chapel Royal and St Paul's), and was succeeded by William Croft. Among the lay clerks at this time were some of the most famous singers of the age—Josias Boucher (1682–1705), John Howell (1691–1708), John Freeman (1692–1736), Leonard Woodson (1697–1716), William Turner (1699–1740), and Richard Elford (1712–14), most of whom sang in the Chapel Royal and at St Paul's as well.

Soon after the Restoration the Abbey bought a set of Barnard's *Church Musick* (1642) and Henry Purcell senior was paid for providing 'books of services for

---

[1] Edward F. Carpenter, 'Restoration and Resettlement', in id. (ed.), *A House of Kings* (London, 1966), 183; William McKie, 'Music in the Abbey', ibid. 416; Pine, *Westminster Abbey Singers*, 114, 121, and 126. Typed lists of minor canons, lay clerks, organists, and masters of the choristers (with dates of service) extracted from Westminster Abbey records are in the Muniment Room.

[2] Zimmerman, *Henry Purcell: Life and Times* (1983), 7–8; Shaw, 331.

[3] Perkins, *Organs and Bells of Westminster Abbey*, 12–13; Pepys, *Diary*, i. 324.

[4] Pine, 120.   [5] Perkins, 14.   [6] Shaw, 331.

[7] Freeman, *Father Smith*, 14, 117.

the choristers' in 1661.[8] The following year Gibbons received payment for an organ-book, but the earliest surviving partbooks for the choir date from the 1670s. None of the early sets is complete, however. The first, comprising tenor and countertenor cantoris partbooks, is mainly in the hand of William Tucker (a minor canon and also, as we have seen, a gentleman of the Chapel Royal). Payments to him in 1677 probably refer to the copying of these books, which cannot be later because of the consistent attribution of numerous anthems to 'Mr Blow'. Apart from Blow, Tucker and Humfrey are the most frequently occurring composers, but six by Purcell are especially interesting as they must be among his earliest anthems (see Ch. 8). The second set is represented solely by a tenor decani book begun by Stephen Bing (a lay clerk, also a minor canon of St Paul's), who died 28 November 1681. He received various payments for copying between 1673 and 1679, and it is possible that the latter date refers to this set of partbooks. Like its predecessor it begins with services, but the works in Bing's hand are all old-fashioned, with only Child and Rogers among living composers. Between them these books give a good idea of the Abbey's repertoire during the years when Purcell was organist. Rather surprisingly, the works of Christopher Gibbons are poorly represented in them, only *The Lord said unto my Lord* being included, though Bing had nine more to hand in his private set of partbooks (the Bing–Gostling Partbooks).

Gibbons, son of the great Orlando Gibbons, was born in 1615.[9] Following his father's death in 1625 he was brought up by his uncle Edward Gibbons, a vicar choral at Exeter, and in 1638 became organist of Winchester Cathedral. In addition to his appointment as organist of the Abbey, he became one of the organists of the Chapel Royal at the Restoration and received various other court appointments. In 1664 he was made Doctor of Music by the University of Oxford, and though he relinquished his Abbey posts in 1666, he lived on for another ten years.

There are fourteen anthems by Gibbons surviving, but he is probably more important as a composer of keyboard and consort music. Most of the anthems are for one or two solo trebles with or without a bass voice and simple choruses in three or four parts between the verses. Three were printed in Playford's *Cantica Sacra* (1674), but the fact that most of his output is in the form of 'chamber' anthems has prompted the suggestion that most may not have been written for liturgical use.[10] Certainly some like *How long wilt thou forget me* (*Harl.* 7340) were in cathedral repertoires, but on the whole they did not circulate

[8] The following is partly based on notes by Margaret Laurie on the Westminster Abbey partbooks and their copyists kept in the Muniment Room at Westminster Abbey. Details of contents are drawn from my own inventories; see also Shaw, *Bing–Gostling Part Books*, 107–11.

[9] *NG* vii. 352–3 (Christopher D. S. Field).

[10] Cheverton, 'English Church Music', 679–82.

widely. It may well be that they were intended for private devotional use, perhaps before the Restoration; their style is certainly early.

William Tucker is one of the most interesting musicians associated with the Abbey in the early years of the Restoration. He even wrung the accolade 'ingenious dilettante' from Burney.[11] As has already been mentioned, he was also a gentleman of the Chapel Royal and employed in both places as a copyist. Moreover, he was quite a prolific composer with numerous anthems in cathedral partbooks far afield—Durham, Ely, Gloucester, Lichfield, Oxford, and Winchester among them. Perhaps only Michael Wise among 'new' composers enjoyed such a wide dissemination of his works at this time, and partly for the same reason, since both wrote modestly and when there was as yet little available in a contemporary idiom for choirs of limited ability. Tucker's circulation was boosted by his own activity as a copyist, for in seeking to obtain up-to-date music by London composers, provincial precentors would contact Tucker to furnish them with suitable material. Thus, in 1669, the Chapter of Peterborough paid £3. 2s. for 'a dozen anthems procured by Mr Dean and transcribed by Mr Tucker of Westminster',[12] in all probability including some of his own.

Possibly he was the son of Edward Tucker, organist of Salisbury earlier in the century, but wherever he came from, by 1661 he was one of the priests of the Chapel Royal and a minor canon of Westminster Abbey. He served in both capacities until his death on 28 February 1679.[13] Three services and at least sixteen anthems by him are known,[14] the most complete source being the Bing–Gostling Partbooks, which contain thirteen anthems, a 'Benedicite Service' in F, and a short Service in D minor. Tudway included two anthems by Tucker in his collection, and Ely and Peterborough were among cathedrals still singing his music in the eighteenth century; indeed, his anthems continued to be copied in the nineteenth century. The most widespread is *O give thanks unto the Lord, and call* (Page, i), a rather four-square full anthem in five parts, competent but lacking the rhythmic impetus and textural variety of the six-part *O clap your hands* in the Bing–Gostling Partbooks, which is actually quite an exciting piece.[15] Most of the others are verse anthems, capably written but musically undemanding. He is particularly fond of verses for two trebles above a bass, the upper voices answering each other in dialogue, then singing together in thirds. There is nothing flamboyant. He shows a firm sense of tonality and his choral writing is effective. His agreeable style is well illustrated by *Wherewithall shall a young man cleanse his way*, the opening of which is given in Example 68.

With Blow, Purcell, and Croft organists of both the Abbey and the Chapel Royal, and many singers common to both, the repertoires of the two places

[11] Burney, *History*, 478. [12] Cheverton, 575. [13] *NG* xix. 247 (Watkins Shaw).
[14] Cheverton, 688–90. [15] Cheverton, 'Musical Supplement', 31–4.

Ex. 68. William Tucker, *Wherewithal shall a young man* (*Ob* Mus. Sch. c. 40)

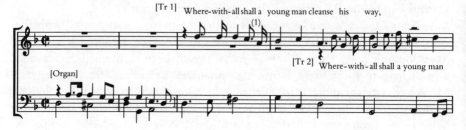

(1) ♪ ♪ in source.

effectively merged. Individual works may have been intended specifically for one or the other, but if so, there is now no telling—except that symphony anthems would not have been performed in the Abbey, other than at coronations. John Church, however, may claim attention as an Abbey composer, for although he also belonged to the Chapel Royal, he served as master of the choristers of Westminster for many years, a post that for present purposes may be taken as determining his principal allegiance.

Church is said to have been born in Windsor in 1675, but whether he was a chorister there or at Oxford (St John's and New College have both been claimed) is not known.[16] He became a gentleman of the Chapel Royal and a lay clerk of Westminster Abbey in 1697. His appointment as master of the choristers dates from 1704 and continued until 1740; according to the Abbey records he died early in 1741. He was principal music copyist both there and at the Chapel Royal. His characteristic hand with its easily identifiable bass clef can be seen in the chapel's early eighteenth-century partobooks (*RM* 27.a.1–15) and the Abbey's 'second' and 'third' set of partbooks, as well as several important secular sources (including the Westminster Abbey copy of Blow's *Venus and Adonis*).

From the contents of the 'third set' of Westminster partbooks it appears that during Church's time more Purcell was added to the repertoire, as well as works by himself and 'Mr' (later 'Dr') Croft. His own output totals at least two services

---

[16] *NG* iv. 383 (Margaret Laurie); see also Rimbault, 225; John S. Bumpus, *A History of English Cathedral Music, 1549–1889* (London, 1908), i. 213; *DNB*.

and twenty anthems, among which *O Lord grant the queen a long life* (*Harl.* 7341) is probably one of the earlier ones, assuming it was written for Queen Anne's accession (1702). Eight others, some carrying dates between 1704 and 1707, are in two Gostling sources (*Ob* Tenbury 1179–81 and *US-Cn* 7A/2). The inclusion of five of these anthems in *Divine Harmony* (1712), which Church may have compiled himself, confirms an early date, while later word-books of 1724 and 1736 add others that may be regarded as 'middle' or 'late'.

Examination of this music (in *Harl.* 7341 unless otherwise stated) shows Church to have been a respectable if unremarkable composer. The judgement seems particularly relevant to the F major Service, which hardly justifies Bumpus's comment that it 'shows great fertility of invention, and proves its writer to have been a thorough master of the resources of counterpoint'.[17] He is certainly rather keen on canons in his services (shades of Purcell), but the observation would have been nearer the mark applied to the E minor Service, in which effectively written verses in up to six parts provide the textural variety lacking in the other work. As a contrapuntist Church can be somewhat unrelenting, but the full anthem *Righteous art thou, O Lord* (Ex. 69), dating from about 1706, provides a competent enough example. Despite its rich C minor, however, there is a lack of harmonic interest and little sense of polyphonic growth, though the piece goes through the proper motions.

Most of the early verse anthems are over-wedded to triple time and the tonic key to be noteworthy for their date, but a work like *I will give thanks unto thee, O Lord* (*Lbl* 30932), which is earlier than 1713, shows more progressive tendencies, particularly in its tonal scheme (C–Em–C–Cm–C) and contrasted movement structure. Ground basses begin to make their appearance, and *Blessed are those that are undefiled* (*Harl.* 7342) has two, one strict, the other modulating. Surprisingly perhaps, virtuoso vocal writing is fairly rare.

There are no surprises in Church's work, no grand gestures—not even empty ones. On the other hand, he does not seem to have been drawn to the pathetic vein, either. The workmanship is sound, the scale modest, the content musical but unadventurous. Technically he was strongly influenced by Purcell, but completely lacked his imaginative qualities.

ST PAUL'S CATHEDRAL

Old St Paul's was destroyed in the Great Fire of London which attacked the cathedral on 3 September 1666. There were plans at first to restore it, as Inigo Jones had done a generation earlier, but it was decided instead to demolish the ruins and build a new cathedral. The foundation stone of Wren's building was

---

[17] Bumpus, 213.

Ex. 69. John Church, *Righteous art thou, O Lord* (Harl. 7341)

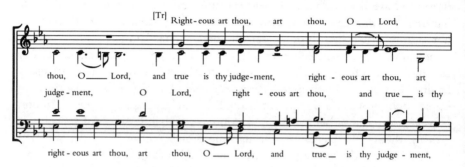

laid in 1675, but although the choir was finished and officially opened on 5 December 1697, it was not until 1710 that the vast building was completed. Over a period of sixty years the cathedral had seen restoration, destruction, and resurrection; so had its music, which by the beginning of the eighteenth century was pre-eminent in the country outside the Chapel Royal. In fact, as we have seen, the most famous names connected with the cathedral at this time—John Blow, William Turner, and Jeremiah Clarke—were gentlemen of the Chapel Royal, as were many of the choir. Their work has been dealt with earlier under that heading.

At the Restoration the choir was reconstituted in accordance with the statutes: twelve minor canons (the three senior of which held the offices of subdean, senior cardinal, and junior cardinal) and six vicars choral.[18] (St Paul's was peculiar in having minor canons and vicars in its choir; both were independent corporations but the minor canons were senior and supposed to be in holy orders, though often they were not.) Presumably the boys were also brought up to their full number of ten. In 1661 the minor canons included Stephen Bing and Randall Jewitt as cardinals, the latter also serving as almoner (master of the choristers). At a later date these well-paid posts became attached to the organist, but at this stage the organist (Albertus Bryne) was still a vicar choral in the first instance. The pre-war organ is thought to have survived to the Restoration despite damage to the organ loft. Repairs, however, were hindered by 'divers persons, [who] to enrich themselves, have sacrilegiously converted to their own private use and advantage, the Organs and Bells . . . and other materials heretofore prepared for the repair thereof'.[19] Nevertheless, from James Clifford's *Divine Services and Anthems* (1663) it appears that the organ was used both for accompanying the choir and playing voluntaries. Pepys was not impressed by the choir at this time; on 28 February 1664 he wrote in his diary 'before and after the sermon I was most impatiently troubled at the Quire, the worst I ever heard'.[20]

Clifford was one of the minor canons, and the second edition of his book (1664) is informative about the repertoire and the way the services were performed in the years before the fire. Among its contents are the words of anthems by a significant number of St Paul's composers, not only Bryne and Jewitt, but others including Richard Price, Lawrence Fisher, and Simon Ives, all of whom were either minor canons or vicars choral.

Of these, Jewitt will be dealt with in connection with Winchester Cathedral, where he went as organist following the Great Fire. Bryne, although he moved to Westminster Abbey after the fire, is more appropriately considered here. He is reputed to have been a chorister of St Paul's and to have succeeded John Tomkins as organist in 1638 'about the age of 17 yeares'. During the Commonwealth he had made a reputation as a 'velvet fingered organist', but at the Restoration he failed to gain appointment as organist of the Chapel Royal, despite petitioning the king for it. Instead he resumed his place at St Paul's, and continued to receive his stipend until 1671, though he had probably died three years earlier.[21] None of the sources of Bryne's music can be positively dated before the Civil War, yet its style is far from progressive. His Service in G

---

[18] David Scott, *The Music of St Paul's Cathedral* (London, 1972), 16; though unreliable see also John S. Bumpus, *The Organists and Composers of S. Paul's Cathedral* (London, 1891). Details of admissions given here are from the Muniment Books (London, Guildhall MS 25664/1–2; 1660–1733).

[19] Scott, 16–17.   [20] Pepys, *Diary*, v. 67.   [21] Shaw, 173–4.

(Arnold, ii) became widely popular—it is one of the most attractive short services of the period—but his anthems do not seem to have achieved general circulation. He is represented most strongly in a partbook, now in the Henry Watson Library, Manchester (BR. M.340 Cr.71), that may have originated at St Paul's as one of a set copied between 1666 and 1669 to replace losses in the fire.[22] It contains four anthems by Bryne, of which *I heard a voice in heaven* and *How long wilt thou forget me* are also in the Bing-Gostling Partbooks. With regard to the first of these, the absence of declamatory elements in the verse-writing suggests a composer steeped in an earlier style, as do the five-part full sections with twin countertenor parts (see Ex. 70).

Following the fire a temporary choir was constructed in the west end of the cathedral in 1667,[23] but as vacancies in the choir arose some were allowed to remain unfilled. As already noted, Bryne and Jewitt went elsewhere, and Stephen Bing departed for Lincoln, though he returned in 1672. Whether or not choral services continued is uncertain, but it seems likely that they did— somehow. The Manchester partbook implies continuity, as does Bing's activity as a copyist in the 1670s after his return. The 'first set' of partbooks (tenor and countertenor only) now in the cathedral library is largely in his hand and contains an extensive range of services, including two by 'Mr' Blow, thus indicating a date of not later than 1677 for their copying at that point. This ties in with a payment on 22 January 1676/7 'To Mr Bing in full [settlement] of his bill for service bookes £7. 19s. 7d.'[24] During the same decade Bing continued to add to his own private set of partbooks, to which John Gostling made further additions after Bing's death in 1682.[25]

The great bass John Gostling was already a gentleman of the Chapel Royal before his appointment as a minor canon of St Paul's in 1681. By then half the vicar choral places were empty, but despite the admission of John Playford as a vicar in 1683, it was ordered 'positively that no more shall be admitted into any petticanons or vicars places until they may be actually admitted into immediate service', which suggests that for the present a full choir was not needed.[26] However, from 1686 steps were taken to bring minor canons and vicars up to full strength. Among the latter were admitted Michael Wise and William Turner. Wise was made almoner at the king's behest in 1687, but his almost immediate death made way for someone even more important to be appointed in his place—John Blow. At the same time, Isaac Blackwell, one of the recently appointed vicars, became organist.[27] He was already organist of St Dunstan's-in-the-West from 1674 and of St Michael's, Cornhill, from 1684. His anthem *O Lord our governor* had been copied into the Chapel Royal partbooks between

[22] Cheverton, 'English Church Music', 394–5; also Sarah Boyer, 'The Manchester Altus Partbook, MS 340 Cr 71', *Music and Letters*, 72 (1991), 197–213.
[23] Scott, 18. [24] Guildhall MS 25707/1, 22.
[25] Shaw, *Bing–Gostling Part Books*, 112–14. [26] Guildhall MS 25738/2. [27] Shaw, 174.

Ex. 70. Albertus Bryne, *I heard a voice in heav'n (Lbl 30931)*

Ex. 71. Isaac Blackwell, *Bow down thine ear, O Lord* (Bing – Gostling Partbooks and *GL* 111)

1670 and 1676,[28] but all that survives is an organ part from Ely (*Cu* Ely 1). Three others are to be found in the Bing–Gostling Partbooks, including *Bow down thine ear, O Lord*, which also occurs in one of the Gloucester organ-books (MS 111) with the note 'finis 1670' (Ex. 71). The declamatory imitative writing in the verses of these anthems is consistent with such dates.

[28] Ashbee, i. 163.

Playford's *Cantica Sacra* (1674) includes three chamber anthems by Blackwell, and four by Playford himself (as well as others by Christopher Gibbons, Benjamin Rogers, John Jackson, and Matthew Locke). In his preface Playford says that they were 'contriv'd . . . both for publick and private use' and claims that they had 'often been Sung in several Cathedral Churches and College Chappels' notwithstanding the fact that they were only for two voices and organ. Playford's are not markedly inferior to Blackwell's and are in a similar vein.

John Gostling was promoted to subdean in 1690. Sometime before 1696 he began copying the 'second set' of St Paul's partbooks, using the Bing–Gostling master copies as his main source.[29] The 'second set', which like the first is incomplete, contains anthems by Blow (16), Child (13), Purcell (11), Wise (10), Tucker (9), Humfrey (8), 'Mr' Turner (6), Aldrich and Rogers (4 each), together with old faithfuls by Byrd (6) and Orlando Gibbons (5). The presence of eight anthems by Adrian Batten testifies to an enduring loyalty to an earlier St Paul's composer.

In readiness for the completion of the choir, a new organ 'bigger and louder than the Temple Organ' was ordered from Father Smith in 1694, for completion by 25 March 1696.[30] Needless to say, it was not finished in time, one of the problems being that Wren's case was not big enough to accommodate Smith's 'confounded box of whistles'. Replete with mixtures of various kinds, it had twelve stops on the great including the (by this time) inevitable trumpet, nine on the chair organ, and six on the echo. Until Renatus Harris's Salisbury organ of 1710 it was the largest organ in England.

The completion of the choir (in the architectural sense) was paralleled (in the musical sense) by some important appointments, such as John Howell, Richard Elford, and John Freeman as vicars choral, between 1697 and 1701, Jeremiah Clarke became organist on the death of Blackwell in 1699 and succeeded Blow as master of the choristers in 1703.[31] With Clarke's suicide in 1707 the mastership passed to Charles King, and Richard Brind became organist, to be followed by Maurice Greene in 1718. Meanwhile the vicars were further strengthened by the addition of Francis Hughes and Samuel Weely in 1710, by which time it was virtually a choir of virtuosos shared with the Chapel Royal and Westminster Abbey. The new repertoire is reflected in a 'third set' of partbooks (and a companion organ-book at Cambridge, *Cfm* 669), again largely in Gostling's hand, covering the years of Queen Anne's reign and extending beyond it. It contains anthems by Croft (18), Greene (18), Blow (13), Aldrich (11, including arrangements), Henry Purcell (8), Humfrey (7), Clarke (6), Charles King, Daniel Purcell and Weldon (4 each), Wise and Turner (3 each).

[29] Ford, 'Minor Canons at Canterbury Cathedral', 276–84.
[30] Freeman, *Father Smith*, 34–5; also Scott, 19 and doc. no. 6.
[31] Shaw, 175–6; Dawe, *Organists of the City of London*, 119.

Of these, the only composer not so far considered (apart from Greene, who hardly comes into our period) is King.[32] Born at Bury St Edmunds in 1687, he was a 'singing boy in Paul's' in 1698, and was apprenticed to Clarke, whose sister he married. By 1705 he was fifth minor canon at St Paul's (his 'demotion' to vicar choral in 1730 was to regularize his position as a layman) and on Clarke's death in 1707 he succeeded as almoner and master of the choristers. The same year he graduated B.Mus. from Oxford. All this was an impressive start for a 20-year-old and must surely have betokened ability, however much charm or influence may have played a part. In addition to his cathedral appointments, which he retained until his death in 1748, he was organist of St Benet Fink from 1714 at a salary of £20 a year.

He wrote at least seven services and nineteen anthems. Tudway included the Service in F and three anthems in volume v of his collection (*Harl.* 7341), among them the five-part *Hear, O Lord, and have mercy* (Arnold, i) which is a companion piece to the service. The other two are *Hear my crying* and *Sing unto God, O ye kingdoms*; all three date from 1712 or earlier because of their inclusion in *Divine Harmony*. The latter is a substantial verse anthem in D major, with organ ritornellos and florid writing for a bass soloist, and a D minor ground in the middle. Further anthem-books of 1724 and 1736 (both entitled *A Collection of Anthems*, etc.) include eight more anthems and probably reflect their order of composition. It cannot be pretended, however, that any consistent stylistic development in these anthems is discernible. In general, King seems to have avoided the influence of Purcell, and for the most part eschewed the flamboyance to which some of his older contemporaries were prone. He was a man of eighteenth-century sensibility.

Maurice Greene was being both witty and wise when he described King as a 'very serviceable man', and it is his services that form the best-known part of his output. There are two in A major (Arnold, ii and iii), and one in each of the following keys: B flat (Tudway, vi, and Arnold, i), B minor, C major (Arnold, iii), D major, and F major (Tudway, v, and Arnold, ii), besides some miscellaneous items. The earliest is probably the one in F major dating from 1706, though its Kyrie and Creed were added 'many years afterwards' according to Arnold. It is the shortest, contains very little counterpoint and almost no verse or triple-time passages. The B minor Service, which possibly came next (*c*.1713) is richer in style. But the stodgy rhythms, easy sequences, and predictable imitations that tend to characterize his full writing are generally all too apparent, despite occasional relief in triple-time verses and some welcome textural changes. Rarely is there any noteworthy effect beyond occasional touches of harmonic colour; featureless competence is the level of King's achievement. This was 'serviceability' with a vengeance, and one can only agree with

---

[32] *NG* x. 65 (Watkins Shaw).

Hawkins, pithy for once, when he said 'his compositions are uniformly restrained within the bounds of mediocrity . . . they leave the mind as they found it'.[33]

Of the five anthems attributed to King's colleague (and Greene's teacher) Richard Brind in *Divine Harmony* (1712) there is now no trace, even in the St Paul's partbooks. One work by a minor St Paul's composer of this period which does appear in the 'second set' is Charles Badham's *Unto thee will I cry*. Badham, a minor canon from 1698 to 1716 and an industrious if unreliable copyist, does not seem to have included his anthem in any of his own manuscripts, however.

Despite the fact that St Paul's was not finally finished until 1710, it had functioned as a kind of national shrine since 1697. The Festival of the Sons of the Clergy was an annual event celebrated there with a performance of Purcell's D major *Te Deum* and specially written anthems, for example, Clarke's *O be joyful in the Lord* (26 November 1706) and Daniel Purcell's *The Lord gave the word* (6 December 1709). Thanksgiving services for Marlborough's great victories were other occasions for special anthems, as we have already seen.[34] When the queen was present, the cathedral in effect became the Chapel Royal and responsibility for the music passed to the chapel—hence Croft usually furnished the music. With so many members in common between the two choirs it made little difference to the personnel involved.

The climax came with the last and greatest of these celebrations, that for the Peace of Utrecht on 7 July 1713, though the queen was absent ill. On that occasion Croft had to be content with providing the anthem only (*This is the day*), for pride of place went to Handel's great 'Utrecht' *Te Deum*. So ended, fittingly, the most splendid period in the musical history of St Paul's.

[33] Hawkins, *History* ii. 798.   [34] See also Scott, 20–1.

Norwich

Joseph Hall, bishop of Norwich, described the desecration of his cathedral in 1643 in the following terms:

Lord, what work was here, what clattering of glasses, what beating down of walls, what tearing up of monuments, what pulling down of seats, what wresting out of irons and brass from the windows and graves . . . what to[o]ting and piping upon the destroyed organ pipes, and what hideous triumph on the market day before all the country, when, in a kind of sacrilegious and prophane procession, all the organ pipes, vestments, both copes and surplices . . . and the service books and singing books that could be had, were carried to the fire in the public market place, a lewd wretch walking before the train, in his cope, trailing in the dirt, with a service-book in his hand, imitating, in an impious scorn the tune, and usurping the words of the Litany, used formerly in the church.[1]

Whatever music may have been lost in 1643 and the years following, the choir was quickly supplied with music after the Restoration. In 1661 payment was made 'for 6 service books at 7s. each book for the Quire' and by 1668 a list of music in the custody of the precentor, Anthony Beck, included several sets of eight, nine, and ten books containing 'divers services', full anthems, verse anthems, 'services for men', etc.—in all more than fifty volumes.[2] At the same time, the cathedral authorities were re-establishing the choir. According to the statutes of King James I, it consisted of six minor canons, one deacon, one epistoler, eight lay clerks, one organist, and eight choristers. The minor canons were to be 'all either priests or at least deacons' and together with 'the Gospeller, the Epistoler, Organist and Clerks should be skilled in singing, expert in voice and talent to serve in the choir'.[3] There was also to be a master of the choristers 'of honourable reputation, honest life, skilled in singing and the playing of musical instruments, and who should diligently devote his time to teaching the 8 boys in their time and supervise the singing of the divine offices'. He was to see not only to their musical education, 'including the playing of musical instruments', but to 'their teaching and training in letters and in Scripture'. Their health was also his responsibility, and four, at least, were to board with him.[4]

---

[1] Percy Scholes, *The Puritans and Music in England and New England* (London, 1934), 251, quoting Hall's *Hard Measure* (1647).

[2] Boston, *Musical History of Norwich Cathedral*, 62, 58.

[3] Cornall, 'Practice of Music at Norwich Cathedral', 153. [4] Ibid. 157.

Throughout our period the number of minor canons was held at six or seven (including usually the organist and master of the choristers), the lay clerks and choristers at eight. Stipends were modest: in 1705 minor canons received £10 with an extra £1 for the precentor; the gospeller (grouped in the accounts with the minor canons) received £9; the epistoler (grouped with the lay clerks) received £8. 10s., and the rest of the lay clerks £8. The organist was paid £20 with a further £8 as master of the choristers, plus £40 for the diet of four boys.[5] There were livings in the town and surrounding country to supplement the minor canons' incomes—though in theory no more than two might be held by statute—and for the lay clerks, a large city like Norwich gave plenty of opportunity to ply a trade, or serve as parish clerk in one of its many churches. The organist, likewise, could augment his income by teaching in town or further afield.

The succession of Restoration organists began with Richard Ayleward in 1661, who served until 1664 when he was superseded by Thomas Gibbs. Gibbs, however, died of the plague in July 1666, and Ayleward was reappointed, but he lived only until 1669.[6] From then until 1689 the organist was Thomas Pleasants, and after him James Cooper, who died in 1721.[7] At first the organ was a small instrument brought over from Bury St Edmunds in 1660 or 1661 at a cost of £45. It was set up temporarily, with a new set of pipes from Lancelot Pease of Cambridge costing £18, pending the erection of a replacement for the one destroyed in 1643.[8] In due course, a contract with George Dallam was signed, and by 1664 a double organ with eight or nine stops had been erected on the screen where the old one had stood.[9] Twenty-five years later Renatus Harris added to the great an 'open diapason of fine metal' to front the west side of the case, a 'furniture and mixture', and, probably, a five-rank cornet, and to the chair organ another 'furniture'. He also added an echo organ of 'six stoppes . . . 150 pipes'.[10] Then, in 1699, the organist James Cooper 'did at his owne charge add a Trumpet stop to ye Organ wch was now finished by Mr Christian Smyth', making, for the time, a substantial three-manual instrument.[11]

Despite the considerable number of choirbooks that were already in existence by 1668, and a continuous record of copying, the cathedral library now contains nothing from the seventeenth century. There is, however, a set of eight partbooks in the Rowe Library, King's College, Cambridge (MSS 10–17) which clearly originates from Norwich. It includes (*a*) works by Richard Ayleward

[5] Details of personnel, stipends, and periods of service have been taken from the cathedral treasurers' account-books now in the Norfolk Record Office, Norwich Central Library. Dates supply the references. Also consulted were Dr A. H. Mann's notes on Norwich Cathedral musicians in the same library (MSS 430–2).
[6] Boston, 71; Shaw, 202–3.　　[7] Boston, 73–80; Shaw, 203.
[8] Boston, 8–9; Gordon Paget, 'The Organs of Norwich Cathedral', *The Organ*, 14 (1934–5), 67.
[9] Boston, 9–12; Paget, 67.　　[10] Boston, 12; Paget, 68.　　[11] Boston, 78; Paget, 68.

dating from the early 1660s, and (b) anthems in a later hand by Norwich composers such as John Connold and James Cooper. The companion organ-book (MS 9), while providing accompaniments for (a) lacks the items in (b), but instead has organ parts for a third group of anthems (c), including works by Hawkins of Ely, Clarke, Croft, and Weldon of the Chapel Royal, and local composers such as William Pleasants (son of Thomas) and Humphrey Cotton that can be assigned to the second and third decades of the eighteenth century.[12] In addition, the 'verse end' contains fifty or more chants, many by Norwich composers.

There are, however, several incomplete sets of eighteenth-century partbooks still in the cathedral. The earliest, 'Old Set 1' (MSS 1–3), was begun in the early 1720s and as such need not concern us here. 'Later' sets, however, preserve an older repertoire, and no doubt replaced worn-out partbooks. To mention only the work of local composers, 'Old Set 4' (MSS 4–10) contains anthems by James Cooper, and a Service in D minor by William Pleasants, lay clerk from 1692 and (concurrently) organist of St Peter Mancroft from 1708.[13]

Richard Ayleward is represented in the Rowe Library MSS by three services and twenty-five anthems. Before the Civil War he had been a chorister under Christopher Gibbons at Winchester, where his father was a minor canon, but his whereabouts during the Commonwealth is a mystery, as are the reasons for the interruption in his period of service at Norwich. His works include a 'whole service' with responses and litany in D major, a *Magnificat* and *Nunc dimittis* in D minor 'for verses', and another Evening Service in F major and triple time throughout. Among the anthems is a setting of *The king shall rejoice* written to mark the coronation of Charles II in 1661, and thoroughly up to date in style. Impressive though it is, there are others which are even more remarkable. Ayleward's anthems are, in fact, quite unlike those of his contemporaries. Most obviously they exceed the modest dimensions of the early Restoration anthem and sometimes make considerable demands on resources. Thus *I was glad* is for three 'meanes' (trebles), three countertenors, two tenors, and four basses, while *Lo, we heard of the same at Ephrata* is for four means, two countertenors, two tenors, and four basses. The verses frequently expand into six, seven, or eight parts, and works like *Blow up the trumpet in Sion* would have taxed any cathedral choir in the land. Its hammered choral declamation brings to mind Carissimi, while the brilliant eight-part trumpet figuration of the opening (over slow-moving tonic and dominant harmony) recalls Monteverdi or Schütz.

More audacious still is *Hark, methinks I hear the trumpet sound*, which begins with a dramatic bass solo and continues with bold gestures throughout. Frequently in these anthems the solo writing is flamboyant in a way that is hardly found before Blow and Purcell. Another striking instance is the bass solo 'The earth shall tremble' from *O Jerusalem, [thou] that killest*, which in range and vocal

---

[12] Clark, *Transposition in Seventeenth-Century English Organ Accompaniments*, 53, 99–104.
[13] William Pleasants was baptized 19 Nov. 1675 and buried 18 Dec. 1717 (Mann MS 432).

Ex. 72. Richard Ayleward, *O Jesu sweet* (*Ckc* 9 - 17)

style anticipates the sort of thing that Gostling later became renowned for. Other voices are not denied solo opportunities, however. More restrained, but equally affecting, are the passages for solo treble in *O Jesu sweet* (Ex. 72). Here and there chromatic inflections play an expressive role in the solos, while choruses exploit the potential of harmonic colouring within a surprisingly wide tonal spectrum. Quirkish effects are rare, and though progressions sometimes lead to sharp or, more often, flat keys far removed from home, the process is controlled and usually convincing. Such passages are rarely contrapuntal in character; the technique is purely harmonic and expressionistic—for example, the section 'Many waters cannot quench love' towards the end of *I charge you, O ye daughters of Jerusalem* (Ex. 73). The opening creates an effect of deep calm centred on G, a calm that represents both the 'waters' and 'love'. After a rest, there is a change from G major to G minor, with more agitated declamation leading to the new, 'brighter' key of B flat major, reaffirming the constancy of 'love' despite the disturbance of the 'floods'. Nothing can conquer love; this is driven home over the next nine bars as the bass, climbing all the time (though it falls back a third for every fourth it rises) finally achieves its climax in a D major cadence. It is a moment of musical truth that underlines the truth about divine love—an exalted state, not just higher (as D is higher than B flat) but transcendent (as D major is sharper than B flat major).

Ayleward's anthems are unusual for the time in that a high proportion are set to poetic texts, rather than passages from the Bible or Prayer Book. Some, such as *O Jesu sweet* have already been mentioned, but others include *Glory to God that hath unsealed mine eyes* (an 'Anthem for the Morning') and a cycle of four anthems, respectively for the Nativity, Circumcision, Purification, and Resurrection. Their imagery and intensity remind one of George Herbert or Richard

Ex. 73. Richard Ayleward, *I charge you, O ye daughters of Jerusalem (Ckc 9 - 17)*

Crashaw, and their metaphysical nature seems almost to rule out their suitability for public performance in a cathedral. That on the Circumcision (*Gently, O gently, father, do not bruise*), for example, with its verse 'Fear not the pruning of the vine', develops a conceit more appropriate to the chamber than the chancel. It suggests the possibility that some of these 'anthems' were devotional music written for domestic performance, or for someone's private chapel during the Commonwealth. In this connection the work of George Jeffreys comes to mind, some of whose sacred music is likely to have been written for the chapel of Sir Christopher Hatton (after 1643 Baron Hatton of Kirby in Northampton-shire). Interestingly, Jeffreys also wrote a cycle of anthems for the major feasts of the church—Nativity, Holy Innocents, Circumcision, Epiphany, Passion Sunday, Easter, Ascension, and Whitsun—to similar poetic texts.[14]

It is difficult to see Ayleward's work within a tradition, either the one he knew as a choirboy or the one which came after him. Perhaps, like Henry Loosemore, he was sheltered by an East Anglian gentleman during the Commonwealth; it would have put him on the doorstep at Norwich in 1660. The fact that, here and there, his work recalls certain Continental composers may suggest foreign influences, or perhaps even travel abroad, though all this is speculative. In any case there are no close models for his work among earlier or contemporary English anthems, and perhaps this may be a reason for suspecting that they were written for some other time and place than Norwich in the 1660s. Significantly, perhaps, the last of his anthems to be entered into the partbooks, and in some respects the most conventional, was the coronation anthem *The king shall rejoice*. Could the others, therefore, have been written before 1661?

Such a line of argument discounts originality, however. No matter how his style was formed, or his conception of the verse anthem took shape, there is no irrefutable reason why these works should not have been written and performed in Norwich—in the case of the services, responses, and litany, this would have been the likeliest reason for their existence. The fact that the anthems and services differ markedly in certain respects is not necessarily surprising, given that the demands of service-setting were quite different from those of the anthem. There are common traits, nevertheless; for example, in the D major Service, the tendency to divide into five or more parts for the verse sections. Still more characteristic are the harmonic transitions and excursions that without doubt make this service one of the most interesting of the period. Flat regions, in particular, are exploited to give expressive effect to certain passages in the *Te Deum*, *Benedictus*, Creed, and *Magnificat*—though almost inevitably 'the sharpness of death' in the *Te Deum* goes in the other direction. A striking illustration is provided in the Creed at the passage beginning 'he suffered and was buried'. By this time the music has moved from D major to F minor, which then changes to F major on the 'third' day, and from that point on builds up towards the triumph of the resurrection and ascension, made all the more overwhelming by the juxtaposition of C major and A flat major at the words 'according to the Scriptures' and the bringing in of the bass to complete the choir at this point. It is a stroke that compels admiration, as does much else in his work (see Ex. 74).

---

[14] Peter Aston, 'George Jeffreys', *Musical Times*, 110 (1969), 776.

Ex. 74. Richard Ayleward, Creed from the Service in D (*Ckc* 9 - 17)

(1) Where it differs from the bass part, the continuo has been given in brackets. The organ part is written a fifth higher than choir pitch.

(2) *g'* in original.

Ex. 75. Anthony Beck, *Behold how good and joyful* (*Ckc* 9 - 17)

Other works by Norwich composers in the same partbooks include anthems, mainly verse, by Anthony Beck, John Connold, James Cooper, John Jackson, and Braithwaite Souter, entered between about 1685 and 1705. Unfortunately, the lack of an organ part for these pieces undermines the attempt to reconstruct them with any degree of certainty—especially when the bass voice is a non-participant. All these composers served at one time or another in the choir at Norwich. Jackson, however, will be considered in relation to the music of Wells Cathedral, where he went as organist in 1674 after being master of the choristers at Norwich from 1670. Of the others, Anthony Beck had been appointed lay clerk at the Restoration, promoted minor canon in 1663 and precentor in 1668; he died in 1674. His anthem *Behold, how good and joyful* reveals him as a capable composer, with an ear for intertwining high voices at the words 'and life for evermore' in the verse 'For there the Lord' (Ex. 75). The presence of another anthem by him in the 'Caroline' partbooks at Peterhouse, Cambridge, points to activity before the Civil War.

Braithwaite Souter's only anthem, *O Lord God of my salvation*, is an unpretentious piece of little technical merit, though not without devotional effect.[15] He became a lay clerk in 1663 and at his death in 1680 left 'one hundred setts of books of Songes composed by divers authors . . . to the Dean and Chapter . . . for the only use of the Canons and Clarks of the Quire when they shall or will

---

[15] Cheverton, 'Musical Supplement', 85–8.

Ex. 76. John Connold, *O God, thou art my God* (Ckc 9 - 17)

(1) The organ bass is editorial.

meet at any time'.[16] What these books can have been—and so many of them—
is an intriguing question. Printed or manuscript (or both), they would have
constituted a valuable legacy of which there now seems no trace.

The two most prolific of this group were John Connold and James Cooper.
Connold is listed among the minor canons in 1675 and drops out after 1690,
though he was rector of Calefield from 1680 and of St Stephen's, Norwich,
from 1683 until his death in 1708.[17] Some of the later cathedral partbooks ('Old
Set 5', MSS 11–14) credit him with two services, one in F, another in G minor,
and the Rowe partbooks contain eight anthems—all verse anthems and thus
difficult to assess, for reasons already stated. There is plenty variety of common
and triple time—the former declamatory, the latter tuneful—but generally
speaking nothing remarkable. Organ preludes introduce the anthems and verses
are frequently rounded off by ritornellos. There are comparatively few trio
verses, though the opening of *O God, thou art my God* is an exception and shows
that he had a serviceable technique (Ex. 76).

However, his general level of competence seems higher than that of Cooper,
who is represented by three services in 'Old Set 5', including a verse Service in
C and a full Service in F, and nineteen anthems (and a Burial Service) in the
Rowe partbooks. Before becoming organist in 1689, Cooper had been a lay

[16] Souter (or Sowter) was baptized 6 Aug. 1612 and died 8 Nov. 1680 (Mann MS 432).
[17] Mann MS 431.

clerk—he is listed as such in 1685—and was in due course to become master of the choristers.[18] Judged by the full anthem *Sing we merrily*, his work is feeble in conception and execution, and there is little in the verse anthems to suggest otherwise. On the whole, such texts as *By the waters of Babylon, I heard a great voice*, and *Why do the heathen* are only trifled with, and create little impact. The choruses, most of which are in triple time, lack distinctive features. In the declamatory solos the usual words receive modest affective treatment, and expressive ornaments—forefalls and backfalls—are a frequent occurrence. Two presumably late works confirm the general impression his work makes. *I waited patiently*, which Tudway included in his collection (*Harl.* 7341), at least has the merit of brevity—more than can be said of *The Lord is King*, an enormously extended anthem for solo treble, and an utterly vacuous attempt at the early eighteenth-century grand manner.

[18] Boston, 76–80.

Oxford

According to Anthony Wood, choral services had been re-established by November 1660 in those colleges where they had traditionally been sung: 'they restored the organ at Christ Church, Magdalen, New, and St John's College, together with the singing of prayers after the most antient way: to which places the resort of people (more out of novelty, I suppose, than devotion) was infinitely great'.[1]

New College and Magdalen College had ancient choral foundations; that at Christ Church had been refounded in 1541, a few years before it became the cathedral church of the new diocese of Oxford. New College had ten conducts or chaplains, three clerks, and sixteen choristers with an *informator*; Magdalen had four chaplains, eight clerks, and sixteen choristers, again with an instructor, while Christ Church had eight chaplains, eight clerks, and eight choristers—a typical 'new' foundation.[2] So far as we know, these numbers were maintained throughout the Restoration period. At St John's College, a benefaction of 1637 had provided for a chaplain, six clerks, four choristers, a master, and organist, but whether the choir was of the same composition after the Restoration is unclear.[3] Thomas Baskerville's account of Oxford in the 1680s makes no mention of it, whereas he confirms details of the choirs at Christ Church, Magdalen, and New Colleges, and even All Souls, where 'The present Warden, Dr James [1665–87] . . . hath 40 fellows, 2 Chaplains, 3 Clarks, 6 Choristers, besides other orders'.[4] Despite the apparent contemporaneity of the report, it probably refers to the original foundation, rather than a choir that was actually functioning. At Corpus Christi College the statutory two chaplains, two clerks, and two choristers were kept at strength throughout the period, though probably not by musicians. At any rate, we know nothing about any music that may

---

[1] Andrew Clark (ed.), *The Life and Times of Anthony Wood Described by Himself* (Oxford, 1891–1900), i. 357.

[2] Harrison, *Music in Medieval Britain* 32, 36, 195; N. Denholm-Young, 'Magdalen College', in H. E. Salter and Mary Lobel (eds.), *The University of Oxford* (The Victoria History of the County of Oxford, iii; London, 1954), 194; M. Maclagan, 'Christ Church', ibid. 235; A. H. M. Jones, 'New College', ibid. 157.

[3] Francis Knights, 'The History of the Choral Foundation of St John's College, Oxford', *Musical Times*, 131 (1990), 446; H. E. Salter, 'St John's College', in Salter and Lobel (eds.), *The University of Oxford*, iii, 255; le Huray, 16.

[4] Humphrey Baskerville (ed.), 'Thomas Baskerville's Account of Oxford, c.1670–1700', *Collectanea*, 4th ser. (Oxford Historical Society, 47; Oxford, 1905), 201.

have been sung there and there was no official organist—nor, indeed, so far as we know, an organ in the chapel.[5]

CHRIST CHURCH CATHEDRAL

Edward Lowe had probably been organist at Christ Church since 1631, certainly since 1641, and at the Restoration was appointed one of the organists of the Chapel Royal as well.[6] He published *A Short Direction for the Performance of Cathedrall Service* in 1661, revised three years later as *A Review of some Short Directions . . . with many usefull Additions according to the Common Prayer Book, as is now established*. The importance of these 'Directions' has already been discussed, but as a composer his work did not receive much attention beyond Oxford and its satellites. The Christ Church partbooks (MSS 1220–4),[7] begun about 1643 though containing mostly Restoration material, include seven anthems by him, six in his own hand entered between 1660 and 1663. Three others are known only from the presence of their texts in Clifford's *Divine Service*.

The only anthem by Lowe entered into the partbooks before the Restoration was *O how amiable*, but with a composing life that may well have stretched back to 1630 it cannot be assumed that the others are all post-Restoration works. Nevertheless, the fact that eight anthems were added to Clifford's second edition (1664) may perhaps suggest a sudden burst of composing activity in the early 1660s. All are verse anthems, but stylistically there is nothing that could not have been written before the Civil War. The verses favour treble and bass soloists and employ an open, imitative texture, with organ introduction and a brief chorus at the end of each verse echoing the concluding words. A more expansive style of counterpoint is reserved for the final chorus, to be seen at its best in the Gloria of *O give thanks unto the Lord* (Harl. MS 7339) or the final Amen of *Turn thy face away*.[8] The latter is preceded by a beautiful passage of chromatic harmony which is both imaginative and controlled (Ex. 77). Lowe succeeded his friend Dr John Wilson as Heather Professor of Music in the University in 1661, and died in 1682.

In 1680, or possibly 1685, a new organ was built at Christ Church by Bernard Smith.[9] We know virtually nothing about the one it replaced, but Smith's specification exemplifies the new principles of tonal design that he helped to establish, eliminating duplicated unison ranks and adding mixtures, mutations,

[5] Thomas Fowler, *The History of Corpus Christi College* (Oxford Historical Society, 25; Oxford, 1893), 423–30; Francis Knights, 'The Choral Foundation of Corpus Christi College', *The Pelican* (1988–9), 25.

[6] *NG* xi. 287–8 (Peter le Huray); Rimbault, 128; Shaw, 210–11.

[7] Cheverton, 'English Church Music', 414–20.   [8] Ibid. 684.

[9] Freeman, *Father Smith*, 20–1; id., 'The Organs of Christ Church Cathedral, Oxford', *The Organ*, 11 (1931–2), 37; Clutton and Niland, *British Organ* (1963), 71.

Ex. 77. Edward Lowe, *Turn thy face away from my sins* (Och 1220 - 4 and Ojc 315)

and reeds to the colour range. Although by no means large, the great organ possessed a full diapason chorus, with twelfth and tierce, a three-rank sesquialtera, and a four-rank cornet (a stop he almost certainly introduced into England), plus a trumpet. The chair had only four stops, however. Lowe's successor as organist was William Husbands, possibly the Husbands listed among the Christ Church choristers between 1673 and 1676.[10] His anthem *Come Holy Ghost* was entered into the Christ Church partbooks in 1688, and there is a setting of *O Lord, rebuke me not* attributed simply to 'Husbands' in a nineteenth-century Tenbury manuscript (*Ob* Tenbury 844).

For their next organist, the authorities looked to New College, where Richard Goodson had been organist since 1682—and Heather Professor after Lowe.[11] His move to Christ Church took place in 1692, and he remained until his death in 1718. Numerous manuscripts in his hand are in the library there, among them autograph scores of four verse anthems—one a setting of *Rejoice in the Lord* with orchestral accompaniment—a Morning Service in C and an Evening Service in F. The one in C is a fine piece with a particularly striking opening and some effective six-part writing, as in the Gloria of the *Jubilate* (Ex. 78).

But the most important composer associated with Christ Church at this time was Henry Aldrich.[12] By any standards he was a man of remarkable versatility,

[10] Cheverton, 419; Shaw, 211.   [11] NG vii. 531 (Watkins Shaw); Shaw, 211.
[12] NG i. 234–6 (Watkins Shaw).

Ex. 78. Richard Goodson, *Jubilate* from the sevice in C (*Cu* Ely 16)

for apart from his career as a scholar and divine (which culminated in being Dean of Christ Church and vice-chancellor of the university), he was a 'gentle-man-architect'—with, among other things, the Peckwater Quad at Christ Church to his credit—and an amateur composer. Born in 1648, he went up to Oxford in 1662 and remained at Christ Church for virtually the rest of his life, becoming a canon in 1681 and Dean in 1689. He died in 1710. Four services and about twenty-five anthems are known by him, in addition to thirty or so English adaptations of Latin works by Palestrina, Carissimi, Tallis, Farrant, etc. Oddly enough, most of the works attributed to Aldrich in the Christ Church partbooks are adaptations. If the choir performed his original compositions then the parts have disappeared, though anthems and services are preserved in several scores, notably the autograph (MS 19). Tudway also included many of Aldrich's anthems in his collection (*Harl.* 7338–40).

Hardly surprisingly in a man who adapted other men's work, he revised a number of his own anthems over the years. His earlier anthems can be identified by their attribution to 'Mr' Henry Aldrich (he became Doctor of Divinity in 1682), and other evidence enables a date before 1680 to be established for such works as *Give the Lord thy judgments*, *If the Lord himself*, *I waited patiently*, *O God, thou art my God*, and *Out of the deep* (Boyce, ii). All but the last are verse anthems characterized by frequent triple-time sections in the modern style, and occasional florid or affective declamatory solo writing. *Out of the deep* was the anthem which achieved the widest circulation in its day. It shows the composer influenced by his study of sixteenth-century music, though more in the spirit than the letter. The opening section, for example, proceeds somewhat in the manner of a Renaissance motet, but the detail mixes archaisms with contemporary idioms such as fully emancipated dominant sevenths, and even diminished sevenths. Hybrid the style may be, but it offered scope for modern harmonic expression in a context that retained the dignity and religious aura of an earlier age.

Later full anthems include *O Lord, grant the king*, with its splendid five-part opening. If it was written to mark the accession of a monarch, then James II is more likely than William III. *God is our hope and strength* is another essay in the antique style but lacks the textual vigour and variety of *Sing unto the Lord, O ye his saints of his*, which owes something to Carissimi. Full credit is nevertheless due to the composer for the way in which 'weeping' and 'joy' are depicted, and the vivid contrast the two create. It strengthens the view that Aldrich, far from being an amateur whose effects owed more to luck than judgement, had a musician's ear and imagination, and sufficient technique to do justice to both.[13]

Nor was he limited to what he picked up from 'old masters'. He kept abreast of contemporary idioms in his verse anthems, showing a marked preference for the solo anthem. He wrote frequently and attractively in triple time, and though his declamation did not approach Purcell's in power, he responded strongly to texts which offered dynamic images. There is a series of striking passages in the anthem *I will love thee, O Lord my strength* beginning with the chorus 'The earth trembled' (Ex. 79), after which the solo bass continues violently ('he bowed the heavens . . . rode upon the Cherubim and . . . came flying upon the wings of the wind . . . the Lord thundered out of heaven . . . he cast forth lightenings and destroyed them'), until triple time assures deliverance at the words 'he shall send down from on high to fetch me, and shall take me out of many waters'.

Each of Aldrich's four services is in a different style from the others. The Benedicite Service in E minor (Arnold, iii) probably dates from before 1676 and is entirely in triple time, while the A major, dating from a few years before 1684, alternates full sections in common time with triple-time CTB verses. Each

---

[13] Excerpt quoted in Spink, 'Church Music II', 116–17.

Ex. 79. Henry Aldrich, *I will love thee, O Lord my strength* (Harl. 7340)

movement begins with a head-motif and the Glorias are all common. Unlike almost all other settings of the *Te Deum*, this one actually has flats at 'the sharpness of death'—much sounder theologically than the traditional sharps, since Christ actually *overcame* the sharpness of death. Similarly, the G major *Te Deum* goes into G minor at this point, thus contradicting 'sharpness' while actually setting the word with an F♯ in the treble (Boyce, i).

This service, written before 1678, was his best-known work and, indeed, he thought it worth publishing *c*.1690. The absence of verse contrast, however, makes it a trifle monotonous, and its repetitiveness, short-windedness, and reliance on clichés point to Aldrich's limitations as a composer. In these respects it compares unfavourably with the more expressive F major Service, in which various verse combinations are supported by an obbligato organ part and the full writing is in five parts. Yet the G major Service is not without some agreeable harmonic touches, and it has an attractive melodic quality. As Watkins Shaw said: 'if not specially distinguished, [it] is no disgrace to a distinguished man'.

Such a comment does not do justice to Aldrich, taking his work as a whole, for he deserves more than the grudging respect he has been given in modern times. Perhaps this is a reaction to his earlier reputation, which probably owed something to snobbishness. As with Parry two centuries later, here was proof that it was not beneath the dignity of a gentleman to show professional competence as a composer. Moreover, he was influential. As a member of the 1689 ecclesiastical commission appointed to inquire into the liturgy to see if some accommodation with Nonconformist views could be achieved (see Ch. 1), he would undoubtedly have argued in favour of maintaining the choral service. And by adapting Latin polyphonic compositions to English words he facilitated their introduction into the cathedral repertoire, and gave direct encouragement to the revival of the 'pure' polyphonic style which came to be regarded towards the end of the century as an ideal for true church music.

MAGDALEN COLLEGE

Robert Dallam's pre-war Magdalen organ, still there in 1654 when Evelyn heard Christopher Gibbons playing on it, was later taken to Hampton Court for Cromwell's pleasure, but brought back in 1660 and re-erected the following year at a cost of £25.[14] Its original specification had been eight stops on the great and five on the chair, all diapasons and flutes with several ranks doubled at the

[14] John Harper, 'The Organs of Magdalen College, Oxford—1: The Historical Background of Earlier Organs', *Musical Times*, 127 (1986), 293–4; see also id., 'The Dallam Organ in Magdalen College, Oxford', *Journal of the British Institute of Organ Studies*, 9 (1984), 62–3.

unison—tonally very old-fashioned, though further work in 1664 and 1665 may have livened it up. The first organist after the Restoration was Theodore Coleby, 'a German' according to Wood, and soon to become organist of Exeter Cathedral.[15] After two stopgap appointments his place at Magdalen was taken by Benjamin Rogers in 1665—already in middle age and with a varied career behind him—who at last seemed inclined to settle down.[16] Born at Windsor (baptized 2 June 1614), he was said by Wood, who knew him well, to have been a choirboy at St George's under Nathaniel Giles and to have become a lay clerk there when he was about 20. From 1638 he was organist of Christ Church Cathedral, Dublin, but 'left the organist place . . . which was but £20 per an., and was prefer'd to be Vicar Choral of Cloyne, where he continued till the Rebellion broke out, and then he went to You[g]all and so to England'.[17] From 1653 he is listed among the clerks of Eton, where he enjoyed the patronage of Dr Nathaniel Ingelo, one of the Fellows. Ingelo's favour was probably behind the award of a B.Mus. degree by Cambridge in 1658, by which time his reputation as an instrumental composer was already high.

Soon after the Restoration his setting of Ingelo's *Hymnus Eucharisticus* was performed at a banquet for the king at Guildhall, 5 July 1660, as a result of which 'he obtained a great name for his compositions and a plentiful reward'.[18] Even so, he had to be content with a lay-clerkship at Windsor, admittedly at an enhanced stipend and further supplemented by an additional 20s. a month for playing the organ when Child, the organist of St George's, was absent at the Chapel Royal. At the same time he was organist and *informator* at Eton, so he would have been quite comfortably off. In 1664, however, he was enticed away to Magdalen College at a salary of £60 a year 'if he forfeit not his place by misdemeanour'—ominous phrase.[19] He graduated D.Mus. at Oxford in July 1669, his exercise being performed at the opening of Wren's new Sheldonian Theatre.

Despite composing the Magdalen 'grace' (*Te Deum patrem colimus*), Rogers did not give the college complete satisfaction. One cause for complaint was 'his troublesome behaviour in the Chapel, where usually he would talk so loud in the organ loft, that he offended the company'. Another was his rudeness to the choir and his refusal to play such services 'as they were willing and able to sing, but out of a thwarting humour would play nothing but Canterbury tune, wherein he minded not the honour of the College, but his own ease and

[15] John Rouse Bloxam, *Register of the Presidents, Fellows, Demies . . . Chaplains, Clerks, Choristers, and other Members of Saint Mary Magdalen College . . . Oxford* (Oxford, 1853–7), ii. 192; Shaw, 381.

[16] J. P. White, 'Life and Vocal Music of Benjamin Rogers (1614–1698)' (Ph.D. diss., University of Iowa, 1973), 9–25; Bloxam, ii. 192–203; NG xvi. 102–3 (Watkins Shaw).

[17] This and the following quotation from White, 8–10, drawing on Wood's notes in *Ob* MS Wood D 19 (4).

[18] Wood, *Athenae Oxonienses*, iv. 307.

[19] Bloxam, *Register*, ii. 197–8 for this and the following quotations.

laziness'. Moreover, he kept his daughter in his lodgings, 'a scandalous creature, and reputed a common ------, contrary to the orders and commands of the President, who several times warned him to dispose of her, and to rid the College of such a lewd creature'. These transgressions resulted in his dismissal early in 1686, though he was awarded an annual pension of £30 which he continued to enjoy until his death at the age of 84 in 1698.

No church music by Rogers survives in pre-Restoration sources, yet it hardly seems likely that he would have written none before 1644, when he was already 30. The fact that two anthems, no longer extant, were in the repertoire of Christ Church, Dublin, in 1662[20] strongly suggests that they date from when he was organist there before the war. Attributions to 'Mr' Rogers in early Restoration sources indicate a date of 1669 or earlier, and these include four of the five services—the well-known 'Sharp Service' in D (Boyce, i), a Service in E minor 'for Verses', another 'for Verses' in G, and a full Evening Service in F. The exception is the Evening Service in A minor, which was one of the services copied into the Chapel Royal partbooks between 1670 and 1676.[21] The most complete source for these early services is the Bing–Gostling Partbooks. In general, the style is severely chordal and akin to that 'for every syllable a note' employed a hundred years before. The Sharp Service, which has already been briefly noted (see Ch. 2), borrows material from Child's of the same name but is shorn of all counterpoint and modernized in harmony—apart from a few false relations and Burney's dreaded chord of 'the lesser sixth and greater third' (augmented triad). Thematic links between the two services are obvious in most of the movement openings, and certainly extend beyond unconscious reminiscence on the part of Rogers, as a comparison of the *Nunc dimittis* in each makes clear (Ex. 80). Rogers, however, has a stronger sense of tonality, and chordal thinking is more evident. The same is true of the full sections of the G major Service, but the turgidity of the style is mitigated in the evening canticles by an obbligato organ accompaniment which permits the verse sections, at least, to open up and flower a bit.

As with the services, so with the full anthems; virtually all are in plain four-part homophony, though here and there simple imitations or staggered homophony provide relief—as in *Lord, who shall dwell* (Page, iii). Fortunately, the small scale of these anthems prevents them from being too tedious, and though *Behold, now praise the Lord* may be dull (and not improved by its concluding Hallelujas), others like *Teach me, O Lord* are more attractive, melodically and harmonically (both are in Boyce, ii). In all there are about thirty anthems, mostly verse anthems. Three chamber anthems together with four Latin hymns by Rogers were published in Playford's *Cantica Sacra* (1674); of the rest, sixteen survive in the hand of Philip Hayes, an eighteenth-century successor of Rogers

---

[20] *Anthems to be Sung in the Cathedral Church of the Holy and United Trinity in Dublin* (Dublin, 1662).

[21] Ashbee, i. 162.

Ex. 80(*a*) William Child, *Nunc dimittis* from the 'Sharp Service' (*Harl.* 7338)
 (*b*) Benjamin Rogers, *Nunc dimittis* from the 'Sharp Service' (*Harl.* 7338)

at Magdalen (*Ob* Mus. c. 96). The Evening Service in A minor, *Te Deum patrem colimus*, and three anthems are holograph in Christ Church MS 21, dated 1677–85.

Establishing a chronology for Rogers's anthems is difficult. On the evidence of the sources the earliest ones include *Behold, now praise the Lord* (the most widespread), *Rejoice in the Lord, O ye righteous*, and *Who shall ascend*. The full anthems show little stylistic variety and reflect his conservatism or caution. A more forward-looking approach is demonstrated in a few verse anthems. The opening of *Bow down thine ear, O Lord* looks conventional enough, but the solo bass verse 'For thou, Lord, art good', and a general willingness to slip into triple time given half a chance, makes the date of 1677 for this anthem given in the autograph credible (*Och* 21)—at least, for that version. The qualification is necessary, for *I beheld and lo*, dated 1678 in the same manuscript, is very different from the cruder but more dramatic version at Durham (MS B.1) which may be a good deal earlier, though admittedly unauthentic. The dates in his autograph are probably those of copying or revision. They certainly cannot be relied upon in establishing a perspective of the composer's development; *O that the salvation*, dated 1684 in the autograph, could have been composed fifty years before.

The overall view of Rogers's church music reveals a composer whose technique was well enough grounded but never fully extended. He accepted modern developments without being in any way experimental. Perhaps he had Puritan leanings which drew him to a severer style, perhaps he just refused to exert himself. Bracketing him with Child, as is usually done, may be justified up to a point, but it needs qualification. Disconcerting transitional elements such as are sometimes found in Child are excluded or assimilated in Rogers, and though his work is less wide-ranging, within its limits it shows sterling qualities.

Probably originating from the closing years of Rogers's tenure is an organ-book in the Magdalen College library (MS 347) which contains services by Tallis, Byrd, Gibbons, Child, Rogers, Blow, and 'Dr' Aldrich, among others, and a unique Sanctus in G attributed to Henry Purcell (Z. D90). One of the most interesting aspects of this manuscript is a highly ornamented version of the Gibbons Short Service, similar to the Tallis *Te Deum* and *Jubilate* found in George Holmes's organ-book already discussed (*Lbl* 31446; see Ch. 4). The written-out accompaniment (here and there supplemented by figures) is ornamented with beats, forefalls, backfalls, and shakes plain and turned, and by divisions, some extremely florid, that must have slowed down the performance to what, today, would be regarded as a very slow speed. Why this particular accompaniment should have been subject to such elaborate treatment whereas others in the manuscript are much less embellished (if at all) is unclear. Francis Knights has suggested that it may have been 'partly to modernise an older repertory';[22] the possibility that such 'worked up' versions may have been used as independent pieces has already been mooted. Their artistic quality would certainly have made them suitable as voluntaries, whatever else their purpose.

When Rogers was dismissed in 1686 his place was taken by Francis Pigott, previously organist of St John's.[23] A list of 'Demies, Chaplains, Clerks and Choristers' dated October 1688 shows him as organist among the statutory complement of chaplains, clerks, and choristers,[24] though by that time he had already left to become organist of the Temple Church in London, where Smith's new organ was being installed. It was undoubtedly a prestigious ap-

---

[22] Francis Knights, 'Magdalen College MS 347: An Index and Commentary', *Journal of the British Institute of Organ Studies*, 14 (1990), 4–8; id., 'A Restoration Version of Gibbons' Short Service', *Organists' Review*, 76 (1990), 97–100.

[23] Bloxam, *Register*, ii. 203; Shaw, 382.

[24] John Rouse Bloxam, *Magdalen College and King James II, 1686–1688* (Oxford Historical Society, 4; Oxford, 1886), 119.

pointment, and in due course Pigott became organist of the Chapel Royal in succession to Henry Purcell.

Meanwhile, Harris had rebuilt the Magdalen organ by 1690.[25] Doubled ranks were thinned out on the great, a twelfth was added, and the chorus brightened with mixtures—a furniture and cymbal. Repairs to the bellows, new keys, and six new stops (among them a 'Cedrine' = Sordun?) cost £167. The organist, by this time, was Daniel Purcell, Henry's younger brother, who took office in 1688. His stipend was £30 a year, but he resigned in May 1695, perhaps to assist his brother in London during the final months of his life—it was he who composed the final Act V masque of *The Indian Queen*.[26] For the next ten years he followed his fortune as a theatre composer and published a good deal of instrumental and vocal music, while serving as organist of St Dunstan's-in-the-East from 1696 and St Andrew's, Holborn, from about 1713.[27] He died in 1717.

Seventeen anthems by Daniel Purcell survive, fifteen of them solo anthems (mostly autograph) in three manuscripts.[28] A service and three further anthems are also known from a report by Stainer of an organ-book at Magdalen College (now missing) from which he edited an attractive Evening Service in E minor, mostly in triple time.[29] Two other anthems that were in the same manuscript, *Hear my prayer, O Lord, and consider* and *Bow down thine ear, O Lord*, fortunately survive elsewhere; but their presence in the missing source probably means that they were composed before Purcell left Oxford. The former, especially, shows his quality, both as to imagination and technique. The opening verse is a fine duet in A minor for countertenor and bass (Ex. 81*a*), followed by a bass solo 'I do remember the time past', with a 'motto aria' beginning that is perhaps too pretentious for the scale of what follows. Next comes another bass solo in 3/2, still in A minor, in which a rising chromatic line illustrates the text 'I stretch forth my hand unto thee'. The ensuing verse, a countertenor solo in D minor, adopts the affective declamatory style of his brother, the phrase 'my spirit waxeth faint' depicted with descending chromaticisms (Ex. 81*b*). The triple-time 'air' which follows ('O let me hear thy loving kindness') is in the same key as the preceding 'recitative'; though not a strict ground bass it shows ostinato features. The final duet sets the verse 'Teach me to do the thing that pleaseth thee'. Reverting to the original key of A minor, it adopts an imitative trio texture with coloratura on 'pleaseth', but concludes somewhat abruptly without even a final chorus. Not only does the work satisfy technical criteria, it forms an aesthetically pleasing whole (the question of a possibly missing final chorus apart), moving from supplication through moods of despair and optimism to final affirmation. There is symmetry and variety of key, movement, texture, and

[25] Harper, 'Organs of Magdalen College', 294.
[26] Bloxam, *Register*, ii. 203–7; *NG* xv. 475 (Jack Westrup).
[27] Dawe, *Organists of the City of London*, 135.
[28] *Lbl* 17841 and 31461, *Ob* Mus. d. 22b.   [29] Dearnley, 234.

Ex. 81. Daniel Purcell, *Hear my prayer, O Lord* (*Lbl* 17841)

timbre, as well as some striking expressive details: comparison with his brother is by no means to Daniel's disadvantage.

When it comes to the solo anthems, comparison with his brother raises questions not so much of quality, for they are attractive and professional pieces of work, but of stylistic disparity. More so than even the latest of Henry Purcell's verse anthems, they are imbued with Italianisms which strongly suggest that few, if any, can have been written before 1695. More probably they date from his years as a city organist, and similarities to John Reading's *A Book of New Anthems* [1715] and John Weldon's *Divine Harmony* [1716–17] suggest that Purcell may have intended to collect and publish a comparable volume, but was prevented by death from doing so. The general plan of these anthems consists of numerous alternating 'recitatives' and 'airs' with contrast of key and movement between sections. *My God, my God*, for example, has ten such movements, beginning in A minor but moving through E minor and C major before returning via E minor to A major. Usually they end with a Hallelujah, solo rather than chorus, but if the latter, a perfunctory one. Such works are appropriately known as 'cantata anthems', though their form is more flexible than the strict recitative–aria–recitative–aria pattern adopted in his self-confessedly Italianate *Six Cantatas* (1713).

Yet despite Italian influences, one hesitates to call them operatic. Passages like this from *I will sing unto the Lord* (Ex. 82) are rare, and for the most part coloratura is absent as a device for spinning out a line. There is, however, plenty of vigorous two-part, tonally directed, motivic counterpoint between treble solo and basso continuo, and sequential writing abounds. Motto aria openings are

Ex. 82. Daniel Purcell, *I will sing unto the Lord* (*Lbl* 31461)

common, as are beginnings which start as ground basses but break off to become free ostinatos. But there are no da capo arias, and the 'recitatives', while occasionally approaching the *secco* style, retain for the most part his brother's florid, rhetorical gestures—indeed, match him at his most extravagant.

It may be that the purposes for which these solo anthems were designed, lying outside the cathedral tradition, encouraged Purcell to adopt a more secular idiom. Nevertheless, the same stylistic features are evident in his anthem *The Lord gave the word* composed for the Festival of the Sons of the Clergy at St Paul's in 1709 (*Ob* Tenbury 310). It is a work conceived on a large scale as befitted the building and the occasion, without quite achieving the same grandeur.

Daniel Purcell, like his brother Henry, chose to make his living and reputation as a theatre composer. As with his brother it was church music's loss, for on the evidence of the work we have been considering he could be regarded as at least the equal of Jeremiah Clarke. His style was more modern, and this in itself may have reflected a lack of sympathy with the cathedral tradition. Significantly, Tudway overlooked him completely in compiling his collection, and that unwarranted neglect has persisted to the present day. Burney may have been right in dubbing him 'a wicked punster', but he was completely wrong in calling him a 'no less wicked composer'.[30]

Purcell's successor at Magdalen was Thomas Hecht, the son of Andrew Hecht, organist of Lincoln Cathedral. He served from 1695 until 1734, but is not known as a composer.[31]

NEW COLLEGE

The first post-Restoration organist of New College was William(?) Flexney, from whom Robert Pickhaver took over in 1662.[32] It is probable that the organ-book now in Christ Church Library (MS 1001), with 'R.P.' on the cover, was his;[33] if so, it may represent the New College repertoire in the years before 1664 when he was superseded by William King. (Pickhaver himself succeeded King's father, George King, as organist of Winchester College in 1665.[34] By 1663 not only was there a new organist, but a new organ. Robert Dallam's original design was for a large organ with sixteen stops on the great ('the bigeste pipe—24 fote long') and eight on the chair (including something called 'the antheme stop', possibly to be tuned at choir pitch for accompanying anthems, etc.), in all twelve hundred pipes. Its mixtures, mutations, and reeds, while possibly reflect-

[30] Burney, *History*, ii. 984.   [31] Shaw, 382–3.
[32] Paul R. Hale, 'Music and Musicians', in John Buxton and Penry Williams (eds.), *New College, Oxford, 1379–1979* (Oxford, 1979), 270; Shaw, 388–9.
[33] Clark, *Transposition in Seventeenth-Century English Organ Accompaniments*, 60, 131–4.
[34] Shaw, 398.

ing the taste of Brittany where he had worked as an organ-builder during the Interregnum, were in advance of their time in England, and either for that reason or because of the expense had to be modified. As it was, the instrument cost £443. 12s. 7d. By 1672 it was in a bad state of repair, but no substantial rebuilding seems to have been undertaken during the period, the largest sum being £35 paid to Harris in 1714 for lowering the pitch 'from Gamut D Sol-re to Gamut proper' (see p. 60).[35]

Before moving to New College, William King had been successively one of the clerks of Magdalen College (from 1648) and one of the chaplains (from 1652).[36] At New College his salary was £50 a year as organist, in which position he continued until his death in 1680, aged 57. The New College partbooks (e.g. *Ob* Mus. c. 48) contain at least eighteen anthems by him, and three further anthems and a Service in B flat are known from other sources.[37] Most are incomplete, but the Christ Church 'Barnard set' from Hereford (*Och* 544–53) enables four anthems to be reconstructed, and we can get a good idea of another ten or so from organ scores now at Gloucester and St John's, Oxford, and from the Berkeley Organ Book (*US-BE* 751), originally from Winchester. Tudway— apparently under the impression that King was organist of Christ Church— included the *Te Deum* and *Jubilate* from the Service in B flat in his collection (*Harl.* 7338).

The anthems that seem to have enjoyed the widest circulation were *O be joyful in God* and *The Lord is king*, both full anthems.[38] Neither retains any significant vestiges of the polyphonic style, and their inelegant homophony compares unfavourably with that of Benjamin Rogers at Magdalen. Some of the harmonic progressions are awkward, though a few make a bold effect. Much the same may be said of the service, which circulated quite widely at the time. The verse anthems are marginally more interesting, however. Solos are sometimes quite florid, and the combination of two trebles is favoured—not unusual in the early Restoration period, as is his propensity for weak concluding Hallelujahs. All in all, it is difficult to see why his music won him such a reputation in the early years of the Restoration, unless for its seeming modernity.[39] The opening of *Now that the Lord hath readvanc'd the crown* shows him at his most convincing (Ex. 83). Its political message suggests a date close to 1660.

King's successor was Richard Goodson, whom we have already encountered as organist of Christ Church. He left New College in 1692 and was followed briefly by someone called Read—a 'young hot-head' according to Wood, who 'ript up his own belly upon some discontent' on Low Sunday, 1694.[40] In his place came John Weldon, an ex-chorister from Eton and pupil of Henry

[35] Andrew Freeman, 'Organs at New College, Oxford', 151–3.
[36] Bloxam, *Register*, ii. 60; Shaw, 389.   [37] Cheverton, 'English Church Music', 395–404.
[38] Cheverton, 'Musical Supplement', 16–17, 23–4; see also 101–3, 175–7.
[39] Cheverton, 694–703, is more impressed.   [40] Hale, 272; Shaw, 390.

Ex. 83. William King, *Now that the Lord hath readvanced the crown*
    (*Llb* 29481 and *GL* 111)

(1) Right hand organ part from here, tails down.

Purcell, whose career was to take him, as we have seen, to the Chapel Royal
in 1701. His works, including some written while at New College, have already
been discussed in that connection. Several are to be found in a manuscript (*US-
BE* 173) inscribed 'Simon Child/Ejus Liber 1716'. Child followed Weldon as
organist of New College in 1702 and served until 1731.[41]

ST JOHN'S COLLEGE

The extent to which the choral foundation at St John's survived following the
Restoration is unclear, though there was certainly some kind of choir in 1663
when 'the quire [of St John's] assisted by the Xt. Ch. quire' officiated at the
funeral of Archbishop Juxon.[42] It seems that a new organ had been erected in

---

[41] Shaw, 390.   [42] Clark, *Life and Times of Anthony Wood*, i. 482.

1660 and William Ellis, the pre-war organist, reappointed.[43] Two organ-books dating from these early years can also be traced to St John's (*Och* 437 and *Ojc* 315—the latter partly in Ellis's hand), and give some idea of the repertoire.[44] Works by Robert Lugge, Ellis's predecessor in the 1630s, and Ellis himself establish the connection, while pieces by Lowe, Pickhaver, and King (in *Ojc* 315) are drawn from the wider early Restoration Oxford scene. Those by Ellis include a setting of *Holy, holy, holy* and three anthems, among them, appropriately, a setting of the collect for St John the Baptist's Day and *This is the record of John*—'for a Tennor alone'. There is nothing here, unfortunately, to rival Orlando Gibbons's setting of these words, written for William Laud, when he was President of St John's half a century earlier, yet there are vestiges of polyphonic thinking, side by side with harmonically static declamatory ingredients.[45]

Little is known about the music at St John's after the early years of the Restoration. Ellis presumably continued as organist until his death in 1674, but his immediate successor is unknown. Francis Pigott, said to have been organist of St John's, would not have been appointed until 1683 or so when he left the Chapel Royal,[46] and, as we have seen, he became organist of Magdalen in 1686. There is some evidence that the choir was maintained throughout the period, however, though its members may have been drawn from other Oxford choirs—as happened in Cambridge. By the same token, services may have been sung only on Sundays and holy days, and then to Anglican chants, of which there is a collection in MS 315.

[43] Bicknell, 'English Organ Building', 16; Salter, 'St John's College', 263.
[44] Clark, *Transposition*, 58–9, 124–8, 68–70, 180–3; see also id., 'A Re-emerged Seventeenth-Century Organ Accompaniment Book', *Music and Letters*, 47 (1966), 148–52.
[45] Cheverton, 'Musical Supplement', 167–9.   [46] Shaw, 382; Ashbee, i. 211.

Peterborough

Simon Gunton in his *History of the Church of Peterborough* (1688) has left us a horrifying account of the destruction of the Peterborough organ in 1643 by soldiers directly under the command of Cromwell:

the next day after their arrival, early in the morning, these break open the church doors, pull down the organs, of which there were two pair. The greater pair, that stood upon a high loft over the entrance into the choir, was thence thrown down upon the ground, and there stamped and trampled on, and broke in pieces, with such a strange, furious, and frantick zeal, as cannot be well conceived, but by those that saw it.[1]

However, with John Cosin briefly as the new dean in 1660 it was to be expected that every effort would be made to return to the old ways quickly. Before the year was out the liturgy was being performed daily so that 'many strangers doe come to toune on purpose to heere us, only wee are in great want of a good organist, and alsoe a good organ'.[2] As for the choir, five minor canons and three lay clerks had survived from before the war, and by 1661 the boys were up to strength. The following year the full statutory number of eight minor canons, eight lay clerks, and eight choristers had been achieved.[3]

David Standish, organist and a minor canon before the war, was reappointed in 1661.[4] Whether or not he answered the 'want of a good organist', the good organ was slow in coming. At first one was borrowed, but although payments to Thomas Thamar, the local organ-builder, over the next twenty years add up to a considerable sum, they hardly represent the cost of a new organ of any size. He was employed to carry out further work in 1680 at a cost of £115, but by 1700 the instrument was again in bad repair and needed another £100 spent on it.[5] In the mean time, William Standish inherited the organist's position from his grandfather, serving from 1677 to 1690, and after him Roger Standish from 1690 to 1713.[6] The following year, James Hawkins, junior, broke the three-generation succession of Standishes, he himself being the son of James Hawkins, organist of Ely.[7]

---

[1] Quoted in Scholes, *Puritans and Music*, 236.

[2] W. A. Roberts, 'Peterborough Cathedral and Its Organs', *The Organ*, 10 (1930–1), 3.

[3] Cheverton, 'English Church Music', 51, 64, 118–19; see also Payne, *Provision and Practice*, 205–11, for the pre-war situation.

[4] Cheverton, 589; Shaw, 220–1; Payne, 266.   [5] Roberts, 3.

[6] Shaw, 221–2.   [7] Ibid. 222.

Throughout the early years of the Restoration there are records of payments for new choir music. In 1663 'a set of Song Books with Anthems prick'd £2' was brought down from London, and 'a dozen anthems . . . transcribed by Mr Tucker of Westminster' cost £3. 2s. in 1669–70.[8] Services by Child and Rogers were copied, but none of these manuscripts is extant. It would be surprising, too, if works by John Ferrabosco and Thomas Bullis from nearby Ely were not also added at this time, since they continue to appear in later partbooks. The earliest of these is a bass partbook (MS 1) begun between 1705 and 1713, and completed after 1717. At one end of the manuscript are ninety or so anthems, strongly representing Ely and Cambridge with anthems by James Hawkins and Thomas Tudway, as well as Chapel Royal composers up to and including Croft. At the other end are thirty-three services by most of the older 'mainstream' composers and a number of modern ones, including 'chanting services' by Hawkins and others by William Norris of Lincoln. The absence of Kyrie and Creed settings may indicate that the communion service was not then sung at Peterborough. The scribe, whoever he was, also compiled *Ob* Tenbury 789— a score containing forty-seven anthems 'bought of Mr John Brown one of the Lay Clerks' in 1725.

Among the services in MS 1 are two by Thomas Mudd, whose picaresque career can be traced from 1631, when he was organist of Peterborough for a year. After the Restoration he seems to have held a series of short-lived jobs, some of which overlapped—minor canon at Peterborough (1662–4), organist of Lincoln (1662–3) and Exeter (1664–5), then master of the choristers at York (1666–7).[9] It is perhaps in connection with Peterborough that his music ought to be considered, however, since, if anywhere, this was home to him. Except for the unlikely possibility that the pre-war Thomas Mudd was of a different generation, we are here dealing with one person, clearly an incorrigible but plausible rogue. It is true that there were others of this name—John, Henry, an earlier Thomas—but the situation is not quite so muddy as it seems, and it is highly probable that the services and anthems attributed to either 'Mr' or Thomas Mudd are, in fact, by this man.

Some, perhaps most, of Mudd's music was composed before the Civil War. Three anthems occur in the Peterhouse, Cambridge, 'latter' set of partbooks (MSS 35–7 and 42–6) dating from the 1630s, among them *Let thy merciful ears, O Lord*, which Fellowes attributed to Weelkes.[10] However, five others are found only in Restoration sources, principally at Durham and Ely. One, an attractive full setting of *God, which hast prepared*, was included by Tudway in his collection (*Harl.* 7340) and is mainly polyphonic;[11] another, a verse setting of *I will always*

[8] Cheverton, 280–1.
[9] Shaw, 110–11, 159–60, 220, 317; also *NG* xii. 758–9 (Susi Jeans).
[10] Thomas Mudd, *Let thy merciful ears, O Lord*, ed. E. H. Fellowes, rev. Walter Collins (London, 1960).   [11] Thomas Mudd, *God, which hast prepared us*, ed. John Morehen (Croydon, 1970).

give thanks, shows little of the declamatory style that might have been expected in the 1660s, though the solos are not supported by imitative accompaniments. The first service in F is strictly chordal; the second service in G is a verse service—with an organ part at Oxford (*Ob* Mus. Sch. c. 39) transposed up a fifth for performance on a '10 foot' organ. All this music shows considerable technical competence, and a conservative technique.

None of the Standish organists is known as a composer, but the tenor part from a setting of *Out of the deep* by Francis Standish, minor canon and master of the choristers from 1667 to 1669, is in the Ely collection (*Cu*).[12] Otherwise, the only Peterborough composer of this period seems to have been James Hawkins, the younger, who was appointed organist in 1714.[13] Hawkins had been a chorister under his father at Ely between 1703 and 1707. Seven or eight anthems are attributable to him, and two services, one in B flat, the other in G. A score of the former survives in his father's hand (*Cu* Ely 9), and is an unpretentious 'short' service with three-part verses in triple time. Five anthems specifically attributed to Hawkins, 'junior', were entered in the Peterborough partbooks between 1713 and 1727. Two of them are in score in *Ob* Tenbury 789, *O clap your hands*, which can be dated before 1713, and *The king shall rejoice*, which may have been written for the coronation of King George I in 1714, and was clearly intended to make a splash. Judged by the four anthems in score, he appears to have been a capable enough composer. The extrovert ones adopt the clichés of the time; C and D major prompt trumpet ritornellos in thirds for the organ, and lively triple-time verses for CTB with dotted-quaver passages abound. There is a modest amount of florid solo writing, particularly for bass. A later anthem, *Lord, let me know mine end*, is quite different. The expression is gentle and devoid of bombast, entirely suitable for a funereal occasion, though the note attached to it in Ely MS 9, 'Mr Hawkins Organist of Peterborough | Sung at his funeral Dec[embe]r 28th, 1728' (in his father's hand) is utterly inexplicable as it stands since the younger Hawkins died in 1750, so far as we know. Three large scores in the Ely collection (*Cu* Ely 17–20) carry the signature 'James Hawkins, Jnr, 1726', but most of the contents are in the hand of Hawkins senior.

[12] Shaw, 221–2; Cheverton, 589.   [13] Shaw, 222.

Rochester

While visiting Chatham on naval business in April 1661, Pepys called in at Rochester 'and there saw the Cathedrall, which is now fitting for use, and the Organ then a-tuning'.[1] During the Civil War the cathedral had served as a stable for General Fairfax's troops and sawpits had been dug in the nave, but the organ, according to Thomas Baskerville, had been preserved in a tavern in Greenwich, and thus spared the depredations of the Roundhead soldiery. He noted that although the cathedral was the 'most ruinated of any I have seen in England . . . the choir is handsomely repaired since our late happy change, and the rest will be with what expedition is possible'.[2] By 1668 it was the turn of the organ and Bernard Smith was engaged to repair it, and add 'a new choyre organ' for £214—his first English organ.[3] Further additions 'of one Furniture stopp into the Greate organ and one flute stop into the Choyre organ' were made in 1677, but by 1709 it was said to be 'altogether useless'.[4]

How quickly the choir was re-established is difficult to determine from the scanty records that remain from the immediate post-Restoration years. According to the statutes there should have been six minor canons, a deacon and subdeacon (gospeller and epistoler), six lay clerks, a master of the choristers, and eight choristers, but the offices of deacon and subdeacon had 'of long tyme bene disused' even at Laud's visitation of 1634, though in their place had been 'always twoe clerkes the more'.[5] From 1672, however, an almost complete series of treasurers' books provides details of personnel and stipends.[6] Minor canons were paid £3 a quarter (with 10s. extra for the precentor), lay clerks received £2. 10s., and choristers 16s. 8d. Except that minor canons usually numbered only five, the choir was maintained more or less at statutory strength and enough money was found to pay the organists quite generously: Charles

---

[1] Pepys, *Diary*, ii. 70.

[2] Plank, 'An English Miscellany', 70, quoting from 'Thomas Baskerville's Journies in England', in *The Manuscripts of his Grace the Duke of Portland* (HMC, London, 1893), ii. 277.

[3] L. S. Barnard, 'The Organs of Rochester Cathedral', *The Organ*, 41 (1961–2), 154; Paul R. Hale, *The Organs and Organists of Rochester Cathedral* (Rochester, n.d.), 1; Percy Whitlock, 'The Organs of Rochester Cathedral', *The Organ*, 8 (1918–19), 66. The usual cost given is £167, but the Chapter records at the Kent Archives Office, Maidstone, give £214 (DRc/FTv 230/101).

[4] Freeman, *Father Smith*, 8, 14; Whitlock, 66; Barnard, 154.   [5] HMC, 145.

[6] DRc/FTb 9–50; information below is drawn from these records without further citation.

Wren received £7. 10s. a quarter, Daniel Henstridge £12. 10s., Robert Bowers and John Spain £10.

At least in the earliest years of the Restoration it seems as if the old organist, John Heath, took up his position again. He had held it since 1614 and was said to be about 60 in 1649, so he was now in his seventies and possibly frail; perhaps the promise of a reversion of the post to William Rothwell in 1661 indicated that the latter substituted for him,[7] though whether or not Rothwell succeeded as organist is not known for certain. By 1672 he was precentor (Heath was still listed as a lay clerk) but the organist by then was Charles Wren, an ex-chorister from Canterbury.[8] In 1673 he became organist of Gloucester, more or less exchanging places with Daniel Henstridge, who took over at Rochester in 1674.[9] Henstridge served the cathedral for twenty-five years, moving to Canterbury in 1699, where he remained until 1736. His time at Rochester was probably the heyday of music there, for he was certainly the most distinguished musician to hold office. New organ and choirbooks were provided in 1683–4 and two guineas given to Dr Rogers for presenting the choir with several services. A number of choristers of that time went on to become organists and choirmen at other cathedrals, among them William Popely of Southwell and Richard Henman, later of the Chapel Royal, and organist of Exeter.

Heath, Wren, and Henstridge are all known to have been composers. Heath, whose work probably dates from before the Civil War, wrote an evening service and a setting of *When Israel came out of Egypt* which displays both technique and imagination. Wren and Henstridge, though presumably active as composers while at Rochester, have been dealt with already in connection with Gloucester and Canterbury. Of their successors at Rochester we know little, still less of any music they may have written, due to the complete absence of any partbooks from the period. Robert Bowers, who became organist and master of the choristers in 1699, had been a chorister under Henstridge and a lay clerk from 1692.[10] Almost certainly he is the 'Mr Bower' represented in the Flackton collection (*Lbl* 30932) by two rather mediocre verse anthems. Short-winded and ever ready to lapse into triple time, they hardly engage the attention, though of the two *O come hither and hearken* offers marginally more interest. For some reason it begins in the major and ends in the minor. His successor, John Spain, was likewise an ex-chorister and lay clerk from 1698.[11]

In the early eighteenth century Rochester suffered the same problems that beset other choirs—absenteeism and general slackness. An attempt was made about 1707 to instil some discipline into the choir, and the rules which the Dean and Chapter laid down give an indication both of what should have been, and, by implication, what actually was.[12] It was ordered, reasonably enough, that

---

[7] Shaw, 234; DRc/Arb 2 fo. 19.
[8] Canterbury Cathedral treasurer's book 1660, 36–8; 1664, 7.   [9] Shaw, 235.
[10] Ibid. 236.   [11] Ibid. 236–7.   [12] DRc/A Ac 5/13.

those in holy orders were 'not to appear in church in their nightgowns but properly habited'. Surplices were to be worn at services, priests and deacons only were to perform the litany—minor canons on Wednesdays and Fridays, while those with no parochial duties were to assist at Sunday litany and communion, or be fined. Minor canons as well as lay clerks were forbidden to be absent without written leave and the chanter was to take note of attendance (though up to fifty absences in any half year seem to have been tolerated). Both minor canons and lay clerks were to take their full part in singing and chanting the services, which were to start punctually. Lay clerks were expected to come in before the psalms had started and attend practices as requested by the organist. They were to sit in the stalls below the minor canons, not among them, unless to accommodate strangers on Sundays when clerks might take over the empty stalls of minor canons serving their parishes. The need for clerks and choristers to practise was again underlined in 1712, and the following year the organist was ordered to transcribe new books for the choir, containing 'six of the best services, twelve verse anthems, and six full anthems'.[13] Modest goals and modest achievements seem to be the implication.

As a melancholy postscript it may be observed that things were much worse at the end of the century. It was reported that in 1790 only one lay clerk attended during the week, while two services (Aldrich in G and Rogers in D) and a total of seven anthems had been in rotation on Sundays for the past twelve years.[14]

---

[13] Shaw, 237.   [14] Ibid. 238.

Salisbury

At Archbishop Laud's visitation in 1634 the choir of Salisbury consisted of 'six vicars chorall, wch are to be in holy orders, seaven singing men, wch are not required to be in holy orders and six choristers of wch seaven singing-men, one is teacher of the choristers, and another organist'.[1] By this time the 'singing men', originally members of the college of vicars, had become mere stipendaries.[2] By September 1661 there were four vicars choral, six lay vicars, and seven choristers; and once the full number had been reached, it was more or less maintained throughout the period.[3] In 1686, for instance, the vicars comprised the statutory six priests and seven laymen (each paid £20 a year), all of whom were said to be satisfactory in their attendance, though most of the priest vicars served parishes close by. At that time the choir was made up of seven trebles, four countertenors, four tenors, and five basses.[4]

Almost immediately on his restoration to the see, the bishop, Brian Duppa, gave £100 towards recommissioning the pre-war organ, by Thomas Harris. With admirable foresight, this two-manual instrument, which was supposed to have been similar to Dallam's old Worcester organ, had been taken down and stored before the plunder of the cathedral by the parliamentary forces in 1644. By 1661 it was in service again and remained so for almost fifty years, when Harris's son, Renatus, built its remarkable successor.[5] The organist, Giles Tomkins, half-brother of Thomas Tomkins of Worcester, was also of pre-war vintage, but he seems to have given less satisfaction than his instrument, for in 1667 he was required to show 'greater diligence . . . in the future' as master of the choristers.[6] However, he ran out of future the following year and was succeeded by Michael Wise, a lay clerk from Windsor, who, for all his talent as a composer, gave even less satisfaction.[7] Following his death in 1687, Peter Isaack from Dublin was appointed, but returned to Dublin in 1692.[8] After

[1] HMC, 129.
[2] Kathleen Edwards, 'Cathedral of Salisbury', in R. B. Pugh and Elizabeth Crittal (eds.), *A History of Wiltshire*, iii (The Victoria History of the County of Wiltshire; London, 1956), 198.
[3] Robertson, *Sarum Close*, 199. I am grateful to Suzanne Eward, Librarian and Keeper of the Muniments of Salisbury Cathedral, for supplying me with lists of vicars choral, lay vicars, organists, etc., and details of their service.
[4] Edwards, 197–8.
[5] Robertson, 199; Michael W. Foster, *The Music of Salisbury Cathedral* (London, 1974), 12–13.
[6] Robertson, 201.   [7] Shaw, 262–4.   [8] Ibid. 264.

him came Daniel Roseingrave, previously organist of Gloucester (1679–81) and Winchester (1682–92); he too left for Dublin in 1698 (though his name remained on the books until 1700).[9] The appointment of Roseingrave might have proved another awkward one for the Chapter, in view of what had happened at Gloucester (and was to happen in Dublin), but he seems to have steered clear of trouble while at Salisbury. However, since most of his compositions survive in manuscripts associated with Winchester, it is in that context his music will be considered. Finally came Anthony Walkeley, whose period as organist and instructor of the choristers lasted from 1700 until 1718.[10] It was during his tenure, in 1710, that Renatus Harris built what was to be, and to remain for many years, the largest organ in England, with four manuals and various coupling devices to permit the great to be 'borrowed' (see Ch. 4).[11]

At this time, too, improving finances enabled the number of choristers to be increased to eight, and in 1713 their stipends were raised from £8 to £12 for the two senior boys, from £7 to £10 for the next two, and to £8 for the remainder.[12] They were to receive a new suit of clothes each year and 'every day frequent the Gram[m]ar School and . . . there continue until ten of the clock in the morning at which time they shall attend the Service of the Church and . . . in the afternoon they shall constantly attend the Instructor Choristarum in his Singing-School until the Bell shall tole to evening prayers'.[13]

There is no music surviving at Salisbury from the Restoration period, but eight of the Barnard partbooks now at the Royal College of Music, London (Printed Music I.A.1) once belonged there—six with extensive manuscript additions, dating from 1668–9 mainly, but continuing intermittently into the next century.[14] Works by local composers include a *Benedicite* by Durant Hunt, vicar choral from 1662 to 1671, previously at Chichester, and a gentleman of the Chapel Royal in 1661.[15] There is also a setting of *I will sing unto the Lord* by a 'Mr London'; Christopher London was lay vicar from 1662 and priest vicar from 1665 until 1703. In addition, there are three anthems in a later hand by Anthony Walkeley.

Significantly, there are fifteen anthems and parts of two services by Wise in the partbooks. In Michael Wise, Salisbury had acquired the foremost young composer of the time, for not even the anthems of Humfrey, Blow, or Purcell achieved such a wide circulation. His date of birth is unknown, but was probably about 1648.[16] He was one of the first choristers in the Chapel Royal after the Restoration, leaving the choir in September 1663 and proceeding to Windsor, where he was a countertenor from 1665 (if not earlier) to

[9] Ibid.   [10] Ibid.
[11] Clutton and Niland, *British Organ* (1963), 77–8; Sumner, *The Organ* (1973), 152–3.
[12] Robertson, 228–9.   [13] Ibid. 229.   [14] Cheverton, 'English Church Music', 374–82.
[15] Rimbault, 128; Ashbee, i. 51.   [16] See Smith, 'Church Music of Michael Wise', 2–24.

1668.[17] In the latter year he became lay vicar, organist, and instructor of the choristers at Salisbury, in which capacity he was expected to board the choristers and teach them music. But this was soon recognized as impractical—his unstable temperament, already apparent at Windsor, no doubt had something to do with it—so the authorities reverted to paying the boys a stipend, enabling them to make their own arrangements.[18] One way and another, Wise continued to cause trouble, and his absences at the Chapel Royal from 1676, when he became one of the gentlemen, no doubt exacerbated the situation. 'Because of his extrordinary skill in Music and his composition of various hymns' he was allowed an assistant to teach the choristers in 1677, and another to play the organ (the latter was probably Stephen Jefferies, another unstable character), yet he continued to give cause for complaint. In 1683 the Chapter alleged that he was 'very shamefully and contemptuously negligent in the performance of his Duty in this Church, and . . . doth lye and labour under a notorious Fame of Prophanenesse, Intemperate Drinking, and other Excesses . . . to the Great Scandall of Religion and the Government of this Church'.[19] At this time a bitter dispute between the bishop, Seth Ward, and the dean, Thomas Pierce, was in progress, and something of the state of anarchy existing in the Chapter had spread to the choir. The bishop of Bristol, visiting Salisbury in 1686, reported to Archbishop Sancroft: 'the day I rested in the town the singing-men refused to sing an anthem which was then desired by the bishop's nephew and Canon Hill, and in the afternoon the organist (which, they say, happens often) was absent, and the prayers performed without the organ'.[20] In January the following year, Wise was appointed organist and master of the choristers of St Paul's Cathedral, but he did not long enjoy his promotion. That August, back in Salisbury, 'he was knock'd on the head and kill'd downright by the night-watch . . . for giving stubborne and refractory language to them on S. Bartholomew's day at night', having apparently quarrelled with his wife and rushed out of the house in a rage.[21]

According to Michael Smith, there are twenty-one authentic anthems by Wise, nearly all verse anthems.[22] Another fifteen or so are probably, or possibly, by him. The earliest would seem to be *Christ rising again from the dead* which, since it sets the pre-1662 Prayer Book text (the 1662 version is 'Christ being raised from the dead'), is likely to date from Easter 1661 or 1662, when the composer was still a chorister in the Chapel Royal. Other early anthems include those in the first Restoration set of partbooks at Windsor (MSS 1–4), dating from before 1666. (Later sources are shown by letters which will be explained in due course.)

[17] Ashbee, i. 54, etc.; Bond, *The Chapter Acts of the Dean and Canons of Windsor*, 255–78.
[18] Robertson, 201.   [19] Ibid. 202–4.   [20] Ibid. 217–18.
[21] Adding Wood's account (quoted by Robertson, 204) to that of Hawkins, *History*, ii. 719.
[22] Smith, 41–101.

Have pity upon me, O ye my friends (also *A, B, C, D, E*)
By the waters of Babylon (also *A, B, D, E*)
O praise God in his holiness (also *E*)
Blessed is he that considereth (also *A, B, C, D, E*)

Soon after his move to Salisbury in 1668, three of the above were added to the partbooks there (*Lcm* I.A.1 = *A*) together with six other presumably recent compositions.[23] (Others were added later.)

Awake, up my glory (also *B, C, E, F*)
How are the mighty fallen (also *B, C, E, F*)
The Lord is my shepherd (also *E, F*)
Hearken, O daughter, and consider (also *F*)
Prepare ye the way of the Lord (also *E, F*)
My song shall be alway (also *F*)

The early date of some of these is confirmed by their presence in the Ely manuscripts (e.g. *Cu* Ely 28 = *B*), where they are placed before items by 'Mr' Benjamin Rogers, and are thus 1669 or earlier.

It seems reasonably certain that all these anthems were written before 1670. Further manuscripts of about that date, originating close to Salisbury, include some of them, together with others in all probability dating from within a few years of 1668. These are contained in two sources: an organ-book at Wimborne (MS P 10 = *C*), and a partbook from Winchester (now *Ob* Tenbury 1442 = *D*). The following anthems may therefore be added to the above lists of early work:

Behold, I bring you glad tidings (*C, F*)
O be joyful in the Lord (*C, F*)
Awake, put on thy strength (*C*)
Glory be to God on high (*C*)
Sing we merrily (*C*)
I will always give thanks (*D*)

Thus, over half Wise's output of anthems can be dated before or around 1670, though this does not preclude the possibility that others are also early works. Dating the remainder is more problematic. Playford printed *I charge you, O daughters of Jerusalem* in *Cantica Sacra* (1674), and other middle-period works from the 1670s probably include those not in the above lists which were copied into the Chapel Royal partbooks between 1670 and 1676 (= *E*) and those of New College, Oxford (e.g. *Ob* Mus. c. 49 = *F*).

[23] Cheverton, 379–80.

> *The Lord said unto my Lord (E, F)*
> *'The Prodigal': I will arise (E, F)*
> *The days of man (E)*
> *O give thanks unto the Lord, for he (F)*
> *O Lord, when thou went'st forth (F)*
> *Open me the gates of righteousness (F)*

A date before 1676 may therefore be assigned to those in *E*; those in *F* are probably slightly later.

Finally, we may speculate about several anthems not in the above lists. Of those regarded by Smith as clearly authentic, the presence of *Thou, O God, art praised in Sion* in British Library, Add. MS 30478 probably puts it among the early ones. No sources earlier than the 1680s are known for the other four: *Blessed is the man that hath not walked* is in Fitzwilliam MS 117 (dated 1683 or earlier); *Behold, how good and joyful* and *I will sing a new song* were entered into the later Chapel Royal partbooks about the same time, while *The ways of Sion do mourn* seems to occur only in posthumous sources.

Though Wise's early anthems could not be said to be old-fashioned, they are more conservative in style than those of his fellow choristers Humfrey, Turner, and Blow. He was certainly no less precocious than they, for some of his best-known anthems were written before he was 20. Despite what we know of his character, his work shows restraint and a sense of decorum. Discord and chromaticism, though by no means absent, are handled cautiously and controlled by an ear which puts musical considerations first. The harmonic language is diatonic and wayward passages are rare. There is even a tendency to use sequences and chord progressions based on the circle of fifths that gives the music a 'modern' if rather bland feel—hence, perhaps, the high regard in which he was held in the eighteenth century.

His writing for chorus is simple yet telling, the word-setting enhanced by expressive touches that are rarely disconcerting. Full sections are used to round off the main divisions of an anthem and punctuate the sequence of verses, sometimes as a recurring refrain, as in *Awake, put on thy strength* (Boyce, ii). In verses, open-textured imitation predominates, so that voices are heard in ever-changing combinations of solo, duet, trio, etc., building up to a full complement towards the end of a section. The declamation is accented naturally and express-ively shaped, avoiding exaggerated affective gestures. Wise is clearly aware of the sonority of his voice groupings, and favours the use of trebles for their ethereal effect and supposed connotations of innocence; the treble duets in *The Lord is my shepherd* (*Lbl* 30932) are a case in point. The bass voice, too, is frequently employed, especially in dramatic contexts, but without recourse to the florid style. The solos in *Thy beauty, O Israel* (Boyce, iii), which do bluster a bit, are actually by Aldrich—the work is an expansion of *How are the mighty fallen* (*Cfm* 117).

We have already compared a brief passage in Wise's *By the waters of Babylon* with settings of the same words by Humfrey and Hall (see under Hereford). It was observed that his solo writing was the least forward-looking of the three, and his harmonic language the most conservative. While it is true that old-fashioned counterpoint forms little part of his thinking, his anthems show few modernisms other than a propensity for triple time. Some of his later works, however, do demonstrate a widening stylistic range and a greater inclination to handle diverse material. *Open me the gates of righteousness* (*Och* 12), for example, is a splendid piece with plenty of panache, and seems to betray the influence of the Chapel Royal, as does *I will sing a new song unto thee, O God* (*Harl.* 7339). This work, one of his latest, goes with a swing worthy of Blow's triple-time anthems, and numerous ritornellos for organ between the verses make it even more reminiscent. The music itself hardly pauses for breath, and is given shape by the return of the opening material as a chorus in the middle and at the end. The beginning of each section is given in Ex. 84; the order in which they occur is as follows (capitals indicate chorus): a–b–A–c–A–d–e–f–e–A.

This work gives a good idea of Wise's more extrovert style, though in general it is not typical. His more reflective vein is well represented by *The ways of Sion do mourn* (Boyce, iii), his best-known anthem and probably his last.[24] Somewhat surprisingly, it seems to have gone to Burney's head:

The first movement . . . is so beautiful and expressive, that I shall give it here as a specimen of grave and pathetic composition for the church, which no Music of other countries that I have hitherto discovered, of the same kind, and period of time, surpasses. The use the author has made of chromatic intervals at the word *mourn*, is not only happy and masterly, but *new*, even now, at more than a hundred years distance from the time when the anthem was produced! The whole composition seems to me admirable; and besides the intelligence and merit of the design, the melody is truly plaintive, and capable of the most touching and elegant expression of the greatest singers of modern times; the harmony too and modulation are such as correspond with the sense of the words, and enforce their expression.[25]

Fellowes agrees, while finding the treble and bass duets 'a little too long, and the combination of these voices, so far apart in compass and quality . . . apt to sound thin'.[26] In this connection it may be pointed out that some sources indicate a tenor rather than treble.

---

[24] *Treasury of English Church Music*, iii. 49–57.   [25] Burney, ii. 357.
[26] Edmund H. Fellowes, *English Church Music from Edward VI to Edward VII*, rev. J. A. Westrup (London, 1969), 152.

Ex. 84. Michael Wise, *I will sing a new song (Harl. 7339)*

(1) *a*(?) in source.

Turning to the services, the earliest source we have is of the *Te Deum* in D minor (*Ob* Tenbury 1442), dating from about 1670. Whether the communion and evening canticles in the same key are contemporary with it cannot be said for certain, but their association in many sources suggests as much. The morning and evening services (*Harl.* 7338) represent the early Restoration verse service at its best. They show considerable technical competence and plenty of variety without having recourse (other than briefly in the *Magnificat* and *Nunc dimittis*) to triple time. Not only is there interesting textural contrast between verse and full sections, but in the *Te Deum*, antiphonal effects between decani and cantoris. The Gloria of the *Nunc dimittis* changes to the major mode and provides a canon 2 in 1 at the fifth between the top two voices—something which Blow attempted in his G major Service at this point, though less successfully (Ex. 85).

Ex. 85. Michael Wise, *Nunc dimittis* from the service in D minor (*Harl.* 7338)

In contrast, the communion service is in triple time throughout, and consequently sounds somewhat lightweight. Indeed, virtually all of Wise's other
service music is in triple time. The evening canticles in E flat have been
published in recent times on the strength of their melodic qualities.[27] Another
Evening Service in E minor may have been the service by Wise copied into the
Chapel Royal partbooks between 1670 and 1676, and, in the case of the *Nunc
dimittis*, still there.[28] Later, between 1677 and 1680 the communion services in
E major and F minor were also entered.[29] We may wonder why Wise appears
to have written two communion services, in such unusual keys, without
morning or evening canticles to go with them. One explanation may be that
they were intended as shorter and lighter alternative-mode substitutes for the
corresponding items in services by other composers in E minor and F major—
Child's for example, both of which were in the repertoire at Salisbury. The
possibility that the *Glory be to God on high* in G may likewise be a substitute
needs to be qualified by the fact that it concludes somewhat redundantly with
a Gloria patri.

Viewed as a whole, Wise's church music presents an attractive picture of new
idioms cautiously absorbed into a fundamentally traditional musical language.
There is no question of him belonging to the school of Child or Rogers;
equally, he stopped short of Humfrey's wholehearted commitment to the latest
styles. Leaving temperament and his natural musical proclivities aside, Wise's
provincial situation probably goes some way to explaining this conservatism,
though the musical fashions of the Chapel Royal may have begun to affect him
after he became a gentleman in 1676. However, he seems to have written little
music after this date. Hardly more than 40 at the time of his death, and on the
threshold of a new stage in his career at St Paul's, he could have been at the
point of new departures that were not to be. Despite the modest scale and
subdued effect of his work, his achievement was considerable, nevertheless, and
deserves greater recognition.

The only other significant Salisbury composer during the period after
Wise was Anthony Walkeley. Presumably he came from Wells, where several
generations of his family served in the choir. There was an Anthony Walkeley
among the vicars choral there in 1632, and another of the same name was
admitted probationer vicar in 1670. This is likely to have been the father or
uncle of the composer; the composer himself died in 1718 aged 45.[30] The name
continued at Wells until 1691 at least, reappearing thereafter in connection with
payments for copying or writing music; for example, in 1704–5 '£1. 1s. 6d. 'to

---

[27] Michael Wise, *Magnificat and Nunc Dimittis* [transposed into F], ed. Christopher Dearnley
(London, 1973).

[28] Ashbee, i. 162; Watkins Shaw, 'A Contemporary Source', 44.   [29] Ashbee, i. 193.

[30] William P. Baildon (ed.), *Calendar of the Muniments of the Dean and Chapter of Wells* (London,
1914), iii. 418; Derek S. Bailey, *Wells Cathedral Chapter Act Book, 1666–83* (London, 1973), 18, etc.

Ex. 86. Anthony Walkeley, *Jubilate* from the sevice in E♭ (*Harl.* 7342)

Mr Walkeley *pro le anthem'* and the same sum in 1707–9 for a service.[31] These later references could be to the composer for copies of his works sent from Salisbury.

Three services and thirteen anthems by him can be traced, though few of the anthems now survive. *Divine Harmony* (1712) gives the words of ten that were no doubt sung at Salisbury while he was there, but of these only *O Lord, thou hast searched me out* is extant (*Cu* Ely 9)—a competent but rather characterless piece for treble and bass soloists. The Salisbury Barnard books (*Lcm*) preserve parts of three others, too fragmentary to reveal much about the music, though furnishing specimens of his autograph.

[31] Baildon, 470, 487, 490.

Walkeley's services have fared better. A verse Service in F seems, on the evidence of its organ score (*Och* 1229), to be a respectable piece of work. The *Te Deum* and *Jubilate* in E flat, which both Tudway and Flackton included in their collections (*Harl.* 7342 and *Lbl* 30933), despite being mainly in triple time, actually achieves a kind of modest grandeur. Some of its writing is quite expansive, and there is a verse in the *Jubilate* ('For he is gracious') which divides into six parts; three on one side of the choir alternate with three on the other, coming together in six real parts at the cadence, not without some Purcellian clashing of seconds (Ex. 86). West mentions a Service in A, 'for long time a favourite at Salisbury', which has not been traced.[32]

[32] West, *Cathedral Organists* (2nd edn.), 102.

Wales

The four Welsh cathedrals of Bangor, Llandaff, St Asaph, and St David's were all 'old foundations', modest in size, poorly endowed by English standards, and geographically isolated. There was even a proposal soon after 1660 that the see of St David's should be moved to Carmarthen due to the 'melancholies and loneliness of the place', but nothing came of it.[1] Indeed, little came of anything. The Welsh church was in decline, and this was reflected in the state of its cathedral music. Lack of money went back to the impoverishment of the church at the Reformation; lack of morale stemmed from the endemic alienation of the indigenous population from the established church.[2] Despite some excellent bishops, and, indeed, some good intentions on the part of deans and chapters in the latter part of the seventeenth century, the clergy lost heart and non-residence made matters worse. Significantly, new endowments for the choirs of Bangor and St Asaph produced hopeful, but short-lived, improvements. No doubt the office was celebrated daily, but the evidence suggests that only on Sundays and holy days were services and anthems sung. It was a struggle even to keep that up, and at Llandaff the struggle had been lost completely by the end of the century.

BANGOR

There was an organist at Bangor before the Civil War, and some kind of choir of men and boys—the latter scholars from the Friars' School comprising 'Glyn boys', 'Hutchings boys', and two further endowed choristers, making perhaps fifteen in all.[3] Following the Restoration a similar arrangement was probably reinstated, though evidence is lacking. Soon after 1666 a new organ was built, thanks to a bequest of £100 by the bishop, William Roberts, and placed in a gallery at the entrance to the choir.[4] Then, in 1685, an act of Parliament secured an augmented income 'for the maintenance of the Choir at Bangor', and this

---

[1] Ian Cheverton, 'Cathedral Music in Wales during the Latter Part of the Seventeenth Century', *Welsh Music*, 8/1 (1986), 8.

[2] Hutton, *The English Church*, 354–60.

[3] Leslie Paul, *Music at Bangor Cathedral* (Bangor, 1975), 6.

[4] Ibid. 3–4; Bishop Roberts died in 1665.

enabled the new dean, John Jones, to set about improving things.[5] In 1690 he wrote: 'I conceive that there are many things wanting . . . particularly the settlement of a Quire, and of a good Organist and of Singing-men.' The following year Thomas Roberts was appointed organist at a salary of £14, rising in stages to £20 by 1698, while the endowments paid for four singing men at £8 each, and four choristers.

In 1701 the practice seems to have been for the choir to be present on Sundays, holy days, and their eves, with an anthem 'every Sunday when the sermon is in English [bilingual services were a feature at Bangor] and in the choir before noon and on the other Sundays in the afternoon'.[6] Tallis's 'Dorian Service' was apparently the staple diet, but in 1703 the organist was ordered 'to teach and practice three other services beside Tallis (whereof two at least to be alternate, or for sides) and that the singing men and boys be obliged to learn and practice the said services, and the Dean and chapter allow them time till Christmas to be perfect in the said services'.[7]

Roberts died in 1705 and was succeeded by (?Nathaniel) Priest, nominated to the post by Henry Hall of Hereford,[8] and promised a gratuity of £5 'if it appear in the year's end that the said Mr Priest hath . . . done much in way of improvement of the choir in point of singing with relation to services, and anthems and chants'. Successful or not in this task, he seems to have left Bangor in 1708, though the name Nathaniel Priest does not re-emerge until 1710 as organist of Bristol (q.v.). Priest, in his turn, was followed at Bangor in quick succession by a Mr Smith (1708), then by someone called Ferrer (1710), and in 1712 by John Rathbone, an ex-chorister from Lichfield, recently dismissed from his lay clerkship at Chester for 'many very great misdemeanours and enormities'.[9] During his incumbency as organist, progress towards enlarging the range of services sung by the choir was slow, judging by the order of Dean and Chapter in 1718 'that the organist be obliged to teach forthwith the Commandments and Nicene Creed, and those in Tallis's and Child's, as soon as they can be had, and to add Bird's service to the other'.

LLANDAFF

In the 1660s and early 1670s a serious, if modest, attempt seems to have been made to build up the music at Llandaff. Whether the pre-war organist, George Carr, survived to the Restoration is not known,[10] but interestingly, two verse anthems by him (*I have lifted up mine eyes* and *Let thy loving mercy*) were included in Clifford's *Divine Services and Anthems* (1664). By 1672 the organist was

[5] Details which follow are from Paul, 6–7; see also Shaw, 21–2.   [6] Shaw, 22.
[7] Paul, 7.   [8] Shaw, 22.   [9] Ibid. 66.   [10] Ibid. 166.

someone called Wrench; his stipend was £4 a quarter (reduced to £3 the following year), as was that of Mr Lewis, master of the choristers. The other six singing men were each paid £5 a year and the four choristers half that. The following year it was ordered that 'the organist and singing men, together with the singing boys, shall meet at the Quire or Lady Chapel of the Cathedral . . . every Tuesday and Thursday weekly by nine of the clock in the morning . . . that they may be further instructed as their teacher shall think expedient'. Records suggest that services were sung only on Sundays and holy days, but even this came to a stop in 1691, when lack of money forced the Chapter to order 'the quire singing to be put down and discontinued'. All that remained was parochial psalmody.[11] Next to go was the fabric. By 1722 the south-west tower had collapsed, the roof of the nave had caved in, and only the Lady Chapel was weatherproof.

ST ASAPH

Although the choir had been re-established at the Restoration, by 1675 it was necessary to warn the vicars, singing men, and choristers that they would be fined if they continued to neglect their duties.[12] By act of Parliament in 1678, certain rectories in the counties of Denbigh, Montgomery, and Flint were appropriated to provide income 'for repairs of the Cathedral Church of St *Asaph*, and the better Maintenance of the Choir there'.[13] About the same time a move was begun to raise money to repair the organ, and between 1682 and 1686 the accounts show that 'one Mr [Bernard] Smith, an Artist therein' was employed to mend the organ, which by that time was more than fifty years old.[14] At the visitation of 1694 the establishment consisted of four vicars, four lay clerks, an organist, and four choristers.[15]

The organists of this period included Thomas Ottey, 'Vicar, Precentor & Organist' (previously a conduct at Chester and before that a vicar at Lichfield), who died in 1671, William Key(s) or Kay (previously organist of Manchester Collegiate Church and later of Chester Cathedral), who served from 1679 to 1686, and Thomas Hughes, who died in 1693.[16] Ottey and Hughes are possibly

---

[11] The above from Shaw, 166, and Cheverton, 11–13. According to Browne Willis the demise of the choir was 'on pretext of applying their Stipends towards repairing the Fabrick', whereas 'their Salaries or Dividends have been, as 'tis commonly reported in these Parts, ever since shared and applied to augment the Income of the abovesaid fourteen Members of the Chapter, notwithstanding they have never resided, and have neglected repairing the Cathedral' (*Parochiale Anglicanum* (London, 1733), 197).

[12] Cheverton, 'Cathedral Music', 9.   [13] Ibid.

[14] Graham J. Elliott, 'The Music of St Asaph's Cathedral' (MA diss., University College, Bangor, 1982), 62; Cheverton, 9; Freeman, *Father Smith*, 30.

[15] Elliott, 10.   [16] Ibid.; Shaw, 243–4.

the composers of two anthems at Worcester, respectively *Have mercy upon me, O God* and *Let my complaint,* although the attributions indicate only surnames, and Ottey had a brother, William, who was master of the choristers at Chester. Hughes's successor was Alexander Gerrard, a chorister in the Chapel Royal under Blow until 1694, whose tenure at St Asaph lasted from then until 1738.[17] West noted that some of his anthems survived in partbooks there—but apparently they are now no longer extant.[18]

ST DAVID'S

In times past, St David's had been foremost among Welsh cathedrals, with as many as sixteen vicars choral and seven choristers in 1504,[19] but these had dwindled to a succentor, eight vicars, two subdeacons, and four choristers, according to the visitation of 1668.[20] As to the music performed we know very little. If local pride played any part in determining what was sung, it should have included music by Thomas Tomkins, whose father had been master of the choristers and who was probably a chorister there himself before the family moved to Gloucester in 1594.[21] However, the two partbooks of *Musica Deo Sacra* (1664) now in the cathedral library are recent acquisitions.[22] A list of services and anthems which the choir was enjoined to practise (for at least one hour a week) in 1707 includes five services, among them Blow 'in E la mi', and ten anthems by unspecified composers. Almost certainly the setting of *Call to remembrance* would have been Richard Farrant's, while the others may have included Weldon's *Hear my crying,* Purcell's *Rejoice in the Lord,* and one or two by Wise and Humfrey.[23]

By this time the cathedral had a new organ. The old one had been out of order for many years, and from 1695 steps were taken to set money aside to pay for a new one. A one-manual instrument of eight stops by Bernard Smith costing £290 was eventually installed in 1704–5, transport from London and sundries adding considerably to the expense.[24] Most of the seventeenth-century organists are unknown, though in 1673 and again in 1684 William Pardoe, one of the vicars, was named as such.[25] He seems to have served until 1697, when

---

[17] Shaw, 244–5.   [18] West, *Cathedral Organists,* 96.

[19] Harrison, *Music in Medieval Britain,* 16.   [20] Cheverton, 8.

[21] Stevens, *Thomas Tomkins,* 25–6.

[22] David R. A. Evans, 'A Preliminary Investigation of an Eighteenth-Century Bass Part-Book from St David's Cathedral', *Welsh Music,* 6/7 (1981), 48.

[23] David R. A. Evans, 'A Short History of the Music and Musicians of St David's Cathedral', *Welsh Music,* 7/8 (1984), 63.

[24] J. Eric Hunt, 'The Organs of St David's Cathedral', *The Organ,* 32 (1952–3), 49; H. Stubbington, 'The Organs of St David's Cathedral', *The Organ,* 21 (1941–2), 2; Freeman, *Father Smith,* 41, 142.

[25] Evans, 'Short History', 61–2; Shaw, 250–1.

Henry Mordant took over for the period up to 1714. At various times he received payments for copying services and anthems (and 'Dr [*sic*] Gibbons Responses'). As Watkins Shaw observes: 'clearly, a substantial effort was being made to keep up the choral services in the Cathedral' during his tenure.[26]

The choir seems to have been held at eight vicars (four priests and four laymen) and four choristers up to the time of the 1736 visitation; one of the vicars, the so-called 'Welsh minister', being responsible for singing the service 'in the Welsh language'.[27] There is no evidence, however, that the choir music was sung in Welsh.

[26] Shaw, 251–2; Evans, 'Short History', 64.   [27] Evans, 'Short History', 61–2, 64.

Wells

At the archiepiscopal visitation of 1634, the Dean and Chapter of Wells stated that under their statutes the choir consisted of 'fowerteene vicars at the least, one organist, six coristars'.[1] Post-Restoration records suggest that it was kept pretty well up to strength, with priests or laymen without distinction varying in number between eleven and fourteen, including the organist.[2] In 1661 this was John Okeover (or Oker), either the one who had been organist and master of the choristers before the Civil War, or his son—one of whom was also organist of Gloucester (q.v.) from 1640. In view of the report that 'widdow Oker' was living in the choristers' house at Wells in 1649 (implying that her husband, the old organist, was already dead), it seems more likely that it was the younger Okeover who was organist of Gloucester before the Civil War, and became organist of Wells after the Restoration. The evidence, however, is not conclusive. Whichever it was, he was dead by July 1663.[3]

The old pre-war organ had been destroyed by Roundhead soldiers one afternoon in May 1643, along with the windows, font, choir stalls, and bishop's throne.[4] A small organ costing £80 was in use soon after the Restoration, but by 1664 a new 'fair, well tuned usefull and beutiful double Organ' by Robert Taunton of Bristol had been erected on the screen for £800. Its specification shows eight stops on the great and six on the chair, very much in the old English style, with neither reeds nor mixtures until a cornet stop was added in 1673. The largest diapason pipe was twelve and a half feet in length, which would have sounded about *FF*.[5]

Okeover died before the organ was finished. His successor was John Browne, on whose death in 1674 'Mr Hall' stepped in for a few months as a stopgap.[6] (This would have been Henry Hall, who later that year became organist of Exeter and subsequently of Hereford.) Next came John Jackson; in 1678–9 he received a £10 stipend as organist, a further £23 'in augmentation', and £20 as master of the choristers.[7] During his time the organ was entrusted to the care of

[1] HMC, 140.   [2] See the lists in Bailey, *Wells Cathedral Chapter Act Book*.
[3] Bowers et al., *Organs and Organists of Wells Cathedral*, 18–20; Shaw, 286–7; also Wyn K. Ford, 'The Life and Work of John Okeover (or Oker)', *Proceedings of the Royal Musical Association*, 84 (1957–8), 71–80.
[4] Bowers et al., 4.   [5] Ibid. 4–5 for above details, including a picture of the case.
[6] Ibid. 20; Shaw, 287.
[7] Bowers et al., 20; Baildon (ed.), *Calendar of the Muniments*, iii. 443–4; Shaw, 287–8.

Renatus Harris, who added two new stops in 1681, and repaired it after Monmouth's 'rebel fanatics' had all but ruined it on 1 July 1685.[8] In 1707 he received £40 'for the eccho stop put in some time since', but in 1708–9 maintenance passed into the hands of Thomas Swarbrick.[9]

Robert Hodge was already a vicar before he succeeded Jackson as organist in 1688, but after little more than two years he left to become a lay clerk at Durham, and soon after that, organist of St Patrick's Cathedral, Dublin (q.v.).[10] John George, who followed him, served from 1690 to 1712; thereafter William Broderip held office from 1713 until his death in 1727, having been made master of the choristers in 1716.[11]

Of these organists, Okeover, Jackson, and Broderip are known as composers. However, the local composer to achieve the widest reputation was Robert Creighton, whose father, also Robert, was dean of Wells at the Restoration, and from 1670, bishop of Bath and Wells. Each had been professor of Greek at Cambridge, but in 1674 the son was made precentor of Wells, which position doubtless afforded plenty of opportunity for him to excerise his musical talent.[12] Bumpus was aware of eleven anthems and nine services by Creighton, not all of which can now be traced.[13] Tudway included two anthems and services in C and E flat in his collection (*Harl.* 7338–9). Another source is an organ-book now at the Royal College of Music, London (MS 673), but originally from Wells, containing further services and anthems, together with works by other Wells composers.[14] This manuscript was begun sometime after 1678 (the year of Creighton's Doctor of Divinity degree, which is accorded him on the first page) and finished in 1685 or soon after.

The surviving versions of Creighton's services show many variants, amounting sometimes to radical revisions that may be explained by the fact that MS 673 and Tudway's collection are separated in time by more than thirty years, and that Creighton himself lived on to 1734. A study of these works, in so far as their incomplete nature allows, shows him to have been a capable composer. From the point of view of melodic and harmonic interest he can hold up his head in the company of Child and Rogers, and the absence of rough edges does not result in insipidity. The E flat Service was widely known in the eighteenth century, and printed more than once in the nineteenth. The verse sections in the Creed illustrate his style at its best, exploiting vocal colour and harmonic expressiveness in a manner which, far from being 'monotonously correct',[15] comes as close to being imaginative as the style will permit (Ex. 87*a–b*). The

---

[8] Bowers *et al.*, 5; Baildon, 445–6, 455–8.   [9] Bowers, 5; Baildon, 488, 490.

[10] Bowers, 20; Shaw, 288.   [11] Bowers, 21; Shaw, 289.

[12] See *DNB* for father and son.

[13] Bumpus, *History of English Cathedral Music*, i. 186–8. *Ckc* 413, a late 18th-c. organ-book, contains four services, including one in F minor.

[14] Cheverton, 'English Cathedral Music', 464–6.   [15] Dearnley, 199.

Wells

Ex. 87. Robert Creighton: (*a*) – (*b*) Creed and (*c*) *Magnificat* from the service in E♭ (*Harl.* 7339)

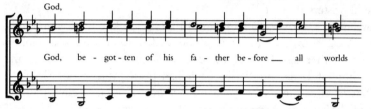

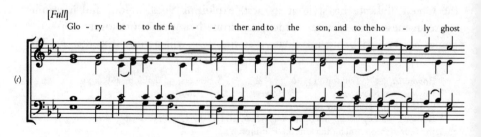

professionalism is a credit to his amateur status; and sometimes he is lucky, as amateurs deserve to be—for example, in the sevenths at the beginning of the Gloria to the *Magnificat*, and the lush harmony that follows (Ex. 87c).

Of the eleven anthems, four are in MS 673, but only as figured basses. Tudway included *I will arise* (Boyce, ii) and *Praise the Lord, O my soul* in his collection, and it is by the former that Creighton is best known. The canonic writing (3 in 1 at the fifth below and fourth above for much of the time) has often been commented on, and so far as it goes—which is not really very far, considering the amount of repetition involved—it works well enough. Modern writers have been somewhat cool on the subject, but Thomas Helmore was evidently of the opinion that no words 'however eloquent, from a preacher can convey the intense humility and sorrowing repentance in which the prodigal returns to his home, as Creighton's touching little anthem'.[16] Creighton's reputation, like that of Henry Aldridge, perhaps owes more to his status among the 'reverend dilettanti' (Burney's term) than to his qualities as a composer. Nevertheless, he is not to be underestimated, and Burney was being no more than fair when he wrote 'though he was not gifted with great original genius . . . yet he has left such pleasing and elegant proofs of his progress in the art, as manifest judgment, taste, and knowledge'.[17] He might, indeed, have called him 'the admirable Creighton'.

John Jackson was appointed organist of Wells in 1674, the year Creighton became precentor.[18] We find him as *informator choristarum* at Ely in 1669, and a lay clerk at Norwich from 1670. At least two services and eleven anthems are attributed to him, besides a Burial Service, the whereabouts of which are unknown.[19] For one of the services composed at Wells he was paid £1 in 1681, with a further £1 as a 'reward'.[20] In all probability RCM MS 673 is in his hand, or mainly so. The presence of treble and bass, as well as figuring and written-out contrapuntal entries, gives sufficient detail to permit an assessment of the two services by him which it contains. They are attractive works in C major and G minor respectively, unified by head-motifs. In general they resemble those of Creighton, but Jackson is more up to date in varying his movement with triple-time sections, and providing greater tonal and textural variety. Changes to the minor at appropriate passages are a feature of the C major Service: for example, at the words 'And was crucified also for us' in the Creed (Ex. 88). The same manuscript contains nine anthems by Jackson in a more sketchy form than the services, though *O how amiable are thy dwellings* can be reconstructed from the Norwich partbooks, now in the library of King's College, Cambridge (Rowe MSS 9–17). Its open-textured declamatory duet-writing is typical of the early Restoration verse anthem.

Several works must date from 1674 or earlier: not only the two in Playford's *Cantica Sacra* (1674), but a further two in the Rowe MSS, given their Norwich

[16] Quoted in Bumpus, i. 189. [17] Burney, *History*, ii. 478.
[18] See above, n. 7. [19] *DNB*. [20] Baildon, 445.

358   *Wells*

Ex. 88. John Jackson, Creed from the Service in C (*Lcm* 673)

Passages in square brackets are editorial.

provenance and the fact he left Norwich that year. The latter include *The Lord
said unto my Lord* (*Harl.* 7338) and *Christ our passover*—a five-part full anthem,
very corrupt and probably misattributed in view of the completely different
version in MS 673. This source presumably contains anthems written after his
arrival in Wells, among them *Many a time they fought*, a thanksgiving anthem for

Ex. 89. John Jackson, *God standeth in the congregation* (*Lcm* 673)

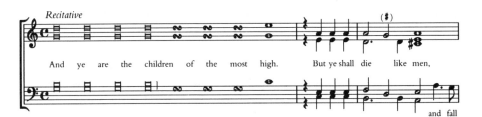

The passages in square brackets are editorial, as is the underlay.

the discovery of the Rye House Plot (9 September 1683), and *I said in the cutting off of my days* for recovery from a dangerous sickness 'Anno 1685'—which, if intended for the king, was somewhat ineffectual. One point of interest in these later anthems is a passage marked 'Recitative' in *God standeth in the congregation*

(Ex. 89). This kind of unmeasured choral declamation is unknown as a device in English church music outside the chanting of psalms and canticles, but striking in its context, and reminiscent of Monteverdi.

The only other composer represented in MS 673 is 'Father Joshua Lasher' (so called), a vicar choral between 1673 and 1702, whose *When Israel came out of Egypt* also occurs in the Berkeley Organ Book from Winchester (*US-BE* 751). In addition to services and anthems, MS 673 contains a set of 'Welles Tunes'— four-part chants (four by Jackson and one by Lasher) set to the *Venite*, but applicable to any psalm.

William Broderip, the last organist of our period, is known as the composer of a service and anthem included by Tudway in the final volume of his collection (*Harl.* 7342). Born 10 July 1683, he was appointed a vicar at Wells in 1701 and became sub-treasurer in 1706.[21] As such his duties were to seal leases, 'receiving 2*s*. 6*d*. for every lease' (having provided the wax), to look after the plate and vestments, and buy bread and wine for every communion 'at the charge of the dean and chapter, receiving for his salary 40*s*. yearly'. He also had to care for the altar linen, 'receiving 2*s*. yearly for washing the same', and see that the candlesticks were 'clean scoured and hung up on All Saints even until the day after Candlemas, for which his fee is 1*s*. 6*d*.'.[22] His anthem *God is our hope and strength* was written to celebrate the Peace of Utrecht in 1713, and is decked out with symphonies and instrumental accompaniments incorporating trumpet idioms appropriate both to the occasion and the key (D major), though the vocal writing is not particularly florid. The service is in the same key and similar in style. There are some briefly impressive moments, but the overall effect is scrappy—not made less so by a disconcerting habit of changing from 'full' to 'verse' (or *vice versa*) in mid-sentence; thus, in the *Nunc dimittis* 'Lord' is sung full, but continues 'now lettest thou thy servant' as a verse duet.

Following Broderip's death, it was ordered that his widow receive 7*s*. a week 'for the support of herself and her 10 children'.[23] Several of these children spread their father's name and practised his profession in various places in the West Country, and as far afield as Canterbury.

---

[21] Bowers *et al.*, 21.   [22] Baildon, 488.   [23] Ibid. 516.

Winchester

WINCHESTER CATHEDRAL

The choir seems to have been quickly reassembled at Winchester Cathedral. Not only was an anthem sung at the proclamation of Charles as king on 12 May 1660,[1] but by the end of the year it was up to strength, apart from four of the six minor canons.[2] The 1638 statutes had laid down a choral establishment of six minor canons, ten lay clerks, and six choristers, with an organist who might also be master of the choristers unless it was felt that one of the minor canons or lay clerks would be more suitable.[3]

By 1662, when Archbishop Juxon made his visitation, there were four minor canons: 'two places of the Peticanons are voyd, because two Peticanons (who are required to be in full orders, yet well instructed in musick) cannot as yet be found'.[4] The Chapter Book for 1660 lists Christopher Gibbons as organist and John Silver as master of the choristers; one of the minor canons was Richard Ayleward, father of the Norwich organist, and rector of St Maurice's in the town. While there were only four minor canons it was ordered that they each receive £30 a year, reverting to £25 when they were up to strength, with £4 extra for the precentor and £2 for the epistoler. By comparison, the lay clerks would seem to have been poorly paid at £13. 10s. each, but between 1660 and 1670 annual augmentations raised their stipends to £21, with extra for the two who served as sub-sacrists. The organist, at least from the time of Randall Jewett onwards, received a comfortable salary of £57. 5s., and the boys £2. 13s. 4d. each.[5]

Christopher Gibbons, who had seen the desecration of the altar, the burning of the choirbooks, and the pulling down of the organ by parliamentary troops in 1642,[6] moved on almost immediately after the Restoration to become

[1] Ian M. Green, *The Re-establishment of the Church of England, 1660–1663* (Oxford, 1978), 3.
[2] Information not otherwise documented in this section is drawn from the Chapter books (1660–) and treasurers' books (1660–) in the Chapter Library, under the relevant dates.
[3] Goodman and Hutton, *The Statutes Governing the Cathedral Church of Winchester*, 55.
[4] W. R. W. Stephens and F. T. Madge, *Documents Relating to the History of the Cathedral Church of Winchester in the Seventeenth Century* (London, 1897), 113.
[5] Details of the above from the treasurers' books; also Stephens and Madge, 112–13, 121–2, 126–35.
[6] Scholes, *Puritans and Music*, 233; Betty Matthews, *The Music of Winchester Cathedral* (London, 1974), 14.

organist of Westminster Abbey, whereupon John Silver succeeded him. It was not until 1665 that the Dean and Chapter took steps to acquire a new organ, although some kind of instrument must have been in use up till then. The contract was with Thomas Thamar of Cambridge to make and set up a 'substantiall good & perfect double Organ' where the old one had been on the north side of the choir.[7] 'The said double Organ shall consist of a faire great Organ and a Chaire Organ', the former with nine stops each of fifty-one pipes 'whose pitch is to be Gam ut in D sol re ... the biggest pipe conteyning thirteene foot in length', the latter with five stops, the whole to cost £720. At 13′, the lowest note would have sounded about (modern) *EE*, but the phrase 'Gam ut in D sol re' indicates an instrument in which the bottom note *G* sounded *DD* (which in the seventeenth century was two or three semitones sharper than today). The organ would thus belong to a group of early Restoration 'transposing' organs such as existed at Gloucester, Salisbury, and Worcester, among other places. It is not known if the pair of carved angels preserved in the triforium belonged to this organ, but if so, it is possible that their movable outer arms were part of some mechanical device to relay the beat to the choir.[8]

While the new organ was being built the plague hit Winchester, and during the second half of 1666 the 'chanting service' was suspended 'by reason of the great increase of the sickness within the City of Winton and the suburbs thereof'.[9] One casualty may have been the organist, John Silver, who died in November 1666. The choral service was resumed after Christmas, but slack attendance caused the authorities to insist that 'there shall be present seven at least of the Petty Canons and Lay Vicars every service. And if the number of seven be not present, then the absent are to be punished twelve pence a peice'.[10]

No music books from this period now survive at Winchester, but J. S. Bumpus seems to have owned several manuscripts of Winchester provenance, notably a bass partbook, now *Ob* Tenbury 1442,[11] and an organ-book in the hands of successive organists, John Reading and Daniel Roseingrave, now in the University of California Music Library, Berkeley (MS 751).[12] The bass partbook is presumably to be dated before and after 'March 25th 1669', which is written on fo. 83ʳ. For the most part it represents an old-fashioned repertoire, but Restoration composers include Bryne, Child, Ferrabosco, Lowe, King, Rogers, Tucker, and Wise. Significantly, there are services and anthems by Silver and Jewett in it. Most of these are also in the Berkeley Organ Book, the early

---

[7] Matthews, *Organs and Organists of Winchester Cathedral*, 5–6; A. Cecil Piper, 'Notes on Winchester Cathedral Organs', *The Organ*, 1 (1921–2), 177–8; G. St M. Willoughby, 'The Organs of Winchester Cathedral', *The Organ*, 9 (1929–30), 2–3.

[8] See Matthews, *Organs*, 7, for picture.   [9] Crook, *History of the Pilgrims' School*, 11.

[10] Stephens and Madge, 117.   [11] Cheverton, 'English Church Music', 404–8.

[12] Clark, *Transposition in Seventeenth-Century English Organ Accompaniments*, 54–5, 105–14; Cheverton, 475–8.

section of which, though generally conservative in nature, includes more recent work by Tucker and Wise, a few anthems by Blow, Humfrey, and Turner, and several by John Reading, in whose hand this part of the manuscript is written. The later section, in the hand of Daniel Roseingrave, is swollen by a considerable number of more up-to-date anthems by Aldrich, Blow, Humfrey, Purcell, Turner, and Wise, including a service and five anthems by Roseingrave himself.

On the basis of these two books it is possible to give some account of the work of Winchester composers in the period up to 1690—John Silver, Randall Jewett, John Reading, and Daniel Roseingrave. Silver had been 'Mr of the Queresters and singing man' since 1638.[13] It is probably to him rather than the younger composer of that name that the service and three anthems in the bass partbook belong. (John Silver, junior, was a lay clerk at Winchester until he resigned in 1663 to become organist of Wimborne Minster, where these works also survive.) Two of the anthems are settings of offertory sentences from the communion service (*Let your light so shine before men* and *Lay not up for yourselves treasure*), the singing of which may have been a Winchester practice at this time.

Randall Jewett was born about 1603 and was a chorister at Chester from 1612 to 1615. In 1631 he became organist at both Christ Church and St Patrick's cathedrals in Dublin. He was briefly organist of Chester on the eve of the Civil War, but returned to Dublin after the siege of Chester in 1646. Later he travelled to London, where he is listed among teachers 'For the Organ and Virginall' in 1651. At the Restoration he was appointed almoner of St Paul's and junior cardinal, but following the Great Fire he moved to Winchester as organist and master of the choristers in 1666. He continued, nevertheless, to enjoy various emoluments from St Paul's up to his death in 1675, aged 72.[14] He is known as the composer of an Evening Service in G 'for verses' and six anthems. Whether they were composed before or after the Civil War is difficult to say. Most of them were in the repertoire at Winchester during his time there, but the fact that several were sung in Dublin (q.v.) within a couple of years of the Restoration suggests a pre-war date of composition. The only one that survives complete, *I heard a voice from heaven*, is found in a pre-war source (Henry Loosemore's organ-book, New York Public Library, Drexel MS 5469), though Tudway provides us with a score (*Harl.* 7339).

John Reading came to Winchester from Lincoln via Chichester. At Lincoln he was a junior vicar and poor clerk (1667), then master of the choristers (1670); at Chichester he was admitted organist and Sherbourne clerk on 28 December 1674.[15] Describing himself as a widower of about 30 years of age, he applied for

---

[13] Matthews, *Organs*, 21; Shaw, 297–8.

[14] Bridge, 'Organists of Chester Cathedral', 84–90; Shaw, 64, 182, 298, 409–10, 417; Scholes, *Puritans and Music*, 166; Matthews, *Organs*, 21–2.

[15] Matthews, *Organs*, 22; Shaw, 76–7, 160, 298.

a licence to marry Ann Mickelthwaite of Lincoln on 20 March 1675. Later that same year he was appointed organist, lay clerk, and master of the choristers at Winchester, attracted there, no doubt, by better pay and an altogether grander establishment. In 1678 he was admonished 'for giving undue and oversevere correction to some of the choristers' and warned 'to take greater care and diligence in the improvement of the Choristers in Musick than hitherto he hath done'.[16] Three years later he resigned to become organist of Winchester College, where he is remembered as composer of the college graces and school song *Dulce domum*. (He has even been credited, erroneously, with the music for *Adeste fideles*.[17])

Seven anthems and a setting of the responses and litany can be attributed to this particular John Reading—at least one other church musician with the same name is known. At Chichester there are remains of an anthem and Burial Service. The rest are to be found in that part of the Berkeley Organ Book which he himself wrote out, but it is difficult to form an opinion of them (other than an unfavourable one) because of their incomplete nature, and (one hopes) inaccurate copying. For much of the time the musical sense is difficult to discern, thus prompting questions as to his musical competence. The A major responses and litany are, however, reassuring, for—judging, at least, by their top and bottom parts—they are attractively and tunefully written in triple time (except for the opening invocations of the litany), and suggest a composer with a sound melodic and harmonic sense.[18]

Winchester was only the second of the five cathedrals that Daniel Roseingrave served as organist, but because his final thirty years at Dublin seem to have been entirely unproductive, and because all his known works occur in the Berkeley Organ Book (which he took over and completed), Winchester rather than Gloucester, Salisbury, or Dublin seems the sensible place to deal with him.[19] His part of the Berkeley Organ Book contains a Benedicite Service in F and five anthems, one of which, *Haste thee, O God*, also survives at Gloucester and is probably, therefore, the earliest. It is simply and effectively written with full and verse sections, in triple time throughout. More varied in texture and movement, and revealing an admirable technique, is *Lord, thou art become gracious*. Luckily, this anthem has been preserved in score (*RM* 20.h.9) and shows that Roseingrave was a cut above his fellow provincial organists as a composer, not least in expressive power. Its well-controlled chromaticism in the closing bars of the first part displays a thorough musician at work, fully capable of shaping means to ends (Ex. 90).

---

[16] Crook, 11.

[17] e.g. Jeffrey Pulver, *A Biographical Dictionary of Old English Music* (London, 1927), 409. The actual composer was J. F. Wade; see Erik Routley, *The English Carol* (London, 1958), 147–8.

[18] *Preces and Responses*, ed. Michael Walsh (London, 1972).

[19] Matthews, *Organs*, 22–3; Shaw, 121–2, 264, 299, 411, 420–1.

Ex. 90. Daniel Roseingrave, *Lord, thou art become gracious* (RM 20.h.9)

Basso continuo is in brackets; otherwise it follows the vocal bass (pairs of quavers on the same note becoming crotchets).

The year after Roseingrave moved to Salisbury, the Dean and Chapter contracted with Renatus Harris to replace Thamar's great organ (and repair his chair organ) at a cost of £450. The new 'usefull substantiall & great Organ' was nothing if not well endowed with mixtures: among its eleven stops were a five-rank cornet, a three-rank sesquialtera, a three-rank furniture, and a two-rank mixture, 'being in the whole nine hundred twenty five speaking pipes of metall and seventy five mute pipes for Ornam[en]t'.[20] It seems surprising that such an instrument appears not to have had a trumpet stop at this time, but we really know too little about the rest of its history to rule out such a possibility. The

---

[20] Matthews, *Organs*, 6–7; Piper, 178–9; Willoughby, 4.

new organist was Vaughan Richardson, who had been a chorister in the Chapel Royal before becoming, briefly, in 1687, a lay clerk at Worcester. What he was doing from 1688 until his appointment at Winchester in 1692 is not known; nor is much more about his life, apart from the fact that he served as organist until his death in 1729. Bumpus possessed a manuscript score, which unfortunately cannot now be traced, containing a service and fourteen anthems by him. In all twenty-one anthems are known, eight of which are complete. Of these, *O how amiable are thy dwellings* (Page, i) is a very short, perfunctory piece, which is probably why it circulated widely. On the other hand, Tudway did well in selecting *O Lord, God of my salvation* for his collection (*Harl.* 7341; also Page, ii). It is a sombre full anthem in C minor, harmonically expressive and alternating contrapuntal full sections with homophonic verses—a fine work which has also been attributed to James Hawkins and Jeremiah Clarke against the bulk of the evidence (Ex. 91).

Further anthems survive in autograph (*Lbl* 42065 and 63490). One, the full anthem *Lift up your heads*, has an effective six-part verse in which the words 'Who is the king of glory?' are treated antiphonally by the two sides of the choir. Of the verse anthems, *The Lord hear thee in the day of trouble* is noteworthy, especially the opening bass solo, and the duet for two trebles ('We will rejoice'), whose easy brilliance is very much of its time. According to Tudway, the Service in C was 'Composed on the Peace [of Utrecht] 1713'. Lively and tuneful, it is mostly in triple time and employs conventional descriptive figures on such words as 'rejoice'. Some of the verses have organ ritornellos, and, needless to say, the *Cantate Domino* calls for the trumpet stop at the verse 'With trumpet also and shawms'—despite its absence from Harris's specification.

WINCHESTER COLLEGE

St Mary's College at Winchester, otherwise known as Winchester College, was not (and is not) the cathedral grammar school, but a distinct foundation comprising a warden, ten fellows, three chaplains, three clerks, seventy scholars, and sixteen choristers, founded in 1394 by William of Wykeham, bishop of Winchester.[21] It was on this general model that Eton College was established almost half a century later by King Henry VI, and just as William complemented his college at Winchester with one at Oxford (New College), so Henry founded King's College, Cambridge, as a sister college to Eton.[22]

Six men and sixteen boys made an oddly balanced choir in the sixteenth and seventeenth centuries. Even with everyone present this meant only one man to a part on each side of the choir in four-part music. During this period, the

---

[21] Harrison, *Music in Medieval Britain*, 31–2.   [22] Ibid. 32–6.

Ex. 91. Vaughan Richardson, *O Lord, God of my salvation (Harl.* 7341)

'Long Rolls' of the college usually list an organist below the three chaplains and above the three clerks,[23] but additional singers were presumably required—whether drawn from college servants, ex-choristers, or the cathedral choir has not been ascertained. Some held places in both choirs; for example, of the three chaplains listed in 1695, 'Rylye' occurs among the minor canons of the cathedral in that same year, and 'Box' among the lay clerks, while a clerk called 'Vander' at the college is probably the Vanderplank who was a clerk in the cathedral. But the organists of the two institutions were certainly distinct until 1729, when John Bishop, already organist of the college, became cathedral organist as well.

The pre-war organ apparently needed only £26 spent on it to put it into working order in 1661, but two years later the college launched into a rebuilding by Thomas Harris at a cost of £145. 6s. 5d.[24] The organist at this time was George King,[25] to whom two anthems are attributed in British Library, Add. MS 30932, though they are more likely to be by his son William, organist of New College. The elder King's successor at Winchester on his death in 1665 was Robert Pickhaver, the younger King's predecessor at New College, where the partbooks contain four of Pickhaver's anthems.[26] Given his lack of reputation as a composer, the fact that his *O sing unto the Lord* is also found in manuscripts associated with Winchester Cathedral (the Berkeley Organ Book) and Wimborne Minster (MS P 14) suggests what might have been guessed on geographical grounds, that to some extent all three institutions shared a common repertoire.[27]

Records of 1673–4 show that Pickhaver's stipend as organist was only £5 a year.[28] He served until 1676, when he was succeeded by 'Mr Jeferies', probably the Stephen Jefferies who had been a lay vicar at Salisbury in 1673, and whose move to Gloucester in 1681 coincided with John Reading relinquishing his post at the cathedral and taking up the college organistship.[29] His salary was set at £50 a year,[30] with the added bonus of a new organ by Renatus Harris costing £225 erected during the early years of his tenure (1683–5).[31] It has already been noted that he was the composer of the Winchester Latin graces and school song *Dulce domum*.

He was followed in the post by 'Mr Clarke' in 1692. Someone of that name had been listed among the clerks since 1670, but this was almost certainly Jeremiah Clarke, who in 1692 left the Chapel Royal on his voice breaking.[32] It was an outstanding appointment, but likely to prove only a stepping-stone to higher things. So it transpired, for by 1696 he is no longer listed as organist,

[23] C. W. Holgate, *Winchester Long Rolls, 1653–1721* (Winchester, 1899).

[24] Jonathan Dawson, 'The Organs of Winchester College Chapel', *The Organ*, 49 (1969–70), 2; E. T. Sweeting, 'The Organs of Winchester College Chapel', *The Organ*, 4 (1924–5), 213–14.

[25] Shaw, 398.   [26] Cheverton, 395–405.

[27] *O sing unto the Lord* is reconstructed in Cheverton, 'Musical Supplement', 162–3.

[28] Sweeting, 214.   [29] Shaw, 398.   [30] Sweeting, 215.

[31] Ibid.; Dawson, 2.   [32] Ashbee, ii. 45.

though as far as we know it was not until 1699 that he became organist of St Paul's Cathedral.

At the college Clarke's place was taken by John Bishop, a chorister at Gloucester during Roseingrave's time, later a lay clerk at King's College, Cambridge, and master of the choristers there in 1688.[33] Jointly with his position at Winchester College he held a lay clerk's place at the cathedral, and succeeded Vaughan Richardson there as organist in 1729, holding both posts in tandem until his death in 1737. Two services and twenty-four anthems by Bishop are known. The bass part of a Service in B flat survives at Worcester, but the D major Service achieved quite a wide circulation, and Tudway included the *Te Deum* and *Benedictus* in the fifth volume of his collection (*Harl.* 7341). It offers plenty of textural variety in the verses, but the imitative full sections are somewhat pedestrian.

Most of his anthems were published in his *Sett of New Psalm Tunes*, which came out in three editions between 1710 and 1730 and was aimed at the market for simple anthems provided by the growing parish church choir movement. Indeed, the four anthems in the first edition were 'Design'd for the use of St *Laurence* Church in *Reading*', among which *Blessed are all they* became one of the most popular parish-choir anthems in the eighteenth century.[34] Such works anticipate the easy, undemanding style of the mid-eighteenth century anthem, and, significantly, those anthems by Bishop that entered the wider cathedral repertoire did not do so until then. In this respect there is almost no overlap between his parish-choir anthems and the half-dozen or so 'cathedral anthems', which are much more Baroque in style. Among the latter group is *O Lord, our governor*, a verse anthem with symphonies and ritornellos which Tudway transcribed (*Harl.* 7341). In view of the instrumental movements one wonders where and for what special occasion it may have been written. It obviously set out to impress, and does so while avoiding the excesses of coloratura and word repetition to which his contemporaries were prone.

[33] Eward, *No Fine but a Glass of Wine*, 338; Shaw, 399.
[34] Temperley, *Music of the English Parish Church*, 163–6, 170.

Windsor and Eton

ST GEORGE'S CHAPEL

King Edward III refounded St George's Chapel, Windsor Castle, in 1348 as the chapel of the Most Noble Order of the Garter. Its constitution was governed by the number thirteen: there were thirteen canons (one of whom was dean), thirteen vicars choral, and thirteen choristers, while the military establishment comprised twenty-six Knights of the Garter (the sovereign and twenty-five) and an equal number of Poor Knights, later reduced to thirteen.[1] However, in the reign of Henry VIII the symmetry was destroyed by the introduction of a body of minor canons, at first eight in addition to the vicars choral, but ultimately absorbing them. Although the legal basis of these developments is obscure, by 1564 not only had the vicars choral ceased to exist—they had never been incorporated by charter—but the minor canons had been reduced to seven.[2]

This was the figure that was taken as the complement at the Restoration, together with twelve lay clerks and eight choristers. It is not known how soon it was before the choir reached full strength, but in view of the nature and importance of the institution it was probably swift, despite 'the insolencyes of mr Cooke (master of the Kings boys) committed lately against this Free Chappell in his stealing away two of our Choristers without any speciall warrant contrary to the priviledge of this place'.[3] In May 1666 fifteen of the men subscribed to a Chapter act for the augmentation of their pay, at the same time renouncing claims for all former perquisites other than 'the benefitt of their houses, the profitt of funeralls from strangers, the fees from knights installed, and the admission money of every Dean and Canon at their first coming in'.[4] Minor canons' stipends were raised from £24 or £25 to £30 a year, and the lay clerks' from £16 to £22. Combined with the salaries many of them also enjoyed as members of the choir at Eton (see below), this represented quite a comfortable living. Later in the period the accounts indicate that the boys received £7. 4s. each, payable to their master for maintenance, in addition to his stipend of £23.

---

[1] Edmund H. Fellowes, *The Vicars or Minor Canons of His Majesty's Free Chapel of St George's in Windsor Castle* (Windsor, 1945), 11.

[2] Ibid. 21.   [3] Bond, *Chapter Acts of the Dean and Canons of Windsor*, 249.

[4] Ibid. 216.

14*s*. and a clerk's stipend of £22. The organist also enjoyed two clerk's places, that is, £44 a year.[5]

At the first meeting of the restored Chapter held on 9 October 1660 Matthew Green was appointed master of the choristers; William Child, whose original appointment as organist went back to 1632, naturally resumed his post.[6] Later that month a new organ was mooted and it was agreed that Mr [?Ralph] Dallam should 'make an organ for the Church & to have £600 for it'.[7] By November 1661 it had been placed on the screen and the case was ready for gilding.[8] In April 1663 a grateful Chapter ordered a further £20 to be paid to Dallam 'for his faithfull discharge of the trust comitted to him in making the Organ'.[9] In fact, Hollar's engraving seems to show two organs: a great organ (presumably Dallam's) facing west, and a chair organ (possibly his father's pre-war organ) facing east, an arrangement which would have necessitated the organist turning round from one keyboard to the other—rather surprising for this date.[10]

While Child was alive—and he did not die until 1697—organist and master of the choristers were separate posts. Green and Child served in their respective capacities throughout the Restoration period, not always amicably. The posts were united under John Goldwin (known officially to the Windsor authorities as Golding but to his fellow musicians as Goldwin), but from 1716 he had the help of Benjamin Lamb in teaching the choristers, Lamb receiving 'half the profits of Master of the Boys' for doing so.[11] At Goldwin's death in 1719, John Pigott succeeded to both positions.[12]

One of the most interesting of the surviving documents relating to the choir at Windsor is a daily attendance record of minor canons and lay clerks at all the services between 1688 and 1693.[13] It is often said that absenteeism was rife in choirs at this period, but at Windsor (if the evidence is to be taken at its face value) this does not seem to have been the case. Analysis reveals some interesting patterns, however. Apart from Thomas Collins, a minor canon marked absent for the entire period (due to his removal to Bedlam some years before), it is noticeable that certain minor canons were usually absent for one or both services on Sunday, no doubt because they held livings which necessitated their presence at their parish church on that day. Thus, Richard Reading and William Jenkinson were respectively vicars of Stoke Poges and Datchet, where they would have conducted services, while Thomas Kellaway, the dean's curate, would have had duties which occupied him otherwise than in the choir on

---

[5] Chapter Library, XV.59.44; accounts for 1682.   [6] Bond, 211, 234; Shaw, 344–6.

[7] Bond, 213; Campbell and Sumner, 'Organs and Organists of St George's Chapel', 147.

[8] Bond, 229.   [9] Ibid. 242.

[10] Clutton and Niland, *British Organ* (1963), 188–9 (also pls. 11 and 12). The specification (with cornet and trumpet) given by Campbell and Sumner, 148, seems dubious for this period.

[11] Wridgway, *Choristers of St George's Chapel*, 49; Shaw, 346. Shaw states that the Windsor records are consistent in calling him Golding, rather than Goldwin.

[12] Shaw, 346–7.   [13] Chapter Library, V.B 3, fos. 89–114 (1688–93).

Sunday mornings.[14] Leonard Woodson, as a gentleman of the Chapel Royal, was also frequently absent, especially during those months when his attendance was required at Whitehall. Likewise, lay clerks Nathaniel Vestment and Nathaniel Watkins alternated with each other in doing their monthly duties at the Chapel Royal. However, the three most important members of the choir were almost never absent. Thomas Cleaver, the succentor, was exemplary in this respect, still more the organist, Child, who despite his great age missed only twenty-five services out of a possible total of 3,652 in the five years between November 1688 and October 1693. Similarly, Matthew Green, the master of the choristers, was absent only seventy-nine times, whereas John Walter was missing on 2,037 occasions—no doubt because he was also organist of Eton. On average, four of the six available minor canons, and nine or ten out of the twelve lay clerks, were present morning and evening throughout the period. With thirteen or fourteen men regularly in the choir, and the eight choristers usually present, there were certainly sufficient forces for the choir to perform the daily round without any serious need for makeshift arrangements, though whether or to what extent the statistics mask the presence of deputies cannot be determined.

Child and Goldwin are, of course, the most important Windsor composers of the period, though others with Windsor (and Eton) connections whose work figures in manuscripts in the library include Benjamin Rogers and Michael Wise, both lay clerks in the 1660s, and John Walters and Benjamin Lamb, organists of Eton before and after the turn of the century. There are three incomplete sets of partbooks at Windsor covering the period 1660–1715. Earliest is a small set containing funeral music bearing the date 1640 on the binding but with post-Restoration additions (MSS 18–20). John Morehen has identified the copyist as Thomas Tudway the elder (hand *A*), father of the man who compiled the Harleian collection of church music.[15] He implies that the same scribe was responsible for the first post-Restoration set of partbooks (MSS 1–4), but examination shows that (disregarding obviously later insertions) two hands are involved: an earlier one which is Tudway senior's (*A*), and a later one (*B*) which, though it overlaps occasionally with *A* before 1663, soon takes over and continues into the 1680s. In fact, *B* is the main hand of this set, *A* probably having dropped out by October 1665, when Tudway was described as 'super-annuated . . . haveing done no service to the Church this Twelvemonth and more'.[16] Hand *B* also copied most of the second set of Restoration partbooks (MSS 11–13), begun sometime after the award of Blow's doctorate (1677) and continuing until about 1715, as well as the earliest organ-book (MS 57), the

[14] Fellowes, *Vicars*, 89, 90, 87.

[15] Clifford Mould, *The Musical Manuscripts of St George's Chapel, Windsor Castle* (Windsor, 1973), 41–2; see Morehen, 'Sources of English Cathedral Music', 368–82.

[16] Bond, 256; Mould, 37–40.

index of which is dated 22 January 1705/6.[17] From page 44 of this organ-book a new hand takes over, identifiable elsewhere as that of Benjamin Lamb, copyist of a further ten organ-books dating from after 1713.

William Child was the country's leading composer of church music in the early years of the Restoration.[18] Already before the Civil War he had a substantial body of work to his credit, and he seems to have continued producing services and anthems that were in tune with the conservative traditions of English church music, yet well adapted to the new situation most cathedrals found themselves in. Not only did he resume his Windsor appointments at the Restoration, he became in addition one of the organists of the Chapel Royal, and served in that capacity at the coronations of Charles II, James II, and William and Mary. Frequent attendance at Whitehall meant absences from Windsor, with the result that in 1662 the Chapter decided that 'Mr. Benjamin Rogers . . . shall receive twenty shillings a month of the Treasurer for every month he plays upon the organs in mr Childs absence to be Deducted out of mr Childs pay to which mr Child Freely consented'.[19] The following year 'Mr' Child received the degree of Doctor of Music from Oxford University.

The Windsor archives reveal numerous details regarding his later life, and growing prosperity. One unpleasant report refers to a vicious assault on him in 1681, when Matthew Green, master of the choristers, 'gave Dr Child uncivill and rude language while he was doeing his duty in playing upon the Organ, and after the ending of the said Divine service did trip up his heeles, and when down, did unhumanly beat him'. In due course Green apologized to all concerned and paid Child £5 and a bond of £40 'for future security of his peaceable behaviour towards him'.[20] In later life Child must have given up his Whitehall duties, but old age did not keep him away from St George's. He died 'the 23d of March, 1696/7 in the 91st yeare of his age'.[21]

Child's surviving church music includes at least seventeen services (besides a Latin morning service 'made for the right worshipful Dr Cosin') and about eighty anthems, not counting *The first set of psalmes of III voyces fitt for private chappelles or other private meetings with a continuall base either for the organ or theorbo newly composed after the Italian way*, which came out in 1639 (and again in 1650 and 1656, the latter renamed *Choise Musick*). As the title indicates, this is sacred chamber music in an Italianate idiom, not (strictly speaking) church music. Much the same may be said of three 'Alleluias', often listed among the anthems, which are in fact settings of poems by 'T.P.' (possibly Thomas Pierce, President

[17] Mould, 40–1, 50.

[18] *NG* iv. 227–30 (Frederick Hudson and W. Roy Large); Fellowes, *Organists and Masters of the Choristers of St George's Chapel*, 44–53; Frederick Hudson and W. Roy Large, 'William Child (1606/7–1697): A New Investigation of Sources', *Music Review*, 31 (1970), 265–84; Shaw, 344–6; Joe M. Zimmerman. 'The Psalm Settings and Anthems of William Child, 1606–1697' (Ph.D. diss., University of Indiana, 1971).

[19] Bond, 235–6.   [20] Ibid. 280–1.   [21] Fellowes, *Organists and Masters*, 49.

of Magdalen College, Oxford). They may be more or less contemporary with the psalms, though their only source is an eighteenth-century one.

Child was best known to his contemporaries as a composer of services, many of which are widely distributed in post-Restoration sources. All the usual keys are represented, sometimes by both full and verse settings, and comprehensiveness may well have been a conscious aim. Inevitably, a degree of confusion exists as to which of two services in the same key certain canticles belong, and indeed, Child's services need (and deserve) sorting out. (The most convenient score versions are the eleven in *Cfm* 117.) The chronology of these works is problematic, but pre-Restoration sources such as Christ Church, Oxford, MSS 1220–4 and the Pembroke College, Cambridge, partbooks (MSS 6.1–6) include the well-known 'Sharp Service' in D (Boyce, iii), which Charles I 'much delighted to hear',[22] the 'flat' verse services in C minor and G minor, and the Service in G 'Made for the Rt. Rev. Matthew [Wren], Ld. Bp. of Ely'. The last contains every sung item in the liturgy, including the *Venite*, all the usual and alternative canticles of morning and evening prayer, and the communion service, including the Gloria in excelsis and an offertory sentence *Charge them that are rich*.

As for when the others might have been written, style (for the moment) cannot be taken as a guide until other preliminary investigations have been carried out. But the fact that there are so many in itself makes it likely that some are post-1660, especially considering the pressing need at that time for new, technically undemanding settings in an acceptable modern idiom. Given Child's position at Windsor, and the general situation, it is possible that the early Restoration partbooks there give us the order in which they were written once the backlog had been cleared, and provide evidence for their dates of composition. It would certainly seem natural that already existing (pre-Restoration) services would be copied in first, together with any of recent date, then others as they became available—with Child on the spot, probably pretty soon after they had been composed. In fact, the order in which they occur in the manuscripts seems to bear out this scenario, and it will be useful to present it here, not only to test the hypothesis, but also to identify the bulk of his output of services. Titles are as given in the partbooks, with the equivalent in le Huray's (unnumbered) list of seventeen services in brackets—counting the evening service for verses 'in A re' as no. 1.[23] The following list is based on the order in MS 2, which seems to be the least disturbed of the set, and (with MS 2a) to have more of hand *A* than the others. Services occurring in pre-Restoration sources are marked★.

---

[22] John Playford, *An Introduction to the Skill of Musick* (London, 1666).

[23] Counting only the English services and disregarding independent items; see le Huray, 358; Ralph T. Daniel and Peter le Huray, *The Sources of English Church Music, 1549–1660* (London, 1972), ii. 93–5.

I. Entered before 1663 (attributed to 'Mr' Child, hand *A*)
    Sharp Service in D★ [= 8]
        (together with *Blessed be the Lord God* and *O clap your hands*, anthems respectively for the morning and evening service)
    Short Service in F [= 15]
        (together with *The king shall rejoice* 'sung at the Coronation', 1661)
    Service in G★ [= 16]
    Flat Service for verses in C minor★ [= 6]

II. Entered between 1663 ('Dr' Child) and before *c.*1665 (hand *A*)
    First [Evening] Service for verses in B flat [= 5]
    Short [First] Service in E minor [= 13]
    Second Service in E [minor] for verses [= 14]
    Service in A [minor] for verses [= 1]
    Short Service in E flat for verses [= 12]
        (*Cfm* 117 has it transposed into C but with 'high clefs' [C$_3$ C$_4$ C$_5$ F$_5$])
    Service in G for verses [= *Cantate* and *Deus misereatur* from 16)

III. Entered after *c.*1665 (hand *B*) and before 1682
    Short Service in A minor [= 2]
        (together with *O Lord God, the heathen are come*★ and *Lord, how long*★)
    Last Service in D minor [= 11]
    Flat Service for verses in G minor [= 17]
    Last Service for verses in A minor [= 3]
    Last Service for verses in B flat [= 4]
        (followed immediately by 'Dr' Aldrich's Service in G)

The association of the coronation anthem *The king shall rejoice* with the Short Service in F points to 1661 as a possible date of composition, and in turn suggests that perhaps it was the *Te Deum* from this service that was sung at Charles II's coronation service in Westminster Abbey. It is one of Child's most disappointing pieces and homophonic from beginning to end. The full services with verses tend to be more rewarding. Of course, verses offered a great deal more scope in terms of contrasting textures and sonorities, thereby helping to maintain interest. Together with antiphonal effects of opposing cantoris and decani choirs and their coming together, sometimes expanding to five or six parts in climactic and specially emphatic passages, all sorts of variety was thus available—verse and full, left and right, high and low—and works like the E minor Service (Boyce, i) or the one in E flat considered elsewhere in this study (see Ch. 2) make imaginative use of them. It is true that there is still little counterpoint, nor are there any passages of triple time to leaven the rhythmic heaviness, but there is considerable harmonic resource and, of course, textural variety. There is more contrapuntal interest in the series of evening services 'for verses' where, perhaps, a more leisurely disposal of the text could be tolerated. Indeed, some of the imitative verse writing in the B flat and A minor Services gives them a distinctly old-fashioned look, as does the written-out organ accompaniments.

Missing from the list of services above is an Evening Service in D minor 'for four means' (= 9)—a seductive sound which fills out to TrCCTB for the full sections. Oddly enough, it does not survive at all at Windsor. There is, however, a service in C (= 7) that occurs in the later set of partbooks (MS 11–13) subtitled 'Dr Wm Child's Last Service in C . . . made for Dr Butler'. (Dr John Butler was canon of Windsor from 1669 to 1682, and precentor from 1670.) His bass partbook, now in the British Library (Add. MS 17784) does not contain this service among the ten by Child systematically arranged in order of key that fill the first eighty or so pages of the book (reversed). These were probably entered between 1670 and 1674, and the fact that the last three services of the above list are also absent from the manuscript may suggest a date of composition for them not earlier than the mid-1670s. In the case of the 'Last Service in C' a date of 1680–2 would be plausible in view of its exclusion from MSS 1–4. It belongs to the category of the triple-time service that was then fashionable; here, at last, we find Child coming to terms with the contemporary idiom, something we shall observe in his anthems at about the same time.

In our present state of knowledge regarding Child's services it is difficult to sum up his achievement. Stylistically there seems to be no strong and consistent line of development from, say, the 'Sharp Service' to his 'Last Service in C', very different though they are from each other. At the lowest level one might merely observe that over a period stretching from when he was a young man to when he was 70 or more, he seemed content to do little more than repeat himself, more or less successfully, in different keys. Yet he was undoubtedly influential. In so far as 'big' services had a role to play in the restored liturgy, the Sharp Service showed what might be done. Less happily, a work like the F major Service provided a baleful model for modest composers working with modest resources, with ultimately dire consequences.

Turning to Child's anthems, it needs to be borne in mind that he was more than twenty years younger than Orlando Gibbons, and more than thirty years younger than Tomkins. He belongs, in fact, to a transitional generation of church composers, and in works written before the Civil War we find elements of the traditional English polyphonic style with its fluid part-writing and uninhibited false relations side by side with Italianate idioms involving homophonic declamation, striking harmonic juxtapositions, and expressive chromaticism. The former is to be seen in *O Lord God, the heathen are come into thine inheritance*, said to have been 'composed in the year 1644, on the occasion of the abolishing of the Common Prayer and overthrowing the constitution in Church and State' (*Harl.* 7338);[24] the latter, poignantly, in *O God, wherefore art thou absent from us*.[25]

---

[24] *Treasury of English Church Music*, iii. 10–21.   [25] Ibid., ii. 248–50.

Again, viewing his anthems as a whole, it is difficult to detect a clear pattern of stylistic development—or so it seems, faced with the considerable number extant, most of which are difficult to date. Joe Zimmerman is of the opinion that nearly all the anthems were written between 1630 and the early 1660s,[26] but it is far from impossible that some were written in the 1670s, or even in the 1680s, without a marked change in style. As with the services (and discounting the Sanctus and Gloria from the G major Service), only four of the twenty-five anthems by Child in the anthem section of MSS 1–4 are known to have been composed before 1644.[27] There is no reason to suppose a date earlier than 1660 for most of the remainder, which, like the services, were probably copied into the partbooks soon after they were composed. In any case, their order of entry may be revealing.

I. Entered into MSS 1–4 before 1663 (i.e. attributed to 'Mr' Child)
   O Lord, grant the king a long life [first setting] (f)+
   The king shall rejoice (f)
   Thou art my king, O God (v)
   If the Lord himself [first setting] (f)+
   O let my mouth be filled★ (v)
   Thy word is a lantern (v)
   O how amiable (v)
   Praise the Lord, O my soul [second setting] (v)
   Turn thou us, O good Lord★ (v)
   O Lord grant the king a long life★ [second setting] (v)

II. Entered after 1663 ('Dr Child'), before c.1665 (hand *B*), and certainly before 1669 ('Mr' Rogers)
   Let God arise (v)
   Glory be to God★ (f)
   Holy, holy, holy★ (f)+
   If the Lord himself [second setting] (f)
   Behold, how good and joyful (v)
      (followed by two anthems by 'Mr' Benjamin Rogers)

III. Entered probably before c.1665 (still hand *A*)
   O sing unto the Lord (v)
   O pray for the peace of Jerusalem (f)
   My heart is fixed (v)
   Praise the Lord, O my soul [first setting] (f)
   O clap your hands [second setting] (v)
   Praised be the Lord (f) ('June 1665', followed by three anthems by Michael Wise)
   Give the king thy judgements★ (v)

IV. Entered probably after c.1665 (hands *B* and *C*)
   The earth is the Lord's (v)

---

[26] Zimmerman, 'Psalm Settings', 205.   [27] Le Huray, 359–60.

O praise the Lord, laud ye (f)+
O that the salvation [second setting] (f)

(f) = full, (v) = verse, ★ = in pre-Restoration sources, + = in Clifford's *Divine Services* (1664)

Although few of the unstarred items above can be dated positively, it may be mentioned that the first two are coronation anthems and therefore may date from 1661, while *If the Lord himself* (Arnold, i) is described as a thanksgiving anthem for 30 September to mark the anniversary of the king's escape at Worcester in 1651. Another thanksgiving anthem is *Praised be the Lord* celebrating 'our late happie Victorie over the Dutch, June 1665'.

Later than the above anthems may be those not in MSS 1–4 but in the later set of Restoration partbooks (MSS 11–13). These include the following, all of which were entered after Blow became 'Dr Blow' (1677); again, there is no evidence that they are much earlier than the mid-1670s. The first was 'Composed for the Right Hon[oura]ble Lady Rachel Hascard', the wife of Gregory Hascard, canon of Windsor from 1671 and dean from 1682 until 1708.

V. Entered into MSS 11–13 after 1676
   O Lord, rebuke me not [second setting] (v)
   I will be glad and rejoice (v)
   Save me, O God (v)
   Hear me when I call (v)
   I was glad (v)

The weakness of this method of dating is clear, for, in default of other evidence, one cannot be sure how close the date of copying is to the date of composition—is it days, weeks, months, or years? But in the absence of earlier sources, there is something to be said for assuming a minimal delay between composing and copying, especially since composer and copyist were in daily contact and the composer was writing directly for the choir in question. It is suggested, therefore, that until evidence to the contrary turns up, the above lists may represent a chronology that would extend Child's composing life well into the 1670s and possibly even into the 1680s. This would be particularly so in the case of anthems in group V. As in the case of the services, further study of the sources and more exacting stylistic analysis will be needed before assertions about date can be made with greater confidence.

The full anthems that Child wrote in the early years of the Restoration are those on which, for worse rather than better, his reputation has largely been based (see Ch. 2). Boyce and Arnold printed some of them, and no doubt their undemanding nature recommended them to the eighteenth century, though modern critics in general have looked for stronger meat and found it lacking.

A more up-to-date side of his work can be seen in the verse anthems. Those which may have been written in the years immediately after 1660 show, as yet, comparatively little use of triple time, and there is nothing that even approaches recitative, though florid word-painting in the duets and trios is quite common. There is no longer a contrapuntally conceived organ part, however, despite plenty of counterpoint on display in the full sections, mostly in five parts, but eight in *Let God arise*. One curiosity is *The earth is the Lord's* with verses for three basses—a sonority which Child's pupil John Goldwin was also to adopt. On the other hand, at least those anthems in group V above do illustrate some modern features. Full passages tend to be simpler and in four parts, and there is considerably more triple-time writing. Significantly, the treatment of the verses is much more dramatic, with expressive gestures involving affective leaps and chromatic harmony that suggest a familiarity with Humfrey's and Blow's early anthems. *Save me, O God* provides several examples of dramatic tension heightened by chromatically ascending declamation (Ex. 92a), and has a passage that comes close to recitative (Ex. 92b).

More powerful still are the affective passages in *O Lord, rebuke me not*. The structure alternates between sections in common and triple time, and is unusual for Child in that the chorus is introduced only at the end—itself a latish sign. Anguished declamation involving awkward leaps and chromaticism characterizes the common-time verses (Ex. 93), while a more optimistic tone pervades those in triple time.

It is interesting to observe Child coming under modern influences in this group of anthems, where style and source evidence both point to a late date. Putting *O Lord God, the heathen are come* and *O Lord, rebuke me not* side by side, it is hard to believe they are by the same man, and shows that, as with the services, he was moving with the times towards the end of his composing life.

In retrospect, however, Child's importance lay more in his role than in his achievement. He carried the pre-Civil War tradition into the Restoration period, adapting to the new situation and serving as a model for younger composers. In so far as it is possible to take an overview of his work at this stage, it must be frankly admitted that it is uneven, though whether what seem to be technical deficiencies are to be put down to the vagaries of the transitional style, personal idiosyncrasies, or inaccurate sources is difficult to say. A provisional judgement might be that despite undoubted successes in his own terms, he wrote too much and somewhat uncritically in a period of changing norms.

Child's successor as organist of St George's was John Goldwin, a chorister himself between 1675 and 1684. He may thus have been born about 1668.[28] In July 1685, having 'attained sufficient skill in music to be capable of performing the duty of the organist, as well as the Master of the Choristers ... the said

---

[28] Fellowes, *Organists and Masters*, 53–6; Shaw, 346.

Ex. 92. William Child, *Save me, O Lord* (Cfm 117)

(1) *A* and *a* in continuo   (2) 𝅘𝅥𝅭 in continuo   (3) *F* in continuo

Golding shall receive monthly from the Treasurer half a clerk's pay, provided he assist the organist upon all necessary occasions and diligently instruct the choristers in the art of singing'. He was admitted to the 'half place of a clerk' in April 1687, and the following year he was listed among the lay clerks of Eton. In 1689 he became a full lay clerk at St George's. He seems to have proved a satisfactory assistant, both as organist and choirmaster, since he was promised the succession to both posts in 1694—which duly came in 1697 and 1704 respectively. He died 7 November 1719.[29]

A service and at least thirty-eight anthems are attributed to Goldwin in various sources. Perhaps surprisingly, only twenty-four of these are at Windsor, mostly in the MSS 11–13 set. Of these, the ten earliest anthems and the service are contained in a score at Christ Church, Oxford (MS 94) together with ten further anthems and a Latin motet, which are probably earlier still. The entire contents of this manuscript are devoted to his work and in the hand of the copyist William Isaac, a colleague of Goldwin at both Windsor and Eton, who died in 1703.[30] Consequently it may be taken as providing a good source of Goldwin's early work, including most of those about to be discussed.

The Service in F 'for verses' is rather pedestrian (Arnold, i). It has plenty of textural contrast but little sense of line or rhythmic subtlety in its contrapuntal sections. Despite certain modern features, the manner is reminiscent of Child, but compared with Goldwin's full anthems, the technique of which should have been adaptable, the result is acceptable without offering much to get excited about. Much more imaginative are the five-part *Hear me, O God* and the six-part *O Lord, God of hosts*, two full anthems with verses included by Tudway in his collection (*Harl.* 7341). Walker thought them 'really fine', an opinion it is easy to agree with.[31] In *Hear me, O God* Goldwin obviously revels in the sonority of the full chorus and the contrasts available within that texture. Like his master, Child, he seeks out rich and surprising harmonic juxtapositions. Close proximity of major and minor chords on the same root are frequent, while root progressions a major third apart, where one note is held between the two chords while another moves chromatically, are clearly expressive devices that appeal. The articulation of the main sections reflects both types of progression: F–F: F m–F: A–F and within the final section we find adjacent major triads on B flat and G, G and E flat, B flat and D. False relations, too, are common, and excursions to flat keys—as at the passage 'Take me out of the mire'—another element in the expressive vocabulary.

As a contrapuntist he shows moments of melodic and harmonic awkwardness, but at his best, for example in the opening section of *O Lord, God of hosts*, he is the equal of Blow and even Purcell in this vein. Writing in six parts does not daunt him; indeed, it brings out the best in him, and shows his sympathy with the old style. More modest in scope, but also more consistent in execution, is

[29] Wridgway, *Choristers*, 48–9.   [30] Holman, 'Bartholomew Isaack'.

[31] Ernest Walker, *A History of Music in England* (Oxford, rev. J. A. Westrup, 1952), 185; see also Anne M. Jones, 'The Anthems of John Golding, Organist and Master of the Choristers of St George's Chapel in Windsor Castle' (M.Mus. diss., Royal Holloway College, University of London, 1985).

Ex. 93. William Child, *O Lord, rebuke me not* (*Cfm* 117)

(1) *d'* in countertenor.

Bow down thine ear. The final section mixes simple homophony with Purcellian polyphony as well as one could wish (Ex. 94).

The absence of triple time, either in verse or full sections of the anthems mentioned so far, is one factor that helps to give them an old-fashioned flavour and a certain strength. In contrast, much of *I have set God always before me* (Boyce, ii) is in triple time and more or less devoid of counterpoint. Though it seems somewhat empty, there is a certain naïve effectiveness in the way moods of steadfastness and confidence in common time are answered by passages in triple time expressing the consolation of faith.

Goldwin's full and verse anthems stand in marked contrast to each other, representing the polyphonic tradition and the new soloistic idioms respectively.

Ex. 94. John Goldwin, *Bow down thine ear, O Lord* (Och 94)

Although the level of technical competence in his verse anthems is above average, one senses an absence of strong individuality. Like many of his contemporaries he is prone to lapse into semiquaver coloratura, dotted rhythms, and easy-going triple time in his verses, while weak, perfunctory Hallelujahs hardly raise him above his fellows. The odd quirk apart, his idiom is firmly diatonic. His choice of extrovert texts limits the scope for pathetic writing, but that it is within his range, various details in *Unto thee have I cried* confirm. Here C minor, with its easy access to F minor, brings out the best in him, as also in the sombre opening verse of *Ponder my words*. Another early work in C minor, *O Lord, my God, great are thy wond'rous works*, provides in its opening a fine example of the florid declamatory style already quoted (Ch. 5, Ex. 13), though it is difficult to imagine a boy singing it convincingly.

Goldwin seems to have had a preference for treble solos and duets, and did not refrain from taxing his young singers' vocal abilities. More writing of this sort, this time for two trebles, is to be found in *O Lord, God of hosts*. By contrast, *Ascribe unto the Lord* is for three basses (used previously by Child in *The earth is the Lord's*); they bring a marvellously portentous air to the opening verse (Ex. 95).

O Lord, God of hosts is one of several anthems with ground bass movements that provide evidence of the structural self-sufficiency which individual sections were acquiring about 1700, with contrast of mood and metre between verses fequently underlined by contrast of key. Large-scale anthems show these features to a marked degree, for example, *O praise God in his holiness* (Page, ii), written

Ex. 95. John Goldwin, *Ascribe unto the Lord* (*Och* 94)

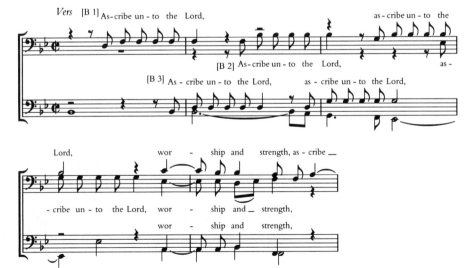

in celebration of the victory at Blenheim (1704). A distinct movement structure
is even more pronounced in *O be joyful in God* (*Harl.* 7342), for countertenor
and bass with plentiful organ ritornellos: its six clear musical divisions, marked
by double bars, are as follows:

> O be joyful in God (C major, **c**):
> > duet with 'Trumpet' organ ritornellos
>
> Be ye sure that the Lord (A minor, $\frac{3}{2}$—leading to C major, **c**):
> > duet with 'Cornet stop' on the organ
>
> O go your way into his gates (E minor, $\frac{3}{2}$):
> > duet with 'Eccho' organ
>
> For the Lord is gracious (C major, **c**—'Slow'):
> > duet with 'Trumpet' and 'Eccho' for organ
>
> O be joyful in God—Hallelujah (C major, **c**):
> > duet
>
> Hallelujah (C major, **c**):
> > 4-part chorus.

The minor-key sections are more lyrical in character than the flamboyant C
major sections which make play with jubilant trumpet motifs—somewhat inappropriate in the fourth verse, where the words are 'For the Lord is gracious'.
The registration indications suggest that it was Bernard Smith's Eton organ of
1701 that Goldwin had in mind when writing this piece. In its way it is a
splendid work, rounded and spacious, full of Baroque self-confidence (and a
certain amount of Baroque self-satisfaction).

Child and Goldwin between them span the whole Restoration period at St
George's. Other composers with Windsor connections include Benjamin Lamb
and John Walter; but as organists of Eton, their work will be considered below.

ETON COLLEGE

The 'College Royal of our Lady of Eton beside Windsor' was founded in 1440
by King Henry VI, together with the 'College Royal of our Lady and St
Nicholas of Cambridge', otherwise known as King's College. The model for
both was William of Wykeham's foundation almost half a century earlier of
Winchester and New College, Oxford, but the scale was grander. The Eton
statutes of 1444 provided for a provost, ten fellows, and seventy scholars, and a
musical establishment of ten chaplains, ten clerks, and sixteen choristers.[32] By the

[32] J. Heywood and T. Wright, *The Ancient Laws of the Fifteenth Century for King's College, Cambridge, and for the Public School of Eton* (London, 1850), 513–19; also C. Maxwell Lyte, *A History of Eton College, 1449–1910* (London, 1911), 580–1.

time of Archbishop Laud's visitation of 1634, the numbers stood at two chaplains, eight clerks, and ten choristers—'for aught wee know thay are full'.[33] This
was the establishment maintained during the Restoration period, as the audit-
books make clear. Each year, listed below the usher (*ostiarius*) are two 'conducts'
or chaplains, then, usually, the organist followed by seven or more clerks (some
sharing places), most of whom are known also to have been members of the
choir of St George's Chapel.[34] Their pay was made up of several elements—diet,
stipend, 'distributions', and livery—but from about 1680 onwards these were
consolidated into £17. 14s. 2d. a year for the conducts, and £17. 6s. 2d. or £15.
9s. 6d. for the clerks.

In considering the Eton choir the question arises as to how distinct it really
was from that of St George's, less than a mile south across the river Thames. In
theory, of course, they were separate; each foundation was independent of the
other, it appointed and paid its own singers, and, at least until 1733, each had
its own organist and master of the choristers. But in practice, the Eton choir was
virtually a sub-group of St George's so far as the men were concerned. At least
during the seventeenth century this does not seem to have been the case with
the boys, however. Officially there were ten, but to what extent they included
boys from St George's cannot be shown, since we do not know their names. A
reference 'to the choir of Windsor and that of Eton' at the funeral of Zachary
Craddock, Provost of Eton (1681–95), implies that the number of singing boys
present was close to the combined forces of the two choirs (ten from Eton, eight
from Windsor).[35] Probably they were distinct until about 1716, when Benjamin
Lamb, the Eton *informator choristarum*, became responsible for the boys of St
George's in addition.[36] The Royal Commission on Public Schools, reporting in
1864, observed that Eton

maintains jointly with St George's Chapel, Windsor, a choir of Twelve. . . . The services, like the support of the boys, are divided between the two establishments a
consequence of which is that there is no choral service at Eton on Sunday or any other
mornings, St George's being deemed to have prior claim. This arrangement . . . has
subsisted for a long time—it is thought since the Restoration.[37]

In this connection it is significant that the Eton organ-books dating from about
1700 contain only evening services.

For present purposes then, the personnel at Eton cannot really be regarded as
distinct from St George's. In 1662 Benjamin Rogers was described in the audit-
book as organist and, jointly with Thomas Tudway senior, as *informator*, but his
links with both Eton and St George's were severed when he became organist of

---

[33] HMC, 147.
[34] Details of personnel, stipends, periods of service, etc., in what follows are derived from the
audit-books, to which dates provide reference.
[35] Wridgway, 50.   [36] Ibid. 49.   [37] Ibid. 80.

Magdalen College, Oxford, in 1665.[38] It is not clear who his immediate successor was at Eton, though his place as clerk seems to have been taken by a Mr Slaughter (presumably Edward Slater of Windsor and later of the Chapel Royal).[39] From 1669 to 1681 the post of organist and *informator* appears to have been held by Edward Sleech, an ex-chorister from Windsor and clerk from 1673. In 1676 he was paid 20s. for teaching the choristers of St George's while their master was out of action due to a 'visitation of small pox at Mr Green's house'.[40] Sleech was followed by John Walter (or Walters), who combined his post at Eton with that of a lay clerk at St George's.[41] He served from 1681 to 1705, though he did not die until 1708, and was succeeded by Benjamin Lamb.[42]

Both Walter and Lamb were composers, and some of their work survives in the Eton organ-books (MS 299, vols. 1–6, 8–10), all that remains of what must have been an extensive collection of choir music, judged by payments for copying recorded in the audit-books.[43] As has already been stated, there are no morning or communion services among their contents, and it is not surprising that composers such as Child, Rogers, Goldwin, and Tudway are strongly represented. Volumes 1 and 2 seem to have been begun by the copyist William Isaac, a clerk at Eton from 1673 to 1703;[44] the continuation appears to be by John Walter, and the conclusion by Lamb. The portion of volume 2 in the hand of Isaac includes four anthems by John Weldon (a chorister at Eton) and a number by Goldwin, including *Praise the Lord, O Jerusalem*, dated January 1701/2. The remaining volumes are in the hand of Benjamin Lamb, and probably follow on in chronological order. The third contains four anthems by Lamb himself and may have been begun around 1705; the fourth contains services and anthems, among which Clarke's *The Lord is my strength* is marked 'Thanksgiving Anthem for June 27, 1706'.

An interesting feature of these volumes is that many of the contents were written first in one key and later transposed up a tone, cross-references leading from one version to the other. This may well reflect a change of pitch in the new organ which Bernard Smith built in 1700–1 at a cost of £789. 2s. 6d. to replace an earlier Dallam instrument dating from 1662–3.[45] The new organ had nine stops on the great, including sesquialtera and cornet mixtures, three on the chair, and four on the echo; both great and echo organs had a trumpet stop.

[38] Shaw, 374–5.   [39] Ibid. 375.   [40] Wridgway, 46.
[41] Shaw, 375.   [42] Ibid. 375–6.
[43] Roderick Williams, 'Manuscript Organ Books in Eton College Library', *Music and Letters*, 41 (1960), 358–9; also Wood, 'Note on Two Cambridge Manuscripts', 310–11.
[44] Wood, 'Note'; also Holman, 'Bartholomew Isaac', 384.
[45] Andrew Freeman, 'The Organs of Eton College', *The Organ*, 4 (1924–5), 160; id., *Father Smith*, rev. Rowntree, 39–40.

Walter had been a chorister in the Chapel Royal under Blow, and in February 1677 was described as 'late child of the Chappel, whose voice is changed and is gone',[46] though where he had gone is unclear since his name does not reappear at Windsor or Eton until 1681. He is known as an important copyist of sacred and secular music by Blow, and others.[47] The manuscript that contains his copy of *Venus and Adonis*—he may have been involved in the first performance in some capacity—also contains the autograph of one of his anthems, *Lord, I confess my sin* (*Lbl* 22100). The first of the Eton organ-books contains a *Magnificat* and *Nunc dimittis* by him, while two further anthems, *O give thanks* and *O God, thou art my God* are at Windsor. A score of the former is in Cambridge, Fitzwilliam Museum MS 117, and shows Blow's influence in the rhythmic vigour of the triple-time section which opens and closes the anthem. Possibly Walter may have written it for the Chapel Royal about 1680 before going to Eton, for the second solo verse requires a bass with John Gostling's full two-octave range. The latter anthem survives in score (*Cu* Ely 6); again, much of it is in triple time, but this time more elegant and polished.

Benjamin Lamb was born on 16 May 1674, the son of Captain Benjamin Lamb, one of the Poor Knights of Windsor.[48] The younger Benjamin and an older brother William were both choristers at St George's, where, in 1680, William became a lay clerk. (There appears to be no connection between him and the organists of that name at Lichfield.) The Eton audit-books list 'Mr Lambe' among the clerks from 1688 (whether William or Benjamin is not stated), but from 1705 specifically mention Benjamin as organist, at first jointly with Walter but alone from 1709. (These are the dates of the audit and thus refer to the previous year.) He composed an evening service and at least eight anthems; the service and four of the anthems are in Tudway's collection (*Harl.* 7341–2). All except one of the anthems pre-date 1712 when their texts were published in *Divine Harmony*, and their position in the Windsor and Eton manuscripts suggests a date of copying soon after 1705. They are typical of the early years of the eighteenth century, especially the use of trumpet and echo effects in their organ accompaniments. These are especially evident in *O worship the Lord in the beauty of holiness*, a conventionally jubilant verse anthem in C major, with plenty of triple-time dotted rhythms, and a florid verse for counter-tenor at the words 'The waves of the sea are mighty and rage horribly'—marked 'Mr Elford's part' at Windsor (MS 12). (The famous Richard Elford was a lay clerk at Windsor from 1701, as well as a vicar choral at St Paul's, lay clerk at Westminster Abbey, and a gentleman of the Chapel Royal.)

Similar idioms are employed in two occasional anthems: *If the Lord himself*, written for the annual commemoration of the discovery of the Gunpowder Plot

---

[46] Ashbee, i. 169.　　[47] Wood, 309–11.　　[48] Wridgway, 40.

Ex. 96. Benjamin Lamb, *I will give thanks to the Lord* (Harl. 7342)

(1) This part is written in small notes above the chorus as if it were a first treble part.

Ex. 97. Benjamin Lamb, *Nunc dimittis* from the Service in E minor (*Harl.* 7341)

(5 November), and *I will give thanks* for the anniversary of the Restoration (29 May)—the triumphal mood of both being relieved in the middle by expressive verses in the minor key. Part of the concluding section of *I will give thanks* gives an idea of the thrilling effect that Lamb conjured up with the help of the new organ (Ex. 96). Reference to 'trumpets', rather than 'trumpet' (i.e. trumpet stop), is presumably a slip of Tudway's pen. In contrast to the general air of rejoicing, *Unto thee have I cried* is a sombre full anthem in E minor, mostly in simple four-part homophony with CTB verses.

The service is a setting of the *Cantate Domino* and *Deus misereatur*, alternating full and verse sections. Despite the key of E minor, opportunities for exploiting the trumpet stop are avidly seized in such passages as 'with trumpets also and shawms' and 'O let the nations rejoice and be glad'—the appropriate modulation, respectively to C major and D major—having taken place. A more traditional aspect of his technique is seen in the closing bars of the service where a superannuated polyphonic cliché is harmonically rejuvenated (Ex. 97).

Worcester

On 20 July 1646 after the surrender of the royalist forces at the siege of Worcester 'the organs were this day taken down out of the cathedral church'.[1] Another three days and the last service according to the Book of Common Prayer was performed; next day the parliamentary army entered the city. Ten years later, the old organist Thomas Tomkins died, having in 1647 commemorated the execution of the Earl of Strafford and Archbishop Laud with elegiac pavans, and the king himself with 'A sad paven For these distracted Tymes Febr. 14. 1649'.[2]

The first choral service after the Restoration was celebrated on Easter eve 1661 (13 April). The previous months had been spent preparing for this event. Ordinary services had restarted on 31 August 1660, ten choristers were on the books by 7 November, and the ten lay clerks were up to strength by 3 April following. For a while it was ordered that the choir should perform only 'on Sundaies and holy daies, Satterdaies in the evening, [and] the eves of hollydaies'.[3] There were to be at least two choir practices a week, but clearly these were interim measures.

That summer it was proposed that George Dallam set up a small organ 'against the King's Ma[jes]ty comeing' to mark the anniversary of the battle of Worcester on 3 September—a visit which in the end did not take place.[4] Plans for a new organ were set afoot the following summer, but after a false start with William Hathaway, a contract was signed with Thomas Harris on 5 July 1666 for a double organ to be erected on the screen with eight stops on the great and five on the chair, very much along the lines of the pre-war organ, and costing £400.[5] As at Gloucester and Salisbury, this was a 'ten foot' organ with a C-keyboard, in other words a transposing organ, the lowest note of which sounded FF when bottom C on the great diapason was played.

By the time the organ was finished, two organists had already come and gone and a third was in post. Giles Tomkins (nephew of Thomas) was found to be

---

[1] Stevens, *Thomas Tomkins*, 18, quoting *Diary of Henry Townshend . . . 1640–1663*, ed. J. W. Willis Bund (Worcester Historical Society, 1920); see also Butcher, *Organs and Music of Worcester Cathedral*, 10.   [2] *MB* 5, nos. 41–4, 57, and 53 respectively.

[3] Ivor Atkins, *The Early Occupants of the Office of Organist and Master of the Choristers of the Cathedral Church of Christ and the Blessed Virgin Mary, Worcester* (London, 1918), 64; Butcher, 10; Dearnley, *English Church Music*, 67–8.

[4] Atkins, 64–5; Butcher, 10.   [5] Butcher, 10–13.

unsatisfactory in 1662 and resigned, Richard Browne had died in 1664, and Richard Davis succeeded him. He served until 1688, with Vaughan Richardson (later organist of Winchester) acting as his deputy from Christmas 1686. Richard Cheriton, an ex-chorister of the Chapel Royal, was appointed in 1688 and gave not entirely trouble-free service until 1724.[6] In the mean time, about 1674, a small organ had been put in the nave. This so-called 'little organ' apparently had its own organist, for which the salary was £3 a year in 1685.[7]

With ten minor canons, ten lay clerks, and ten choristers, the choir at Worcester was unusually large, and from May 1662 onwards these numbers were pretty well maintained.[8] It was unusual, too, in that minor canons and lay clerks were paid the same: £16 a year, with £4 each for the boys and £32 for the organist and choirmaster.[9] A minor canon, of course, could augment his stipend by holding additional livings, and it certainly seems as if frequent absences were tolerated. Indeed, of the ten minor canons listed in 1671, John Sayer, Philip Tinker, Andrew Trebeck, and George Yardley were all simultaneously gentlemen of the Chapel Royal—in Tinker's case, precentor of Westminster Abbey as well. Clearly his place at Worcester was something of a sinecure since he was also 'Confessor of his Majesties household' (which should have been a full-time job in itself), while Trebeck managed to combine being precentor of Worcester with his London commitments.[10]

The pre-war music for the choir did not survive the Civil War, since soldiers under the Earl of Essex in 1642 'tore in pieces the Bibles and service books pertaining to the quire'.[11] A set of Barnard's *Church Musick* was bought in 1661 for £12. 15s. 6d., and in the same year a manuscript containing 'variis canticis describendis in usu ecclesie' from one of the Cambridge Loosemores. Four of the Barnard partbooks are still in the library, as are four of Tomkins's *Musica Deo Sacra* (1668).[12] The Restoration repertoire is contained in a set of partbooks (MSS A.3.1–6), unfortunately, but not unusually, lacking treble parts. Of particular interest are numerous works by local composers such as Richard Browne, already mentioned, John Badger, and William Harvard, to be noticed in more detail below. James Hawkins, a chorister at Worcester in the 1670s,[13] also had some of his work included. Indeed, he may have been the copyist of the earliest and largest portion of MS A.3.1—an enormous bassus cantoris partbook with almost 700 pages beginning with services and continuing with anthems. The sequence as it now appears is periodically interrupted by later insertions, but the entries in the main hand give us a good idea of the cathedral's music in Charles II's reign. Among the services are the usual early ones—Bevin, Byrd, Gibbons, Mundy, Patrick, and Strogers—though none by Tomkins (five were available in *Musica Deo Sacra*, however). Later services include nine by Child, four by

---

[6] For the organists see Shaw, 306–8.   [7] Butcher, 14.   [8] Atkins, 20, 61.
[9] Treasurer's Accounts, (A XXVII) 1686–7.   [10] Rimbault, 15, 49, 94, etc.
[11] Butcher, 35.   [12] Atkins, 63; Butcher, 35–6.   [13] Atkins, 34.

Rogers, two by Wise, and one each by Aldrich, Tudway, and William King, while local composers are strongly represented with five by Badger, two by Hawkins (who may be regarded as local at this youthful stage in his career), and one each by Richard Davis and William Harvard. All these works were entered before December 1684.

The anthems, too, begin with early ones—Byrd, Farrant, and Mundy, etc.—and continue with a generous number by Blow (29), Wise (15), Purcell (13), Child and Hall (11 each), Aldrich, Humfrey, Rogers and Tucker (10 each), etc. Again, local composers are present to a remarkable extent. Richard Browne, for example, has six anthems in MS A.3.1. and though at least one other composer of this name is known (organist at Wells before Okeover in 1620), it seems likely that this man is of a younger generation. They include *By the waters of Babylon* and *Unto him that loved us*, the second of which is listed by Clifford (1664).[14] Browne's successor as organist, Richard Davis, is represented by a Service in C major and thirteen anthems.[15] His verse anthem, *Thou, O God, art praised in Sion*, can be reconstructed fairly confidently from an organ part at Gloucester (MS 111) and countertenor, tenor, and bass parts originally from Hereford but now at Oxford (*Och* 544–53). Its straightforward, undemanding style is typical of the early Restoration verse anthem as practised by provincial composers (Ex. 98).

Equally prolific was John Badger, born in 1645 and a BA from New College, Oxford, where he probably came under the influence of William King. He was appointed a minor canon in 1668, and, in addition, vicar of St John's, Worcester, from 1676 until his death in 1690.[16] There are twelve anthems and services in B flat, C minor, D major, E flat, and G major by him in the Worcester partbooks, as well as a setting of the Gloria in excelsis.[17] Four of the services were written before 1680, judging by the dates in MS A.3.2, but, as with Browne and Davis, little can be convincingly reconstructed owing to the lack of treble parts. The *Magnificat* and *Nunc dimittis* in C minor do survive in one of the Ely organ-books (*Cu* Ely 3), but even this does not seem to make much sense. William Harvard, represented by a Service in G in the partbooks, was also a minor canon, serving from 1669 to about 1680.

Later partbooks include a number of works by William Davis, son of the organist Richard Davis, a chorister in the 1680s and lay clerk from 1693. He was successively organist of the Little Organ and master of the choristers from 1721 to 1745.[18] A book of keyboard pieces belonging to him has already been discussed (*Lbl* 31468; see Ch. 4), though it does not seem to contain any organ music by him. Parts of a Service in G minor and a *Jubilate* in D minor (dated

[14] Cheverton, 'English Church Music', 618–20.   [15] Ibid. 620–1.
[16] Ibid. 621.   [17] Ibid., 'Musical Supplement', 154–5.
[18] A. Vernon Butcher, 'Worcester Cathedral Library: Catalogue of the Music Collection of the Cathedral' (MS, 1982) 62; Shaw, 319.

Ex. 98. Richard Davis, *Thou, O God, art praised in Sion* (*Och* 550 and *GL* 111)

1715) survive at Worcester, the latter bearing the legend 'To Mr Bevan'—not
a dedication but indicating a substitute for the *Benedictus* in Elway Bevin's
'Dorian' service. Among his twelve anthems are *Praise the Lord, O Jerusalem*,
written for the Peace of Ryswick, 1697, *O Lord, make thy servant Anne* for the
accession of the queen in 1702, and *The word of the Lord is tried* for the
thanksgiving after the battle of Ramillies in 1706. In contrast to these works of

Ex. 99. William Davis, *Let God arise* (*WO* A.3.8)

jubilation there is a setting of *Cry aloud* marked 'An anthem for Days of Humiliation'.

Fortunately, one of his anthems survives in score. Dated 1709, his setting of *Let God arise* is a forceful, extrovert piece, owing much—especially its duets and trios—to the Italian church sonata style of Corelli, then at the height of its influence in England. As one would expect, sequential writing is plentiful, and

dotted coloratura passages expressing such words as 'scattered', 'fly', 'joyful', etc., abound, but the technique is sufficient to lift the piece from empty routine. The organ ritornellos are copiously ornamented, and marked with indications of 'loud' and 'soft' (and 'cornet' in one place). In terms of key and texture the movements are well varied, with excursions to the tonic and relative minors, and there is a nice sense of balance in the overall structure. Basically, it is in two parts, each ending with a chorus in C major—the second an extended version of the first. In the first part, the C minor trio 'Like as the smoke' has some strong chromatic progressions, while, in the second part, the declamatory countertenor solo 'O God, when thou went'st forth', has typically expressive detail (Ex. 99a). By contrast, the trio which follows, 'He is a father of the fatherless' (Ex. 99b), is characterized by tender lyricism, until C minor triple time gives way to C major retorted common time (Ex. 99c). Whether or not the piece was written for a special occasion such as the victory at Malplaquet, and why it alone of Davis's anthems survives in score, is unclear. On this evidence the composer would seem to be one of the more talented of Croft's contemporaries—which makes the incomplete nature of the rest of his output particularly disappointing.

York

One of Thomas Mace's great musical experiences occurred at York in 1644 during the siege.

Now here you must take notice, that they had then a *Custom in that Church*, (which I hear not of in any other *Cathedral*, which was) that always before the *Sermon*, the whole *Congregation sang a Psalm*, together with the *Quire and the Organ*; And you must also know, that there was then a most *Excellent-large-plump-lusty-full-speaking-Organ*, which cost (as I am credibly informed) a *thousand pounds*.

This *Organ*, I say, (when the *Psalm* was set before the *Sermon*) being let out, into all its *Fulness of Stops*, together with the *Quire*, began the *Psalm*.

But when *That Vast-Conchording-Unity* of the whole *Congregational-Chorus*, came (as I may say) *Thundering in*, even so, as it made the very *Ground shake* under us; (*Oh the unutterable ravishing Soul's delight!*) In the which I was so *transported*, and *wrapt* up into *High Contemplations*, that there was no room left in my *whole Man*, viz. *Body*, *Soul* and *Spirit*, for any thing below *Divine* and *Heavenly Raptures*; Nor could there possibly be any *Thing* in *Earth*, to which *That* very *Singing* might be truly compar'd, except the Right apprehensions or conceivings of *That glorious and miraculous Quire*, recorded in the *Scriptures*, at the *Dedication* of the *Temple* . . . where *King Solomon* (the wisest of men) had congregated the most *Glorious Quire* that ever was known of in all the world.[1]

So much for 'the unutterable Excellency and Benefit of a Psalm Rightly sung', as Mace describes it. Later that summer the parliamentary forces entered the city. The choral service ceased, even if psalm singing continued, and in June 1646 the organ was pulled down.[2]

The authorities were quick off the mark at the Restoration. Already by 26 August 1660 it was reported that 'the singing men and organs are preparing', though apparently two sackbuts and two cornetts were still needed to support the choir in May 1663—and continued in use at least until 1676 when Roger North noted the fact.[3] A visitation of 1662 helped to enforce standards and root out vestiges of Puritanism. It was even ordered 'that upon Wednesdays and

---

[1] Mace, *Musick's Monument*, 19.

[2] Peter Aston, *The Music of York Minster* (London, 1972), 9; see also Payne, *Provision and Practice*, 86, 113, 188–90, 224–5.

[3] Dorothy M. Owen, 'From the Restoration until 1822', in G. E. Aylmer and Reginald Cant (eds.), *A History of York Minster* (Oxford, 1977), 233–7; Peter Aston, 'Music since the Reformation', ibid. 408–9; Wilson (ed.), *Roger North on Music*, 40; Nicholas Thistlethwaite, 'Rediscovering "Father" Smith', *Musical Times*, 128 (1987), 404.

Fridays in Advent and Lent the whole morning prayer with Latin only is to be used'.[4] The organ was to be made ready by Michaelmas 1663. This was probably Dallam's 'excellent-large-plump-lusty', etc. pre-war organ, refurbished and re-erected in a loft on the north side of the choir. At the same time the choir was re-established with five vicars, seven singing men, and six choristers—numbers which still held in 1730.[5] The vicars paid the singing men £10 a year each from their rents, but their own profits were modest, despite some bumper years.[6] It was accepted that they needed additional livings; thus, when John Bell was admitted vicar in 1663, it was stipulated 'that his ordinary Salary be made up [to] £30 p.ann. out of the Vicars money untill he can be provided of a Vicarage in town or otherwise'.[7] The organist, too, was paid £30 a year, the master of the choristers an additional £8, and the boys £4 apiece.[8] These were the rates in 1698, but they probably applied through most of the period. Considering that the Minster was the seat of an archbishop and one of the largest and most magnificent buildings in Europe, it is surprising that it had such a small and poorly paid choir—certainly in comparison with its rich northern neighbour, Durham. Indeed, York was musically the poor relation, and even something of a satellite.

The choir music that had survived the Civil War was in tatters. According to a report of the vicars choral (1663–7), a set of Barnard's *Church Musick* was in poor repair ('10 bookes printed in folio of services and anthems which are something rotted and decayed'), likewise the manuscripts ('our written bookes are very old and much torne').[9] Of the latter, one depleted Jacobean set containing services—including Byrd's 'Great Service'—is still in the library (MS M.13.S). Most of whatever else survived must have perished in the great fire of 1829, though some music associated with the choir remains from the early eighteenth century.[10]

The pre-war organist, John Hutchinson, had died in 1658, but no doubt his music continued to be sung.[11] Several anthems by him are at Durham (where his father had been organist), but Restoration partbooks now in the Henry Watson Library, Manchester (MS 340 Hy 21) and probably originating from York contain a service (lacking the *Nunc dimittis*) and ten anthems by him. Three were still being sung at York in the early eighteenth century, among them *Behold how good and joyful* which Tudway included in his collection (*Harl.* 7340).

[4] Owen, 237.

[5] Frederick Harrison, *Life in a Medieval College* (London, 1952), 210, 334; Aston, *Music of York Minster*, 9; L. W. Cowie, 'Worship in the Minster', in P. M. Tillott (ed.), *A History of Yorkshire: The City of York* (London, 1961), 352.

[6] Harrison, *Life*, 256–8, 332–3; Cowie, 350.   [7] Harrison, 334.

[8] Owen, 240.   [9] Harrison, 327.

[10] David Griffiths, *A Catalogue of the Music Manuscripts in York Minster Library* (York, 1981).

[11] Shaw, 316–17.

Who the organist was immediately after the Restoration is not known, but in August 1666 the disreputable Thomas Mudd, having left Exeter under a cloud, was appointed master of the choristers (and probably organist), only to be replaced little more than a fortnight later by Thomas Preston.[12] The latter served until 1691 and is credited with a solitary anthem, *Sing aloud unto God*, in the York books (MS M.2/3.S)—a late eighteenth-century score. Other works attributed to Thomas Preston are more likely to be by Thomas Preston, junior, who was organist of Ripon. Contemporary with him was William Greggs, a singing man from 1670 and master of the choristers from 1677, who moved to Durham in 1681. The partbooks there contain six anthems by him, which have already been briefly mentioned in that context.

Towards the end of Preston's time at York the organ was in need of attention, and in January 1691 Bernard Smith undertook 'to make & set up a new great chair & eccho organ . . . within the space of twelve moneths'. The great was to have ten stops (including cornet IV, sesquialtera II, mixture II, and trumpet), the choir six stops (including vox humana), the echo a cornet. It took longer than twelve months to build, but by 1693 it had been installed on the screen.[13]

The new organist was Thomas Wanless, who became, in addition, master of the choristers in 1692.[14] From the word-books of anthems 'as they are . . . Sung in the Cathedral and Metropoliticall Church of St Peters in York' published by Wanless in 1703 and 1705, the repertoire seems to have been both extensive and growing during his period, comprising fifty-seven anthems in 1703, and seventy-nine in 1705, full anthems in the latter outnumbering verse anthems roughly two to one. The full anthems include well-established pieces by Byrd, Parsons, Hooper, Gibbons, etc., while the verse anthems present a selection by Blow, Humfrey ('Mr Umphreys'), Purcell, Tudway, and Turner—and, significantly, sixteen by Wanless himself in the 1705 edition. However, only his 1698 Cambridge B. Mus. exercise, *Awake up my glory*, survives complete. It is a lively piece in C major for two trebles and a bass, with parts for two violins, though technically it shows no great accomplishment.[15] The part-writing is awkward and the modulation restricted. Other surviving material includes his 'York Litany' (MS M.8.S), undistinguished but serviceable, and a simple homophonic Burial Service about which the same may be said (*Lbl* 17820). In 1702 he published *The Metre Psalm-Tunes, in Four Parts* 'for the use of the parish-church of St Michael's of Belfrey's in York'—unusual for the time in that the tunes are in the treble rather than the tenor.[16] Wanless died in 1712 and was succeeded by

---

[12] Ibid. 317; Aston, *Music in York Minster*, 9. Mudd has been dealt with under 'Peterborough'.
[13] Thistlethwaite, 'Rediscovering "Father" Smith', 403–4; Freeman, *Father Smith*, 195–9.
[14] Shaw, 318–19; Aston, *Music in York Minster*, 9.
[15] See Aston, 'Music since the Reformation', 412.
[16] Temperley, *Music of the English Parish Church*, 126, 369.

Charles Murgatroyd, known only as the composer of one or two chants in the cathedral manuscripts. He died in 1721.[17]

From the present point of view the most important manuscripts in the York library are several large score-books in the hand of John Cooper, a singing man from 1721 to 1730.[18] One book (MS M.14/1.S) contains morning and communion services by composers ranging from Tallis and Byrd to Goldwin and Charles King; a companion volume (MS M.14/2.S) contains the corresponding evening services. Another (MS M.8.S) includes thirty-six anthems by Purcell (7), Tudway (6), Blow (5), Humfrey (5), etc., the most recent being two by 'Mr' Croft. Works in score by Clarke, Croft, Goldwin, Goodson, Holmes, Walkeley, and Weldon also survive in his hand. A collection of 'Psalm tunes sung in York Cathedral' (MS M.11. S) dated 1712–18 contains chants by Blow, Purcell, and Tudway, as well as various local composers, among whom John Tomlinson, a vicar choral between 1681 and 1714, appears the most prolific.

Others whose work is to be found in these sources include the 'gentlemen amateurs' Edward Finch (1664–1738), fifth son of Heneage Finch, Earl of Nottingham, and Valentine Nalson (1683–1723), eldest son of the historian and pamphleteer John Nalson. Finch was a Cambridge man who, having briefly represented the university in Parliament, was subsequently ordained and appointed a canon of York in 1704, where his brother Henry was dean. Tudway's collection includes a *Te Deum* in G minor by Finch (*Harl.* 7342), together with a short setting of the collect *Grant, we beseech thee, merciful Lord.* Both are in five parts and severely chordal, but not without harmonic interest (and a fair degree of beginner's luck in dealing with the inner parts). The prayerful mood of the collect's opening is well caught, while some rich harmony in the Amen suggests, at least, a musical ear (Ex. 100). An autograph manuscript at Glasgow University (Euing MS R.d.39) dates the *Te Deum* 17 August 1708, though a companion *Jubilate* is dated 6 December 1721. The same manuscript contains another *Te Deum*, this time in G major, which does little more than confirm his amateur status.

Nalson graduated from Cambridge in 1702 and was subchanter of York from 1708. There is a litany in eight parts by him at York (MS M.103), but his best-known work is the six-part Service in G, which, according to Tudway, was written 'on the Thanksgiving for the Peace [of Utrecht], 1713' (*Harl.* 7342). It survives in several sources; one in the hand of James Hawkins (*Cu* Ely 16) is sprinkled with approving comments such as 'Sweet Mr Nalson', 'Excellent Mr Nalson', 'Admirable Mr Nalson'. It does indeed have its moments, and is a remarkable piece for such a person to have composed, even remembering the achievements of Creighton of Wells and Aldrich of Christ Church. Most of the

---

[17] Shaw, 319.

[18] See indexes of Griffiths, *Catalogue.* The Bing–Gostling Partbooks, though belonging to York Minster Library (MS M.1.S), did not originate there; see Shaw, *Bing–Gostling Part Books*, 4.

Ex. 100. Edward Finch, *Grant, we beseech thee* (*Harl.* 7342)

(a)

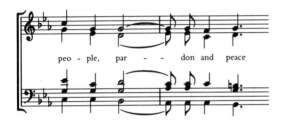

(b)

writing is in six parts, not faultless but more than adequate. The general style is old-fashioned 'short service', but there are also passages in the modern 'figural' style. As an example of the former 'Vouchsafe, O Lord' from the *Te Deum* may be cited (Ex. 101*a*); of the latter, the Gloria from the *Nunc dimittis*, its vigorous double counterpoint well deserving its 'admirable' from Hawkins. The movement closes with the Amen given in Example 101*b*.

Before we get carried away with such music it is well to bear in mind that some of the anthems attributed to Nalson are adaptations of motets by Pietro Antonio Fiocco (*c.*1650–1714) and his son Jean-Joseph (1686–1746). In this respect he was a follower of Henry Aldrich, though his models were very much in the modern style. A setting of *Give thanks unto the Lord* in Bodleian MS Mus.

Ex. 101. Valentine Nalson: (*a*) Te Deum and (*b*) Nunc dimittis from the Service in G
(*Cu* Ely 16)

(1) C 2 has *e'*.   (2) C 1 has *d'*.

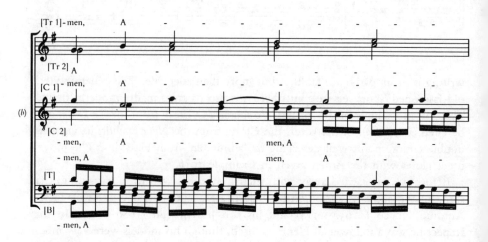

c. 58 carries the note 'The Musick by Fiocco Senior. The words fitted to it by Mr Valentine Nalson, Subchanter of York and Prebendary of Ripon', while the York anthem-book of 1715 states that *O most blessed, who can praise thee* has 'musick by Fiocco Jnr. and fitted . . . by the Rev. Mr Nalson'. In the light of this evidence the advanced technique of *Thou, O God, art praised in Sion* and [*O*] *clap your hands* begins to look suspect, and perhaps we should also be cautious about accepting the more florid writing in the service as Nalson's. Furthermore, it seems unlikely that a mass (Kyrie and Gloria in ten parts) ascribed to Nalson at York (MS M.146) can be by him, so the possibility that he may have been something of a magpie should be borne in mind. It is worth adding that there is a considerable amount of music by both Fioccos in manuscript at York.

Collegiate Parish Churches

In addition to the cathedrals of England and Wales, and the collegiate chapels of Oxford, Cambridge, Winchester, and Eton, there were four foundations with choirs of vicars (or chaplains), clerks, and choristers endowed to perform the cathedral service despite their status as parish churches. Manchester, Ripon, Southwell, and Wimborne had all been collegiate foundations in the Middle Ages, and though they were suppressed under the Chantries Act of 1547, gradually, for different reasons and in different ways, they reacquired choral establishments during the reigns of Queen Elizabeth I and the first two Stuart kings. There was no logical reason why Southwell and Ripon should have been restored and not Beverley, nor Wimborne rather than Crediton, Tattershall, or any other parish church that had once boasted a collegiate foundation. They were anomalous, and remained so until the nineteenth century, when three of them became cathedrals—Ripon in 1836, Manchester in 1847, and Southwell (having lost its collegiate status for a while) in 1884. At Wimborne, on the other hand, the foundation was disbanded in 1876, and the church has remained a parish church to the present day.

Their peculiar constitutions apart, these establishments had little in common with each other, though their second-class status rather cramped their style, and made them, Ripon and Wimborne especially, satellites of their larger and richer neighbours. With the Restoration, each set about re-establishing itself for the second time in a hundred years as best it could, organs were repaired and re-erected, choirmen and choristers recruited, music bought and copied.

MANCHESTER COLLEGIATE CHURCH

At Manchester Parish Church, charters of 1578 and 1635 led to the re-establishment of 'Manchester College', first under the name of Christ's College, then as the 'College of the Blessed Virgin Mary of Manchester'. About 1720 it was described as consisting 'of [a] Warden and 4 Fellows, who supply all the turns of Preaching, and 2 Chaplains, who read Prayers and doe all the other Duty of the whole Parish, and . . . 4 Singing Men, 4 Choristers, and an Organist, who perform Cathedral Service'.[1] According to statute, the chaplains were to receive

---

[1] Francis Gastrell, *Notitiae Cestriensis* (Manchester, 1849), 57.

£17. 10s. per annum, the singing men £10, and the boys £5.[2] By 1662, the choral service had been re-established, and a visitor recorded that on St Stephen's Day 1665 'we went to church and looked about us, and anon the quiristers came and we stayd [to] morneinge prayer. I was exceedinglie taken by the mellodie.'[3] Among the early organists were William Carter, who had been appointed in 1638 and survived the Civil War, William Turner (1666–70)—not to be confused with his more famous namesake, at that time master of the choristers at Lincoln—and William Keys (1669–79), later of St Asaph and Chester.[4] His successor was Richard Booth (1679–96), and it was during his period of tenure, in 1683, that a new organ of eight stops was ordered from Bernard Smith at a cost of £100.[5] No music survives from this period, but it appears that the choral service was maintained, while 'parochial services' were held in the nave. Edward Betts, the organist from 1714, published _An Introduction to the Skill of Music_ in 1724, containing several pages dealing with the rudiments of music, and a selection of 'Anthems in two, three and four parts'. Although unattributed, they can mostly be identified as being by Humfrey, Hawkins, Purcell, etc., and probably reflect the choir's repertoire in the early eighteenth century.

RIPON MINSTER

Successive charters in 1604 and 1607 re-established Ripon with a dean, subdean, six Prebendaries, and a choir of two vicars choral, a parish clerk, six lay clerks, an organist, and six choristers.[6] By 1663 the establishment was up to strength.[7] Henry Wanless—an ex-chorister of Durham and possibly the father of Thomas Wanless of York—was organist from about 1662 to 1674, though from 1668 his duties were taken over by a Mr Wilson because of deafness.[8] His successor, Alexander Shaw, was also from Durham and soon returned there as organist in

---

[2] William Farrer and John Brownbill, 'Manchester', in Farrer and Brownbill (eds.), _The Victoria History of the County of Lancaster_, iv (London, 1911), 193.

[3] A. W. Wilson, 'The Organs of Manchester Cathedral', _The Organ_, 12 (1932–3), 1; Plank, 'An English Miscellany', 69.

[4] Shaw, 184–5; Henry A. Hudson, 'The Organs and Organists of the Cathedral and Parish Church of Manchester', _Transactions of the Lancashire and Cheshire Antiquarian Society_, 34 (1916), 129–30.

[5] Hudson, 119–20; Shaw, 'Stray Notes on "Father" Smith', 26.

[6] J. T. Fowler (ed.), _Memorials and Chapter Acts of the Collegiate Church of SS Peter and Wilfrid, Ripon_, ii–iii (Surtees Society, 78, 81; 1886, 1888), iii, p. xviii; for vicars and parish clerks see ii. 324–5, 354.

[7] Temperley, _Music of the English Parish Church_, 351.

[8] Shaw, 227–8; also Cheverton, 'English Church Music', 187–8.

1677.[9] While at Ripon he made manuscript additions to their set of Barnard's *Church Musick*—or so it would seem, in view of the apparent Ripon connections of a surviving bassus decani partbook now in the British Library (K.2.e.7).[10] Its contents include Shaw's anthem *I will sing unto the Lord*, together with others by northern composers such as Hutchinson, Wilkinson, and Foster. Later additions include five services and six anthems by Thomas Preston, one service signed 'Tho Preston jnr' by the composer himself. It seems probable, however, that all are by Thomas Preston, the younger, organist of Ripon from 1690 to 1730, rather than Thomas Preston, the elder, organist of York from 1666 to 1691. This is suggested by the presence of *When the Lord* [sic] *came out of Egypt*, attributed to plain 'Mr Tho Preston' in the partbook, but known from pre-1693 Durham sources to be by Preston, junior. Significantly, the anthem *Sing aloud unto God*, known from York sources to be by Preston, senior, is absent from the Ripon partbook.

Thomas Preston of Ripon, therefore, seems to have been quite a prolific composer, though the fragmentary nature of his extant work makes assessment difficult. Two of his services were triple-time services, and the fact that he set the words of the preface 'Therefore with angels and archangels' throws an interesting light on the way the communion service may have been performed at Ripon. Presumably the two Prestons were father and son (another Thomas Preston succeeded at Ripon in 1731), though how they may have been related to William Preston, organ-builder of York, is not clear. Back in 1677, the Dean and Chapter of Ripon had paid William 'the sume of Tenne pounds, for making the Organ in the s[ai]d Collegiate Church, to have five stops'—a sum which must refer to repairing or enlarging an already existing organ.[11] By 1695 a new organ was needed and there is some evidence that Gerard Smith may have been the builder. Damage caused 'by the fall of the Trumpett Stop amongst the other small pipes' in 1708 was repaired by Thomas Preston for £10.[12] At various times between 1696 and 1708 he was paid for copying music into the choirbooks,[13] though nothing now survives unless the references are to the Barnard partbooks.

As has already been suggested, music at Ripon was strongly influenced by its two neighbours, Durham and York. Inevitably it must have shared their conservatism, at least until Preston's incumbency as organist. No doubt this reliance continued into the eighteenth century, and we can assume that works by

---

[9] Shaw, 228; Crosby, *Durham Cathedral Choristers*, 24; but see also Charles H. Moody, *Ripon Cathedral Organ: A Short History and Description, including Miscellaneous Notes from the Cathedral Records* (Ripon, 1913), 21.

[10] Cheverton, 'English Church Music', 367–9.

[11] Moody, 4; Laurence Elvin, 'The Organs of Ripon Cathedral', *The Organ*, 46 (1966–7), 137.

[12] Freeman, *Father Smith*, 162–3; Moody, 5.

[13] Temperley, *Music of the English Parish Church*, 351.

Heseltine of Durham and Wanless of York joined those of Thomas Preston in the Ripon repertoire, together with an increasing number of works by mainstream composers, filtered perhaps through Durham and York.

SOUTHWELL MINSTER

At Southwell, new statutes in 1585 established a dean, sixteen prebendaries, and a choir of six vicars choral, six singing men, an organist, master of the choristers, and six choristers—a cathedral in all but name.[14] By early 1663 the choir was almost up to strength, though it lacked one vicar and one singing man 'because we cannot yet get fit persons'. Daily services were 'duelie and reverently performd', holy communion was celebrated monthly, and sermons preached on the appointed days.[15] The vicars were paid £15 a year each, the singing men £10, the choristers £2. The first organist after the Restoration, Edward Chappell, received £15 as vicar, £15 as organist, and £5 as master of the choristers.[16] Steps were taken early to obtain a new organ. Even before April 1661 Chappell had travelled up to London 'about the Organ' but further visits do not seem to have borne fruit.[17] In the end it was a local man, Mr [Edward] Darbie of Lincoln, who built the instrument, completing it by February 1663 at a cost of £140. The picture is not entirely clear, for almost immediately the maintenance of the instrument passed to Mr Preston—presumably one of the Prestons just encountered at Ripon. Records of repairs to the organ continue over the years, but it seems likely that around 1700 a new organ was built, perhaps by Bernard Smith. Repairs were needed after 'the South Spire was fird with lightning and burnt at the Antiquire and Organ' in 1711.[18]

Chappell was succeeded as organist by his son George in 1689, and by William Popely in 1696.[19] Popely had been a pupil of Daniel Henstridge at Rochester, where he was a chorister in the years around 1680. Foster lists three anthems by him said to be in one of Bumpus's manuscripts, but no longer identifiable.[20]

WIMBORNE MINSTER

In some ways the most remarkable of these collegiate parish churches was at Wimborne, where the church governors obtained a renewal of their 1562

[14] Alan Rogers, *Southwell Minster after the Civil Wars* (Nottingham, 1974), 5–6.
[15] Ibid. 22.   [16] Ibid. 35.   [17] Ibid. 30.
[18] Freeman, *Father Smith*, 157–9; William L. Sumner, 'The Organs of Southwell Cathedral', *The Organ*, 14 (1934–5), 12–13; ibid. 51 (1971–2), 89–90. See also Rogers, 31.
[19] Shaw, 275–6.
[20] Myles Birkett Foster, *Anthems and Anthem Composers* (London, 1901), 79.

charter from King Charles I at a cost of £1,000, establishing 'three Priests and three Clerks to celebrate divine service in that place, and four choristers, two precentors [their role is unclear], and one organist'.[21] It is here that we can see the influence of great neighbours most strongly; in terms of personnel and repertoire this small Dorset foundation clearly looked to Winchester and Salisbury. The fact that so much of its music has survived is particularly fortunate, since is confirms what otherwise might not have been guessed, that such an establishment took itself seriously with regard to its duty to perform the cathedral service.

The immediate post-Restoration organist was John Silver, son (presumably) of John Silver, organist and master of the choristers of Winchester Cathedral up to 1666. The younger Silver had been a chorister there before the Civil War and was appointed lay clerk in 1661, resigning to take up his post at Wimborne in 1664. His contract stipulated that he was to be paid £22 a year 'provided allwayes that the sayd John Silver shall make his continuall abode within the p[ar]ish . . . and shall discharge the duty of an Organist there, and shall diligently from tyme to tyme teach and instruct the singingmen choristers and other servitors of the sayd Church in the art and skill of singing'.[22] Later that year a new 'payre of Organs' by Robert Hayward of Bath was erected at a cost of £188. 15s. 6d. and placed on the screen where the old organ had stood. Incidental charges included £5 paid to Giles Tomkins, organist of Salisbury, and John Silver (probably the elder) for 'Comming over . . . To prove the Organ'.[23]

Silver remained organist of Wimborne until his death in November 1694, and was succeeded by George Day in 1695 and John Filer in 1713.[24] Day had previously been a lay vicar at Salisbury but had been dismissed in 1693 after what was possibly an unsatisfactory probationary year. Filer is likely to have been a chorister at Salisbury, since one Samuel Filer was succentor there between 1683 and 1703.[25]

Silver, Day, and Filer are each represented as composers in the Minster partbooks, though probably the Service in F and five anthems attributed to Silver are by his father. Day has two services and eight anthems, Filer a service and a single anthem. Unfortunately, the sources are too fragmentary to tell us much about the music, but they are revealing in other ways. Most interesting is an organ-book (MS P 10) bearing the date 1670 and the initials 'D.S.' on the binding. It is impossible to tell at which stage the date was added (or, at present, what the initials stand for) but the fact that Michael Wise is described as 'Org: of Sarum' near the beginning suggests that the book was begun in or after 1668,

---

[21] Quoted from a translation of the charter in the Minster Library.

[22] Betty Matthews, *The Organs and Organists of Wimborne Minster, 1408–1972* (Bournemonth, n.d.), 19.

[23] Ibid. 6.   [24] Ibid. 20.

[25] Information kindly supplied by Suzanne Eward, Librarian and Keeper of the Muniments at Salisbury.

while the presence of a psalm-chant by 'Mr' John Blow several pages further on puts it before 1678. It therefore seems likely that 1670 is about right and that, consequently, several anthems by Michael Wise in the first part of the book can be regarded as early works—which other evidence also suggests. As he was organist of Salisbury, the presence of so many pieces by him comes as no surprise. After him, the most frequently represented composers are Child with three anthems, and John Ferrabosco, organist of Ely, with two. The last few anthems, however, were entered in another hand (almost certainly Day's) towards the end of the century, and include Purcell's *My song shall be alway*— one shudders to think how badly its solos could have been sung. At the other end of the book (reversed) are organ pieces by Frescobaldi, Richard Portman, and Christopher Gibbons, followed by organ parts to various services, mainly by composers from the earlier part of the century. Among later additions are a *Magnificat* and *Nunc dimittis* by George Day, again in his own hand.

The earliest of the vocal partbooks may date from before 1670, but the chronology and original collation is confused by a multiplicity of hands, missing pages, and later in-filling. However, here and there one can recognize runs of quite early pieces: for example, in manuscript P 14 (tenor decani, fos. 71ᵛ–89ʳ), probably in the hand of Silver himself. Most of the living composers here had Winchester connections, not only Silver, but also William King and Robert Pickhaver. Immediately following this early series, the hand changes (fos. 89ᵛ– 102ᵛ) to that of Day, who entered another sequence of anthems mainly by Wise, but including several of his own. Finally, a closing section contains anthems by Clarke, Hawkins, Humfrey, Purcell, and Weldon, two by John Bishop, organist of Winchester College, and one by Anthony Walkeley, organist of Salisbury.

Even though these partbooks do not form complete sets, their interest is considerable. Quite apart from the fact that they supply otherwise missing parts for two of Thomas Weelkes's services (Weelkes had been organist of Winchester College in the late sixteenth century), they help us to identify some of the early anthems of Michael Wise. More importantly for present purposes, they tell us what was actually sung at Wimborne during the period—and, indeed, in the case of an ornamented bass partbook (MS P 17), how it was sung. At the same time they bring works of local composers to our attention, despite problems of reconstructing the music from incomplete sources.

APPENDIX A

Directions for Singing Services at Ely, 1702 – 1708

(Ely Dean and Chapter MS [Cu] 10/12b)

Begin the Sentences or exhortations in a reading tone which being ended, Elevate your voice to a Moderate pitch & begin the confession, in as even a voice as you can keeping your voice steadfast in the same tone, after this manner

Almighty &

Al - migh-ty and most mer - ci - ful fath - er

Then proceed to the absolution with the same Elevated voice, which being done, begin the Lord's prayer in the same tone, which the Choire will take from you & finish,

Then proceed to petitions & responses thus,

& our mouths [&c]

O   Lord op - en thou our lips

O Lord &c

O   God make speed to save us

Glo - ry be to the fath - er, and to the Son, and to the Ho - ly Ghost

As it was &c

The Lords name be praised,

praise yee the Lord

at the end of ev'ry pray'r end thus

Through Je - sus Christ our Lord

or thus

through Je - sus Christ our Lord

At the end of the Apostles Creed, which is allways Chanted by the Choir, Elevate *your* voice as at first, or to such a pitch as you can best keep your voice to, without varying, & proceed after this manner;

at the end of the Lord's Pray'r you are at Liberty to take a new pitch, & proceed after this manner

Who ever goes out with you to the Litany, let him pitch the beginning about E la mi, or F fa ut, for fear of leading you, out of the compas of your voice.

The Litany

O God &c   The same of all the rest of the three petitions.

Remember not Lord our Offences nor the Offences of our forefathers neither take thou
vengeance of our Sins Spare us good Lord Spare thy people whom thou hast redeemed with
thy most precious blood,

& be not Angry      and so of the end of ev'ry one.

The Litany being ended, you must begin the first sentence of the Lord's Pray'r, with an
Elevated voice, which the Choir will take from you, & finish, then raise your voice as
before, & proceed;

   *neither reward us*

   *O Lord arise &c*

   *O Lord arise &c*

As it was &c

From   our   en - e - mies de - fend us   O   Christ

Graciously look &c

Pit - ty - ful - ly be - hold the sor - rows of   our   Hearts

Mercifully forgive &c

Fav - our - ab - ly with mer - cy hear   our   pray'rs

O Son of David &c

Both   now   &   ev - er vouch - safe   to   hear us O   Christ

Graciously hear us &c

O   Lord let thy mer - cy be   shew - ed up - on   us

After this, if you find your voice well pitch'd, proceed to the rest of the pray'rs; But if you find your self to have deviated from the pitch you began with, take a new pitch & proceed to the end of the first Service

Let   us   pray &c

The 2d Service begins the Lord's Pray'r with a pretty Elevated voice, but not so high but that you may raise your voice higher at the Pronouncing of the Comandments, & so, keep to that Pitch up to the Epistle & Gospell, which being ended Give the Pitch to the Choir, for the Nicene Creed; &c

APPENDIX B

Dean Paul's Articles of Inquiry into the Vicars Choral of Lichfield, 1663

(Lichfield and Staffordshire Record Office: MS DC/C/1/2)

Directions & Articles of Enquiry given in charge to Zachary Turnpenny Succentor of the Cathedrall Church of Lichfeilde John Johnson Sacrist Michael East Vicar Chorall elected & approved inquisitors by the Company of Vicars Chorall there In the Primary Visitacion of the said body, & all the Commorantts within the precincts of the said Close Anno domini 1663 By William Paule D D Deane of Lichfeild & the Chapter of the same Whereunto particuler presentment is to be made by the said Inquisitors onerated with an oath speciall And by any other of the said body upon his oath generall according to good conscience &c

1 What good benefactor gathered you (when in a dispersed condicion) into this place of comfortable cohabitacion? for it concernes you to honor his memory And to remember what an obbligacion lyes upon you to serve God most devoutly and continually for such excellent accomodacion by his divine guidance.

2 It concernes you to search out your severall charters from previous princes & if the originalls be lost to gett Coppyes against a time of need to prove you are a corporacion by Charter as well as prescripcion And it were very commendable in you to renew them now in the time of his gracious Majesty.

3 Have you in your new buildinge a muniment house wherein to keepe safe under severall keyes all your munniments evidences leases and statutes (if you have any) which are now to be exhibited, your Accounts alsoe, and all other writeinge that may import you?

4 How many persones are you by originall statutes & foundacion And how many by latter indulgence? Is your number full? Who governes your body within itselfe And distinguish the number of the Vicars that have surviv'd the late calamities from those that are newly added to you That the mercy of God in giving you by his sacred Majesties favour, a new being (a mercy never to be forgotten) may remaine upon record to posterity.

5 How many Vicars Chambers are voyde? & how long have they bin for? are they in dilapidacione? who dwelles in them & of what quality? by what authority? Upon what rents? And how hath the same (if any) bin paid out? have any Vicars Chambers bin lately alienated? And is there any Inhabitante within your colledge or without, that ought to give the Deane & Chapter caution for theire familyes & have not?

6 Are your 2° quadrangles, & the great Close or Churchyarde &c within consecrated ground kept cleane, healthfull & decent, without nasty cattle, insanous dunghills & is the mulct gathered for such offence to the use of the fabricke?

7 Have you all those officers in being, by due choice, that you had before the wars for collecting your rents, payments & other services. Are they sworne (as formerly) to all fidelity, the rest to fidelity & secrecy, as touching strangers & Chapter corrections? And doe they faithfully discharge theire truste & duties?

8 Have you providently surveyed your houses and lands? & booked the surveys for the benefitt of Succession? How many houses & other buildings have you new raised, or repaired within the Close; or without? and to what charge? what good freinds have you found? And how many houses remaine tennantles and in deplorable ruine, upon the score of your loyalty: what improvemente of rent have you made? And what may your remediles losse of rente & Commons in arreare amount to duringe the late unhappy warre And what prejudice have you susteined in the right of Patronage of any Church appropriate belonging to your body. And what is the now Incumbent as to loyalty & the Church & religion established & declare the same in order to the reestablishment of your right, And also declare what augmentacion hath bin made by you or your feefarme tennant for the Curate, or Vicar (or whatsoever his title is) that serves at Chesterton?

9 You are to remember to goe the perambulacion or procession (which you have this last & many yeares omitted, to the great prejudice of the Church) the three dayes before the ascension of our Lord by the law & our locall statutes. Let the Subchanter remember to give directions therein hereafter, unto whose affair it doth belonge.

10 Doth the said Subchanter perform laudably (as we doubt not) his office in the Quire? & in the hall? Are the Statutes that concerne you read & hearkened to as oft as is appointed? Doth he governe the musick Schoole & children of the Quire under the high Chanter by his best iudgment & advise to the officiall or Master And doth he publiquely every Saturday order the Service of the whole furthre weeke in writeinge or Table?

11 Doth the Sacrist perform his duty as far as possible? Doth he receive the moneyes which his predecessors used to receive? Doth he find the lights according to the antient honor of this Church and make due provisions for the holy sacrament according to antient frequency? Doth he adorne the holy table on the Eves before each Sunday & holyday according to antient custome? And doth he cause the sexton to discharge his office according to his obbligacion And pay his wages?

12 What are the names of the Vicars, that by theire stalls ought to serve as hebdomadaries under the Five Prebends that are the Chaplaines of dignity? Are they in the holy order of Preisthood, That they may serve at the Altar or holy Table? Doe they upon solemne festivalls request a Canon to officiate there? Or at least provide that the gravest person under a Canon doe execute on such daies? And is the accustomed money weekly paid to the Assistants in that Service by them, as formerly? viz, vjd per weeke.

13 Are your whole body present in due time at the morning & evening services not haveing mist & allowed impediment? What remember you concerning your sixe a Clocke prayers in order to the Restoration thereof when God shall please to fitt the Church?

14 Have you one of your Company worthy trust assigned by the Deane & Chapter (or you must have such a one soe assigned) to be Intitulator & to note the defaults and absences of all his bretheren; and that upon speciall oathe, and to notice the same to the deane & Chapter from time to time?

15 Doth the Subchanter write downe in a table every weeke the Preist that is to be hebdomadary for that weeke, with a Deacon & one other Vicar, to minister at the holy

table, especially upon solemne feasts? Doe you begin that service in due time or pay the mulct? And the like for those that are appointed to singe; And doth any person soe mulcted contumaciously forbeare the service of the Church for three dayes after?

16 If any Vicar request another to read or singe, or doe any other office in his stead, and the requested Vicar failes The Intitulator is to notice the names of both to the deane & Chapter in order to double correction?

17 Doe any more than 2 Vicars of a side at most request the liberty of the sergine daies and that but once a month? And that not on the Lords dayes or festivalls, And is any permitted to goe out of towne till the other 4 are returned home?

18 Doth any Vicar carry the Church bookes forth of the Quire or Vestry without the license of the Sacrist?

19 Doth any Vicar presume to enter the Quire after the first Gloria Patri? or to depart before the blessinge? except for sudden infirmities sake, or naturall necessity, And doth he in that case presently returne? And doth every Vicar that hath such causes declare the same to the deane, senior Cannon, other Cannon or Subchanter upon the mulct appointed.

20 Is the Hebdomadary constantly ready to begin morninge and evening prayers in due time? or mulcted? And the like for him that shall be requested by him to officiate in which case both are to be corrected.

21 Doth every Vicar enteringe the Quire first reverently incline or bow to God towards the holy table? & next to the Bishop? And in his absence to the Deane? And doe they enter the Quire gravely and leasurely, not croudingly and rudely? And doe they depart with like decency? Doe the like reverence when they passe from one side of the Quire to the other?

22 Doe the whole Quire kneele at the Confession, & all prayers, converted or turned towards the holy table? as also at all the Collects? Doe they stand up at the creedes so converted? Doe they bow at the blessed name of Jesus? also they soe turne at the beginning of Te Deum? when the Gospell is read? doth the Quire turn towards the Gospeller? And likewise at Gloria Patri? & Glory be to God on high, Turne towards the Sacred table?

23 Doth the Organist play a Voluntary before the first lessone after the Psalmody as hath bin anciently accustomed? And is it grave or apt? For ye know how he hath bin accused that hath bin in that office.

24 Is the Chorus written faire & hung alternly, one weeke on the decani side & two weekes on the Cantoris side?

25 Doth any Vicar misbehave himselfe in the Quire by murmuring whispering laughing upon whatsoever occasion? or talkinge? Or doth any one use any words more than necessary? or any other rudenes?

26 Is the interessem or perdicion money distributed amongst the present persons only?

27 Doth any Vicar offer to reade any lesson, Epistle or Gospel before private & preparatory auscultacion or reading? upon the shame decreed by statute? And doe the said Vicars bringe theire bibles, and reade with the Lectors? or theire latine testaments if they understand the language.

28 Doth any Vicar presume to bury any person (not being of the Quire) in the Churchyard without license from the deane or the Canon Resident present upon the Paines?

29 Doe any of the Vicars forbeare the Sacrament whensoever it is celebrated without lawfull excuse for that time? or receive Commons for any day when he is absent at his own pleasure?

30 Do all & every of the Vicars demeane themselves to all & every of the Canons in generall with devout reverence (as the statute phrases it) without insurreccion, without detraccion? doeing theire accustomed duty for theire wages, at their going to & from Church, deske or pulpitt? And are all stall wages justly paid? or what doth hinder? sett down your knowledge concerning the Nedicions [*tradicions?*] And all other good & laudable customes of the Quire.

31 Doth or hath any Vicar taken giftes or bribes of new Vicars, for a favourable testimony, (an old fault) forbidden by Statute? whereby both sufficient and insufficient persons are received, & sufficient persons (contrary to oath) are repelled?

32 Can you tell what became of the Mansion or house at Stow, whither Vicars broken by or with age or infirmity might retire & enjoy theire Commons dureing life?

33 Doe all your company constantly come into the Quire in theire Chorall habitts?

34 Do any Vicars that are at variance with theire bretheren or neighbors runne to law without endeavouring first the severall wayes of composement & reconciliacion commanded by Statutes?

35 For as much as the Vicars of dignitaries have larger allowance for a certaine ornament now growne out of use, some other distinctive order, as a tippett blacke but not of silk, according to the Cannon may be enjoyned to be worne upon theire surplices.

36 Doe any women resort to the Chambers of unmarried Vicars without the company of other good women, as wittnesses of their conversacion?

37 You are to give a perfect Catalogue of all persons whatsoever old and younge that live in your vicaridges or the Close? Also theire quality & course of life And how they stand affected to the King's Majestie & the Church of England?

38 What persons & how many sell ale within the Churches liberties? how are they licensed? doe they keepe and suffer disorders in their houses by day or night, especially at service times? do any of your body haunt them? to the dishonor of the Church & theire own discredit?

39 Do any of your Society (which God forbid) or any other commorant in the Close lead ungodly, unrighteous, unchaste, unsober lives, tipling away theire pretious time? Are any blasphemers? swearers? perjured persons? quarrelsome? brawlers? fighters? Gamesters in any kind or any the like inordinate & scandalous livers? Town walkers without necessary business? outlyers? frequenters of infamous and suspected places? Present them in the fear of God &c.

40 You are to make a schedule of your owne laudable customes.

41 Do you know, or have heard of any Church utensils, ornaments, plate, bookes of any kind, Records, materialls of the Church, Palace, deanery, Canonicall or other houses, Iron or lead of the Church, Aquaduct, Cisternes, Pipes that have bin by any private person taken or conveyed away, sold or converted toe theire own use? name them.

You are to present to all these particularities, Both, you the Inquistors upon your oath speciall, and the rest of the society by theire generall oath of fidelity to the Church, so shall we & you also deliver your owne soules.

APPENDIX C

Lichfield Cathedral Statutes, 1694

(Lichfield and Staffordshire Record Office: MS D. 30)

CHAPTER 8. CONCERNING THE VICARS

The order of the Vicars in the choir is this the Subchanter is allways to be the chief &
to have the first place the Deans Vicar the second the Chancellors the third & so on in
the same order as they are plac'd in the table at the end of the last Chapter but one.

For some of these we must make some rules by themselves as for the Subchanter the
Sacrist & the Organist & some for all of them together.

The Subchanter hath allmost the same place among the Vicars as the Dean hath
among the Canons that is the first & Chief for he it is that is the proper Vicar of the
Precentor, whose office & authority doth particularly regard the government of the
Choir, & therefore those duties which we have above assign'd to the Precentor, do all
of them in his absence devolve upon the Subchanter. Most of them allso he shall
perform when the Precentor himself is present & shall appoint him so to do so that it
allmost allways lyes upon the Subchanter in the Services at all times of publick prayers
to prescribe what services shall be used, to appoint the Anthems, to make the weekly
table, & allso to take care that as well his fellow Vicars as the Choristers in time of
Divine Service be decently apparelled & behave themselves attentively & devoutly
according to the holiness of the place & things in which they are concerned, & to keep
both Vicars & Choristers in their duty as well there as elswhere as far as it shall be in his
power, & if they any way offend either against the rules of their office or good manners
he shall admonish them according to their offence either privately or publickly in the
Vicars Hall, & if they do not take notice of his admonition he shall complain of them,
of the Vicars to the Dean & Chapter of Resident[iary]s to be punished as shall be
appointed in these statutes & of the Choristers to their Schoolmaster to be corrected by
him. He is allso to set up the citation of the Prebends every one in his own stall at the
command of the Dean or President & to do all other things that are any where assign'd
him in these our statutes. And for the performance of those things the Subchanter shall
receive of every one of the Canons whom he shall install 6s–8d & of every one whom
he shall cite & send them letters to certify them of it one shilling sixpence.

The Sacrist is the Treasurers Vicar & as the Treasurer is among the Canons, so is he
to be reckoned the fourth among the Vicars These dutys we lay upon the Sacrist He is
to perform all the Divine Service in the Cathedrall both for weddings & Christnings &
Churchings & burialls whether in the Church or in any other part of the Close, unless
either the Bishop or the Dean or any of the other Canons have a mind to perform any
of these offices. He is allso to Register faithfully in a parchment booke which he must
buy at his own charge all the weddings Christnings & burialls which shall be perform'd
by himself or any one els in the Cathedrall or Close. He is alsoe to keep in good order

all the bells that are or shall be hung up in our Church, & so provide at his own cost the rope & iron work & whatsoever els is necessary for them, as allso candles for publick prayers bread & wine for the Sacrament, & coales & basses & matts for the Church; he is allso at his own perill to keep & to make clean all the flaggons cups candlesticks cushions books & other such things. He is at his own cost to repair the ornaments of the Church & by himself or his Subsacrist to take care that the font be fill'd with clean water when there's occasion & that the whole buildings both roofs windows walls—pavements & all the other parts thereof & allso the seats be swept & kept clean, & that the Church doors be kept open at the appointed church times & when theres any other occasion & that at all other times they shall be kept shut, that those graves which by these our statutes we permit be dug in the Church or Churchyard without any further leave but no other graves but by the permission of the Dean or the Canon that is in Residence, & lastly that the bells of the Church be rung in such order & for so long time as is requisite whether for giveing notice of prayers or sermons to be there, or for welcoming the Bishop or funeralls in the Close or weddings or upon holy days or other solemn times. but never els unless it be by the command of the Bishop or with the leave of the Dean or any other Canon that is in Residence.

We give to the Sacrist all the fees that arise from marriages Churchings or burialls that are perform'd by any one whomsoever in the Cathedrall or Close & allso the fees that are due for Registring the said marriages Christnings & burrials: We appoint allso for the Subsacrist a yearly pension of forty eight sillings to be paid out of the revenue of the Dean & Chapter of Residentiarys.

We appoint one Organist & the same to be a lay Vicar in our Cathedrall Church, that in those parts of the Services which are onely to be sung he may joyn with the rest, & in those where the organ is to be used he may play upon that: the Organist is allways to have the same places among the Vicars as the Canon that made him his vicar had amongst the Canons, for salary the Organist shall yearly receive of the Dean & Chapter of Residentiarys four pound & six shilling eightpence for an organ blower.

As to other things which concern him as he is a Vicar as allso the Sacrist & Subchanter the following statutes are for them in common with the rest of the Vicars

The Dignity of every one of the Vicars is that they perform the sacred functions & in this do as it were represent the turns of the Canons; it is from hence that they have their names & that they take their places among one another, as the Canons do among themselves, according to the table that is put down at the end of the Chapter about the Canons, Except onely the Subchanter, who though he be onely the Precentors Vicar, that is in the rank of the second Canon yet hath a peculiar right over all the rest as we above ordained.

Wherefore we charge & require every one of the Canons themselves to be affable & show a due respect to each of the Vicars Choralls according to his degree, unless they shall otherwise deserve, and the Residentiarys allso as we above ordered, to use them hospitably, & that neither the Dean nor any of the Residentiarys ever pretend out of Chapter to turn out any of the Vicars for any cause whatsoever, nor that he attempt to do it in Chapter, unless, which God forbid, the Vicar either have done something that is very ill, or shall have committed the same fault thrice for which he hath been first admonish'd, & then hath received severer punishment in Chapter, or unless he shall be condemned by the appointment of any of these our statutes.

We do moreover allow free burying place in the Cathedrall Churchyard to the Vicars that dy in the close whether they be past service or dye in their duty.

And to each Vicar that hath perform'd his duty, we allow 3 days in a moneth either together or at different times to be absent from publick prayers without any punishment, yet upon these conditions that none of them shall ever make use of this Indulgence either upon Sundays or Festivall days, & that neither the Organist nor any other that hath any service appointed him in the weekly table shall stir without getting somebody to supply his place for him, & that more than two of the same side shall never be absent at once. But if any of the Vicars shall upon any pretence soever be at any time absent from morning or evening prayers otherwise than is here allowed, unless he be kept away by sickness or any other extraordinary occasion approved of by the Dean if present, or in his absence by the Chief in the Church that is present, or unless he shall first have obtained leave of the Dean, or the Chief that is present in the Church he shall for every time that he is absent forfeit a shilling out of his Commons or Salary to be distributed once a month to the rest of the Vicars that were then assisting at publick service. But if any one happens to be sometimes absent upon any other occasion besides those above mentioned & be neither detained by any such impediment, nor permitted or excused as is aforesaid he shall toties quoties forfeit two pence besides his Commons to be laid out upon the Fabrick of the Cathedrall as we above ordained in the Chapter of the Dean.

But we ordain that no Vicar shall be by any means turned out or corrected but by the Generall Chapter or the Major part of them, or at least by the unanimous consent of the Dean & all the Residentiarys themselves present & not by their proxys; unless it be in the two cases before mentioned in the Chapter about the Dean.

And to the end that the Dean & Chapter of the Residentiarys may have notice as often as any of the Vicars is absent from publick prayers, they shall as often as they think fit choose one of them under the title of Intimator, who according to an oath to be administred to him to that purpose by the Dean or President shall observe & signify such absences every weeke to the weekly Chapter.

For it is the Chief or Sole Office of the Vicars to attend the Celebrating the Divine Worship, to apply themselves with diligence to the service of the Choire & to do their utmost in those parts of it which are appointed them in their places by the Precentor, or Subchanter, either by word of Mouth, or in the weekly table.

And this is the way & manner of makeing the weekly table that in it on every Saturday before morning prayer there shall be appointed, one of the Lay Vicars to read the first lesson both at morning and evening service all the week following beside two others in the same tone either to chant or read the Litany as far as the Lords prayer on the days that it is appointed to be done & one of the Vicars in holy Orders to read the Epistle at the Communion Table as oft as there is occasion & another to perform all the rest of the publick service, if either the Lord Bishop or Dean or any of the Canons do not read any of it for the whole week who from thence hath the name of Hebdomadary

The Vicars are moreover to keep & preserve in repair all their buildings in the close if Common or Empty, at the common charge, but if belonging to any one of them at the owners charge, & if they are in tenants hands, they are to take care that the Tenants do the same; nor shall they for the future ever let out any of the aforesaid buildings either empty or publick or private, for any term of years or for one or more lives without first obtaining the speciall leave of the Dean & Chapter of Residentiarys for it under their hands & seal. And it is ordained in the Old Statutes that every one of the Vicars, as often as they come into the Choire on the East or West side to Divine Service, must first make a bow toward the Altar & then to the Bishop, or in his absence to the Dean, & that as oft as they crosse the Choire or any part of it in service time they must bow toward the Altar only, in which we have not thought fit to alter any thing without the command of our Superiors.

The Vicars are moreover to be very intent at their devotions & to observe the behaviours & rites that are prescribed, & to abstain from any laughing or noise or undecent postures, or talking, & allso from the reading of any private books as much as is possible, & to carry themselves in all respects reverently and religiously, & to be obedient to the Canons as their Masters, & love one another with Mutuall Kindnesse.

Moreover we assign equall commons to all the Vicars, deducting what is to be deducted, that is 3d per day to each, but to every one his own Salary according to the portion appointed for that stall to which he is Vicar, as it is in the Table in the Chapter about the Canons. And as to all other both offices & rights & whatever els belongs to the Vicars, whether to all in Generall, or to some of them in particular, we leave them all to their own private statutes & customes as far as they are not against the laws of the land, or do not contradict these statutes of ours.

We forbid any of the Vicars Choralls to appear in the Choire at the time of Divine Service without a Surplice on unlesse he be just come into or going out of town, he that doth otherwise as allso he that does not come in till after the psalms are begun, & he that goeth out before prayers are done unless he goes out to ease nature & comes in again, or he that goes without leave from the Chief then in the Church shall be accounted as absent, & have the very same punishment

We strictly enjoin that no one of them offer any injury or affront to the Dean or any of the Canons, If any one doth, let him be turned out of the Church by the Dean & Chapter according to the Method above prescrib'd untill he have made satysfaction to the Dean or that Canon.

APPENDIX D

Domestic Statutes of the Vicars Choral of Lichfield, 1694

(Lichfield and Staffordshire Record Office, MS. D. 30)

Statutes of the Subchanter & Vicars of the Cathedrall Church of Lichfeild agreed upon by themselves & presented to the Right Reverend father in god William Lord Bishop of Coventry & Lichfeild & to the Dean & Chapter for their allowance & confirmation at his lordships primary visitation Mar. 8 1693.

1 Imprimis We ordain & appoint that every Vicar upon his admission shall pay to the community of vicars twenty shillings without any delay before he be admitted to commons amongst them, or to share in the division of their common goods or profits: and that he shall take the oath following to be administred by [blank]

> I N. will be true & faithfull to the Subchanter & the company of Vicars of the Cathedrall Church of Lichfield, I will diligently to my power preserve love in my selfe & with all my fellows & I will faithfully stand by both them & their honest concerns against all according to my power as may be reasonable, their counsells as well in the Hall as at the Desk or those things that are or shall be imparted to me as secret I will not knowingly reveal to any one to their damage, & allso I will keep safe & indemnify'd all & every of their writeings that I shall be intrusted with, I will keep their statutes & ordinances when I shall know them or they be read & publish'd to me, so help me god & these holy Gospells of god.

this is to be done as often as any Vicar shall leave his place in the Quire & be readmitted anew, to wit he must pay the 20s & swear as is aforesaid.

2 We ordain & appoint that it shall be in the power of the Subchanter to call a Hall or Desk as oft as there shall be occasion at both which every Vicar upon Notice shall be bound to attend without a reasonable excuse to be allowed by the Subchanter & the rest of the Vicars, or the major part, upon pain of one shilling to be deducted out of his dividend & to be distributed amongst the rest of the Vicars.

3 We ordain and appoint that dureing such desk or Hall every Vicar shall behave himself decently to the Subchanter & with due respect to the rest of his brethren, giveing no uncivil or provoking language, or any other disturbance under pain of one shilling toties quoties to be distributed as aforesaid.

4 We ordain & appoint that no Vicar shall disclose to any person but to his own brethren, any thing that by the major part of the Vicars shall be declared a secret at either desk or Hall under pain of five shillings to be distributed amongst the rest of his brethren.

5 We ordain & appoint that if any of the Vicars raiseth any discord among his brethren or give any cause or occasion of discord, or contendeth with abusive, scandalous,

injurious, & dishonest words or by giveing the lie or the like he shall forfeit 12d to the Society, but if any man by the others giveing this occasion fall into the same offence then the first that gave the occasion shall forfeit double that which the last shall.

6 We ordain & appoint that if any Vicar shall make or disperse or cause to be made or dispersed any scandalous libell, or any other thing in writeing to the disgrace of any of his brethren or to the lessning of their credit [he] shall pay 20s to be divided as aforesaid

7 We ordain & appoint that if any of the Society shall violently touch or strike another, whether with offensive arms or by any other means shall draw blood of him he shall forfeit to the Society 6s–8d to be paid as above & shall make reparation to the endamag'd party according to the determination of the Society

8 We ordain & appoint that if any Vicar shall draw or unsheath any knife dagger or sword & lift them up or a staf against any of his fellows with a design to strike him he shall pay to the Society ten shillings. And if he shall strike or draw blood of any of the Society, with any of the aforesaid arms he shall pay 20s to the said Society to be distributed amongst them without any excuse whatsoever, & shall further satisfy the endamag'd party according to the Judgment of the Community.

9 We ordain & appoint that no Vicar may wear a dagger or sword or any knife of an unlawfull size, unless he wear a sword in his goeing out of town or returning home, under the penalty of six shillings & eight pence to be distributed as aforesaid.

10 We ordain & appoint that no Vicar upon any difference ariseing among them shall bring any person or persons to take his part or shall reveal it to any one till it is decided among themselves if it be possible or before the Dean & Chapter if it cannot be otherwise under pain of 10s to be paid as aforesaid.

11 We ordain & appoint that no one of the Society shall prosecute another for any fault or offence done in the Hall or within the precinct & gates of the close before laymen or in a secular court to have reparation made him; but shall first desire of the Subchanter & of the community to have his injuries redress'd and if they shall be careless he shall go to the Dean & Chapter to do him justice in that matter & if they allso shall neglect him he shall go to the Bishop for a remedy & if after haveing observ'd this method the matter be not determin'd then let him prosecute him that has done him wrong in the common form of law as shall seem most expedient to himself

12 We ordain & appoint that no Vicar shall stand privately near another chamber or house to peep or endeavour to hear what is said or done in it; neither shall he hearken to them that backbite his fellows nor have any communication with such by any means under forfeiture of five shillings toties quoties to be paid as above

13 We ordain & appoint that no Vicar shall bring into their company at any publick meeting any one whom he knows for certain to be an enemy to any of his brethren under forfeiture of 1s toties quoties to be paid as above

14 We ordain & appoint that no Vicar shall empty a chamber pot any where but in the place appointed for that use under forfeiture of 1s to be paid to the Society toties quoties

15 We ordain & appoint that no Vicar shall presume to play in the common hall or in any other place within the precincts of the Vicars either at dice or tables or any other game forbidden to clergy men for money or drink but onely for recreation sake neither shall he introduce into their company any other person into their common Hall

to play for such purposes, under pain of 6s–8d toties quoties to be distributed as aforesaid

16 We ordain & appoint that no Vicar shall bring suspected women or any woman whatsoever that may give suspition & scandall day or night to his dwelling or into any chamber within the gates or precinct of the Vicars be the pretence what it will or shall permit them or any of them to continue there under payn of paying 13s–4d to the community of the Vicars toties quoties in such manner as is abovesaid.

17 We ordain & appoint that no Vicar shall keep or feed at the table or within the gates or precincts of the Vicars, Grey hounds or hunting dogs or any other dog under payn of paying 1s for every day that he shall so keep any dog to be payd to the Community

18 We ordain & appoint that every Vicar shall be carefull according to his power to keep his own house within & without from fire & water & shall competently repair it, & not change his house untill it be competently & sufficiently repaired in the Judgment of the Dean & Chapter & the community abovementioned

19 We ordain & appoint that whereas the said Vicars have at present one Bailiffe or officer whose duty it is to gather the rents belonging to the Subchanter & Vicars & to receive the pensions due to the said Subchanter & Vicars & the fines & seal money due for the granting & sealing of any lease or leases made by the said Subchanter & Vicars & likewise the said Bailiffe or officers duty is to disburse all cheif rents pensions or other payments charged upon the Vicars estates likewise to give account every quarter of all the rents received belonging to the said Subchanter & Vicars & all the necessary disbursments to be made out of the said rents, for the collecting of which said rents & makeing of which said accounts the said Bailiffe or officer is to receive from the said Subchanter & Vicars every quarter the summe of 20s, that the said offices of collecting the rents & makeing up the accounts which have been formerly invested in two persons shall & may be so again when the Subchanter & Vicars shall find it convenient

20 We ordain & appoint that the officer for the time being shall receive the Fines due for the granting & sealing of every lease made by the Suchanter & Vicars & to account the share of every Vicar not present at the sealing of any lease so granted & sealed as aforesaid under the penalty of answering & paying out of his own pocket the proportion or proportions of the absent Vicar or Vicars share or shares of the aforesaid fines when the said share or shares of the Fines shall be by the said Vicar or Vicars to whom they belong, demanded

21 We ordain & appoint that the Bailiffe or officer for the time being shall pay to every Vicar without delay any part of his proffits that he shall have received for him under payn of 2s–6d toties quoties to be distributed as aforesaid.

22 We ordain & appoint that the said Bailiffe or officer shall within two months after every quarter day give up his accounts to the company of Vicars in the Vicars Hall & pay to every Vicar that proportion of his dividend as shall be due to him under the pain of ten shillings toties quoties to be distributed as aforesaid.

23 We ordain & appoint that the officer of the Subchanter & Vicars shall upon the sealing of every lease by them granted immediately put the counter part of the said lease into the muniment house upon forfeiture of ten shillings to be divided as aforesaid.

24 We ordain & appoint that the said person shall immediately Register the heads of every particular lease (as before granted) in a booke for that purpose provided by the

company, within two days after the sealing thereof under pain of five shillings to be divided as aforesaid.

25 We ordain & appoint that the Bailiffe of the Subchanter & Vicars shall upon the payment of every pension from them to the King, Dean & Chapter, or any other persons whatsoever immediately put the severall acquittances into the muniment house under pain of five shillings to be divided as aforesaid

26 We ordain & appoint that if any Vicar shall at any time be found to imbezill or take away out of the muniment house any counterpart of any lease or acquittance or any other writeing whatsoever without leave of the Company he shall forfeit five pounds to divided as aforesaid.

27 We ordain & appoint that the Respective Intimator of every year shall without delay pay to every Vicar so much of his commons as he shall receive under pain of 1s to be distributed as aforesaid.

28 We ordain & appoint that when any one of us is deputed by the rest to excercise any office according to the course used among us, he shall give such sufficient security for his fidelity in the administration of it, & for giveing us a faithfull account of it afterwards as shall seem most expedient to us.

29 All these statutes & orders & all others which upon emergent occasions shall hereafter be ordained for the glory of god & the establishment of our Society we do promise for ourselves & oblige our successors truly & faithfully to observe; and if any shall refuse to keep them let him be remov'd by the Dean & Chapter as unfit to be a member of our Church & Community.

30 & That the forementioned statutes & ordinances may be better kept in memory we ordain that every quarter on the last friday of the quarter all the Vicars Chorall shall meet after evening prayer in the Vicars Hall, & that all these statutes which they are oblig'd to keep shall be audibly & publickly read in English before them from which no Vicar shall absent himself under forfeiture of 1s unless he have a reasonable excuse which shall be approved by the Subchanter & major part of the Company & this shall be performed by the Subchanter or some other deputed by him

31 We appoint & ordain that all these statutes shall be written in one table to be hung up in our common hall that they may be at any time perus'd by the Vicars, that no man may plead ignorance of all or any of the premises, & it is ordained that if any of the aforesaid penalties be not raised by the Subchanter & the rest of the Vicars as is above ordered that then the Subchanter or in his absence the steward or senior of the Society shall give notice of it to the Dean & Chapter that they may cause the said penalties to be raised & to be layd out upon the fabrick of the Cathedrall Church of Lichfield. In witness whereof, We have hereunto put our Common Seal the day and year above written.

APPENDIX E

Extracts from Ely Cathedral Statutes, 1666

(Ely Dean and Chapter MSS [Cu])[1]

STATUTES OF THE CATHEDRAL CHURCH OF ELY
GRANTED BY THE MOST HIGH AND MIGHTY
KING CHARLES II

Chapter 1

Of the number of those who are to be maintained, or receive a stipend, in the Church of Ely

First of all we decree that there shall be perpetually in the said church, one dean, eight canons, five minor canons, one reader in theology, four chaplains, with the cure of Holy Trinity and St Mary's churches and the chapels of Chetsam and Stunteney, one deacon, eight lay clerks, one master of the choristers, one organist, eight choristers, two teachers of grammar for the boys (one to be preceptor, the other subpreceptor), twenty-four boys to be taught grammar, six poor men, two sub-sacrists, one registrar, one seneschal, one auditor, one janitor, one barber, one caterer, one cook, one keeper of the bridges, one bell-ringer and clock-winder, and seventeen bailiffs of the manors, and these are all to serve diligently in the same church in the numbers prescribed (each in his own degree) according to our statutes and ordinances.

Chapter 19

On the quality, choice and admission of the minor canons and clerks

Because we have decreed that in this our church, God is to be worshipped with hymns, psalms, and perpetual prayers, we decree, determine, and desire that those five priests whom we call minor canons, and the eight lay clerks, as well as the deacon who reads the epistle (all of whom we have appointed to sing the praises of God constantly in our cathedral church), shall be, so far as possible, educated, of good report and decent speech, and lastly, skilled in singing; a thing which we wish to be established by the judgement of those in the same church who are well versed in the art of music. And they will be chosen, when their places are vacant, by the dean, or in his absence, by the vice-dean and chapter. Further, at the time of their admission, they will swear an oath of this kind. [The oath follows as Chapter 20.]

---

[1] I am grateful to Mr John Carter for allowing me to use (and slightly tamper with) his translation of the statutes as they affect the choir.

Chapter 21
Of the residence of the ministers

We ordain and desire that the minor canons, the clerks, and all others ministering in our church should be permanently resident. No one shall be allowed to be absent from our church for an entire day or an entire night unless permission has first been obtained from either the dean or, in his absence, the vice-dean; and whoever does otherwise shall be fined by the dean or, in his absence, the vice-dean, a sum to be determined. And if any minister of the choir is so discourteous as to leave our church without giving the dean or, in his absence, the vice-dean, three months' notice, we desire him to forfeit three months' stipend. Also, if any of the minor canons is absent from morning prayers, he is to lose a penny. Whoever is absent from evening prayers is to lose a halfpenny. If anyone fails to enter the choir before the end of the first psalm, he will lose a farthing. Whoever fails to perform a duty laid upon him in the choir by the precentor shall lose twopence. But the fine for the clerks is to be determined after consideration by the dean and the majority of canons present, and the clerks are to abide by their decision. The total of fines for absence will be distributed at the end of each term to those present in equal proportion to the number of days on which they have attended, so that those who have attended on more days receive a larger share, but those who have attended on fewer, a smaller. And further, so that the minor canons and priests of our church may more diligently perform their duties, we permit them to enjoy no other ecclesiastical benefice than as chaplains of Holy Trinity and St Mary's churches and the chapels of Chetsam and Stunteney, and we desire them to be content with the emoluments assigned to these chaplaincies by the Dean and Chapter.

Chapter 22
Of the precentor and his duties

We decree and ordain that one of the minor canons who is older in years and more distinguished in character and learning should be chosen as Precentor by the dean or, in his absence, the vice-dean and chapter. His duty will be to maintain good order among the singers in church, and set an example to the others with his voice, and to be, as it were, a leader so that no dissonance arises in the singing. All the minor canons and clerks, and the rest who come into the choir to sing, shall obey him, so far as concerns the business of the choir. Whatever he prescribes to be read or sung, they must obey promptly. And furthermore, without malice he shall record the presence of the dean and canons at divine service, and the absence of all who serve in the choir, every fortnight rendering a faithful account in the chapter house before the dean or canons present. And if any of the minor canons or clerks show cause for his absence, it ought to hold good if it be approved by the dean or, in his absence, by the vice-dean. In addition, he shall see that the books allotted to the choir are well cared for and preserved. Finally, whenever he shall chance to be absent himself from our church, he shall designate another to carry out his duties faithfully. All this he shall promise by a solemn oath faithfully to perform.

Chapter 23
Of the sacrist and sub-sacrists

We decree and desire that from the minor canons one man who is industrious and trustworthy be chosen by the dean or, in his absence, the vice-dean and chapter, who is to be called the sacrist, to whom will be entrusted the care of the cathedral, the altar, the chapels, the vestments, cups, monuments, and other ornaments: and he shall receive them all from the receiver by indentures in the presence of the dean or vice-dean and the canons present, and he shall return them in like manner. He shall also ensure, with the advice of the receiver who happens to be in office, that there be no lack of wine, water, or wax for candles required for the celebration of divine service in the aforesaid cathedral at the appropriate times. Furthermore, the said sacrist shall visit the sick in the said church of ours, and he shall diligently and reverently administer the sacraments to the infirm as well as to the firm, as often as the need arises, or the nature of the time requires. He shall also receive the offerings, if there be any, in the cathedral, and shall keep them to be handed over for the use of our church. We desire, moreover, that he may have under him two good and industrious men, to be nominated by the dean or, in his absence, the vice-dean and chapter, who are to obey the instructions of the sacrist himself, fold the vestments, light the candles, prepare the altar, see that the cathedral is swept and cleaned, and ring the bells, or see that they are rung, at the hours prescribed by the dean or vice-dean. It will also be their duty to carry a staff in front of the bishop, if he be present, or in his absence in front of the dean, when he enters the cathedral or departs from it, and to conduct preachers to and from the pulpit. Finally we desire that the sacrists, when they chance to be away from our church, find others to take their places and perform their office faithfully while they are absent. And these sacrists and sub-sacrists shall be bound by an oath to perform their duties faithfully.

Chapter 24
Of the choristers and their master

We decree and ordain that in our said church there shall be, according to the choice and designation of the dean or, in his absence, the vice-dean and chapter, eight choristers, boys of tender years with tuneful [*sonoris*] voices well suited to singing, who shall serve the choir, minister, and sing. To instruct and imbue these with modesty of behaviour no less than with skill in singing, we desire to be chosen by the dean, or in his absence the vice-dean and chapter, besides the eight clerks previously mentioned, a man of good reputation, upright life, skilled in singing and playing the organ, who will give his time with zeal to the instruction of the boys and the singing of the divine offices. But if he is found to be negligent, or lazy in teaching, he is to be removed from his post after the third warning. And he is to swear an oath also that he will perform his duty faithfully.

Chapter 25
Of the grammar-school boys and their teachers

So that piety and good learning may always bud, grow, and flower in our church, and in due season bear fruit for the glory of God and the advantage and ornament of the nation, we decree and ordain that there be always in our church of Ely, according to the choice and designation of the dean and chapter, twenty-four poor boys, of natural aptitude (so far as possible) for learning, and for the most part without the help of friends, who are to be supported from the property of our church. But we do not wish them to be admitted amongst the poor boys of our church before they have learned to read and write and have some knowledge of the first rudiments of grammar, as judged by the dean or, in his absence, by the vice-dean and the headmaster. And we desire these boys to be brought up at the expense of our church until they have acquired a reasonable knowledge of Latin grammar, and have learned to speak Latin and write Greek: for this the space of six years will be allowed, or if the dean and headmaster think fit, at the most seven and no more. We desire, however, that no one, unless he be a chorister of our church of Ely, be chosen as a poor pupil of our church if he has not completed the ninth year of his life, or passed the fifteenth year of his life, nor do we wish anyone to remain any longer in our school if he has passed his eighteenth year. But if any of the boys be notable for uncommon slowness and dullness, or naturally averse from learning, we desire him to be expelled by the dean or, in his absence, the vice-dean, and placed elsewhere, so that he does not, like a drone, devour the honey intended for the bees. And in this connection, we charge the conscience of the teachers, that they give as much effort and attention as they can to see that all boys make progress, and become proficient in their studies, and that they do not allow any boy who is clearly marked with the fault of slowness to remain uselessly for any considerable time with the others, without reporting his name at once to the dean, so that on his removal a more suitable boy may be chosen in his place by the dean and chapter. We decree furthermore that there is to be chosen by the dean or, in his absence, the vice-dean and chapter, one who is learned in Latin and Greek, of good report, of godly life, and endowed with the ability to teach, who will bring up in piety and adorn with learning not only these twenty-four boys of our church, but any others who may be drawn to our school to learn grammar. This man is to hold first place in our school, and is to be headmaster, or chief teacher. Again, we wish there to be chosen by the dean and chapter a second man of good report and godly life, learned in Latin and endowed with the ability to teach, who will, under the headmaster, teach the boys the first rudiments of grammar and will be called the undermaster or second teacher. We desire these teachers of the boys to observe diligently and faithfully the rules and order of instruction which the dean or, in his absence, the vice-dean and chapter shall prescribe. But if they are discovered to be lazy or negligent or not suited to teaching, after the third warning they are to be removed by the Dean and Chapter and lose their office. They will promise by oath that they will faithfully perform everything which relates to their functions.

Chapter 28
Of the stipends of the ministers in our church

We decree and desire that from the common property of our church stipends may be paid to all the ministers of our church, through the hands of the receiver, in equal portions at the end of each term, in the following way: viz., to each minor canon as his share fifteen pounds, to the principal teacher of grammar eighteen pounds, to the assistant ten, to the organist twenty pounds, to the master of the choristers ten pounds, to the deacon eight pounds, to each clerk ten pounds, to the sub-sacrists, whomever, six pounds, to the caterer six pounds, to the janitor six pounds, to the barber six pounds, to the cook six pounds, to the choristers four pounds, to the boys of the grammar school three pounds thirteen shillings and four pence, to each of the six poor men six pounds thirteen shillings and four pence, to the vice-dean five pounds, to the receiver ten pounds, to the precentor forty shillings, to the seneschal or clerk of the estates five marks [£3. 6s. 8d.], to the auditor six pounds.

Chapter 29
Of the celebration of divine services

So that petitions and prayers may constantly be made in our church in a fitting and proper manner, and every day the praise of God may be celebrated with song and jubilation, we decree and ordain that the junior canons [minor Canons] and clerks together with the deacon and master of the choristers shall perform divine services every day in the choir of our cathedral according to the custom and ceremony of other cathedral churches. But we do not wish them to be obliged to sing services at night. We desire further, that on all the principal feast-days the dean, if he is present and business permits, and on the other feast-days (Sundays excepted) the other canons, each in order, shall conduct holy prayers. We decree also that none of the canons or others who serve in the choir should enter the choir at the time of divine service without the dress appropriate to the choir. We desire in addition that both teachers of grammar should be present in the choir on feast-days, with dress appropriate to the choir and to their rank; of whom one shall have a place in the choir above the minor canons, the other below them, unless he be a Master of Arts, when he shall sit above the minor canons. Furthermore, we wish the grammar-school boys who are maintained in the church to attend in the choir on feast-days wearing surplices, and to perform diligently the duty laid upon them by the precentor, unless they be instructed otherwise by the headmaster. These boys we also order to be present in our cathedral church on each working day of the year for morning prayers at five o'clock.

Chapter 32
Of the correction of offences

So that integrity of character and behaviour may be preserved in our church, we decree and desire that if any of the minor canons, clerks, or other servants has committed a petty offence, he is to be punished by the decision of the dean or, in his absence, the vice-dean; but if his offence be more serious, he shall be expelled by the dean, if this be judged fair. If, however, any of the canons shall be found guilty of any offence or crime from which serious scandal could arise against our church, he shall be reprimanded by the dean; and if, after the third warning, he has not reformed his behaviour, he is to be charged before the bishop, his visitor, and be punished according to his decision. But in the case of the poor men, however many times they may offend, we reserve their punishment to the dean, and if they remain incorrigible they are to be expelled from our church by the dean with the agreement of the chapter, and forfeit all advantage from it.

APPENDIX F

Prefaces to Thomas Tudway's *Services and Anthems* (1715–20)

(London, British Library, Harleian MSS 7337–42)

(i) VOLUME I (1715)

A | COLLECTION | OF THE | MOST CELEBRATED | SERVICES | AND | ANTHEMS | USED IN THE | CHURCH | OF | ENGLAND | FROM THE | REFORMATION | TO THE | RESTAURATION | OF | K. CHARLES II. | COMPOSED BY THE | BEST MASTERS, | AND COLLECTED BY | THOMAS TUDWAY, D.M. | MUSICK-PROFESSOR | TO THE | UNIVERSITY OF CAMBRIDGE | A.D. MDCCXV.

To The Right Honourable
Edward Lord Harley

My Honoured very Good Lord

I shall think my self much Honoured & very happy, if any endeavours of mine, in Obeying your Lordships commands, may contribute anything to your Pious designe, of rescuing from the dust, & Oblivion, our Ancient compositions of Church musick; at this time, so much mistaken, & dispis'd.

The Pious Reformers of our Church, from the Errors of Popery, haveing settl'd the Doctrines therof, thought it very necessary, & advisable allso, to appoint a standard of Church Musick which might adorn the dayly Service of God, by such a solemn performance, as might best stir up devotion, & Kindle in mens hearts, a warmth for devine worship.

I dare affirm my Lord, that there cou'd never have been any thing better devis'd, than what was compos'd first of that Kind, by Mr Tallis, & Mr Bird. They were both Servants, & Organists, to her Majesty Queen Elizabeth, & employ'd by her in composing for the Service of her Chappell Royall; & though both of them Papists, have sett an inimitable Pattern of solemn Church musick, which no one since, has been able to come up to, & remains to this day, a demonstration of their exalted Genius; of which two excellent persons, give me leave to give your Lordship some further Account. Mr Tallis was the Senior, & began to appear eminent, in Harry the 8th. & Edward the 6ths time; But the greatest part of his compositions, were made in Queen Elizabeths time, & for the use of her Chappell, as I have allready mention'd.

Mr Bird was his schollar, & allso a Contemporary with him; He imitated so well the copys his master set him, that tis a hard matter to know which exceeded;

I think Mr Bird outliv'd his Master, & was Servant & Organist to King James the 1st.

Your Lordship will find in this Collection, the works of all that liv'd at the same time, with these Excellent men; such were cheifly, Dr Tye, Dr Bull, Dr Giles, Mr Barcroft, Mr Stonard, Mr Morley, with severall others; These, no more than those who succeeded them, cou'd ever make appear so exalted a faculty in compositions of Church Musick; I must here however, except, that most Excellent Artist, Mr Orlando Gibbons, Organist & Servant to King Charles the 1st, whose whole Service, of *Venite Exultemus, Te Deum, Benedictus, Kyrie Eleyson, Credo, Magnificat, Nunc Dimittis,* with severall Anthems &c, are the most perfect peices of Church Compositions, which have appear'd since the time of Mr Tallis, & Mr Bird; The Air so solemn, the fugues, & other embellishments so Just, & Naturally taken, as must warm the Heart of any one, who is endu'd with a Soul, fitted for devine raptures.

I must allso further acquaint your Lordship, that this Standard of Church Musick; was not left at random, to the fancy & invention of the Composers of those times; But was circumscrib'd, among other Ecclesiastical matters, by Authority; As your Lordship will find, by a Book entitl'd Reformatio Legum Ecclesiasticarum; which has been publish'd three severall times; first in the reign of Queen Elizabeth, And twice by King Charles the 1st; The Original Mss, of which, is in the Harlyan Library, as I'm inform'd, by the most Ingenious and Learned, Mr Humfrey Wanley, your Lordships Librarian, the first proposer of this work.

The Governours of our Church in those dayes, wisely forsaw, that any deviation in matters of Church Musick, woud soon destroy, the cheif designe, & use therof; And therefore, guarded against all innovations, & encroachments, of the Composers of Musick; They prohibited all vibrative, & operose Musick; things perfectly secular; And ty'd 'em down, as near as possible, to the Planus Cantus; That those who sung, as well as such as hear'd, might have the Benefitt of the result, in their Pious Exercises, & stir'd up to a devout sence, & frame for religious worship.

They knew well, that operose, or Artificiall Musick, woud have no effect, to inspire true devotion, but wou'd rather excite delight, and Pleasure; And therefore not fitt, or proper to be admitted, within the doors of the Church; They kept closs therfore, ev'n to the Character, or Notes, long before us'd in Church Musick; viz: Breif, semebreif, minum &c, & forbid the makeing use of Notae deminutionis, that they might not in any wise, mix devine musick, with Secular.

Your Lordship will find therfore, through this whole Collection, the same Style, & Character, as at first appointed to be us'd, & which lasted without deviation, for above a 100 years; How we are come to a Kind of Theatrical, & Secular way, in our Modern Compositions of Church Musick, I shall presume to acquaint your Lordship, in my Collection, of the next volume, which I intend to present to your Lordship; beginning at the Restauration of King Charles the 2d.

Thus by makeing an Everlasting Memorial of these allmost forgotten compositions, of Ancient Church Musick; & by allowing them a place among so many, & inestimable Antiquities, & Manuscripts, as are Collected in your Lordships Library, will rendre your Lordships Piety, & Patronage of learning, & learned men, conspicuous to all the world. That your Lordship may live, many, many, & very happy years, will be ye constant prayers, of all good men, & more particularly of my self, as in duty bound, who am

> My Honoured very Good Lord
> your Lordships most Faithfull
> Obedient Humble Servant,
> Tho: Tudway.

(ii) VOLUME II (1716)

A Collection of the most celebrated | Services and Anthems | both Ancient and Modern used | in the CHURCH of | ENGLAND beginning at the | Restauration of K. CHARLES. | II Compos'd by the best Masters And | Collected by Tho. Tudway DM | and Musick Professor to the University | of Cambridge AD MDCCXVI

To The Right Honourable Edward Lord Harley

My Honoured & very good Lord

I here present your Lordship with a 2d volume, after the maner, both of Ancient & Modern Church Music, which I promis'd to give your Lordship some Account of, in the dedication of my 1st volume as also the reason, as I conceive, how we are fall'n into this Theatricall & Secular Style, in our Compositions of Church Music.

King Charles the 2d being restor'd to his Just Rights, & with him the Church of England to its Ancient use, & dissipline; The 1st thing thought of, was to settle the divine service, & worship, in his Majestys Chappell Royall, after such a Modell, as the Cathedralls in England, and Ireland, were to Establish theirs by.

The Horrible devastations, the sons of violence had committed, on all things sacred, in the time of the Usurpation, had disfurnish'd all the Cathedralls throughout both Nations of their Organs &c, so necessary for the solemnization of divine service, in Singing of Hymns, & Psalms. Twas in those dark & Gloomy days, The Church of England was sad, & disconsolate, & Robb'd of all its Melody; Twas then the Church of England, was in the same afflicted State, as the Jews were in the Babilonish Captivity, when they Hung their Harps upon the trees, & coud not sing the songs of Sion in a strange land; But as soon as the King was restor'd, the Church reviv'd, And Cathedral worship, was again Establish'd.

In the beginning of the year 1662, the first Organ was Erected in his Majestys Chappell in White Hall; The King took great delight in the Service of his Chappell, & was very intent upon Establishing his Choir, and had the goodness to make such an addition, as almost to double the number of Gentlemen, & Children of the Chappell which it consisted of before the Rebellion, to make room for those, who had bin Sufferrers, & had surviv'd the wars, & allso for the best voices that were then to be found.

The Standard of Church Music, begun by Mr Tallis & Mr Bird, &c was continued for some years, after the Restauration, & all Composers conform'd themselves, to the Pattern which was set by them;

His Majesty who was a brisk, & Airy Prince, comeing to the Crown in the Flow'r,

& vigour of his Age, was soon, if I may so say, tyr'd with the Grave & Solemn way, And Order'd the Composers of his Chappell, to add Symphonys &c with Instruments to their Anthems; and therupon Establish'd a select number of his private music, to play the Symphonys, & Retornellos which he had appointed.

The King did not intend by this innovation, to alter anything of the Establish'd way; He only appointed this to be done, when he came himself to the Chappell, which was only upon Sundays in the Morning, on the great festivals, & days of offerings; The old Masters of Music viz: Dr Child, Dr Gibbons, Mr Low, &c Organists to his Majesty, hardly knew how, to comport themselves, with these new fangl'd ways, but proceeded in their Compositions, according to the old Style, & therfore, there are only some Services, & full Anthems of theirs to be found.

In about 4 or 5 years time, some of the forwardest, & brightest Children of the Chappell, as Mr Humfreys, Mr Blow, &c began to be Masters of a faculty in Composing; This, his Majesty greatly encourag'd, by indulging their youthfull fancys, so that ev'ry Month at least, & afterwards oft'ner, they produc'd something New, of this Kind; In a few years more, several others, Educated in the Chappell, produc'd their Compositions in this style, for otherwise, it was in vain to hope to please his Majesty.

Thus this Secular way was first introduc'd, into the Service of the Chappell, And has been too much imitated ever since, by our Modern Composers; After the death of King Charles, Symphonys, indeed, with Instruments in the Chappell were laid aside; But they continu'd to make their Anthems with all the Flourish, of interludes, & Retornellos, which are now perform'd, by the Organ.

This However, did not Oblige the Cathedrals throughout England, to follow such an Example; for indeed such an Example was very improper for their imitation; because they had none of the fine voices, which his Majesty had in his Chappell, to perform light Solos, & other slight Compositions, And therfore it had been much better for them, to have kept close to the old, Grave, & solemn way; which such voices as they had, were more capable of performing; But the Composers of those, and later times, being Charm'd, with what they heard at White Hall, never consider'd how improper such Theatrical performances are, in religious worship; How such performances, work more upon the fancy, than the passions, and serve rather to create delight, than to Augment, & actuate devotion; And indeed all such light, & Airy Compositions, do in their own Nature, draw off our minds, from what we ought to be most intent on, & make us wholy attend, to the pleasing, & Agreeable variety of the sounds, and from hence sprang all that contempt, which Cathedral Service is fall'n into; The fanaticks, & other enemies of our constitution, seeing the bungling work, that many, if not most of our Cathedrals made of the Service, by following a Style, which was neither suitable to devotion, nor capable of being perform'd by Ordinary voices, have had the confidence, to preferr their own heavy, & indeed shocking way, of Psalm Singing, to the best of our performances; Wheras, such Compositions as are Grave, solemn, & fitted to devotion, have allways been valu'd, & esteem'd, ev'n by our enemies, for that they naturally have a mighty force, & Energy to excite & heighten all our passions, which are devotionall; The Notes seeming so Adapted to the words, that they do in some measure, express the Seriousnes of the matter, which goeth along with them, which make strange impressions upon a mind religiously affected, & make it more in Love, with those things, about which it is conversant.

This is that Harmony, that doth not only strike, & please the Ear, but is from thence carried to our spirituall facultys, & is wonderfully efficacious, to move all our affections, & oftimes, ev'n to draw forth tears of devotions. This is that Harmony, which as a Divine of our Church expresses it, warms the best blood we have within us, & is fitt for a Martyr to sing, & an Angel to hear.

These are the Compositions my Lord, which your Lordship has had the Piety & Goodnes to encourage a Collection of, & therby vindicated, & rescu'd from the dust & Oblivion; And by taking them into your Patronage, you not only declare to the world, the great regard, you have, for things of this Nature, But you mightily enhance the value of them; you hereby do allso, a great Honour to the memory of the Composers of Church Music, & make their skill, & wisdom in that faculty, appear to all succeeding generations.

My Lord, after I had begun this volume, there are come to my hands a great many important peices of the Ancient Church way of Composition; & allso an Anthem of Harry the 8ths Composing for his own Chappell; I judg'd it necessary therupon, to begin my 3d volume, with a Royall Composure, & with such other peices of Ancient Church Music, as were come to my hands before, & then proceed to add such further Modern Compositions, as I had not room for, in this; I am with the Utmost duty, & most profound respect

My Honoured Good Lord
your Lordships most faithfull &
Obedient Humble Servant
Tho: Tudway

(iii) VOLUME III (1716)

A Continuation of Ancient | & Modern Church Musick | Being a Collection of the most | Celebrated Services and Anthems | Used in the Church of England, before | & since the Restauration of King Charles | the IId. | Compos'd by the best Masters, And | Collected By Tho: Tudway. D.M. | Music-Professor | To the University of Cambridge | AD MDCCXVI | VOL III

> To the Right Honourable
> Edward Lord Harley

My Honoured very Good Lord

This 3rd volume of Church Music which I here present to your Lordship, is a further Collection of Ancient & Modern Compositions, which ev'n Emperou[r]s, Kings, Popes, & great Drs of the Church, have not thought beneath 'em, to be concern'd in. St Gregory the Great, compos'd what we now call the responses, or the Chanting of the Service, & which we at present retain. King Henry the 8th, compos'd in Latin, the Anthem which is prefixt at the beginning of this volume; And caus'd it to be perform'd in his own Royall Chappell, which has been Translated, or Set to English words by the most ingenious, & incomparable Dr Henry Aldrich, late Dean of Christ Church in Oxford; And the late Emperour Leopald is famous for haveing had severall Te Deums, of his own Composeing, sung in his own Royall Chappell at Vienna.

If any shou'd Cavil, as if these Kinds of Exercises, were not proper for Kings, & Princes, to busy themselves about, & in makeing themselves Masters of; They may be better satisfied, when they shall call to mind, That neither King Henry, nor the late Emperour Leopald, were born to the Regal Dignity, having both of them Elder Brothers, And therupon were each design'd for Ecclesiasticks; King Henry, to be Arch Bishop of Canterbury, And Leopald, whatever the Interest of the Emperour his father, could procure for him in the Church; They were both for this purpose, educated among the Jesuists, those famous, & expert Masters in all Sciences & facultys; it was by this means, these two Royall Princes, came by their Skill in Music.

Since the Reformation, I am not able to say how many great men of the Church of England, have Honoured Music with compositions of this Kind, before King Charles the 2ds time, when, we meet with the Revd. Dr William Holder, Subdean of the Royall Chappell, Residensiary of St Pauls, & Prebendary of the Church of Ely, a Composer of a Service, & Severall Anthems. The Revd. Dr Robert Creighton, formerly Greek-Professor to the University of Cambridg, & at present Canon, & Precentor of the Church at Wells, hath composed, severall whole Services, & many Anthems, which are inserted in these volumes; But above all, The Revd. Dr Henry Aldrich Dean of Christ Church, with great Judgment, hath translated, or Set to English words, not only a great many Latin Anthems or Compositions, by the best Italian Authors, as Charissimi, Palastrina, Stradella. &c, But besides of his own, he hath Compos'd, Services & Anthems, near forty, which are all recorded, by your Lordships particular commands, in these volumes.

And indeed it has never been thought, by the greatest Personages, below their Dignity, to have a Competent share of knowledg in Music; The Statutes of many Colleges in both Universitys, enjoine it, & make it a Qualification for fellowships &c, to be *Mediocriter Doctus in Musica*, or at least skillfull *in plano cantu*; which was to be sure, that by that means, they might be able to direct & Govern Choirs, &c when they shoud arrive, or be promoted to be Deans, Prebendarys, Precentors of Cathedrals, &c. By this is not meant, that part of Music, which is us'd for secular purposes; no, the faculty in Church Music, appears not only in its self, far different from secular, But also, by severall distinguishable marks of Honour & respect. First, as aforemention'd, That Kings, Princes, & great men, have thought it, not beneath their Dignity, to exercise their facultys therin, ev'n so long ago, as King Davids time, in the Jewish Church.

I dont pretend to urge as an Argument here, the skill which King David was endow'd with on the Harp; nor the Operations, or effects therof, which we must allow to be inspir'd, by God himself; But it is certain he appointed Masters in that faculty, to take care of the music assign'd for the daily Service of the Jewish Church, As we may see by the Titles of many of the Psalmes of David, where, he directs his Compositions to the cheif Musicians, or Masters, to take care of the solemn performance therof. 2dly

For the encouragement of Study in this faculty, were degrees conferr'd in both Universitys, upon the Professors therof; I do not mean upon professors of music in Generall, But upon such only, who had & shoud attain, to a faculty in composing Music, for the Service of the Church; This is further evident, from the words of the Statutes which enjoines the exercise, or tryall of ev'ry one, that was to be admitted to such degrees, viz: *ut canticum, in Sacris Componat.*

Thus my Lord, I have endeavour'd to give your Lordship, some Account of the Dignity of Church Music, above the Secular; And as your Lordship has had the goodnes to think me worthy & equall to such an undertaking, I lay hold of this opportunity, most Humbly to make the best of my acknowledgments, for the Honour & favour you have done me herein, & to assure your Lordship, of my unfeigned zeal, & Attachement to your Lordships Service, being both by duty, & inclination,

My Honoured very good Lord.

Your Lordships most Oblig'd,
faithfull, & Obedient Servant
Tho: Tudway

(iv) VOLUME IV (1717)

A | Continuation of the most Celebrated | Services & Anthems both Ancient & | Modern, us'd in the Church of England | from the Reformation to the Restauration | of KING CHARLES II down | to the Accession of QUEEN | ANNE, Compos'd by the best | Masters And Collected by | Tho: Tudway D.M. Musick | Professor to the University of Cambridge | A.D. MDCC[X]VII

To the Right Honourable
Edward Lord Harley

My Ever Honoured & very Good Lord

This 4th volume which I here present to your Lordships hands, finishes my Search after Ancient Compositions of Church music, In which I think I may boast, in the success I've had, that there is Scarse a Cathedrall in England, from which I have not drawn some Copys or Mss. or hardly an Author, or Composer of Church Music, from the Reformation to the Restauration of King Charles the 2d Of whose works, I have not in these volumes, recorded, more or less of their Compositions. Of the most Celebrated, I have not Omited, any one peice; Those less famous, I have taken of theirs, more Sparingly; enough to keep their names, in Everlasting remembrance.

It was not possible for me, to furnish out, so many Compositions of Ancient Church Music only, as would have fill'd these 4 volumes, neither coud I enter them all in Order, & point of time; The Copys comeing from so many remote places, that I must have Stay'd for them, And therby retarded, very much, the great work, I had undertaken;

I have therfore, throughout these three last volumes, been forct to mix, Ancient and Modern together, as they came to hand, which I have mention'd, in the Title of Each volume, viz: A Continuation of the Collection of Ancient, & Modern Church Music &c from the Reformation, of the Church of England, to the Restauration of of [*sic*] King Charles the 2d. down to the Accession of Queen Anne; The blessings, & wonderfull Events, of whose reigne, have produc'd so great, & so many voluminous peices, as will take up two volumes more, as large as any of the preceeding, & yet I shall Omit, very many, which may be Judg'd frivolous, & common peices.

Having finish'd, as I have allready said, my Search after Ancient Compositions of Church Music, Be pleas'd my Lord to allow me, to give your Lordship, some further Account of them, and how much better it had been, for the promotion of Divine worship as well as Honour to the Authors of such Compositions, as were made for the Service of the Church; If all the Composers, since the Restauration, had thus distinguish'd their works, from the Secular, by Keeping up to the Standard of Mr Tallis, Mr Bird, & Mr Gibbons &c;

The Composers of Church Music in their time, had all the Knowledge, the skill, & Art of Music; they were Educated, & excercis'd in all the intricate, & abstruse parts of Composition; such as Canons, of 2. 3. & 4 parts; 2. 3. & 4 in one; Compositions, *per Arsin et Thesin*, with severall others; which did plainly evidence their Knowledge, & skill in Music, in composeing of parts;

The devideing the scale into, Base part, Tenor, Contratenor, & Treble, were all contriv'd for Church Music, And Adapted to each part of the scale, according to the Naturall voices of men; some voices being fitted Naturally to sing the Base, or Lowest part; others the Tenor; others, thô very few, the Contratenor; The Treble, or highest part, is allways sung by Boys, or women, and hereby is the whole scale compleated, by these 4 parts, or divisions of the Scale; And ev'ry thing that was set in Church Music, & sung by the Choir, was compos'd in 4 parts at least; often in 5, & 6, & sometimes, in 8, 10, & 12 parts, as the Ability of the Composer, would allow of;

If the Composition was of 5 parts, they commonly made two Contratenors, one Base, one Tenor, & one Treble; If in 6 parts, often 2 Trebles, 2 Contratenors, one Tenor, & one Base; And if in 8 parts, they usually doubl'd all the 4 parts; You must not my Lord, understand here, that doubling of any part, was only, that instead of one mans Singing a part they therupon set two, to Sing the same part; No, my Lord, in Music, when there are two or more Counter parts Compos'd, as it is, when all the parts are doubl'd, Ev'ry one of the said 8 Parts, Moves in a sphere of its own, And all conspire together, to make the Harmony; which I take to be a most wonderfull, & surprizing result of the Art of Composing of parts, and therfore, best fitted, for divine uses.

This was most properly call'd *Componere*, to compose, because of the puting, or seting of parts, one against an other; When the learning, knowledg, or Skill in Music, was in this Situation, The bus'nes of Secular composers, was only, to furnish out Tunes, for Masks, & dances, for interludes, & the like; Their skill usually reach'd no further, than makeing different sorts of Tunes, fitted, for such & such purposes of danceing &c; They woud have been too much fetter'd, and Hamper'd, with many parts, with Canons &c; Their bus'nes of Tunes, & Madrigals, or Songs, was to be free in their inventions, & flights, and not ty'd down to intricate rules of Composition &c; In a word my Lord, tis not above a Century since, there was Nothing compos'd of Music, in parts, But what was made for divine Uses; For the result of Music, in many parts, especially for voices; carrys, such a Solemnity with it, as makes it extreamly Suitable to the devotion, it was design'd to inspire; And wou'd men come to, the Cathedralls, or places of Worship, where tis best, & most Solemnly perform'd, with devotional, & religious intents, they woud soon find, the difference, betwixt those, & the Theatrical Anthems of these dayes; Where people are accustom'd to expect, what will rather divert, & delight 'em, than that, which ought to serve, as helps to their devotion;

An instance of the former, I shall give your Lordship, in the last Anthem, of this volume; Compos'd by Mr Henry Purcell, after the old way; & sung at the interrment of Queen Mary in Westminster Abby; A Great Queen, & extreamly Lamented, being there to be interr'd, ev'ry body present, was dispos'd, & serious, at so solemn a Service, as indeed, they ought to be, at all parts of divine Worship; I appeal to all that were present, as well such as understood Music, as those that did not, whither, they ever heard any thing, so rapturously fine, & solemn, & so Heavenly, in the Operation, which drew tears from all; & yet a plain, Naturall Composition; which shows the pow'r of Music, when tis rightly fitted, & Adapted to devotional purposes; I think I need say no more but this, to evince, what I have been endeavouring to prove, that woud men come to Church, so prepar'd, with a pious, & devout disposition, The old compositions, of Tallis, Bird, Gibbons, with Such as have imitated them, woud have the same Effect, as this of Mr Purcells, I've just now given an instance in.

My Lord, I have insisted more largely on this Head. because your Lordship has been pleas'd, to declare your self, A Lover of the solemn Church music, above all other; And therupon has had the goodnes, to make an Everlasting Memoriall of it, By Ordering a Collection of Church Music to be made, and laid up, for all succeeding generations; If your Lordship shall be pleas'd, to accept the Service, which I may have render'd to your Lordship herein, I shall think my self very happy in haveing been able to bring to this period, a work, in which your Lordship receives, any Satisfaction.

My Ever Honoured & very Good Lord.
Your Lordships Most devoted
and most Obedient Servant
Tho: Tudway

(v) VOLUME V (1718)

Continuation of the most | Modern celebrated Services, | and Anthems, us'd in the | Church of England, at this | day, Compos'd for the most | part, in the Reigne of her | Majesty Queen Anne, | by the best of Masters | And Collected | by Tho. Tudway D.M. | Music Professor to the | University of Cambridge | A.D. MDCCXVIII | Vol. V

To The Right Honourable
Edward Lord Harley

My Ever Honoured & very Good Lord

Haveing in the 4 first volumes, according to the best of my Skill, & pow'r, conducted this affair, down to the Reign of her Majesty Queen Anne; I have in this 5th volume, confin'd myself, to the works of liveing Authors only, except the famous Te Deum, & Jubilate of Mr Henry Purcells; the first of that Kind, ever made in England, which I have plac'd in the Front; with some peices, of one, or two more, who dy'd Since this volume was begun;

I have reserv'd, for the 6th & last volume, cheifly, such peices, as were made upon the great Events, & occurrences of her Majestys Reigne, wherin most of the Composers of Church Musick, in all Cathedrals &c as well as those of her own Chappell, were desirous to signalize themselves, on those Publick occasions; The voluminous peices of this Age, on the Account, of so many instrumental parts, accompanying the voices, will swell these two last volumes, into a greater bulk, than any of the preceeding; And I find by the Copies, which I have allready by me, of such Anthems, & Te Deums &c, only, as were made for St Pauls Church, as often as the Queen came in ceremony thither, woud alone, make a considerable volume; I have therfore in this, enter'd whatever I cou'd procure of liveing Authors, with which, I have fill'd up this Collection, reserving only some of 'em, as I cou'd not find room enough to insert here, for the next; I can aver to your Lordship, that I have not Omitted, to my knowledg, one peice, which may be Judg'd valuable, throughout the whole Collection; & by that time, I have compleated the 6th & last volume, I shall be able to boast, I hope with reason, that there is no such Manuscript, of this Kind in being, nor ever was; I shall at the end of the last volume, give your Lordship a Catalogue, of the Names of such persons, who compose ev'ry distinct volume; as well Ancient, as Modern, & therby do an Honour to their Memorys, which few of 'em, perhapps any other wayes, woud have been entitl'd to; I shall not detain your Lordship, any further in this dedication, But shall reserve to my next, what may be said Historically, relateing to the whole work; I'm glad of ev'ry occasion, wherby I may have an opportunity, of testifying the unfeigned zeal, and affection, I have for your Lordships Service, being

My ever Honoured & very Good Lord

your Lordships most devoted & Obedient

Humble Servant

Tho: Tudway

(vi) VOLUME VI (1720)

VOL: the 6th & last | A Continuation of the most Modern | Celebrated Services & Anthems, us'd | in the Cathedral Churches, & Chappells | of England, at this day Compos'd, | Cheifly, in the Reigne of her | Majesty, Queen Anne, by the | best Masters | And Collected | By Tho. Tudway D.M. | Music Professor to the | University of Cambridge | A.D. MDCCXX

To The Right Honourable
Edward Lord Harley

My Ever Honoured & very Good Lord

I have, with the Blessing of God, brought to a conclusion, a Collection of all the most eminent Church Music, which has been compos'd, for the use of the Church of England, as well the Services, as Anthems, from the Reformation, to the end of the reigne of our late Souvereigne Lady Queen Anne; which coud not be contain'd in less, than a thousand Sheets; Your Lordships known Piety & zeal, for the Honour of Cathedral Service, I make no question, inspir'd you with thoughts, so peculiar to your Lordships religious disposition, of makeing an Everlasting Memorial of these sacred Compositions; The Glory of the Church of Englands publick worship, particularly at this time, when Cathedral Service, lyes under so many & great discouragements & disregards; Nay ev'n when, (so little is Church Music understood), it is much to be feard, the use of it, may soon be going to be laid aside;

The Revd Dr Holder in his Treatise, of ye Naturall Grounds and Principles of Harmony sayes, that Music, is so Essential a part of worship, & Homage, to the divine Majesty, that there was never any religion in ye world, Pagan, Jewish, Christian, or

Mahometan, that did not Mix Some Kinds of Music, with their devotional Hymns, of Praise & Thanksgiving . . . .[1]

. . . Henry the 8th, haveing an Elder Brother who was to inherit the Crown, He was by his father, Henry the 7th design'd for an Ecclesiastick, & being brought up in their semenarys, became skillfull in Music; we have an Anthem at this day, said to be his. which was compos'd in Latin, and which they say, was sung in his own Chappell, when afterwards King of England;

The King thus Honouring this Science, we may be sure, that others took great pains to approve themselves Artists in composing of Church Music; However, there are few, or no compositions to be met with of that standing; what Dirges, or Te Deums, Jubilates &c there might be, was compos'd in Latin, for the Service of the Romish Church, & therfore, not within the Compass of this Collection, which begins at the reformation of the Church of England; I believe the improvement both of Church Music, as well as Secular, did somewhat advance in this Princes time, He being a proficient himself in the one, & keeping a splendid Court, with Music, danceings &c for the encouragement of the other; Notwithstanding which, there is nothing extant to be found before, or in his time, but what woud be dispis'd by our Artist at this day, either for Skill in Seting, or the Air, or Style therof; So that we must Date the beginning, & improvement, of Church Music Especially, from the Reign of Queen Elizabeth, to the decease of Queen Ann, where this Collection ends;

Queen Elizabeth haveing then Establish'd the reformation of the Church of England and appointed the dayly Service of the Church to be said, & sung in English, it was altogether necessary, that the Hymns of Morning, & Ev'ning Service, as well as the Anthems, shoud be all compos'd anew, in our own Language; Those, first employ'd in this work, were Mr Tallis, & Mr Bird, two of the Queens own Servants, who, it is own'd at this day, set an incomparable Pattern of Church Music, in a Style, befitting the Solemnity of the Service; Their composition, are all in 4 parts, except, some Anthems in five; The adding of this 4th part, gave a wonderfull Harmony, to the whole Chorus, wheras before, they never aim'd at above 3 parts, for which there were 3 cliffs establish'd, suited to each part; But these skilfull Artists, finding, there might yet be a higher part, than a Tenor introduc'd, betwixt ye Tenor & Treble; compos'd a 4th part, calling it Contratenor; In these 4 parts, were all the compositions for the Church cheifly made in that time; But as men of Head, & skill in composition of this kind, came on, we have seen Hymns, & Anthems compos'd, of 4. 5. 6. 7. 8 &c parts[;] But these appear'd, rather as an Exercise of their Art, than use in the Church.

These 4 parts then, viz: Base, Tenor, Contratenor, & Treble, were fix'd, as sufficient to make the fullest & compleatest consonancy, & Harmony, their ratios, being all contain'd, as I've said in an Octave, the most compleat System;

These compositions of Mr Tallis, & Mr Birds, were us'd many years along in the

---

[1] Tudway continues, as promised, with 'what may be said Historically, relateing to the whole work', beginning with the music of the Jews as revealed through the Bible (fos. 2–6). It is a digest of what passed, in literary circles, as a history of music at that time. (See Hogwood, 'Thomas Tudway's History of Music'.) A section on Greek music and theory follows (fos. 6ʳ–8ᵛ). 'As to the Romans, they were never famous, in any Musical performances', regarding which a solitary paragraph leads into a garbled account of the music of the Christian church, from apostolic times down to King Henry VIII (fos. 9ʳ–10ᵛ).

Church, without admitting any others; However, in that Queens time, severall eminent men, for compositions in Church Music, rose up, viz: Mr Parsons, one of the gentlemen of the Queens Chappell, Mr Morely, the greatest Artist in fugues, Canon, & such like Exercises, of figurative Music, that ever was; Dr Bull, Organist to her Majesty, the most famous of his time, & Dr Tye, both Batchelours, and Drs of Music; these have Compos'd also for the Church, but without any great effect, or success; I think never the less, I ought not to omit the mentioning, in this place, an Anthem of Dr Bulls, being the Collect for the Feast of the Epiphany, commonly call'd the Star Anthem, which for Art, & Air, & other Excellent dispositions, hath maintain'd its ground, ev'n to this day; it being still perform'd, on that occasion, in many of our Cathedrals;

In King James the first's time, there were Severall Eminent composers of Church Music, particularly, Dr Giles, Mr Bevin, famous for the Art of Composing many parts, Mr Shepherd, Mr Lugg &c. The Elaborate works of these, & many others; are now allmost forgot, The new Style prevailing in all our Cathedrals, & places, where the Singing of Divine Service is us'd;

I shall pass on to name some of the most eminent in King Charles the first's time, viz: The Tomkins's, 3 Brothers; very skillfull Organists, Mr Henry & Mr William Laws, both Brothers, all Servants to his Majesty; the 2 Laws's dy'd in the feild, in the Service of that Prince; But above all, I must never forget to mention, Mr Orlando Gibbons, first Organist to his Majestys Chappell, who, throughout all his compositions, has alone maintain'd, the Harmony, & dignity of the Church Style, & I think I may Justly say, comes little, if at all short, of the Pattern Set, by Mr Tallis, & Mr Bird; Thus I have given your Lordship some Account of the beginning of Church Music, from the Reformation; with the Characters of the cheifest Composers, down to the restauration of King Charles the 2d; when Music, & ev'rything praiseworthy, was again restor'd, & introduc'd, into the Service of the Church;

I gave your Lordship in a former Epistle to one of my volumes, some account how, the Alterations in the Church Style began, with the probable reasons, which occasion'd it; I may now with more assurance, tell you, that, by what I have met with, I find, there is hardly any flights in Music, ev'n of the Stage, that some Composer or other, has not introduc'd into the Church; I have seen the most extravagant repetitions imaginable, ev'n upon a single word, repeated, eleven times, which coud never be tollerable, but on the account of some fantastical humour, or other, which I'm sure, was never consistant, with divine Service; The words, *all, now, ever, Never*, &c have had their share likewise, in these musical tautalogies; I forbear mentioning Authors; But above all; to the corruption of that solemn, & grave Style, which was Establish'd as only proper to be us'd in divine Service, there are composers, within the compass of this Age, that I defye the stage, to outdo, in Levity, & wantonnes of Style; The reason of this must needs be, the little care that is taken, to inspect Compositions, before they are addmitted into the Church Service; The compositions of Mr Tallis, & Mr Bird, were so, & approv'd of, by Authority, before they were admitted within the doors of the Church; But now, ev'ry one is become a Composer of Church Music, and I verily beleive, since the Restauration; there are no fewer, than 500 Anthems compos'd, & have been perform'd in divine Service, beside the Hymns, of Morning, & Ev'ning pray'r, in abundance; wheras, from the Reformation, to the Restauration, in 1660, there is hardly forty Anthems to be found, & perhapps not half of them ever sung in the Church; such sorry,

& injudicious compositions, as before mention'd, instead of assisting, & improveing, the performance of the Service, as is pretended, by a greater variety, do but bring a disreputation, & contempt upon it, & is the occasion of that irreligious behaviour, which most people make appear at Cathedral Service, where they come, rather to be entertain'd, & diverted, than with a sence of Religion, or devotion; for finding such turns, & Strains of Music, As they have been accustom'd to hear at the play House, think it but reasonable, to make the Same use of it in the Church; And this I conceive to be the very reason, why Church Music, has lost, so much of its former respect, & reputation, as well as the Composers therof, viz: by departing from that peculiar gravity of style Appropriated to it; If this had been strictly adher'd to, people had not come to Church, for diversion, but to say their pray'rs, which Cathedral Music, was design'd, to assist them in;

However, there are other reasons of the decay of this institution, for in all Cathedralls where Choirs were first founded, I dare say then, their Stipends were a maintenance; But Deans, & Chapters, since the Reformation, tyeing their Clerks down to the same allowance, now, when money is not a 5th part, in value, to what it was then, have brought a general neglect of the Service, & a very mean, & lame way of performing it, for want of encouragement; I can't forbear to say, it was an oversight at the Reformation, to constitute a dayly Service, for Chanting, & Singing of Hymns, &c, & not provide a sufficient maintenance for those, upon whom the performance of that duty lay, wheras, before the Reformation, their Clerks were provided for, in their way, in the Colleges, & Cloysters, &c in which they were Establish'd, & had their meat, drink, lodgings, &c provided; they were by that means at leisure to practice & prepare, what was necessary for divine Service in Publick, & were not encumber'd with familys to provide for; This insufficient provision, I take to be, the Sourse of the decay of Cathedrall Service with us; and what makes this, yet more Evident, is, that where there is encouragement, or a maintenance, as at the Royall Chappell, St Pauls, Westminster Abby &c, they abound in good voices, and the service is perform'd, with such decency & solemnity, that God is truely worship'd, as of old, in the beauty of Holines;

My Lord

The Service of the Church of England, thus Suitably Compos'd, & decently perform'd, is that Sort of Music, which your Lordship hath vouchsaf'd to become the Patron of, in these Collections; and which may truely be esteem'd, such a peculaiar rarity, & curiosity, as no one, but your Lordship, in any Age, hath pitch'd upon, to make a Memoriall of; And I hope therfore will not be reckon'd the meanest, among the Harleyan Manuscripts.

How it comes to pass, that Church Music only shoud be so little regarded, in an Age, when Music in generall, is come to Such a heighth of improvement as I appeal to all the musical world, is incomparably beyond what ever was before, must proceed, from much the same reason, as that of religion, viz: that in this Age, also, when there was never so learned a Clergy, nor learning at so great a heighth, Religion itself shoud be so boldly attack'd, & Orthodoxy, in beleif, & worship, so impudently oppugn'd. As to Church Music, I'm afraid, some have mixt too much of the Theatrical way, thinking therby to make it more Elegant & takeing; But by this means, the peculiarity, & gravity of Style is lost, wherby it was always, worthily distinguish'd from the Secular; The truth of all this is; the Skill of Composeing is much more generall, & greatly improv'd, And the composers of secular Music, are become much greater Masters, than ever was known before; The Art of composeing Operas for the Stage, is a very great, & Masterlike performance, which they may have had in Italy, three score, or four score years, thô scarse in such perfection as at this day; I must, thô I shoud offend some of my Country men, needs say; to Compose an Opera, is a very great & Masterlike work, & the greatest of all Secular performances in Music; which few genius's ev'n among the Italians, can reach; But I don't in the least question, by that time these musical representations, have been a few years longer in England, & the present engouragement continues, by the Countenance of so great a Number of our Nobillity, & Gentry, it will appear, we have Genius's in England strong enough for that work; However, this can't be done, by despising of 'em, as many of our Masters do, who obstinatly deprive *them*selves of the means of obtaining to the perfection of them;

Our Country man, Mr Henry Purcell, who was confessedly the greatest Genius we ever had, dy'd before these musical representations, came upon the Stage in England; He would have been so far from despising them, that he woud never have ceas'd, till he had equall'd, if not out done them; And did by the pow'r of his own Genius, contrive very many, & excellent compositions of divers kinds for the stage; But that which Set Mr Purcell eminently above any of his contemporarys, was that Noble Composition, the first of its kind in England, of Te Deum, & Jubilate, accompanied with instrumentall Music; which he compos'd principally against the Opening of St Pauls, but did not live till that time; However, it was Sung there, Severall times Since, before her Majesty Queen Anne, upon the great Events of her Reigne; I needed not perhapps to have mention'd this, Since tis inserted in these Collections, but to observe to your Lordship, that there is in this Te Deum, such a glorious representation, of the Heavenly Choirs, of Cherubins, & Seraphins, falling down before the Throne & Singing Holy, Holy, Holy &c As hath not been Equall'd, by any Foreigner, or Other; He makes the representation thus; He brings in the treble voices, or Choristers, singing, To thee Cherubins, & Seraphins, continually do cry; and then the Great Organ, Trumpets, the Choirs, & at least thirty or forty instruments besides, all Joine, in most excellent Harmony, & Accord; The Choirs singing only the word Holy; Then all Pause, and the Choristers repeat again, continually do cry; Then, the whole Copia Sonorum, of voices, & instruments, Joine again, & sing Holy; this is done 3 times upon the word Holy, only, changeing ev'ry time the Key, & accords; then they proceed altogether in Chorus, with, Heav'n, & Earth are full of the Majesty of thy glory; This most beautifull, & sublime representation, I dare challenge, all the Orators, Poets, Painters &c of any Age whatsoever, to form so lively an Idea, of Choirs of Angels Singing, & paying their Adorations;

Dr Crofts, and Mr Hendale, both by the Queens Order, have likewise with great Art And good Success, compos'd the like peices, of Te Deum, & Jubilate, which were perform'd before her Majesty, on Publick Occasions, with great Applause; These 3 compositions, are all of this kind at present were ever made in England; Your Lordship, will distinguish, that such like peices as these, are only proper in the Church, for great Occasions of Publick Thanksgivings; &c, These Compositions therfore, are not Stricktly call'd Church Music, although, they are upon the same divine Subject; I have been the more particular upon them, because, they are the production of this Age only, at least in England; There remains for me to add, some Account of that most Noble Instrument, an Organ, whose Artificiall breath, will nere expire, whilst the vital breath of Singing in Choirs, remains; they seem to be made for each other, & will hardly Subsist asunder; And as Organs have been infinitely improv'd, since 50 or 60 years, by additional Stops, which imitate almost e'vry instrument of pipe, or String; so are they become, in less than an Age allso, a very Ornamental, and the most beautifull Structure, that was ever Erected in the Church;

The word Organum, is of so extensive a Signification, that 'tis almost impossible to guess what maner of instrument, a Musicall Organ, so often mention'd in Scripture, was; it is certain that Organs, whatever they were, have not been us'd in the Western Christian Church, above 4 or 500 years, & tis as certain, that the inventors therof. made but a small progress, in comeing to any perfection;

A Church Organ consisted then, but of 5 or 6 stops, which might perhapps take up, 200, or 250 pipes of wood; wheras, tis nothing now, to have Organs of 15, or 20 Stopps, all, or most of Metal, consisting of 1200, or 1500 pipes; Besides those Stops, properly call'd Organical, our Modern Artists, have invented Stops, which imitate the Cornet, Trumpet, flute, Vox humane, Ecchos, Bassones, Violins &c with Severall others, less frequent; To dissect this Noble Machine, woud require a volume, rather than the compass of a Dedication; but by what I have been able to say of it, Your Lordship may perceive, how much an Organ exceeds, all other instruments, And cannot be deny'd, ev'n by the profest enemys of that, & Church Music, to be the greatest, & most Noble instrument of Music, that was ever in the world, & the most worthy of all others, to accompany the service of God in his Church;

Thus, my Lord, I have endeavoured to the best of my pow'r to give your Lordship, what may be gather'd from Scripture, of the divine use of Music, among the Hebrews; and I think, I have not mistaken them, in representing them as knowing Nothing of Harmony, or the propertys therof; Sounding Brass, & tinckling Cymbals, is a Character, which St Pauls [*sic*] gives of those instruments; & I beleive will Serve, for most of their Musical instruments; However, the Harp, & Tabret are indeed mention'd in Scripture, with Epithets of Melody, & pleasantnes of sound, which need not be deny'd; But for any Skill, or Science, in the use of Music, I must insist upon it, they were altogether Ignorant; Yet, might delight themselves with it, as knowing no better; Science in Music, came in afterward, by the Greek Philosophers, and theirs, seems more a Mathematical, & Philosophical knowledge, than any exquisitenes in performance; If they knew nothing, as before hath been observ'd of the Harmony of parts, as many Authors confess they did not, their solitary music, of tune alone, can never come into competition, with the Harmony that results from a Composition in parts; Tune alone, may indeed be call'd Melody, but can't, with any Propriety, be styl'd Harmony; which I presume is made, from the Agreement, & adjustment, or the Severall parts, of a Composition; I have likewise brought Music, down, to the use of it, in the Christian Church, but with little more knowledg for Severall Ages, than a Bare Chanting or Elevation of Voice; I'm sure, they have left us no tracts, or footsteps wherby to Judg of them; But, as I've said, about Harry the 8ths time, Church Music, began to make some figure; He being himself a Composer of Church Music in parts; But that which brought on the Search after knowledg, & skill in that way was, The thorough Reformation of the Church, under Queen Elizabeth, when, as I've said, the Hymns, & Anthems, were all to be compos'd anew, in our own Language, and degrees in music, began then, again to be more

frequently taken in both Universitys as an encouragement & recompence, for Composing the Hymns of the Church; what progress, & improvement, hath been made, down
to this time, I leave to Ages to come, to make a Judgment of, from the Severall
Compositions, both Ancient, & Modern, Collected in these volumes; After this breif
recapitulation, there remains only, for me to add, with great truth,

My Ever Honoured and very good Lord.
The Honour your Lordship hath done Church Music, & the Composers therof, by this
Memoriall of it, I dare not take upon me, to draw a discription of; This I dare say, with
great assurance, that all true Lovers of the good old constitution, of Singing the Service
of God, in the Church, will bless your name, & Memory for it; The Professors of this
faculty, are infinitely Honoured by your Lordships Patronage; And as to the Unworthy
Collector of these volumes, he hath no greater Ambition, than your Lordships favourable acceptance, & approbation of them; Haveing great assurance in your Lordships
goodnes, I beg leave to subscribe as in duty bound;
My Ever Honoured & very good Lord

Your Lordships most faithfull and most
Obedient Servant.
Thomas Tudway

BIBLIOGRAPHY

Anthems to be Sung in the Cathedral Church of the Holy and United Trinity in Dublin (Dublin, 1662).

ARDRAN, G. M., and Wulstan, David, 'The Alto or Countertenor Voice', *Music and Letters*, 48 (1967), 17–22.

ARKWRIGHT, G. E. P., 'Purcell's Church Music', *Musical Antiquary*, 1 (1909–10), 63–72, 234–48.

—— 'The Chapel Royal Anthem Book of 1635', *Musical Antiquary*, 2 (1910–11), 108–13.

—— *Catalogue of Music in the Library of Christ Church Oxford, Part 1: Works of Ascertained Authorship* (London, 1915).

ARNOLD, SAMUEL (ed.), *Cathedral Music*, 4 vols. (London, 1790); ed. E. F. Rimbault (London, 1843).

ASHBEE, ANDREW (ed.), *Records of English Court Music*, 6 vols. (Snodland, Kent, and Aldershot, Hants, 1986–93).

ASTON, PETER, 'George Jeffreys', *Musical Times*, 110 (1969), 772–6.

—— *The Music of York Minster* (London, 1972).

—— 'Tradition and Experiment in the Devotional Music of George Jeffreys', *Proceedings of the Royal Musical Association*, 99 (1972–3), 105–15.

—— 'Music since the Reformation', in G. E. Aylmer and Reginald Cant (eds.), *A History of York Minster* (Oxford, 1977), 395–429.

ATKINS, IVOR, *The Early Occupants of the Office of Organist and Master of the Choristers of the Cathedral Church of Christ and the Blessed Virgin Mary, Worcester* (Worcester Historical Society; London, 1918).

ATKINSON, MONTE, 'The Orchestral Anthem in England, 1700–1775' (Ph.D. diss., University of Illinois, Urbana, 1991).

BAILDON, WILLIAM P. (ed.), *Calendar of the Muniments of the Dean and Chapter of Wells*, iii (Historical Manuscripts Commission, 12th Report; London, 1914).

BAILEY, DEREK S., *Wells Cathedral Chapter Act Book, 1666–83* (Historical Manuscripts Commission, Joint Report, 20; London, 1973).

BAKER, Sir RICHARD, *A Chronicle of the Kings of England* (London, 1665).

BALDWIN, DAVID, *The Chapel Royal: Ancient and Modern* (London, 1990).

BALDWIN, OLIVE, and WILSON, THELMA, 'Alfred Deller, John Freeman and Mr Pate', *Music and Letters*, 50 (1969), 103–10.

BANNISTER, ARTHUR T., *The Cathedral Church of Hereford* (London, 1924).

BARNARD, JOHN, *The First Book of Selected Church Musick consisting of Services and Anthems such as are now Used in the Cathedrall and Collegiat Churches of this Kingdome* (London, 1641; facs. edn., Farnborough, 1972).

BARNARD, L. S., 'The Organs of Bangor Cathedral', *The Organ*, 34 (1954–5), 113–22.

—— 'The Organs of Rochester Cathedral', *The Organ*, 41 (1961–2), 153–63.

BARRETT, PHILIP, *The College of Vicars Choral at Hereford Cathedral* (Hereford, 1980).

BASKERVILLE, HUMPHREY (ed.), 'Thomas Baskerville's Account of Oxford, *c.*1670–1700', *Collectanea*, 4th ser. (Oxford Historical Society, 47; Oxford, 1905), 175–225.

BEEKS, GRAYDON, 'Handel's Chandos Anthems: The "Extra" Movements', *Musical Times*, 119 (1978), 621–3.

—— *The Chandos Anthems and the Te Deum of George Frideric Handel (1685–1759)*, 2 vols. (Ann Arbor, Mich., 1981).

—— 'Handel's Chandos Anthems: More "Extra" Movements', *Musical Times*, 62 (1981), 155–61.

BELL, G. K. A., *The Statutes of the Cathedral and Metropolitan Church of Christ, Canterbury* (Canterbury, 1925).

BENNET, F. G., CODRINGTON, R. H., and DEEDES, G., *Statutes and Constitutions of the Cathedral Church of Chichester* (Chichester, 1804).

BENTHAM, JAMES, *The History and Antiquities of the Cathedral and Conventual Church of Ely* (London, 1771).

BETTS, EDWARD, *An Introduction to the Skill of Music . . . Anthems, Hymns and Psalm Tunes in Several Parts* (London, 1714).

BICKNELL, STEPHEN, 'English Organ Building, 1642–1685', *Journal of the British Institute of Organ Studies*, 5 (1981), 5–22.

—— 'The Transposing Organ', *Journal of the British Institute of Organ Studies*, 8 (1984), 79–81.

BISHOP, JOHN, *A Sett of New Psalm Tunes* (2nd edn., London, [1722]; 3rd edn., London, [1730]).

—— *A Supplement to the New Psalm Book* (London, 1725).

—— *A Choice Collection of Eleven Anthems* ([Birmingham], 1754).

—— *A Choice Collection of . . . Thirteen Anthems* ([Birmingham], 1780).

BLOW, JOHN, *Thirty Voluntaries*, ed. Watkins Shaw (London, 1958; rev. edn., 1972).

BLOXAM, JOHN ROUSE, *Register of the Presidents, Fellows, Demies . . . Chaplains, Clerks, Choristers, and other Members of Saint Mary Magdalen College . . . Oxford*, 2 vols. (Oxford, 1853–7).

—— *Magdalen College and King James II, 1686–1688* (Oxford Historical Society, 4; Oxford, 1886).

BOND, SHELAGH, *The Chapter Acts of the Dean and Canons of Windsor, 1432, 1523–1672* (Historical Monographs Relating to St George's Chapel, Windsor Castle, 13; Windsor, 1966).

BOSTON, NOEL, *The Musical History of Norwich Cathedral* (Norwich, 1963).

BOWERS, ROGER, COLCHESTER, L. S., and CROSSLAND, ANTHONY, *The Organs and Organists of Wells Cathedral* (Wells, 1951; 7th rev. edn., 1979).

BOYCE, WILLIAM (ed.), *Cathedral Music*, 3 vols. (London, 1760–73); ed. Joseph Warren (London, 1849).

BOYER, SARAH, 'The Manchester Altus Partbook MS 340 Cr 71', *Music and Letters*, 72 (1991), 197–213.

BRADSHAW, HENRY, and WORDSWORTH, CHRISTOPHER, *Statutes of Lincoln Cathedral*, 3 vols. (Cambridge, 1892–7).

BRAY, JULIE, review of *Christopher Gibbons: Keyboard Compositions*, ed. C. Rayner and J. Caldwell, *Early Music*, 21 (1993), 121–7.

BRIDGE, JOSEPH C., 'A Great English Choir Trainer, Captain Henry Cooke', *Musical Antiquary*, 2 (1910–11), 61–79.

—— 'The Organists of Chester Cathedral', *Journal of the Architectural, Archaeological and Historical Society for Chester and North Wales*, 19 (1913), 63–124.

BROWN, JAMES W., 'An Elizabethan Song-Cycle', *Cornhill Magazine* (1920), 572–9.

—— 'Caroline Music Books from Carlisle Cathedral', in *Round Carlisle Cross—Old Stories Retold* (Carlisle, 1921).

BUMPUS, JOHN S., *The Organists and Composers of S. Paul's Cathedral* (London, 1891).

—— *A History of English Cathedral Music, 1549–1889*, 2 vols. (London, 1908; repr. 1972).

BURNE, R. V. H., 'Chester Cathedral after the Restoration', *Journal of the Architectural, Archaeological and Historical Society for Chester and North Wales*, 40 (1953), 25–53.

—— 'Chester Cathedral in the Eighteenth Century, 1701–1740', *Journal of the Architectural, Archaeological and Historical Society for Chester and North Wales*, 41 (1954), 39–61.

BURNEY, CHARLES, *A General History of Music from the Earliest Ages to the Present*, 4 vols. (London, 1776–89); ed. Frank Mercer, 2 vols. (London, 1935; repr. 1957).

BURROWS, DONALD J., 'Handel and the 1727 Coronation', *Musical Times*, 118 (1977), 469–73 (see also p. 725).

—— 'Some Misattributed Eighteenth-Century Anthems', *Musical Times*, 121 (1980), 521–3.

—— 'Handel and the English Chapel Royal during the Reigns of Queen Anne and King George I' (Ph.D. diss., Open University, 1981).

—— *Handel and the English Chapel Royal* (London, [1984]).

—— 'Handel's "As pants the Hart"', *Musical Times*, 126 (1985), 113–16.

BUTCHER, A. VERNON, *The Organs and Music of Worcester Cathedral* (Worcester, 1981).

—— 'Worcester Cathedral Library: Catalogue of the Music Collection of the Cathedral' (manuscript, 1982).

BUTLER, CHARLES, *The Principles of Musik in Singing and Setting* (London, 1636; facs. edn., New York, 1970).

BYARD, HERBERT, 'The Rebuilt Organ in Gloucester Cathedral', *The Organ*, 51 (1971–2), 133–47.

—— 'New Sounds and Sights at Wells Cathedral', *The Organ*, 53 (1973–4), 89–97.

CALDWELL, JOHN, *English Keyboard Music before the Nineteenth Century* (Oxford, 1973).

CAMPBELL, SIDNEY, and SUMNER, W. L., 'The Organs and Organists of St George's Chapel, Windsor Castle', *The Organ*, 45 (1965–6), 145–56.

CARDWELL, EDWARD, *A History of the Conferences and other Proceedings connected with the Revision of the Book of Common Prayer from the Year 1558 to the Year 1690* (3rd edn., Oxford, 1899).

CARPENTER, ADRIAN, 'William Croft, 1678–1727' (Diss., University of Birmingham, 1970).

—— 'William Croft's Church Music', *Musical Times*, 112 (1971), 275–7.

CARPENTER, EDWARD F., 'Restoration and Resettlement', in id. (ed.), *A House of Kings* (London, 1966), 179–205.

The Cathedral Magazine; or Divine Harmony being a Collection of the Most Valuable and Useful Anthems in Score, 3 vols. (London, c.1775).

CHANTER, J. F., *The Custos and College of the Vicars Choral of the Choir of the Cathedral Church of St Peter, Exeter* (Exeter, 1933).

CHEVERTON, IAN, 'Captain Henry Cooke (*c.*1616–72): The Beginnings of a Reappraisal', *Soundings*, 9 (1982), 74–86.

—— 'English Church Music of the Early Restoration Period, 1660–*c.* 1676' (includes 'Musical Supplement') (Ph.D. diss., University of Wales, Cardiff, 1985).

—— 'Cathedral Music in Wales during the Latter Part of the Seventeenth Century', *Welsh Music*, 8/1 (1986), 6–17.

CHURCH, JOHN, *An Introduction to Psalmody* (London, *c.*1723).

CLARK, ANDREW (ed.), *The Life and Times of Anthony Wood Described by Himself*, 5 vols. (Oxford Historical Society, 19, 21, 26, 30, 40; Oxford, 1891–1900).

CLARK, J. BUNKER, 'A Re-emerged Seventeenth-Century Organ Accompaniment Book', *Music and Letters*, 47 (1966), 148–52.

—— 'Adrian Batten and John Barnard: Colleagues and Collaborators', *Musica Disciplina*, 22 (1968), 207–29.

—— *Transposition in Seventeenth-Century English Organ Accompaniments and the Transposing Organ* (Detroit, 1974).

CLARKE, W. K. LOWTHER, and HARRIS, CHARLES (eds.), *Liturgy and Worship: A Companion to the Prayer Books of the Anglican Communion* (London, 1964).

CLIFFORD, JAMES, *The Divine Services and Anthems usually Sung in His Majesties Chappell, and in all Cathedrals and Collegiate Choires in England and Ireland* (London, 1663; 2nd edn., 1664).

CLUTTON, CECIL, 'The Organ at Chichester Cathedral', *The Organ*, 11 (1931–2), 71–8.

—— and NILAND, AUSTIN, *The British Organ* (London, 1963; 2nd edn., 1982).

COCHERIL, M., 'The Dallams in Brittany', *Journal of the British Institute of Organ Studies*, 6 (1982), 63–77.

COCKER, NORMAN, 'The Organs of Manchester Cathedral', *The Organ*, 22 (1942), 49–62.

CODRINGTON, R. H., et al., *Statutes and Constitutions of the Cathedral Church of Chichester* (Chichester, 1804).

A Collection of all the Anthems Daily Us'd in Divine Service, throughout the Year . . . in Cambridge (Cambridge, 1706).

A Collection of Anthems, as the Same are now Performed in his Majesty's Chapels Royal, &c. [compiled by Edward Aspinwall] (London, 1724).

A Collection of Anthems, as the Same are now Performed in his Majesty's Chapels Royal, &c. [compiled by George Carleton] (London, 1736).

Collection of Anthems, as the Same are now Performed in the Cathedral Church of Durham [compiled by Christopher Hunter?] (Durham, 1749).

CONWAY, MARMADUKE P., 'The Organ in Ely Cathedral', *The Organ*, 11 (1931–32), 193–9.

COOK, D. F., 'The Life and Works of Johann Christoph Pepusch (1667–1752)' (Ph.D. diss., London University, 1982).

COOPER, BARRY, 'Did Purcell Write a Trumpet Voluntary?' *Musical Times*, 119 (1978), 791–3, 1073–5.

—— 'Keyboard Sources in Hereford', *Royal Musical Association Research Chronicle*, 16 (1980), 135–9.

—— *English Solo Keyboard Music of the Middle and Late Baroque* (London and New York, 1989).

COOPER, BARRY, 'Keyboard Music,' in Ian Spink (ed.), *Music in Britain: The Seventeenth Century* (Blackwell History of Music in Britain, iii; Oxford, 1992), 341–66.

—— 'Problems in the Transmission of Blow's Organ Music', *Music and Letters*, 75 (1994), 522–47.

CORNALL, ANDREW, 'The Practice of Music at Norwich Cathedral, *c.* 1558–1649' (M.Mus. diss., University of East Anglia, 1976).

COTTON, Henry, *Fasti Ecclesiae Hibernicae: The Succession of the Prelates and Members of the Cathedral Bodies in Ireland*, 4 vols. (Dublin 1849).

COWIE, L. W., 'Worship in the Minster', in P. M. Tillott (ed.), *A History of Yorkshire: The City of York* (London, 1961), 343–57.

COX, GEOFFREY, 'John Blow and the Earliest English Cornet Voluntaries', *Journal of the British Institute of Organ Studies*, 7 (1983), 4–17.

—— *Organ Music in Restoration England*, 2 vols. (New York and London, 1989).

CROFT, WILLIAM, *Musica Sacra*, 2 vols. (London, 1724).

—— *Complete Organ Works*, ed. Richard Platt, 2 vols. (London, 1976; rev. edn., 1 vol., 1980).

CROOK, JOHN, *A History of the Pilgrims' School and Earlier Winchester Choir Schools* (Chichester, 1981).

CROSBY, BRIAN, 'An Early Restoration Liturgical Music Manuscript', *Music and Letters*, 55 (1974), 458–64.

—— 'A Seventeenth-Century Durham Inventory', *Musical Times*, 119 (1978), 167–70.

—— *Durham Cathedral Choristers and Their Masters* (Durham, 1980).

—— 'A Service Sheet from June 1680', *Musical Times*, 121 (1980), 399–401.

—— letter, 'Purcell in G minor', *Musical Times*, 123 (1982), 746.

—— *A Catalogue of Durham Cathedral Music Manuscripts* (Oxford, 1986).

DANIEL, RALPH T., and LE HURAY, PETER, *The Sources of English Church Music, 1549–1660*, 2 vols. (London, 1972).

DAWE, DONOVAN, *Organists of the City of London, 1660–1850* (Padstow, Cornwall, 1983).

DAWES, FRANK, 'Philip Hart and William Norris', *Musical Times*, 110 (1969), 1074–6.

DAWSON, JONATHAN, 'The Organs of Winchester College Chapel', *The Organ*, 49 (1969–70), 1–7.

DEARNLEY, CHRISTOPHER, *English Church Music 1660–1750, in Royal Chapel, Cathedral and Parish Church* (London, 1970).

DENHOLM-YOUNG, N., 'Magdalen College', in H. E. Salter and Mary Lobel (eds.), *The University of Oxford* (The Victoria History of the County of Oxford, iii; London, 1954), 193–202.

DENNISON, PETER, 'The Church Music of Pelham Humfrey', *Proceedings of the Royal Musical Association*, 98 (1971–2), 65–71.

—— 'The Stylistic Origins of the Early English Church Music [of Purcell]', in F. W. Sternfeld, Nigel Fortune, and Edward Olleson (eds.), *Essays on Opera and English Music in Honour of Sir Jack Westrup* (Oxford, 1975), 44–61.

—— *Pelham Humfrey* (Oxford, 1986).

—— Review of John Blow, *Anthems II: Anthems with Orchestra*, ed. Bruce Wood, in *Music and Letters*, 67 (1986), 100–1.

DEUTSCH, OTTO ERICH, *Handel: A Documentary Biography* (New York, 1955; repr. 1974).

DICKSON, W. E., *A Catalogue of Ancient Choral Services and Anthems, Preserved among the Manuscript Scores and Partbooks in the Cathedral Church of Ely* (Cambridge, 1861).

—— 'Early Organs in Ely Cathedral', *The Organ*, 1 (1921–2), 61–3.

Divine Harmony; or a New Collection of Select Anthems, Us'd at Her Majesty's Chappels Royal, Westminster Abby, St Paul's, Windsor, both Universities, Eaton, and most Cathedrals in Her Majesty's Dominions [compiled by John Church] (London, 1712).

Divine Harmony. Six Select Anthems for a Voice alone . . . The 2d Collection being Select Anthems for a Voice alone as also some for 3 and 4 Voices . . . 2 vols. (London, [1716–17]).

DOEBNER, R., *Memoirs and Letters of Mary, Queen of England* (Leipzig, 1886).

EDEN, CONRAD, *Organs Past and Present in Durham Cathedral* (Durham, 1970).

EDMONDS, BERNARD B., 'The Chayre Organ: An Episode', *Journal of the British Institute of Organ Studies*, 4 (1980), 19–33.

—— 'John Loosemore', *Journal of the British Institute of Organ Studies*, 5 (1981), 23–32.

EDWARDS, KATHLEEN, *The English Secular Cathedrals in the Middle Ages* (Manchester, 1949).

—— 'Cathedral of Salisbury', in R. B. Pugh and Elizabeth Crittall (eds.), *A History of Wiltshire*, iii (The Victoria History of the County of Wiltshire; London, 1956), 156–210.

ELLIOTT, GRAHAM J., 'The Music of St Asaph's Cathedral' (MA diss., University College, Bangor, 1982).

ELLWAY, THOMAS, *Anthems . . . as they are now Perform'd in the Cathedral and Metropolitical Church of St Peter in York* (York, 1736).

ELVIN, LAURENCE, 'The Organs of Bristol Cathedral', *The Organ*, 42 (1962–3), 71–9.

—— 'The Organs of Ripon Cathedral', *The Organ*, 46 (1966–7), 137–46.

EVANS, DAVID R. A., 'A Preliminary Investigation of an Eighteenth-Century Bass Part-Book from St David's Cathedral', *Welsh Music*, 6/7 (1981), 48–54.

—— 'A Short History of the Music and Musicians of St David's Cathedral', *Welsh Music*, 7/8 (1984), 50–66.

EVANS, WILLA McCLUNG, *Henry Lawes, Musician and Friend of Poets* (New York, 1941; repr. 1966).

EVELYN, JOHN, *The Diary of John Evelyn*, ed. E. S. de Beer, 6 vols. (London, 1955).

EWARD, SUZANNE, *No Fine but a Glass of Wine: Cathedral Life at Gloucester in Stuart Times* (Salisbury, 1985).

FALCONER, DAVID, *Bath Abbey: Its Choirs and its Music* (Bath, 1984).

—— 'The Two Mr Priests of Chelsea', *Musical Times*, 128 (1987), 263.

FALKNER, J. MEADE (ed.), *The Statutes of the Cathedral Church of Durham* (Surtees Society, 143; Durham, 1929).

FARRER, WILLIAM, and BROWNBILL, JOHN, 'Manchester', in eid. (eds.), *The Victoria History of the County of Lancaster*, iv (London, 1911), 174–338.

FELLOWES, EDMUND H., *Organists and Masters of the Choristers of St George's Chapel in Windsor Castle* (Historical Monographs Relating to St George's Chapel, 3; Windsor, 1939).

—— *English Church Music from Edward VI to Edward VII* (London, 1941); rev. J. A. Westrup (London, 1969).

—— *The Vicars or Minor Canons of His Majesty's Free Chapel of St George's in Windsor Castle* (Historical Monographs Relating to St George's Chapel, 5; Windsor, 1945).

FINNEY, THEODORE M., 'A Manuscript Collection of English Restoration Anthems', *Journal of the American Musicological Society*, 15 (1962), 193–8.

FIRTH, C. H. (ed.), *The Clarke Papers* (Camden Society, 3; London, 1899).

—— and RAIT, R. S. (eds.), *Acts and Ordinances of the Interregnum, 1642–1660*, 3 vols. (London, 1911).

FORD, ROBERT F., 'Minor Canons at Canterbury Cathedral: The Gostlings and Their Colleagues' (Ph.D. diss., University of California, Berkeley, 1984).

—— 'A Sacred Song not by Purcell', *Musical Times*, 125 (1984), 45–7.

—— 'Henman, Humfrey and "Have mercy"', *Musical Times*, 127 (1986), 459–62.

—— 'Purcell as His Own Editor: The Funeral Sentences', *Journal of Musicological Research*, 7 (1986), 47–67.

FORD, WYN K., 'The Life and Work of John Okeover (or Oker)', *Proceedings of the Royal Musical Association*, 84 (1957–8), 71–80.

—— 'The Chapel Royal at the Time of the Restoration', *Monthly Musical Record*, 90 (1960), 99–106.

FORTUNE, NIGEL, and ZIMMERMAN, FRANKLIN B., 'Purcell's Autographs', in Imogen Holst (ed.), *Henry Purcell, 1659–1695* (London, 1959), 106–21.

FOSTER, JOSEPH, *Alumni Oxonienses, 1500–1714* (Oxford, 1891).

FOSTER, MICHAEL W., *The Music of Salisbury Cathedral* (London, 1974).

FOSTER, MYLES BIRKETT, *Anthems and Anthem Composers* (London, 1901; repr. 1970).

FOWLER, J. T. (ed.), *Memorials and Chapter Acts of the Collegiate Church of SS Peter and Wilfrid, Ripon*, ii–iii (Surtees Society, 78, 81; Durham 1886, 1888).

FOWLER, THOMAS, *The History of Corpus Christi College* [Oxford] (Oxford Historical Society, 25; Oxford, 1893).

FRANKLIN, DON, 'The Anthems of William Turner (1652–1740): An Historical and Stylistic Study' (Ph.D. diss., Stanford University, 1967).

—— review of *Pelham Humfrey: Complete Church Music*, ed. P. Dennison, in *Journal of the American Musicological Society*, 28 (1975), 143–9.

FREEMAN, ANDREW, 'The Organs of Bristol Cathedral', *The Organ*, 2 (1922–3), 65–73.

—— 'The Organs of the Abbey Church at Westminster', *The Organ*, 2 (1922–3), 129–48.

—— 'The Organs of Lincoln Cathedral', *The Organ*, 2 (1922–3), 193–200.

—— 'The Organs of Gloucester Cathedral', *The Organ*, 4 (1924–5), 1–10.

—— 'The Organs of Eton College', *The Organ*, 4 (1924–5), 157–71.

—— *Father Smith* (London, 1926); ed. with new material by John Rowntree (Oxford, 1977).

—— 'The Organs of Exeter Cathedral', *The Organ*, 6 (1926–7), 100–12.

—— 'The Organs at King's College, Cambridge', *The Organ*, 8 (1928–9), 128–38.

—— 'The Organs at New College, Oxford', *The Organ*, 9 (1929–30), 149–56.

—— 'The Organs of Christ Church Cathedral, Oxford', *The Organ*, 11 (1931–2), 36–42.

—— 'The Organs of Chester Cathedral', *The Organ*, 13 (1933–4), 129–39.

FRERE, W. H., *The Use of Sarum: II. The Ordinal and Tonal* (Cambridge, 1901).

FRITH, BRIAN, 'The Organists of Gloucester Cathedral', in *The Organs and Organists of Gloucester Cathedral* ([Gloucester], 1971), 45–67.

GASTRELL, FRANCIS, *Notitiae Cestriensis* (Chetham Society Publications, 19; Manchester, 1849).

GEE, HENRY, and HARDING, WILLIAM J., *Documents Illustrative of English Church History* (London, 1910).

G[EE], H., *The Statutes of Gloucester Cathedral* (London, 1918).

GIBBON, REGINALD H., 'Small Beer of History', *Church Quarterly Review*, 113 (Oct. 1933), 100–16.

—— 'The Account Book of the Dean and Chapter of Ely, 1604–1677', *Church Quarterly Review*, 115 (Jan. 1933), 210–33.

GIBBONS, CHRISTOPHER, *Keyboard Compositions*, ed. Clare G. Rayner, rev. John Caldwell (Corpus of Early Keyboard Music, 18; Neuhausen-Stuttgart, 1989).

GILES, PETER, *The Counter Tenor* (London, 1982).

GILLINGHAM, MICHAEL, 'The Organs and Organ Cases of Gloucester Cathedral', in *The Organs and Organists of Gloucester Cathedral* ([Gloucester], 1971), 1–31.

GOODMAN, ARTHUR W., and HUTTON, WILLIAM H., *The Statutes Governing the Cathedral Church of Winchester Given by King Charles I* (Oxford, 1925).

GRAYSON, JOHN H., 'The Organs of Durham Cathedral', *The Organ*, 13 (1933–4), 65–73.

GREEN, IAN M., *The Re-establishment of the Church of England, 1660–1663* (Oxford, 1978).

[GREENING, ANTHONY J.], *The Organs and Organists of Ely Cathedral* ([Ely, 1972]).

GRIFITHS, DAVID, *A Catalogue of the Music Manuscripts in York Minster Library* (York, 1981).

—— 'The Music in York Minster', *Musical Times*, 123 (1982), 633–7.

GRINDLE, W. H., *Irish Cathedral Music: A History of Music at the Cathedrals of the Church of Ireland* (Belfast, 1989).

Grove's Dictionary of Music and Musicians, 5th edn., ed. Eric Blom, 10 vols. (including Supplementary Volume) (London, 1954–61).

GWYNN, DOMINIC, 'Organ Pitch in Seventeenth-Century England', *Journal of the British Institute of Organ Studies*, 9 (1985), 65–78.

[HACKETT, MARIA], *A Brief Account of Cathedral and Collegiate Schools, with an Abstract of their Statutes and Endowments* (London, 1824).

HALE, PAUL R., 'Music and Musicians', in John Buxton and Penry Williams (eds.), *New College, Oxford, 1379–1979* (Oxford, 1979).

—— *The Organs and Organists of Rochester Cathedral* (Rochester, n.d.).

HAMPSON, ETHEL M., 'Choir Schools', in L. F. Salzman (ed.), *A History of the County of Cambridge and the Isle of Ely*, ii (London, 1948), 335–8.

HARDING, ROSAMOND E. M., *A Thematic Catalogue of the Works of Matthew Locke* (Oxford, 1971).

HARLEY, JOHN, *Music in Purcell's London* (London, 1968).

HARPER, JOHN, 'The Dallam Organ in Magdalen College, Oxford', *Journal of the British Institute of Organ Studies*, 9 (1984), 51–64.

—— 'The Organs of Magdalen College, Oxford—1: the Historical Background of Earlier Organs', *Musical Times*, 127 (1986), 293–6.

HARRIS, B. E., 'Chester Cathedral', in id. (ed.), *A History of the County of Chester* (Victoria County History of Cheshire, iii; London, 1980), 188–95.

HARRISON, FRANK Ll., *Music in Medieval Britain* (London, 1958).

HARRISON, FREDERICK, *Life in a Medieval College* (London, 1952).

HART, PHILIP, *Organ Works*, ed. Frank Dawes (Tallis to Wesley, 37; London, 1973).

HARVEY, S. W., 'The Organs of Canterbury Cathedral', *The Organ*, 3 (1923–4), 1–19.

HAVERGAL, F. T., *Fasti Herefordenses* (Edinburgh, 1869).

HAWKINS, JOHN, *A General History of the Science and Practice of Music*, 5 vols. (London, 1776; 2nd edn., 2 vols., London, 1875; repr. 1963).

HAYES, W., 'Rules Necessary to be Observed by all Cathedral-Singers in this Kingdom', *Gentleman's Magazine*, 35 (1765), 213–14.

HEYWOOD, J., and WRIGHT, T., *The Ancient Laws of the Fifteenth Century for King's College, Cambridge, and for the Public School of Eton* (London, 1850).

HINE, WILLIAM, *Harmonia Sacra Glocestriensis, or Select Anthems . . . and a Te Deum and Jubilate, together with a Voluntary for the Organ* ([London, 1731]).

HODGSON, FREDERIC, 'The Contemporary Alto', *Musical Times*, 106 (1965), 293–4.

HOGWOOD, CHRISTOPHER, 'Thomas Tudway's History of Music', in C. Hogwood and R. Luckett (eds.), *Music in Eighteenth-Century England: Essays in Memory of Charles Cudworth* (Cambridge, 1983), 19–47.

HOLGATE, C. W., *Winchester Long Rolls, 1653–1721* (Winchester, 1899).

HOLMAN, PETER, 'Bartholomew Isaack and "Mr Isaack" of Eton', *Musical Times*, 128 (1987), 381–5.

—— *Four and Twenty Fiddlers: The Violin at the English Court, 1540–1690* (Oxford, 1993).

HOWARD, P., and CLUTTON, C., 'The Organ in Llandaff Cathedral', *The Organ*, 39 (1959–60), 157–64.

HUDSON, FREDERICK, 'Thomas Bullis, Father and Son', *Musical Times*, 114 (1973), 420–1.

—— and LARGE, W. ROY, 'William Child (1606/7–1697): A New Investigation of Sources', *Music Review*, 31 (1970), 265–84.

HUDSON, HENRY A., 'The Organs and Organists of the Cathedral and Parish Church of Manchester', *Transactions of the Lancashire and Cheshire Antiquarian Society*, 34 (1916), 111–93.

HUNT, J. ERIC, 'The Organs of St David's Cathedral', *The Organ*, 32 (1952–3), 48–51.

HUTTON, WILLIAM H., *The English Church from the Accession of Charles I to the Death of Queen Anne (1625–1714)* (London, 1934).

JEBB, JOHN, *The Choral Service of the United Church of England and Ireland* (London, 1843).

—— *The Choral Responses and Litanies of the United Church of England and Ireland* (London, 1847).

—— and PHILLOTT, H. W., *The Statutes of the Cathedral Church of Hereford, promulgated A.D. 1637* (Oxford, 1882).

JOHNSTONE, H. DIACK, review of THOMAS F. TAYLOR, *Thematic Catalog of the Works of Jeremiah Clarke*, in *Music and Letters*, 59 (1978), 55–61.

JONES, A. H. M., 'New College', in H. E. Salter and Mary Lobel (eds.), *The University of Oxford* (The Victoria History of the County of Oxford, iii; London, 1954), 144–62.

JONES, ANNE M., 'The Anthems of John Golding, Organist and Master of the Choristers of St George's Chapel in Windsor Castle, 1697–1719' (M.Mus. diss., Royal Holloway College, University of London, 1985).

KETTLE, ANN J., and JOHNSON, D. A., 'The Cathedral of Lichfield', in M. W. Greenslade (ed.), *A History of the County of Stafford*, iii (London, 1970), 140–99.

KIRWAN, A. LINDSEY, *The Music of Lincoln Cathedral* (London, 1973).

KNIGHTS, FRANCIS, 'The Choral Foundation of Corpus Christi College [Oxford]', *The Pelican* (1988–9), 22–6.

—— 'The History of the Choral Foundation of St John's College, Oxford', *Musical Times*, 131 (1990), 444–7.

—— 'Magdalen College MS 347: An Index and Commentary', *Journal of the British Institute of Organ Studies*, 14 (1990), 4–9.

—— 'A Restoration Version of Gibbons' Short Service', *Organists' Review*, 76 (1990), 97–100.

KRUMMEL, DONALD, *English Music Printing, 1553–1700* (London, 1975).

LAURIE, MARGARET, 'The Chapel Royal Part-Books', in Oliver Neighbour (ed.), *Music and Bibliography: Essays in Honour of Alec Hyatt King* (London, 1980), 28–50.

LAWLOR, HUGH J., *The Fasti of St Patrick's, Dublin* (Dundalk, 1930).

LEGG, L. G. WICKHAM, *English Coronation Records* (London, 1901).

—— (ed.), *A Relation of a Short Survey of 26 Counties . . . 1634* (London, 1904).

LE HURAY, PETER, *Music and the Reformation in England, 1549–1660* (London, 1967).

LEWIS, ANTHONY, 'English Church Music: Purcell', in Anthony Lewis and Nigel Fortune (eds.), *New Oxford History of Music*, V (Oxford, 1975), 526–37.

LOCKE, MATTHEW, *Modern Church-Musick Pre-accus'd, Censur'd and Obstructed* (London, 1666).

—— *The Present Practice of Musick Vindicated* (London, 1673; repr. 1974).

—— *Seven Pieces (Voluntaries) from 'Melothesia' (1673)*, ed. Gordon Phillips (Tallis to Wesley, 6; London, 1957).

—— *Organ Voluntaries*, ed. R. T. Dart (Early Keyboard Music, 7; London, 1957; 2nd edn., 1968).

—— *Melothesia*, ed. Christopher Hogwood (Oxford, 1987).

LONG, KENNETH R., *The Music of the English Church* (London, 1972; repr. 1991).

LOWE, EDWARD, *A Short Direction for the Performance of Cathedrall Service* (London, 1661; 2nd edn., *A Review of a Short Direction*, London, 1664).

LYTE, C. MAXWELL, *A History of Eton College, 1449–1910* (London, 1911).

MACE, THOMAS, *Musick's Monument* (London, 1676; repr. 1966, with commentary by J. Jacquot and transcriptions by A. Souris, 2 vols., Paris, 1958–66).

McGRADY, RICHARD, 'Captain Cooke: A Tercentenary Tribute', *Musical Times*, 113 (1972), 659–60.

MACKERNESS, E. D., *A Social History of English Music* (London, 1962; 2nd edn., 1966).

McKIE, WILLIAM, 'Music in the Abbey', in E. F. Carpenter (ed.), *A House of Kings* (London, 1966), 416–45.

MACLAGAN, M., 'Christ Church', in H. E. Salter and Mary Lobel (eds.), *The University of Oxford* (The Victoria History of the County of Oxford, iii; London, 1954), 228–38.

MADDISON, A. R., *A Short Account of the Vicars Choral, Poor Clerks, Organists and Choristers of Lincoln Cathedral* (London, 1878).

—— 'Lincoln Cathedral Choir, A.D. 1640 to 1700', *Lincoln and Nottingham Architectural Society*, 20 (1889), 41–55.

MAHAFFY, ROBERT P. (ed.), *Calendar of State Papers, Domestic Series, 1702–3* (London, 1916).

MANNING, ROBERT, 'Purcell's Anthems: An Analytical Study of the Music and of Its Context' (Ph.D. diss., University of Birmingham, 1979).

—— 'Revisions and Reworkings in Purcell's Anthems', *Soundings*, 9 (1982), 29–37.

MASON, W. MONCK, *The History and Antiquities of the Collegiate and Cathedral Church of St Patrick's near Dublin* (Dublin, 1820).

MATTHEWS, BETTY, *The Music of Winchester Cathedral* (London, 1974).

—— *The Organs and Organists of Winchester Cathedral* (Winchester, 1964; 3rd rev. edn., 1975).

—— 'The Influence of the Organists of Salisbury Cathedral', *The Organ*, 61 (1981–2), 114–22.

—— 'The Dallams and the Harrises', *Journal of the British Institute of Organ Studies*, 8 (1984), 58–68.

—— *The Organs and Organists of Exeter Cathedral* (Exeter, n.d.).

—— *The Organs and Organists of Wimborne Minster, 1408–1972* (Bournemouth, n.d.).

MENDEL, ARTHUR, 'Pitch in Western Music since 1500', *Acta Musicologica*, 50 (1978), 1–93.

MOODY, CHARLES H., *Ripon Cathedral Organ: A Short History and Description, including Miscellaneous Notes from the Cathedral Records* (Ripon, 1913).

MOREHEN, JOHN, 'The Sources of English Cathedral Music, *c.* 1617–*c.* 1644' (Ph.D. diss., University of Cambridge, 1969).

—— 'The English Anthem Text, 1549–1660', *Journal of the Royal Musical Association*, 117 (1992), 62–85.

MOULD, CLIFFORD, *The Musical Manuscripts of St George's Chapel, Windsor Castle* (Historical Monographs Relating to St George's Chapel, Windsor Castle, 14; Windsor, 1973).

Musica Britannica (Royal Musical Association; London, 1951–).

   7. *John Blow: Coronation Anthems with Strings*, ed. Anthony Lewis and H. Watkins Shaw (1953).

   33. *English Songs, 1625–1660*, ed. Ian Spink (1971; 2nd edn., 1977).

   34–5. *Pelham Humfrey: Complete Church Music*, ed. Peter Dennison (1972).

   38. *Matthew Locke: Anthems and Motets*, ed. Peter le Huray (1976).

   50. *John Blow: Anthems II* (Anthems with Orchestra), ed. Bruce Wood (1984).

   64. *John Blow: Anthems III* (Anthems with Strings), ed. Bruce Wood (1993).

NOBLE, JEREMY, 'Purcell and the Chapel Royal', in Imogen Holst (ed.), *Henry Purcell, 1659–1695* (London, 1959), 52–66.

OWEN, DOROTHY, M., 'From the Restoration until 1822', in G. E. Aylmer and Reginald Cant (eds.), *A History of York Minster* (Oxford, 1977), 233–71.

PAGE, JOHN, *Harmonia Sacra: A Collection of Anthems in Score*, 3 vols. (London, 1800).

PAGET, GORDON, 'The Organs of Norwich Cathedral', *The Organ*, 14 (1934–5), 65–74.

PARROTT, ANDREW, 'Grett and Solompne Singing: Instruments in English Church Music before the Civil War', *Early Music*, 6 (1978), 182–7.

PAYNE, IAN, 'Instrumental Music at Trinity College, Cambridge, c.1594–c.1615', *Music and Letters*, 68 (1987), 128–40.

—— *The Provision and Practice of Sacred Music at Cambridge Colleges and Selected Cathedrals, c.1547–c.1646* (New York and London, 1993).

PAUL, LESLIE, *Music at Bangor Cathedral* (Bangor, 1975).

PEARCE, ERNEST H., *The Sons of the Clergy: Some Records of Two Hundred and Seventy Five Years* (London, 1924; 2nd edn., 1928).

PECKHAM, W. D., 'The Vicars Choral of Chichester Cathedral', *Sussex Archaeological Collections*, 78 (1937), 126–59.

PEPYS, SAMUEL, *The Diary of Samuel Pepys*, ed. R. C. Latham and W. Matthews, 11 vols. (London, 1970–83).

PERKINS, JOCELYN, *The Organs and Bells of Westminster Abbey* (London, 1937).

PHILLIPS, GORDON (ed.), *John Blow and His Pupils John Barrett and John Reading* (Tallis to Wesley, 21; London, 1962).

PINE, EDWARD, *The Westminster Abbey Singers* (London, 1953).

PIPER, A. CECIL, 'Notes on Winchester Cathedral Organs', *The Organ*, 1 (1921–2), 176–9.

PLANK, STEVEN E., 'An English Miscellany: Musical Notes in Seventeenth-Century Diaries and Letters', *The Consort*, 41 (1985), 66–73.

PLAYFORD, HENRY, *The Divine Companion . . . being a Collection of New and Easy Hymns and Anthems* (London, 1701; 2nd edn., 1707; 3rd edn., 1709, etc.).

PLAYFORD, JOHN, *An Introduction to the Skill of Musick* (3rd. edn., London, 1666; 7th edn., 1674, facs. edn., Ridgewood, NJ, 1966; 12th edn., 1694 'Corrected and amended by Mr. Henry Purcell', facs. edn., New York, 1972).

—— *Cantica Sacra: Containing Hymns and Anthems for Two Voices to the Organ, both Latine and English. Composed by Richard Dering, Dr Christopher Gibbons, Dr Benjamin Rogers, Mr Matthew Locke, and Others* [including Isaac Blackwell and Playford himself] (London, 1674).

PLUMLEY, NICHOLAS, and LEES, JOHN, *The Organs and Organists of Chichester Cathedral* (Chichester, 1988).

POPE, R. A. D. 'The Organs of St Patrick's Cathedral, Dublin', *The Organ*, 15 (1935–6), 201–8.

PRESCOTT, J. E., *The Statutes of the Cathedral Church of Carlisle* (Carlisle, 1879; 2nd edn., London, 1903).

PULVER, JEFFREY, *A Biographical Dictionary of Old English Music* (London, 1927).

PURCELL, HENRY, *The Works of Henry Purcell*, 32 vols. (Purcell Society; London, 1878–1965; rev. 1974–) [PS]

  6. *Harpsichord and Organ Music*, ed. W. B. Squire and E. J. Hopkins (1895).

  13. *Sacred Music, Part I: Nine Anthems with Orchestral Accompaniment*, ed. Peter Dennison (1988).

  14. *Sacred Music, Part II*, ed. Peter Dennison (1973).

  17. *Sacred Music, Part III: Seven Anthems with Strings*, ed. H. E. Wooldridge and G. E. P. Arkwright, rev. Nigel Fortune (1964).

  23. *Services*, ed. A. Gray (1923).

  28. *Sacred Music, Part IV: Anthems*, ed. Anthony Lewis and Nigel Fortune (1959).

  29. *Sacred Music, Part V: Anthems*, ed. Anthony Lewis and Nigel Fortune (1960).

  30. *Sacred Music, Part VI: Anthems*, ed. Anthony Lewis and Nigel Fortune (1965).

  32. *Sacred Music, Part VII: Anthems and Miscellaneous Church Music*, ed. Anthony Lewis and Nigel Fortune (1962).

—— *Organ Works*, ed. Hugh McLean (London, 1957; 2nd edn., 1967).

QUANTZ, J. J., *Versuch einer Anweisung die Flöte traversiere zu Spielen* (Berlin, 1752); English trans. by Edward R. Reilly (London, 1966).

RAVENSCROFT, THOMAS, *A Briefe Discourse of the True (but Neglected) Use of Charact'ring the Degrees* (London, 1614; facs. edn., New York, 1976).

READING, JOHN, *A Book of New Anthems . . . with a Thorough Bass Figur'd for the Organ or Harpsichord with Proper Retornels* (London, *c.*1715).

RIMBAULT, EDWARD F. (ed.), *Cathedral Music Consisting of Services and Anthems Selected from the Books of Different Cathedrals* (London, [1847]).

—— *The Old Cheque-Book, or Book of Remembrance of the Chapel Royal from 1561 to 1744* (Camden Society, NS iii; London, 1872; repr. New York, 1966).

RISHTON, TIMOTHY J., 'An Eighteenth-Century Lichfield Music Society', *Music Review*, 44 (1983), 83–6.

ROBERTS, W. A., 'Peterborough Cathedral and Its Organs', *The Organ*, 10 (1930–1), 1–10.

ROBERTSON, DORA H., *Sarum Close: A History of the Life and Education of the Cathedral Choristers for 700 Years* (London, 1938).

ROGERS, ALAN, *Southwell Minster after the Civil Wars* (Nottingham, 1974).

ROGERS, BENJAMIN, *Complete Keyboard Works*, ed. Richard Rastall (Early Keyboard Music, 29; London, 1972).

ROUTH, FRANCIS, *Early English Organ Music from the Middle Ages to 1837* (London, 1973).

ROUTLEY, ERIK, *The English Carol* (London, 1958).

ROWNTREE, JOHN, 'Bernard Smith (c. 1629–1708) Organist and Organ Builder: His Origins', *Journal of the British Institute of Organ Studies*, 2 (1978), 10–23.

SALTER, H. E., 'St John's College', in H. E. Salter and Mary Lobel (eds.), *The University of Oxford* (The Victoria History of the County of Oxford, iii; London, 1954), 251–64.

SALTMARSH, J., 'King's College', in J. P. C. Roach (ed.), *A History of the County of Cambridge and the Isle of Ely*, iii (London, 1959), 376–408.

SAYER, MICHAEL, 'Robert Dallam's Organ in York Minster, 1634', *Journal of the British Institute of Organ Studies*, 1 (1977), 60–8.

SCANDRETT, ROBERT L., 'The Anthems of William Croft (1678–1727)' (Ph.D. diss., University of Washington, 1961).

SCHOLES, PERCY, *The Puritans and Music in England and New England* (London, 1934; repr. 1969).

SCOTT, DAVID, *The Music of St Paul's Cathedral* (London, 1972).

SHAW, H. WATKINS, 'A Collection of Musical Manuscripts in the Autograph of Henry Purcell and other English Composers, c. 1665–85', *The Library*, 5th ser., 14 (1959), 126–31.

—— 'A Contemporary Source of English Music of the Purcellian Period', *Acta Musicologica*, 31 (1959), 38–44.

—— 'A Cambridge Manuscript from the English Chapel Royal', *Music and Letters*, 42 (1961), 263–7.

—— 'The Autographs of John Blow', *Music Review*, 25 (1964), 85–95.

—— 'Some Stray Notes on "Father" Smith', *The Organ*, 51 (1971–2), 25–8.

—— *The Organists and Organs of Hereford Cathedral* (Hereford, 1976).

—— *A Study of the Bing–Gostling Part Books in the Library of York Minster* (Croydon, 1986).

SHAW, H. WATKINS, *The Succession of Organists of the Chapel Royal and the Cathedrals of England and Wales from c.1538* (Oxford, 1991).

SIKES, J. G., and JONES, FREDA, 'Jesus College', in J. P. C. Roach (ed.), *A History of the County of Cambridge and the Isle of Ely*, iii (London, 1959), 421–8.

SIMPSON, CHRISTOPHER, *A Compendium of Practical Musick* (2nd edn., London, 1667); ed. Philip J. Lord (Oxford, 1970).

SMITH, MICHAEL J., 'The Church Music of Michael Wise' (D.Mus. diss., University of Edinburgh, 1970).

SNOW, HERBERT, 'The Organs of Lichfield Cathedral', *The Organ*, 12 (1932–3), 98–104.

SPELLER, JOHN, 'Bristol Organs in 1710', *The Organ*, 57 (1978–9), 85–90.

—— 'Some Notes on Thomas Swarbrick', *The Organ*, 59 (1980–1), 87–90.

SPINK, IAN, 'Playford's "Directions for Singing after the Italian Manner"', *Monthly Musical Record*, 89 (1959), 130–5.

—— *English Song: Dowland to Purcell* (London, 1974; 2nd edn., 1986).

—— 'Church Music II: From 1660', in id. (ed.), *Music in Britain: The Seventeenth Century* (Blackwell History of Music in Britain, iii; Oxford, 1992), 97–137.

SPURR, JOHN, *The Restoration Church of England, 1646–1689* (London, 1991).

SRAWLEY, J. H., *The Origin and Growth of Cathedral Foundations as Illustrated by the Cathedral Church of Lincoln* (Lincoln, 1965).

Statuta et Consuetudines Ecclesiae Cathedralis Lichfieldiae (London, n.d.).

STEPHENS, W. R. W., and MADGE, F. T., *Documents Relating to the History of the Cathedral Church of Winchester in the Seventeenth Century* (Publications of the Hampshire Record Society, 14; London, 1897).

STEVENS, DENIS, *Thomas Tomkins, 1572–1656* (London, 1957).

STRUNK, OLIVER, *Source Readings in Music History* (London, 1952).

STUBBINGTON, H., 'The Organs of St David's Cathedral', *The Organ*, 21 (1941–2), 1–4.

SUMNER, G., 'The Origins of the Dallams in Lancashire', *Journal of the British Institute of Organ Studies*, 7 (1983), 4–17.

SUMNER, WILLIAM, L., *The Organ* (London, 1952; 4th edn., 1973).

—— 'The Organs of St John's College, Cambridge', *The Organ*, 36 (1956–7), 28–35.

—— 'The Organs of Southwell Cathedral', *The Organ*, 14 (1934–5), 12–21; also ibid., 51 (1971–2), 89–98.

SWEETING, E. T., 'The Organs of Winchester College Chapel', *The Organ*, 4 (1924–5), 211–20.

SWIFT, JONATHAN, *The Correspondence of Jonathan Swift*, ed. Harold Williams, 5 vols. (Oxford, 1963).

TATNELL, ROLAND STUART, 'Falsetto Practice: A Brief Survey', *The Consort*, 22 (1965), 31–5.

TAYLOR, THOMAS F., *Thematic Catalog of the Works of Jeremiah Clarke* (Detroit, 1977).

TEMPERLEY, NICHOLAS, *The Music of the English Parish Church*, 2 vols. (Cambridge, 1979).

—— 'Organ Music in Parish Churches, 1660–1730', *Journal of the British Institute of Organ Studies*, 5 (1981), 33–45.

THISTLETHWAITE, NICHOLAS, 'Notes Relating to the Organization of Organ Building in England, to c. 1740', *Journal of the British Institute of Organ Studies*, 5 (1981), 46–51.

—— 'Rediscovering "Father" Smith', *Musical Times*, 128 (1987), 401–4.

—— 'Music and Worship, 1660–1980', in Dorothy Owen (ed.), *A History of Lincoln Minster* (Cambridge, 1994), 77–88.

THOMAS, ROBERT D., *A History of the Diocese of St Asaph: General, Cathedral and Parochial* (London, 1874).

THOMPSON, ROBERT, 'George Jeffreys and the "Stile Nuovo" in English Sacred Music: A New Date for his Autograph Score, British Library Add. MS 10338', *Music and Letters*, 70 (1989), 317–41.

TILMOUTH, MICHAEL, *A Calendar of References to Music in Newspapers published in London and the Provinces (1660–1719) (RMA Research Chronicle, 1 (1961))*.

TOMKINS, THOMAS, *Musica Deo Sacra* (London, 1668), ed. Bernard Rose (Early English Church Music, 5, 9, 14, 27, 37, 39; London, 1965–92).

Treasury of English Church Music, ed. G. H. Knight and W. L. Reed, 5 vols. (London, 1965)
  2. *1545–1650*, ed. Peter le Huray.
  3. *1650–1750*, ed. Christopher Dearnley.

TURNBULL, EDWARD, 'Thomas Tudway and the Harleian Collection', *Journal of the American Musicological Society*, 8 (1955), 203–7.

VAN TASSEL, E., 'Purcell's "Give sentence with me, O God"', *Musical Times*, 118 (1977), 381–3.

WALCOTT, MACKENZIE E. C., *Cathedralia: A Constitutional History of Cathedrals in the Western Church* (London, 1865).

WALKER, ERNEST, *A History of Music in England* (Oxford, 1907; rev. J. A. Westrup, 1952).

WANLESS, THOMAS, *The Meter Psalm-Tunes in Four Parts, Compos'd for the Use of the Parish-Church of St Michael's of Belfry in York* (London, 1702).

—— *Full Anthems and Verse Anthems as they are . . . sung in the Cathedral and Metropolitical Church of St. Peters in York* (York, 1703; 2nd edn., 1705).

WEBER, WILLIAM, 'Thomas Tudway and the Harleian Collection of "Ancient" Church Music', *British Library Journal*, 15 (1989), 187–205.

WESLEY, JOHN, *The Journal of the Rev. John Wesley, A.M.*, 4 vols. (London, 1827).

WEST, JOHN E., *Cathedral Organists Past and Present* (London, 1899; 2nd edn., 1921).

WESTRUP, J. A., *Purcell* (London, 1937; rev. edn., 1968).

—— 'Cathedral Music in Seventeenth-Century England', in *Festschrift Friedrich Blume* (Kassel, 1963), 375–80.

WHITE, J. P., 'The Life and Vocal Music of Benjamin Rogers (1614–1698)' (Ph.D. diss., University of Iowa, 1973).

WHITLOCK, PERCY, 'The Organs of Rochester Cathedral', *The Organ*, 8 (1918–19), 65–72.

WHITWORTH, REGINALD, 'The Organs of Carlisle Cathedral', *The Organ*, 15 (1935–6), 65–71.

WILLIAMS, RODERICK, 'Manuscript Organ Books in Eton College Library', *Music and Letters*, 41 (1960), 358–9.

WILLIS, BROWNE, *A Survey of the Cathedrals of York, Durham, Carlisle, Chester, Man, Lichfield, Hereford, Worcester, Gloucester and Bristol*, 2 vols. (London, 1727).

—— *Parochiale Anglicanum* (London, 1733).

WILLIS, BROWNE, *A Survey of the Cathedrals of York, Durham, Carlisle, Chester, Man, Lichfield, Hereford, Worcester, Gloucester, Bristol, Lincoln, Ely, Oxford, Peterborough, Canterbury, Rochester, London, Winchester, Chichester, Norwich, Salisbury, Wells, Exeter, St David's, Llandaff, Bangor, and St Asaph*, 3 vols. (London, 1742).

WILLOUGHBY, G. St M., 'The Organs of Winchester Canthedral', *The Organ*, 9 (1929–30), 1–10.

WILSON, A. W., 'The Organs of Manchester Cathedral', *The Organ*, 12, (1932–3), 1–4.

WILSON, JOHN (ed.), *Roger North on Music* (London, 1959).

WILSON, RUTH M., 'Anglican Chant and Chanting in England and America, 1660–1811' (Ph.D. diss., University of Illinois, Urbana, 1988).

WOOD, BRUCE, 'A Note on Two Cambridge Manuscripts and their Copyists', *Music and Letters*, 56 (1975), 308–12.

—— 'John Blow's Anthems with Orchestra' (Ph.D. diss., University of Cambridge, 1977).

—— 'Cavendish Weedon: Impresario Extraordinary', *The Consort*, 33 (1977), 222–4.

—— 'A Coronation Anthem, Lost and Found', *Musical Times*, 118 (1977), 466–8.

WORDSWORTH, CHRISTOPHER, *Statutes of Lincoln Cathedral*, 3 vols. (Cambridge, 1897).

—— and MACLEANE, DOUGLAS, *Statutes and Customs of the Cathedral Church of the Blessed Virgin Mary of Salisbury* (London, 1915).

WRIDGWAY, NEVILLE, *The Choristers of St George's Chapel, Windsor Castle* (Windsor, 1980).

WULSTAN, DAVID, 'Vocal Colour in English Sixteenth-Century Polyphony', *Journal of the Plainsong and Medieval Music Society*, 2 (1979), 19–60.

YOUNG, PERCY, *Lichfield Cathedral Library: a Catalogue of Music, 1. Manuscripts* (Birmingham, 1993).

ZIMMERMAN, FRANKLIN B., *Henry Purcell, 1659–1695: An Analytical Catalogue of His Music* (London, 1963).

—— 'Purcell's "Service Anthem" O God, thou art my God and the B-flat Major Service', *Musical Quarterly*, 50 (1964), 207–14.

—— *Henry Purcell, 1659–1695: His Life and Times* (London, 1967; rev. edn., Philadelphia, 1983).

—— 'Anthems of Purcell and Contemporaries in a Newly Rediscovered "Gostling Manuscript"', *Acta Musicologica*, 41 (1969), 55–70.

—— 'The Anthems of Henry Purcell', *American Choral Review*, 13/3–4 (1971).

—— (ed.), *The Gostling Manuscript* (facs. edn., Austin, Tex., 1977).

ZIMMERMAN, JOE M., 'The Psalm Settings and Anthems of William Child, 1606–1697' (Ph.D. diss., University of Indiana, 1971).

INDEX